ALSO BY COLIN FLETCHER

The Man from the Cave (1981)

The New Complete Walker (1974)

The Winds of Mara (1973)

The Man Who Walked Through Time (1968)

The Complete Walker (1968)

The Thousand-Mile Summer (1964)

THE COMPLETE WALKER III

$12

THE *Complete*
WALKER III

*The joys and techniques
of hiking and backpacking*

THIRD EDITION, REVISED,
ENLARGED, AND UPDATED

COLIN FLETCHER

Illustrations by Vanna Prince

ALFRED A. KNOPF

New York   1989

THIS IS A BORZOI BOOK PUBLISHED BY ALFRED A. KNOPF, INC.

Copyright © 1968, 1974, 1984 by Colin Fletcher
All rights reserved under International and Pan-American Copyright Conventions.
Published in the United States by Alfred A. Knopf, Inc., New York,
and simultaneously in Canada by Random House of Canada Limited, Toronto.
Distributed by Random House, Inc., New York.
Library of Congress Cataloging in Publication Data
Fletcher, Colin.
The complete walker III.
Rev. ed. of: The new complete walker.
2nd ed., rev., enl., and updated. 1974.
Includes index.
1. Backpacking.   2. Hiking.
I. Fletcher, Colin.
New complete walker.   II. Title.
III. Title: Complete walker 3.
GV199.6.F53   1984   796.5'1   83-48870
ISBN 0-394-51962-0
ISBN 0-394-72264-7 (PBK.)

MANUFACTURED IN THE UNITED STATES OF AMERICA
THIRD EDITION, REVISED

Published June 13, 1984
Reprinted Three Times
Fifth Printing, June 1989

TO MY MOTHER

who understood that walking for fun
is no crazier than most things in life,
and who passed the information along.

Author's Note

Several fibers woven into this book have been plucked from *The Thousand-Mile Summer,* published by Howell-North Books, and from *The Man Who Walked Through Time* and *The Winds of Mara,* both published by Alfred A. Knopf. To protect readers of these books from echo trouble, I have identified the rare passages in which I found it necessary to reuse any lengths of fabric.

A few strands also come from articles of mine that have appeared in *Field & Stream, Sports Afield, Reader's Digest* and the San Francisco *Chronicle,* and I wish to thank their publishers for permission to rework the material.

For a listing of the many individuals who helped me compile this edition, see page 645.

Contents

Preface to the Third Edition

What I tell you three times is true.

Lewis Carroll,
The Hunting of the Snark

The second edition of this book appeared because the first was five years out of date. This revision is therefore doubly due: ten more years of backpacking revolution have rolled over us.

Above all, hi-tech has hit. Pile, polypropylene and Gore-Tex have transformed the clothes closet. Boots have begun to break old bonds, packs to mutate and tents to take off. Meanwhile we face packfuls of better traditional mousetraps. And the marketplace has modulated accordingly. New firms have sprouted and, like Apple in the wider world, borne instant fruit. Some old stalwarts have pulled a Braniff and crashed; others, following in the footsteps of U.S. Rust, have suffered serious corrosion. The decade has brought peripheral supplements too—from fresh medical truth about mountain sickness to new judgments on the depraved current foodways of bears. On top of all this, I have garnered what I choose to see as a few additional droplets of wisdom.

"Ah, yes," you say, much as you did ten years ago. "But is this really a revised edition, facing such changes? Or do we just have a cosmeticized rehash?"

Once again I have revised—perhaps even more copiously than last time.

The boots chapter is virtually new. Ditto the one on packs. The core of the "Kitchen" has been rebuilt. And so it goes throughout the book, in varying degrees. Here and there I have injected new sections—including one on operating in heavy rain (something I had rightly been accused of short-changing you on).

This revision, like the last, has been enriched by feedback from readers. As one wrote: "You have been thrust (inadvertently perhaps) into the unique and important role of national (and international?) collator of suggestions from a very diverse and dispersed lot of walkers." This is a heady and rather terrifying assessment; but down the years I've certainly received many letters—ranging from bloody silly to brilliant.

An Illinois reader wrote: "Dear Sirs, Would you please send me any information about backpacking and campping too." Many other people requested data easily plucked from a local library. The useful letters mostly dealt with specific and mundane equipment matters or with techniques. But some commented pithily. (A California wail against the onslaught of hi-tech: "Next thing you know there will be boots with five gears and reverse.") And a few letters soared. One, from a mature New Mexico youth of eighteen, ostensibly concerned hang-gliding. This sport, developed only a few years ago by pioneer backyard experimenters, has already ossified, my correspondent complained, to the stage at which it has become impossible to learn anything about it except through organized and accepted institutions, run by the Elect. God recently appointed these Elect, "taught them how to fly hang-gliders without getting themselves killed. . . . then charged them with guarding his knowledge faithfully, making sure no one deviates from the true way. (Anyone foolish enough to do so is certainly insane, and most likely a threat to the health and well-being of society, and should promptly be put away.)" By implication, my correspondent detected a tendency toward similar ossification in the backpacking body. And I think maybe he's right. Certainly, schools and seminars have proliferated (page 26). See also my bleat about NFS and USFS backcountry permits (page 45). But I am appalled to learn that earlier editions of this book may have helped spread a subtle form of the disease. A Rhode Island reader reports that while pausing in a public campground, preparing for a backcountry trip, he overheard a young couple arguing over some detail in setting up their camp. Finally the girl said, "Well, what does the —— —— [expletives deleted] say about it?" Her husband reached into his pack, pulled out a well-worn copy of *The Complete Walker,* consulted it—and was proved "right." So this time around I have tried to accent even more strongly than before that I seek to inscribe no gospel, only to suggest guidelines.

The past decade has also brought changes in the backcountry: at first a continuation of the explosion in our numbers; then, it seems, a leveling off or even a slight contraction. This welcome easing of pressure may be due in part to the negative feedback of the overcrowding and of the permit systems that have evolved to meet it. Walkers who love the backcountry because it offers silence and solitude soon become disenchanted at finding their favorite and once remote campsites encircled by other people; and they'll likely balk at the strictures imposed by the need to obtain a permit for entering what was once free—in the non-economic sense of furnishing an antidote to civilization's linear thoughtways. The people pressure has also been dampened by a widening of perceived options: those who once restricted their wilderness activity to backpacking may now also or alternatively raft rip-roaring rivers, canoe more placid waters or cross-country ski. A former backpacker, pushing forty and now heading his own camp-equipment company, promulgated another fetching if befogged vision: "People of my age are too busily involved in real estate, Mercedes, wine and drugs, buying art and taking luxury cruises; now that we're actually working instead of rioting in the streets, we must face the reality of having to work to support our habits —and we're not about to take two weeks to go out and backpack." Perhaps the people pressure has also been mildly mitigated by a further reinforcement of the "new ethic"—the understanding that we must treat wilderness with tender loving care. But although people now pay louder lip service to the concept, most of them have, unfortunately, not yet broadened it to include a comprehension that trail guides and other signpost writings about unfrequented and attractive places infallibly corrupt and probably kill the remoteness and therefore much of the attractiveness. In this edition I have tried to embody, even if only obliquely, all such modulations that the decade has wrought.

I have also restruggled to bring everything else up to date: prices, practices, even prejudices. The illustrator has furnished 64 new and 34 amended new drawings, and has more than kept the faith: no one but me knows how heroically she has grappled. Throughout the book I have again tried to improve any writing that no longer satisfied me. Finally, I have refurbished all appendices, painfully and prodigiously.

But in the end it is the core of the book, the main text, that matters most. When my editor first saw the fruits of my two and a half years' labor, he said, "Why, it's seventy or seventy-five percent new!" And the finished product turns out to have grown from 470 to 647 pages. So I think I can safely claim, once again, that this is a genuine, organic revision.

Yet in a sense nothing I wrote about has changed since the second edition appeared. I do not mean only that my publishers have foiled me again by vetoing, amiably but firmly and no doubt rightly, a new subtitle I was hankering for: "The Pre-ante-penultimate Complete Walker." I do not mean only that although much equipment has mutated, a great deal has not; and that principles of construction persist. Or that techniques evolve only slowly. I mean, as I have said repeatedly, that equipment and techniques are mere means to an end, and the things I was writing toward are timeless. Cloud shadows still scud across sunlit peaks. Fleeing lizards still corner frantically around creosote bushes, flinging out little spurts of sand. I now have another hilltop—different from and yet not different from the flat, grassy one mentioned on page 9—to which I can conveniently drive and walk, and on which I can sit for two days when I need space and beauty and silence so that I can sweep the daily clutter aside and penetrate surfaces and consider what I want to do with the rest of my life; or perhaps only so that I can wrestle with the preface to a new edition of an old book. A few years ago, beside a remote Alaskan river, I met my first moose and then, minutes later, still high from that experience, had a caribou stroll up to within eight paces of where I stood upright and in the open. The caribou eyeballed me with a long and rather glassy stare; then it began to angle slowly away—and I saw the huge, suppurating wound on its haunch, probably bear-inflicted, that had no doubt glazed the poor beast's mind. Just last month, snow-shoeing for a week in the Sierra Nevada, I sat at 10,000 feet, cradled in the silence and softness and harshness of a cupped basin, and watched its rocky slopes as the sun of yet another turning summer beat down from a cloudless sky and began to cleave and slough off into the past, in massive cake chunks, the rich white legacy of what we humans had regarded as an extraordinarily stormy winter. No, if you back off just a little ways, nothing much has changed since I wrote the last edition. Essentially, the old writ stands.

So here, once again, is the old-new book.

C.F.

Summer 1983

WARNING! PRICES

As this edition goes to press in late 1983, prices
are no longer rising quite fast enough to make a
bear blush; but the recent decade-long restlessness could return, and you may have to extrapo-
late from the figures I quote.

WHY WALK?

Now shall I walk
Or shall I ride?
"Ride," Pleasure said:
"Walk," Joy replied.

W. H. Davies

Why Walk?

Sanity is a madness put to good uses.

George Santayana

I had better admit right away that walking can in the end become an addiction, and that it is then as deadly in its fashion as heroin or television or the stock exchange. But even in this final stage it remains a delectable madness, very good for sanity, and I recommend it with passion.

A redeeming feature of the condition is that no matter how heavily you have been hooked you can still get your kicks from very small doses.

Ten minutes' drive from my apartment there is a long, grassy ridge from which you can look out over parkland and sprawling metropolis, over bay and ocean and distant mountains. I often walk along this ridge in order to think uncluttered thoughts or to feel with accuracy or to sweat away a hangover or to achieve some other worthy end, recognized or submerged. And I usually succeed—especially with the thinking. Up there, alone with the wind and the sky and the steep grassy slopes, I nearly always find after a while that I am beginning to think more clearly. Yet "think" does not seem to be quite the right word. Sometimes, when it is a matter of making a choice, I do not believe I decide what to do so much as discover what I have decided. It is as if my mind, set free by space and solitude and oiled by the body's easy rhythm, swings open and releases thoughts it has already formulated. Sometimes, when I have been straining too hard to impose order on an urgent press of ideas, it seems only as if my mind has slowly relaxed; and then, all at once, there is room for the ideas to fall into place in a meaningful pattern.

Occasionally you can achieve this kind of release inside a city. One day some years ago, when I had to leave my car at a garage for an hour's repair work, I spent the time strolling through an industrial area. I crossed a man-made wasteland, then walked up onto a little-used pedestrian bridge over a freeway. Leaning on its concrete parapet, I watched the lines of racing, pounding vehicles. From above they seemed self-propelled, automatic. And suddenly, standing there alone, I found myself looking down on the scene like a visitor from another planet, curiously detached and newly instructed. More recently I have discovered a sandhill near the place I now take my car for repair. This desiccated oasis among encroaching industriana still supports on one flank a couple of windswept pines. Its center cradles dips and hummocks that are smooth and flower-decked. And there, while the twentieth century ministers to my horseless carriage, I can lie and read and lunch and doze, cut off, in a quiet urban wilderness. Most cities offer such veiled delights. In walking, as in sex, there's always a very good chance that you'll find, almost anywhere, given time, something that wows you.

But no one who has begun to acquire the walking habit can restrict himself for long to cities, or even to their parks or less intentional enclaves. First he explores open spaces out beyond the asphalt. Then, perhaps, he moves on to car camping and makes long, exploratory, all-day treks. But in due course he is almost sure to find his dreams outreaching these limitations. "For the human spirit needs places where nature has not been rearranged by the hand of man." One of the joys of being alive today is the complexity of our human world. We have at our fingertips more riches than anyone has ever had: books by the zillion; records and movies and TV by the ton; the opportunity to move around almost as we please. But in time the sheer richness of the complexity can sandbag you. You long for simplicity, for the yin to that yang. You yearn—though you may not openly know it—to take a respite from your eternal wrestling with the abstract and instead to grapple, tight and long and sweaty, with the tangible. So once you have started walking down the right road, you begin, sooner or later, to dream of truly wild places.

At this point you are in danger of meeting a mental block.

Even in these mercifully emancipated decades, many people still seem to become alarmed at the prospect of sleeping away from officially consecrated, car-accommodating campsites, with no more equipment than they can carry on their backs. When pressed, they babble about snakes or bears or even, by God, bandits. But the real barrier, I'm sure, is the unknown.

I came to comprehend the reality of this barrier—or, rather, to recomprehend it—almost twenty years ago, during a four-day walk through some coastal hills. (I was walking, as a matter of fact, in order to sort out ideas and directions for the first edition of this book.) One warm and cloudless afternoon I was resting at a bend in the trail—there was a little triangular patch of shade, I remember, under a rocky bluff—when some unexpected tilt of my mind reexposed a scene that I had completely forgotten. For all the vividness of the vital features, it remained a curiously indistinct scene. I was not at all clear when it had happened, except that it must have been more than fifteen years before.

I still do not even remember for sure whether it happened in Africa or America. But the salient contours stand out boldly. I had come to some natural boundary. It may have been the end of a trail or road, or the fringes of a forest or the rim of a cliff, I no longer know which. But I do know that I felt I had gone as far as a man could go. So I just stood there looking out beyond the edge of the world. Except for a wall of thick, dark undergrowth, I am no longer sure what I saw, but I know it was wild, wild, impossible country. It still looms huge and black and mysterious in the vaults of my memory.

All at once, without warning, two men emerged from that impossible country. They carried packs on their backs, and they were weatherbeaten and distilled to bone and muscle. But what I remember best of all is that they were happy and whole. Whole and secure and content.

I talked to them, briefly and in considerable awe. They had been back deep into the wilderness, they said, away from civilization for a week. "Pretty inaccessible, some of it," admitted one of them. "But there's a lot of beautiful country in there—some of the finest I've ever seen." Then they walked away and I was left, still awestruck, looking out once more into the huge, black, mysterious wilderness.

The awe that I felt that day still hangs in my memory. But my present self dismisses it. I know better. Many times in recent years I have emerged from wild country, happy and whole and secure and content, and have found myself face to face with astonished people who had obviously felt that they were already at the edge of the world; and I know, now I have come to consider the matter, that what I have seen on their faces is exactly what those two men must have seen on mine, many years ago on the edge of that other wilderness. And I know now that the awe is totally unwarranted. There is nothing very difficult about going into such places. All you need is the right equipment, a reasonable competence in using it, a tolerable degree of physical fitness and a clear understanding of your own limitations. Beyond that, all you have to do is overcome the fear of the unknown.*

Once you have overcome the fear of the unknown and thereby

---

* You will see that I tend to write of walking as if it is something that must be done alone. Most people prefer company, and by all reasonable standards they are right. For efficiency and comfort and the rewards of sharing, and above all for safety, a walking party, like a political party, should consist of at least two or three members.

But I like to walk alone. And therefore, when I am being honest, that is how I tend to write. It does not matter, though: if you choose, sensibly, to travel in twos or threes or twenties, just about everything I have to say still applies. You miss something, that's all. You never quite learn, for instance, that one of the riches a wilderness has to offer is prolonged and absolute silence.

There is one notable exception to my rule. When you and your companion are newly in

surmounted your sleeping-out-in-the-wilderness block, you are free. Free
to go out, when the world will let you slip away, into the wildest places
you dare explore. Free to walk from dawn to dusk and then again from
dawn to dusk, with no harsh interruptions, among the quiet and sooth-
ing cathedrals of a virgin forest. Or free to struggle for a week, if that is
what you want at that particular time, toward a peak that has captured
your imagination. Or free, if your needs or fancies of the moment run
that way, to follow a wild river to its source, fishing as you go, or not
fishing. Free, once you have grasped the significance of this other reality,
to immerse yourself for two months in the timeless silence of a huge
desert canyon—and to learn in the end why the silence is not timeless
after all.

But long before the madness has taught you this kind of sanity you
have learned many simple and valuable things.

You start to learn them from the very beginning. First, the comforting constants. The rhythm of boots and walking staff, and their
different inflections on sand and on soil and on rock. The creak of harness
as small knapsack or heavy pack settles back into place after a halt. And
the satisfactions of a taut, controlled body. Then there are the small,
amplified pleasures. In everyday life, taking off your socks is an unnoticed

---

love, the two of you walk with minds interwoven, and the bond enriches everything you see.
And that is the best walking of all.

But be warned that solitude, for all its sweet sound, is not everybody's bag. I know one
woman, very experienced at backpacking in groups, who discovered that when she at last
ventured out on her own, as she had long been dreaming of doing, she was too nervous to
sleep more than fitfully. And when she told other people about her fear she found that a
surprising number of them shared it. Several, faced with the reality, the first night out from
roadhead, got the shakes and hightailed for home. Some people seemed to feel the problem
was almost universal. One man commented that "even Colin Fletcher says he takes two or
three nights to get over it." This is a masterpiece of misinformation. I have my fears, but
sleeping alone in wilderness is not one of them. Very much the reverse.

Then there are those who only talk solitude. Not long ago, traveling cross-country at
10,000 feet in the Sierra Nevada, following a faint game trail and a train of thought that I'd
been trying to board for a long time, I met a young couple strolling near their rockbound
lakeside camp. They crowded around me—which takes some doing when you have only two
bodies at your command—and began talking. Wasn't it wonderful up here away from
everybody? So peaceful. Why, only yesterday they'd been on the main trail, over the other
side of that crest, and they'd met fourteen people inside of two hours. Fourteen! That was
simply too crowded, so they'd struck away from the trail. And now it was wonderful, being
out here on their own. Why, I was the first person they'd seen all day. . . . I began to ease
on around the lake. My companions eased with me, still talking. Hoping to catch up with
the fast-vanishing train of thought, I dropped a couple of hints. They fell on stony ground.
When, in desperation, I was gently but firmly explicit, my companions looked surprised,
almost shocked—and sorely disappointed.

Although "solitude" and "loneliness" describe identical physical conditions, the mental
states stand poles apart.

chore; peeling them off after a long day's walk is sheer delight. At home a fly is something that makes you wonder how it got into the house; when you are lying sprawled out on a sandbar beside a remote river you can recognize a fly as something to be studied and learned from—another filament in the intricate web of the world. Or it may be a matter of mere money: five days beyond the last stain of man, you open the precious little package of blister-cushioning felt pads that is marked "$1.29" and discover, tucked away inside, a forgotten and singularly useless $20 bill. Yet two days later you may find your appetite suddenly sharp for civilized comforts that a week earlier had grown flat and stale. Once, toward the end of a week's exploration of a remote headwater basin, I found my heart melting at the thought of hot buttered toast for breakfast. And in the final week of a summer-long walk I even found myself recalling with nostalgia the eternal city hunt for parking.

But well before such unexpected hankerings arise, your mind as well as your body has been honed. You have re-remembered that happiness can have something to do with simplicity. And so, by slow degrees, you regain a sense of harmony with everything you move through—rock and soil, plant and tree and cactus, spider and fly and rattlesnake and coyote, drop of rain and racing cloud shadow. (You have long ago out-grown the crass assumption that the world was made for man.) After a while you find that you are gathering together the whole untidy but glorious mishmash of sights and sounds and smells and touches and tastes and emotions that tumble through your recent memory. Then you begin to connect these ciphers, one with the other. And once you begin to connect, only to connect, nothing can stop you—not even those rare moments of blackness (when all, all is vanity) that can come even in the wilderness.

When you get back at last from the simple things to the complexities of the outside, walled-in man-world you find that you are once more eager to grapple with them. For a while you even detect a meaning behind all the complexity. And that of course is the way it has to be. We are creatures of our time; we cannot escape it. The simple life is not a substitute, only a corrective.

For a while, I said, you detect new meanings. For a while. That is where the hell comes in. In due course the hot buttered toast tastes like damp sawdust again and the parking hassle is once more driving you crazy and the concrete jabs at your eyes and the din and the dirt sicken you, and all at once you realize that there is no sense to be discovered, anywhere, in all the frantic scurryings of the city. And you know there is only one thing to do. You are helplessly trapped. Hooked. Because you know now that you have to go back to the simple things.

You struggle, briefly. But as soon as the straight-line world will let you slip away, or a little sooner, you go. You go in misery, with delight, full of confidence. For you know that you will immerse yourself in the harmonies—and will return to see the meanings.

This is why I recommend walking so passionately. It is an altogether positive and delectable addiction.

Naturally, not everyone understands.

A smooth and hypersatisfied young man once boasted to me that he had just completed a round-the-world sightseeing tour in seventy-nine days. In one jet-streamed breath he scuttled from St. Peter's, Rome, via the Pyramids, to a Cambodian jungle temple. "That's the way to travel," he said. "You see everything important."

When I suggested that the way to see important things was to walk, he almost dropped his martini.

Walking can even provoke an active opposition lobby. For many years now I have been told with some regularity that by walking out and away I am "escaping from reality." I admit that the statement puts me on the defensive. Why, I ask myself (and sometimes my accusers as well) are people so ready to assume that chilled champagne is more "real" than water drawn from an ice-cold mountain creek? Or a dusty sidewalk than a carpet of desert dandelions? Or a Boeing 747 than a flight of graceful white pelicans soaring in unison against the sunrise? Why, in other words, do people assume that the acts and emotions and values that stem from city life are more real than those that arise from the beauty and the silence and the solitude of wilderness?

For me, the thing touched bottom when I was gently accused of escapism during a TV interview about a book I had written on a length-of-California walk. Frankly, I fail to see how going for a six-month, thousand-mile walk through deserts and mountains can be judged less real than spending six months working eight hours a day, five days a week, in order to earn enough money to be able to come back to a comfortable home in the evening and sit in front of a TV screen and watch the two-dimensional image of some guy talking about a book he has written on a six-month, thousand-mile walk through deserts and mountains.

As I said, I get put on the defensive. The last thing I want to do is to knock champagne and sidewalks and Boeing 747s. Especially champagne. These things distinguish us from the other animals. But they can also limit our perspectives. And I suggest that they—and all the stimulating complexities of modern life—begin to make more sense, to take on surer meaning, when they are viewed in perspective against the more certain and more lasting reality from which they have evolved—from the underpinning reality, that is, of mountain water and desert flowers and soaring white birds at sunrise.

Here endeth the lesson.

But perhaps you are an unbeliever and need proof—a no-nonsense, show-me-some-practical-results kind of proof.

I can tell you now that I have had an unholy awful time with this introductory chapter.* I wrote it a dozen times, over a period of several months, and a dozen times it utterly refused to say what I wanted it to say. In the end I drove an hour out of town, parked the car on a dirt road, heaved the pack onto my back, walked for another hour, and then camped on the flat, grassy summit of a familiar hill. That was two evenings ago. I am still there. In front of me the long grass is billowing like the sea. Far beyond it and far below sprawls the city. It is very gray. But here on my hilltop there is only the grass and the wind and the sky.

From time to time since I climbed up here I have strolled around my domain. Once I went down a few hundred feet with the pack on my back and filled all four canteens at a spring. But mostly I have sat up here in the shade of my poncho awning. I have looked at the billowing grass. I have looked beyond it at the sprawling gray city and have listened to the roar from a freeway that feeds it. I have consulted with a number of hawks, mice, beetles and trees. And this morning—after two nights and one day of bitter, bitter struggle and many, many words—I suddenly relaxed and began to write. I do not say that I am yet satisfied with what I have written. But I think it will do.

I am down off my hilltop now, but before we move on to consider the ways and means of walking I must point out two pitfalls that you should bear in mind, always—or as always as you can manage.

First, make sure the ways and means remain just that. They will always be threatening to take over. They will tend, particularly at the start of a trip, to imprison your thoughts on a treadmill of trivial worries: "Is that a blister forming on my right heel?"; "If the storm breaks, will that little tarp really keep me dry all night?"; "My God, is the water going to last out?" And any sudden small problem is liable to inflate without warning and fill the horizons of your tight little world. It all sounds very silly, I know; but anyone who has traveled on foot, especially alone, will recognize the syndrome. I should like to report that experience cures such nonsense. Unfortunately, it doesn't. It helps; it helps a

---

* I have let this little story stand as it appeared in the first edition, because that is the way it happened, sort of inside the book.

lot. But I still find, especially on long trips with a sharp physical challenge, that I need at least a few days of "shakedown cruise." On a two-month journey I once made through Grand Canyon it took me all of two weeks to break free.

Whether you like it or not, the trivia are always there. Never underrate them: either you subdue them or they subdue you. A single blister can blacken the most shining day. And if you are miles from anywhere, soaked through and shivering and with no confidence in your ability to contrive a warm, dry shelter for the night, you will be deaf to the music of raindrops drumming against your poncho and blind to the beauty of clouds swirling around sawtooth peaks.

The important thing, then, about running your tight little outdoor economy is that it must not run you. You must learn to deal with the practical details so efficiently that they become second nature. Then, after the unavoidable shakedown period, you leave yourself free to get on with the important things—watching cloud shadows race across a mountainside or passing the time of day with a hummingbird or discovering that a grasshopper eats grass like spaghetti or sitting on a peak and thinking of nothing at all except perhaps that it is a wonderful thing to sit on a peak and think of nothing at all.*

The second pitfall is more subtly camouflaged. Naturally, your opinions on equipment and technique must never fossilize into dogma: your mind must remain open to the possibilities of better gear and to new and easier ways of doing things. You try to strike a balance, of course—to operate efficiently and yet to remember, always, that the practical details are only a means to an end. But I am not altogether convinced that after years and years of it—when you have at last succeeded in mastering most of the business and people have begun to call you an expert and someone may even ask you to write a book on the subject—I am not at all sure that it is then possible to avoid the sobering discovery that you have become, ex officio, a very tolerably accomplished fuddy-duddy.

If you recognize these minor pitfalls and are careful and lucky, so that you don't tumble into them too often, you will discover as the years pass that walking becomes a beautiful, warm, round pumpkin that sits up on a shelf, always ready to be taken down. There are moments, sure, when you worry if time hasn't tamed it, just a touch. Moments when you fret that perhaps it has turned into something safer, like a self-

* It would probably be a good thing if you reread this paragraph at least once—and tried to remember it. This is essentially a "know-how" book, but we must never lose sight of the fact that what matters in the end is the "feel-how" of walking.

replenishing bank account. But most of the time, when you look up and see it sitting there on the shelf, waiting, it remains round and warm, a magical thing to have around the place. You wonder, sometimes, what in God's name you would have done with your life if you had failed to fall victim to the addiction.

It wouldn't be the same round and personal pumpkin, of course, if you hadn't grown it yourself. Because in the beginning it was not like that at all.

In the beginning, for one thing, there was all that worrying before-hand about the damned equipment. The hassle could smother the important things, the things that mattered. It could even screen them off when you thought you had left the man-world far behind. But as time went on you got better at that game. The things that mattered would gleam and flash sooner, more and more often, more and more momentously: sunrise behind Spanish moss; aching feet in a cool, caressing creek; a moose, chomping knee-deep in marsh, that in profile had been a harmless and rather comic creature but that suddenly swung its head up, alert, and looked directly at you and instantly became a very large and very serious and potentially menacing citizen; or that focused moment in which a perfectly ordinary scrub jay decamped from an oak limb, refolded its wings, like the scarabs, and as silently swooped away—blue and smooth-gray and white, at ease and elegant, provoking you to sudden envy.

As the years rolled by, your ground-rule worries faded. You fretted less and less not only about equipment but about just where you'd go and how long it would take and where you'd camp. You still took care, mind. Still went carefully through your checklist beforehand—for long trips, went through twice, maybe three times. Still retained a habit of watchful but nonparanoid attention to detail. But you always knew, now, with more than thin logic, that these were only means. And you were able, easily and naturally, to go out longer, higher, remoter, farther into what was once jeopardy. So there were glaciers and deep desert canyons and mountaintops with views to the edge of the planet, of yourself.

Perhaps, if you found it suited you, you learned about solitude. Real solitude. Not the kind with two or ten or twenty other tarps strung up beyond the next tree bole. Not the kind where for half the day you talk with other humans instead of with the rest of the world, with yourself. But the kind where you feel cheated if you meet more than two people a week, a bit bruised if you have to exchange more than one-word greetings. The kind in which you learn about silence and peace and the wider circles.

You still don't do silly things, of course—whether you decide that solitude is for you or not. As the years go by, in fact, you play it closer and closer. You still checklist equipment, preview the mountain cold or desert heat, and finger the five-day forecast; and you take fewer and fewer risks, particularly when you're on your own. But you know a bit more about what you're doing now, so you are freer for the things that matter, for the meanings. They are still the same: the roughness of granite; good, clean, voluntary sweating, unprodded by money or other master; a big-horn materializing out of mist, momentarily close and understood, weathered gray and green, sagacious, magnificent; or just sunlight slant-ing through junipers. Still the same. But you know how to reach them now.

For in the end it is always there, sitting up on the shelf, round and warm and shining, waiting to be taken down. The flat, logical sector of you tends to think of it as therapy. So sometimes, as I say, you wonder if the years haven't tamed it a touch. But you know, if you stop to think, that at any moment, just when you least expect it, a lily or a thunder-storm or a moose, or just more sunlight slanting through different juni-pers, will tingle you into goose pimples. Or a rockface or river, a snake or sudden snowstorm will up and scare the arse off you—to the immense benefit of your little universe. So it's never really tamed, thank God. And it's always sitting up there on the shelf—that big, beautiful pump-kin—just waiting for you to wave the wand and turn it into something much more magical than a carriage.

HOUSE ON YOUR BACK

Meticulously organized, the flower of complex and collective thought, the loaded pack—like the space module—is fully a vehicle of our century's last quarter, and sits squarely on contemporary shoulders.

Bruce Berger,
The Mountain Gazette

Ground Plan

As long as you restrict your walking to one-day hikes you are unlikely to face any very ponderous problems of equipment or technique. Everything you need can be stuffed into pockets or if necessary into a convenient little pouch slung from waist or shoulders. And if something should get left behind, why, home is always waiting at the end of the day's road. But as soon as you start sleeping out you simply have to carry some kind of

A house on your back.

Obviously, there is a difference between the kind of house you need to carry for a soft, summer weekend in the woods and for a month or more in wild mountain country. But it is convenient and entirely possible to devise a standard structure that you can modify to suit a broad range of conditions. In past editions I tried to instruct mainly by describing in detail the fairly full-scale edifice, very simply modifiable, that I had evolved over a considerable number of years. If some of the architecture seemed too elaborate for your needs, all you had to do was simplify toward harmony with those needs. Similarly, I discussed most techniques as they applied to trips of at least a weekend. Often I talked in terms of more ambitious journeys. And again, if my suggestions were too intricate for what you had in mind, you simply simplified.

Basically, my method stands. But things have grown more complicated. The range of equipment now available means that my house tends to get more markedly modified for different kinds of trips than it did in the past. I'm certainly more likely to switch from one kind of pack to another—thereby altering not only what goes inside but some details of how I operate. And the sheer volume of new and mutating gear means that I can no longer try out a representative cross-section. It has therefore become necessary for me to discuss, rather more often than in earlier editions, equipment I have not adequately tested.

In spite of these changes the book remains highly subjective—a book that will give many experienced walkers a whole slew of satisfying chances to snort with disagreement. And I make no apologies. For backpacking is a highly subjective business. What matters to me is what suits me; but what matters to you is what suits you. So when I describe what I have found best, try to remember that I am really saying that there are no truly objective criteria, and the important thing in the end is not what I or some other so-called expert happens to use or do, but what you find best. Even prejudice has its place: a technique or piece of equipment that you have devised yourself is much more satisfying to use than an "import"—and in your hands it may well prove more efficient. In fact, the whole game lacks really set rules. Two equally experienced backpackers may under the same conditions carry markedly different gear. I am always being amazed at the very wide variation in the ways people operate. Again, one of the most important things for a backpacker to be able to do is extemporize—mostly in the field but sometimes even in planning. And extemporizing is something that cannot really be taught— though the right mindbent can, I think, be encouraged. Given all this, then, the most a book can do is suggest guidelines.*

Guidelines are all I can offer for another reason too:

The current state of the mart.

In 1968 I wrote in the first edition of this book that backpacking was "in a stimulating if mildly confusing state of evolution—or perhaps I mean revolution—in both design and materials" and also in distribution methods. In the second edition I noted that "the ev- or rev-olution continues." Now the process has spun into high gear. Bootmaking has begun to throw off century-old traditions. Cold-weather clothes are slanting out in new directions. So is raingear. And almost all fabrics—for tents, sleeping bags and packs as well as clothing—are now stronger and lighter and come with more effective coatings. Drastic changes have swept through the peripheries too, from compasses to flashlights.

All this not only means that my choices and practices, like many people's, are presently in a state of flux; it also means that some of my solemn, carefully updated advice will soon be outmoded yet again. That matters less than it may seem to. Although I shall often be describing

---

* Frankly, my advice to those genuinely interested in walking has always been to forget the books and to get out and get on with it, relying on the two finest teachers in the business —trial and error. I'm not at all sure a piece of me doesn't still stand by that advice.

specific items, the essence will lie not so much in the items themselves as in the principles that govern choice—those vital factors an intelligent backpacker should keep his eyes skinned for.

Custom suggests that I avoid trade names. But only by discussing brands and models can I adequately indicate the details. And if I recommend one pack or jacket over another it is because I find it suits my needs better, not because, for crying out loud, I'm mad at Mr. Madden or starry-eyed for Ms. Moonstone.

In the past decade the giddy pace of product evolution has wrought something like a quantum change among manufacturers and retailers—from the roots up. Ten years ago equipment was still mostly made and sold by backpackers with a flair for design or retailing who had come to learn the manufacturing or selling business as a necessity. They might have become very efficient in their niche but somehow they seemed to remain backpackers rather than manufacturers or salesmen. Today that is not necessarily so. Even oldtimers have had to swing with the tide. Their talk now reverberates with such phrases as "company philosophy" and "the industry"—which means "the backpacking industry" or even, by God, "the wilderness industry." Reaction to a new, seminal notion is less likely to be "Hey, that's a great idea for a piece of equipment, let's go build it" than "But how about its marketability right now?" The criterion for continued production is not "It works best" but "It sells these days." These mercenary factors always weighed, of course. They had to. But the shift of emphasis has been radical. I for one find the mutation sad, going on nauseating. It is not always easy to pin down just what sticks in the craw—though the Golden Age of Sententious Crap can be pretty hard to take. (Mind you, not even the advertising hype is all-pervading. Why, just the other day I saw an ad for a bandanna that did not claim it was being tested on Mount Everest.) These changes are perceived and often regretted by those who appear to be happily embedded in the industry. "Something has been lost," one of them said to me recently. "The bigness and the dominance of economics have killed something. There used to be . . . oh, a sense of adventure." On a purely intellectual level, of course, results have often been beneficial. Fierce competition has generated more varied products of keener design at a larger number of sources. Technological and workmanship standards have, by and large, risen to new high levels. The pressure is so great that virtually every product niche has been filled and you are pretty sure to be able to find something appropriate to your particular needs. In fact, it's now easy to find good equipment, while to pick up really bad stuff you almost have to put your mind to it, at least in reputable "mountain shops"—that pleasant and useful misnomer for "backpacking stores." Of course, some models are better than others—and probably more expensive. In other words, we are better served—economically, anyway. This state of affairs is known, I understand, as capitalism.

The organizations that implement capitalism inevitably reflect, in their natures and structures, the sea changes of the past decade (though "reflect" may possibly be the wrong word). I do not mean only internal adjustments, such as a growing tendency to concentrate corporate energies on production and to rely for technical design, especially of such complicated items as tents, on outside consultants—who may also design for competitors. The most far-reaching change has been the rush to conglomeration (a.k.a. merging). General Mills, for example, bought Eddie Bauer, Franklin Mint absorbed Eastern Mountain Sports—and were in turn absorbed by Warner Communications. Meanwhile, Johnson's Wax ingested Camp Trails (packs), Eureka (tents), Silva (compasses) and Holubar (down gear and wide-spectrum retail)—though they have now disgorged Holubar onto The North Face.*

I guess conglomeration benefits somebody: the trend continues. But I find it increasingly difficult to enthuse. Ski Hut–Trailwise for many years offered perhaps the fullest range of backpacking equipment, and were pace-setters. In 1974 Boss Glove Company of Illinois took them over. The Ski Hut declined, dropped their prestigious catalogue and countrywide mail-order service, and were eventually sold to a general sporting-goods chain. The name persists, but the place is no longer a real mountain shop or of much interest to backpackers. Trailwise, the manufacturing branch, though maintaining their high quality standards, have for years produced very little new—though there are signs that this may change. Sierra Designs, conglomerated in 1973 by Charles M. Leighton, an investment corporation, have undergone similar travails—though their tents have remained in the forefront of innovation. Other conglomerees have quavered too. You can argue, of course, that the take-overs did not cause the quaverings. And you may be right. Yet misgivings often surface from within. "One trouble is," an executive of a conglom-

---

* "They," referring to "Johnson's Wax," is no accident. I regularly peeve at radio commercials that bellow: "Snodgrass Chevrolet (or Fat Foods or Moron Mountaineering) *is* offering *their* latest . . ." Agreed, a company can be singular or plural: there's something to be said on both sides. But to switch decisions in midsentence seems gratuitously fickle, going on feeble-minded. And in this book I propose to do something about it: I shall make all companies consistently plural. My missionary effort will no doubt fail, but at least I will have tried.

I recognize that my constructions may clang in certain ears, especially with such upcoming toughies as the singularly singular Ski Hut. If your ears suffer, feel free to dismiss the whole thing as the pedantic quibble of an ex-Limey who, after a quarter-century of happy Americanization, remains imperfectly detribalized.

By the way, if you find you're damned well not interested in details of what goes on in "the industry," skip to "Helpful literature," page 22.

erated outfit said to me recently, "that the *big* decisions get made by people who are not backpackers."*

The few sizable firms that remain independent seem to have prospered. But if they grow markedly they too often begin to suffer—from the confusion that sheer size can bring. Beyond a certain point the company's energies can become dissipated. The best available minds tend to lose sight of consumers' use of the end-product and to become bogged down in such administrative problems as warehousing (which can loom huge) or even, in the most enlightened firms, in ways to subvert these barriers to efficiency that bigness spawns. As in most fields, though, bigness can work. Provided the organization stays nonsclerotic, it can keep costs down as well as build up valuable experience. In fact, some makers of good or even excellent equipment go under, or at least feel the pinch, because big buy-in-bulk outfits outsell them with products that may be inferior. But a small, specialized company drawing its energy from the dream of a single obsessed and energetic individual can still thrive remarkably—provided it maintains high quality. Specialization has its own pitfalls, though. Its products may, as a competitor testily remarked, "move a step beyond practicality and verge on trickery."

It is not easy to translate these generalizations into specifics, naming names. And I don't mean only that the situation fluctuates daily. It is difficult to avoid comparing apples and oranges, packs and parkas. Some major retailers sell only direct, others mainly by mail order; others may manufacture as well, mainline or on the side. Again, some manufacturers do not retail at all, while some sell wholly or mostly under other people's labels (here, the interfaces can get pretty incestuous). Then there is a whole casserole of specialists, often unclassifiable, even *sui generis*. And in all this salmagundi, size and success and quality do not necessarily bear any discernible relationship to each other.

Still, I suppose I must attempt a summary—even though nobody is likely to agree with all my classifications.

I would guess that most backpacking equipment is still sold direct, through small, local, one- or two-store companies. But in the West there are two big retailers: The North Face, with 16 stores (including those still labeled Holubar), and Recreational Equipment Incorporated (REI), a Seattle cooperative that now has eight stores between Anchorage and Minneapolis (and recently swallowed Mountain Safety Research and began to boost the manufacturing side, accenting innovation). In the

---

* Freeman Dyson, in *Disturbing the Universe,* detected the same process in the designing of nuclear reactors—and saw therein the real roots of the industry's present problems: ". . . the fun went out of the business. The adventurers, the experimenters, the inventors, were driven out, and the accountants and managers took control."

East the dominant retailer is Eastern Mountain Sports (EMS), now with twenty-one stores, including an emigrant in Denver. REI and EMS operate extensive mail-order services. So do L. L. Bean in the East and Eddie Bauer out West, though both are generalists with only one foot in backpacking. Eddie Bauer now have twenty-nine stores, coast-to-coast and Canada. North Face's mail-order business is small, but they are now probably the biggest makers of a wide range of backpacking gear, and tops among major suppliers to the industry. Others, in addition to Trailwise and Sierra Designs, include Wilderness Experience (first company in the industry to "go public") and Camp 7—and also JanSport (always striving to improve) and Kelty, both moving again after languishing in doldrums. On the fringe of this group stand Marmot Mountain Works (determined innovators), Sierra West and Alpenlite (both emerging fast from specialization into a broad range of ultralightweight equipment), and Black Ice (innovative tents, sleeping bags and clothing, primarily for mountaineering, much of it made overseas). Somewhere between broad-spectrum and specialization stand two very different outfits: Stephenson of New Hampshire, long producers of high-quality idiosyncratic equipment; and the relatively new Peak 1 division of the old-established Coleman Company (except for the popular Peak 1 stove, their gear still appears more often in upper-level sporting-goods stores than in mountain shops). The long and constantly changing list of specialists embraces subspecies ranging from major producers to little one-man outfits and from highest-quality innovators to almost unabashed commercial copycats. The spectrum includes, in various fields: packs— Gregory, Lowe, Madden, Camp Trails, Adventure 16, Caribou, Dolt, Synergy Works (back in business after defunction) and Antelope; tents —Moss and Eureka!; sleeping bags and/or quilted garments—Moonstone (who also produce excellent vapor-barrier and other severe-weather gear), Blue Puma and Bristlecone, and three more small outfits that welcome special orders, Down Home (superb, spare-no-pains-or-expense quality), Western Mountaineering ("We'll do anything if someone's got a valid project for us") and Bugaboo ("We'll custom-make any gear for outsize people"); clothing—Patagonia, Robbins, Alpine Adventure (mainly mountaineering) and Mark Pack Works (high-quality pile clothing as well as packs). There are also many other small specialist firms with little present impact. But remember that this is how most giants began. Wholesalers of importance, whose own labels sometimes appear on their goods, include Chouinard Equipment (mainly mountaineering), Donner Mountain Corporation (DMC) (boots and clothing), and Liberty, Pacific Mountain Sports and Coughlan's of Canada (accessories). Then there are what have been called the "lifestyle purveyors": Early Winters and The Yak Works, whose retail mail-order offerings include interesting and often new backpackish items.

The do-it-yourself field, after a period of boom, has sharply contracted. Frostline, sole major survivors, have cut their far-flung stores to four—three in Colorado, one in Minnesota; and although their continuing mail-order service still offers some backpacking gear (and also such raw materials as Cordura fabric [page 122]), it now concentrates on general outerwear. I have never grappled with a do-it-yourself kit of any kind, but there seems to be a reasonable consensus that if you are on the all-thumbs sewing team you might be wise to conscript a pinch hitter; that if you know how to operate a sewing machine you should be able to cope with a relatively simple challenge like a down vest; but that for such creations as sleeping bags you need unlimited time and patience, a genius's infinite capacity for staking pins, and—above all—an ability to follow written instructions accurately and to the last letter.

In some cities there are "swap shops" at which you can trade or buy used backpacking gear.

For boot repairers, see page 74; for food suppliers, Appendix II, page 614.

Outfits that offer logistical support to backpackers seem to come and go. But Stow-A-Way Industries of Massachusetts (see Food Suppliers, Appendix II) continue to mail prearranged food packages to convenient post offices for people making extended trips along the Appalachian Trail and elsewhere.

For details of many firms I have mentioned, and others, see Appendix II—a list of retailers throughout the United States and Canada who specialize or deal extensively in backpacking equipment and maintain countrywide mail-order services.

Many of the firms listed in Appendix II issue catalogues. In the second edition of this book I described the best of them as "quite a phenomenon." I have just thumbed through the batch filed away years ago for comparison in the rewriting of this paragraph—and I find that "phenomenon" was right. Especially sumptuous were the encylopedic works of art and instruction issued by EMS from 1971 through '74. But such creations are now memories (though a recent Early Winters issue, with its 24-page magazine section, was a heart-warming innovation). The Ski Hut catalogue, for many years the standard, has gone. The current EMS offerings * have joined the vast majority that reek of slick merchandising techniques. They're often indexless, for example: ruffled, you have to riffle. No doubt they sell stuff, but they're no longer seminal

* *Later:* Their Fall '83 catalogue shows a welcome if only partial healing.

sources of ideas and information. Perhaps the litmus tests for usefulness to backpackers, if not to sales managers, are—apart from a really full listing of equipment—the presence of an index and of weights for each item. REI's catalogue still qualifies. So does Campmor's—even more richly, in spite of its unsumptuous format. (I have used their latest as source for many quoted prices—with REI's as general backup.)

The catalogues of general outdoor merchandisers such as L. L. Bean mostly retain their character; but I find the decline at the specialist summit a sad minor straw in the onsetting wind of the Industrial Devolution.

Catalogues, of course, are only the beginning of the

Helpful literature.

In the last fifteen years backpacking has drawn upon itself a demilibrary of new books. Many of them try, roughly speaking, to do what this book tries to do. I shall not attempt to review them. After all, only a fool would accept me as a disinterested critic. If you covet a list— exhaustive to the numbing point—of books and pamphlets, ancient and modern, on walking and allied matters, write to *Walking News* (see Appendix II, New York), enclosing $.20 for postage, for a free copy of the condensed version of *The Great Outdoors Book List* (499 titles).

The magazine field has contracted sharply.

From its birth in 1973 until its engulfment by Ziff-Davis in 1979, *Backpacker* Magazine stood as something close to the backpacker's periodical "bible," a handsome, beautifully produced magazine with well-researched and often provocative articles and equipment reports—though it soon scrapped its original policy of *not* telling people where to go. But conglomeration corrupted it. After the first sickness there was some recovery, and today it shows signs of what may be the bloom of full health. I hear in mountain stores, though, that few people now come to shop, as they often did, with it tucked under their arms. And I'm appalled to see in a recent issue an ad for a fat-tired cross-country motorcycle designed to take you "across sand dunes and streams . . . or up to sharp gullies." * ($2.95 a copy. Subscription: $16 a year, six issues; P.O.

---

* Prediction: The world being what it is, do not look for ecstatic reviews of this revised book in *Backpacker*. But I must acknowledge a continuing debt to the magazine for helping keep me up-to-date on equipment changes, especially in the realm of small, often nonessential delectables. I must also point out once again that there is one task that such magazines as *Backpacker* can perform better than anyone else—at least in a narrow and time-restricted way. There are now so many models of equipment items, and they change so fast, that, as I have

Box 2784, Boulder, CO 80322.) *Backpacker* is not widely available in libraries. In California, for example, only 10 libraries out of 500 list it —and rarely from the first issue. But you can get electrostatic copies, at a price, from University Microfilms International, Article and Issue Reprint Dept., 33 North Zeeb Road, Ann Arbor, MI 48106: $.20 a page, but minimum order $20.

Many other magazines have, since OPEC, folded their presses and silently faded away. Sadly, that includes the literate, unglossy, unhidebound *Mountain Gazette.** Also *Camping Journal* and *Better Camping.* And *Wilderness Camping* was swallowed by *Backpacker.* Among those that dealt with the outdoors in general and backpacking as part of it, *Adventure Travel* was also Ziff-Davised, then sickened and died, while *Mariah* merged with *Outside*—which also consumed *Backpacking Journal.*

Outside remains perhaps the most vital survivor. Its scope runs from solo Atlantic crossings through hang-gliding to cycling. But the backpacking component, though minor, is generally good, imaginative, realistic, well-researched stuff. And it reflects a healthy, informed attitude toward the earth.

Nationally, the old stalwart magazines—*Field & Stream* & Co.— have always run occasional backpacking articles. And at least one local backpackers' newsletter has prospered and grown. *Signpost* (started 1966) is now published monthly. It concentrates on Washington State but also covers news and trails of neighboring states and provinces. It maintains an "Outdoor Bookstore" and a formidable list of hiking and similar clubs, and of businesses, government agencies and individuals concerned with trails. (Subscription, which includes sundry side benefits: $16 a year; $28 two years. Editor: Ann Marshall, 16812 36th Avenue W., Lynnwood, WA 98036.)

There are, I believe, a number of local commercial outdoor publi-

---

already suggested, one man can no longer pretend to have meaningful experience with even a representative selection. And interested and competent groups who could and sometimes do produce books tend to be beholden in some way to a manufacturer or distributor, or at least a region. A book has a built-in time lag, anyway. But a magazine, with a staff at its command, and timeliness an ever-present spur, can conduct a somewhat objective and vaguely scientific survey of many models and maybe make some kind of sense. *Backpacker* has long done just that with most equipment items. I'm by no means happy that walking—our simple, delightful, intended-to-be-liberating-from-the-straightline-coordinates-of-civilization pastime—should have reached this pass, but there it is.

I hasten to add that one experienced man may still be well qualified to describe in detail the equipment he uses—not necessarily to make you buy any particular model, but to point out important things to look for. And I regard that as a valid alternative instructional approach. Hell, I have to.

* *Later:* News just received that *Mountain Gazette* hopes to re-surface in May 1984 as a bimonthly, minimum 48 pages ($2 a copy, $10 a year; Box 307, Crested Butte, CO 81224).

cations, coast-to-coast, but some of them, insofar as they recognize back-packing, are liable to do so by offering the impossible. One invites you to learn about "a little-used trail . . . a virtually *unknown* backpacking area . . . uncrowded trails just a short drive from [a major metropolis]." This is stupid, destructive claptrap: if it's true and anyone reads it, it will no longer be true.

Two rather surprising sources of information about new equipment are the trade magazines *NOON* (National Outdoor Outfitters News), published in Illinois, and *Outdoor Retailer,* published in California. Though written purely for "the industry," their words often filter out to "consumers": a salesman may quote and display a copy—or be called away and leave it on the counter, irresistible browse-bait.

There remain two other sources that are neither magazines nor exactly books.

The Next Whole Earth Catalog (608 pages, weighs a ton, $14, Sausalito, CA, 1980) is hysteron-proteron successor to *The Last WEC.* It again offers nutritious and delightful "access to tools." The 62-page "Nomadics" section subheads into not only Outdoor Gear, Camp Skills, Foraging, Survival, Expeditions and Trout Fishing but also Mountains, Winter, Alaska, Knots, Hunting, Knives and Mushrooms.

The new and enlarged *Explorers Ltd. Source Book* (Harper and Row, NY, 1977, 413 pages, half a ton, $13.95) devotes 32 pages specifically to Backpacking but many more to such ancillary matters as Wilderness Areas and Trails, Pathfinding, Provisioning in the Field, First Aid and Medicine, Survival and Photography.

Books on backpacking with children

As a firsthand authority I rank right up there with W. C. Fields; so all I can legitimately offer—beyond a few scattered thoughts (see index) —are book recommendations. They are mostly secondhand recommendations too—though from people who seem to know what they're talking about. For basics: *Backpacking with Babies and Small Children* by Goldie Silverman (Signpost Books, Edmonds, WA, 1975, 6 ounces, $5.95); *Backpacking with Small Children* by James and Ann Stout (T. Y. Crowell, NY, 1975, 16 ounces, $7.95), and *Starting Small in the Wilderness: The Sierra Club Outdoors Guide for Families* by Marlyn Doan (1979, 11½ ounces, $6.95). I've looked through *Kid Camping from Aaaaii to Zip* by Patrick F. McManus (Lothrop, Lee and Shepard, NY, 1979, 16 ounces, $7.25) and found it full of good fun and some wisdom. For metabasics, I got one ecstatic personal rave about *Sharing Nature with Children: A Parents and Teachers Nature Awareness Guide Book* by Joseph Bharat Cornell (Ananda Pubs., Nevada City, CA, 1979, 6 ounces,

$4.95): "The games honestly do teach intuitive awareness . . . a real eye-opener . . . makes learning fun—and really makes it sink in."

Come to think of it, I do have one shred of advice to offer—culled from observations of friends. As in certain other pursuits, the first time is supremely important. So when you plan that initial outing with the kids, set yourself ridiculously low logistical targets. If they have to slog along all day, and arrive at camp wet and tired with no time for their accustomed play, they'll probably never want to go again. But if the first day turns out to be a gentle stroll with little or no load (beyond a token for pride) and plenty of rest hours for cowboys and Indians or Star-warring or whatever, then they'll likely ask for more—and may eventually shed the play brought in from the outside world and discover the delights of the new world around them.

The current state of the Ms.

Very few women now regard themselves as second-class backpackers. And rightly so. They apparently buy around 70 percent of backpacking clothing—though not necessarily all for backpacking. Much of the advertising now courts them. Many makers—notably Patagonia in clothing and Lowe in packs—have made efforts to fit them. And "fit" is the crux: function, not fancy fashion pandering, is what women backpackers want and are now getting—though difficulties linger with pack yokes and boots. They have also gotten several books by and for women backpackers, such as *The Backpacking Woman* by Lynn Thomas (Doubleday, NY, 1980, 11 ounces, $6.95). Yet the demand for these books, say the mountain shops, is small. The reason given: there is really not all that much difference between backpacking for women and for men. Of course. The barrier was mainly in the mind. There have long been plenty of women who backpacked because they wanted to, did so very happily, thank you, and were fully accepted by all except dyed-in-the-down male-chauvinist pigs. And now, after a rough interlude, we are, thank God, pretty well past the stage of the true-believing female-chauvinist sows. They have played their role. Women are back into being wonderful women instead of pale copies of us overrated men. Along the way they have learned, en sort of masse, that if they want to they can backpack. (As if anyone with any sense ever doubted it.) In other words, they have liberated themselves from the walls of their own expectations. That is no mean achievement. Would that we all succeeded, up and down our prisons. For the rest follows.

And now, after that interval of pulpiting—which will surely earn me neckloads of new true-believing enemies—what about this book? As in the past, I can only say, fondly, that everything I write applies equally to both men and women. Well, almost everything. And almost equally. See page 393. And 541.

Women are certainly not short-changed in one relatively new back-packing field:

Schools and seminars.

It's not just that they are as a matter of course encouraged to participate; many seminars and at least one school are tailored specifically for them. And, as far as I know, the rest welcome both sexes.

The seminars—and to some extent the schools—tend to cluster around universities, but they have now spread clear across the country.

I had intended to add a list of schools to Appendix III, but I find they are so metamorphic that it seems far more useful to refer you to the ads in the back of *Outside, Backpacker* and other magazines. Even as I do so, though, certain words about the appointed Elect (Preface, page xii) sound faintly in my ears.

But it's time to get our eyes back on the trail.

When planning a house on your back, the weightiest matter is

Weight.

The rules used to read:
1. If you need something, take it.
2. Pare away relentlessly at the weight of every item.

Basically, these rules still stand. But you should know, and probably do, that a tide race has set in toward ultralightweight gear. Its practitioners, surfing out over the mountains on the crest of the craze, have even been called "The New Wave." And in their rules the emphases have shifted. They strive to reduce to a minimum the number of items they carry (often by sensible multiple usage); and then they gossamerize every item toward vanishing point. Result: loads that by old standards are featherweight.

Up to a point the New Wave represents both common sense and genuine progress. In fact, you could almost say that technological changes made it inevitable. Radically new boots and vapor-barrier clothing produce, under the right conditions, semirevolutionary weight savings. Pile and Gore-Tex have wrought pregnant changes. And most fabrics have been fined down without loss of strength. A tent with 1.5-ounce taffeta walls and 2.2-ounce floor can now be as tough as one made five years ago with 1.9- and 2.6-ounce fabrics. Such apparently minor gains, applied across the board—to tents, sleeping bags and clothing—can save pounds. Add (or rather subtract) refined manufacturing techniques, and you have an almost automatic paring of loads. The process has been going on for years. But the New Wave leaders have crystallized it. They look with horror and pity on those of us who still go out for a week in the mountains with a load of 50 pounds or even more. They can do it comfortably, they claim, at around 30 pounds. And for weekends they can cut the figure to below 20.

Which is better, the New Wave or the Old? The answer seems quite clear: neither.

One recent October I went for a week into the High Sierra. Because I went alone, at a time when the first winter storm could force me to hole up for a long spell, and because I planned to spend time at around 12,000 feet, I skimped on nothing—and carried a pack weighing 55 pounds. Basic clothing, binoculars, and staff raised the total to 65 pounds, from the skin out (FSO). I do not think I could with safety and reasonable comfort have pared another pound off this load—which my new internal-frame pack rendered astonishingly unburdensome. The only man I spoke to, up at timberline, clearly knew what he was doing—and he carried a 65-pound pack.

A few weeks later, in early December, I made a two-day, one-night trip into some California coastal mountains. Although I again went alone, I knew that in spite of a mild rain threat the weather was unlikely to turn very surly and that, as I planned to go no higher than 3500 feet, temperatures would probably not drop much below freezing. I also knew the country intimately. And because I was going partly for therapy and partly for some ongoing repair work, I would never move off trails or be more than three hours from roadhead. So I made my first real attempt at something like New Wave lightness.

The prospect of heavy pick-and-shovel work meant I could not skimp on food. And the rain threat forced me into carrying a rather heavy tarp rig that was the lightest I happened to have at the time. Yet somewhat to my surprise I managed to set out with a 19-pound pack and 26-pound-FSO load. Everything worked out fine. And the light load was a joy, especially uphill and obstacle-crossing.

For rough data on the 65-pound one-week load and details of the 26-pound weekend experiment, see Appendix IA, page 604.* But in

---

* Do not dismiss these examples as anything at all special. I have recently repeated both, in essence though not detail. On a week-long Sierra snowshoe trip in late May (with snow still 10 feet deep at 10,000 feet) my pack's starting weight was 58 pounds—including 5 or 6 pounds of special gear for testing.

Then, two months later, going ultralight on a recover-from-mental-exhaustion trip into evaluating the New Wave load, bear in mind that I knew I would not have to carry water at any time (a contingency that can make a hash of lightweight plans) and that I deliberately chose to go with no margins for safety or error. (I emerged with barely 3 ounces of food and the stove's tiny cartridge almost empty.)

I am still not fully practiced in New Wave techniques (though I have now used some of "their" equipment, especially clothing, for a fair span); but I have reached some tentative conclusions. It presently seems to me—and to many others I have consulted—that if you never attempt more than weekends in smiling or familiar country and hug frequented trails or always have companions to bail you out of trouble, then equipment failure due to marginal reserve strength or the lack of a nail may be a mere nuisance, a risk well worth taking; and if you so choose you can safely and advantageously ride the New Wave. But if you know you may find yourself alone in a mountain storm, three days from roadhead, then false weight-economy could prove fatal; and you had better forget the gossamer game and lean heavily toward Old Wave ruggedness. In between, you can wallow rather comfortably in the interwave trough, making graduated compromises in response to conditions and experience, and using such new and efficient spin-off gear from the New Wave as pleases you and your purse.

Do not underestimate these spin-offs. And remember that they apply to minor as well as major items. Prompted by my research into New Wave gospels, I recently tooth-combed through my accessories and replaced a 4¾-ounce compass I'd carried for years with a new ¾-ounce model that did just as good a job (page 482), a 1¾-ounce metal-cased magnifying glass with a plastic ½-ounce version (page 218) and a 3½-ounce smoke bomb with one weighing only 2¾ ounces (page 499). The 6 ounces cut by this minipurge may not sound a lot, but it's a 60-percent saving. Such nudgings toward periodic review and pruning of *all* gear may well be the greatest practical contribution the "lightweight revolution" can make to those of us who walk for pleasure, not the restricted if real one of equipment nuttery.

Note, by the way, that both old and new systems tend to be self-reinforcing. If you follow the traditional rules and launch yourself along a gear-selecting curve that opts for safety and comfort, then no matter how hard you think you are paring away at each item your choices are calibrated for a "heavy" regimen, and no matter how short the trip you mostly end up with a load that demands a capacious and rugged pack

---

coastal mountains, carrying plentiful food for four days and also a book that weighed almost 1½ pounds, I got by with a pack of just 26 pounds at the start, 19 pounds (with all garbage) on return.

that may weigh 6 pounds or more. You have to go heavy-footed too: you need stout, old-style boots that will support your feet under the extra load. Conversely, if you are New Waving with sharp, eliminate-and-pare-to-gossamer criteria for each choice, you probably aim all the time toward cramming the entire load into a small, ultralight pack and therefore are always trying to reduce bulk—an aim that in itself reinforces the weight-paring. And you will almost certainly travel light-footed: your feet can handle the light load in boots that are close cousins to running shoes. In other words, once you start serious weight-cutting, the effect snowballs.

All this is good news. But the New Wave gospel must be carefully scrutinized. Two experts recently made a much-publicized 4½-day, 92-mile summer trip in rugged Oregon mountains carrying just 15 pounds each, FSO. What they did is valuable. It shows what can be achieved if you push to the limit. There is a danger, though, that other people will expect to do the same—forgetting that the experiment bore the same relation to a normal backpacking trip as an Indy 500 car does to a Chevy Chevette. What has been learned at Indy may have helped improve your Chevette; but you hardly expect to bash the poor thing all day at 200 mph. On that Oregon trip, for starters, the hikers ate only 1 pound of food a day—though they carried 1.3 pounds—and in those 4½ days one of them lost 10 pounds. They carried only one monumentally sketchy 0.8-ounce first-aid kit between them. Although the genuine practicality of some of the gear is difficult to assess—both men are innovative makers of some of the best hi-tech backpack clothing and other equipment around, and they used special prototypes—they certainly pared to the bone, if not the marrow. As a challenge and experimental test all this was fine—and must have been great fun. As a practical procedure for normal mountain use I suggest it would be neither. And it is important that people recognize the fact.

A parallel though different caution should be exercised in contemplating all the more extreme New Wave advocations. Reading some of the hype, it's difficult to avoid a suspicion that at least part of the impetus is mercantile rather than backpackerly: after all, the gospel opens up such inviting prospects as two or three different packs in every backpacker's closet. Again, some of the genuine, practicing enthusiasts tend, while extolling undoubted advantages, to gloss over uncomfortable facts. Pleasure, they say, is a lighter load. Sure, a lighter load helps. Helps a ton. But, as I've already suggested, that is not the whole truth, so help me God. Backpacking is not all traveling. It is also sleeping and loitering and eating, for example. So backpacking pleasure is also comfortable sleep, cozy warmth at all times and perhaps a few heavy luxuries—short of the complete works of Sherlock Holmes (page 503)—not to mention a full belly. I note that many light-gear enthusiasts seem to skimp on the food. Yet there is general, though not total, agreement that to stay healthy and fully active the average person needs a daily ration of around 2 pounds of dehydrated food; and some stories of ultra-Spartan rations (page 186) frankly sound a lot harder to swallow than the food. Beware, too, of seduction by convenient, short-trip figures. Reducing equipment by a third—to 20 pounds, say, from 30—sounds dramatic. And is. For a full weekend, with 4 pounds of food, that's 24 against 34. But for a week, still at 2 pounds of food a day, and with a stingy allowance of only 2 more pounds for extra stove fuel, toilet paper et al., that's 36 against 46—well worth doing, certainly, but in percentage terms no longer so earth-shaking. Finally, remember that real pleasure demands, above all, gear that has enough reserve strength (and sometimes reserve items too —see page 428) to tide you over those inevitable occasions when Murphy's Law—"If things *can* go wrong, they will"—exerts its stern sway. Perhaps this is the nub. A very experienced all-weather backpacker who works for a leading mountain shop said to me recently, "Yes, I've played the ultralight game—and backed off a ways. For a week's trip, now, I'm generally back at fifty pounds, or close to it. The trouble is, as you go lighter, so the chances of failure increase. Some merchandisers say, 'Well, maybe it won't last ten years, like the old heavy stuff.' But that's not the real point. What matters is the danger of being let down in the field. Soon that risk grows too big. And there's more to it than safety, of course. When you go light, you travel more miles. Fine—the first day. But you're likely to be rather less comfortable around camp, so you don't rest quite so well—and next day you're less efficient on the trail. By the way, the go-light guys often don't mention cost—and although we can make things much lighter now, the price difference is often huge. Don't forget that."

There is another thing too. In all this talk about pounds on your back, don't let mere figures blind you. They have their uses, sure. Remember, though, that they are just an attempt to quantify grief. And the correlation, though broadly valid, is imperfect. Particularly for packs. You may find that a good, frameless, pared-to-the- seams, 1½-pound pack makes all kinds of sense for a load up to 25 pounds. But for a three- or four-day trip when conditions demand that you hump, say, 32 pounds on your back, then a switch to a stouter pack with an advanced hip suspension may increase the statistical load by 3 pounds or even more, yet reduce the grief by a dozen groans.

It is also essential, I think, to examine very closely the advantages of lightening loads, even as far as actual travel is concerned. Any reduction in weight seems pure gain. But the purity turns out to be sullied. If, as I did for years, you use the same pack for all loads (thereby saving money), and if you make no great effort to cut weight for short trips, you reap the advantage of keeping yourself in better shape for long trips when you'll be heavy-laden—not only because your body gets used to carrying fairly heavy loads but also because it (and especially its hips) are conditioned at precisely the right stress points. In the past I've often been aware of this advantage. Now that I've experienced the pleasure of ultralight loads under suitable conditions I'll probably stick with them when I can—and thereby gain a great deal; but I recognize that for conditioning purposes I shall suffer a small loss.

Another debit is less easy to express. When I did my first New Wave trip last December with an FSO load of 26 pounds instead of the 40 I would probably have lugged under my old regimen, I found to my surprise that beneath the pleasure lurked some slight disappointment. It was almost as if I had cheated. What I felt, I think, was the loss of the catharsis that comes from good, honest, voluntary sweat. For although I walked somewhat faster I expended less effort. That, of course, was great. But my sense of cleansing and honing weakened. And that was not so great. Although this admission lays me wide open to cries of "Masochist!," the criers from beside pop couches will have missed the point. I do not really enjoy suffering under heavy loads (and suffering is sometimes the right word): when I can, I'll go light. I must concede, though, that the gain I choose to take levies yet another peripheral toll.

Now look, please do not construe these last few cautionary pages as a vote against the trend toward lighter loads. Far from it. In spite of my caveats I think we should welcome the New Wave with open packs. The Wave may turn out to be plain ongoing evolution rather than a revolution; a highly helpful hop rather than the claimed quantum leap. But when it loses its first fine frenzy and recedes to the point of being embraced with perspective instead of true belief it will leave our shoreline a cleaner and more beautiful place.

Wave or trough, you will always find yourself paring away at your gear. In doing so, look after the ounces and the pounds will look after themselves. Any good catalogue will list the weight of each article to the nearest ounce, and every good mountain shop used to keep an accurate arm-scale handy. No more, unfortunately. (Can it be because, as one honest retailer said, "Everybody lies about weights"?) So when shopping in mountain shops nowadays I often take along a postal scale and weigh every item like gold dust, as I have long done in other stores. (I still like to remember the bewilderment of one sales damsel when I produced my scale and insisted on comparing the weights of two rival pairs of jockey shorts.)

I find that the paring process never ends. At home many foods get repacked from heavy store wrappings into plastic bags (which can be a snare in themselves: even midsize ones may weigh almost half an ounce —and they add up). And nowadays I always extract the cardboard core from toilet-paper rolls. Then, at roadhead, I trim margins and unneeded areas from new maps. Later, when I'm laboring along under a knee-buckling load, I'm never really happy until I've eliminated the last eliminable fraction of an ounce. Once or twice, in really frenetic moments, I've even found myself tearing the labels off tea bags.

Unfortunately it seems impossible to predict just what your load for a given trip will be. No matter how carefully you plan, you have to wait for an answer until you batten down the fully furnished pack. The only thing you can be sure of in advance is that it will weigh more than you had hoped. If you want a meaningful figure don't rely on the way the pack feels; get it onto a trustworthy scale. I have at last bought one and find it distinctly useful. A scale, by the way, cuts the ambient bull quotient: when it comes to talking about the loads they carry, lamentably few backpackers seem to restrict themselves to confirmed, objective, unembroidered fact.

People such as Himalayan Sherpas, who have toted huge loads all their lives, can carry almost their own weight all day long. And even a halfway-fit, fully citified man can pack a very heavy load for short distances, such as canoe portages. Again, people whom I trust implicitly talk of having to carry 80 or 100 pounds or even more on slow and painful approach marches of five or ten miles at the start of mountain-climbing expeditions. But this kind of toil is hardly walking, in our sense. The heaviest load the average person can carry with efficiency and enjoyment for a long day's walking seems to vary within rather wide limits, but a rough guide would be "up to one third of bodyweight for a man, perhaps one quarter weight for a woman—because of her muscle structure." Naturally, these figures assume an efficient pack and a reasonably fit and practiced body. Practiced, mark you. The only way to get used to heavy loads is to pack heavy loads (though see page 37 for reasonably short-circuiting facsimiles.)

Age imposes limits on what you can carry—both prepuberty and again as you shuffle toward senility—but the effects are often exaggerated. See page 39.

Don't forget, by the way, that the start of any trip brings the worst of the grief (unless you have to carry a lot of water a little later on). Each day you use up not only food but also such items as stove fuel and toilet paper. And beyond each water-refill point the load diminishes steadily, hour by hour. By the end of a week that began with a 55-pound pack you may be carrying barely 30 pounds. Your body will likely be honed sharp too. And although modern packs have eliminated a lot of the early grief, the reduced load still makes a tremendous and welcome difference.

After all my words about ounce-paring I shall undoubtedly be taken to task again for the weight of this bloated third edition. Even in paperback it's a bit of a tome. But it is intended primarily for prewalking study. Of course, if you want to put it in your pack . . .

Cost

The only really satisfactory way to approach the price problem is to ignore it. Good equipment always seems expensive, but whenever you find yourself scowling at a price tag in a store try to remember that out in the wilds, where money is meaningless, the failure of a single item can easily ruin a trip. It may even endanger your life.

"Ignore the cost" is easier said than done, of course (though I should like to add, at the risk of sounding smug, that even when I used to live on what many people regarded as the smell of an oily rag, I would not think of walking away from my ancient car with any equipment in my pack that fell short of the best available). In the end, naturally, everyone has to establish his own standards, with due consideration for other responsibilities. But when it comes to such critical items as sleeping bags, the only safe rule is to buy the best you can afford—and then another grade better.

In the course of researching this edition I have been interested and heartened to hear in mountain shops that people now seem more ready to spend money on quality products that will last. "Makes sense," said one salesman. "After one big failure the poor guy may never go out again."

In this edition I have once more indicated a price for almost every item I mention. Generally speaking, the figures represent averages for late 1983; but—as I have warned in the note following the preface—inflation is still with us and you may have to do some sums.

A few mountain shops have stopped pricing things at "$2.49" or "$9.99" and have substituted the more honest "$2.50" or "$10," and where applicable I have followed this courageous lead.

When you are in the market for a specific item you can narrow the field by accepting my prejudices or those of some other writer or of an acquaintance—or your own, if you have chalked up enough experience to achieve prejudices. You can heed the makers' passionate pleas. Or you can check a dependable and informed magazine survey. But sometimes the best way to confirm your choice before buying outright may be through a trial run by

Renting.

If you live near a good mountain shop you may be able to rent certain items such as packs, tents and sleeping bags—and possibly, though improbably, boots. Because of liability insurance problems, few stores except REI now rent crampons or ice axes.

Renting also makes sense, of course, if you want a tent, say, for only a week or two in a year.

Sample rental rates: two-man tent—$12–$15 for a weekend (Thursday evening through Monday evening), $28 for two weeks; pack —$10–$15 a weekend, $18 for two weeks.

It would probably be a good thing to take a brief look, here, at the general considerations to be borne in mind when deciding on

EQUIPMENT FOR A SPECIFIC TRIP.

Most decisions about what to take and what to leave behind will depend on the answers you get in the early stages of planning when you ask yourself "Where?" and "When?" and

"For how long?"

We have already looked (on page 27) at the kinds of differences that can arise in equipment choice for a weekend as opposed to a week. Beyond a week the problems change. Food is the trouble. For ten days, most people need around 20 pounds of it; for two weeks, almost 30. And such weights reach toward the prohibitive. I do not think I have ever traveled—as opposed to operating from a base camp—for more than ten days without food replenishment. (For replenishment methods—by outposts of civilization, caches, airdrops, etc.—see pages 541–9.)

As far as equipment is concerned, then, even a very long journey boils down in essentials to a string of one- or possibly two-week trips. Besides replenishable items, all you have to decide is whether you'll be aching too badly before the end for a few extra comforts. A toothbrush, a paperback book and even camp footwear may be luxuries on a weekend outing, but I imagine most people would think twice about going out for two weeks without them.

What makes a very real difference is that the longer the trip, the greater the uncertainties about both terrain and weather; but here we begin to ease over into

"Where and When?"

The two questions are essentially inseparable (see, again, page 27; and for planning from maps, see page 474). Terrain, considered apart from its weather, makes surprisingly little difference to what you need carry. The prospect of sleeping on rock or of crossing a big river may prompt you to take an air mattress, as opposed to an insulating pad for snow, or nothing at all for sand (page 331). In cliff country you may elect to take along a climbing rope, even when on your own (page 501). Glaciers or hard snow may suggest ice axe and crampons (page 83). But that is about all. And snow and ice, in any case, come close to being "weather."

In the end it is weather that governs most of the decisions about clothing and shelter. Now, weather is not simply a matter of asking, "Where?" and answering, "Desert," "Rainforest," or "Alpine meadows." You must immediately ask, "When?" And from the answer you must be able to draw accurate conclusions.

In almost any kind of country the gulf between June and January is so obvious that your planning allows for it automatically. But the difference between, say, September and October is not always so clear—and it may matter a lot. (One of my advisors calls it "transition weather.") The most convenient source of accurate information that I know is the series of booklets issued by the U.S. National Climatic Center under the title *Climatic Summary of the United States—Supplement for 1951 Through 1960.* Each booklet covers one state (exceptions: one booklet each for New England, Maryland-Delaware, Hawaii and the Pacific area, and Puerto Rico–Virgin Islands–West Indies). For every weather station with records for more than five years, the summaries list monthly figures for total precipitation, snowfall, and temperature (mean, mean maximum, mean minimum, highest, lowest, and mean number of days with readings below freezing and above 90° F.). Where records exist prior to 1951, averages are given. An index locates each station on a sketch map and gives its latitude and longitude and elevation. These booklets are available, at prices ranging from $.25 to $33 ($3 minimum order), from the National Climatic Center, Federal Building, Asheville, NC 28801–2696. (Booklets periodically go out of print, but Xeroxes are then available at about twenty times booklet cost.) From the same source you can get a lot more weather literature, including *Climates of the States* ($.50 for each state; $3 minimum order), that offer some nonessential but possibly useful information. Now available: a one-page precipitation report for several stations along the Appalachian Trail. Please note that all NCC prices are under review, and likely to change. Write or phone for current figures (phone is changing too: check under "U.S. Government, Department of Commerce"). The National Park Service sometimes has weather data for the larger parks.

In Canada the equivalents to the U.S. *Climatic Summary* booklets are *Temperature and Precipitation Tables* (one booklet each for British Columbia, Yukon and the Northwest Territories, the Prairie Provinces, Ontario, Quebec, and the Atlantic Provinces [$6 each]) that give roughly the same information but unfortunately include no maps for identification of the weather stations. The booklets are available from the Assistant Deputy Minister, Atmospheric Environment Service, 4905 Dufferin Street, Downsview, Ontario M3H 5T4 (checks payable to the Receiver General of Canada). From the same gentlemen you can get two volumes covering all Canada for 1951–80: *Temperature Normals* ($7.20) and *Precipitation Normals* ($9.60). Also a free list of *Selected Publications in Climatology* that summarizes many local and general information sources.

Monthly figures can never tell the whole story, but these booklets (or at least the U.S. ones, which I use regularly) can be a great help in planning a trip. In deciding what night shelter you need, it may be critical to know that the lowland valley you intend to wander through averages only .10 inch of rain in September (20-year high: .95 inch) but 1.40 inches in October (high: 6.04 inches). And decisions about what sleeping bag and clothing to take on a mountain trip will come more easily once you know that a weather station 8390 feet above sea level on the eastern escarpment of the 14,000-foot range you want to explore has over the past thirty years averaged a mean daily minimum of 39° F. in September (record low, 19°) but 31° in October (low, 9°); by applying the rough but fairly serviceable rule that "temperature falls three degrees for every 1000-foot elevation increase," you can make an educated guess at how cold the nights are going to be up near the peaks. Remember, though, that weather is much more than just temperature. See especially "windchill" chart, page 575.

A wise precaution before any trip that will last a weekend or longer is to check on the five-day forecast for the area. Such forecasts are given every few minutes on National Oceanic and Aeronautical Administration (NOAA) VHF radio stations that now form a network covering most of the country. You can buy small sets that receive them, starting at 6 ounces and $13. Failing such a resource, you can try the weatherman at your nearest international airport. Or check the telephone book under "U.S. Government, Department of Commerce, National Weather Service."

But the finest insurance of all is to have the right friends. Or, to be more exact, the right friend. I have one who is not only a geographer with a passion for weather lore but also a walking computer programmed with weather statistics for all the western United States and half the rest of the world. I try to phone him before I go on even short trips to unfamiliar country. "The Palisades in early September?" he says. "Even close to the peaks you shouldn't get night temperatures much below twenty. And you could hardly choose a time of year with less danger of a storm. The first heavy ones don't usually hit until early November, though in 1959 they had a bad one in mid-September. Keep an eye on the wind, that's all. If you get a strong or moderate wind from the south, be on the lookout for trouble." By the time he has finished, I am all primed and ready to go.

For keeping an eye on the weather during trips, see page 586.

Unless you have the only infallible memory on record, you ought to have a couple of copies of a

Checklist of gear.

It should be a full list, covering all kinds of trips, in all kinds of terrain, at all times of year. On any particular occasion you just ignore what you don't want to take along.

Eventually everyone will probably evolve his own list. But many local and national hiking organizations (see Appendix III) are happy to supply beginners with suggestions. So are some commercial firms. Appendix I of this book (page 601) is a very full list that might be a useful starter. You can Xerox it and check from the loose pages, conveniently buttressed by a clipboard. But as soon as experience permits, draft your own list.

FURTHER PLANNING

Unless you are fit—fit for backpacking, that is—you should, at least as early as you start worrying about equipment for a trip, worry like hell about

Getting in shape.

I repeat that the only real way to get used to heavy loads is to pack heavy loads—though what you mean by "heavy" will depend on your experience, ambition, frame, muscles and temperament. I certainly try to fit in one or two practice hikes in the week or two before any long wilderness trip. Sometimes I even succeed. Whenever possible, I make this conditioning process seem less hideously Spartan by stowing lunch in the pack and eating it on a suitable peak, or by adding typewriter and papers and setting up temporary office under a tree. Or I may carry the pack on one of the walks I regularly take in order to think, feel, sweat or whatever (page 3). As far as the exercise goes, I find that it makes no difference—well, not too much difference—whether I walk in daylight or darkness.

Even if your regimen does not permit such solutions, make every effort to carry the pack as often as you can in the week or two before you head for wilderness, if only to prepare your hips for their unaccustomed task. Details of distance and speed are your affair, but take it easy at first and increase the dose until at the end you are pushing sweaty hard. If possible, walk at least part of the time on rough surfaces and up hills. Up steep hills. Not everyone, of course, has the right kind of terrain handy, but at a pinch, anywhere will do. The less self-conscious you are, the freer, that's all. You may blench at the thought of pounding up Main Street with a 40-pound pack (all those damned traffic lights would wreck your rhythm anyway), but, pray, what are city parks for? And many big metropolitan areas now have nearby hiking trails (see Appendix III, page 617).

If the pressures of time, location, family and *amour propre* combine to rule out fully laden practice hikes, attack the problem piecemeal. Your prime targets are: feet, legs, lungs and shoulders. (In the last edition I included "skin"—and advised preguarding against sunburn by exposing "yourself to the sun as often and as flagrantly as you can . . . in the days and weeks before you leave for desert or seashore or mountains or almost anyplace else." But current medical truth suggests that such exposure is dangerous: it encourages or perhaps almost ensures skin cancer, twenty or thirty years down the line. So it's probably better just to take great care with suntan lotion . . . [page 492].)

Legs are best conditioned by walking, jogging or running. Especially running. And especially up hills. For those with limited time at their disposal, running is currently the most popular and perhaps the most efficient answer. I suspect that a not inconsiderable number of those pent-up citizens who pant around Central Park Reservoir at their various rates and gaits may be preparing for a week or weekend along the Appalachian Trail. I know at least one who often is. Nowadays there are "par courses" in some cities: you run from one exercise station to the next, do your chosen stint there, and discipline and improve yourself by monitoring the overall torture time. Frankly, I find a much more pleasurable, though possibly less effective, regimen is tennis—singles, not doubles

—played often and earnestly. It's rather less hard on knees and backs. An alternative that's even gentler on those fragile members is running in place (and doing other fun exercises) on a small trampoline, indoors or out.

The finest conditioner for your lungs—probably even better than carrying loads—is, once again, running, especially up hills, up steep hills.

Because all the weight of a pack used to hang from the shoulders, people still connect backpacking with "sore shoulders." There is a certain residual truth in the idea: any but the very best modern packframes, properly adjusted, can leave unready shoulders a mite stiff. But with the hipbelt that is the crux of today's pack suspension (page 107) it is on your hips that the real load bears. And, brother, does it bear! I go for sumptuously padded belts and I'm fairly often in harness, but I still find, on the second morning of most trips with heavy loads, that I wince as I cinch the belt tight—the way it must be cinched—on hip muscles still complaining about yesterday. And on that second morning, if not earlier, any hips that have never undergone the waistbelt trauma under a heavy load, or have not done so for a long time, are just about guaranteed, I hereby warn, to complain fortissimo. Until recently there was no way I knew of to prepare shoulders and hips for a load except—wait for it—a load, preferably carried in the pack you expect to use; but an escape hatch may just possibly have appeared in the form of the latest Gregory hipbelt (page 138).

When you are young such preparations may be less important, but with age you grow less resilient and must pay more attention. (Mind you, that's no excuse for hunkering down into an armchair. There are ways to avoid, or at least mitigate, the tolls of time. Just before reaching 60, Fletcherheit, I underwent a cautionary conversion, and now, at 16 Celsius, I find I'm still going reasonably strong. And I'm a kid compared with some walkers who have simply kept at it. In the course of researching my last book I made contact with a Spanish-American War veteran who at 99 still walked three or four miles every day.)

I'm afraid all these strictures end up sounding ferociously austere. But Arcadian ends can justify Spartan means. Many a beautiful backpacking week or weekend has been ruined at the start by crippled, city-soft muscles—because their owners had failed to recognize the softness, or at any rate to remedy it.

Harbor no illusions about how much difference fitness makes to backpacking. A study conducted at the University of Texas at El Paso in 1974 indicated that "physical fitness appears to be more closely related to pack-carrying performance than is either age or weight." I buy that.

There is a certain forest to which I retreat from time to time for a two-
or three-day think-and-therapy walk. Normally I go when mentally exhausted from work and muscularly out of practice. I start, mostly, in the
evening. I am glad to camp a little way up the first, long hill and then
to plod on next morning until I reach a little clearing on the first ridge,
where I often stop to brew tea. Sometimes it is by then time for lunch.
But once, in order to think out the shape of a book, I went to my forest
only ten days after returning from a week spent pounding up a Sierra
Nevada mountain. I was therefore fit and alert. And that purgatorial first
hill flattened out in front of me. I stayed in high gear all the way;
although I had as usual started toward the end of the day, I reached the
ridge clearing in time to choose a campsite by the last of the day's light.

So even if you cannot manage practice hikes, try to do something.
Start early. Start easy. Work up. You may find that you actually enjoy
what you are doing, especially if you organize the right palliatives (hilltop lunches, subarboreal offices, daydreams, tennis). And when you
stride away from roadhead at last, out into Arcady, you will very likely
discover that getting in shape has made the difference between agony and
ecstasy.

Getting in shape for high altitudes

Up high, your body works less efficiently, especially at first. There
is wide variation: some people tolerate high altitude well, others poorly.
And the more practiced you are, the better you tend to play the game.
But current gospel maintains that physical condition has no effect—at
least on the more serious forms of distress, known as "acute mountain
sickness." In fact, fitness may make you drive too hard, and so overtax
your body.

Symptoms of what could properly be labeled "acute mountain sickness" rarely occur below 8000 feet. (For much, much more on that
subject, see page 577.) But if your body is tuned to operate at sea level
you may well experience as low as 6000 feet enough mild initial distress,
such as shortness of breath, to impair your efficiency and enjoyment. And
a little higher you may begin to suffer headaches. You can dampen such
distress almost to extinction if you acclimate correctly—that is, give
your body time to make adjustments (mainly increasing the depth and
rate of breathing) so that it can perform properly under the new conditions. If you are making your first energetic trip into high mountains
and do not know what your threshold of tolerance will be, pay particular
attention to this acclimation process.

The body does most of its adjusting in the first three days, with the first two the most important. So those are the days to watch. I seem to tolerate high altitude fairly well, at least up to 16,000 feet, but if I'm going over about 10,000 I take pains to arrange that I cannot get out of the car and immediately, with my body still tuned for sea level, start to walk toward those beckoning peaks. When checking gear at home I leave such details as rebagging food and waxing boots to be done at roadhead. Other things being equal, I cdhoose a roadhead as high as possible—at 6000 or 7000 feet or more. And I tend to drive until late at night to reach it. Sometimes I drive clear through the night. Then I more or less have to sleep up high for at least one night, or part of a night (or day); and by the time I've slept late and then gotten all my gear ready there is normally only an hour or two of daylight left—just enough for a leisurely walk and then another night's sleep up high before I can even begin serious walking.

Not everyone will want or even be able to apply my particular built-in brakes at roadhead, but try to devise your own version. If time and terrain permit, it is naturally better to start low and let the body adjust slowly, as you gain elevation. But the slope must be reasonable or the pace slow, or both. I know one family that on its first Sierra backpack trip ignored warnings and tried too much, too high and too early, so that everyone suffered headaches and the other malaises of "mountain sickness" and came down vowing never to set pack on back again. Even when you ought to know better you can still do stupid things. Only a few years ago, after sleeping one night at a 9000-foot roadhead and a second night just above it, I pushed too hard on the third day, with a very heavy load, and was pretty tired, as well as somewhat dehydrated, by the time I camped at dusk on a 13,000-foot peak. That night, for the only time in my life so far, altitude ruined my sleep. All night I kept coming awake to find myself gasping for breath. It was not pleasant. And as soon as dawn broke I betook my shaken self down a talus slope that ended at 10,000 feet. There I camped. All day I sat. Next morning I felt fine. For the rest of that week—walking along a ridge, camping twice at 13,000 feet, only once below 12,000—I experienced no further distress. I had learned, vividly, what I had long known in a general way: for the first three days up high, you take things easy. (I now know that this "periodic breathing" or "Cheyne-Stokes syndrome"—in which you repeatedly stop breathing for as long as ten or fifteen seconds—is common under such conditions and *in the absence of other symptoms* appears quite harmless. See page 578.)

Even after the first few days of adjustment you must still take things much easier than at sea level. But that is a walking rather than an acclimating matter, so see page 97.

Be prepared, by the way, for your body to make readjustments when you return quickly, as you often will, to sea level or thereabouts. For two or three days you may feel somewhat sleepy.

Pretrip sickness

If you are what laymen call a hypochondriac but perceptive doctors classify as someone merely overaware of how the old organism is functioning, and if you're in the throes of planning a really challenging trip, funny things can happen.

In order to deal with them you must first get yourself a good doctor —the kind you've come to trust down the years, so that eventually you can call him and say, "Look, Glenn, I feel this and this and this. Am I ill or have I got Fletcheritis?" *

Almost twenty years ago, just before embarking on my two-month, length-of-Grand-Canyon walk, I was deep in the pit of logistics, economics, equipment, permissions and all the other hassles when I was laid low by some new and inopportune affliction. For two days, or maybe three, I languished in bed, weak as a winter butterfly, sweating intermittently, deeply depressed at the prospect of the year's postponement that would result from a two- or three-week delay. At last I phoned my Doctor Glenn, described the symptoms and put the Fletcheritis question.

"Are you afraid of this trip?" he asked.

"I don't think so. Not beyond a reasonable awareness that there's a physical challenge."

We talked a bit more, and eventually the doc rather tentatively suggested that perhaps I should not go.

Within half an hour, still bedridden, I had made the one phone call needed to bring preparations to a grinding halt.

Within another half-hour I found myself out in the garden standing in brilliant sunshine, throwing a golf ball in the air and catching it and generally beaming at the world. The moment I realized what I was doing I rushed back indoors and rephoned the doctor.

---

* Fletcheritis is a recurring and scurvy condition (typically, a horrendous slump with variegated symptoms, uniformly exhausting and dire, or semi-dire) that oozes into existence at such moments of crisis as the onset of a new book.

A different doctor, whom I had acquainted with the correct medical terminology, once told another patient, "Hm, in my opinion you've got Fletcheritis."

The patient stared, round-eyed. "My God, what's that?"

"Well, the way to cure it is to go away and get drunk. And if possible, laid. Then call me tomorrow and tell me how you feel."

The patient duly called. "You were dead right," he said. "I feel great."

"It was just the pressure of all the perishing hassles, wasn't it?" I said.

"Probably."

"And there isn't a damned thing wrong with me."

"No. But it might come on again, down in the Canyon, you know."

"It won't," I said.

And it didn't.

The moral of this story is, I guess, that every walk of life falls under the sway of the Testicular Imperative: "Either you have the world by them—or it has you."

The planning question that seems to haunt almost all inexperienced hikers is

"How far can I expect to walk in a day?"

For most kinds of walking, the question is wrongly put. Except along flat, straight roads, miles are just about meaningless. Hours are what count.

Naturally, there is a connection—of sorts. I have only once checked my speed with any accuracy, and that was more or less by accident. It was during my summer-long walk up California. One afternoon I followed the Atchison, Topeka and Santa Fe for 9 arrowlike miles into the desert town of Needles. It so happened that I began at a mileage post, and I checked the time and jotted it down on my map. I traveled at my normal speed, and I recall no difficulty about stepping on ties (as so often happens when you follow a railroad track), so it must have been straightforward walking on a well-banked grade. I took a 10-minute halt at the end of the first hour; and exactly 1 hour and 55 minutes after starting I passed the 6-mile mark. I would guess that this 3-miles-per-roughly-50-minutes-of-actual-walking is about my norm on a good level surface with a pack that weighs, as mine probably did that day, around 40 pounds. In other words, 7 hours of *actual walking* is roughly the equivalent of a 20-mile day on the flat, under easy walking conditions—provided you are fit, practiced and motivated.

But on trails you will rarely come close to 20 genuine miles in 7 hours. Mostly, 2 miles an hour is good going. Off trails, over really rough country, the average can fall below half a mile. The nonsense that hikers commonly talk about mountain miles walked in one day is only equaled, I think, by the drivel they deliver about loads.

But if you now ask the amended question, "How many hours can I expect to walk in a day?" it remains difficult to give a straightforward answer. The thing is seamed with variables. On any given day—provided you are well rested and not concerned with how you will feel next morning—you can, if you are fit and very powerfully motivated, probably keep going most of the 24. But what really matters in most cases is what you are likely to keep up, fully laden, day after day. Even a rough estimate of this figure demands not so much a grasp of arithmetic as an understanding of human frailty. I have published elsewhere a table representing a typical day's walking on the desert half of my California trip —a day on which, beset with all the normal and fascinating temptations of walking, I pushed tolerably hard, though not even close to my limit. Mildly amended to fit more general conditions, that table may help explain the difficulties of computation:

	Hours	Minutes
Walking, including 10-minute halts every hour	7	
Extension of half the 10-minute halts to 20 minutes because of sights, sounds, smells, ruminations and inertia		30
Compulsive dallying for photography and general admiration of the passing scene— 4²/₇ minutes in every hour		30
Photography, once a day, of a difficult and utterly irresistible object (this will seem a gross over-estimate to nonphotographers, an absurd underestimate to the initiated)	1	
Conversations with mountain men, desert rats, eager beavers or even bighorn sheep	1	
Cooking and eating four meals, including tea	3	30
Camp chores		30
Orthodox business of wilderness traveler: rapt contemplation of nature and/or navel		30
Evaporated time, quite unaccountable for		30
Sleep, including catnaps	8	59
Reading, fishing, additional rest, elevated thinking, unmentionable items and general sloth		1
Total	24	

Nonwalks, sort of

Please do not assume from all this talk of miles and hours that sheer walkery lies at the heart of every backpacking trip. Even when you set out with walking as your prime aim, things do not always turn out that way. Sometimes you find that what you really want to do is loiter along or even just loaf around a camp that you thought was just an overnight stop. Or planned extraperambulatory activities (page 513) may hold the walking to a subservient, get-me-there niche. A special case, growing in popularity, is physical do-gooding. Mostly, that means making or maintaining trails—a task that leaves me philosophically unexcited, to say the least. But there are other forms of helping the wilderness. For several years now I have, with one or two others, been going up from time to time into what was once untouched wilderness and slowly repairing a small section of the damage inflicted by bulldozers as they "fought" a forest fire. The practical impact of any such project on your equipment and planning may be small—a need for work gloves, stout boots if you're shoveling earth, maybe pack modification to carry tools, even including a chain saw (if you have permission to use one); but I very much want to inject a word about projects of this kind. I strongly recommend them as good for the soul: to my surprise, the work we undertook has turned out to be one of the most rewarding things I have ever done. Frankly, I like to operate in parties of one or maybe two, and find that things glow warmer when free of help from any organization. I'm aware, though, that most people prefer to work in groups and may have difficulty in matching their desires with suitable tasks. Local walking clubs, including Sierra Club chapters (see Appendix III), may be able to help with such matching. And many public libraries apparently have a 16-page directory, *Helping Out in the Outdoors,* that lists interesting volunteer jobs in parks and forests, and although the majority are administrative, some include backcountry work. Copies of the directory are also available, $3 postfree, from 16812 36th Avenue W., Lynnwood, WA 98036.

Permits and other controls

A new and increasingly intrusive element in planning is the system that now meters backcountry visitors in many national parks and forests. You cannot legally go backpacking in them without a permit. To make sure of getting permits for the most popular places you may have to apply far ahead of time. If you arrive unheralded at the entry station you may be turned back. And the thing does not end there. Before you go in you'll likely have to specify not only your route but also the location of each night camp. For all its good intentions, the system is already a pesky affliction. It threatens to become a plague.

The reason for the system is clear and understandable: so many people now want to go into the backcountry that, in order to protect it and also the visitors' enjoyment, entry must be controlled.

The trouble lies in the nature of the controls. Most people, whether they recognize it or not, go into backcountry because they want to leave behind for a spell the human-dominated world, ruled by linear thinking: by immersing themselves in a world of curves that operates on quite different grids of meaning—or perhaps I mean webs of meaning—they hope to emerge with broader perspectives. Almost anyone who has spent a few days in wilderness, alone or in quiet company, understands the antithesis between the two worlds. And it's there, though not always so clearly recognizable, in any backcountry journey.* But present control methods are the aggressively linear kind that will be the obvious and inevitable first choice of almost any human organization: to make absolutely sure of getting a permit you must delineate your plans weeks or even months ahead; and to satisfy the permit ranger you may have to set in concrete—or pretend to do so—even what you will do once inside and "free." In other words, this key does not fit this door. The system is, I suggest, self-defeating.

Its shortcomings reach out far beyond the philosophical: it generates traumas and hassles that range from minor to monumental. Many permit rangers perform their duties with perception and restraint, and the instructional sermons they deliver with the permits may even succeed in helping teach the uninitiated how to treat the backcountry; on the other hand, the system also guarantees employment for the kind of person who has reveled in rasping domination of his fellows since long before Shakespeare bewailed "the insolence of office"—the arrogant broad-brimmed Gauleiter who can, single-handed, tarnish anyone's entry into what was meant to be a beautiful experience. Most of us have brushed with such fauna. But many of the system's failures derive from its very nature, not from warts on its enforcers. With time precious as pearls, you have ignored speed limits and generally busted your ass in order to reach roadhead by midafternoon—but still arrive half an hour after the permit ranger has shut up shop: if you're going to be legal you have to hang around until opening time next day. (True, if you can phone ahead and if you hit a cooperative ranger you may be able to get a permit pinned to a bulletin board; but that's big "if" country.) In the summer of 1982 two experienced backpackers with only three days' free time set up a double trans-Sierra trek: at journey's end each would take the other's car. The one who planned to start from the mountains' eastern flank arrived

---

* I have just come across a passage in Joseph L. Sax's 1978 Albright Lecture: "There is something about the idea of an encounter with nature that has a powerful hold on the American imagination—an idea of independence, of self-reliance, self-sufficiency and autonomy. These are ideas that lie very close to the heart of the cultural values we prize most, and that seem to be most threatened by the style of modern, urban, industrial society."

at his entry point to find its daily quota filled, and was told he would have to wait for twenty-four hours. He remonstrated: a day's delay would mean canceling the trip, and his partner would already have started; besides, one additional hiker who knew how to operate would surely have close to zero impact on the country. The permit ranger remained unmoved. The frustrated visitor eventually decided, "The hell with it," and went. Next day a backcountry ranger asked for his permit and served him a $40 ticket. The recipient was not happy. Although that may be an extreme case, the present system clearly causes a whole slew of rather less infuriating but very real and far more frequent lacerations. As time passes and pressures increase, it will inflict even more. And something needs to be done, fast.

A valid alternative system, it seems to me, would radically reduce or eliminate all piecemeal, man-contrived controls and replace them with a natural, more or less self-regulating arrangement that still protects both the land and human experience. Now, devising such a system is not easy. Nor is embracing it. Out in the civilized, linear world where the relevant decisions must be made, it is difficult to retain a grasp of the curved, weblike modes of thinking at stake—even though you vividly remember the feel of the values they generate. In addition, our political and legislative machinery remains unpracticed in such solutions. And any plan that fits is almost sure to run head on into the often unintentional but still undeniable tendency of bureaucracies, including the National Park and U.S. Forest Services, to extend their fiefdoms.

Still, somebody has got to try.

The filter-by-natural-obstacles system I propose is not new, at least in essence. But it has not, I think, been seriously put forward in print. Its salient measures:

A. Move roadheads back as far as possible, or at least as far back as is necessary to reduce usage and protect the land.

B. Reduce and if necessary eliminate trail maintenance of the kind that encourages easy access (broadening, making easy grades, removing all encroaching brush and, especially, fallen trees and rocks). Continue minimal maintenance to prevent erosion at specific points.

C. Force the Park and Forest Services to quit advertising. That is, to eliminate or at least radically reduce their well-intentioned efforts to tell people "what is out there." They do so not only with maps and brochures but also with strategically placed rangers trained to dispense information—and graded on how well they do it. Such a policy was once valid. For "social," human-dominated areas served by roads, such as the floor of Yosemite Valley or Cade's Cove in the Smokies, it still is. But for today's pressured backcountry it makes no sense. After all, what goes on, essentially, is that one public hand encourages an influx of backpackers while the other hand tries to impose a curb because the numbers have grown too big.*

Please note that I am *not* advocating a simple dropping of the permit system and throwing open of the backcountry. That would be crazy. I suggest replacing the present controls with others, of an entirely different, nearly self-regulating nature, that would remove the current and growing barriers to human enjoyment *while still protecting the land.*

I also do not suggest that the permit system be abandoned everywhere, overnight. That would cause chaos. But I do believe that it should be replaced as soon as possible in suitable trial areas—which probably means large, rugged tracts where cessation of trail work would quickly make access a lot more difficult. Then, when the new system had been tried and its worst bugs swatted, we should consider extending it, perhaps in modified form, to many or even most backcountries. It may well turn out that no filter-by-natural-obstacles system will work in certain easily accessible areas, such as those used or overused by weekenders—who demand easy access and may be perfectly happy to pay for it with the permit hassle. I am sure there will be teething difficulties anyway. And I do not pretend to have fine-focused all ramifications and implications. Frankly, I lack the technical expertise. I suggest, though, that once the plan's essence and the changed mode of thought behind it have been genuinely accepted, then details of application and such related matters as fire-protection policy, rescue stance and backcountry ranger stations could be hammered out. Others would solve themselves.

The plan is not perfect, of course. Like our form of democracy, it may be the worst system you could imagine—except for all the others that have been tried. But at least its key fits the backcountry door. Naturally, it would not solve all problems in all situations, neatly and quickly. Some backcountry lacks both trees and unstable rock, and it may well be that you need a few tree trunks or good-size rocks, left where they fall across trails, to deter the fainthearted. Again, some existing roadheads almost defy manipulation. But the beneficial results of a largely self-regulating setup would, I think, prove overwhelming:

1. The present cumbersome and unsatisfactory permit system,

---

* Lumping the National Park Service and U.S. Forest Service together, as I have done for simplicity, is not really fair. Managing visitors forms only a small part of the USFS's job, and that fact often shows. But the NPS is deeply and basically concerned. It mostly does a superb job of running the roadbound, straight-line parts of its domain. Unfortunately the same principles and mindsets tend to guide its backcountry management. And that goes so gratingly against the grain that I sometimes feel the whole permit system, if not unconstitutional, damned well ought to be. If the Founding Fathers were around now, with roadless country so shrunken and precious, perhaps it would be.

which is barely enforceable and encourages law-breaking, would be scaled down and perhaps eventually eliminated.

2. The number of users could still be controlled, within reason (by adjustment of trail maintenance and roadhead siting), so that the land would be at least as well protected as it now is.

3. Backpackers would earn their right to enter not, as now, by an ability or willingness to lay plans far ahead, or by the lottery of first-come-first-served, but in the coin of the realm: ability to operate in relatively uncombed backcountry (or willingness to learn how to do so); and ability and willingness to put out genuine physical effort.

4. People might often find to their surprise that they derived deeper and more satisfying rewards than they do now—cushioned as they often are, even in backcountry, by so much outside-world "convenience," the beguiling but insidious modern canker that leaves most victims unaware of their corruption.

5. It is possible, though unprovable, that people so selected would move into closer harmony with the land and therefore treat it with greater respect.

6. Eliminating entry controls and reducing trail maintenance would save minidollops of taxpayers' money.

7. We have been ruled and regulated enough, say the reigning rascals—and here is a case in which we can march alongside them without reservation as we take a small but significant step toward getting the government off our backpacks.

Objections to any such plan will, of course, pour in thick. To answer four in advance:

a. Step B and result 2 will provoke choruses of that modern shibboleth "Elitist!" from those who enjoy shouting "Elitist!"—and who ignore the uncomfortable fact that you cannot achieve quality, anywhere, without some form of culling. It would certainly be pleasant if we could still encourage everyone to go into the backcountry. But such a time is past. That is why we are discussing the future. And while the plan undoubtedly selects among applicants and thereby creates (if you must use the word) an elite, I repeat that this elite earns its entry in an appropriate local currency and not, like the present elite, in the foreign, "outside" coin of money or friends at court or an ability or willingness to plan every damned thing way ahead, linearly, yea unto the last campsite.

b. "Park and Forest Service polls among users show that they favor the permit system." But the alternative presented is apparently no control at all. Besides, such polls are biased because they are inevitably conducted among those who have acquiesced to the permit system and exclude the growing number who have been repelled by it.

c. "It won't work." But reducing impact by moving roadheads

back and radically cutting trail maintenance has been successfully tried, de facto, in remoter parts of a few National Parks—albeit with permits still required. (Has been tried so successfully, in fact, that one park superintendent who did exactly that was attacked for trying to reduce the number of visitors. Poor guy!) The system, more or less unintentionally imposed because of budget cuts, has even worked on a once-busy trail in Yosemite Valley.

d. "Because the concept runs contrary to the thoughtways of the Park and Forest Services, and because it poses a threat to the built-in and often unconscious tendency of bureaucracies toward self-perpetuation and expansion, it will draw opposition from the powerful bureaucratic arm of government." Sure. But that's no reason for abandoning the plan. Perhaps we can even convince both Park and Forest Services that the budgetary savings from a largely self-regulating system might salvage more visible projects in areas of denser use.

I recognize that this proposal will, at least at first, be unpopular. It will no doubt provoke derision. But I repeat that the plan, though imperfect, is a key that fits its door. And it is necessary, in some form. We sorely need to devise some valid alternative to the present permit-and-handcuff system of control. It strikes at the core of what people go into wilderness to find. With the best of intentions it destroys, as the army once destroyed a certain Vietnamese village, the very values it seeks to save.

Letting some responsible person know where you're going and when you'll be back

Please see page 524.

Two veiled elements of planning that are often overlooked

When you leave civilization and enter wilderness you need time to convert from the linear coordinates of the human world to the softer web of wilderness. The interval required for fairly full recovery from this jolt —which is really an extreme case of "culture shock"—commonly runs to about three days. That is what I find, anyway. And until you complete your readjustment to the new "culture"—or, rather, to the lack of culture—you do not operate well. You tend to stumble on loose stones, select inefficient routes, hestitate or even balk at mildly challenging scrambles, and spend twice as long as normal choosing campsites. But after three days, give or take some, this nonsense passes and you are back in stride.

When you leave wilderness and reenter civilization you must, of course, reconvert. And you weather a corresponding withdrawal period. If you reenter by car, for example, you are likely to find that for twenty minutes after leaving trailhead you drive poorly, even a little unsafely. And although your eyes are newly and widely opened, what you see—or at least what you do with what you see—may remain strangely unfocused. I have learned that, back home, I can soon go about routine business halfway adequately but that it will be three days before I have readjusted well enough to do serious, delicate work.

I am almost sure I have never read anything explicit about these dual phenomena, but I do not think there can be any doubt about their existence. Any experienced backpacker to whom I mention them immediately recognizes the reality. "Yes," said one friend who moves frequently between the two worlds, "I guess you could say I live in a perpetual state of maladjustment."

It seems to me that the two-way condition could usefully, if a little cutely, be called "trail lag." It should certainly enter—by any name you like—into your planning calculations.

There is another phenomenon you might do well to consider, too. An expectancy barrier is a superbly efficient human device—either self- or other-induced—for ensuring that an experience falls thuddingly short of its billing. The condition runs rampant in such fields as mutual friends ("Oh, you must meet John—you two will get on like a house on fire") and movies ("The funniest show since Genghis Khan—promise me you won't miss it"). And an expectancy barrier also lurks on the preboundaries of almost every backpacking trip—ready to cast its shadow over the round and beautiful pumpkin that sits waiting up there on the shelf. I can suggest no antidote beyond an alert and ongoing skepticism. But I think you should be warned.*

---

* A valued critic questioned the need for this paragraph: "I think most people know that life is like that." I'm by no means sure I agree. Besides, there's more involved than sheer information. I coined the phrase "expectancy barrier" some years ago, sprang it on the world in print, and waited for the English language to embrace the pearl with gratitude and accompanying hosannas. Not a peep. So I'm running it up a more visible flagpole. But you'll understand, I'm sure, that nothing would compel me to admit such an ulterior motive.

Foundations

The foundations of the house on your back are your feet and their foot-wear, and the cornerstone is a good pair of

BOOTS.

In choosing these boots we now face a wild spectrum of options, for bootmaking has in the last decade broken free from the chains of an almost medieval tradition. Korea is replacing Western Europe as the prime high-volume manufacturing center. And new mass-production techniques have generated viable boots markedly cheaper than those produced by traditional, labor-intensive methods. The new-tech boots are much lighter too. They also offer other advantages—and disadvantages. Above all, though, they are different in revolutionary ways. For the new techniques have challenged and often demolished long-standing assumptions: that in backpacking boots, heavier is better; that only stitched soles stand up to brutal wear; that leather makes the best uppers; that new boots must be stiff and will therefore need breaking in; and that the higher the upper, the more support it provides. The challenge to these assumptions has been almost entirely successful, and as a result we now have boots of so many kinds that they fill just about every imaginable backpacking niche.

All this sounds mildly exciting. When you look closely, though, an uncomfortable fact emerges: boots, though basic, are boring. And there is another thing too that makes . . . Well, I guess I may as well come clean. Eighteen months ago, when I originally wrote this revised chapter, I explained the various new techniques at some length. But now, with the rest of the book drafted, I have reread what I wrote—and found it both dreary as afternoon TV and also already out of date. Techniques seem sure to continue evolving very rapidly, so in rewriting I shall include only enough technical detail to clarify important practical matters.

Before surveying the boots now available we ought to consider some nontechnical fundamentals:

What a boot is meant to accomplish. The upper must be pliant enough to let your foot bulge slightly under load but must give it the necessary support. It must conform to the foot's minor idiosyncrasies, preferably without being broken in. It must protect the foot. It must repel water. It should, to some degree, breathe. *The sole* must be joinable to the upper in a waterproof, nonseparating way. It must provide safe traction on all expected surfaces—but, ideally, do so in a way that will not damage fragile land. It must cushion your foot against the worst sole-bashing it is likely to sustain. It must support that foot when it is bearing an unusually heavy load. Yet it cannot be too rigid because it must encourage, or at least not unduly impede, the foot's complex natural walking movements.

We will consider most of these criteria later, piece by piece, but we must take a look right now at an important word used twice in the last paragraph.

Support, as applied to boots, is difficult to define. In a general sense it probably means something like the holding-together-against-abnormal-strain that professional athletes achieve when they tape their ankles, or that we mortals achieve with Ace or Champ bandages. More specifically, it seems to mean three discrete things: First, sufficient lateral rigidity to prevent feet from twisting severely under loads on uneven surfaces. Second, arch support of a kind that will prevent flattening under overload yet leave boots longitudinally flexible enough "to let your feet work"; that is, will mimic, at least to some degree, the spring action of your arches—an action vital to the feet's cushioning effect on the rest of the body. (Such flexible reinforcement of the natural arch is normally achieved by inserting between midsole and insole a contoured shank, typically steel and about 3½ inches long—perhaps a quarter the length of the boot. In hiking boots, such a shank more than half the length of the boot tends to make it too stiff. Shanks also help protect arches from stones and uneven ground.) Finally, the boots must have stiff heel counters that reinforce your muscles below the anklebone. This seems to be the critical area for ankle support. Note that most running backs in the NFL now wear low-cut shoes; but those shoes undoubtedly have strong heel counters—and the ankles under them will be heavily taped.

Weight is even more important on the feet than on the back. In his classic 1906 book, *Camping and Woodcraft,* Horace Kephart calculated the results of wearing boots just one pound too heavy: "In ten miles there are 21,120 average paces. At one extra pound to the pace, the boots make you lift, in a ten-mile tramp, over ten tons more foot gear." In 1953 the successful Mount Everest expedition came to the conclusion that in terms of physical effort one pound on the feet is equivalent to five pounds on the back. A consensus of informed opinion now seems to support that assessment. Anyway, today's trend is certainly toward lightness.

In describing the many kinds of boots now available I shall have to divide them into categories. But although separate categories do indeed exist they are already cross-breeding, madly. So please try to bear in mind that, although description demands classification, what we now have is really a continuum.

Let us assume five current categories:

1. *The sneaker cousins* (which can be broadly seen as having evolved from tennis and basketball shoes) started the roll toward revolution. They remain popular—though on the lowest rung on the ladder in both serviceability and price (up to $45).

Their uppers, originally canvas, may now be made of Cordura (heavy woven nylon fabric) or even split leather (page 64). Water repellency therefore ranges from nillish to fair. Uppers and soles are typically joined together by vulcanizing (a.k.a. autoclave): the entire sole assembly is cold-cemented to the uppers, then heat-pressed in a process similar to that once used for tire patching. Vulcanizing is the cheapest way to mass-produce a durable, watertight bond between sole and upper. And it can make a reasonably light boot—but not one with the kind of lateral rigidity and foot support needed in boots for heavy hiking.*

Sneaker cousins are fine for city use and for unladen walking in wilder places, probably adequate for strong-footed people who carry light loads and stick to trails or smoothish terrain, and even seem to satisfy some stalwarts out beyond these confines. A New York friend recently wrote me that he's "using $10 Spanish boots called Chirucas, rubber-soled and with canvas uppers that can be waterproofed, within reason, by spraying with silicone from time to time. The tongue is terrible. But they are said to be good for 500 to 600 miles . . . and [seem] just fine for Eastern backpacking."

---

* Normally, I avoid the word "hiking." To me, it suggests a macho march from A to B—head down, face tight, brain blinkered. The very different act of traveling to taste the joys that lie between A and B is far better served, I feel, by "walking." But in this chapter, for clarity, I've had to succumb. "Walking boots" are not the same as "hiking boots."

"Heavy hiking" is, in my book, the sort of thing done by serious but not necessarily solemn backpackers who sometimes carry heavy loads or strike away from trails across rough terrain.

Leading makers of sneaker cousins include Donner Mountain, Inter-Footwear and Palladium.

2. *The running-shoe cousins.* In 1981, Nike and New Balance and other running-shoe makers moved into the hiking-boot market—and brought the nascent revolution to a boil. The new boots are constructed very like their running-shoe antecedents: uppers of Cordura or some other nylon fabric or even Gore-Tex, reinforced at wear points with leather; and soles cemented on by a cold-pressure process made possible by vastly improved new glues. The boots retain at least a vague "running-shoe look" but within certain limitations make excellent hiking boots. They need virtually no breaking in. Proper treatment can make them reasonably water-repellent. And unlike heavy leather boots they quickly dry out. The cemented-sole-attachment construction permits the building in of enough strength and stiffness at toe cap, midsole and heel counter to provide the foot support necessary for light loads and easy terrain. Above all, though, the boots are light. Even ankle-length models average only 2¼ pounds—or about half as much as traditional leather hiking boots. And low-cuts such as the Nike Lava Dome weigh only 1¾ pounds. So they have all been embraced with joy by New Wave ultralightweight enthusiasts. But they're also popular—more popular than their sneaker relatives—with people who carry heavy loads on trails or even pack cross-country.

For a closer look at the model I have chosen, see page 65.

Running-shoe cousins—made by Rocky, Asolo, Donner Mountain and a growing number of others, in addition to Nike and New Balance —currently cost from $45 to $100. This places them neatly, in price as well as serviceability, on the next rung above the sneaker cousins. But the category leaks. On the down side, a Nike copy that may or may not stand up to heavy wear now sells at $26. And the uppers of one Nike model are all-leather, of another mainly Gore-Tex (page 405)—and this could be seen as putting them halfway into the next category, which I shall call

3. *The emerging lightweights.* I hope this vague heading suggests a broad spectrum of boots that under the stimulus of new materials and ideas are in the process of evolving from current models. For that is what we now have. Construction of these boots may take almost any form: sole attachment may be by vulcanizing, cementing or injection molding—a process in which completed uppers are held in a contained mold and the liquid that will form the sole is forced in under pressure, either hot or cold, and then solidifies, firmly fixed to the uppers. Other innovations are surely lurking. In other words, this category embraces every lightweight from the tried-but-not-yet-proven, through the still secret and semisecret, to the barely born.

The only members now clearly visible are those with Gore-Tex uppers—usually leather-reinforced at wear points. Although the makers of Gore-Tex like to claim otherwise, these boots still stand in the tried-but-not-yet proven class. It remains unclear whether even Gore-Tex II (page 406) is resistant enough to the inevitable abrasion and heavy soiling that a boot must withstand. And seams continue to present problems. So does the attachment of soles to uppers. Time—not to mention Life, Fortune, Money and People—will tell whether these difficulties can be overcome. Meanwhile some users seem very happy, others malcontentious.

Good Gore-Tex boots start around $75 and average about 3½ pounds. Danner (most successfully, so far), Nike, Donner Mountain and Herman Survivors were early experimenters, and others are now following.

The rest of this emerging category remains largely nebulous—a swirling mist of tomorrow's successes and failures.

4. *Traditional boots* are all-leather-uppered and built for long, rough wars and therefore usually heavy as hell—though there's a lightweight division, often featuring suede uppers. Traditionals retain a viable if limited niche and will probably continue to do so. In my opinion—and in the opinion of most, though not all, experienced backpackers—no other boot yet in sight provides the support and protection you need for heavy loads and rough terrain.

Traditional boots have during the last thirty years been slowly but steadily evolving. Hard thermoplastics radically improved toe caps and heel counters. "Regenerated leather"—a conglomerate of resin and leather scraps, bearing the same relationship to leather as a Prestolog does to wood—gave us midsoles that were more waterproof, resilient and heat resistant. But the boots' basic character persisted. You still had to break them in, slowly and often painfully. And not even the best made for effortless walking. Recently, though, an apparently minor innovation—a sole with a marked "rocker" action that rolls with your foot—has made possible stout, heavy boots that need very little breaking in and that indeed seem to make walking easier and more comfortable. We will discuss reasons for and details of this pleasant phenomenon when we examine the traditional boots I now use (page 66).

Traditional heavy-duty boots probably average around 4½ pounds and close to $150, but the cost range is wide. You can get good, serviceable if rather light models for around $75. Most of these are Korean-made. They often embody the latest improvements but their leather is not yet always of the highest quality. European-made high-quality boots now mostly start at around $100. Widely available makes include the Italian Pivetta and Fabiano and Asolo, French Galibier, Swiss

Raichle and Yugoslavian Tyrol. Kastinger of Austria have a new and interesting boot. Vasque (now essentially domestic rather than Italian) and Danner of Oregon compete very successfully.

Superb custom-made boots come from Limmer of New Hampshire, Hunkidori Bootmaking of Colorado and Randall Merril of Utah (wait times, four to ten months; $130–$300).

5. *The coming synthetics.* Hard-shelled plastic boots have virtually blown away old-style leather competitors for skiing and mountaineering, and Koflach have recently been advertising their Viva model as suitable for hiking. But it is essentially a mountaineering boot: rock-hard shell, pivoting ankle socket, felt liners. And such boots lack any flex in the sole and would therefore be damnably uncomfortable for protracted walking on hard surfaces. They also cannot breathe at all. The makers, queried, tend to agree that these are serious drawbacks but say the boot has its place for cold, wet-weather backpacking. I would have to question that —though I must accent that I do not yet have firsthand experience of any such boots. For the moment I think we must accept that the viable hard-shelled plastic hiking boot lies, if anywhere, in the future. Meanwhile informed rumor has it that soft synthetic materials may challenge leather for uppers in about five years.

Costs in this category average around $?! Weights ditto. Makers include Quien Sabe, Sijui and Çanefaitrein.

The question arises: "Will new-tech boots totally replace traditionals?" It's difficult to say. My guess is that there will be more inter-breeding but that traditionals will continue to hold on to a limited backpacking niche. Their ruggedness is proven, under all conditions. And although they reflect conservative thoughtways their hand-made nature makes it fairly easy for makers to incorporate design changes, item by item. On the other hand, the mass-production methods necessary to make new-tech boots economically viable make their designs, once set, relatively inflexible.

The one change that might drown traditionals would be the discovery of a truly waterproof boot that fulfilled all the other criteria for a rugged but comfortable heavy hiking boot.

Certain features are obviously common to all categories of boot.

Lacing and laces

Three distinct systems are commonly found on hiking boots: grommeted eyelets; D-rings (attached by the straight sides to swiveling clips that are fixed to the outside of the uppers); and open hooks (similarly attached). The miniature tunnels of "speed lacing" are now rare, though you still see them occasionally. The systems often come in combinations —especially with hooks at the top of the boot.

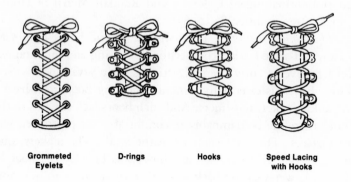

| Grommeted Eyelets | D-rings | Hooks | Speed Lacing with Hooks |

Grommeted eyelets are almost indestructible. And even if a grommet wears through or works loose (something that has never happened to me) the hole remains usable. But eyeleted boots are not always quick or simple to take off or put on: all the alternatives are better. Indeed, if you are wearing big gloves in severe cold, open hooks at the top of the lacing may be the only practical system. On the other hand, all the alternatives to eyelets can, at least in theory, pull out or break off and leave you miles from God knows where with an imperfectly laced and therefore ill-fitting boot that lets water in like a sieve. What's more, hooks can snag on undergrowth and other bootlaces—a misadventure that has never happened to me in several years of recent use but which I still cannot totally banish from my mind. I suspect that many of us generate such half-acknowledged biases. Try to squelch them. You'll probably find you adapt easily enough to any lacing system.

Whatever system you use, do not lace too tightly at the bottom: the pressure can block the necessary wiggle-freedom of your toes and may even constrict circulation. But on the near-vertical part of the boot the lace must be tight enough to keep your foot from sliding forward under the kind of pressure you generate when walking downhill. You can block the transfer of tension from tightly to loosely laced sectors by crisscrossing the laces two, three or four times at the changeover point.

Calf-length boots—now rare for backpacking, except under special conditions (page 68)—should be laced up to the ankle in the same way as ankle-length boots; but the calf section, especially when of soft leather, should be left rather loose to provide better ventilation and less muscle constriction. One reader suggests using separate laces, top and bottom.

Laces are now mostly braided nylon. They're very strong: I've never had one break on me. They do not rot, absorb water, dry out stiff or become brittle in extreme cold. Unlike leather laces, they are never eaten by mice or their allies. And the flat kind have largely overcome the old, round version's tendency to slip out of top eyelets when your boots are unlaced—an annoyance some people overcome by knotting the lace ends.

I used to follow tradition and carry a spare pair of laces, but long ago decided to rely on a length of my ubiquitous nylon cord (page 518).

Velcro-closured boots, already used for Nordic skiing, may be on their backpacking way.

Tongues

The critical area is at the base of the lacing system: the inevitable meeting place of two or more segments must meld neatly, and any stitching must be stout. The tongue gussets should be waterproof and also fold down without abrasive lumps or ridges. Fold-over flaps on top clearly aid waterproofness, particularly in snow, but seem likely to impede cooling in hot weather.

Linings

Most hiking boots except the lightest now have soft "glove leather" linings that shield your feet from any stitching in the main uppers, improve fit, reduce friction and absorb sweat. The leather may soon be replaced, though, by Cambrelle, a woven synthetic fabric developed by Danner that is comfortable, somewhat absorbent and, above all, "wears like iron." In heavier boots, foam padding around the ankle sections increases comfort, especially during breaking in, and keeps feet warmer —though in hot weather that may mean "hotter." Foam also absorbs water and dries slowly.

Scree collars

Once rather clumsy addenda at the boot top—sometimes even miniature gaiters—scree collars have now been refined to well-padded, bulging rolls that no longer do much to keep out fragments of scree and gravel but look nice to a buyer—and on stiff boots certainly reduce the ankle agony if you have not been wearing them for a spell. In some very good traditional boots the outside of the collar is now part of the main upper, and therefore almost immune to wear. In others it is far from immune.

Soles

Most heavy hiking boots—and many medium- and lightweight ones too—still come with black, high-carbon lugged soles made by Vibram: the lighter, shallower-lugged Roccia or the heavier and more deeply lugged Montagna. But the similar Galibiers are still around. And Kastinger now have an interesting new sole.

For the extreme rocker sole, see page 67.

Sneaker and running-shoe cousins and the emerging lightweights come with a wild variety of soles, most of them more lightly lugged than was traditional (for a specific case, see page 66). Although they may grip less well under certain conditions, they are much lighter—and offer another important advantage.

A few years ago loud voices began to complain about damage done to the land, and especially to trails, by standard, heavily lugged soles. The question is clearly legitimate, and is not answered, except emotionally, by the valid countercharge that far more damage is done to trails by horse traffic—usually a couple of horses per person, always four legs per horse, and every one steel-shod and digging. Yet the voices seem to have died away. The trouble is, I think, that although we have many miles of flat, smooth trail on which lugged soles are both unnecessary and unnecessarily damaging, there's at present no effective alternative to deep lugs for the steep, rough terrain and trails over which many people, especially in the West, do at least some of their walking. But the new lightweights offer hope. Their soles tend to be less deeply lugged, sometimes even nonlugged. And they are most suitable for precisely those places in which deep-lugged soles are often both unnecessary and most damaging. Alternatives to deep-lugged soles are available from Vibram, even for heavy boots, but do not sell well. Vibram say that is because they do not have "the climbing look." But they also wear out more quickly. One suggestion I have not yet tried: fill deep-cut grooves between your lugs with Boot Patch (page 74).

Choosing your boots

First, hold the objectives tightly in mind: you want to walk in comfort; you do not want to get unnecessarily tired; you want to keep your feet as dry as possible. To achieve these ends you must balance weight against support and protection. In the past, boots probably tended to be too heavy, but today the trend is toward lightness (and longitudinal flexibility, so that your foot can "work"). And you should certainly not buy a tank when a VW will do. But don't forget that the nature of your feet, your load, the terrain or the weather may sometimes demand a tank.

Second—because there is now a boot for almost every backpacking niche—you must know just what you will be demanding of the pair you choose.

If you intend to walk only in cities or suburban parks, unladen, then—provided you have strong feet and ankles—you can probably get by with tennis or running shoes. Some people even use them for much rougher walking. (I wore running shoes not long ago for a day hike on Mongolian grasslands, but the place had been grazed lawnlike and I had no more suitable footwear within 10,000 miles.) Sneaker cousins or running-shoe cousins, low-cut or ankle-length, are certainly fine for such jaunts—and for fair-weather work with light loads on trails or across friendly terrain. If you have suspect ankles or rain seems likely or the terrain gets rough you may want to forget the sneaker cousins and go with only ankle-length, top-of-the-line running-shoe cousins or with emerging or even traditional lightweights. And if the weather promises to be really foul or if the load gets over, say, 35 pounds (though that figure will vary prodigiously person to person) then you may prefer heavy, top-grain traditionals. Here, ability and experience count. An athletic and experienced walker may be able to carry heavy loads over rough terrain wearing lightweight boots that on a tyro would mean courting injury. But, generally speaking, if you are what I have called a heavy hiker (page 54), you should stick with traditionals, titrating their heaviness against the heaviness of your hiking. Avoid "climbing" or "mountaineering" boots: the necessary stiffness of their soles makes them murderous for long-distance walking.

These are only guidelines, of course. No two people have the same feet—or mindset. A few happily pack 40-pound loads across talus while wearing low-cut cheapies. Others get out their backcountry heavies for a stroll around the park. And it's important to recognize that, even beyond such personal preferences, every choice is a compromise: no single boot will work best in all situations. Finally, if you find my guidelines fudgy to the brink of uselessness, remember that, as I said at the start, we are really looking at a continuum of boot styles, not a series of sealed-off categories.

Once you have decided what you will be demanding of your boots and go to a store to buy them, try to have your decisions ready to put into words. A good salesman recently told me, "We try to tailor sales to customers' needs, but we have to work with the information they give us —and it's often pretty vague." No matter how experienced you are, you'll probably find that in the store you still, like me, feel the need for guidance through the thickets of current brands and models. Even if you hike like crazy, all year round, you buy new boots only once every few years, and you tend to forget the rules. But the salesman is at it all day and every day. So if you feel confident that the one you get is an experienced backpacker and knows what he is talking about, lean heavily on his advice. In the end, though, you have to rely on your own judgment, feelings and even hunches. So the more you know, the better shod you'll be.

In making your choice, the first criterion should be quality.

If, like most of us, you lack technical competence, judging a boot's quality is largely a matter of common sense; of impression rather than specifics. But remember that a maker who cuts corners is likely to cut all corners. So, in both new-tech and traditional boots, examine the stitching on uppers. If it is weak-looking, beware.

For more on the rather specialized subject of judging the quality of uppers and also sole attachment in traditional boots, see page 63.

In new-tech boots the nub question is the sole attachment's reliability. But the answer seems to be that, beyond gross and obvious deformity, looking will not tell you much. Other than rely on the maker's reputation, all you can do is wear the damned things and see if they hold up.

The second criterion in choosing your boots is fit.

The third criterion is fit.

And the fourth criterion is fit.

When trying on boots in the store, take along the socks you plan to wear "on the trail" (a phrase I loathe, but which has its uses, I guess). Alternatively, buy some socks of the kind you "borrow" from the store when you fit the boots (most mountain shops have a basket of socks ready for that job). But don't be too inflexible about your sock requirements: a slight change in your usual sock combination may allow you to buy the pair of boots that really fits you best.

If you favor insoles you must, of course, put a pair in each boot you try—unless it's the kind that has a special built-in insole.

In fitting the boots, think of yourself as trying to put a glove on your foot. But do not picture a skin-tight glove. What you need is a boot that fits snugly at the broadest part of the foot (the trick is deciding exactly what "snugly" means, and in the end you always have to make your own decision, based on experience) but which leaves one finger's width of free room in front of the toes. You can check this toe space by unlacing the boot, standing up without a pack and pressing forward until your toes meet the end of the boot. If you can just slide a forefinger down into the gap left at the heel, that part of the fit is about right. With the boot laced there should be room to wriggle your toes fairly freely, and you should not be able to kick them forward so that they bear uncomfortably on the front of the boot (the shape of the toe cap is important; for most feet, the broader and squarer, the better). On the other hand, it is vital that, with the boot laced tightly up the vertical part, there be as little movement as possible at the heel, upward or sideways (though see page 67 for an apparent exception). The difficulty is that with wear all boots mold themselves to the shape of your feet. With light new-tech boots the change is minor. But heavy traditional boots are mostly stiff when new, and you simply have to guess how much change will take place—how much the sides will "give" and how well that stiff-feeling heel will conform to the contours of your particular foot. Generally speaking, cheaper boots alter more than good-quality ones, especially if they are unlined; buy them a little on the tight side. In modern high-quality boots with first-rate leather, soft linings and foam padding, a good fit in the store seems to mean a good fit on the mountain.

Do not, by the way, pay rapt attention to sizes. Base your decision on the feel of the boot. If the size is not the same as last time, it doesn't matter a damn. Different boots marked as the same size may vary appreciably.

Similarly, try to ignore advertising hype about "American," "Italian" or "French" lasts. A last is simply a boot manufacturer's idea of what a human foot looks like. It is crazy not to try on a boot just because it's not advertised as being built on an "American" last. What matters is how the damned thing fits your foot.

Even if cost has to loom large in your decision, beware of false economics: heavy traditional boots may cost twice as much as lightweight new-tech models but will probably outlast two or three pairs of them. A $120 boot that lasts ten years is, at $12 a year, cheap transportation. Someone recently figured out that typical lightweight new-tech boots cost 17 cents a mile, heavy traditional ones ½ cent. (Estimated cpm for comparison only. Your costs may vary depending on speed, walking habits, trip length, terrain and weather. Highway and talus figures lower.) In weighing the economics, try to remember as usual that money may loom large in the store but will shrink to frippery on a blizzardous mountaintop.

As these protracted pages of instruction suggest, choosing a new pair of boots is a long, slow business. I still find it often takes me an hour or more. But it's time well spent. An ill-fitting boot can cripple a trip, single-footed.

Judging quality in traditional boots

is a somewhat specialized matter.

First, scrutinize the uppers' leather. It should be pliable but tough and have a rich texture that will absorb waterproofing materials. And the closer the upper comes to being a single piece—as in some of the very best boots—the more likely it is to be of high quality. A one-piece upper will certainly be stronger: seams, no matter how good, are a potential weakness.

Leather thickness obviously makes a difference (though I'd have difficulty in imparting any quantitative guidelines) and Asolo now state the thickness for all their boots.

There's one partially valid question that's often asked about leather uppers: "Are they full-grain?" Unfortunately, "full-grain" is a misnomer: except for some inferior belly cuts, full-thickness cowhide is too thick and rigid for modern boots, and the inner part of the hide is almost always removed. So "full-grain" should really be "top-grain"—and that term may in fact be taking over. Anyway, the question remains: "Does the leather still have its vital smooth outer skin that—if it is intact—provides the prime water barrier?" Obviously, any smooth-side-out boot is top-grain: the skin stares you in the face. With "rough-outs" (rough side outermost) you frankly have to rely on the maker's reputation. Arguments still rage, smooth-outs versus rough-outs. "Cows wear the skin outside" goes one refrain, "and they must know something. Besides, with smooth-outs I know I've got genuine top-grain, and cuts and blemishes in the skin can't be hidden by the lining." The counterchant runs: "But in smooth-outs the vitally important skin gets broken by every little nick. And although rough-outs may be less resistant to abrasion, the skin is protected from all but really deep cuts." I have worn both smooth- and rough-out boots, and frankly there seems little to choose between the two. In the end, what matters is the quality of the leather. Generally speaking, if it's good, so is the boot.

Not all uppers are made of top-grain leather. Split-grain hides have had the skin side removed. They are cheaper, lighter and more flexible than top-grain, and if of high quality make good uppers for medium-weight boots not expected to last for years or be very waterproof.

Suede is generally the inside half of a split hide and therefore has two rough sides, one of which has been further roughened by an abrading machine. Good suede makes good lightweight boots. Dressings will render it reasonably water-resistant, but will destroy the cosmetic nap.

The new sole-attachment methods have not yet been successfully applied to heavy-duty leather boots—and may never be. So stitching still rules. For years, in bull sessions and books (including earlier editions of this one), argument has roiled around the relative merits of the two main methods of sole attachment: turned-in (or Littleway) and stitched-down (or Norwegian or Goodyear). But the facts seem to suggest that the differences between them are now academic. Given high quality, any modern stitched-on sole should work fine.*

Many reputable stores will let you try out your boots for a limited period—if you treat them properly. An excellent little pamphlet by REI advises: "For the next week or so wear your boots around the house or office, *on carpeted areas only.* Any signs of wear will interfere with a return for a full refund. . . . *Boots worn outside or treated* will be handled as used boots." You really can't ask for more.

If you live far from any dealer that carries the kind of boot you want, you may have to mail-order. I hear that the best firms are very good at matching outline sketches of feet. Follow their instructions meticulously, that's all—particularly in making the foot sketches. And deal only with reputable people who offer what seems to be an honest guarantee.

My choices

Until recently I owned only heavy traditional boots and wore them for all walking, near and far, heavy- and un-laden. Note that there was a method behind this meagerness: the boots were worn in to my feet and my feet were worn in to the boots, and wearing them as often as possible helped keep things that way. Then, last year, I bought a pair of New Balance Rainiers, mainly to make footsense under ultralightweight loads (page 27). The Rainiers' uppers are blue Cordura, massively reinforced with supple pigskin leather. The boots have D-ring lacing, glove-leather lining. Soles are lightweight Vibrams with a special pattern of lugs that look like miniature tank barriers. They are said to be self-cleaning—and sometimes oblige. The soles are heavily beveled at the heels (see Easy Hiker, below) and mildly rockered at the sturdily reinforced toes. The thick, shock-absorbing, one-piece synthetic midsoles are cemented to the uppers. The overall look is mildly "running shoe" and not, to my eye, particularly pleasing (though more so than that of most competitors). But the result is certainly light: my size 11s weigh 2 pounds 6 ounces. Cost: $70.

* Only when preparing this revision did I discover to my horror that an illustration on page 35 of the previous edition, purporting to show a "standard or Goodyear welt," reeked with error. In addition, my use of the word "welt," in text and caption, was incorrect. And it's no real excuse that I followed a usage that is for some reason prevalent in hiking-boot literature.

In bootmaking, a welt is correctly "the strip of leather stitched into the seam between sole and upper, to strengthen the joining." It does not mean, as I—and many others—have implied, the general area of junction between sole and upper. So there is, for example, no such thing as "a Littleway welt," only a "Littleway attachment." I apologize.

Before using my Rainiers for the first time I waterproofed the leather with Biwell and sprayed the Cordura with silicone. Then I wore them, with no breaking in at all, on a two-day, one-night trip with a 26-pound from-skin-out load (page 27): three-plus hours up a faint, steep trail with no rain but much wet undergrowth and frequent stone-hopping creek crossings; two half-days shoveling soil and other rough and unfair work; then almost three hours down, with some submomentary lingering at creek crossings, boots just awash, to give them a mild test. Result: complete comfort, total dryness and distinct joy at the lightness of foot. Ditto on all later trips.

The Rainiers have one-level soles, without a step at the forward edge of the heels. The lack of a ready-made place to hold gaiter cords is more imagined than real: I find that you can without too much trouble lay the cords into the lug pattern so that they hold well and without disastrous wear. But although the flat sole offers greater traction area than the standard in-stepped kind, its shallow lugs and lack of that step at the forward edge of the heel mean that it cannot bite effectively into such surfaces as deep carpets of dead leaves. When the carpets are sloping, that can be dangerous. I have several times slipped a little. But I'm learning to walk softly in such terrain, angling in with the edges of the boots, and carrying my staff ready for instant help.

Although the boots have so far proved very cool for walking they seem for some reason to be a little hot for sitting around in. And trials under various conditions suggest that, as I expected, they probably won't remain waterproof in heavy rain but that they will handle loads of up to at least 40 pounds on good surfaces. So while I've not yet used my Rainiers enough to deliver a round, pontifical verdict I have to report that this jury, though still out, is certainly leaning toward approval.

For twenty-odd years my heavy traditional boots have been a series of Italian-made Pivettas, developed by Donner Mountain of California. I came to them by the orthodox route: a combination of chance and whim and experience and personal prejudice, mitigated by a salesman's advice. I used successive models in daytime temperatures ranging from 20° F. to over 110°, on snow and sand, in places as different as Grand Canyon and Kilimanjaro. And I was satisfied. But the model I was using until recently, the 4¾-pound Eiger, has fallen victim to Herblock's Law: "If it's good, they'll stop making it." With the trend to lighter boots for backpacking and also for "in" wear around campuses, demand fell too low to justify continued production.

For the last two years I have been using a pair of Italian-made Easy Hikers from Pacific Mountain Sports of California. The boots are reasonably priced ($88) and mediumweight (size 8s rated at 4½ pounds—though my size 11s, now heavily loaded with wax, weigh 5½ pounds).

Uppers are one-piece, top-grain rough-outs. Beneath the laces, each upper double-folds over a heavily foam-padded tongue, and a small Velcro patch on the tongue mates with one on the underside of the bottom flap to prevent the tongue from slipping sideways. Lacing is by D-rings and hooks. The first pair of hooks, located very low in a soft leather insert, almost at the anklebone, help you to pull the boot snug around your foot.

The Easy Hiker's glove-leather linings are foam-padded around the entire ankle area, and the scree collars are even more heavily padded. The boots come with contoured foam insoles. Sole attachment is Norwegian. But the boot's outstanding feature is the extreme "rocker" sole—an asymmetrical refinement developed from modern running shoes. The sole is curve-beveled at heel and toe, to help the foot roll your weight in a more natural way at each step, across the ball of the foot to the big toe; and this action is further aided not only by slight increases in thickness of the sole beneath both heel and ball of foot but also by a rigid but contoured nylon shank that runs the full length of the boot—not just a quarter of its length, as in most hiking boots.

The makers maintain that all this adds up to a revolution: "By reducing the pressure as well as resistance on the lower shin bone, heel, achilles, ball of the foot and instep, your foot does not experience the tightness and fatigue it usually does. Therefore it will normally allow you to walk further more comfortably or, as we say: you'll get more miles per effort (MPE)." The sole design also means, they maintain, that the need to break the boots in virtually vanishes. Now, I've heard a lot of this kind of hype. And I began testing the boots with acid cynicism.

I found that they did not grip my heels firmly, the way boots are traditionally meant to (the makers later told me that the sole construction makes really tight gripping unnecessary, and this reduces the pressures on feet, especially with new boots); but after barely three hours' testing I was so impressed with their comfort that I wore them on a week's trip in the High Sierra. I went in early fall, with a 50-pound pack. From the start the boots felt good. On the fourth morning I descended rather hurriedly for about three hours in the face of an apparent storm threat, from 11,300 to 9000 feet, cross-country, over mostly rocky and very steep terrain. My feet suffered no discomfort. Then, on the last day, I came down about 3000 feet, all on a fast trail, in a seven-hour stint divided into two parts, with a boots-off rest at lunchtime. I reached roadhead at around six o'clock—and at eleven o'clock, after a leisurely meal and a long talk with a ranger, suddenly realized that I had not even loosened my boots. True, the ranger was slim and decorative; but she can hardly rob the boots of the main credit. Since that trip the Easy Hikers have become my standard heavy-load boots. They still don't really grip the back of my heels. But they remain extremely comfortable. And I'm very inclined to think that they do indeed make walking rather less tiring.

Boots for special conditions

Special conditions may call for special boots.

Twenty-five years ago, two summers of slogging through trailless tracts of western Vancouver Island convinced me that for cross-country travel in rainforests, where your route often lies over or along slippery fallen tree trunks and where undergrowth is always snatching at your legs, the only satisfactory footwear is a pair of calked knee boots. By no means everyone agrees. But I understand that although some loggers have now switched to triple-soled Vibram soles, those who work "in deep woods and on very steep slopes" still use calked boots.

Another summer in the muskeg-and-lake country of Canada's Northwest Territories taught me that in such places you need a stout and roomy pair of leather-topped rubber boots. At that time the Maine Hunting Boot by L. L. Bean was standard for such conditions, and for wet snow. Such boots are reportedly admirable for much Eastern wilderness—the sort of flat, soggy terrain in which old tote roads skirt or even transect spruce and cedar swamps. They're especially good when hiking is largely a means to camping or hunting or fishing, and a day's backpacking may amount to no more than five miles and is unlikely to exceed twelve. The Maine Hunting Boot has now evolved, and in many places the current standards for soggy conditions—for ski operators in the West, for example—are calf-length boots by Sorel of Canada with leather uppers, injection-molded lug soles and thick, removable felt liners that can be washed. You can dry the liners off overnight, in your sleeping bag if necessary, or can carry a spare pair.

For lacing calf-length boots, see page 58.

In certain parts of the country—because of local conditions or innate human conservatism or both—a specific style of boot may remain as traditional as the dialect. You can always ask a reputable dealer about parochial preferences. Of course, there's no law that says you have to take his advice.

In bitterly cold weather, especially at high altitudes, even extrathick traditional boots (a size or two larger than usual, to accommodate more sock) may not protect you. Vapor-barrier socks worn over inner socks are said to help a great deal (VB socks by Duckabush: 2 ounces, $13; by Chouinard: 1½ ounces, $7.50. For discussion of VB principles, see page 387). Plastic bags make practical substitutes. Overboots exist too. And Army surplus Mickey Mouse boots have long been popular. The hard-shelled plastic boots with pivoting ankle sockets that have taken over for skiing and mountaineering are indeed waterproof, but in their present form they are not for long-distance walking (page 57). Until they have been successfully modified for general backpacking or some other totally waterproof design emerges, our feet are in worse shape than any other part of the body to cope with long spells of abysmally wet weather. No matter how stout or "waterproof" any current viable hiking boots may be, a few days of heavy rain or wet snow will assuredly soak them—if not through uppers, then by seepage through tops. Gaiters certainly help, but they do not work miracles (though see below). In prolonged, really wet conditions you always seem to end up with damp or even soaking socks, and then, if the temperature is low, your feet at some point get cold. Again, VB socks or plastic bags may help. But the boots remain soggy. And drying them without ruining them (page 74) is a protracted business, normally impossible in the field until the sogginess lifts. In other words, there is so far no high-tech defense against wet feet, as there is against wet torso (page 377). One possible approach has now surfaced, though, among

Gaiters.

In heavy rain, long gaiters provide the only halfway viable protection against "run-down" into boots. But while they give some protection to uppers they will not in the end keep them from getting soaked. A recent advance offers hope. The knee-length Yeti gaiter by Berghaus (2 pounds, $60) has around its foot a 1½-inch-deep rubber seal that grips the boot sole tightly enough to exclude all moisture. In theory, anyway. And I hear some good reports. The idea certainly sounds interesting. Breathable neoprene wet-suit material has also been used in the lower sections of gaiters, by Pacific Ascente and others, but is apparently rather liable to damage by gouging.

Most gaiters are made of coated nylon fabric. Gore-Tex is not only too expensive but also unlikely to withstand the abrasion and extreme soiling inevitable around ankles; but it is sometimes used for the upper sections of knee-length models, to improve ventilation.

Less ambitious, ankle-length gaiters perform a multitude of functions, with long or short pants. They give at least some protection against snow, rain and wet undergrowth. They blunt cold winds. They're good in country infested by ticks or clinging grass seeds, both of which delight in socks but are defeated by nylon. And they're even better when you're boulder-hopping across creeks: they'll ward off a surprising amount of splashing and even brief immersion. Nowadays I almost always carry a pair of short coated-nylon gaiters with elastic inserts top and bottom to grip legs (or pants) and boots. Cords fit under the instep (see page 66 for instepless soles) and stop the gaiters from riding upward. Zippers make them easy to put on and take off, and Velcro-stripped flaps protect the zippers. (Height 6 inches, 3 ounces, $10.)

Insoles

In recent years insoles seem to have become much more popular among walkers of all kinds. A prime reason may be that Spenco Medical Corporation of Texas have brought out a first-class product. "Nitrogen bubbles introduced into neoprene sheets under intense pressure," says their blurb, produce an "extraordinary shock absorption system [that] absorbs side-to-side friction as well as vertical pressures." It seems to work too—without roasting or even simmering your sole. The distinctively green-lined insoles are described as "sanitary, decay resistant, odor proof, washable, never flatten out and will far outwear other products" (1¾ ounces [size 10–11], $6). You can trim them to fit your foot. Spenco also make a variety of heel cushions and arch supports embodying the same nitro-bubbly.

For several years I used Spenco insoles in my boots with gratitude (but do not need them in my current Rainiers and Easy Hikers). Similar insoles that I have not tried include Early Winters's Blue Prints ($5—similar to Spenco's but with blue lining) and Cosmic Feet ($8). Sorbothane insoles, made of a fleshlike, visco-elastic polymer, are thick and heavy and very expensive (⅜-inch at heel, ¼-inch in forefoot, 6 ounces a pair, $16) but seem to do an excellent cushioning job.

Around 1974 a New Jersey doctor patented an "energy-conserving rubber insole" that, according to *The New York Times,* embodied bands in the insole which stretched when the boots bent during a step and then, when the walker lifted his foot, contracted and helped straighten the boot. Reputed result: a slight speed-up in walking and a decrease in fatigue. An Army laboratory was said to be evaluating. I regret to report that I've heard no further news.

For emergency use—when sole-stitching protruded and chafed my feet—I have tried cardboard cutouts from cereal boxes (they last about six hours), regular foam-rubber insoles of the kind you can pick up at a drugstore (intolerably hot) and makeshift devices fashioned from asbestos gasket sheeting bought at a wayside garage (effective, though they tend to curl).

There is some advantage to gluing insoles into your boots. If they are left loose, though, you can transfer an old pair, already molded to the contours of your soles, into a new pair of boots and so dampen the grief of breaking them in. Boots dry better without insoles in them too.

If you intend to use insoles, you must obviously wear them when you fit a new pair of boots. And remember that they can even be used as an aid in fitting a pair of boots that, alone, are a tad too roomy; also, with old boots as compensation for changing to thinner socks.

Dog boots

In 1973 a Seattle outfit came up with laced "suede leather" coverings for dog paws, complete with holes for two front claws and adjustable for a wide range of paw sizes. Said to be the kind worn by real "working sheepdogs and cattle dogs." Sadly, the firm seems to have faded away. But I'm told that some dogs, under certain conditions, really do get immobilized by compacted snow building up on the hair around their paws; also that springcorn snow can cut canine pads.

For other considerations when taking your dog along—if you decide doing so is reasonable—see page 147.

Breaking in new boots

Most new-tech boots and some evolving traditionals (page 67) need little or no breaking in. But most old-style leather boots, especially if they're heavy and stiff, must be slowly and carefully footbroken. Until some of the stiffness has gone and insoles and uppers have begun to conform to the contours of your feet, they are almost sure to be uncomfortable. And they'll be great at generating blisters. I have heard people advise: "Just put your new boots on and soak them in water for a while and then go out and walk. You'll never have any trouble." It sounds like pretty drastic treatment to me, and I have never tried it. One experienced mountaineer I know, who had always felt as I do about the soaking theory, once tried it out as a crash program and found that it worked, but perhaps it's relevant that he says he hasn't repeated it. The difficulty with the method lies in the drying out afterward. Water is the enemy of boots, heat even worse: wet leather, if heated, tends to harden and crack; stitching pops; and soles, midsoles and uppers shrink differentially and often separate. Another, more reasonable watery way to hasten breaking in is to fill the boots with hot water ("Oh, please no!" exclaims an experienced boot man in my ear), pour it out almost instantly, then put the boots on and wear them until dry. The effect is said to be much like sweating into your boots over a long haul. And if you condition the boots with Biwell or whatever (page 74) immediately after walking them dry they'll reputedly suffer little or no damage.

Frankly, all I have ever done is to take short, easy walks, with little or no load at first, and gradually increase load and distance. At the very beginning, even wearing the boots around the house helps. Naturally, boots should be well waxed or oiled as soon as you buy them (page 73).

For a major backpacking expedition—the kind that threatens to wear out a pair of boots—you obviously have to start with new ones. After all, you wouldn't set out on a transcontinental road rally with worn tires. For such expeditions, breaking in the new boots can present a problem. The theory is simple: the boots will take care of themselves during those practice hikes you plan to take for several weeks beforehand in slowly increasing doses that will painlessly harden your feet and muscles. But I have found that in practice the press of administrative arrangements just before the start rises to such a frantic peak that there is no time for any practice hikes worthy of the name. So you start with flabby muscles, soft feet—and stiff boots. And this is no laughing matter. It is not simply that sore feet soon take the joy out of walking. They can make walking impossible. Just before my Grand Canyon trip, while putting out a food cache and at the same time trying rather belatedly to harden my feet and soften a new pair of boots, I attempted too much in a single day, generated a blister, developed an infected heel and had to postpone the start for a week. Fortunately I had planned an easy first week's shakedown cruise. But even with an old pair of insoles in the boots my feet barely carried me through the second critical and much harder week of the trip. I offer no solution to this kind of problem (which can also crop up on shorter journeys) but I suggest that you at least make every effort to allow time for a gentle shakedown cruise at the beginning. As we have seen (page 9), there is an even more important reason for such an arrangement. See also page 86.

Care of boots

Some new-tech boots need little or no maintenance beyond decrudding after a dirty walk. But any leather used to reinforce wear points must be treated occasionally (see below) to keep it in condition. To increase the water-repellency of my new Rainiers (page 65) I put Biwell on the pigskin and silicone on the Cordura nylon. Silicone spray is said to be safer than sloshed-on liquid because appreciable amounts dripping down onto the sole can delaminate glued attachments. A felt-pad-on-wire applicator attached to the stopper, as in Meltonian Shoe Dri (4-ounce bottle, $2), obviates that difficulty. But Thompson's Sport Spray (12-ounce can, $5.50) is also good. If you have nothing else around, silicone fluid for floating dry flies seems to work fine.

Traditional boots demand regular care. Leather uppers must be conditioned with wax or oil. But which conditioners should be used and which avoided on what kinds of leather is something that dissolves experts into raucous disagreement. As far as I can make out, the tentative current gospel reads: on chrome- or vegetable-tanned leather (which forms the uppers on most hiking boots), use wax and/or silicone, *but never use oil or grease;* on oil-tanned leather (which is normally softer and more flexible, as on the upperworks of many calf-length boots), use oil or grease. Moral: when you buy new boots, make sure you know what treatment they demand.

For summer use, the ideal is to apply the conditioner lightly so that your feet can "breathe" through leather that will be reasonably water-repellent. In snow or wet, condition heavily. The leather will become waterproof; but it cannot then "breathe." That's the theory, anyway. Frankly, I find that in hot weather I need plenty of conditioner to keep the bloody boots soft.

At one time I used Kiwi neutral wax but found that my boots tended to dry out too fast on long journeys even though I applied an average of one 2½-ounce can a week. For many years I used Sno Seal, a wax that keeps leather supple for very much longer. The old version, which required heating the boots before application, probably led to much damage by enthusiasts who invoked hair driers and even ovens. With the present, improved product you just leave the boots in sunlight for a while and the wax is absorbed. The new version is also silicone-free and therefore does not damage toe or heel counters. For years Sno Seal ruled (7½-ounce can, $3.50; 4-ounce tube, $2.50). Now it has been challenged and is perhaps being superseded by Bee Seal Plus, a beeswax-and-lanolin compound that conditions and tends to waterproof (7½-ounce can, $4) and, for pure waterproofing, by Biwell, a nonsilicone conditioner from Austria (4-ounce tube, $2.50). Alternatives to Biwell: Water Seal (2-ounce jar, $2.89) and REI's Ultra Seal (2-fluid-ounce jar, $2.75; 4-fluid-ounce jar, $4.95). Many people, including me, now use Bee Seal on newish or very dry boots, Biwell as conditioner on old ones.

Sno Seal now make high-adhesion Welt Seal for waterproofing exposed stitching (2-ounce tube, $2.50; 2-ounce bottle, $3.50). Alternatives: Stitch Lock, Ultra Seam Guard, Seam Sealer and Boot Patch.

Standard conditioners for oil-tanned leather uppers are L. L. Bean's SuperDry (8 ounces, $3.25) and REI's Ultra Seal (see above). Neat's-foot oil, once standard for all uppers, attacks modern thermoplastic toe caps and counters if used too liberally. Some experts also say it oversoftens leather. "You have a choice," says one. "A boot or a baseball mitt." Neat's-foot remains useful for softening the tops of stiff boots.

Whenever your boot uppers show the slightest sign of needing lubrication, and also when you get home after a trip of any magnitude, clean and dry the boots and rub the chosen dressing well into the leather with fingers or a rag.

If your boots get thoroughly wet, dry them *slowly,* at air temperature or, at most, in sunlight. Packing them loosely with newspaper or toilet paper helps absorb internal moisture. *Never* put wet boots close to a fire or—back home—over a radiator or foot air register.

The interiors of boots left standing for any length of time may sprout a green mold. Cure, or even prevent, by spraying with a fungicide powder (BFI, Quinsana, Desenex). Boot Guard contains a high-density silicone oil to keep the insides of boots soft and supple and reduce sweat penetration, and also a fungicide to prevent mildew or rot. You can use Kiwi wax too.

If your soles wear badly, get them replaced before midsoles begin to wear. A reputable backpacking store should be able to tell you which local repairmen do a good job on hiking boots. For serious repairs, inquire with diligence. Steve Komito of Colorado has a reputation as repairman par excellence, but usually his waiting list for appointments is several weeks long. Wheeler and Wilson Boots of California now offer reputable mail-order service. For addresses of both, see Appendix II.

Please do not expect advice on how long a pair of boots should last. Obvious variables include toughness of boot and of terrain. Less obvious but at least as variable is the way the wearer walks. As with cars, spouses and daydreams, so with boots: some people are gentle on them, some downright murderous.

SOCKS

For years I wore only one pair of socks at a time. But some while back I succumbed to the currently more popular theory that you reduce friction and remove more sweat if you wear two pairs: a thin inner, thick outer.

For thick outer socks, wool is the material on almost every count: resilience, insulation, general comfort—and dissipation of sweat. Unlike other materials, wool works moisture upward along its fibres, out of the boot, where air can dispel it. The ribbing on most socks' upperworks is designed to aid this process. Nylon reinforcement—a small percentage throughout, with a boost at heels and toes—increases durability without detracting appreciably from other qualities.

The socks I now use are the Norwegian Ragg that are, in some form, almost standard Western hikers' wear (average of various versions: About 4 ounces, $6). They come in 100-percent wool or with 15-percent nylon. (A reader suggests that with needle and monofilament thread— or maybe dental floss—you can reinforce any wool socks at such wear spots as toenails and heel.) Luxury versions have now flowered, including two in the Early Winters catalogue: the Thousand-Mile Socks, which I've tried with satisfaction but which no longer appear, and the Million-aire's Socks (6 ounces, $25; guaranteed for life of original owner). Such socks are generally preshrunk wool-with-nylon woven around an elastic spandex or Lycra core. Opinion on them seems to vary from "genuine value" to "pure hype."

For a time, some years back, I used the two-layered Wick-Dry socks (4½ ounces, now $4), in which an inner layer of moisture-repellent Orlon and nylon is designed to wick perspiration to the outer layer of moisture-absorbing yarn (the socks are 10-percent cotton). But after a while—for no stunningly convincing reason beyond a suspicion that they tended to be rather hot—I went back to wool. Wick-Dry have their uses, though, notably for those unfortunates allergic to wool.

Thin inner socks come in wool (usually nylon-reinforced), cotton, silk and polypropylene (Olefin, Qiana, etc.). When I consulted three experienced and observant users, I found that all three had experimented

—and come to firm conclusions: one went for wool, one for silk and one for polypropylene. A doctor reader with perennially sore feet has written describing Qiana polypropylene socks as "a small miracle." And a friend who has backpacked a prodigious number of miles simply grunts, "I guess, only wool or cotton." As my own experiments tend to bear out these nonconclusions, the only honest advice I can currently offer is: "Consult your own feet." Most thin inner socks weigh around 1½ ounces. Typical current prices: wool, $3.50; cotton, $3; silk, $7; polypropylene, $3. One word of warning: do not use polypropylene inners alone, without wool or other absorbent outers. Polypropylene wicks moisture outward but not upward. Sweat therefore lies soggy on the lining of your boot and may cause blisters (page 88).

A reader has suggested that because most socks are constructed with at least one eye on cosmetics, heel and toe seams face inward—and at their termini provide "considerable bumps of stitching" to rough up your feet. Solution: wear such socks inside out. Wise words, maybe. But remember that some socks, such as those with a layer of terry looping on the inside, must not be reversed.

Whatever socks I'm wearing, I want them long enough to turn down over my ankle boots when I'm wearing shorts—which is almost always. An ordinary rubber band helps keep stones and dirt from falling down between socks and ankle. For protection of socks from such infuriating environmental hazards as dry grass seeds, see "gaiters" (page 70).

On journeys of a week or more, and often on shorter trips, I carry three sets of socks. In very hot weather I often used to change socks every hour but nowadays I rarely seem to do so more than once a day, and in cool weather often seem to wear the same pair several days in a row. To air dirty socks or dry those that have been washed I tie a three-foot length of nylon cord somewhere high on my pack, secure the tops of the socks with a clove hitch and tuck them under the pack's closure strings to prevent them from slipping off to one side. (Well, usually prevent.) If a pair of dirty socks has to go inside the pack for any reason (such as rain or snatching tree branches or recently washed socks that monopolize the outside drier) I segregate them hygienically in a plastic bag.

A pair of socks no doubt lasts longer for some people than for others. In the six months and thousand-plus map-miles of my California trip (many more on the ground) I wore out nine pairs of mediumweight (4-ounce) wool socks, worn without liners.

Care of socks

Woolen socks must be washed carefully. Some backpackers carry packages of Woolite, specially made for washing wool in cold water. But you eliminate one item and do almost as good a job if you use soap, which may be in your toilet gear anyway. Avoid detergent: it removes vital oils from the wool. Trak and other biodegradables (page 488) are safe for wool and are convenient maids-of-all-work. But, whatever you use, rinse the socks thoroughly. An advantage of Wick-Dry socks is that you need exercise less care. Ditto polypropylene undersocks.

If no washing agent is available, plain rinsing out of dirty socks, even in cold water, does a surprisingly good job.

Strictly speaking, socks should be dried away from the sun and lying flat rather than hanging, but even with wool I have often broken both rules without apparent penalty. I find, in any case, that drying out socks on top of the pack as I walk is often the only way I get to dry them out at all. (Warning: wet socks are heavy and when spread out to dry on a rock will stay put in moderate winds; but as they dry out so the tendency to flight increases. Solution: hobble them with rocks, full canteens or what have you.)

Try to wash your socks fairly often. In hot weather that may mean once a day. Dirty socks, especially wool socks, insulate poorly, absorb little sweat and, because they are no longer soft and resilient—and because wet skin quickly softens—can cause abrasions.

The only time I wore a hole in a sock while out and away, I patched it with a small foam-rubber disk cut from a sheet of "moleskin" (page 89). The repair turned out to be astonishingly effective.

CAMP FOOTWEAR

Wearing boots around camp is usually a nuisance, can often be uncomfortable and may even amount to a serious inefficiency. (Toward the end of my first week's traveling in Grand Canyon my feet became so sore that I rested a day and a half beside a spring. Because I had moccasins, which slip off and on very easily, I was able to expose my feet almost continually to the air and never to the painful pressures of boots. If I had had to wear the boots for the many small chores that always need doing around camp I am sure my feet would not have recovered as quickly as they did.)

Unless you feel confident that conditions will allow you to go barefoot in camp—and they almost never will—the only answer is to carry lightweight campwear.

For years I used moccasins with soft, lightweight, ¼-inch, off-crepe composition soles that grip most surfaces (wet or dry), wear well, keep out thorns and blunt the cutting and bruising edge of almost any stone. (Buffalo-hide Moccasins made by the Minnetonka Moccasin Co., of Minnesota, *not* available direct; 17 ounces, $25.) If the weight problem became acute I substituted light unsoled moccasins (average 9 ounces, now $21). But stony country savages the unprotected leather soles. A pair I carried in Grand Canyon just about lasted out the two-month trip.

Three or four years ago, needing camp shoes that would also serve for frequent expected creek crossings, I bought a pair of garish-looking yellow-and-blue synthetic-uppered shoes with small leather inserts at toe and heel and a ½-inch, three-layer sole. Although I did not realize it when I chose them—in a hurry—they were fairly typical modern racing shoes (Onitsuka Tigers [now called Asics Tigers]; 18 ounces, now $40 and up). Many backpackers have apparently adopted such shoes or rather heavier standard jogging models as campwear. I found my Tigers excellent. Their well-patterned, soft composition soles grip well, even on wet surfaces, so they're great for river crossings. They dry out quickly. They're at least as comfortable as moccasins. And although the laces can be a minor nuisance they make it even easier than with moccasins to adjust the fit: loose for slipping on and off sore feet in camp; firm and safe if the feet are in good fettle and take me exploring. I guess they would, as an advisor comments, "make excellent back-up shoes for feet that can't bear to look at boots, third or fourth day out." All in all, you could hardly ask more of camp shoes—except that they be warm, which these are not, and that in dry grassland they repel spiky seeds instead of collecting them, as these do. When such things look like being important, I may still take my moccasins.

When your feet are really sore, even moccasins or racing shoes can feel uncomfortable, particularly if new. One solution: pad toes and heels with toilet paper.

For down booties—and electric socks—see pages 416–17.

AIDS AND ATTACHMENTS

Walking staff

Although the vast majority of walkers never even think of using a walking staff, I unhesitatingly include it among the foundations of the house that travels on my back. The other day I was solemnly advised that doing so is "even further out of the mainstream" than when I wrote the last edition of this book. OK, call me Eddy. But I still take my staff along almost as automatically as I take my pack. It is a third leg to me —and much more besides.

On smooth surfaces the staff helps maintain an easy rhythm to my walking and gives me something to lean on when I stop to stand and stare. Over rough going of any kind, from tussocky grass to pockety rock, and also in a high wind, it converts me when I am heavily laden from an insecure biped into a confident triped. It does the same, only more so, when I have to scramble across a chasm or a big boulder or a mildly obstructive stretch of rock and keep reaching out sideways for a balancing aid or backward for that little extra push up and over. And it does the same thing, even more critically and consistently, when I cross a steep, loose slope of talus or gravel or dirt, or wade a fast-flowing creek or cross it on a log. In marshland or on precarious rock or snow, and in failing light or darkness anywhere, it tests doubtful footing ahead. It reconnoiters bushes or crevices that I suspect might harbor a rattlesnake. It pushes or slashes aside poison oak or ivy. It's useful for pushing up and pulling down balanced bundles of food hoisted into trees to foil bears (page 568). After rain it knocks water off leaves that hang wetly across the trail. It often acts as the indispensable upright needed to rig a shelter from rain or sun with fly sheet (page 318) or groundsheet or poncho (pages 324 and 325). Occasionally, held down by a couple of heavy stones, it serves as ground anchor for the windward side of such a shelter (illustration, page 326—in lieu of canteen). When I have camped in some casual and unconsecrated place I often use the staff, just before leaving, to rough up the ground where I have slept so that no one, but no one, could see the signs. It has also performed successfully as a fishing rod. It has acted as a marked measuring stick, to be checked later when a rule is available, for the exact length of fish, rattlesnakes and other dead animals. It forms a rough but very ready monopod for steadying binoculars if my hands are shaking from exertion, or for a camera if I need to shoot with a shutter speed slower than 1/60 second. It is, of course, invaluable whenever I meet a unicorn: deftly placed, it helps disguise me as a conspecific, and therefore as acceptable company. And day in and day out, at almost every halt, it props up my pack and gives me a soft and stable backrest (page 150). (As I am lazy enough to believe that being able to relax against a soft backrest for even a ten-minute halt is no minor matter, I am almost inclined to regard this function of my staff as one of its most vital.) It may well be, too, that the staff also gives me a false but subconsciously comforting feeling that I am not after all completely defenseless against attack by such enemies as snakes, bears and men.

Down the years, my various staffs have surprised and pleased me from time to time by accomplishing new and unexpected chores. Once I decided halfway up a short rockface that it was unclimbable with the heavy pack on my back. I slipped the pack off and held it with knee pressure in a sloping crevice and took a short length of nylon cord from an outside pocket and tied it to the head of the staff and then to the packframe. Then I jammed the foot of the staff on a convenient ledge and angled its head up against the bottom of the pack so that it held there without my knee and thereby freed the knee and the rest of me for the short and relatively simple climb (unencumbered) to the top of the rockface—where I had a safe stance from which to reach down without difficulty and pull up the pack and attached staff. One cool and windy afternoon when I was booted and fully clothed, the staff rescued, with about an inch to spare, an empty plastic water canteen that the wind had blown into a river no less wet than any other river and a good deal bigger and stronger than most. One night when I was camped in a cave I tied the staff onto the nylon cord from which my candle lantern (page 451) was suspended—and thereby furnished myself with a convenient handle by which I could, without moving my lazy butt an inch, adjust the candle lantern into the various specific positions I wanted it for cooking, writing notes or contemplating cave or universe. And very recently, one super-soggy morning, it enabled me to stay fully inside my tent while I reached out and with its tip dug a shallow diversionary ditch in spruce needles so that the tent alcove, in which I was about to cook breakfast, gradually changed from a lake into a mere morass.

Of course, other writers have extolled the virtues of staffs, directly or indirectly. J. R. R. Tolkien, in *The Two Towers,* wrote: "I have no fitting gifts to give you at our parting. . . . But take these staves. They may be of service to those who walk or climb in the wild." And Carlos Castaneda's Don Juan hints at an additional transcendental use: "By forcing the hands into a specific position," he says, "I was capable of greater stamina and awareness."

For a long time I used a bamboo staff with an average diameter of $1\frac{3}{8}$ inches—just right for a firm but comfortable grip. Eventually small cracks developed up and down its whole length, some of them decidedly threatening. Mostly, they stopped when they came to a knot mark, and the general structure remained sound. But each end section had split so severely that, left to itself, it would flap like an empty banana skin, and over the years I bandaged the wounds with several rings of Rip-stop tape (page 511). Yet I had to confess that when I looked at the bamboo's weatherbeaten surface, and especially at the brown patina that had formed around the second knot, where my hand usually gripped, I felt sad at the thought that it would not last forever. In other words, I had come to regard the staff with a warm affection. I suppose some people would call it soggy sentimentality.

But a dozen years of grinding toil wore away the foot of the staff, inch by inch, until at last it measured only 3 feet 10 inches. Reluctantly, I retired it. For a while I used a replacement bamboo, but it did not last long. Today I own three staffs. One is a thin ash model with leather wrist thong, bound at the foot with a tapered brass ferrule that's fitted with an abrasion- and slip-resistant urethane tip. This staff or others very similar appear erratically in stores and catalogues (53½ inches, average weight 13 ounces, $18). My second staff, heavier but with a more satisfying girth for the hand, and pretty indestructible, is fiberglass—and now has an endearing bow and even a provisional patina. It's no longer commercially available. The third staff is, somewhat to my surprise, the one I now tend to use: a two-piece aluminum-alloy job with choice of four different handles, ranging from 12 to 35 inches, all covered with moisture-absorbent neoprene. They screw into a 34-inch, bare aluminum, rubber-tipped lower section. Out in the green world, the bare metal looks gross, but I've spray-painted it dark brown with a plastic finish reputed to withstand God Almighty abrasions. It doesn't, I find, and I hope to come up with a better camouflager—though a dark-brown anodized version of the staff, now being tested by the makers, sounds like a better answer.* This Nomad staff reeks with cunning. Its high-strength aluminum head is tooled to take the handle of a Sierra Club cup, which slips in and is held firm, so that you can dip water out of otherwise inaccessible places, such as small creeks in deep snow (though it will not work with the bent-handle modification to the cup, page 212). Holes in the head and at the top of the lower section allow lashing with cord or rope (or even pinning with the pike, below) so that the disassembled staff can act "as structural members for a variety of applications (tent frame, camera bipod, splints, hammock support, traps, snares . . . limited only by ingenuity of user)." Stainless-steel, screw-in options include a three-pronged, barbed fishing gig, a ball-joint camera mount for the top (usable with staff standing as monopod or rigged as tripod—see page 469) and a 3½-inch pike for either end that can be used with a plastic snow basket for snow walking, snowshoeing or even skiing. (I've tried it on a week-long snowshoe trip, and yes, it really works, though pike and basket are liable to detach unexpectedly.) A saw attachment may soon appear. Frankly, I find I mostly ignore the options. But the staff is beautifully made, and being able to break it down into two pieces is a real advantage in car or plane or when climbing or scrambling (page 83). Above all, its balance and "feel" are excellent: I'm surprised to find that with the 27-inch Backpacker handle I mostly use, it weighs as much as 18 ounces. (With the 12-inch Flatlander handle that I'm beginning to use for light loads the total weight is only 12 ounces.) The neoprene handles and rubber crutch tip are good insulators, but the staff might not be entirely safe in thunderstorms—though probably no more dangerous than an aluminum-frame pack. (Nomad staff: now available in some stores or from LL Engineering, P.O. Box 1708, Thousand Oaks, CA 91360. The three shorter staffs, $50; the 69-inch

---

* I have now seen and tested a sample, and it is indeed far better.

longest, $60. Options range from ½ to 1 ounce, $4.50 to $20 each. Spare crutch tips, $1.40. A new, one-piece staff, the Explorer, will cost around $35.) After initial repulsion at the gross technological look of the thing, I've come to feel considerable affection for my Nomad—not the warm sentimentality I lavished on my old bamboo, but a solid respect for a good, functional tool.

I gather that my staff fixation has generated a bemused merriment among many readers of earlier editions. But by no means among all. Several have sent messages of support, both pragmatic and sentimental. Others supplied new stavic suggestions. One who recommends a yucca staff, cut about September, adds that he has used it in groups as a makeshift, largely psychological "railing" (held between two stalwarts) to help nervous people past exposed sections of trail, and also as a "yucca belay" by lowering it to where a scrambler in difficulties can grasp it. Another reader writes that "a broomstick makes a very serviceable and cheap staff, and if you leave the end on and happen to be hiking around October 31st, can speed your travel considerably." A third reader, who totes a 134-cm piece of hickory ("bound with nylon thread to stop a split"), finds "the big rubber tip a remarkably prehensile organ for picking up bits of plastic, foil or paper which litter the trail"; he had always wondered, he says, about "carrying 20 ounces for a little stability and a few gimmicky uses, but it gradually dawned on me on [one] trip that the staff takes a tremendous load off my feet. And when I got home I pressed the staff down on a scale in the manner I would engage while vigorously climbing a steep slope, and discovered I was intermittently taking 30 pounds off my feet. While modern suspension systems take the load off my shoulders and back, nothing else takes any weight off my feet, which are, after all, the part of me that feels by nightfall as though a hippopotamus had been jumping up and down on them all day." Now, why didn't I think of that really beautiful justification?

One small but constantly recurring matter: you cannot conveniently lift a pack onto your back while holding a staff. Where possible, lean the staff against something before you lift the pack so that once you're loaded up you can easily take hold of it. But even in open places there is no need to waste the not inconsiderable energy expended in bending down with a heavy load on your back; just hook one foot under the staff, lift it with your instep and take hold of it when the top angles up within reach of your hand. With practice you'll probably find yourself flipping the head of the staff up with your foot and catching it at apogee. You'll soon get used to laying the staff ready for this maneuver on a low bush or stone or across a depression in the ground before you hoist up the pack, so that afterward you can slide a toe under it. If you forget the precaution and can't get a toe under, simply roll the staff onto your instep with the heel of the other foot. It sounds gymnastic but is really very simple.

There are, I admit, times when a long staff, unless it breaks down like the Nomad, becomes a nuisance.

If you have to swim across a fast river, for example, it can tangle dangerously with your legs. In calm water it's easy enough to pull the staff safely along behind on a length of nylon cord (illustration, page 533). But when a fast-water situation was plainly going to arise on one trip beside the Colorado River I left my regular staff behind and on the first day cut a four-foot section from the stem of a dead agave, or century plant. With the thicker end carefully rounded it made a very serviceable third leg. During river crossings it tucked conveniently out of the way in the bindings of my packframe, protruding only very slightly at the top (page 535). The odd thing was that by the end of two weeks I was feeling for this little staff the same kind of affection that I lavished on my regular bamboo one—so much so that when it broke on the next-to-last day and I had to cut a fresh length of agave I stuffed the scarred, foot-long stub into my pack and carried it all the way home. I guess "soggy sentimentality" is about right.

A staff is also a nuisance, even a hazard, if you have to do any climbing that demands the use of two unencumbered hands. Occasionally, on short and unexpected pitches, I've pulled the staff up after me on a nylon cord, or lowered it ahead. If you know you're likely to face some rock climbing it may be worth leaving your regular staff behind and cutting a temporary one that can be discarded and replaced (climbing was a contributory reason for my doing so on that Colorado trip). If you expect to do very much climbing, there are three solutions: do without a staff; use one that breaks down into two or more sections; or take along an

Ice axe.

You may carry an axe on certain trips because you know you may need to cut steps in ice or hard snow or, more likely, to self-arrest in case of a fall on steep snow or ice (I was very glad of one on an April ascent of Mount Fuji); and even if you use the axe little if at all for ice or snow work it will serve as a reasonably efficient staff, even in the pack-prop role. It is also, incidentally, a splendid instrument for extracting stubborn tent pegs from packed snow (page 312)—and in its old age, I'm told, for gardening. When not in use it straps conveniently onto your pack.

Traditional ash shafts on ice axes have now almost given way to metal or fiberglass or fiberglass-graphite. The standard and cheaper poly-vinyl-covered aluminum shafts are fine for marginal backpacker use, with 80-cm. probably the best length. Forged heads (as opposed to the stamp-outs now favored for technical climbing) will be entirely adequate. Such axes, weighing just under 2 pounds, now start at about $50. Many axes no longer come with glide ring and wrist strap. For the kind of nontech-nical use we are talking about, it's probably worth installing them.

Rubber protectors for base tips can be used on hard surfaces, and definitely should be used when the axe is in the car or at home (1 ounce, $.95). You can also get rubber covers for the axe head (1½ ounces, $1.95).

It is generally though not universally agreed that the way to hold an axe when walking is by the head, with its pointed pick forward, so that in case of a fall the danger to you is reduced.

The technical use of an ice axe does not fall within the scope of a walking book.

Two other walking aids that lie close to the fringes of walking deserve brief mention:

Crampons

Although crampons are essentially ironmongery for climbers they are sometimes worth carrying if you expect to cross ice or hard snow. And not only steep snow. A flat snowfield that has weathered hard may develop basins and ridges and even savage pinnacles that in naked boots create considerable and potentially dangerous obstacles. I once discovered by accident, when I climbed out onto the lip of an ice-covered gully on Mount Shasta, that when you are carrying a heavy load crampons can transform a sloping slab of very soft rock from a nasty barrier into a cakewalk.

For use with hiking boots, make sure you get crampons that are somewhat flexible as well as adjustable for length. Almost all are now twelve-point. Suitable models average about 23 ounces, $40. Take pains to ensure that crampons fit your boots exactly, for both width and length. A loose pair can be highly dangerous. Make sure, too, that you learn how to strap them on properly. I will not try to describe the correct method: it is a complicated thing to verbalize but very simple to learn by demonstration. Rubber protectors for points of 12-point crampons: 5 ounces, $5. Because of liability problems, few stores now rent crampons (or ice axes). An exception: REI.

Always exercise great care with crampons. Some experts even sug-gest that a novice may be better off with an ice axe alone.

Convenient, lighter, cheaper and rather safer halfway-house alternatives to crampons are "trail paws"—small aluminum plates with serrated down-facing teeth that strap under your insteps (10 ounces, $12). I'm told they work on hard snow, sort of.

Weighed down with stones, crampons make excellent tent pegs on hard surfaces that more orthodox pegs refuse to penetrate.

The most joyous and efficient way to travel over snow is on skis. But that lies outside our orbit: on skis you are no longer walking. There is an alternative, though, that lies around about the limits of walking, and is appropriate or even necessary for certain times and places and people—people like me, for example, who are inexperienced and shaky performers on skis and who tend to travel alone, with heavy loads:

Snowshoes.

My experience is still meager, but I have learned that snowshoes permit you to move with a heavy pack over the very surface of snow into which your booted legs plunge knee-deep—and that immediately after a storm they will allow you to travel (sweating hard, but sinking in less than a foot at each step) across snow into which you would otherwise go on sinking forever if God had not arranged that human legs eventually converge. I have also learned that with a heavy load, unless you are in practice, four hours' actual snowshoeing a day is plenty. That if you are carrying a pack it pays to use ski poles. That if you have an old hamstring injury, then big, old-style snowshoes may let you in for some nagging discomfort. Also that, short of a shovel, there is nothing like a snowshoe for digging out your tent during and after a storm.

But for real information, read the generally accepted "bible" on the subject: *Snowshoeing* by Gene Prater (2nd edition, 1980, paperback, 176 pages, 7½ ounces, $6.95: The Mountaineers, 7918 Pike St., Seattle, WA 98101); or *The Snowshoe Book* by William E. Osgood and Leslie J. Hurley (1975, paperback, 8 ounces, $7.95: Stephen Greene Press, P.O. Box 1000, Brattleboro, VT 05351).

In the last five years, violent revolution has overtaken snowshoes. Traditional ash-and-thong shoes have been rendered almost obsolete by anodized aluminum frames with solid, neoprene-coated-nylon decking. Tubbs of Vermont still make wooden models, but even they have ventured into aluminum. Black Forest of California make all types: wood, aluminum, plastic—even kits. I recently used an aluminum pair by Sherpa on a week-long Sierra trip in May, on snow still deep from a stormy winter, and found them a vast improvement over the old, more eye-pleasing wooden kind. They tend to "track" better—and the serrated "claw" or minicrampon binding that is standard on many models greatly improves traction on packed snow and ice. They can also be put on and taken off more quickly. They are smaller and tougher—and lighter. And, finally and stunningly, they need no maintenance.

The pioneering Sherpa snowshoes that I used are generally accepted as current "state of the art." Two popular and versatile models: the Featherweight (8 by 25 inches, 2 pounds 15 ounces, $125, with bindings) and Lightfoot (9 by 30 inches, 3 pounds 11 ounces, $155). (Assemble-yourself kits available, $92 and $100.)

CARE OF FEET

Some people seem to have naturally tough feet. But even those not so blessed can improve their situation. Some years ago a reader advised me: "If you go barefoot whenever you can, you'll most likely develop lovely leathery feet." She was right. Whenever possible I now go around with nothing on my feet (and et cetera, which also feels nice), and because of that—or maybe because of improvements in boots or a lowering of ambitions or something entirely different—it is years since I had real foot trouble. The fact remains, though, that human feet are delicate instruments: they embody 52 separate bones (about one-quarter of the body's total), along with related muscles and tendons; they sweat through some 250,000 glands. And for all but the most blessed tough-foot, it pays to take stringent precautions before and during any walk much longer than you are currently used to, or with a load much heavier than you have very recently carried. If you do not yet understand the value of such precautions, then you've never generated a big, joy-killing blister with many miles still to go.

Getting your feet ready

This vital task is best achieved by practice—by taking time out beforehand to work up slowly from a few gentle miles, unladen (if you are in really bad shape), to a long day's slog with a load as big as you mean to carry (page 32). But somehow (page 72) you rarely seem to have the time to take out, and even more rarely the determination to take it. For years the only substitute I've known—and a poor one at that—has been to toughen up the skin (soles, toes and heels particularly) by regular applications of rubbing alcohol for a week or so beforehand. (If you put the alcohol bottle beside your toothbrush it is not too difficult to remember this simple half-minute chore, morning and night.) But recently I've been told that tincture of benzoin (available in most drugstores: 2-ounce

bottle, $1.88) works better. My limited experience suggests that it does
—though it is a little messier to use. If you cannot get out for any serious
walking during the preparation period it helps to wear your boots—
especially new ones—as much as you can for a week or so beforehand,
even if only around the house.

Some people who habitually get blisters in certain places on their
feet say they ward them off by covering the sites in advance with tape,
moleskin or Adhesive Knit (page 89).

On the march

The important thing is to begin easily. People who backpack into
the bush for once-a-year vacations all too often find the whole week or
fortnight ruined at the very beginning by too much ambition and too
little discretion. Their feet never recover from the pounding of the first
day or two. A gentle shakedown cruise (pages 10 and 72)—a day or a
week, depending on the total length of the trip—can make all the
difference. On my thousand-mile California walk, although I began with
stiff new boots and soft city feet, I suffered only one blister—a minor
affair generated by an ill-advised insole experiment. During the first
week, though, I averaged less than seven miles a day, over very easy
going. In Grand Canyon my feet fared less well. But I began with a
barely cured infected heel and because of it had worn nothing but moccasins for almost two weeks. If it had not been for two days of easy
ambling at the start and a further four days of taking it fairly easy, I
should probably have been crippled before I got fully started.

It's essential that you continue to take precautions until your feet
are comfortably lasting out the longest day and the heaviest load—even
with steady downhill work, which gives them a much more brutal hammering than they get on the level or uphill. On long, hard treks I rarely
seem to reach this point for at least a week or two. Until then I go on
applying rubbing alcohol. For years I carried about 5 ounces of it in a
flat plastic bottle but have now switched to one of those little plastic
squeeze-bottles that drugstores sell for use with all kinds of liquids, from
hand lotion to insect repellent. These bottles (¾ ounce, $.59) have long,
thin, internal tubes attached to their caps, and when squeezed they eject
liquid contents in a fine spray. They are therefore much more economical
than open-mouthed bottles, which tend to slosh too much alcohol (or
tincture of benzoin) onto your feet. For a normal week's walking I find
the 2-ounce bottle adequate. But there are larger sizes. Before you pass a
bottle for "combat" duty, try it in every position, including upside
down, to check that the spray cap never leaks. (For use of rejects, see
footpowder, below.) A technical advisor assures me that "a useful source

for good bottles (for this and other uses) is the nasal-spray counter. The inner tops come out, they are the right size, and you can always pour the junk down the drain." My alcohol bottle travels, immediately accessible, in an outside pocket of the pack (page 528). Normally, I rub my feet with a little alcohol morning and night, and in hot weather or when my feet are really sore I may do so several times a day.

I also carry footpowder in the same pocket of the pack, and always sprinkle the insides of my socks with it in the morning. I may do so several times during the day.

The smallest Scholls' footpowder containers now hold 3 ounces. If this seems too big and heavy for your purposes, decant some into a convenient small container, such as a failed alcohol-squeezer (see above). I now use a film can with salt-shaker top (page 215).

Many experienced hikers deplore all this messing around. "Unless something is seriously wrong," I once heard an expert advise a beginner, "keep your boots on until you stop for the day. You'll have far less trouble with your feet that way." No doubt such advice is sound enough for some people. But I still tend to remove boots and socks at protracted halts. And in blisteringly hot weather I may even take my boots off at each halt and let air get at the perspiring feet. When my feet got really sore I used to anoint them with alcohol and powder at almost every hourly halt and then change socks, repowdering the pair that had been drying out on top of the pack. I sometimes used, if water was available, to wash my feet at almost every halt—a practice that a lot of people regard as skin-softening idiocy. I am now inclined to regard it—with considerable conviction, on the flimsiest of evidence—as skin-softening idiocy.

Taking your boots off and airing your feet whenever you can certainly makes good theoretical sense. Heat is the cause of all blisters—though softening of the skin by unwicked-away sweat may also contribute. Locally, the heat comes from the friction of a rucked sock or an ill-fitting boot. But it seems reasonable to suppose that the overall temperature of your feet makes a big difference. I certainly find deserts the hardest places on feet. And it is not really surprising: few people realize how hot the ground underfoot can be. In Grand Canyon I repeatedly checked air and ground temperatures. With air temperature about 85° F. I would get a ground reading on unshaded rock (and that meant just about any rock) of around 115° or 120°. On unshaded sand the mercury would go well past the last gradation of 120°. When air temperature climbed over 90° I had to be careful where I left the thermometer, for fear the mercury would blow off the top.*

---

* An article by A. Court in the *Geographical Review* (1949, No. 2, pp. 214–20) gives these figures for extreme conditions in American deserts: air at 5 feet (which is where official

A reader recommends as "freaking marvelous" this simple exercise for tired feet after you have removed your boots: slowly flex them forward; wiggle at extreme extension; flex fully backward; rewiggle; repeat as often as needed. My interim evaluation: "freaking marvelous." A sort of miniservice version that I find useful on the march for any forefoot discomfort, especially when going downhill, is simply to wiggle your toes occasionally.

Remedial treatment

If, in spite of all your care, your feet need doctoring, start it early. The moment you feel what may be the beginnings of a blister, do something about it.

First remove any obvious and rectifiable local irritant, such as a fragment of stone or a rucked sock. Then cover the tender place. Cover it even if you can see nothing more than a faint redness. Cover it, in fact, if you can see nothing at all. Being a "hero" is being a bloody fool. The covering may only be needed for a few hours; if you take it off at night and let the air get at the skin you may not need to replace it next morning. But if you do nothing at the first warning you may find yourself inside the hour with a blister that will last a week.

For covering, a piece of surgical tape or a Band-Aid will do at a pinch, provided its adhesive surface is efficient enough to prevent rucking —a requirement not always met when the trouble is on your toes. But for years now I have, like most backpackers, patched with the oddly miraculous devices known as "moleskins." The original Scholls' Mole-skins—sheets of white felt, adhesive on one side, that you can cut to suit your blister or sore spot—are sold in most drugstores. Now, it used to be that a moleskin was a moleskin was a moleskin. No more. Scholls some years ago put out four variants: Kurotex (flesh-colored), Kuro Felt (flesh-colored and double thickness), Adhesive Foam (latex) and Mole-foam (felt over latex). I have still failed to extract from the makers any coherent information about the advantages and disadvantages of each— and I note that mountain shops, which always carry Moleskins, mostly don't seem to stock the variants. A possibly viable alternative to Mole-skins has now appeared: Spenco Adhesive Knit—a breathable synthetic knit that stretches to cover curved and mobile surfaces. I have not tested

---

readings are taken), 125° F.; at 1 foot, 150°; at 1 inch, 165°; at ground, 180°. This kind of heat layering is by no means confined to deserts. See, for example, page 510.

Interesting temperatures recorded during World War II at a naval research center in Imperial Valley, California, on a day when the official air temperature touched 120° F., include 145° in the gasoline in a 50-gallon drum left in the sun, 155° in the vapor above the gasoline, and 190° on the seat of a jeep.

Adhesive Knit. And I'm damned if I'll go get blisters deliberately, just for your edification, buster (or, of course, bustress). But it is beginning to appear in stores and catalogues. So is another Spenco product, 2nd Skin—a gel-like sheeting said "to remove all friction between two moving surfaces, clean wounds by absorbing secretions and relieve pain and itching of burns and rashes—including sunburn and poison ivy." Because 2nd Skin will not stick to either normal skin or wounds, you must hold it in place with Moleskin, Adhesive Knit or adhesive tape and gauze. But, properly used, it may well prove just the thing for really excruciating blisters.

Standard Moleskins come in sheets, 7 by 10 or 7 by 30 inches, or, far more commonly, in packages of four 3-by-4-inch strips (1 ounce net, $1.29). Adhesive Knit comes in a package of six 3-by-6-inch sheets: 1 ounce; $2.95; 2nd Skin, 3 by 13 inches, in a plastic container, 1½ ounces, $3.50. And Spenco now produce a Blister Kit—"enough for over 50 treatments"—that includes 2nd Skin (three 3-inch squares, twelve 1-inch squares), adhesive knit (three 3-by-5-inch pieces, twelve 3¼-by-2½-inch pieces), Supersorb padding (3 by 4 inches), antiseptic first aid cream, two sterile needles, three pre-cut ovals of stick-on padding (3-by-5-inch) and "blister-related first aid instructions"; all in 4½-by-6-inch packages, 5½ ounces, $9.95).

Moleskins—and, I assume, the variants—stick to skin like glue, even after your feet get wet. In fact it is sometimes quite a business peeling the thin protective layer of plastic off new patches. (The makers leave a helpful projecting band of this layer and advise you to remove the plastic before cutting patches to the required shape. But in order to preserve the adhesive qualities—which can be rather easily damaged by handling—I shape the patch first with a pair of scissors, carefully beveling all edges, then lever up one corner of the plastic with the scissors' point, and peel it off.) Mere adhesion does not begin to explain the extraordinary efficiency of moleskins. I suppose their secret has something to do with the resilience and sideways-sliding quality of the felt. Anyway, I know for a fact and with gratitude that they can stop embryonic friction trouble dead; can stifle the pain from any surface blister and often keep it from getting worse; and can even, apparently from mere cushioning, deaden the worst pain from those deep, dismal, often invisible blisters that occasionally form under heel or ball of foot. My moleskins travel in my "office" (page 506).

If you generate a blister in spite of all your care—or because you were not careful enough—and if it is either very deep or is not yet very bulbous, the best treatment is probably just to cover it. If the blister is close to the surface and has already inflated you will need to burst it before you can walk with comfort. Pierce it with a needle, from the side, down near the base of the balloon, so that all the liquid can drain away. (I carry several needles, primarily for repair work, in my waterproof matchsafe [page 217].) Sterilize the needle first, in a sterilizing agent if you carry one (rubbing alcohol won't do) but, failing that, in a flame— far better than nothing, in spite of the carbon deposits. If you have got to keep walking and if the loose skin of the balloon does not ruck up when deflated it is probably best to leave the skin in place and cover it, and to cut it away only when the skin beneath has had time to harden. If you can rest long enough for the skin to harden—which it does more quickly when exposed to air—or if the deflated outer skin puckers so badly that it seems likely to cause further damage as you walk then you should remove it by scissoring carefully around the edges of the blister. Take care to keep the exposed area clean. And leave no dead skin likely to cause new chafing. Once the newly exposed skin has dried, hasten hardening with tincture of benzoin or even rubbing alcohol. If you must keep walking, and apply a moleskin or other adhesive cover, use a thin fragment of gauze—or perhaps 2nd Skin—to prevent the cover from sticking directly to the still tender skin. A sprinkling of footpowder can also help reduce friction, and so can an antiseptic of a kind that will lubricate as well as reduce the danger of infection.

But never forget that a blister is a sign of failure. The efficient way to deal with foot trouble is to avoid it. Preharden. On the march, and especially in the early days of a trip, attend assiduously to preventive measures. And nip tribulations in the bud.

THE FOUNDATIONS IN ACTION

A book on walking should no doubt have something to say about the simple, basic, physical act of walking.

On the most fundamental level, advice is probably useless. Anyone old enough to read has almost certainly grown too set in the way he puts one foot in front of the other to alter it materially without devoting a great deal of time and determination to the task.*

---

* I am no longer convinced that this is so. At least, the necessary time and even determination may be a lot less than I imagined. A course of Rolfing has demonstrated to me that it can alter your gait as well as stance—while also giving you a new and effective tool to deal with certain nagging back and other anatomical problems.

On the other hand, it is very easy to improve by a little conscious thought what I regard as the most important single element in the physical act of walking: rhythm. An easy, unbroken rhythm can carry you along hour after hour almost without your being aware that you are putting one foot in front of the other. At the end of a really long day you will be aware of the act all right, but as long as you maintain a steady rhythm very little of your mind need be concerned with it. And your muscles will complain far less than if you have walked all day in a series of jerky and semicoordinated movements, sometimes pushing close to your limit, sometimes meandering.

With experience you automatically fall into your own rhythmic pace. (At least, mostly you do. There will still be days when you have to fight for it, and not always with total success.) But when you first take up real walking you may have to think deliberately about establishing a stride and a speed that feel comfortable. And both stride and speed may be rather different with and without a load.

You will almost certainly have to concentrate at first on the important matter of not disrupting the rhythm unless absolutely necessary. This means stepping short for a stride when you come to some minor obstacle such as a narrow ditch, or even marking time with one foot. I cannot emphasize this unbroken-rhythm business too strongly.

A Massachusetts reader writes: "You are right to stress rhythm, but it can be improved with coordination of breathing, arm movement and a [simple] mantra . . . [that] quickly becomes unconscious, bringing the whole self to a deeper unity."

Of course, rhythm is not always a simple matter of constant stride and speed. In fact it remains so only as long as you walk on a smooth and level surface. The moment you meet rough going underfoot or start up or down a gradient, you have to modify stride or speed or both.

Climbing a gentle slope means nothing more than a mild shortening of stride, though leaning forward slightly may help too. But long before a mountainside gets so steep that you start reaching out for handholds, stride becomes a meaningless word. Now you put your feet down almost side by side at one step, a foot or more apart at the next, depending on the immediate local gradients and footholds. Even the rate at which you move one leg past the other—slowly and deliberately and almost laboriously, though not quite—may vary in response to changes in the general gradient. Yet the old rhythm persists. I am not sure where the relationships lie. It is not—though I have sometimes thought so—that you continue to expend the same amount of energy. Steep climbing takes more out of you, always (page 157). But the fact remains that although you must change gear in an almost literal sense at the bottom and top of a steep hill you can maintain the deeper continuity of the old rhythm. The pulse is still there, somewhere, if you know where to feel for it.

Downhill walking, though less sweaty than climbing, is less easy than it ought to be. In broad theory you merely relinquish the potential energy you gained with such labor as you climbed; but in practice you do no such thing. At every step you expend a great deal of effort in holding yourself back—and this effort too demands a deliberate change of gear. If the gradient is at all severe you reduce both stride and speed as much as you think necessary to prevent yourself from hammering hell out of knees and ankles and feet (especially feet). Again, though, you find with practice that it is possible to maintain the essence of the old rhythm.

You may also have to apply a conscious effort to maintaining your rhythmic pace when you come to certain kinds of rough going—soft sand or gravel that drags at your feet like molasses; talus that slides away from under your feet like a treadmill; rough rock or tussocky grassland that soon disrupts an even stride; or prolonged sidehill work that puts an abnormal strain on foot and leg muscles and may also present something of a problem in balance.

Walking after dark, especially on pitch-black, moonless nights, can also destroy your customary rhythm. If you have been walking in daylight and simply keep going, little trouble seems to arise. But if you get up in the middle of the night and hike out into darkness you may have a surprise in store. I wrote in *The Thousand-Mile Summer* about the only time I traveled at night on my California walk. It was in Death Valley. The first night inside the Valley I had no sleeping bag, and I failed, dismally, to stay asleep (see page 354, this book). At 3:30 I got up from the gully in which I had camped and headed north into the darkness. There was no moon. From the start I found myself walking in a curious and disturbing state of detachment. The paleness that was the dirt road refused to stay in positive contact with my feet, and I struggled along with laborious, unrhythmic steps. All around hovered hints of immense open spaces and distant, unconvincing slopes. Time had lost real meaning back in the gully; now it lacked even boundaries. When dawn gave the landscape a tenuous reality at last I was still two hours away from my next cache. In those endless two hours I completely failed to reestablish my usual rhythmic pace.

Next night I was on the move by 9:30. This time, bright moonlight made the physical world something real and conquerable. I could plant my feet firmly and confidently on the solid white road. But soon after eleven o'clock the moon set. The world narrowed to hints of colossal open space, to a blur that achieved reality only through jabbing at my feet.

Distance degenerated into marks on the map. Time was the creeping progress of watch hands. All through the long and cold and dismal night that followed I had to struggle to hold some semblance of my usual daytime rhythm. I succeeded only marginally. But I succeeded far better than on the previous night. In recent years I seem to have had no such problem at night. I guess it's just practice.

A delicate sense of balance is vital to good walking, day or night. And it's not just a matter of being able to cross steep slopes without tightening up. Your body should always be poised and relaxed so that you put down your feet, whatever their size and whatever your load, with something close to daintiness. Before I walked through Grand Canyon I met the one man who seemed to know much about hiking away from trails in its remote corners. Trying to get some idea of whether I would be able to cope with the rough, steep country that he crossed with such apparent ease, I asked him to tell me, honestly, if he was a good climber. "No," he said, "definitely not. I'd say I was a very mediocre climber indeed. But in the Canyon it's mostly walking, you know, even though it can be pretty tricky walking at times." He smiled. "I guess you could say, come to think of it, that maybe I don't dislodge quite as many stones as the next guy." I knew then that he was a good walker.

One of the surest ways to tell an experienced walker from a beginner is the speed at which he starts walking. The beginner tends to tear away in the morning as if he meant to break every record in sight. By contrast, your experienced man seems to amble. But before long, and certainly by evening, their positions have reversed. The beginner is dragging. The expert, still swinging along at the same easy pace, is now the one who looks as though he has records in mind. One friend of mine, a real expert, says, "If you can't carry on a conversation, you're going too fast."

The trap to avoid at all costs, if you want to enjoy yourself, is spurious heroism—the delusion that your prowess as a walker rests on how dauntlessly you "pick 'em up and lay 'em down." It's a sadly common syndrome.

The actual speed at which you walk is a personal and idiosyncratic matter. Settle for whatever seems to suit you best. It is really a question of finding out what you can keep up hour after hour in various kinds of terrain carrying various loads. Until you know your own limits, aim for a slow, rhythmic, almost effortless pace. You'll be surprised, I think, at the ground you cover. The miles will come to meet you. In time you'll learn that, generally speaking, the way to hurry is not to hurry but to keep going. To this end I have two walking speeds: slow and slower. See also page 43. Note (page 158) that the energy expended in walking doubles, roughly speaking, with each mile-per-hour increase in speed;

and that the best way to prevent a build-up of lactic acid in the muscles is to walk more slowly.

For a different look at the basic facts of walking, see an excellent article by James Tabor in *Backpacker* Magazine, Vol. 9, No. 2, April/ May 1981. It propounds, in more scientific terms, more or less what I have said here; but it also adds new insights into the extraordinarily complicated act of walking.

The halts you choose to take are a matter of personal preference, but frequent and irregular halts are a sure sign of an inexperienced hiker. Unladen, it may be a good thing to keep going hour after hour without disturbing your rhythm. But if you're carrying a sizable pack you will almost certainly find that, no matter how fit you are, you need to get the weight off your back for a short spell about once an hour. I halt every hour with fairly mechanical regularity, modifying slightly to suit terrain. I like to get to the top of a hill before I stop, for example; and I often halt a few minutes early or late to take advantage of convenient shade or water or a pleasing view. In theory I rest for 10 minutes. (In the first 5 to 7 minutes of rest the body flushes out about 30 percent of the lactic-acid build-up in muscles, only 5 percent in the next 15 minutes.) But it is horribly easy to let a halt drift on for 20 or even 30 minutes, and as protection I often set at zero as soon as I halt the expired-time dial on the scuba diver's wristwatch that I presently wear. In the past I would often, when I had a map, mark on it the halting place and also pencil in the exact time I stopped: I am no longer sure why I began doing so but

I went on doing it because the penciled figures on the map acted as a reminder and spur. They also helped me judge how I was progressing across a given kind of country and made it easier to estimate how far I should be able to travel in the next hour or afternoon or day or week. In fact I still sometimes pencil in halt sites and times for that purpose.

At each halt I take off my pack and prop it against a rock or a tree or the staff and lean against it. I try to relax completely. Sometimes, warding off the attractions of scenery, animals and the map, I quickly succeed. If I fail I may use Selective Awareness (page 99); I may even doze off for a few minutes. Getting started again may demand considerable willpower, especially toward the end of a long day; but within a few paces I slip back into the old, regular rhythm. And mostly I will hold it, unbroken, for another 50 minutes.*

For a time I considered adding to this revised edition some sapient advice on both

Winter and desert walking.

But when I buttoned my mind down to the task I decided that almost everything I had to say was either common sense or appeared elsewhere in the book or both; and that in the case of winter walking it eased over, anyway, into snowshoeing or ski touring—which both lie at or beyond the limits of this book.

Still, here are a few ill-assorted snippets.

In snow country, in any but flat terrain, learn as much as you can about avalanches (page 580). And in extreme cold—except at high altitude, where the need for every available oxygen molecule may rule it out —consider using a cold-air mask. Such masks are made by Spenco and also by Edwards Ski Products, 2109 W. 2300 S., Salt Lake City, UT 84119.

In deserts, think "water" incessantly. At times you may need to carry two gallons of the stuff, or even more. You must certainly plan every move with known sources in mind; and remember that a spring marked on a map is *not* a sure and certain source unless confirmed by recent firsthand evidence from a person you feel sure you can trust (for hints on calibrating trustworthiness, see page 486). For more on water —dehydration, conservation, how much to carry, how often to drink, sources, purification, desert stills, caches and canteens—see pages 189—

* "Any other man stops and talks,
  But the walking man walks."
          Song, "The Walking Man," popular mid-'70s.

208. In low desert, except in midwinter, consider walking early and perhaps late in the day, or even at night—but don't ignore possible rhythm difficulties (page 93) and rattlesnakes (pages 552–3). Desert walking in winter or early spring can be delectable; but you must still think "water" all the time.

A Southern California reader offers some interesting thoughts: "Most of my walking is done in the desert and much of that when it's hot. Why? The challenge (if snow, ice and subfreezing temperatures are allowable obstacles for the climber, then why not obstacles of the other extreme?), the virtual assurance that one will escape from ORVs and (I confess it) other hikers, and—I like hot weather. Yet there are times when one wants and needs shade. I have tried a space blanket (silver side up) and six aluminum tent poles—three for each prop—for protection on lava fields and the like. A bit unsteady in a wind but even a droopy awning gives shade. . . .

Walking at high altitudes

Even if you acclimate properly (see page 40) you must, once you get up high, walk differently. "How high" is not really answerable with a figure: your body, on any given day, will respond more accurately. But as a guideline it is probably safe to say that most people will have to adjust over 10,000 feet, and that many will have to do so a lot lower.

First, you must learn to modulate your rhythm—to dead slow. Even at sea level there's nothing so becomes a walker as modest slowness and languidity;

> But when the mountain air blows in your ears,
> Then imitate the action of a tortoise;
> Slacken the sinews, throttle down the blood,
> Deflect ambition with delib'rate pace,
> And lend the legs a loitering aspect;
> Let them creep through the hours of the day
> Like a brass clock; let the body dawdle
> As languidly as doth a smoker
> Drag slow-foot through the grass, like a tippler
> O'erfilled with mild but tasteful potion.
> Now ope the teeth, and stretch the nostril wide;
> Draw slow the breath, and suck down every intake
> To his full depth!—On, on, you noble Walker,

whose blood is thin from scaling this full height, and remember that not only during the first three days of your body's readjustment but on, on, into the fourth and fifth, Henry, and beyond that for as long as you stay up high, you must strive to keep moving in this consciously imposed, almost ludicrous slow motion. If you do it properly you will not get breathless unless you go very high indeed. And your heart will not pound. (I maintain that if your muscles feel the strain of walking when you are up high then you are asking too much of your heart.) If you forget to hold your legs in check, and revert to something like your normal pace, you will probably begin to gasp and to feel your heart triphammering. You will therefore rest—and lose time and momentum. But if you tortoise along you can often keep going for the full regulation hour with no more distress than at sea level. (For a discussion of "acute mountain sickness," see page 577.)

Remember, always, about those deep, slow breaths—preferably taken in rhythm with your steps. (Up high, try taking more breaths to the step.) By dragging each breath down into the full depths of your lungs you will at least in part make up for the reduced oxygen in the air. If you find your brain is not functioning very well—and up high there will assuredly be times when it does not—stop and drag down several extradeep breaths that expel every lurking unoxygenated residue from your lung cellars. You may begin to think better at once. And this treatment will as often as not remove or at least moderate the headaches that are apt to afflict you for a spell. I keep at headaches with such deep breathing, and it is many years since I needed to resort to aspirin.

Once you have mastered these simple lessons you will be ready to sample the simple joys of walking around on top of the world.

There remains the matter of what you do with your mind while your body walks. Mostly, I find that everything takes care of itself. My mind soars or grubs along or meanders halfway in between, according to the sun or cloud, the wind or rain, the state of my metabolism, the demands of the hour or other elements beyond my control. But there are times when, in the interests of efficient walking, you need to discipline your thoughts. If the way ahead looks long and tiresome, and above all if it slopes steeply and inexorably upward, on and on, then you are liable to find that the prospect presses heavy on your mind and that the depression acts as a brake on your body and that its lethargy further depresses your mind—and so on. The syndrome is pandemic to mountains, and especially to those high enough for the thin air to brake directly on mind and body. Some years ago, in early November, I went up Mount Whitney. I wandered up, acclimating slowly, savoring the emptiness and silence of the country (I had chosen November for horde avoidance); but I was carrying a considerable load—my plan, eventually scuttled by weather, was to camp on the summit—and on the long, final pull each step became a wearisome, mind-demanding effort. Ahead, the trail curved on and up, on and up. As I climbed, the air grew thinner, even less sustaining. My mind sagged under the burden of step-by-step effort. And then I remembered something. My paperback for the trip was *Zen in the Art of Archery,* and while reading it in my tent the night before I had decided to try applying one of its lessons. I immediately began to do so. "I am the summit," I told myself. "I am the summit. I am the summit." I focused my mind on the statement, close. And very soon, very easily, I believed it: my insignificant self and the apex of that huge blade of rock *were* the same thing—or at least they occupied the same point in space and time. Yet the space was in another sense still above me. The time, I think, was a nudge ahead in the future. Or perhaps it was the present. Anyway, I held the concept tight and firm, so that there was no room for anything else. (Excluding other ideas was not difficult: at 14,000 feet you can rarely cope with more than one at a time.)

It seemed to work. The effort of climbing—of pulling self and load on and up, on and up, step by laborious step—faded away. To say that I floated upward would, I guess, be hyperbole; but when I reached the summit in a physical sense I was, I think, less tired than I have ever been at such a high and crowning moment.

That experience on Whitney turned out to be only a start. In the years since I have employed for all manner of purposes—from nonanes-thetic dentistry through giving up smoking to controlling pre-tennis-tournament nerves—a technique devised by Dr. Emmett Miller that he calls "Selective Awareness." It is not altogether unlike Transcendental Meditation: you put yourself into a kind of hypnotic trance that is really no more than a controlled focusing of the mind and relaxing of *all* muscles. Selective Awareness has often proved invaluable to me on walks. Not long ago, as I was coming down from a week-long trip into some familiar mountains, darkness fell when I was still a couple of hours from roadhead. In itself, that did not matter: moonlight illuminated a trail I knew well, and I had a good flashlight. But it had been a hard week, and when I stopped for my final rest, barely an hour from the car, I felt suddenly exhausted. Directly ahead, beyond a creek, the land rose precip-itously for what I knew was the last, ten-minute climb before a long, steep descent. For a few moments I wondered how the hell I was going to make it up and down that final ridge. Then it occurred to me to rest with Selective Awareness, the way other people apparently do with Yoga. After five minutes, or maybe ten (time seems suspended when you are in that state), I emerged feeling totally refreshed. I went up the hill as if it were a plain and I a lightly loaded gazelle. And then I glided happily down to the car.

Walls

Next to your boots, no item of equipment is more likely to make or mar your walking than the pack that forms the walls of your house. For the pack is more than a shell that contains and protects everything else. It also embodies the crucial interface between you and your load: that artful combination of hipbelt and shoulder harness known as the suspension system. And there grief can lie—unless you get everything just right.

If a trip will last only a few hours, of course, you may not need a pack. You can stuff everything you want into pockets. Or you may take one of those small pouches—not really houses at all, just pottering sheds —that are known as

DAY PACKS.

Mountain shops—and many other stores too—now sprout whole forests of day packs in almost imperceptible gradations of size, conformation, zippering and pocketing. (For one version, see left center, illustration.) Most models rely on simple shoulder-strap harnesses, adequate for light loads. A recent worthy development: foam pads up the forward wall. They increase comfort somewhat and although hardly making the packs cooler at least shield their contents from sweat. A few bigger models have hipbelts and even rudimentary internal frames. Eagle Creek of California make day packs (and belt bags, see below) with reflective fabrics; though primarily for town use, they might be a comforting safety element as you reenter vehicularized civilization after dark at the end of a long day's hike. Good day packs come from all major packmakers and from specialist firms like Caribou and Cannondale, and you'll find whole woodlots of others. Many house-label models are made by such reputable wholesalers as North Face. But lemon trees grow here too. So once you have settled on the size you need, vet contenders stringently for quality, especially at seams and zippers. Shoulder a few for comfort checks. And in the end try to pick one that pleases your aesthetic sense. You want to live happily together.

Day packs vary widely in size and weight. Costs run from $11.50 to $65. And you can pick up a svelte little Louis Vuitton from Saks Fifth Avenue for a mere $275.

If your load is very small, an alternative is a

BELT BAG OR FANNY PACK

that simply straps around your hips. The multitude of models are all, size and quality apart, essentially the same. (For one, see lower right center, illustration opposite.) Capacities run from about 200 to 400 cubic inches; prices, $9–$35. New Wave ultralightweights cost a hell of a lot more ($20–$50). One reader recommends "From your Friendly Neighborhood Surplus store, a nylon GI belt pouch for four M-16 clips . . . 10 to 25 cents in excellent condition, complete with the dingus that permit the pouch to be installed or removed from the belt without loosening the belt itself."

If everything will fit in I prefer fanny packs to shoulder pouches. They put the load in the most comfortable place. On long treks they can be useful for away-from-camp strolls, and I sometimes take one along in my big pack—though my new internal-frame pack has a detachable top that doubles in this role. At home, fanny packs are perfect for those begging letters that clog your mail: you can put all your begs in one ass kit.

Once you decide to stay out overnight or longer you'll find you must carry a genuine house on your back.

A few years ago that house was virtually always a pack with a large and clearly visible tubular aluminum frame as its central feature: the kind of pack now called "external-frame." But soon after the last edition of this book appeared, so did successful "internal-frame packs." They begat "travel packs." And now "ultralight packs" have arrived. So we need some definitions.

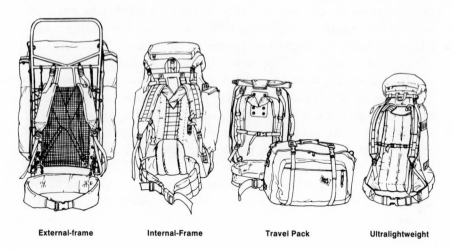

External-frame   Internal-Frame   Travel Pack   Ultralightweight

External-frame packs evolved from the old wooden-frame Yukon packboards, and although aluminum tubing replaced the much heavier wood, their structure remained essentially unchanged: a roughly rectangular frame with a bag attached to one side and a harness to the other. Down the years variations have visited the frames (including a few departures from aluminum), the bags have matured (some to the brink of senility) and harnesses have grown far more sophisticated and efficient. But the E-frame's essential architecture endures.

Internal-frame packs evolved from long, soft, frameless, back-snuggling mountaineering packs that hampered a climber's free movement and delicate balance as little as the load permitted and had no protuberances to be damaged by or to interfere with the pack's being dragged up rockfaces—but which rode imperfectly and were abominably hot on the back. Then somebody inserted a rudimentary frame inside the pack bag to hold its forward surface just clear of the wearer's back yet still follow the back's contours. Today the frames remain rudimentary. Mostly, they consist of two flattened but curving aluminum stays arranged either in X form or running parallel up and down the back. Either arrangement radically improves the pack's ride and also holds it clear of your back so that cooling air can circulate—while retaining at least some of a mountaineering pack's clean-lined, nonsnagging qualities. Suspension systems on the best current I-frame packs are even more sophisticated and efficient than on equivalent E-frames.

Travel bags evolved from I-frames in response to the growing popularity of "adventure travel." The travelers' needs range wide. People planning backpack treks in distant places want something that will do the job on the trail but can without suffering or causing damage be slung hard and often into cab or bus and will even withstand the ravages of the human and mechanical gorillas who handle airplane baggage. At the other extreme are those "adventurers" who stride out for exotic, mildly roughing-it trips all over the world: their prime concern is luggage they can load without tears on dhow or camel or spaceship and can conveniently hump on their backs around airports or even along short trails. Intermediate demands abound. So we now face a continuous spectrum of devices ranging from near-expedition I-frame packs to modified suitcases.

Ultralightweight packs germinated with the New Wave (page 26). All therefore pare ounces to the practical limit, or beyond. Most are enlarged but gossamer day packs, with simple suspension systems and some back-contouring stiffener, such as a foam pad. But an emerging variation is a standard I-frame model shorn and abraded toward ethereality. At a guess, another wide spectrum of choices is about to materialize. Lightweight fanny packs (page 101) form a subgenre.

DECIDING WHAT KIND OF PACK OR PACKS YOU NEED (OR WANT)

The question used to be simply, "What kind of pack will suit me best?" One set of walls, it was assumed, would serve for any version of the house on your back. That was how most people operated. I certainly did. But, as with boots, complexity has opened things up or—if you prefer to see it that way—taken its toll.

You can, of course, still stick to one pack. Most people probably will. But if you do much backpacking of varied kinds you may now decide that you need more than one—because today, much more clearly than yesterday, no one pack is "best." Under different conditions each type offers specific advantages. "The industry," of course, rejoices. Its profound sociological aim: "three or four packs in every American closet." And I, for one, have succumbed. Mind you, my downfall—or uplifting—has been helped along. Some makers regard me as a pro and occasionally send me new products to test. So when you make your own decisions you should probably, in weighing my personal example, bear that dollar-relevant factor crisply in mind.

The prime decision, for most people, will be choosing between an E-frame and an I-frame pack.

Before we get down to tidy objective evaluations we must consider an element that is entirely subjective and singularly elusive. For reasons not presently understood—and probably hidden forever from our pawing minds—I-frame packs hang on some human bodies like church pews but fit others like gloves. And the glovelike mesh may occur with somebody who church-pews it in an E-frame. (A very experienced mountaineer/ backpacker/salesperson tells me she finds I-frames tend to fit women better than E-frames do, perhaps in part because the frames can be made to conform to their spines' curvature, which is generally greater than men's.) Again, two apparently similar I-frames may ride quite differently on the same body. So it pays to shop around. Try several packs, both E- and I-frames, at least in a store and preferably in the field—perhaps by renting. With I-frame packs especially, a great deal depends on correct fitting (page 131), so even more than with most gear you should seek out a good salesman—one who is genuinely competent to make the necessary fine adjustments in what are often rather complicated suspension systems. Be forewarned that at present very few people really qualify.

Another eminently unpinnable element tends to color any choice between E- and I-frames. Most people, from personal experience or simply from seeing others with packs, still regard E-frames as the natural and safe choice. They may also have been scared off by once-common stories of early I-frames that rode like bears—probably because of incorrect fits. Now, I am not trying to imply that I-frames are essentially better. At least, I don't think I am. I just want to issue a warning about the likelihood of built-in bias. For, as usual, battle lines are being drawn. It is easy enough to change someone's religion; but it has already almost come to pass that for true believers in either E- or I-frame packs, conversion to the opposing camp is not only as monumental a task as with stoves but also something likely to be regarded as apostasy.

On a rather more manageable level, your decision may mostly revolve around what you expect to be doing.

If you travel a lot an I-frame pack is definitely preferable (opposite page). If you often use a tent remember that an I-frame is less liable to damage it. If you plan to walk much in very hot weather note that E-frames tend to leave more room for air to circulate around and so cool your back—though the best new I-frame packs seem to come close, if not neck and neck, and one has a specific "desert" antidote for heavy sweating (page 139). Terrain can make a lot of difference too. If you stick to manicured trails or flat and level land, no big deal. But a well-designed and properly adjusted I-frame, like the mountaineering and ski-touring packs from which it evolved, hugs the contours of your back much more snugly and therefore comes closer to being a part of the body instead of a mere appendage. In addition, a properly loaded I-frame tends to bring the pack's center of gravity lower. These mechanical advantages mean that you are better balanced. So if that seems likely to be important—if you expect to do much bouldering or rock-hopping, to travel cross-country over any but the most level terrain or even to use precipitous trails (after all, just where does "climbing" end?)—then you should at least consider an I-frame. Remember, too, that the lack of a bulky, extruding external frame allows you freer movement. And the stream-lined pack is not only less likely to snag vegetation (as almost any E-frame will, constantly, if you have to bushwhack) but is also far less apt to throw you dangerously off balance by bearing unexpectedly and rigidly against tree trunks, rock or ice.

The basic and pivotal question remains: "Yes, but for pure load-carrying in open, not too precipitous country—which is, after all, where most people do most of their backpacking—are I-frames as good as E-frames?" There is as yet no consensus. Many people answer: "For light loads, maybe I-frames are better. For middling loads, no difference. For heavy loads, the E's still have it." But a growing band of cognoscenti claim that a *first-class,* properly adjusted and loaded I-frame carries even the heaviest load better than will any E-frame. And I agree with them. Initially, I viewed the newcomers with skepticism. But I am now a convert. My present I-frame (page 136) takes the sting out of 55-pound loads, even cross-country. Not long ago, carrying just about that weight, I angled for almost an hour across a steep sidehill, through intermittent brush and over occasional rocky outcrops, with my mind very much on route-finding, and realized when I halted that I had been virtually oblivious to the load on my back. I do not believe that would have been the case with any other pack I know.

There are, mind you, a few things about I-frames that I do not like: the need to stuff my sleeping bag into the bottom of the bag (page 139); a certain lack of convenience in managing my gear (page 137); a misera-ble performance as backrest (page 150). But these are muted complaints, all eminently superable. And at the moment I am yoke over hipbelt in love with my I-frame, especially for heavy loads or over rough terrain.

In assessing my personal endorsement, don't forget all those wise things I said at the start about heeding the demands of your own very idiosyncratic bend of body and bent of mind. The first two or three I-frames I tried on in stores struck me as rather less comfortable than my E-frame. Then I slipped into the one I now own. It was love at first feel. And the glow is still there. I cannot imagine that it will ever cool. But then, isn't that how things are at the start of every affair?

If you travel at all you know that bulky and fragile E-frames can be a drag. No one likes taking them in cab or bus. Airlines eat them. And I-frames, though markedly better, are imperfect. (For ways of protecting them, and even E-frames, see page 141.) The answer that has evolved—the whole spectrum of travel bags (page 102), from near-expedition I-frames to modified suitcases—means that in theory all you have to do is select the right point on the spectrum: you determine your luggage needs, then buy a backpack that meets them.

Gadget freaks will probably find this lure irresistible. But in practice an iceberg looms. One immutable law of the universe has it that the more functions a device is designed to perform, the less perfectly it can perform each of those functions. No adjustable wrench works as well as a closed-end wrench on its designated nut. And no near-suitcase is going to fit and ride as efficiently as a sophisticated I-frame. So any travel bag involves compromise. Sometimes that may be fine. If you are making a Tuesday-so-it-must-be-Belgium tour of Europe, say, but hope to squeeze in one weekend of light-load backpacking afterward, then something down toward the Samsonite end of the spectrum might suit you admirably. If, on the other hand, you are planning some serious backpacking in the mountains of southern China but cannot determine just how you and your equipment will be transported to base camp you will probably be well served by a near-expedition I-frame with certain travelwise modifications (page 140).

But the problem is rarely as simple as that. For one thing, your needs probably fluctuate from year to year, trip to trip. And in the end your decision will no doubt ride on the range of your activities and the depth of your pocket. If you spend half your life backpacking and mountaineering and ski touring and canoeing and adventure traveling, in roughly equal doses, and if money is no object, then you should probably own a dozen different packs, each perfect for its own niche, including two or three along the travel-bag spectrum. If, on the other hand, you are appreciably poorer than Croesus, do a fair amount of backpacking in varied terrain and are now dreaming of a cut-rate trip to Nepal you should probably look very seriously at a travel bag that's a mildly modified I-frame expedition bag.

In between—and in between is where most choices will no doubt lie—you just have to make your own assessments about where you'll come down among the many makes and models that are strung out along the travel-bag spectrum. For which, see page 140.

If all or even most of your backpacking takes the form of short trips —one to four days—in warm weather, then you should probably consider one of the new ultralightweight bags. They often fill that bill perfectly. For an example of how one did so for me, see "Weight," page 27. But see that same section (page 30) for a view, not shared by everyone, about limits beyond which paring pounds with such packs may make no sense at all. On the other hand, do not doubt that if you can refine the house on your back enough to enclose it safely in such flimsy walls then you will enjoy a new, lightfoot freedom.

For makes and models of ultralight packs, see page 142.

Before we look closely at each breed of pack we had better consider

SUSPENSION SYSTEMS.

The suspension system forms the core of every pack. And the marrow of almost every suspension system is now

The hipbelt.

Things were not always so. When Kelty pioneered aluminum-frame packs in the 1940s they inherited from the wooden Yukon packboard, essentially unchanged, the ancient and obvious method of hanging a load on the human body: a pair of simple shoulder straps. For years almost the sole advance was a little padding on the straps. Then, in the early 1960s, Trailwise introduced a belt that did more than attempt—as had a few earlier, flimsy affairs—to reduce a pack's sway. At first the new hipbelts were unpadded and rather narrow. But they revolutionized backpacking. A nonhiking friend once slipped my E-frame pack on when it held about 55 pounds and was appalled at the dead weight on his shoulders. I told him to fasten the belt—one of the early, narrow, unpadded kind. "Why," he said when he had done so, "it practically takes the sting out of the load!" It does too. The belt removes almost all the weight from the shoulders and puts it on your hips.

That is where it belongs. The human backbone has evolved from a system designed primarily for horizontal use, with the weight taken at anchored end-points. Our newfangled upright stance has therefore assured us a rich legacy of back trouble. Packs with suspension systems consisting only of a shoulder harness imposed fierce vertical pressure on the easily damaged spine. They also put a heavy strain on the muscles of shoulders, neck and back, hastening fatigue. A hipbelt removes this pressure and strain and transfers the weight to the simple, strong and well-muscled structure of hips and legs. It also lowers your center of gravity.

For two decades the hipbelt has evolved slowly toward bigger and mostly better things: from a simple 2-inch-wide belt of cotton or nylon webbing, through broader Ensolite-padded affairs covered with nylon fabric, to sumptuous foam creations, 4 inches deep or more at the back. If you carried heavy loads you welcomed each advance: the broader and better-padded the belt, the less sting to the load, and the less second-morning hipbelt trauma (page 39).

We seem to be reaching a limit, though. It is not only a limit imposed by added weight and increased heat in the small of the back. For some time the trend in the best packs has been toward broad, contoured or "curvilinear" belts designed to fit snugly on the hips. But practical difficulties have emerged. The new belts look magnificent. They feel fine too—in the store. Yet I have found, in common with many people, that under a heavy load most of them tend, after a while, to slide downward in a way their contouring is specifically designed to prevent. The result is crampingly uncomfortable. At first I thought the trouble might lie in my shape. Everybody's hips and arse are idiosyncratic. (Women, with their broader hip design, have the belt advantage, statistically, over us straighter-up-and-down men.) It seems, though, that I am far from alone. And some kind of consensus on the reason is now building.

After years of doubt, two fundamental facts of belt design now seem to be generally, though still not universally, accepted. First, a fully encircling belt works better than sidestraps from the base of frame or bag. Second, the essential element in a fully effective encircling belt is a continuous, unbroken base of some semistiff material such as webbing. The explanation may be obscure but the pragmatic evidence has grown overwhelming. Unfortunately it seems to be difficult, going on impossible, to sew broad webbing around a curve so that it lies naturally. There are ways around the problem, but they involve such labor-consuming measures as padding layered with foams of differing consistency—and the finished products, though dulcet, are therefore expensive. As a result, at least one man at the heart of equipment research and development thinks that only the most expensive packs will persist with broadly padded curvilinear belts; the majority will go with well-padded straight belts incorporating a single piece of continuous, unbroken webbing. Naturally, not everyone agrees. Packs with good reputations still feature non-encircling belts. And you can still buy medium-priced curvilinears with a pieced, rather than continuous, base. Meanwhile, high-friction coverings (page 138) seem to carry us a quantum step forward. The whole picture may change tomorrow, but that seems to be how matters rest at the moment. Make no mistake, though: compared with all our yesterdays they rest remarkably comfortably, no matter what the details, right where they should, on our hips.

When the hipbelt appeared and initiated the surge toward that happy state of affairs,

The yoke or shoulder harness

at first remained unchanged, even though its function had become quite different: instead of taking the full load, it was now called upon—with a properly designed and adjusted suspension—only to hold the upper part of the pack fairly close to and in harmony with the body, moving in sync with its rhythm. Old-style, single-pin shoulder harnesses, fixed at top and bottom of the frame and adjustable only for length, did this job poorly. Trailwise soon introduced a system tailored for the new task. The main suspension straps are attached to the frame's lowest crossbar near its outside edges. They cross at the middle of your back (behind a mesh panel), curve over the shoulders in padded arcs, and are attached to the frame again at the front low-points (illustration, page 114). At your shoulders a short strap stitched to the padding at each collarbone runs directly back to the shoulder-level crossbar (same illustration). Any harness of this kind has three separate adjustments. One need be set only the first time you put the pack on, and ensures correct fit at the shoulders. The other two can be changed, even when you are on the move, to allow for variations in load, slope, slippage, expansion, sagging muscles and any of the other mysterious but undeniable factors that can affect the way a pack rides on your back. And as you walk the whole harness flexes with your body. With really heavy loads in particular, the Trailwise pack rides better than any other E-frame I know.

For a long time, though, there were doubters. There still are. In fact, most E-frame packs still have simple, old-style, single-pin shoulder straps—though you may be able to adjust them laterally by using spare holes in the crossbar and vertically, a very little, by moving attachment points above or below the bar (illustrations, page 116). But several sophisticated E-frame models other than Trailwise's—including all of Wilderness Experience's and some by Camp Trails—now incorporate the sliding-crossed-strap system. And most I-frame packs have harnesses that are essentially this system modified for the new structures. As perfect fit and frequent fine-adjustment are crucially important with I-frames, that seems conclusive endorsement.

Mark Pack Works have now introduced on some of their travel and day packs "a breathable mesh harness system which is lightweight and extremely comfortable"—and looks very interesting.

A suspension system includes three other major components: sternum strap; backbands (in E-frames) or lumbar pad (their rough equivalent in I-frames); and hipbelt buckle.

Sternum straps

A sternum strap attaches at each end to one shoulder strap at such a height that it meets across your sternum or breastbone (illustration, page 132). It separates amidships at an easily adjustable clip buckle, and when you tighten this adjustment you pull the shoulder straps toward each other and reduce shoulder fatigue. In some packs the sternum strap also transfers a significant portion of the load away from shoulders and even hips onto your chest. But the strap must be properly fitted. First, adjust the movable attachments on the shoulder yoke. (A few packs have sternum straps that cannot be moved up and down on the yoke. Women, in particular, should avoid them. Note, though, that because women tend to have narrower shoulders than men, and a properly adjusted sternum strap pulls the yoke strap inward, it often makes a pack fit them better.) With an adjustable sternum strap, move its attachments to the yoke until the strap crosses your chest about 2 or 3 inches above the portion of your chest that expands the most. This will bring it near the top of your breastbone but *not* high enough to bear in any way on neck tendons. Then, by trial and error, tighten the strap at the joining buckle until it feels most comfortable. You can either leave it at that tension or, as some people prefer, tighten and loosen intermittently to alter load distribution.

Sternum straps may be only gravy, but make no mistake, they work. And although only introduced fairly recently, on I-frames, they now appear on most packs of all kinds.

Note that a sternum strap seriously impairs the usefulness of a quick-release belt buckle—unless you are prepared for an emergency, as when crossing a creek, and disconnect the sternum strap in advance.

Backbands

In all E-frame packs some system of tautly stretched support holds the frame away from your back. It cushions the pressure and applies it at strategic places—and also ensures ventilation between back and pack.

The most common arrangement is still a pair of woven nylon bands, 4 or 5 inches wide. One rests against your shoulder blades, the other across your hips. The gap between the bands is normally about 8 inches, and in this gap air can circulate freely. In hot weather, if you walk bareback or with only a thin shirt, such ventilation can make a world of difference. But with loads of more than about 40 pounds the lower band may begin to press uncomfortably; sometimes it even rucks.

Now, when the weather is even mildly warm I like to walk stripped to the waist; and where weather and privacy are both right I like to strip to hat, socks and boots. When Trailwise replaced the double-band arrangement some years ago with a single nylon-mesh support, 17 inches high, I at first resisted the change because I feared the harsh-feeling material would rub a bare back raw and, in spite of the open mesh, would prevent adequate ventilation. When I tried out the new support, though, I found that even in temperatures well over 100° F. my fears on both counts proved unjustified. The long single support vastly improves the pressure distribution on your back. Some people maintain that with a shirt it seriously reduces ventilation. But nowadays, if I try a pack with the old double-band support, I find myself longing for the extended-mesh system. And several makers have adopted it in some form. If you buy a pack with one, make sure the mesh (or, for that matter, any other back support) comes down far enough for it to rest against the hipbelt under heavy load. Otherwise its lower edge may cut into you.

On packs with a single long nylon-mesh backband, keep it drum-tight, or at least near-tympanic. On packs with double bands, keep the lower one that way too. If you keep the top band tight you will improve ventilation behind your back; if you slacken it a shade you may improve the riding qualities of the pack slightly by angling the frame somewhat farther forward.

For weight distribution in packs, see pages 125 and 130.

Lumbar pads

Most I-frame packs have a pad, often quite bulky and protuberant, in the middle of the back of the hipbelt. This lumbar pad, though structurally quite different from the backband on an E-frame, performs much the same function. It absorbs shock. And it also transfers as much load as possible to the small of the back.

Many lumbar pads look distinctly awkward (see the hourglass-shaped one on my I-frame, page 137). But they work. As with hipbelts, high-friction coverings (page 138) seem to make them work even better.

Desert panel

A sort of upper-back lumbar pad, designed to improve ventilation. See page 139.

Hipbelt buckles

Most belts now have quick-release buckles. "People demand it," says the industry. "If you don't have it, they don't want your pack." The principle is clearly sound: in any emergency you can snap your belt free in an instant and can probably wriggle out of the shoulder harness and so rid yourself of the encumbering pack—though note the near-nullifying effect of a sternum strap unless you are prepared (opposite page). But the buckle must work.

The trouble is, not all of them do. Some simple-interlock kinds will under a heavy load twist and jam—and become very slow-release indeed. This does not happen with the two-pronged black plastic Fastex buckles, in various sizes, that are now almost standard. But with a Fastex I find myself struggling to cinch the belt tightly enough—which is a serious matter (page 127). Besides, I'm unimpressed with the quick-release coefficient. It seems to me that in the twirly-bang of a genuine emergency you'll be damned lucky, brother, if your thumb and forefinger zero in first time on the partially recessed release points.

On the other hand, the metal Kelty buckle quick-releases with a single flip of a fingertip on a protruding flange. More important, it makes belt-cinching simple. That is why I like to replace a Fastex with one, even though it is heavier (2½ ounces, against 1½). (My slightly out-of-date Trailwise has a simple, non-quick-release metal buckle that cinches tight very effectively, and I notice that I have made no attempt to change it.) I know at least one packmaker who would use Kelty buckles if he could; but it is current Kelty company policy not to sell them within the industry for original use on non-Kelty packs. A pity. You can order buckles, though, from dealers—but not direct from Kelty—as "replacement parts" ($4.75).

An alternative to a buckle is a Velcro-stripped belt that passes through a plain metal loop and then presses into holding position. This system, introduced by Synergy and now used on some North Face packs, may not be ultraquick-release but the free belt end is eminently grabbable in an emergency, and the low-friction passage through the loop makes for easy belt-cinching. I understand the Velcro wears out in time and needs replacing. And some people say it tends to clog with snow.

In everything except their suspension systems, E-frame and I-frame packs differ appreciably. We will therefore consider them separately.

The design of

EXTERNAL-FRAME PACKS

now seems to have stabilized. Most continuing improvements amount only to variations on an established theme.

The frames

are roughly rectangular and usually made of aluminum tubing (exceptions, page 118), which is rigid and extremely light and much stronger than it looks. Some cheaper models are straight, but most now contour in a gentle S that echoes the curve of the spine and holds the load closer to your body, where it exerts the least leverage on muscles. Such curvature leaves plenty of air space between load and back for ventilation. And the pack's outward-curving lower ends never bear on your rump in the uncomfortable way those of a straight frame can.

The suspension system goes on one side of the frame, the load on the other. Normally, the load is a packbag. But you can remove the bag and tie on a slaughtered deer or a five-gallon can containing a cache of food or water (pages 203 and 543). By lashing on a kiddie seat (page 146), you can even convert the frame into a sumptuous rickshaw for Junior.

Makes and models of E-frames

All the leading pack makers—JanSport, Kelty, Trailwise, Camp Trails and Wilderness Experience—make such frames. So do many others. And even within this suborder of packdom you face a back-boggling array. Most models sold in reputable mountain shops (but not necessarily in all general sporting-goods stores) are now viable units and fair value. Some are more viable than others, of course. And some are fairer value. By and large, as in most walks of life, you get what you pay for.

Frames are rarely sold alone, without bags; but the weights and current costs of complete E-frame packs range from about 3¼ pounds and $50 for the smallest, most fundamental, stripped-down versions up to 6¼ pounds and $175 or even more for top-quality expedition models.

There is one injunction you should bear steadily in mind when choosing a frame. It applies to all equipment—and to techniques as well —and it advises: "Keep things simple." Backpacking, even more than most human activities, is Murphy-ridden. Much of today's equipment is so finely developed that improvements, especially in zealot hands, can develop into bad cases of over-engineering; and when you see an alluring packframe that's a jury rig of split rings and couplings and other adjustable festoons, you should instantly weigh its Murphy quotient. Ask yourself, "Yes, but *could* things go wrong?" Ask the question several times, searchingly. And ask it early—in the store, not in the teeth of a mountain storm.

For many years, most high-quality models were heliarc-welded at the joints, which are potential weak points. (You can identify heliarc welding by its uneven, obviously handmade look, distinctively different from the smooth, machined finish of standard spot welds.) Heliarc remains the most popular system (Kelty, Wilderness Experience, Alpenlite, Universal, Adventure 16 [in part] and the more expensive Camp Trails models). Trailwise employ a variation, tungsten-inert-gas or TIG welding, which they claim produces a less brittle junction. Other alternatives include arc welding, soldering and brazing (certain cheaper REI and Camp Trails models), adjustable bolts (Antelope) and—for flex and adjustability—cast-aluminum couplings (JanSport).

We can examine E-frames in general by looking closely at the only one I know intimately.

A quarter of a century ago a great deal of chance, a little prejudice and almost no informed opinion put a Trailwise pack on my back. I used the original frame, with successive improved bags, for more than ten years, and it did me proud. It withstood three long treks totaling about twelve months of walking. Every year it came on a couple of week- or two-week-long wilderness trips, perhaps half a dozen two- to four-day jaunts, and many one- or half-day walks. It also endured, fully loaded and without murmur, untold heavings into and out of cars, buses, airliners and those sadistic airline conveyors. I don't think I treated the frame particularly brutally but I took no very great care of it and it never gave me a moment's trouble. At the end of the ten years it was still in perfect condition, and I would probably still be using it had Trailwise not produced a new model. In the improved current equivalent Model 82, the frame (without bag) weighs 2½ pounds, costs $105.

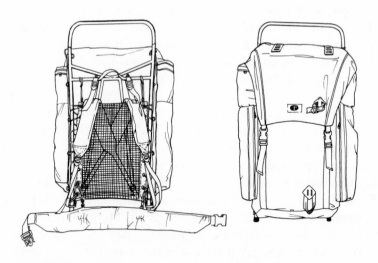

Like the original, the frame is ¾-inch aluminum-alloy tubing, TIG-welded, S-contoured, tapering slightly from shoulders to waist. It is simple and very well constructed.

An optional extension bar (4 ounces; $9.50) can conjoin the protruding top ends of the frame—and I have now fitted one, primarily to prevent the frame ends from snagging vegetation. Principal loss: the protruding ends from which I used to hang binoculars, cameras and, sometimes, hat (pages 145 and 463). Compensation: straps and buckles, grommeted to pins in holes drilled in extension bar (see, just, in illustration page 125), over which binoculars, etc., can be hung—though not very securely. Bonus gain: increased carrying capacity for articles lashed to the bar in a good, forward-on-the-body's-center-of-gravity-line position, where they cannot flop onto my neck as they sometimes will if tied to the top of the pack. Extension bars are removable, but I'd guess that mine will stay on. I'm told that most customers seem to like them, on all brands of packs—in part because grasping the bar makes it easier to lift a pack onto your back and, especially, onto someone else's back.

I always lift my Trailwise by a small nylon hand strap on the top crossbar (illustration opposite). You may, like me, dismiss it at first glance as an effete fussyism but I assure you that it turns out to be a jewel. Many packs, I- as well as E-frame, now incorporate them.

Small plastic buttons plug the open ends of the frame at its foot, and also at the top when no extension bar is fitted. Such buttons are now standard on most tubular E-frames. You need them, particularly at the bottom: open ends pick up samples of any soft ground you put the pack down on, and when you walk on again the samples neatly decant, if you are wearing shorts, into waiting sock tops. And the buttons protect not only the frame but also tents, cars and homes. On my Trailwise the bottom buttons have now been enlarged so that they fit over the frame. Rubber caps that slide over them not only further protect tent, car and whatever but also reduce the chance of slippage on slick surfaces. In addition, they absorb much of the shock that is transmitted to any frame each time it's put down hard or dropped. A reader has suggested removing an end-button and using a section of the frame as a kind of "mailing tube" for storing such items as hacksaw blades. I'm not sure the idea is furiously practical but it does open up fragrant possibilities. For carrying spare buttons, see "Odds-and-Ends Can" (page 522).

In other packs the most common system for anchoring packbag to frame is a series of clevis pins that run through pairs of holes bored in the side tubes. Grommeted holes along the edge of the packbag are then secured to the pins by a variety of cunning or bizarre methods. Most of them presumably work. In Trailwise frames the anchoring is effected by ten small eyebolts that screw into recessed devices called Riv-nuts. A special expansion tool secures the Riv-nuts in position in single holes. Trailwise claim that the frame is less weakened than by the standard double-drilling for clevis pins and that the expanded Riv-nuts restore even the single holes to virtually full strength. The system certainly works: I've never had a Riv-nut pull out. And the eyebolts, which very rarely seem to snag on anything, are occasionally useful as lashing points.

The Trailwise hipbelt is so designed that it hangs upside down on the frame and can be a minor nuisance: when the pack is set down the belt drags and may suffer damage from the frame; and it has to be flipped up each time you put the pack on. The solution, now standard on all Trailwise packs: a miniature bungy-cord loop attached to a convenient backband cord (illustration, page 114).

Although each packframe has its own idiosyncrasies, similar to those I've described for my Trailwise, almost all are built on the same basic, roughly rectangular, aluminum chassis. But there are several genuine

Variations on the theme of E-frames.

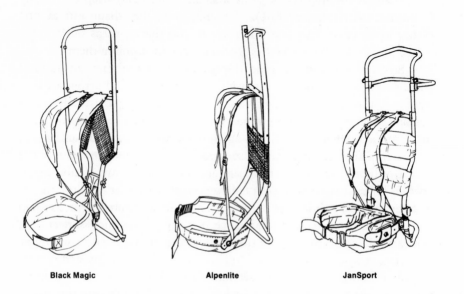

Black Magic   Alpenlite   JanSport

One interesting stray from the norm is the North Face Back Magic. Bolted through the isthmus of its hourglass frame is a nylon joint that "flexes from side to side but not from back to front." The idea is that your hips and shoulders, instead of being "in a splint" the way a normal E-frame holds them, are free to swivel laterally in opposite directions—as they do in the unfettered act of walking. Yet the frame's vertical rigidity remains unimpaired. Result: reduced fatigue. At least, that's the theory.

The hipwrap is a more common and now well-established variant.

According to Murry Pletz, originator of JanSport packs, the germ of the hipwrap system surfaced in 1878 in a pack patented by Henry Merriman of Connecticut. For almost a century the idea lay dormant. But in the last decade it has bloomed.

The basic idea of the modern version is to extend the foot of an E-frame forward in some way and suspend the waistbelt from points level with the hip sockets (junction of pelvis and thigh bones). The line

joining these sockets is the axis around which pivot the major movements
of the walking human body, and with a packframe suspended from the
hipbelt at approximately these points so that it also pivots around that
axis, frame and back move together, in harmony. And that is clearly the
way things ought to be. Well, fairly clearly, I guess.

Hordes of people have now guessed so, anyway. The simplest and
perhaps strongest fixed-wrap version—and certainly the most popular—
is the Alpenlite. But the projections inherent in any such frame will
necessarily project, and therefore be liable to damage when the pack is
off your back—not only at rests and campsites but also, even more
achingly, when being man- and machine-handled into and out of cars,
pickups and airplanes.

The Stephenson Golite pack has—among many unusual features—
a very long, swinging hipwrap system that reaches forward to the front
of the body.

Makers of some fixed-hipwrap models claim that their packs stand
upright, unassisted. On such flat surfaces as living-room floors and some
meadows, they will. But on typical wilderness surfaces they often will
not. Then the projections become a minor nuisance. They also make it
difficult to lean the pack backward against a tree or other convenient
prop. And for me—because I regularly convert the pack into a backrest
by propping it against my staff (page 149)—this is a serious drawback.
One reader writes that he simply reverses the pack—and leans against
the harness.

A difficulty with hipwrap frames has always been that the metal
projections, to function properly, must lie close to your hip sockets, and
fit is so critical that a slightly wrong size, or even putting on bulky
clothes, can throw things awry. Result: muscle cramps or even "hipwrap bruises." But a cunning new variant may at last have solved this
problem.

JanSport, for years in the forefront of innovation, have now produced hipwrap bars (see illustration) that rotate on beveled cams and can
be fine-tuned with set screws so that they exert slight outward pressure
and will therefore "give" long before inducing muscle cramps or bruises.
They are also said to "improve the mechanical transfer of energy." The
bars will fold flat against the pack. They can even be detached. The
arrangement looks highly Murphoid (it is, I hear, indeed rather liable to
damage) but apparently works well. And after five years on the market,
and many important improvements, it seems to have struck a chord
among backpackers. JanSport D Series packs that embody it are in some
stores the currently best-selling E-frames.

Another variant has now appeared in the new Adventure 16 Hip
Hugger packs. The hipwrap takes the form of a single, curved, flexible

spring. Educated people seem to speak highly of it. I tried one pack in a store and it certainly felt good (Expedition model, 3815 cubic inches, 6 pounds 10 ounces, $214).

Alternative materials for packframes

A few years ago Segan Pax of Oregon produced a laminated wood frame (illustration page 100, right center, rear). Other materials were mostly natural too: leather-and-felt shoulder harness and hipbelt; varnished, woven-rush backband. The result was a work of art. But as a practical load carrier it could not quite compete with modern technology's best. And the company has folded. Sad.

Coleman have reached the other way with their Peak I plastic frames. Early models were reportedly liable to break, but a change from straight-link-chain polymer plastic to cross-linked ditto has apparently

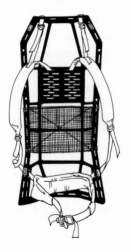

cured the problem. The frame is light (33 ounces in the original plastic; 42 ounces in the new and tougher material) and has what Coleman call "controlled flexibility." That is, "it moves, bends and flexes with your body." The multislotted frame certainly makes it highly adjustable—and therefore suitable for use by groups such as Scouts, for rentals or for bean-stalking youngsters. The Peak I packs are very competitive ($59–109). But they lack some of the sophistication of state-of-the-art models and therefore tend, like many Coleman products (other than the Peak I Stove, page 236), to be sold more often in upper-level general sporting-goods stores than in mountain shops.

Other frames for children (beyond the many small, soft day packs that may do for the very young). Strong and adjustable packs specially designed or particularly suitable for children include: the Antelope Little

Hiker 2000 (2 pounds, complete with bag, $33.50), that can be used by 4- to 9-year-olds and "grow" along with them; other Antelope models, similarly adjustable, for 9–90-year-olds, including growing teenagers ($46.50–$160); the Kelty 4C (1½ pounds, $64), also with an adjustable frame; for preteens, the Wilderness Experience Little Big Man (2¼ pounds, $70) and JanSport Rover 2 (1¾ pounds, $45); and for teenagers the JanSport Rover 1 (3 pounds, $75).

Back- and front-packing (middle-packing)

The Bal-Pak "is designed for carrying heavy loads on trails for extended backpacking trips and for packing in supplies" (Bal-Pak, 10860 Scotsman Way, Rancho Cordova, CA 95670; 6½ pounds, $100).

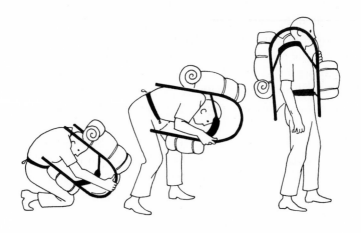

Packbags for E-frames

Any good packbag is tough enough to withstand years of the roughest wear you'll give it, as close to waterproof as you can make it and big enough to meet your most expansionist needs. It should also, except under special conditions (page 123), be multipocketed.

In my opinion, the bigger a pack, the better. A cavernous sack weighs only a few ounces more than an equivalent middle-class job, and it will accept and protect all your chattels—as a good house should— even on winter snow trips, when the bulk problem looms largest. So you rarely find yourself struggling to cram everything in—or traveling with the overflow so festooned around the pack that it looks like a newlyweds' getaway car. Such festooning is surprisingly common. But it makes for poor load distribution (page 126). And in rain it courts disaster. Some people maintain that a small packbag helps you prune the load's weight. There's probably some truth in the idea; but not, for me, enough. And although the trend has for years seemed to be toward "the smallest possible pouch," that may be changing. A mountain-shop manager recently told me that "people now want the most cubic inches per dollar."*

Beyond such basics you face three major, overlapping packbag choices:

1. Three-quarter-length bag (sleeping bag goes underneath)
   or all-embracing full-length-of-the-framer;
2. Top-loader *or* panel-loader;
3. Compartmented bag *or* single-bloody-great-sack.

1. The three-quarter-length bag has for years been so overwhelmingly popular that some firms no longer make full-lengthers. And the tucked-down-below sleeping bag became, for some people, the only way to go. I was once starting on a wilderness trip when a young boy—golden-haired, bright, "almost eleven"—walked with me a few hundred yards toward the reservoir he was going to fish. When I responded to one of his questions by saying that I'd be back in the wilderness for several days, he looked hard at my bulging pack and said: "Oh, I see—I didn't think you were staying overnight, but you must have your sleeping bag inside."

I remain skeptical about the three-quarter-bag-with-sleeping-bag-underneath system. It's not only that I have yet to be convinced about the load-distribution advantages most makers claim (page 125). I dislike the loss of valuable space. And long before I suffered my first wet sleeping bag (page 431) on my first trip with an I-frame pack—which, for reasons we'll discuss later, more or less demands that you carry the sleeping bag at the bottom—I rebelled against the idea of strapping mine on at the foot of the packframe. No backpacker's sleeping bag is a robust article, and it is the one piece of equipment you just have to keep dry. It also seemed to me, and still seems, that every time you put your pack down, a sleeping bag strapped to the foot of the frame receives the maximum quota of both wear and moisture. Stuff sacks may be protective and waterproof when new but under this kind of treatment will not remain so for long. I therefore continue to use a full-length-of-the-frame pack-

* Measuring the cubic capacity of irregular items like packs presents problems. I'm advised that some manufacturers "fill test models with Styrofoam balls, popcorn or peanuts, then pour the contents into graduated cylinders." Choice of medium no doubt depends on whether the maker is into mailing, movies or monkeys.

Users face different difficulties. One reader complains, "I've searched every shop and can't find any cubic inches to put in my pack. It must be important, though, because every packmaker says you need them."

bag. When rain threatens—and often when it doesn't—I pack my sleeping bag carefully into its mid-maw, deep and safe.

Recent reports suggest that full-lengthers are now coming back into favor.

2. Panel-loading bags—in which all or almost all the back of the pack zippers open—have become very popular. If you lay the pack flat you can open it up like a suitcase and get at any item without fuss. At least, so the catalogues say. But the zippers come under repeated heavy strain and tend to "break, bend or rip from the fabric" (quote from a thrice-unhappy user). A response by many makers has been to affix compression straps that relieve zipper strain when the pack is full. And that no doubt helps. I still stick with old-style top-loaders, though. If you use reasonable foresight in packing them (page 527) you very rarely have to dive and fumble for any item. You also gain extra strength and waterproofness—and un-Murphy-ridden simplicity.

If you use a top-loader do not underestimate the importance of the method by which the pack's flap is battened down. You probably open and close your pack many times a day, and if you have to bend or kneel down every time to the foot of the bag—perhaps into mud or snow—in order to release or retie a knot your back and language will soon reflect the exercise. Current available systems run from good through fair to diabolical. For years I used the system found in Kelty packs: nylon cords adjusted by small, simple, spring-loaded toggles that you can fit on any bag. But plastic Fastex side-release buckles (illustration, page 114) are now taking over. And once you get used to them they are good.

Many top-loading packs—and some panel-loaders too—now have a rigid aluminum hold-open bar that keeps the pack's mouth squarely open, for easier loading. (Also, perhaps, for easier selling: it makes the bag look very neat and shipshape.) I've removed my bracket—because it prevents me from reaching back and down into the lower fastnesses of the bag when the pack is propped up behind me; because it ruins the empty pack as a backrest; and because discarding it saves 2 ounces. The bracket also hinders rather than helps in the struggle to get everything in when the pack is full to overflowing—as most packs manage to be most of the time. On this score, and also for protection from rain, I still like the old sleeve-and-drawstring system with which you simply push down on everything with one hand while pulling the drawstring tight with the other. At least in theory, such devices—sometimes called snow-cuffs—can even convert the bag into an emergency bivouac (page 149).

A pure top-loading pack—without panel-loading lower sections—can hardly be compartmentalized. And a pure panel-loader almost always is. So the second of our gnawing packbag choices merges into the third: to have or not to have compartments.

3. The theory of compartmentalization is fine: your house comes with neat little "cupboards" for keeping everything tidy. But my first experience with simple dividers (and some packs run to a half-zillion) convinced me that they were a perishing nuisance: many bulky though light items I always carry simply would not fit in. Yet a majority of bags now feature at least upper and lower compartments. There are even multilayered jobs, like midrise parking lots. I look on such structures with horror. I have never used one, and I base my contempt squarely on prejudice. Don't ignore that. The savage divergence of views among experienced backpackers on this subject (and oh so many others!) may stem from accidents of evolution as well as common human orneriness: if you developed your gear and techniques while using a multipocketed marvel you'll likely look with supreme contempt on my cavernous, undifferentiated sacks. And vice versa.

No matter which style of bag you choose, its fabric must be tough enough to withstand the sudden grabbing onslaughts of the sharpest rock outcrop and the most viciously pointed branch. It must not crack in extreme cold, as some of the older synthetics did. The bottom must resist constant scuffing. And the fabric itself should be water-resistant and must be compatible with an inner coating that will make it waterproof —though, as we shall see, there is more to waterproofness than that.

Three woven nylon fabrics are currently used in packbags. Packcloth or Parapac is, at 400 or 420 denier, the lightest and most closely woven and therefore most water-resistant. ("Denier" is a relative measure of a fabric's density: in an X-denier cloth, 1000 meters of the thread used to weave it weigh X grams. Fabrics are also measured in ounces per square yard of finished product: "8-ounce Packcloth," for example.) The more coarsely textured Cordura and Oxford Cloth (600 denier and up) resist abrasion better, water less well. The relatively new Ballistic Cloth (about 1000 denier)—so called because originally developed for bulletproof vests—is extremely strong and tear-resistant, but heavy. Most good packbags are currently made of Packcloth, often with Cordura patches around the foot and at wear points. Ballistic Cloth, though largely still restricted to packs that suffer extreme abrasion, as in rock-climbing, may soon find broader use. And the fabric field is growing. Every day brings new variations that are lighter and stronger and take coatings better.

Unfortunately, even waterproof-coated fabrics that stand up to hard wear do not ensure a waterproof bag: most untreated seams can be waterproofed but it is a tedious job that must be done by hand—though factory-sealed seams may be coming. Meanwhile, in downpour country —and also if you may have to swim across a river (page 531)—you should certainly do the job yourself with one of the specially made solutions suitable for the fabric of your particular bag. You will probably be wise to do it anyway. If you mean to do a good job—and no other kind is worth considering—do not expect to get through with a brush-on solution in under an hour or two. Frankly, I remain unconvinced that any such waterproofing job, no matter how carefully done, stays totally waterproof for very long. But you should certainly strive to make your pack as water-repellent as possible. Sealants that come in roller-top "de-odorant-style" bottles are apparently appearing, and make the job easier. And waterproofing tape may be just over the horizon.

Unfortunately, "water-repellent" can, like "hi-fi" or "psychoso-matic," mean almost anything or almost nothing. And in the end the safest solution may be to carry waterproof nylon shells, now available from several makers (about 4 ounces; $15), that slip over the entire pack. A cheaper but less robust alternative is a heavy-duty plastic trash bag, suitably trimmed to fit over your particular pack or kept whole and therefore stronger and used as an internal liner (for big packs, 30-gallon size, 3-mil bags, 3½ ounces; $.28). (For subsidiary uses of the trash bag, see page 521.)

Unless you expect to bushwhack through clutching vegetation or do something else that makes outside pockets inadvisable, you can hardly have too many of them. They house all the things you are continually wanting, plus the items you may need in an emergency, such as a first-aid kit; also a stack of small articles that you could never lay hands on if they languished at the bottom of the main sack (for suggestions on packing, see page 526). A few makers now offer loose pockets for attach-ment to the main bag. See page 125 for bright thoughts on color-coded pockets.

The pocket zippers on most good packs—and also on other equip-ment—are now usually nylon. They run more smoothly than metal ones and do not so easily become iced up—though they will fuse if you somehow succeed in dropping a hot coal on them. Continuous-coil zip-pers, at last strong enough for use on pack pockets, are replacing the toothed kind. They have no teeth that can pull out—and they're more or less self-repairing (page 347).

People who operate in very cold weather and therefore have to wear large and clumsy gloves will sometimes thread loops of nylon cord through the zipper tabs of their pack pockets. The advantages are obvious —though it is difficult to imagine a more efficient way to snag trees or bushes or damn near anything than by festooning your pack with five or six loops of nylon cord. A reader has suggested circumventing that dan-ger with long, single-strand thongs.

For more than twenty years I used, almost exclusively, an evolving series of simple, top-loading, bloody-great-sack packbags by Trailwise. The illustration on page 114 delineates the main features of the current, improved version with contoured top hood and extension bar, which is now standard (#82, 6394 cubic inches, 5 pounds 2 ounces complete; $185). All down the years I was more than satisfied. But when John Foley of New Hampshire—a math teacher by trade but recently a part-time professional equipment-maker for a spell—kindly offered to make a bag to my exact specifications I jumped at the chance. I have now looked his gift horse sternly in the mouth—and I like what I have seen. So I guess the results reflect my current vision of the ideal packbag—within those constraints imposed by the frame, today's materials, my layered prejudices and Mr. Foley's considerable ingenuity.

His general approach was "to try to retain the general 'feel' of the bag which you've become used to." The result is above all simple and big: a basic bloody-great-sack, innocent of compartments, with the only seams (other than for pockets) running around the sides and reinforced foot (main sack, 6038 cubic inches, pockets 1368 cubic inches, total 7406 cubic inches; weight, 2 pounds 7 ounces).

Main sack and all pockets are 8-ounce nylon taffeta Packcloth. Eleven-ounce Cordura reinforces the foot. All fabrics were cut with a hot gun to preclude unraveling.

The pack's very wide mouth has grommets set at 3-inch intervals along its hem, and the drawstring threaded through them can be pulled tight to form what is essentially a snow-cuff. A huge flap battens down over this cuff.

The flap is double-thickness—to meet my request for an easily accessible map pocket without inviting seepage through seams right up there on top where the rain pounds hardest. The bottom layer of the flap is seamless. The upper one—"available for a pincushion"—has the pocket sewn onto it. (To be honest, I'm still not sure if the extra weight of the double layering is worthwhile. Years ago I complained bitterly when Trailwise, because of seam seepage, discontinued their map pocket. I had gotten used to it. But with time I had adjusted to the loss. And now I'm frankly undecided about the pocket's value.) The flap battens down with two plastic Fastex-type side-release clips. Two sets of female clip halves—at lower- and mid-bag—make closure easy whether the bag is full or almost empty. And I can adjust more finely with somewhat complicated slide-through-leather-buckle arrangements on each strap.

The two side pockets on one side are the same dark green color as the main sack but the other pair are pale buff. I stipulated this arrangement—first suggested by JanSport, I believe—because any pack, when off your back, can face two ways, and I am often unsure of which pockets contain what. That confusion has down the years been a minor but by no means negligible frustration, because one of the upper pockets houses the goodies I nibble at almost every halt (page 528). But the pale buff pockets show up clearly in any light and signal to me, instantly, "Here is your food." Or, if I'm looking for some other small article, they say, "It's on the other side." The color coding works, I assure you.

All pockets close with continuous-coil zippers, and the zipper pulls have short loops of nylon lacing tied on, for easier grasping. Both upper corners of all pockets have a small loop of ¾-inch nylon webbing sewn into them: I can grasp one with my free hand for easier zipping or unzipping; they are strong enough to use as lashing points; and they could be pressed into service for compression-strap anchors, to hold the load close to my back when the sack is less than full.

Near the foot of the bag are two strong leather lash tabs of the kind now common on many commercial packs. They will take straps to secure anything I feel the need of attaching: foam pad, crampons, stirrups for exhausted companions, spare bottles of champagne, unicorn fodder.

Weight distribution in external-frame packs

It is too early to consider details: we have not yet discussed the furniture. See page 526. But we should at this stage review general principles.

It was always said, and I think rightly, that with the old shoulder-load packs you should keep the weight as high as possible. Most makers maintain that, even with a hipbelt, high loading remains an advantage. That is one reason they make three-quarter-length bags: the main load rides high; your sleeping bag, which for its bulk weighs precious little, sits at the foot. It is undoubtedly true in theory that, because most packs ride most of the time with their tops tilted slightly forward, a high load rides closer to your center of gravity; but I remain in a state of mild skepticism about any practical advantage. Rough-and-ready experiments with 20 pounds of full canteens shifted as high and then as low as they would fit into an otherwise normally loaded pack failed to convince me that there was any real difference. On the other hand, carrying the load low obviously lowers your center of gravity, and the greater stability can be important: in snowshoeing, climbing, crossing rugged terrain, even when battling high winds. In fact, several makers of three-quarter-length bags recommend that under such conditions you consider carrying the sleeping bag on top and refastening the packbag on the lower part of the frame.

But there is no doubt about the value of keeping a load close to your back. Many years ago I fell for a time into the habit of tying my sleeping bag on the back of the pack in a large, unlovely, unstuffed lump. When rain forced me to put it inside again one day I was amazed at the improvement in the way the pack rode. As far as possible I now stow all heavy articles close to the packframe, or at least keep them away from the back of the bag.

Fitting a new external-frame pack

First, select the right size for your torso. This means matching the distance between upper shoulder-strap connection and hipbelt on the packframe with the distance between your shoulders and hips (most frames come in at least three sizes). Any halfway competent salesman will set you straight. An adjustable frame (page 114) accommodates everyone, at least in theory.

Choosing the make and model that works best on your particular body has to be a matter of trial and error. Hip shape may be one big factor, body length another; but the rest tail away into such barely quantifiable subtleties as dynamic muscle relationships and idiosyncratic gait.

When trying out a pack in the store you must, to judge it properly, fit the suspension system to your body. Many packs come with specific fitting instructions. Follow them meticulously. In particular, do so with Trailwise-type sliding-crossed-strap suspensions. Procedures with them are rather more complicated than those I'll outline. They come much closer, in fact, to those for I-frames (page 131).

The general rules for fitting E-frames—though they may be superseded by any pack's specific instruction sheet—are as follows:

First, load the pack with at least 20 pounds and preferably with as much as you habitually carry. (Most good mountain shops now have sand-filled sacks calibrated in multiples of 10 pounds for this job.) Slip the pack on. If it has several holes in the shoulder-level crossbar, use them to space the tops of the yoke into the most comfortable position. With the hipbelt undone, adjust the yoke until it just holds the pack against your back but not too tightly. Next, hunch your shoulders so that the pack lifts a little, and cinch the hipbelt tight. Really tight. To achieve that end, pull firmly. Then shrug the pack even higher and tighten again. Now take a deep breath and pull even harder. If the belt hurts a little it's about right.

Once the load has settled down on your back, the belt will bear on the protruding hipbones, not on your waist, and will slant slightly upward and forward. On some packs you can adjust the belt so that it bears in the right place by moving the belt attachment to the frame up or down. In others you adjust the yoke-to-frame attachment point. In some you can adjust at both sites.

With the hipbelt tight and settled down on your hips, readjust the yoke so that it takes little or none of the load but just bears enough to prevent the pack from swaying. When you have a pack fitted to your frame, walk about the store. Try several packs. Decide which feels most comfortable. If it meets all your requirements, including nature and capacity of packbag (page 119), buy it. Or, better yet, rent it for a trial.

Adjusting an E-frame suspension in the field

With a heavy load you may at first find that the tight belt, taking almost the whole weight of the pack, tends to constrict your hip muscles. It may even cause mild cramp pains. But persevere. In a day or two the muscles will accept their new work. And the ease with which you now find yourself carrying the load will soon make you forget any temporary discomfort. If you want to, you can ease the strain from time to time by loosening the belt and returning the load to the shoulders. At least, I understand that is the theory. In practice I find I very rarely do so. Not deliberately, that is. But with most packs and most people there comes a time after a prolonged bout of walking with a heavy load—after nearly an hour's solid slogging, say—when you find that everything has settled down a shade and you are taking more weight on your shoulders than you would like. So you stop, or at least break stride, and hitch the damned pack back up higher and maybe try to tighten the hipbelt another quarter-inch. It should not happen like that, but it all too often does. In fact, the sight of another hiker stopping in his tracks and wearily hitching everything upward is perhaps one of the most lasting human-meeting memories that we carry away from the backcountry. Or has been. Today's big hipbelts and sophisticated harnesses, if properly adjusted, can make that settling-sinking feeling a thing of the past.

Deliberate transfer of some of the load to your shoulders from time to time is a different matter. Some people like to ring the change regularly. With simple, old-style shoulder harnesses, all you need do—in fact, all you can do—is tighten the one buckle on each shoulder strap. Later, when you've had enough of the increased load on your shoulders, you slacken it off again.

Trailwise-type, sliding-crossed-strap E-frame harnesses offer essentially the same broader options you get when fine-tuning I-frame suspensions. (page 131).

INTERNAL-FRAME PACKS

In most places you still meet far more backpackers carrying E-frames than I-frames. But retailers tell me that in current sales the newcomers have almost pulled level. It's certainly worth noting that although some of the very best I-frame packs come from new specialist firms, just about every established packmaker has climbed aboard the saleswagon.

I-frames are succeeding in spite of some immediately visible drawbacks that hit potential converts in the buying eye. The best I-frames tend to be rather heavier than E-frame equivalents. Rather more expensive too. Note that I say "the best." In I-frames the differences between the mediocre, the good and the superb seem to me to lie, even more than with most equipment, in the accretion of small but significant details, meticulously considered and constructed. The resultant complexity not only accounts for the heaviness and expense of the best models, it also underlies what may be an even greater impediment to wholesale conversion of backpackers: a widespread failure to understand that in order to make an I-frame pack work you must first fit it to your body like a custom-made suit and thereafter must drive it as you would a Ferrari, not an automatic-shift Chevy. It will not drive itself; but once you have learned how to handle it the rewards are rich. That could be why you meet both evangelistic I-frame enthusiasts and bitter debunkers. Sometimes the gulf between them may yawn only because of those elusive and unquantifiable personal statistics that we have already discussed (page 103). But I suspect that the I-frame enthusiast often enthuses because his pack was meticulously fitted in the first place and he then learned how to drive it, while the debunker debunks because he had the new pack draped sloppily onto him and he was not even told he had to drive it. You all too often see such unhappy people on the trail with malad-

justed I-frames hanging from their backs like ill-tempered baboons—
and their natural complaints (the bearers', not the baboons') no doubt
echo down backpacking's word-of-mouth corridors.

It was certainly an expert fitting and proper driving instruction that
initiated my conversion from doubter to enthusiast.

But before we can examine fit and driving technique (or fine-tuning)
of I-frames we must take a closer look at essential structural elements
other than the suspension systems we have already surveyed (page 107).

I-frames are still in an early stage of evolution and details change
with every tide, but the main lines seem to have been drawn.

The frames

mostly consist of nothing more than two aluminum stays, like emaciated
tire levers, running parallel on either side of the spine or, alternatively,
arranged in X-form across the back. But parallel stays may be joined by
a crossbar at or near their tops. And X-form stays may be left floating or
be pinned in some way at the crossing point. In both systems the stays
must be bent to conform to the curvature of your particular spine, but
this fitting is more important with parallel stays (page 131). One maker
now offers lighter, more efficient graphite stays that must be custom-
made to fit your back (page 139).

I-frame packbags

Most of what I said about E-frame packbags applies (page 119):
fabrics, pocketing and zippers are identical; you can choose top-loaders
or panel-loaders, compartmentalized wonders or single-bloody-great-
sacks, even combinations thereof; and you can still choose almost any
capacity you want. But there are differences too.

The more closely the bag conforms to the curvature of your back,
the better it carries its load. So the very best I-frame bags are contoured
and rather complicated structures—and thereby impose, as part of the
price for load-carrying efficiency, some loss in packing and access convenience. Because the bag must, or at least should, hug your back as closely
as ventilation and comfort permit, compression straps that pull the load
in tight against the frame are much more important than in E-frames.
Most I-frame packs have two or three sets of such straps spread along the
length of the bag, and only a fool ignores them. Another requirement,
or near-requirement, imposed by I-frames' back-hugging nature is one I
dislike: it is almost necessary that you pack your sleeping bag in the very
foot of the bag. In part, this is to enable you to wrap the foot of the bag

more snugly around your hips. (In the more sophisticated packs, pull straps enable you to cinch the soft, sleeping-bag-filled corners in really tight. This cinching does not make for hotter walking, as might be imagined, because that portion of the bag overlies the hipbelt.) But the main reason for carrying your sleeping bag in the foot of the bag hinges on the demands of

Weight distribution in I-frame packs.

Because the bag hugs your back and becomes almost an integral part of you, the way you arrange your gear in the bag is also more important than in E-frames. In fact, it is critical.

Makers differ mildly in their recommendations (for two, see illustration)—no doubt because of idiosyncrasies of their packs, gaits or theories. But they agree on general principles that, with one exception, echo those for E-frames. The exception is that the foot of the pack must not carry a heavy load. And I-frame makers all agree that the way to achieve this end is to put your sleeping bag there. Some even provide separate zippered basement compartments with compression systems that coerce your sleeping bag into the most efficient conformation. One maker now offers an optional contoured sleeping-bag stuff sack that fits the pack's foot the way a sock fits a boot (page 139).

To keep the load close to your back you must, of course, pack heavy items well forward in the pack, or at least at the top, where the bag's natural lean and curvature will bring it closest to your balance line. Above all, avoid heavy items low down and far back.

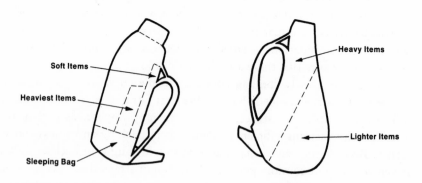

Because the bag will, if properly adjusted, travel closer to your back than an E-frame bag, you must take even greater care not to pack protruding articles along the forward surface where they might gouge your back. Instead, stuff in soft or flat and not-too-rigid items.

The final touch to an efficient loading job is pulling tight on all compression straps.

Such touches are important. Just as meticulous attention to rather complex details of I-frame construction seems to make the difference between mediocre, good and superb results, so does meticulous attention to the rather complex details of "driving" I-frames. Paying such attention would seem to mean some loss of simplicity and convenience. And maybe it does. But the loss is very slight. Rather to my surprise, I find the gain overwhelmingly worth it.

Fitting a new internal-frame pack

As with loading, so with fitting: it is both more important and more complicated than with an E-frame.

Unless you adjust the suspension properly when you first try the pack on, it will hang there like one of those ill-tempered baboons. You're unlikely to give the wretched thing real consideration, let alone buy it. And if you are foolish enough to buy it you'll probably never get the slightly-mixed-metaphor monkey off your back.

If you are shopping in a store, seek out help. Perhaps more than with any other backpacking item, you need the assistance of a salesman you can trust. Failing such trust—or if you shop by mail—read the instructions that come with the pack. Read them carefully. At first they may seem rather daunting. But the procedure is easy enough once you grasp the principles. I shall have to consider the more sophisticated kinds of suspension, so if you're eyeing a simpler pack, just cut some of the complicated cackle.

You can probably select the right-size pack by heeding such maker's recommendations as "medium for people 5′ to 5′7″; large for people 5′8″ to 6′3″." A more accurate method is to measure the distance between the base of your spine and the point your shoulders meet your neck, and then to check that the pack's harness can be adjusted so that the bottom of the lumbar pad and the arch of the shoulder straps are this same distance apart.

With all I-frames—but more essentially with parallel stays than X-forms—the first step is to remove the stays from their holding sheaths inside the bag and bend each of them so that it conforms to your back contour. Conforms exactly. Many small, merging bends will do the job better than a few large bends. Make the bends over your knee, or over the rounded edge of a kitchen table or counter top. Keep bending each stay until it lies flat along your spine when you are leaning very slightly forward in a normal backpacking stance. (Details of where stays should start at the base of your spine and of how to bend the portion that protrudes above the nape of your neck may vary from pack to pack. Check instructions.) When both stays are accurately bent, replace them in their sheaths.

Load the pack with at least 25 pounds and preferably with as much as you normally carry. Do not, as with E-frames, use only such heavy items as sand-filled sacks. Instead, follow the loading instructions above. Stuff a sleeping bag or reasonable facsimile into the foot of the bag. And try to put light and heavy items in their appropriate places. If you have only heavy items like sandbags make sure that when you cinch up the compression straps you pull them very tight.

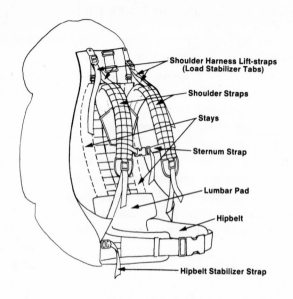

Shoulder Harness Lift-straps
(Load Stabilizer Tabs)

Shoulder Straps

Stays

Sternum Strap

Lumbar Pad

Hipbelt

Hipbelt Stabilizer Strap

Put the pack on. Adjust the main shoulder straps until they are firm but not uncomfortably tight. Then cinch the hipbelt tight—really tight (see page 127). Its upper edge should ride about an inch above the top edge of your hipbones. If the pack has hipbelt stabilizer straps (see illustration) cinch them tight too.

The next step is, like the stay-bending, a once-only operation, but it can be a bitch: you must check that the torso-length adjustment is correct. (With some more sophisticated packs the instructions will show you how to do this, at least approximately, before putting on or even loading the pack.) The check consists of seeing whether the upper ends of the shoulder-harness lift straps (sometimes called load-stabilizer tabs) ride in such a position that they slope down at the proper angle to their junction with the shoulder straps. In most packs this angle is about 45°. If the top of the strap rides too high you must shorten the torso adjustment; if too low, you must lengthen it. The method of altering the torso adjustment varies from pack to pack but usually involves broad nylon webbing with cross-straps and a Velcro securing pad. Alternate points of attachment to the packbag may permit fine adjustment of the lift-strap position.

On some packs the torso adjustment also takes care of what may seem a minor matter but is absolutely critical: the point of attachment between each main shoulder strap and its lift strap must be directly on top of your shoulders, in line with the collarbone. (Somewhat too far forward is all right; a touch too far back is not.) On more sophisticated packs you make this adjustment separately, with some system of holding cross-straps.

These matters taken care of, you fine-tune shoulder and lift straps until the pack rides in the most comfortable position and does not sway, no matter how swaggeringly you walk. Then you adjust the sternum strap's attachments to the yoke (page 110) until the strap lies in the right position across your breastbone. Finally you tighten the sternum strap, very gently, until it too is playing its part and you suddenly realize that the whole schmozzle has bloomed into as close an approach to comfort as it's possible to imagine with such a goddam load on your back.

Now look, I know these instructions are not limpidly clear. They can't be. The procedures are not limpidly simple. Not first time through, anyway. And they're further blurred because I've tried to make them apply across the board, to most I-frame packs. But I hope what I have written will help people who are buying packs without the assistance of adequate instructions or of a salesman they trust. I also hope, beyond that, to have emphasized to everyone the critical importance of first-time fitting if an I-frame is to be a boon rather than a baboon.

Next along the pathway to satisfaction there stands—second in importance only to that initial fitting—the daily, ongoing, hour-by-hour business of

Fine-tuning (or driving) an I-frame pack.

Coldly stated like that, the thing may sound like a hassle. But I have found—like most experienced people I've consulted—that with very little practice the process becomes almost automatic, demanding precious little time or thought.

There are, I guess, five somewhat separate ways in which you can fine-tune or drive your pack. Once you've fully grasped the underlying principles they are all matters of common sense, and really very simple. Please note that when I speak of adjusting some strap or fitting, the alteration is almost always very small. A ⅛-inch movement in a strap buckle may bring about a marked change in the way the pack rides.

The first fine-tuning procedure comes at the start of a trip or when you radically change the loading of your pack. At such times you must run quickly through the last few items of the fitting procedure. That is, you: Loosen all adjustments. Put pack on. Tighten shoulder straps to firm position. Cinch hipbelt tight. Tighten belt stabilizer straps. Possibly readjust shoulder straps. Adjust lift straps. And, finally, fasten and adjust sternum strap. The more sophisticated the pack, the longer all this will take; but even with the most sophisticated it need consume no more than about a minute.

You go through the second procedure, a sort of miniversion of the first, every time you put the pack on: Cinch hipbelt tight. Tighten belt stabilizer straps (if any). Possibly (but improbably) readjust lift straps. Fasten sternum strap. Walk. Elapsed time, maybe 30 seconds.

The third kind of tuning is another miniversion of the first. When you put the pack on after a camp or halt, as above, you find that because of some overlooked change in load or loading (lots of food eaten, or an item of a companion's gear taken aboard, or merely some rearrangement of your own gear) the pack does not sit quite correctly. The response is simple: Slacken off lift and sternum straps a touch, readjust shoulder straps until the load feels right, then readjust lift and sternum straps. A sub-version of this procedure may be needed on the move, particularly with a new pack: while you walked, hipbelt or harness has shifted a shade, and the fit is no longer exact. Your response will obviously vary with what feels wrong. Sometimes a simple readjustment of lift straps will be enough. But if the hipbelt has slunk lower you must hunch your shoulders to lift the pack higher and then recinch the belt. (As I've said, we see this all too often; but it should not happen with a really good pack, properly fitted.) Once the hipbelt feels right, you will probably have to readjust shoulder lift and sternum straps just a touch.

The fourth tuning procedure also occurs on the move. You have been walking for half an hour and, because you are out of practice or new to the game, the muscles taking most of the load have begun to rebel. Mostly, with a properly fitted pack, this means that the hipbelt is so tight it's crucifying your hips. But some people like to take part of the load on their shoulders, and it may be the shoulders that are aching. If so, all that's needed may be a very slight tightening of the sternum strap, to change minutely the places the shoulder straps bear. If more is needed, you adjust matters accordingly. That is, you manipulate the controls of your pack (which you can by now do with about as little conscious thought as you apply to manipulating the controls of your car) so that part of the load transfers from hip to shoulder, or vice versa. With a good pack you no more think of halting to make this readjustment (unless it involves tightening the hipbelt) than you think of stopping your car to change gear.

Now, the difference between these four tuning procedures and those for E-frames is only one of degree, in adjustment and result. But the fifth is the one that adds the final elegant touch to I-frame efficiency (though it can be applied with similar if rather lesser benefits to E-frames that have sliding-crossed-strap harnesses). This fifth procedure is a response to changing terrain. Mostly, that means hills. When you walk uphill with a load you tend to lean forward. So in order to keep the pack balanced on your hips you slacken off the lift straps very slightly. And when you're going downhill and tending to lean farther back than when on the flat, you cinch up the lift straps just a touch. The difference this simple adjustment can make is astonishing. I now find I often make it—without even breaking stride, of course—even for an uphill stretch that's no more than 50 yards long. You can also adjust the lift straps—and perhaps the shoulder straps as well—in response to other changes in terrain. For rock-scrambling or boulder-hopping or crossing any rough country, tightening them will draw the pack more firmly against your back and reduce any tendency it may have to sway and so throw you off balance.

But perhaps I have already passed the point at which discrete quanta of logical responses are useful. In the end, fine-tuning boils down to something less obviously cerebral. If you use a sophisticated pack you'll probably find that with a little experience you repeatedly make minuscule readjustments almost without thought and often without quite knowing what you're responding to—and then, even when you stop to consider the matter, you're still not really sure whether you were responding to new terrain, wearying muscles, changes in the pack's conformation or some combination of these. After all, that's mostly how you drive a car, isn't it? And when you reach that point with your pack, you're driving it. If you are not by that time halfway in love with it, then that pack is probably not for you.

MAKES AND MODELS OF I-FRAME PACKS

The evolution of I-frames is still in too early a stage for design to have settled down, and current choices range across a mildly dazzling array. The most immediately obvious difference between candidates is the least important: bag shape can run anywhere from more or less simple-sack rectangular—easiest for loading and managing your gear—to back-con-touring and therefore complicatedly curvaceous—most efficient for load-carrying. Less obvious but more vital are details of the suspension system. Chief of these is the nature of the frame (page 129)—parallel-stay or X-form. And backpackingdom has now, of course, divided into two camps, each fiercely defended by both makers and users, each issuing resonant claims of soaring superiority for its nominated stay arrangement. Currently, packs with parallel-stay frames come from Lowe Alpine Systems, Gregory Mountain Products, Madden Mountaineering, Kelty, JanSport and Caribou; packs with X-form frames from Robertson/Synergy Systems, Wilderness Experience, Trailwise, Alpenlite, Camp Trails and Dolt (though Dolt are really into travel packs rather than straight I-frames).

Lowe were pioneers in the field and their popular packs remain at or near the cutting edge of design. Like nearly all makers, they offer models with different capacities. Their Lhotse—the biggest and most stalwart—accepts 7350 cubic inches (5 pounds 6 ounces, $248). A series labeled Nanda Devi is designed specifically for women's shorter torsos, narrower shoulders and smaller backs but is also good for smaller-torsoed men—who are not necessarily small men.

Madden make packs of quality materials, well put together with deliberate lack of frills: "Our philosophy is simplicity in design. This is not to say that our packs are unsophisticated, they are merely uncluttered and consummately functional." And although my accretion-of-small-sophistications view of I-frame efficiency tends to hold me rather far from the Madden crowd, I note that there does indeed seem to be a crowd. (The Extra Large size of the Mountain Pak, Madden's biggest model: 6000-inch capacity, 6 pounds, $193 [illustration page 100, right].) Madden make a simple waterproof-nylon raincover for their packs, with reinforced bottom and drawcord closure. I have used it and it works well (7 ounces including protective stuff sock, $25 plain, $34 camouflaged).

Synergy were X-form pioneers, and a few users I have met waxed enthusiastic to the brink of ecstasy. The original California firm unfortunately sank, but has now resurfaced in Colorado as Robertson/Synergy. (Their largest pack, the 9.2TL [for 9.2-liter top-loader]: 5600 cubic inches, 6 pounds 2 ounces, $212; five optional and detachable pockets add 1490 cubic inches, 1¾ pounds and $65.)

All the other makers, and no doubt a few I have omitted, can claim supporters who like the fit, price, flexibility or some other features of their packs; but I'm afraid I can offer no meaningful firsthand reports.

Once again, we will examine details of the genre through the piece of equipment I know best.

The I-frame pack I use—the one that provoked me to love at first feel—is Gregory's largest model, the Cassin. Gregory, though compara-

tive newcomers in the field, are already leaders. The company philosophy, as enunciated by Wayne Gregory, resident dynamo, is simple,
complex, obsessed and altogether productive: "I want to build the best
damned pack there ever was." The outcome is a series of packs so sophisticated that detractors label them "over-engineered"; so meticulously
constructed that their weights and prices provoke raised eyebrows; so
continually evolving that—just as Wayne Gregory intended—no model
seems to remain unchanged in all details for more than a month (or is it
a week?); and, as a result of all these things, so efficient—on my body,
anyway—that I can not merely overlook but happily ignore both the
weight and the kind of complexity I normally decry in any equipment.
In that first moment when a Cassin, fitted by a highly competent salesman, first caressed the contours of my back, I think the store moved.
And after many miles with heavy loads, the light that filled me then has
not dimmed. I do not say the pack is perfect. I still find it appreciably
less convenient than my E-frame for packing and managing gear and for
leaning against at halts and in camp (a more important matter than you
might think: page 150). But I recognize that had my techniques evolved
with an I-frame they would probably not now be suffering such abrasions
(see page 122). In newer models the pack's few physical imperfections
have been remedied, so our affair burns on. I still say, a little breathlessly, that for heavy loads my Cassin is "the best damned pack there
ever was."

The Cassin is a top-loading, mildly mitigated bloody-great-sack.
(For mitigations, read on a ways.) Including the pocket embodied in its
rooflike top (which detaches and can be used as a fanny pack), the basic

pack has a capacity of 6125 cubic inches. Four optional side pockets, attachable by buckles (and I always attach them)—or an alternative arrangement of two side pockets and one large back pocket—bring the total to about 7200 cubic inches. That satisfies even me. The pack alone weighs 5¾ pounds; but with all four pockets and an optional office-on-the-yoke the complete rig climbs close to 7 pounds. At least, mine does. And no complaints. The naked pack costs $225. Small pockets are $12 each; large pockets, $20.00; office, $15.

The Cassin's suspension system is its core and joy. The current hipbelt is an even more complicated and efficient creation than the one that originally wooed and wowed me. A continuous-circle belt of 30-mil semistiff polyethylene, 3 inches wide, provides the support base. But it is cushioned by a broad, tapering, hip-encircling, curvilinear pad constructed of three layers of foam—5-pound Olefoam, 2½-pound Ethafoam and 2-pound Etherfoam—progressively softer from outside to in. Most padded belts are covered with Cordura fabric. But Cordura is rather slick. That may be, in part, why hipbelts tend to slip down your body as you walk. But in new Cassin models the fabric is 8-ounce Packcloth (lighter, less bulky, and more waterproof) and the Packcloth has an inner-side covering of nylon mesh with high-friction coating. This mesh resists slippage on any clothing and even skin (painlessly too). It looks rather fragile but will probably wear well: the mesh is used by truckers to sling over amorphous loads and hold them in place, largely by friction. Even if it eventually wears out it is fairly easily replaceable. (Gregory have christened this covering Gription Mesh—following the "good ol' boy" Southern stock-car driver who, after crashing, explained that his tires "weren't getting no gription.")

The entire hipbelt assembly, though it passes under the lumbar pad, is removable. You can therefore select the size belt that brings the padding around to the correct point on your hips, so that it does not bear bruisingly on the forward, bony projections, where it can in some people constrict an artery that serves the leg—and cause numbness. The hour-glass-shaped lumbar pad looks distressingly awkward but in fact conforms very comfortably indeed to the curves of the human body at the spine-arse junction. The pad is covered with the same Gription Mesh as the belt. All this rather complicated construction adds up to extreme simplicity and comfort in use—especially with the easily cinched Kelty buckle (page 112) that I have installed in place of the plastic Fastex.

The shoulder harness embodies all the sophisticated details I have mentioned (page 108). And two interchangeable sizes of padded, contoured shoulder straps ensure a fit for almost everyone. The original arrangement for altering the height of the upper end of the lift straps—

three holes in each aluminum stay and in the packbag, which were horribly liable to admit water (and once did, for me [page 431])—has been replaced by a sounder two-buckle system.

Two newly available options refine the suspension even further. You can now buy graphite stays ($70) to replace the aluminum standards. The 22-layer graphite weighs less than half as much as aluminum, is stronger and reverts more readily to its original shape; also, and perhaps most importantly, it twists as well as flexes. (Gregory maintain that "graphite stays allow the pack to move *with* your body when it twists rather than hinder your movements. Remove one of the graphite stays from your pack, grip it at each end and twist the ends in opposite directions. Perform the same test on an aluminum stay—and suddenly you begin to understand what graphite stays are all about.") My graphite stays weigh 4 ounces; my aluminum, 11 ounces. (To ensure satisfaction, Gregory require that the buyer wear his aluminum stays on at least three backpacking trips to confirm their fit. Then an authorized dealer will trace their outline for exact copying.) The second new option is a Desert Panel—a sort of mini-lumbar-pad (but with no fabric between Gription Mesh and foam—for good ventilation and sweat absorption). The panel attaches to the harness up near your shoulder blades and is designed to hold the pack a smitch farther away from your body and thereby increase air ventilation in hot weather (3 ounces; $10). A half-day test suggests that it works. It goes on and off fairly easily. It indeed holds the pack farther away from your back, and so permits better ventilation. But I also found—or imagined I found—that the load therefore rides a touch less well.

Although the packbag is, functionally, a bloody-great-sack, it is carefully contoured to fit the human back, not a refrigerator. It is this anatomical molding that makes the bag rather less easy than a single-sack E-frame to load and unload. Two mitigations help offset the difficulty. Both do their jobs and do them well, but each exacts a small counterprice. The first mitigation is a pair of 15-inch zippered slits that run down each flank of the bag and improve access. (They are absent in the two smaller top-loading Gregory models, which are otherwise essentially scaled-down versions of the Cassin.) These slits provide an undeniable convenience but I regard them as slightly Murphoid: the zippers are liable to gape and admit rain—though see the Madden raincover, page 136. (Gregory now have their own raincover, predictably more complex but probably even more effective [7 ounces; $20.00].) The second mitigation is the basement compartment: a width-of-the-sack zipper allows you to inject your sleeping bag there and to stuff it deep and firm into the corners of the pack so that it forms an integral, hip-wrapping part of the suspension system. (A new, optional, waterproof pouch for the sleeping bag helps protect that precious item. It is shaped to fit sweetly in the hip-hugging compartment, weighs 4½ ounces and costs $16.50.) A floating flap that forms the top of the compartment lets you adjust its size to suit your sleeping bag. The compartment's flanks are reinforced by semistiff plastic inserts that help improve load-transfer to the hipbelt. Outside them, pockets with drainage holes will cradle tent poles for tenters, avalanche wands for winter wanderers, horsewhips for flagellants. A stiffish foam pad that runs the length of the bag's forward wall cushions the stays and the area between them. An ample snow sleeve with drawstring at the mouth of the sack means that, no matter how full you stuff it, all gear remains protected. The main bag of 8-ounce nylon Parapac (420 denier) is reinforced around its foot with 11½-ounce waterproofed Cordura (1000 denier). The pack's bottom is canted "to help direct the load towards the hipbelt." There are no raw-edged seams anywhere in the pack: all are protected against raveling back of the fabric by nylon binding tape. And Gregory guarantee that if any seam on any of their equipment comes apart they will repair or replace the item, free. You really couldn't ask for much more.

In fact, I really couldn't ask much more of my Cassin in any respect —except for those minor operating inconveniences. And when I sing its praises I am far from a voice crying in the, uh, wilderness. A growing chorus of backpackers seems to be joining in the Gregorian chant.

TRAVEL PACKS

For definitions, see page 102; for discussion of uses, page 105.

Down at the suitcase end of the travel-pack spectrum sit models that are essentially squared-off items of soft luggage with rudimentary harnesses, and maybe hipbelts, that can be covered or tucked out of harm's way. At the other extreme—which really interests us more— stands the fully functional backpack modified for travel. Typically, its sophisticated suspension system can be completely covered with a zippered flap, and it has a detachable carrying strap, often with a leather hand-grip that may be adjustable into a shoulder sling (see illustration page 100, center). Most such packs are panel-loaders, for suitcasing, and have lockable double-slider zippers. Lowe, Gregory and Madden all make models that look as if they carry as well as their pure-pack equivalents. JanSport, Wilderness Experience and others offer compromises, on down the scale. Dolt specialize in travel packs and produce quality models over the whole range except the modified pure-pack. In framed versions the suspension is X-form. Other travel-pack makers include Caribou and Mountain Equipment.

Capacities, weights and prices of travel bags vary so widely that any sample figures would be meaningless. Consult catalogues.

TRAVEL ALTERNATIVES TO TRAVEL PACKS

If backpacking is the prime reason for your journey you won't want to compromise with a pack that may glide angelically through airports and bus stations but will assure at least some degree of agony once you start walking. And you may be unable or unwilling to buy a sophisticated-suspension pack with travel features. Or you may, with considerable wisdom, refuse to trust anything but your old and well-tried favorite. Provided you take the right precautions, though, you can still get by.

First, if you feel you really must carry an E-frame pack, remove the frame and carry it, if that's at all possible. Second, pack for the journey, not the trail. Put fragile items at the core and pad the periphery with software. Tighten all straps and tuck their conveyor-snagging ends out of the way. If necessary, tape them to the bag. For protection and also to discourage pilfering, try to empty all outside pockets. And carry on your person such valuables as camera and binoculars. Just in case baggage labels pull off, put a card with your name, address and destination inside.

But the safest precaution is to encapsulate the whole pack, mildly or monumentally. One cheap, simple and marginally effective capsule is a heavy-duty plastic trash bag, tied at the mouth and strapped tightly around the pack. If you travel a lot, though, you may want to consider a canvas version. And if your pack has to be an E-frame, do as I finally did some years ago: have a sailmaker construct a stout canvas cocoon with a rigid metal band around its circumference. (A simple canvas sack would do for an I-frame.) The earliest version of my case failed to prevent one airline from denting the metal band and damaging a frame's projecting lower end; but a modification with reinforced corners and padding at each end to take the worst shock off the frame verticals seemed to do the trick. The pull-back panel cover of my case has double-slider zippers that lock together with a small combination padlock; also compression straps to hold everything firm and an all-around-the-circumference web belt, secured to the metal by studs, that has several small handles. A simple shoulder harness lets me carry the rather bulky device on my back. One advantage of some such case—though little consolation on an outward journey—is that, although airlines have become leery of compensating for damage done to E-frame backpacks, I found them willing to accept responsibility when I had taken such reasonable precautions.

ULTRALIGHTWEIGHT PACKS*

For definitions, see page 102; for a few words on usage, page 106; for a fuller discussion on how such packs fit into the New Wave trend toward ultralight gear, pages 26–31 and Appendix 1A.

The purest form of ultralightweight pack is an enlarged but gossamerized frameless day pack in which the overriding design target has been paring ounces to the practical limit. Sierra West pioneered. Alpenlite followed. Capacities of such packs range from 2000 to 3350 cubic inches, weights from 16 to 27 ounces, prices from $70 to $120.

The model I use is the Half Dome, Sierra West's biggest frameless lightweight (3350 cubic inches, 1 pound 11 ounces, $120).

The Half Dome carries up to 25 pounds far better than you might expect from its simple design—which includes an "exclusively reinforced" closed-cell foam pad running the length and width of the forward

* IMPORTANT LATE NOTE: Things have changed radically. The Ultralightweight-pack movement seems to have largely burned out in one season. Sierra West have stopped production of such packs. Alpenlite apparently continue. Even those lightweight packs that are fined-down versions of regular models seem to have vanished. Gregory, for example, no longer make their Superlight series. But it is now impossible to rewrite the text, and rather than cut it I shall let it stand: As usual, my object was to instruct by example, not guide you by the nose. At worst, regard this section as a small historical notation—though by no means without practical interest.

Pack evolution continues, of course. JanSport have now revealed a pack with a very narrow, miniature external frame, said to ride like an I-frame, ventilate like an E-frame.

wall. The pad indeed seems to "add stability and forms a malleable internal structure which conforms comfortably to the wearer's back while retaining pack shape." The sternum strap also makes an appreciable contribution. But I find that with loads over 25 pounds the Half Dome's efficiency begins to fall off, and although the pack is said to cope with up to 40 pounds you would at that point probably be dreaming of a couple of helium balloons to share the burden. The uncoated 3.4-ounce nylon Rip-stop fabric is not waterproof but the bag comes with a "weatherproof shower cap" of 1.5-ounce nylon tent-fly fabric (5 ounces, included in pack weight above). It drawstrings snugly over the pack and seems to work well. All Sierra West ultralightweights come with such shower caps. (Alpenlite equivalents [see illustration page 100, one from left] go the orthodox route with coated nylon Rip-stop fabric, said to be waterproof.) I color-code one side pocket of my Half Dome by replacing the gray nylon loop provided—in lieu of a metal tab—with a red nylon loop. (For color-coding rationale, see page 125.)

Whether gossamer packs of this kind stand up to prolonged use probably depends on how you treat them. But my experience with the Half Dome suggests that within certain limitations—one- to four-day trips in warm weather, and loads to about 25 pounds (or whatever seems to be the comfort limit for you and your pack)—they make a valuable and indeed essential contribution to the lightfoot freedom that New Wave techniques can bring.

Beyond a certain comfort limit, as I have said (page 30), it seems to me to make sense to switch to a rather stouter pack with a sophisticated suspension system. Sierra West's new Phantom Pack with an external X-form aluminum frame, foam backpad, 3.4-ounce uncoated fabric bag (8-ounce coated bottom) and shower cap might be an answer (for loads to 45 pounds; 4000-cubic-inch capacity in large size, 2½ pounds, $165). Another choice with perhaps broader range of use might be one of the lightweight packs now put out by many makers that are fined-down versions of their regular models. Among them are three by Gregory—none of which I have tested. Their suspensions are identical to those on standard models, and therefore impose no load limit, but fabrics are 4-ounce instead of 12-ounce. The largest of them is the Superlight Snow Creek (5046-cubic-inch capacity; 4 pounds 6 ounces with aluminum stays, 4 pounds with graphite; $189.50).

For most people that last figure hits. And perhaps we have passed the reasonable limit of specialization. It's all very well for makers to dream of three or four packs in every backpacker's closet. At some point, though, the backpackers are going to revolt. In part, it's a question of simplicity. But money comes into it too. Like hell it does.

MODIFICATIONS AND AUXILIARIES

Office-on-the-yoke

Because I often walk without a shirt and therefore without a front pocket, I long ago had a 5-by-6-inch pocket sewn onto the front of my yoke or shoulder strap, roughly where the shirt pocket comes. Into it go notebook and map, and sunglasses when not in use. Pen, pencil and thermometer (page 509) clip onto the rear, between pocket and strap, where they are very securely held—not, as they used to, in front, where removing map or notebook can flip them out unnoticed. I cannot imagine how I ever got along without such a pocket. Mine is made of ordinary blue-jean material, but anything stout will do.

Removable pouches based on this idea now keep appearing in catalogues. They run from simple nylon-fabric envelopes (light but rather slick, and don't hold pens and pencils too securely) to multicompartmented edifices that seem to offer a nook for everything including map, credit cards and your will. Mostly, they're equipped with little straps that Velcro or press-stud around a shoulder strap, but I tend to tie mine on with fine nylon cord, for insurance. Such pouches can also be used on a belt or even slung by a cord around your neck so that they hang under one arm.

With my Sierra West ultralight Half Dome I use a simple 1-ounce nylon envelope by Moor and Mountain ($7.75). My Trailwise E-frame still bears a faded blue-jean pocket. And to my Cassin I have, a little to my surprise, attached a Gregory Pocket Office (folds to 5½ by 8½ inches, 3 ounces, $15). When I first saw this stoutly built creation with taped edges that opened up to reveal six compartments (one Velcroshuttable for "valuables," two transparent for maps) I judged it grossly over-engineered. Yet when I tried it on a couple of week-or-longer trips I found it collected a surprising amount of furniture (including my miniature camera [page 465]) and held everything instantly available and also protected from all but torrential downpours.

For which side to put your office-on-the-yoke, see page 148.

Belt pouches

for hipbelts keep appearing in catalogues too. It seems to me they'd get in the way, especially when putting the pack on. But I could be wrong.

Binocular bump-pad

When I used an open-topped E-frame pack my binoculars used to travel slung on a short cord over the projecting top of the frame, at my left shoulder. At each step they bumped, very gently, against the frame. For years I accepted the slight metallic sound without thinking about it. Then, one summer when I was out with a party in the Washington Cascades, a young fellow who had been following close behind me for several days said, "You know, I can't understand how you tolerate the rattle of those binoculars just behind your ear. Even walking several feet back of you like this, it nearly drives me crazy." After that, of course, it began to drive me crazy too, so I finally stuck a thick wrap of air-mattress patching fabric around the frame's upright and crossbar just where the binoculars bumped. Soon I was happily back to not noticing the muffled sound. I imagine fewer animals were scared out of my view too. A reader has suggested cementing a loop of heavy elastic to the frame and slipping it over the binoculars to hold them snug.

Now that I have an extension bar on my E-frame and cannot loop the binoculars' carrying strap over the projecting end, a bump-pad is useless. Binoculars are lighter these days too, and I mostly carry mine slung around my neck. For more on the matter, see page 463.

Tumplines

A tumpline is an adjustable band that runs around your forehead and attaches to packframe or bag—the lower the better—and helps take some of the strain of heavy loads. A friend of mine who occasionally uses one says it is an appreciable help, especially on steep upgrades. Unfortunately, he says, you cannot really use one effectively until your neck muscles have grown accustomed to the unfamiliar strain.

Tumplines can also be used alone, with any tied-together bundle.

Women in parts of Africa use them that way all the time for huge loads. So do the Nepalese. I had always looked on such use by Westerners in this day of sophisticated packs to be purely an emergency measure. And maybe I still do. But Yvon Chouinard, the well-known climber, has become a convert. Although he began using a tumpline only because of an old back injury, he now says he "would never go back to conventional packs—with or without my back problems." (Though it may be relevant that he has, he says, very small hips and has "never been able to fully utilize modern packs.") Chouinard now uses "a 2-inch-wide piece of soft webbing that goes over the head and narrows down to ¾-inch webbing with an adjustment strap. This goes along the sides of any soft or frame pack and then around the bottom. I like the strap to go across the top of my forehead so that I can press forward and build up my neck muscles, although for minimum effort it should be slightly more on top of the head. I use shoulder straps to carry about 20 percent of the load on flat or uphill stretches and tighten them down to carry most of the load for downhill bits. Otherwise, the jarring effect of going down a steep slope is too much for my weak knees and neck muscles. Also, shoulder straps stabilize the load from side-swaying." The greatest advantage, says Chouinard, comes at high altitudes, "where lung expansion is totally unrestricted. You can breathe with a smoother rhythm and breathe deeper without shoulder straps. . . . Your enjoyment of load-carrying will increase, especially if you take pleasure in being out of step with the technological age."

To help you take those different-drummer steps, Chouinard Equipment offer a commercial tumpline (3½ ounces, $5.50). So now you can happily ignore just about everything I have written in this chapter.

AUXILIARIES

Child Carriers

Standard, these days, is the Gerry Kiddie Pack: aluminum frame, padded yoke, portable stand; cotton-duck carrier, with room for sub-buttock storage; new generation sits facing forward close to parent's center of gravity—and ready, during temper tantrums or bouts of curiosity, to tear at proffered hair (1¼ pounds, $30). Foam-filled hipbelt further cushions load (5 ounces, $6).

For newborns through 3 years there is also the Snugli I, a frameless carrier that can be used as backpack, front pouch or nursing sling: padded yoke; heavyweight corduroy with corduroy inner bag and mouth-high flannel patch that absorbs baby's bubbles; also tucks and darts that release to allow expansion along with baby's; machine washable, yet (1 pound 7 ounces, $49). The similar Snugli II—65 percent cotton and 35 percent polyester brushed denim—weighs the same but costs only $34. (Replacement bib: $1. Rain cape for enthroned baby: 3 ounces, $11.)

For very long hauls—or children grown agonizingly heavy—you can lash a framed carrier to your regular packframe.

A dog's life

Although not always easy to find, a number of doggie packs now exist. The Wanaha comes in four sizes: extra small, for dogs 25–40 pounds; small, 40–60; medium, 60–95; large, 100 and up (weights and prices ascend to 2 pounds 2 ounces and $37 for large size). Packs come with complete instructions and hints on how to accustom hound to them. If you do it right, I'm told, he soon wags his tail and jubilates when you produce the pack, the way he does when you show him the leash. Other doggie packs come from Caribou and Adventure 16.

Remember that in much backcountry, especially in National Parks, dogs are forbidden. In others, such as USFS wilderness areas, they are permitted only if kept on a leash. In others they must be "under control."

I am at best ambivalent. Cases clearly occur in which dogs harass wildlife. Barking dogs can be a pain, especially at night. Even someone repeatedly calling dogs to heel can disturb the peace and silence you have gone to find. That happened to me just last month. But I recognize that some people's trips are enriched by being able to take their pets along. And I guess there is something to be said for the practice—in the right places, and if extreme care is exercised to prevent the dogs from interfering with wildlife or with other backpackers.

A Vermont reader who took me to task for giving "short shrift to dogs" has put the case very well indeed—at least for Eastern backcountry. "I have been backpacking with my dog for seven years," she writes. "Besides her own food she carries two 1½-quart canteens, maps, guidebook and sundries. The point I wish to make is that dog owners should follow some basic rules, e.g.:

"1. Keep the dog on leash *always,* day and night. It takes a little trouble first thing in the morning and just before bed, but it is worth it.

"2. Never let the dog run up to—much less jump up on—other hikers.

"3. At meal times, especially when with a group, tie the dog away where it won't get into food or knock the stove over.

"4. Only bring a quiet dog. Several times after a night in a shelter with others, they have remarked, 'Your dog is so quiet. She never barks.' Well, she does bark if other hikers approach after we have settled in, and growls if another animal approaches. (She scared off a large porcupine one night.)

"5. The dog owner must know how much weight his dog can carry (one quarter to one third of body weight) and get the dog in shape just as he does himself. He must also be as sensitive to the dog's need for *water* and shade as he is himself. And last, he must realize that a dog cannot travel consistently the long distances a human can."

Now if everyone behaved that way . . . .

I hear that tincture of benzoin (page 86) is good for hardening dogs' paws for talus-jumping and hard snow. For dog boots, see page 71.

There is a book, *Taking Your Dog Backpacking* by Alan and Joan Riley (1979, hardcover, 8½ ounces, $4.95 from TFH Publications, P.O. Box 427, Neptune, NJ 07753-0427).

THE WALLS IN ACTION

Getting the pack onto your back

You carry out this operation in the field many times each day, and the total energy consumed is considerable. At the end of an exhausting day it might even be crucial. So it pays to give the matter some thought.

The easiest way to load is to use a loading platform—a convenient rockledge or bank or fallen tree trunk—and just slip into the yoke.

Failing a loading platform—and rest assured that you will mostly fail—you can sit down, enyoke, and then stand up with an easy if inelegant sidle. With a back-breaking load this is about the only possible method. I believe it is the one the time-and-motion sages agree is the least expensive in energy.

Yet for all but the very heaviest loads I find that the simplest method is to hoist the pack up into position with an easy swinging motion, one hand gripping a shoulder strap and the other the small nylon hand strap that is now fitted to most good packs. Swing the pack up from whichever side comes naturally; but if you use an office-on-the-yoke (page 144) make sure you put it on the strap that slips onto your shoulders first. On the other side it will infallibly foul things up.

The question remains: "At what stage should I switch from the easy-swing-up to the sit-and-enyoke method?" My own answer is: "Not until somewhere around 60 pounds, and not even then for sure." I find that by swinging even a very heavy pack up onto a raised upper leg first, and then onto the shoulders without ever quite stopping, you use sur-prisingly little energy. Yet one experienced friend of mine sits-and-enyokes with a load as low as 40 pounds. To find out what suits you, experiment.

THE WALLS AS NONWALLS

Your more or less empty pack may from time to time act as windbreak on one side of a tent or bivouac, as ground insulation for your feet when they protrude out beyond a three-quarter-length air mattress or pad, or even as a pillow. If it is big enough, and uncompartmented, it could make a water- and windproof cover for the foot of your sleeping bag—though you would have to check that it did not soak the bag in the moisture escaping from your body. It could certainly make an emergency footsack in the horrendous event you burned or otherwise lost the use of your sleeping bag. On such occasions sleeve-with-drawstring tops are obviously best.

But for my money by far the most important auxiliary use is

The pack as backrest.

If you prop a full E-frame pack against something, it makes a very comfortable chairback. When the bag has been emptied or part-emptied it works better with the luxury padding of an air mattress or foam pad.

When you can, simply prop the pack against a tree or rock. But if, like me, you believe in resting on the smoothest and softest piece of ground in sight there will nine times out of ten be no such convenience. So mostly you use your staff as the prop. It soon becomes almost auto-matic, the moment you halt—even for a 10-minute rest—to look for a rock or crevice or a tree or even just a clump of grass to wedge the butt of the staff against. Failing all these—and here again you will fail regu-larly—just angle-prod the staff down into the soil until it holds firmly, with or without an assist from a stone, and then jam the top of the staff between the yoke and the top crossbar of the pack, hard up against the bag. (A hand strap holds it perfectly.) Fine-adjust the angle of the pack-frame, sit thankfully down and lean back. But lean so that your back thrust is along the staff's axis. Otherwise the pack will assuredly skew. It will skew anyway, from time to time, no matter how careful you are. But care helps. This all sounds rather complicated, I know; but after a while the whole operation takes about 4 seconds—and virtually no con-scious thought (unless your packframe has a rounded foot that skews and skids at a touch on almost any ground: no amount of conscious thought will teach such mavericks a lasting subservience).

With a hipwrap frame (page 116) you lean against harness rather than bag—as you can, of course, with any pack.

An I-frame makes a scurvy backrest. Especially with a staff prop. Even when it's full you can rarely lean against it for more than about 30 seconds before it swivels and falls. And unpacked it's about as useful as a waterless waterbed. I find this a sad defect of character in such a noble item of equipment, and the first person to proffer a solution that really works for me gets an autographed copy of this book in glorious black and white.

PACK, SWEET PACK

Whenever I am out on my own, free from civilization, and my pack is in every way my home, containing everything on which my continued existence depends, I find that I develop a reluctance to move very far from it. Even a sidetrip of an hour or two involves a battle with this reluctance—an almost physical tearing away. For a long time I assumed that mine was an idiosyncratic caution, but I find—hardly to my surprise, come to think of it—that other lone backpackers quickly arrive at the same sensible state of mind.

Kitchen

FOOD

Backpackers in embryo sometimes dream of just walking out and away and living off the land. There is a delightful simplicity about the idea, of course, and its allure is stiffened by obvious practical advantages: no heavy food in your pack; constant variety; fresh, vitamin-rich products at every plucking. It seems as if you could hardly ask for a more perfect fusion of romance and efficiency.

Forget it. Above all, forget the efficiency. There are no doubt a few places in which certain select souls could live off the land and still find time to do one or two other things as well, but my advice is to leave the happy dreams to those who have never tried it.

That does not mean ignoring what the land drops into your lap (see, especially, Euell Gibbons's *Stalking the Wild Asparagus* and other books; Phyllis Glick's *The Mushroom Trailguide* [Holt, Rinehart & Winston, 1979, paperback, 13 ounces, $5.95]; and two little decks of cards—one for *the Western States,* one for *the Eastern States*—with color photographs and text on *Edible and Poisonous Plants* [each deck 3½ ounces; $5.95 post free from Plant Deck Inc., 2134 S.W. Wembley Park, Lake Oswego, OR 97034]). I often supplement my regular rations with trout, and occasionally with mushrooms or watercress or a few wild strawberries. And not long ago I came close to eating my first rattlesnake steak. But in most cases and places the time and energy you would have to expend in shooting, snaring, catching or otherwise gathering in a day's food and then preparing it are simply better applied elsewhere. Anyway, such hunting and cropping have little place in today's pressured wilderness: even where not illegal, they're mostly immoral.

An emergency is a different matter (see, for example, page 552 for rattlesnakes as emergency rations). And a deliberate attempt to live off the land may be well worth it for the spiritual effect of sheer primitive simplicity. But for normal walking, when one of your objects is to get somewhere or to do something when you get there, like climbing or looking or lazing, I recommend unequivocally that you carry just about everything you expect to need.

In choosing what foods to take, consider:

1. Nutritional values
2. Weight
3. Ease of preparation
4. Palatability
5. Packaging (with a special thought for litter)
6. Cost

Some people carry fresh food for the first day or two out, and perhaps a package of sprouts for later germination (page 180). These are certainly sound nutritional practices. But the only practical answer for any trip of more than a couple of days—and the simplest answer for shorter ones too—is dehydrated food. Most mountain shops now carry a wide selection of freeze-dried items. They are tasty and said to retain most of their nutritional value, and they have largely, though not entirely, replaced vacuum-dried foods. Both kinds are stable: provided water content remains below 5 percent, neither bacteria nor mold will grow on them and insects will not even snack. Such foods are not perfect, of course. They tend to be expensive and to make you fart like a bull, and they come in air-excluding foil or polyethylene envelopes that cannot be completely burned and therefore must be packed out. Other dehydrated foods, such as oatmeal, soup powders, spaghetti, rice and couscous, line supermarket shelves. But read the cooking instructions before you buy them, resolutely reject those that must be cooked for an hour (unless you cook on an open fire and love it) and think twice about any that must be soaked overnight.

Less than 2¼ pounds of properly dehydrated food will satisfy your nutritional needs for a highly energetic day. Many people seem to function on far less. And you can adjust the cuisine to suit personal tastes and current conditions. You can concoct complicated, multiflavored dishes or can keep the cooking childishly simple and still have a nourishing and palatable meal. Palatable, that is, for its time and place. A steaming mix of meat bar, rice and gravy may hardly be the kind of dish you would want to find on the table at home, but I assure you that at the end of a 20-mile hike it can taste better than a filet mignon in any restaurant.

In America, at least, we now have such a wealth of special backpacking foods, and of other foods eminently suitable for backpacking, that there is no longer any real problem about finding something that will do, only about making suitable decisions. But before we dip into our cornucopia we had better examine some general considerations.

There are two possible approaches to backpacking gastronomy:

Trial and Error, in which you follow personal preferences and are guided only by rules of thumb; and

The Scientific Nutritional Method, in which you calculate in calories and try to balance intake against energy output.

Trial and error

The advantage of this approach is that, although it involves a lot of built-in chance, your answers begin with a bias toward your individual requirements and evolve along the same axis. This is important, physiologically and psychologically. Each individual's alimentary system works in its own idiosyncratic way. And different people have very different philosophies of outdoor eating. Some like to make a meal out of making a meal. Some almost seem to make each trip one long making of meals. Then there are those who, like me, were born British and therefore, as far as food goes, barbaric. (Hell has been described as a place in which the politicians are French, the policemen German and the cooks British.) And at the extreme there sit—or stand or maybe even walk—those who never cook in the field or who even subsist entirely on pills (page 183).

I began, the way most people do, with the trial-and-error method. That is, I stood and looked at the packages in the stores and listened to a little advice and even took some of it. If I found I was at all hungry on a trip I took a bit more next time. If—as was far more likely—I had a lot left over, I retrenched. If an item tasted good and/or seemed to keep my legs going like pistons, I tended to take it again. If not, not. Anything that turned out to be a nuisance to prepare, I promptly dropped. Continually, though never lavishly, I experimented. And in the course of time I developed a well-tested backpacking menu, entirely adequate for a barbarian.

But one day it occurred to me that the logical approach was the strictly rational, quantitative,

Scientific nutritional method.

It seemed to me that by tailoring a diet to my exact nutritional requirements under specified conditions and by paring vigorously away as usual at the half-ounces I could hardly fail to come up with the most economical menu—economical, that is, in terms of weight and energy. I might have to allow for a few personal fads and fancies, but that was all.

I chose, at that time, to ignore vitamins and minerals. But I examined fat and protein requirements closely. The gospel of the moment was that fats should constitute at least 20 percent of total caloric intake and could run to 35 percent or even more; and that you needed 45 grams of protein per day per 100 pounds of bodyweight (though your body could not assimilate the protein properly if you ate the full requirement at a single sitting).

Now, fats contain approximately 9 calories per unit of weight compared with 4 calories in the same weight of protein or carbohydrate, and they therefore form by far the most efficient food in terms of calories per unit of weight. Although no meaningful figures exist (the technical literature hedges, even cites "fast and slow stomachs"), it seems to be accepted that the energy from fats and protein is released over longer periods than that from carbohydrates, and that they are therefore less efficient for booster snacks but eminently suitable for what might be called all-day or all-night background. The body has to work hard to digest them—much harder than with carbohydrates—so they should in general be avoided during or immediately before very strenuous exercise.

Fats can also raise palatability problems. At high altitude (and in extreme heat too) anyone's appetite is liable to falter, and you may find yourself revolting against the very thought of fats. A possible reason: fat needs more oxygen to "burn" than do other foods. But up high you may also abhor the thought of protein. The elevation at which such awkward things happen varies widely from person to person, even from trip to trip. It may start as low as 8000 or 9000 feet. It's apparently rather likely to happen above, say, 17,000. Slow acclimation helps but does not necessarily cure. All you can really do is take along a fair variety of foods and hope there's always something in your pack that appeals to you. Sweet things are probably the best bet, but the range of sudden demands is unpredictable. Frank Smythe, struggling on and up, alone, toward the summit of Mount Everest, longed for frankfurters and sauerkraut; Ed Hillary, high on Cho Oyu the year before he climbed Everest, for pineapple cubes. I had always thought these reports a bit farfetched. But on one trip I found myself feeling, at a mere 14,000 feet, the same craving for pineapple. Such vagaries of appetite are the results of a particular kind of stress. A soldier may face a similar situation, and the U.S. Army Food Service recognizes the palatability problem that can arise under combat stress. They have a saying, "It doesn't matter how many calories you give a man if he won't eat." In the mountains the trick is to guess right—short of pineapple cubes—and still keep your menu practical. It's as simple as that. And as difficult.

With these preparatory considerations out of the way I turned, in my search for a scientific nutritional method, to the first part of the basic problem: computing total energy supply.

First I set about learning how to calculate the nutritional content of various foods. Almost at once I discovered *Agricultural Handbook No. 8: Composition of Foods,* published by the U.S. Department of Agriculture. I recommend this book to anyone at all interested in a scientific approach to outdoor eating (or, for that matter, indoor eating). Most of its 190 pages consist of two vastly comprehensive tables headed "Composition of foods, 100 grams, edible portion" and (better still for our purposes) "Nutrients in the edible portion of 1 pound of food as purchased." These tables analyze in detail the nutritional make-up of everything from aba-lone (raw and canned), through muffins, to zwieback. It is worth remem-bering, though, that the figures for many foods can be only approximations. As a nutrition expert warned me: "No two wheat germs are quite alike." (See, I suspect, the rather surprising figures the table gives for different kinds of trout.)

The book also contains several supplementary tables (Table 6 gives accurate calories-per-gram figures for selected foods) and some mildly useful notes. It does not contain, as it should, the information that 1 gram = .0357 ounce, and that therefore 100 grams = 3.57 ounces; or that 1 ounce = 28.35 grams. Even if you are not about to use these full and rather forbidding figures, you need a rough conversion rate.

Public libraries—except, perhaps, very small ones—are likely to have reference copies of *Handbook No. 8.* There is sure to be one in the nutritional-science library of any university, and with luck you'll be able to buy a copy from the student-union bookstore or its equivalent. Failing that, you can, in the due course of bureaucratic time, get one for $7 from The Superintendent of Documents, U.S. Government Printing Office, Washington, D.C. 20402. There is also a new series of seven ancillary publications, all looseleaf for updating, of which the most interesting seem to be those on the nutritive values of dairy and egg products (#8–1, $7), spices and herbs (#8–2, $6.50), fats and oils (#8–4, $7), poultry (#8–5, $9.50) and soups, sauces and gravies (#8–6, $8).

By studying *Handbook No. 8,* consulting various manufacturers and reading much small print on many labels, I managed to calculate the caloric, protein and fat content of each item on my standard food list for a 7-day period—the normal basis on which I plan.

Because the nutritional gospel, not to mention my tastes and the available foods, are now radically changed, I will not bother you with the item-by-item table from the first two editions of this book. The important thing is that the theoretical daily intake came out to 3830 calories, of which 900 were from fat.

At first glance the caloric total struck me as a little low, but I postponed judgment. Naturally, I was relieved to find that my diet provided more than the guideline minima then in vogue for both fats and protein: fats, 23.5 percent of total caloric intake as against a recommended minimum of 20 percent; protein, 152 grams as against the recommended minimum of 85 grams, based on my bodyweight (190 pounds).

With these intake figures established I turned to the second part of the food-to-output tailoring process: calculating what my body needed for maintenance and exercise under various conditions. If I had been starting from scratch, without a food list to evaluate, I should probably have begun on this tack. I'm glad I didn't.

I soon learned that for maintenance alone (basal metabolism) the average person needs about 1100 calories per day per 100 pounds of bodyweight. In city-slob shape—which is the way I seem to start just about every backpacking trip—I weighed around 190 pounds. So mere maintenance drained off 2090 calories from my daily total of 3830.

During the process of digestion the body consumes a certain amount of energy as heat. This factor is called, for some reason, "specific dynamic action." It fluctuates between 6 percent and rather more than 10 percent of the total caloric intake. For simplicity, it is usually averaged at 10 percent. So in my case specific dynamic action accounted for another 380 calories, 2470 of the total gone; 1360 left. I began to wonder.

Next I got down to assessing energy output over and above these constants. I quickly ran to earth a table of fascinating figures. The moment I began to read the table I thought, "Ah, *this* is the answer. Now nothing can stop me."

THE ENERGY COST OF ACTIVITIES*
(exclusive of basal metabolism and influence of food)

	Calories per 100 lbs. per hour
Walking: on hard, smooth, level surface, at 2 mph	45
at 3 mph	90
at 4 mph	160

(For walking on rough trails, multiply each figure
by a very arbitrary factor of 2.)

* Most of these figures are derived from T. M. Carpenter: *Factors and Formulas for Computing Respiratory Exchange and Biological Transformations of Energy* (Carnegie Institute, 1948 edn.), p. 136.

	Calories per 100 lbs. per hour
Standing relaxed	30
Sitting, quietly	20
Eating	20
Dressing and undressing	30
Lying still, awake	5
Sleeping (basal metabolism only)	0
Shivering, very severe	up to 220
Sawing wood	260
Swimming, at 2 mph	360
Writing	20
Dishwashing	45
Doing laundry (light)	60
Singing in a loud voice	35

This table lists several other activities that make interesting reading, and all of them might, at a pinch and on a highly diversified walking trip, become ancillary pursuits:

Typewriting, rapidly	45
Driving an automobile	40
Bicycling (moderate speed)	110
Horseback riding, walk	65
trot	200
gallop	300
Running	320
Boxing	520
Rowing	730

Come to think of it, campfire concerts often feature harmonica and recorder accompaniment, and I suppose there is no reason why it should stop there. So:

Violin playing	25
Cello playing	60
Piano playing, Mendelssohn's songs	35
Beethoven's *Appassionata*	65
Liszt's *Tarantella*	90

Almost all walking includes some uphill work. And it seems that, assuming a body efficiency of 30 percent, you use about 110 calories in raising every 100 pounds of bodyweight each 1000 feet of elevation. For practical purposes you can add the weight of your pack direct to bodyweight.

Armed with all these figures (but already suffering misgivings) I began to work out energy sums for an average fairly hard day's wilderness walking. I pictured myself, at 190 pounds, carrying a 50-pound pack, walking on a rough trail for 7 hours (with halts), gaining a total of 3000 feet in elevation and otherwise doing all the things you do on an average day. Juggling with the figures I had gathered, and trying to pin down the hours of a wilderness day along the lines of the table on page 44, I came up with:

	Calories
Basal metabolism (190 lbs. @ 1100 cals. per 100 lbs.)	2090
Climbing 3000 feet (240 lbs. @ 110 cals. per 1000 ft.)	792
6 hours actual walking, at 2 mph (240 lbs. @ 45 cals. per hour per 100 lbs., times a factor of 2 for roughness of trail)	1296
3 hours dishwashing, laundering (light), making and striking camp, photography, compulsive dallying, and unmentionable activities (average: 50 cals. per 100 lb.-hours)	285
3 hours dressing and undressing, standing (relaxed), singing in a loud voice, cooking, and such items as evaporated time (quite unaccountable for) (average: 30 cals. per 100 lb.-hours)	171
3 hours eating, writing notes, and sitting quietly (halts, rapt contemplation, worrying, elevated thinking, general sloth) (average: 20 cals. per 100 lb.-hours)	114
1 minute lying still, awake (to nearest cal.)	0
8 hours 59 minutes sleeping (including catnaps)	0
Total	4748
Plus specific dynamic action, 10 percent	475
Total day's energy output	5223

Even before I arrived at this figure and stopped to contemplate with dismay the gulf between it and my theoretical daily food consumption of 3830 calories, I knew something was going wrong with my neat little sums. Some of the figures in the energy-output table were obviously very rough approximations indeed. The efficiency with which you walk, saw wood, do laundry (light) or sing in a loud voice may vary drastically from day to day, even from hour to hour. And you perform most wilderness activities much more efficiently after you have been out for a week. Altitude tells too. And an arbitrary reclassification of the trail as "smooth" cuts the calorie total by 700 (including specific dynamic action) —which makes a huge difference.

But the biggest variable is the individual. All the figures are for average people, and although rough theoretical allowances can apparently be made for discernible differences due to age, build, sex and even race, the critical question remains, "How do I, personally, function?" The spread, even between apparently similar individuals, can be wide. About 70 percent of people fall within a fairly narrow central efficiency range; but if you belong to the 30 percent in any one function—and the chances are that you do—then any computation may give highly misleading results.

At this point in my investigations I began to suspect that the right approach to the food question was, after all, *trial and error* and not the strict, rational, quantitative, *scientific method.* With considerable misgivings I voiced this thought to several experienced research workers in the field of human nutrition. To my surprise, they tended to agree. Present knowledge, they said, left too many variables for any very meaningful quantitative balancing of energy input and output. The best way was to "get out in the field and establish bases for your own personal nutrition requirements." To do, in other words, just about what I had done in the first place.

Now, the last thing I want to suggest is that the scientific method turns out to be useless. If I thought so I should hardly have inflicted 6 pages of it on you. Nowadays, with a markedly changed nutritional gospel, and different foods available, I still routinely apply what I have learned to make rough calorie counts and even estimates of protein and fat content for almost any food list I assemble. And I'm convinced that even a little knowledge of the principles of human nutrition can be an invaluable aid to anyone striving to evolve a backpack diet that suits his needs. Had I known what I know now, my early trials would have been less tribulatory, my errors less gross.

So please do not write off my energy-input and -output tables as stillborn theorizing. Apart from anything else, what I've learned about nutrition in the course of preparing them has helped me build some solid-looking bridges across the gap they have revealed between my actual intake and apparent needs. And down the years it has continued to color my thinking.

On long trips I usually take one day of almost total rest in every week of walking. Often I take two. On these days I normally eat less than on the others. So for the days that really demand energy I have rather more than the standard quota available—more than 4000 calories, almost certainly.

In addition, I tend to nibble away at small quantities of food throughout the day, and this little-and-often kind of intake turns out to be the most efficient, especially for quick-burning carbohydrates.

But the really big factor, in more ways than one, may be my spare tire. I know from happy experience that my midriff begins to deflate after just a few days of walking with a load. On the California and Grand Canyon trips the tire vanished. The Grand Canyon trip was the only time I have ever done a before-and-after weighing, and in those two strenuous months I dropped from 194 to 174 pounds. I am fairly sure that almost all the loss came in the very strenuous first half—a conclusion borne out by nutrition experts who say, "Weight loss is usually most marked at the start of any stepped-up exercise." I lost, then, something approaching 20 pounds in 30 days. Up to two-thirds of this loss, or about 14 pounds, is likely to have been fat. (Water would account for most of the balance.) Now, it seems that the body uses this fat just as efficiently as it does fat ingested by mouth. That is, it extracts 9 calories per gram, or about 4000 calories per pound. In other words, my 14 pounds of fat gave me an additional 56,000 calories in 30 days, or close to 2000 calories per day! Too many imponderables are involved in reaching this rather astonishing figure for us to accept it as at all accurate. But, to say the least, it makes the theoretical daily gap of 1300 calories between my apparent needs and actual intake yawn a great deal less capaciously.

In conclusion, then, it seems to me that the way to work out a good backpacking diet is to go on a shakedown cruise and find out by trial and error what suits you. If this sounds too unscientific for your temperament, call it "going out in the field and establishing personal nutritional bases." A good starting point is the U.S. Army allowance of 4400 calories per man for heavy work. (Allowance for "normal" work, 3600; for sedentary jobs, 2800.) To translate calories into ounces of food, consult *Agricultural Handbook No. 8* or some simplified list. Remember that most backpackers, including me, tend to err on the side of taking too much food. From there, play it by ear. But keep one ear cocked in the direction of calories and their constituents. Think like a rough-and-ready computer. And don't forget to sing in a loud voice.

A dozen years have passed since I made these sagacious calculations. Today the energy-output figures still stand. But nutrition is one of those fields of human ignorance now in a state of extreme flux; in fact, like almost every damned thing connected with backpacking, it has been undergoing sea changes. So although this is no place for a treatise, we must reassess matters in the light of current scientific "truth."

The basic tenets of this year's gospel, highly simplified, read: *

---

* The dogma of the month varies, of course, from expert to expert. But I have passed my deliberately general summary before the eyes of three very different savants—an academic nutritionist, a consulting nutritionist and a doctor who specializes in preventative medicine

1. *Complex carbohydrates should form the bulk and basis of your diet.* Complex carbohydrates, or starches, include all carbohydrates except the sugars. They tend to be seriously under-represented in the modern American diet, which consists of 60–70 percent fats and sugars. Unlike proteins and fats, complex carbohydrates burn fast and "clean" in your digestive system, leaving few toxic residues. As with all foods, "natural" forms are best: grains should be whole, including the vital trace components embodied in their outer shells; whenever possible, vegetables should be fresh—and lightly cooked.

Note that as you get progressively more tired, so your muscles apparently need more and more carbohydrate, as opposed to protein or fat.

2. *Treat sugar as a condiment rather than a food.* (I speak primarily of sucrose—common sugar; but everything I have to say applies, though sometimes less stringently, to the other sugars—glucose [or dextrose] and fructose.) There is nothing intrinsically wrong with eating sugars— only with eating a lot of them, especially alone. But they now occur in alarming percentages in most processed foods. Read labels and learn.

Large quantities of sugar are not something the human organism evolved to stomach. As recently as the fourteenth century, according to Dr. Ballantine, a pound of sugar cost more than a week's wages for a European servant ("It was a rare delicacy, available only on the tables of royalty"); then extraction and refining became industrialized, and since 1815 per-capita annual consumption in the Western world has rocketed from 15 to 120 pounds. This abrupt and pitfallous turn in habits has meant trouble in Liver City. Sugars provide what are now called "empty calories": in digesting them you must draw on your stored reserves of vitamins and minerals, even of fats and proteins, and you thereby "incur a debt." A meal or snack rich in sugar will boost your energy (and curb hunger pangs); but unless you follow it within about two hours with other kinds of food your blood sugar may drop sharply, and if it does you will suffer the sudden and severe exhaustion known as hypoglycemia. My

---

and dotes on diets—and each has at least acquiesced to the summary. I have also read, marked and inwardly digested *Diet and Nutrition* by Rudolph Ballantine, M.D. (Himalayan International Institute, Honesdale, PA., 1978; 2 pounds, $10.95 in paperback) and have checked with the author that nothing I say flouts his beliefs too blatantly.

Throughout, I have retained a healthy skepticism of extremists—the hyperhypoglycemites and -hyperlipidians, and the over-holy "holistics" who in reality have often been dazzled by a single beam and can no longer focus the whole. But I do my best to listen. Wisdom often underlies the chaff.

Above all, I have studiously ignored all currently popular, widely touted diets, ranging from old-style high-protein hymnals to restrictive, soul-cramping, Pritikin-like regimens that proclaim, roughly speaking, "Eat what you like, provided it isn't food."

old backpacking menu was grossly overloaded with sugar, and I indeed used to sink into occasional sudden hollows of exhaustion. I now carry far less sugar—and the hollows have flattened out. But sugar, even alone, as in candies, can provide needed spurts of energy. Just remember that unless you can supplement the boosts fairly soon with other food—or keep pushing the sugar in—you must expect to pay for it.

Contrary to current folklore, all refined sugars, whatever their hue and granulation, are created about equal. And honey and dried fruits are only marginally more equal.

3. *Too much protein is bad.* Other drawbacks aside (they include an increased need for water, and financial and ecological wastefulness), protein "burns dirty," leaving toxic nitrogen residues that may overload the body's cleansing system. (*Note:* By no means all experts agree with this statement.) You indeed need a certain amount of protein, and while opinions on the exact figure vary, a vague consensus seems to settle at no higher than 3 ounces a day. Optimum intake seems to be little, if any, higher than this minimum. The protein must contain all eight amino acids that the body cannot synthesize and are therefore called "essential." (Here again, some experts balk; virtually all foods, they say, contain a full complement of amino acids.) Meat, fish and dairy products are the most widely recognized protein sources but not necessarily the best (see fats, below). Legumes provide protein (raw beans average 25 percent; cooked beans, 18 percent; soybeans, raw or cooked, 32 percent). So do nuts (average, 9 percent; but 82 percent fat). Also grains and fruits, in small but significant amounts. "Provided you keep the fats and sugars down," says the doctor on my advisory panel, "you'll have difficulty in *not* getting enough protein."

4. *Reduce fat to vanishing point.* Today's typical American diet contains 45 percent fat—as against 10 percent in China and Japan. And fats, like sugars, are "empty calories." In addition, excessive fat, even polyunsaturated, seems linked with several pathological conditions, including gallstones and some cancers. And the current hyperlipid scripture (which shows signs of settling down after two decades of oscillation) affirms that saturated fats increase the chances of dangerous plaque build-up in the arteries of everybody, no matter what their age. The process, even if it occurs, can take years to manifest as a heart attack; but it may well pay to start cutting fats as early in life as possible. Note that it is very difficult to keep fats low when you eat meat—even "lean" meat; that natural plant fats (nuts, avocadoes, olives, soybeans) work just as efficiently as animal fats and do less harm; and that fats are helpful in cold weather.

5. *Take adequate vitamins and minerals.* Both are best ingested in fresh foods, not as additives, let alone supplements. In fact, the average

healthy person living on a good and varied diet almost certainly needs no supplements at all. So although some backpackers maintain, a little breathlessly, that you should never venture away from roadhead without a half-ton of pill supplements in your pack, it seems safe to say that for all but the most prolonged expeditions (page 179) you can forget the whole thing. I do—except for Vitamin C for cold-fencing (again, page 179). Knowledge of vitamin and mineral requirements is still building, but this week's verities attribute possible toxic effects to overdoses of Vitamins A (in tablet form), D and E.

6. *Transmute your ideas of a balanced diet.* For years we have been taught to think of four groups: meat, milk, fruits/vegetables and grains. Substitute three major groups: grains, legumes (including certain seeds and nuts) and vegetables. Add two minor groups: the B_{12} series (meats, fish, dairy products, eggs and such fermented bean products as tofu) and raw foods (fruits, vegetables). Try to eat plenty of grains, and emphasize the other groups in roughly the order given.

7. *Eat as many different kinds of food as possible.* This studied complexity seems to be as important as any single facet of diet. It will help fill not only potholes we can see but those that surely lurk outside our present vision. Some statistics suggest that, provided a diet is healthy and varied, otherwise dangerous components may prove harmless.

For the low-sodium caper, see page 178.

Some of these simplified guidelines may need a little modifying if they're to be incorporated into the house you carry on your back.

A carbohydrate-rich diet, for example, does not stick well to most people's gut. So you have to keep snacking. And while that's often just a matter of remembering to do so, it can under certain conditions prove inconvenient, going on impossible. Boosting your intake of protein and fat, which you metabolize slowly, will take care of that difficulty. These days I try to follow the new guidelines; but after ruminating on past experiences I still tend, in spite of the alleged bad effects, to eat rather more protein and fat when backpacking than I do at home. ("Me too," says my doctor-advisor—to my surprise and pleasure.)

I hope you will pay some attention to the scientific pearls I have silk-pursed before you; but I also hope you nurture a healthy cynicism about all new knowledge, and can thereby, while slushing happily around in it, retain some semblance of wisdom. Bear in mind, constantly, that this whole field of nutrition is shot through with uncertainty. Figure-fouling idiosyncrasies do not end with wheat germs and humans. I once saw on a blackboard in the nutritional-sciences department of a famous university: "Lipids are inscrutable." But someone had struck out "lipids" and substituted "guinea pigs."

Although not all the new, revised nutritional precepts can be applied, pure, to backpacking, they provide useful guidelines; and with them firmly in mind we can at last consider

Dipping into the food cornucopia.

You must buy backpacking food differently from and much more carefully than the food you use at home.

The current propaganda permeating modern, crazy, industrialized life tends to view calories as something to be avoided, or at least pared down. In backpacking, because you will be exercising strenuously and carrying everything on your back, your object must be—within other constraints—to pack the maximum number of calories into the minimum number of ounces. So you compare all net weights (not the reconstituted weights of reputed servings, which depend on how much water you add). You check packaging for weight too—and for toughness and disposability (page 181). You read cooking instructions and choose the simplest (remembering, though, that meals with mixed ingredients and slightly complex cooking methods may taste better than those to which you just add water). You ignore cost to the limit of purse and temperament. You also ignore the "zesty richness" and "tangy flavor" and other alluring horseradish printed on the packages. What you want to know, in most cases, is how quick and easy this particular item is going to be to prepare when you're tired and hungry, how much better it is going to make you feel and how long it will go on making you feel better. Advice on this score is useful only up to a point: what really matters, remember, is how the food suits *you*. And the only way to decide that is to experiment.

For our experimentation we now face a palate-boggling array of choices.

Freeze-dried foods have largely replaced vacuum-dried: they retain nutritional values better and are tastier and simpler to prepare. They also cost more. And, once opened, they must be used fast: exposed to air, their taste and nutritive values soon deteriorate.

Competition has generated a rich potpourri of complete meals, separate courses and individual items. Mountain House foods, dominant for several years, are now being challenged by Weepak's tasty, high-quality packagings. Dri-Lite still produce popular items. And Richmoor, once the leaders, are coming back with their very palatable, nonpreservative Natural High meals. All four brands are widely available in the West and patchily over the rest of the country. The East produces Stow-Lite (by Stow-A-Way), Speedy Chef, Seidel and an EMS line. Some interesting items also come from smaller firms. In Canada, where U.S. brands are always costly and often unobtainable, the best-known labels are Magic Pantry, World Famous and Coughlin's.

Several small "organic foods" firms now put out neat packages of soups, vegetables and supporting items, all more or less guaranteed to be innocent of preservatives, chemicals, chocolate and James Watt. At least two outfits—Natural Food Backpack Dinners and Alpineaire—market fairly full lines. You can't help feeling a great deal of sympathy for the ideas, or at least emotions, that prompt this revolt against industrial buggering about. But it becomes a little wearying to be warned ad nauseam that consuming polluted "commercial" food is the reason you have warts, are impotent and died last week. And organic food seems to generate not only energy but also haloes—the same appallingly human haloes that always lurk, ready for conspicuous wear, behind the knowledge that you have "seen the light," and it makes no difference whether your "truth," hidden from all lesser eyes, concerns "natural food," Islam, the Moral Majority, the cooperative movement or "ecology." Anyway, the point is that the "organic" movement generates a backlash. I confess that I sometimes find it difficult, faced by certain food purists, to stop their goddam haloes from blinding me to real advantages that "natural" foods may offer. But if you are immune to such choler, or can survive it, and want to live on a preservative-free, unpesticided, health-and-halo-inducing diet, and also to backpack, then know ye that the world is full of little packaged jewels.

Do not forget—especially if cost is a major consideration, or if you live far from any special store—that today's supermarket is a part of our cornucopia. You'll find plenty of examples in the next dozen pages. For short trips, when weight is not such an overburdening problem, you really need not shop anywhere but at a supermarket. Read all about it in *Supermarket Backpacker* by Harriett Barker (hardcover, 194 pages, 9½ ounces, $6.95, 1977, Contemporary Books, 180 N. Michigan Ave., Chicago, IL 60601).

Many people still tend to select backpacking foods purely for flavor and to assume that the nutritional values are there. They are wrong. Read all labels carefully—and remember that ingredients are listed in descending order of occurrence, by weight. Also that if the package bears a USDA stamp, which it certainly should, then the big-type title of a complete meal tells you a lot. "Beef Stroganoff," for example, must contain a minimum of 45 percent beef, while "Noodles and Stroganoff Sauce with Beef" may have only 21 percent and "Beef-Flavored Stroganoff Mixed with Freeze-Dried Beef" less than 1 percent. Similarly, "Chicken and Rice" means more chicken than "Rice and Chicken."

Note that unless your soul warps at the prospect you can dehydrate some of your own foods. You can remove 90 percent of the moisture that way, as compared with 96 percent in vacuum- or freeze-dried items. I understand that Mirro's dehydrator works, and so does Jack's Food Dehydrator by Stowline Enterprises of Washington State. Stowline also distribute *Home Food Dehydration* by emme Wheeler (160 pages, $4.95). Another beginner's instruction book, said to be good, is *Dry It, You'll Like It* by Gen MacManiman (paperback, 7 ounces, 1973, $4.95, Madrona Publishers; obtainable from Gen MacManiman, Box 546, Fall City, WA 98024). For packaging, and storage desiccants, see page 181; for making your own beef jerky, page 175.

Finally, remember that dehydrated foods are not the whole story. Some people say, "Eat as fresh as you can for as long as you can"—and they carry fresh vegetables, meat and other items for the first few meals (see page 180 for a "Take-Along Garden"). While I certainly agree with the fresh-food principle, I never seem to follow it in practice. I have not experimented, as I've intended to do, with fresh bread. And in the following meal-by-meal review of present backpacking foods I'm afraid I rather ignobly tend to ignore fresh-food alternatives.

The review, though it seems necessary, poses difficulties: I am undoubtedly ignorant of many first-class items, particularly those sold only in the East; taste is perhaps the most wildly idiosyncratic corner of the idiosyncratic backpacking field; and attitudes toward meal-making run it a close second. So while I shall follow my normal practice of stating personal preferences you'll find that I try to take a rather more objective view than usual. Remember too that personal tastes and attitudes toward meal-making can change. I remain, at rock belly, a Britannic barbarian. But the years have taken their toll: America has corrupted me. I have to confess that at times, even far from civilization, I now yearn for particivilized food. And I often pander to this treasonable weakness. So my needs have evolved—but not necessarily progressed. A backpacker with a cuisine that is simple going on depraved can perhaps claim survival advantages.

Breakfast

I find this the most difficult meal. The basic requirements are at odds with each other. Nutritionally, you want something that will keep you going through a long morning's walking; but you often want to start walking immediately after eating, so the slow-digesting fats and proteins that fill the first requirement are the very items that, because of their demands on the body's energy output (page 154), should be avoided immediately before strenuous exercise. Even more to the point, the meal should, except on rest days, be very simple to prepare. I find that I eat most breakfasts in at least a mild hurry, sometimes in darkness, and nearly always in that pseudo-catatonic post-eye-opening period when no one in his right mind would describe me as awake. And I have yet to discover the perfect meal to accompany the hot tea that is the only catalyst reasonably sure to jolt me toward interaction with a new day.

For years I ate 4 ounces of cold dehydrated fruit, soaked overnight. Later I alternated it with one of the Swiss-type cold-cereal-fruit-and-nut mixtures (Fini, Familia, Swissy, Alpen). But eventually I tired of the cloying sweetness, and now, if I want cold cereal, which is also useful as an odd-time filler, I use a sugar-free brand or mixture of brands (Grape-Nuts, small Shredded Wheat, for example; read supermarket labels for others. Familia now comes in a "no-added-sugar" version). All-Bran can be helpful in the first days of a trip if, because of the suddenly changed way of life, your bowels need prompting. (An alternative, I'm told, is dried fruit, especially white figs.) Often I spice up the cereal with Familia-or-similar. And I almost always add a protein booster.*

For some time now my standard breakfast, especially in cool weather, has been one or two 1-ounce envelopes of Quaker Instant Cereal (the regular flavor has no added sugar) with protein booster and, often, a sprinkling of Swiss cereal or gorp (page 174). Occasionally I substitute a 3-ounce package of ramen (Oriental noodles), boosted to taste (current "in" brands: Top Ramen for the upper crust and Smack Ramen for the S-M set). Both oats and ramen are cheap supermarket standards and very simple to prepare. But lately, as a variation and on hurry-up days, I have been experimenting with wads called Bear Valley Fruit-'n-nut Pemmican (successor to Running Bear's Pemmican: malt, nonfat milk, honey,

---

* A low-cost protein formula based on defatted soybean and known as MPF was for several years my protein booster for breakfasts and all other meals too, as needed. But it has, in obedience to Herblock's Law (page 66), just gone out of production. The makers kindly suggested as a replacement either soy flour (comparable to Fine MPF) or soy grits (comparable to Coarse MPF) from supermarkets or health-food stores. But the untreated soy products are not stable, like MPF: even in a refrigerator they last only a few weeks; in a pack, only a week or so. Worse, some of them have a pervasive taste—and it's a sound principle, likely to avert considerable suffering, that if some items of your diet are frequently repeated you should try for bland-tasting versions that will be swamped by other ingredients. Several protein powders now meet this criterion. Plus Formula 398, based on milk and soy, has 86 percent protein by weight, no fat or carbohydrate, and a list of vitamins and minerals that stretches from here to Zanzibar (12-ounce can, $7). Tiger's Milk—36 percent protein, 7 percent fat, 57 percent carbohydrate (12-ounce can, $5.50)—is self-effacing enough in the "natural vanilla" flavor and can be found in many supermarkets, though not among the cat foods.

Important note: Nutritionists, with considerable reason, quantify the protein, fat and carbohydrate content of foods as percentages of total calories, not of total weight. I have followed their lead. So my figures will differ from those you find on packages. They normally show grams-per-serving of each commodity. To convert into nutritional terms, multiply protein and carbohydrate figures by 4, fats by 9 (that is, by the number of calories per gram); then reduce to percentages. I hope you have more fun doing so than I did.

wheat germ, walnuts, soy flour, raisins, grape juice, soy oil, wheat bran, pecans; 17 percent protein [including all eight essential amino acids], 28 percent fat, and 56 percent carbohydrates; 3¾ ounces; 420 calories; $.98; by Intermountain Trading Company of California [see Appendix II, page 615]. New variants, with same weight, similar contents: carob, 470 calories; coconut almond, 415 calories; sesame lemon, with bee pollen, 435 calories). The wads, though hardly a gourmet's delight, need no cooking: you just eat, right out of the wrapper. And they seem to keep me going for hours. (See also "Lunch," opposite page.)

Other breakfasts I've tried include some surprisingly palatable bacon bars (by Westland, 2 ounces, 147 calories, 10.5 percent moisture, 40 percent protein, and 38 percent fat by weight, $2, distributed by Rich-moor; and 3-ounce bars by Right Away foods, $3). You can goo them up with a little hot water and perhaps a dash of onion flakes and herbs, or even eat them raw, like a banana. ("Barbarous!" says one advisor.) Either way, the bacon tends to keep burping up all morning; but it keeps your legs pumping. In the past I've sometimes substituted meat bars, but those currently available are neither very nutritious nor bland enough to swamp with other ingredients (page 167, footnote). I often intend to beef up breakfast with jerky, but my glazed morning mind almost always seems to overlook the overnight intention.

Other alternatives include Carnation Instant Breakfasts (130 calories per 1¼-ounce envelope, 10 envelopes for $3.49; 22 percent protein, 7 percent fat, and 71 percent carbohydrates), but although I occasionally carry one I find I can rarely face it. (And purists recoil in horror from the additives in such fare.) On rest days, of course, when there's no need for speed, you can let yourself go: my favorite is small trout, caught either the evening before or, better still, that same morning. But don't kid yourself that trout are fuel fit for long-distance walking.

Now, I'm aware that many people turn up their noses at my kind of breakfast and demand bacon and eggs or some stalwart equivalent— which has the advantage of giving your stomach what it's used to, back home. Fresh bacon and eggs and bread are certainly feasible for the first day or two of a trip—if you're willing to pay by carrying extra weight and devoting extra cooking time. (Precooked, vacuum-packed cans of bacon by Westland: 4 ounces, 9–12 slices, $3.50. For carriage of fresh eggs, see page 216.) Note that freeze-dried menus offer not only "eggs with real bacon bits," but "Western" and "Mexican" omelettes, and also "hash browns," "blueberry flavor pancake mix" and other resistibles.

But the important thing is to follow your own fresh or freeze-dried star, tailoring each breakage of a night's fast to suit your own mind and gut and the particular day that fans out ahead. A Texas reader speaks glowingly of grits. And a New York couple recommend "at close of breakfast" (as well as at bedtime) a 1-ounce package of Swiss Miss—a "really dynamite cocoa" laced with nonfat dry milk and malt.

Lunch

Hot food seems to recharge me best. So for years I have lunched on soup. Although Maggi is good, I now mostly use Knorr-Swiss: it comes in light, burnable, waxed-paper packages (discard the outer cardboard box), is easy to prepare and seems to satisfy me more than others I have tried ($.89). (Both Knorr and Maggi packages vary somewhat in weight and markedly in calorie content, according to flavor.*) But sometimes I replace the soups with 3-ounce packages of ramen (page 167). Alternative cooked lunches: chili, sausage patties.

If, like many people, you make the lunch stop little more than an excuse to get the pack off your back for rather longer than usual, you can —as I seem to have been doing a lot lately—just sit down and devour part or even all of a Bear Valley Pemmican bar (page 167). Or you can carry bread and spread peanut butter or other goodies on it to your stomach's content. If it's a gourmet stomach, consider the slightly de-lectable Mountain House shrimp cocktail (1¾ ounces, $6)—which also makes a good two-person aperitif, pre-lunch or -dinner—or even Early Winters's Caviar-in-a-Tuna (3¾ ounces, $1.85) ("not caviar in the classic sense, but a tasty pâté of lightly smoked Norwegian cod roe").

Or you can make lunch no more than another helping, perhaps bigger than normal, of your routine "trail snacks" (page 174). Or just dip into a bag of corn tortillas. In practice you often have to operate this way, like it or not. I find myself doing so, for example, if it is too cold to stop for long without making camp or if I am pushing for miles and the days are short.

If, on the other hand, you can afford and also appreciate a medium-long halt but do not want to cook, you may like to try freeze-dried salads

* KNORR-SWISS SOUPS:	oz.	cals.
Green Pea	2⅞	330
Oxtail, Leek, Mushroom, Minestrone	2⅝–2¾	300
Noodle Chicken, Beef Barley, Asparagus	2¼–2⅝	270
Napoli	2⅜	240
Onion	2	180
Vegetable	1⅝	150

Caloric constituents vary, but average 10 percent protein,
12 percent fat, and 78 percent carbohydrates.

(chicken, tuna, cottage cheese, for example); mostly, they demand only cold water, mixing and a 5- or 10-minute wait. Beware of gelatin-based salads that need hot water to dissolve them and then chill to a jelly. I do not mean only that the process takes time. Or even that one of my advisors classifies gelatin as "utterly worthless." I regret to be able to inform you on the best possible authority that although it would seem difficult to do anything too disastrous with such a mixture you can, given enough sun and stupidity, spread a tenacious goo over roughly one-quarter of your equipment.

Britannic afternoon tea

Most people can let four o'clock pass without stopping everything (as I am still unable to—despite American citizenship and more than a quarter-century's U.S. residence); but few backpackers fail to drink tea or its nutritional cousin, coffee, at some point in the day. So I'll take this opportunity to air a few minor facts and one scurrilous innuendo.

First, the "facts." A little to my surprise, I find plain, straightforward Lipton tea best for sheer resuscitation power. Thirty bags see even me through the thirstiest week. I normally include a few fancier jobs, mint- or orange- or cinnamon-flavored, for rest-day kicks. Several readers have registered horror at my use of bags. One suggests instant tea, because "tea bags are simply unnecessary deadweight." A "lover of tea and hater of tea bags" counter-recommends a blend of genuine leaves (3 parts Darjeeling, 3 parts Keemun, 1 part Ceylon and a dash of Lapsang Souchong) which, he avers, can actually be smoked and "will cure all ills, including future smoking of anything."
You carry such loose tea in a Ziploc plastic bag and steep by means of a lightweight metal teabasket. A tea sock—cotton, with stainless-steel rim (½ ounce; $2.45 from Early Winters)—can also be used for coffee. (Genuine "fresh roasted" coffee—not instant or freeze-dried—is now available occasionally in bags that are twins to tea dittos.) "Iced" tea, in crystal form, is more quickly and easily concocted than hot tea—add the coldest water around, then stir—but does not seem to pack the same wallop.

The resuscitative power of both tea and coffee stems, of course, from caffeine. And this is where the innuendo lurks. I am indebted, or something (what *is* the antonym of "indebted"?), to a Texas reader for a 1974 report by Dr. R. M. Gilbert, published in *Addictions,* the quarterly publication of the Addiction Research Foundation of Ontario. (Note the tainted source.) This report turns up some mildly interesting facts: "Caffeine" has its origin in the Arabic word "gawah," which once meant wine. Tea leaves and coffee beans both contain about 1.5 percent caffeine, but because of preparation methods an average cup of coffee "is believed to contain" more than an average cup of tea (100–150 mg. as against 50–75 mg.). Tea, unlike coffee, also contains a related drug (another xanthine alkaloid) that neutralizes some of caffeine's rather complicated effects on blood vessels. Many soft drinks also contain caffeine (Coca-Cola: 43 mg. per can), and so does chocolate ("about 25 mg. per 10-cent bar"). "Thus, a 70-lb., 10-year-old kid who consumes four bottles of Coke and three chocolate bars a day could be ingesting more caffeine per kilogram than a 170-lb. man whose daily liquid intake includes seven cups of coffee." Further, "it is probable that a childhood dependence on caffeine in the form of cola or chocolate becomes translated into an adult dependence on coffee or tea." The effects of caffeine on human behavior have been confirmed experimentally. "Five studies conducted at California's Stanford University in the 1960's indicated that caffeine in coffee both prevented and disturbed sleep, and elevated mood but not performance. It also caused characteristic dysphoric symptoms such as irritability, inability to work effectively, nervousness, restlessness, lethargy and headache when taken by non-users, or not taken by regular users." This hodge-podge of alleged effects, labeled "caffeinism," "is said to be current among intellectual workers, actresses, waitresses, nocturnal employees, and long-distance automobile drivers. Illness otherwise unexplained may be caused by excessive ingestion of the xanthine alkaloids, including those in coffee, tea [and] cocoa. . . ."

Now, coffee and cocoa are mere foods. But such calumnies against the good name of tea are enough to depress the mood, if not the performance, of an Un-British Activities Committee. And worse follows. Dr. Gilbert (sounding more like Mr. Sullivan) calls caffeine "a drug of concern." Perhaps its most insidious effect, he says, lies in the consequences of its withdrawal. "Many early morning blues are quite likely caffeine withdrawal symptoms. Inability to rise, the empty feeling behind the eyes, irritability, headache and fragility are all relieved by caffeine, but only at the cost of staying on the drug. Often too little may be self-administered and the withdrawal state may persist into the working day, at least until the coffee machine can be encountered. . . . Studies with rats have shown that the after effects of caffeine on behavior (i.e., the withdrawal effects) are much more profound than the direct effects of the drug, even after one day's administration."

"Ain't this a bitch?" comments my reader-informant. It is indeed. All I can personally hope for is that Hades has at least a caffeine-maintenance program. Otherwise it'll be just hell down there. Meanwhile all this emotional stuff has gotten to me, and I must pause for my second fix of the day.*

Dinner

Even more than at home, this is the main meal of the day, and probably your main protein intake: the day's walking or exploring or fishing or what-have-you is over and you have both time to cook and also freedom from the inhibiting prospect of immediate strenuous exercise. The catalogues offer a wild array of dinners (full menus, single courses, separate items) and most now come with fairly simple cooking instructions—though they range from "add boiling water and take five" to shepherding several ingredients through the maze of stirrings and simmerings beloved of do-it-yourself gourmets. Freeze-dried dinners often taste remarkably good: in Weepak's Shrimp Creole, for example, the shrimps actually taste like shrimps. With all dinners—and other meals too—ignore such printed fiction as "serves four." Maybe—at the feeding of the five thousand. But if you need the kind of evening meal I do you should allow a total of around 7 ounces, dry weight, and include adequate protein for sure and maybe some fat. If you travel solo and find a dinner pack too big, use only half and rubber-band the balance away for another day.

Alternatively, you can concoct your own dinners. Supermarket standards such as spaghetti, couscous or lentil pilaf (though it needs a lot of simmering) can form the grain or legume backbone. So can the convenient envelopes of straightforward, unjazzed-up freeze-dried vegetables by Weepak and others. Or you can buy in bulk and repackage: Mountain House put up such vegetables, and many other foods too, in #10 and #2½ cans (available in the East through Stow-A-Way), and both Weepak and Seidel bulk-pack their products. Bulk "survival" foods, such as those by Neo-Life (available through local agents), are also possible sources. (For repackaging techniques, see page 181.)

The obvious protein source has for years been meat bars. But Wilson's bar, long my standby, has vanished—another victim of Herblock's Law. And its successor, by Westland, has too intrusive a taste for frequent use and is sadly adulterated (16 ingredients listed). The best meat protein sources I know at present are the Weepak envelopes of diced beef

---

* One of my advisors insists that tea and its cousins, taken alone, produce the same boom-and-bust effect—though less severe—as empty-caloried sugar (page 161). Well, OK. I've just taken some gorp along with my fix.

and diced chicken (2 ounces, $2.83). Textured vegetable protein (TVP) has over the past few years made great strides toward palatability and is now often used in foods that can replace meat as your protein source. It is cheaper, eliminates fat and placates vegetarians.

Your personal melding of 3 ounces of protein in some form with 4 ounces of vegetables (or whatever amounts seem to suit you) can form the foundation of dinner every night for a week, with very little pain. For the switcheroos are almost limitless. You can vary both protein and vegetable, and the mixtures thereof. You can ring gravy changes. You can shuffle and reshuffle your herbs, spices and other trimmings. And you can modulate the amount of water so that you serve yourself anything from thickish soup to amorphous meat loaf. Mostly, though, you end up with what can only be called "stew." Some such variant—which one backpacking companion labeled Fletcher Stew (Boeuf Gallois Alfresco)—was for years my dinner, six days out of seven. I still fall back on it fairly often, particularly when I'm tired and want an easily prepared meal. But everyone evolves his or her own standbys. A Texas damsel maintains that "a supply of bouillon cubes, gravy bars, Italian herb mixture, tomato sauce (in squeeze tubes), rice and elbow macaroni mixed into various concoctions and eaten with beef jerky or beef sticks will provide light-weight, varied, fully satisfying meals."

Gravy masculates any stew. My current favorite is Knorr Hunter Sauce Mix, but choices are wide, and include soups. A reader stresses the value of chili and curry powders as antidotes for any mistakes one might make.

Herbs, spices and other trimmings can vivify any lunch or dinner. I carry three very small bags of herbs on each trip, ringing the changes on ground cumin seed, oregano, thyme, sage and Italian herb mix. Other bags may hold garlic powder, dried onion flakes and imitation bacon chips. Sometimes I add a ½-ounce package of dried mushrooms ("Refresh in cold water 2 to 3 hours. Use the same as fresh mushrooms"). And I've recently learned that a sprinkling of roasted sunflower seeds imparts a subtle taste and texture to many meals.

But the vital element in dinner trimmings is variety: handle them properly and you'll dine off a different dish every night, even if the basics remain unchanged. Well, a vaguely different dish, anyway.

Desserts rarely grace my dinner menus, but you'll find fruits and other goodies in every food catalogue. Try freeze-dried "ice cream" in solid form (not too much like ice cream, perhaps, but it sure as hell tastes good—though it lingers on fingers as well as palate). Another delectable: freeze-dried strawberries flavored with banana chips and a little sugar and lubricated with water and powdered milk. Failing a dessert, you can round off dinner very satisfyingly by a little judicious thieving from your stock of

Trail snacks,

which should be small, conveniently packaged items that do not melt, crumble or make you unduly thirsty. They travel in an accessible pocket of the pack ("nibble pocket," page 528) or clothing. I nibble at every halt, except perhaps the first of the day. And now that I have cut down on fat and protein I tend to nibble big.

At the moment, in harmony with this Friday's nutritional gospel, I also curb my sugar intake. Curb, but not eliminate. I no longer use the mint-cake candy that for years was my staple snack; but I always carry

Hard candies—the boiled kind, individually wrapped. (But beware of flimsy little wrappers that slip off more easily than a nightdress, creating sticky pockets and furry candies.) I also mix in a few specials such as toffees and mints to pamper my post-dinner palate. The candies' straight sugar is particularly useful, I find, toward the end of a morning or day, when I need a sharp energy boost and know I'll be eating a meal within an hour or two. But I may use the candies—sparingly, and buffered with more-balanced snacks—at other halts.

Gorp has become my basic snack. The term embraces a wide spectrum of mingle-mangles, usually based on dried fruit and nuts, sometimes with chocolate or carob. In many supermarkets as well as natural-food stores you can now make your choice from a line of intriguing drums and ladle out as much as you need. I'm currently enamored of a supermarket concoction called Tropical Trail Mix (date pieces, raisins, sunflower seeds, coconut chips, pineapple pieces, banana chips, papaya, almonds and peanuts); but this is a field in which you can switch inamoratae (or inamorati) as often and unguiltily as you like. Make sure, though, that the loved one is somewhat nutty and not too sugary. Then life together should be satisfying and not a switchback of ups and downs.

You can, if you like, make your own gorp. One reader suggests this recipe: "I throw raisins, dates, coconut, figs, prunes, pecans, walnuts and filberts in a heterogeneous mixture into the food chopper. I pack the dubious-looking mess which the chopper spews out into a 1-inch metal tube, ramming it down hard with a close-fitting rod. When the tube is nearly full, I lay it on waxed paper and push the cylindrical rod of 'gorp' out, wrap it in the paper, wrap that in foil, and stow it in the refrigerator. I suppose it would go rancid eventually at summer temperatures but I haven't noticed it after it has been out a week or so. On a hike one merely peels it like a banana."

Mixed nuts in small quantities also make good trail snacks, though I find they more often serve to fill odd corners after a meal, especially at night, when their 82-percent fat content can be easily digested—and will help keep you warm. Note that deermice love nuts with deermonic passion and in order to gratify it will penetrate all manner of obstacles, including layers of thick plastic tucked under your knees at night.

Semisweet chocolate contains about 35 percent fat and in theory is therefore unsuitable for use during or just before strenuous exercise. The balance is mostly sugar, laced with caffeine. I find that chocolate does not, in practice, produce any "heavy" effects—and always tastes good, under any conditions. As a result, I almost always carry it—and always finish it, down to the last morsel. So, I gather, do most walkers, theory or no theory. Convenient 1-ounce Hershey bars of "tropical chocolate" are back again, after a hiatus in production. But half-pound bars of supermarket semisweet chocolate, used mainly for cooking, are cheaper, just about as good and only marginally less convenient. Both kinds melt less readily than ordinary chocolate. Still, they melt. Try to keep out of direct sunlight. In deserts, avoid.

Banana chips are nutritious, easily digested, rich in potassium, mid-dle-income in minerals and delectable alone or conglomerated. Note that if prepared with coconut oil they can "go bad."

Beef jerky makes a protein- and fat-rich snack for any time of day, or for dropping into soup or stew—though it will not rehydrate because, unlike most dehydrated foods, it has been heated past the point at which tissue structure is irreversibly damaged, and no amount of soaking will soften its leathery soul. One pound reputedly equals 3½ pounds of fresh steak, but quality seems to vary widely and I can offer no logical testing criteria.

A Pennsylvania reader who "fell in love with biltong in South Africa" gives this recipe for making your own jerky: "Take several pounds of good beef and soak it for 3 hours in salt water. A little fat left on adds to the flavor. Hang up in *dry* wind (cold is fine; just has to be dry), shielded from flies. Let dry for 2 days. Take down and pound peppercorns and any other spices you feel like adding into it. Hang up again to dry until the stuff is hard as a rock. It can be refrigerated and kept forever (or frozen) but will also keep *for weeks* without refrigeration. You will need very strong teeth to deal with the stuff, or preferably a strong knife (you can precut it before you hike) but it is delicious. The Boers thrived on it."

You can make low-fat jerky by using flank steak. And I'm told you can dry the stuff by laying on cookie sheets in an oven, on pilot. If you slice thin, along the meat's grain, the job takes only 12–24 hours.

Alternative snacks

Fancy little bars, conveniently packed and bearing such titles as Aplets and Cotlets, now crowd the catalogues. Supermarket substitutes that I've tried with happiness include: Life-Savers (kept in pants pocket as instant reserve); raisins (to avoid goo-coated fingers, buy the dry type always); marzipan (Odense of Denmark make luscious 7- and 3-ounce candles—sugar, almonds, liquid glucose, certified color added, but by appointment to the Royal Danish Court, no less); and halvah ("a Turkish confection"—though a plant that has grown in Brooklyn produces 1⅛-ounce bars packing 183 nicely balanced calories—"consisting of a paste made of ground sesame seeds and nuts mixed with honey"). Do not ignore Bear Valley Pemmican (page 167) as a snack, even if you spurn it as a meal. My recent successful experiments include Glenny's Spirulina Sunrise bars (unsulfured natural dates, barley malt, unsweetened coconut, carob powder, pure spirulina powder [page 183], nonfat dry milk, palm-kernel oil, soya lecithin, natural vanilla and Glenny's special care; 1½ ounces, $.79; name catches in craw but bar doesn't); and Japanese-style dried seaweed (one package of 10 sheets, ¾ ounce, $1.59, is a hell of a lot, tastes good either munched alone or added to soups, etc. and reminds you of the fresh vegetables you'd like to be eating).

But there is really no end to this subject. And trail snacks, remember, are not only for trail snacks: they may form your entire lunch; they can round off any meal; and for people who dine early they make the most convenient warming-effect-last-thing-at-night snacks (page 354). So whenever need strikes, delve into your personally evolved nibble bags of trail snacks, come up with whatever catches your fancy, serve to taste and continue singing in that loud and cheerful voice.

A few words on some staple items:

Milk. Adding cream to nonfat milk (that is, milk from which the cream has been removed) sounds crazy; but with Milkman dried milk it seems to work. At least, that is what Foremost say they do before drying their product; and the resulting powder dissolves at least as quickly as the Carnation Nonfat I used to favor, tastes distinctly better, contains about 25 percent more calories and somehow seems to go appreciably further in normal use. A single foil envelope (3.44 ounces; 380 calories; 37 percent protein, 12 percent fat, 51 percent carbohydrate, battalions of vitamins; 12 envelopes for $5.89) makes 1 quart of reconstituted milk (butterfat: .5 percent), neatly fills (with a little shaking down before the final topping up) my plastic milk-squirter (page 217) and unless used ultralavishly lasts me rather more than a single day.

A Maine reader waxes semi-ecstatic over Meadow Fresh, a whey product laced with corn and coconut and a long line of additives. It is lower than Milkman in cholesterol and possibly sodium but, to my taste buds, rather less inviting.

Granulated sugar. Use as a condiment, not a food (page 161). For a week I now take no more than 6 ounces, rather than the 1½ or even 2 pounds I once did.

Margarine (rather than butter, because it keeps) improves almost any dish. And because it is almost pure fat it has a higher energy/weight ratio than almost any food you can lay sticky hands on (204 calories per ounce—compared with 203 for butter, 159 for sunflower seeds and for halvah, 144 for semisweet chocolate, 112 for Milkman dried milk, 109 for granulated sugar, 105 for spaghetti, 99 for dried red pinto beans, 74 for caviar, 28 for raw brook trout [flesh only], 14 for raw brook trout [whole] and also for yogurt made from partially skimmed milk, 3 for watermelon [raw, whole] and 120 for zwieback. (But note that lard packs 256 calories; salad or cooking oil, 251.) In spite of the antifat strictures in the gospel of the hour (page 162), I usually take 2 or 3 ounces of margarine for a week's trip. In trout country I often carry an extra 4 ounces, for frying.*

Fruit-drink mixes used to mean Wyler's or Kool-Aid or similar in some flavor that pleased you. (One reader wrote that he had heard grape juice was the best thirst quencher, but I suspect his informant of being a straight-faced W. C. Fields.) Such sugary concoctions are pleasant quick-energy sources that disguise the taste of unappetizing water. But what you drink at halts can now, much more importantly, also be a means of replenishing the electrolytes (potassium and sodium, and chloride radicals) that you lose in sweating. Gatorade, in crystal form, will do the job. But I find that Gookinaid ERG (Electrolyte Replacement with Glucose, developed by Bill Gookin, a marathon runner) does it even better and seems to lie much more lightly on the stomach. (In hot weather I drink a quart of the stuff per set of tennis singles, and thrive.) ERG comes in 1.8-ounce envelopes (makes one quart, $.65), 7.1-ounce envelopes (makes one gallon, $1.65) and 35-ounce plastic tubs (makes 5 gallons, $5.50). The potassium-sodium ratio of ERG is reputedly calibrated with that of the average human sweat according to the manufac-

---

* This paragraph set me toying with the idea of a new appendix listing calories per ounce for a wide range of backpacking foods. In the end I decided "no." And not only because the job would be a pain in the butt. Such a list might dangerously mislead earnest people who ignored such vital factors as nutritional balance, minimum protein requirements, upper fat and sugar limits, vitamin and mineral requirements and the need for some fiber and at least some variety—not to mention the vagaries of taste. Anyway, if you really want such figures, consult *Agricultural Handbook No. 8* (which, as you have no doubt zwiebacked out, is what I did). Scan Table 2, Column D, and divide by 16.

turers, human sweat ranges from 31 to 47 percent potassium, 18 to 37 percent sodium; and ERG provides 42.1 percent potassium, 32.4 percent sodium—while Gatorade has 9.8 percent and 48.3 percent, respectively. The degree of dilution of the ERG powder (one 1.8-ounce envelope to a quart of water) is therefore important. If you need or are prepared to carry a full quart canteen, no problem. Otherwise, eye-stimate one-quarter of an envelope to a cup or baby bottle (page 207). This leads us into the whole question of

Electrolyte replacement. When you sweat you lose not only water but also the electrolytic salts, potassium and sodium chloride (see above), and without them in the right proportions, electrical processes within the body become impaired. Unless you replace both water and salts you may suffer from heat exhaustion.

In the past, electrolyte replacement was seen as a matter of "salt" replacement. That is, replacement of sodium chloride. Hence the popularity of salt tablets—which actually often contain potassium chloride too. But although the whole subject remains controversial it now seems generally accepted that, except possibly for people on very stringent low-sodium diets, no one is likely to suffer from sodium deficiency, no matter how much sweat pours out. (Note that most backpacking foods are riddled with salt.) Potassium deficiency after heavy sweating is entirely possible (though the matter is complicated by the possibility that the body can, with considerable consumption of energy—which helps to cool it—transmute sodium to potassium).

On a practical level, then, the response to heavy sweating should be replacement of *all* lost materials. First and most important, the water—if possible, in small, frequently consumed quantities, so that no serious deficiency arises. Second, along with the water, potassium in the form of the chloride. And third and least important (mainly for the transmutation process rather than direct replacement), the sodium. ERG accomplishes these aims perfectly, provided its concentration is right. Salt tablets, the old standbys, should probably be avoided, not only because the potassium/sodium ratio is wrong but also because consuming them without the right amounts of water can insult internal balances and cause serious illness. In cases of suspected heat prostration, Lite Salt (with half the sodium of regular salt and much more potassium) or No Salt (rich in potassium, almost sodium-free), taken in large quantities of water, is safer and more effective than tablets. As a preventive measure, use Lite Salt or No Salt in your shaker (as I have done for years) and sprinkle profusely over meals.

Some authorities now deny that any such precautions are necessary. Supply a little potassium, they say, and you can't get electrolyte deficiency. Along with a lot of people, I disagree. Twice—once backpacking in desert, once after a long summer day's tennis—I have suffered what I still cannot see as anything but electrolyte deficiency. On the other hand, there seems little doubt that individual requirements vary widely. Years ago, when salt tablets were still standard, a Death Valley ranger told me, "When it reaches 110° F., I take one tablet a day. I need that one, but my stomach won't accept more. Yet there's a guy at Park HQ who has to take twenty a day. If he doesn't he ends up in the hospital."

Important footnote: It now seems generally accepted that too much sodium, at least in some people, raises blood pressure and can increase the likelihood of heart attacks. And do not assume that such strictures apply only to old crocks with marginally high blood pressure. There is some evidence that it pays to reduce sodium intake as early in life as possible.

Vitamins. See page 163. Some people backpack with the whole quinque-alphabet in tablet form. To improve performance on long high-altitude expeditions, others take Vitamin E or Stress Potency C and D complex. I continue to rely on my fresh-food-at-home body reserve, plus additives in the dehydrated foods and maybe dried seaweed. The one exception: Vitamin C. Although the medical establishment still seems to scorn Linus Pauling's *Vitamin C and the Common Cold,* some doctors, the general public and I find we have to go along. When backpacking I take one 500-mg. tablet every day I don't forget; and I carry a reserve so that if a cold strikes a couple of days out from the civilization that passed it along, I can suppress the effects with a first dose of 1000 mg. and then 500 every few hours. Of course, nobody, but nobody in his right rutted mind believes Pauling's assertions that Vitamin C can also curb or even cure cancer. Well, almost nobody: I see that Blue Cross of California now suggest that it may nullify the cancer-causing effects of sodium nitrite— a preservative often used in cured meats such as bologna and, that's right, meat bars. So maybe even the ruts are being overrun.

I have recently been experimenting with spirulina—a vitamin source but also much more. See page 183.

Emergency ration. It is probably wise to carry a small emergency ration of some sort, just in case of trouble. I now carry, in lieu of the vanished Wilson's meat bar, an extra Bear Valley Pemmican (page 167).

Morale-boosting: goodies. If you have been living on dehydrated food for days or weeks or months you will not hesitate, given half a chance, to call in at a cafe (as I could occasionally on the California walk) and order a red-blooded steak or whatever your fantasies have been featuring. Even under more Spartan conditions you may be able to engineer a change of pace, beyond such delicacies as small trout so fresh that it's a problem to keep them from curling double in the frying pan: consult your palate and pack along one small, fully hedonistic meal.

If you really pine for fresh greens, consider Sprout Packs. Described as a "Take Along Garden," the seeds come in a large "tea bag" sealed inside a Ziploc bag. "Keep the tea bag dry," say the directions, "and the seeds keep indefinitely. But if you soak the seeds overnight, drain them, seal them in the Ziploc bag and put them in a dark place in your pack, they'll grow as you go. By the third day on the trail you'll have a bag of tasty, crunchy alfalfa, radish, sunflower and azuki sprouts to munch. Take several Sprout Packs and keep one growing all the time for fresh food all during your trip." (About 1 ounce; $1.95 each; The Sprout Pack Co., 2145 Everding, Eureka, CA 95501.) This sounds, at the very least, an interesting idea for successive rest days. Similar packs, under such names as Kitchen Crisp, are now appearing in health stores and even supermarkets.

On my Grand Canyon walk I included in each cache and airdrop one can of delectables—oysters, lobster, cocktail meatballs, fish appetizers or frog's legs—and a small bottle of claret. The goodies were great. But the claret, oddly enough, did not really fit in. And I decided that you simply didn't need alcohol in the wilderness. Not when you were on your own, anyway. Yet nowadays I find that I often, but not always, take along a snort of bourbon. This change no doubt indicates a heightening of common sense, mellowness or depravity.

Purists still maintain that the only satisfactory container for booze is glass, but I find that the little hip flasks made of special hard plastic

(10-ounce capacity; 2 ounces; $2.75) leave bourbon unblurred. A reader writes that "Lemon Hart or Hudson's Bay Demerara rum, at 151 proof, gives you twice the mileage for half the weight." The math seems murky but the idea sound.

Even if you deplore solitary drinking there's no denying that a little

Scotch or bourbon (or potent rum) can be very welcome in a group at the end of a day. Especially in a group of two. A bottle, or even half-bottle, of champagne carried secretly in a male chauvinist's pack and then produced with a flourish from a cold creek at lunch or dinnertime may just possibly help melt a damsel's heart. And there is absolutely nothing, of course, to prevent a damsel chauvinist from trying her delicate hand at male-heart-melting.

Packaging—and repackaging

The foil envelopes in which freeze-dried foods come (because air must be rigorously excluded until they're used) have a very long shelf-life; but they will sometimes crack under bottom-of-the-pack buffeting —though the best are now becoming very tough indeed. The foil cannot be burned, cannot be burned, cannot be burned and must be packed out, must be packed out, must be packed out (page 269). Note, for paranoid weight-saving moods, that the edges of many foil packages can be trimmed, especially up top, where holes for store display live.

The polyethylene that houses most vacuum-dried foods—and that also forms standard supermarket plastic bags—gives the illusion of being burnable. But in fact there is always a residue, and I now pack out such empties. Polyethylene is moisture-proof for reasonable periods but there is some degree of porosity (for an alternative, see below). In damp climates the packages should if possible be stored or cached in airtight cans, preferably with some desiccant such as silica gel or Drierite (anhydrous calcium sulfate), which come with moisture indicators and can be regenerated by baking. (Silica gel from VWR Scientific Company, Box 3200, San Francisco, CA 94119; Drierite from them too, and from W. A. Hammond Drierite Company, Xenia, OH 45385.)

If you choose to buy in bulk (page 172) and repackage you must take certain precautions. Because of the very short storage life of freeze-dried foods after opening you cannot satisfactorily repack them. But if you buy vacuum-dried products in bulk you can repackage into small amounts that suit your requirements by buying small polycell heat-seal bags and sealing along the open edge by pressure with a warm iron. Ditto if you dehydrate your own foods (page 165). The plastic called Mylar affords a better air-and-moisture barrier than polyethylene, which is somewhat permeable. But Mylar is not readily heat-sealable. Laminated Mylar/polyethylene bags, eminently heat-sealable, can be bought in ½-pint, 1-pint and 2-pint sizes in some department stores. The current Sears, Roebuck catalogue lists (on the same page as the electric toasters, fry pans, etc.) a small household heat-sealer machine for about $25.

.   .   .

I am not menu-minded. The meticulous culinary briefings that beguile so many people leave me emotionally inert, intellectually repelled. But there is no doubt about the general beguilement. Backpacking magazines and books steam with menus. One recent magazine classified read: "FOOD PLANNING DONE! Prepackage for whole season. Nutrition tips. 3 week menu, shopping list, recipes for lightweight, inexpensive, spoilage-free eating. $3.25." And another: "DELICIOUS vegetarian backpacking menu and recipes. Detailed menu for 7 days. Send $3.00." Then there are three recommended paperback books expressing attitudes quite different from mine: *Simple Foods for the Pack* by Vikki Kinmont and Claudia Axcell (Sierra Club Books, 1976, 8½ ounces, $5.95)—consisting of practical natural-food menus that are meatless, sugarless, chemical-free and inexpensive; *Backpacker's Cookbook* by Margaret Cross and Dean Fiske (Ten-Speed Press, Berkeley, CA, 1974, 8 ounces, $3.95)—good, common-sense instructions, including menus, for "eating well from your pack"; and an attractive newcomer, *The Hungry Hiker's Book of Good Cooking* by Gretchen McHugh (Knopf, 1982, 15 ounces, $8.95).

As I say, this is not my bag. And my immediate reaction to the prospect of compiling a current, personal

Specimen food list

was to say, "The hell with it!" But there remain valid reasons for doing so, and I guess I had better have a go this time around too.

No perfect food list for every trip exists, of course. It's not only that we have to meet the varying demands of weather, terrain, load and trip length: our theories, tastes and prejudices change; and most of us experiment. So I specifically do not say that my list shows what I am nowadays likely to carry for a typical week's trip. But it includes only things I have tried and found satisfactory. It is offered primarily as an up-to-date starting point from which beginners can work out their own salvations, and the selection is designed to suggest ideas and sources and at the same time to convey as much information as possible about quantities, nutritional values and costs of items fairly readily available to Western backpackers. Easterners, I'm afraid, may need to translate a few items.

For the list, see pages 184–5.

My menu and cooking methods place me, I guess, somewhere around midway on the scale of current backpackers' eating systems.

At one extreme on the scale (upper or lower, take your pick) crouch the fancy cookers, simmering, steaming, sautéing, baking and otherwise gourmeting; all terribly civilized. I'm afraid I have nothing of value to offer in this field—beyond drawing your attention to a couple of fancy utensils (page 211).

At the other extreme march

The New Wave eaters.

Naturally, there is wide variation within this subdivision: all that its members share, really, is the burning desire to pare their loads. But some hard-core New Wavers (and even a few Old Wavers) never cook.

You can, of course, forgo cooking and still ingest just as many calories as a gourmet. In my sample menu Bear Valley Pemmican, cold cereal, salads, trail snacks and staples demand no cooking; and with a little imagination you could increase and augment them into a 4000- or 5000-calorie diet. Starting from scratch it would be even easier. It all depends on how austerely you are willing to eat. A few New Wavers have pushed austerity to the limit: they apparently subsist, largely or even entirely, on a form of black magic, blue-green in color.

Spirulina (spear oo LEE nuh) is a blue-green algal plankton now being commercially harvested, mainly in a Mexican lake, and sold in pill, capsule and powder form. Although a vegetable organism, its 70-percent protein content is said to be "higher than [that of] any other known natural food." And the protein, which includes all 21 amino acids, is 80–95 percent digestible. Spirulina is also rich in Vitamin A, in the entire B Complex and in iron, phosphorus, zinc, potassium, magnesium, and calcium. It has traces of selenium and chromium. There is "no evidence of any side effects or complications" from heavy ingestion of spirulina; it is 4 percent nucleic acid (RNA and DNA), which "some scientists suggest may be dangerous to the human body"—but others maintain that such amounts are no greater than those in most vegetables we eat, and lower than those in yeast and cheese (and at least one doctor recommends nucleics to counteract the aging process). Spirulina can be stored up to seven years with practically no protein loss. It is a very concentrated food and if taken regularly demands plenty of water drunk throughout the day. Digestibility is high: you experience both a long-lasting and an immediate energy boost.

Now, I must warn you that everything I have said so far about spirulina is based foursquare on sales blurb. But the figures, if not the hyperbole, appear on every label and have presumably been eagle-eyed

Net wt. oz.	Quantity	Item	Brand	For # days	Energy value calories[a]	Calories Prot.	Calories Fat	Calories CH	Protein grams	Cost $	Based on price of
		BREAKFASTS									
6	6	Instant oatmeal (pkgs.)	Quaker	2[b]	600	111	102	387	8	.95	1.59/10
8	—	Cereal mix (cold)	Familia	1[b]	904	112	166	626	28	1.24	4.99/2 lbs.
6	2	Ramen	(Supermarket)	2	792	80	288	424	20	.50	.25 ea.
3.75	1	Bear Valley Pemmican	Intermountain	1	420	68	104	248	17	.98	.98 ea.
2	1	Bacon bar	Richmoor	1[c]	267	80	179	8	20	2.25	2.25 ea.
		LUNCHES									
5	2	Soups (Green Pea, Leek)	Knorr	2	630	106	184	340	22	1.78	.89 ea.
6	2	Ramen	(Supermarket)	2	792	80	288	424	20	.50	.25 ea.
2.75	1	Tuna salad	Mountain House	1	440	104	232	104	24	2.80	2.80 ea.
7.5	2	Bear Valley Pemmican	Intermountain	2	840	136	208	496	34	1.96	.98 ea.
		DINNERS									
6.5	1	Chicken and Rice	Weepak	1	761	160	253	348	37	5.85	5.85 ea.
7	1	Sweet and Sour Shrimp (Natural High)	Richmoor	1	624	124	80	420	31	4.39	4.39 ea.
7.6	2	Chili Mac with beef	Mountain House	2	1000	196	296	508	48	5.60	2.80 ea.
3.5	—	Minute Rice	(Supermarket)	1	382	38	—	344	10	.40	1.59/14 oz.
1.5	1	Peas	Weepak		139	38	5	96	10	1.50	1.50 ea.
2	1	Diced chicken	Weepak		213	130	83	—	37	4.20	4.20 ea.
3.5	—	Couscous	(Supermarket)		331	46	18	267	13	.40	1.19/lb.
1.5	1	Carrot slices	Weepak	1	139	9	4	126	3	.90	.90 ea.
2	1	Diced beef	Weepak		275	134	141	—	32	4.25	4.25 ea.
5	—	Spaghetti	(Supermarket)		500	65	29	406	17	.22	.70/lb.
0.5	—	Tomato sauce (powder)	(Supermarket)	1	43	6	3	34	2	.18	1.26/3.5 oz.
2	1	Meat bar	Richmoor		319	108	211	—	27	2.25	2.25 ea.
3	—	Pinto beans	(Supermarket)		290	75	9	206	19	.06	.33/lb.
2	1	Diced beef	Weepak	1	275	134	141	—	32	4.25	4.25 ea.
2	1	Corn	Richmoor		236	24	18	194	6	1.95	1.95 ea.
1	—	Gravy powder	(Supermarket)	2 +	100	20	10	70	5	.39	.39/1 oz.
1	—	Herbs, spices and trimmings	(Supermarket)	7	—	—	—	—	—	—	—

Net wt. oz.	Quantity	Item	Brand	For # days	Energy value calories[a]	Calories Prot.	Calories Fat	Calories CH	Protein grams	Cost $	Based on price of
		TRAIL SNACKS[d]									
16	—	Gorp	(Supermarket)	7	2208	230	928	1050	58	2.97	2.97/lb.
28	—	Semisweet chocolate	(Supermarket)	7	3887	135	2163	1589	34	7.63	1.09/4 oz.
12	7	Candies	(Supermarket)	7	1313	—	31	1282	—	1.04	1.39/lb.
10	—	Nuts (mixed)	(Supermarket)	7	1800	190	1380	230	50	3.31	2.15/6½ oz.
	—	Banana chips	(Supermarket)	7	193	9	4	180	3	.18	1.47/lb.
3.38	3	Halvah (or similar) bars	(Supermarket)	7	541	53	329	159	14	.63	.21 ea.
0.75	1	Strawberries (sliced)	Mountain House	7	52	4	—	48	1	2.35	2.35 ea.
2	—	Beef jerky	Richmoor	7	220	156	64	—	19	4.39	4.39/2 oz.
		STAPLES									
6	—	Granulated sugar	(Supermarket)	7	663	—	—	663	—	.21	1.09/2 lbs.
17.2	5	Milk powder (envelopes)	Milkman	7	1900	706	228	966	175	2.47	5.89/12
3.5	—	Protein powder	Plus Formula 398	7	319	319	—	—	83	2.02	6.95/12 oz.
2.5	—	Margarine	(Supermarket)	7	515	2	512	1	1	.16	.99/lb.
2.5	ca. 25	Tea bags	Lipton et al.	7	—	—	—	—	—	.94	1.80/48
12.5	—	Drink mix	Gookinaid ERG	7	1332	—	—	1332	—	1.93	5.50/35 oz.-tub
3	—	Salt (or salt substitute), pepper	(Supermarket)	7	—	—	—	—	—	.16	60/11 oz.
1	ca. 30	Vitamin C (tablets)	(Supermarket)	7	—	—	—	—	—	.71	11.79/500
1	28	Spirulina tablets (750 mg.)	(Health-food store)	7	77	77	—	—	1	2.66	9.50/100
14 lb. 0[e] oz.		→ Total for One Week			26,332	4065[f]	8691[f]	13,576	961	83.51	
2 lb. 0 oz.		→ Average Daily Total			3762	581	1242	1939	137	11.93	

a. You can quibble forever, happily but quite fatuously, about precise calorie contents. My sources: manufacturers or *Agricultural Handbook No. 8*.

b. Preferably boosted with protein powder and perhaps modified to taste with trail snacks, especially gorp, bananas, chocolate. Cold cereal also for snacks and boosting other breakfasts.

c. Carbohydrates added to taste from cereal, trail snacks.

d. Often used with meals too—mixed in or as corner-fillers.

e. Gross weight (with packaging) probably about 1½ pounds extra.

f. Despite all my fine words about cutting fat and protein intake, these fat and protein percentages turn out to be marginally higher than in the last edition's sample menu. I am surprised—and tempted to tamper. But I'll let the figures stand as certificates of the difficulty of achieving what remains a worthy intent. I'm confident, anyway, that even if you had noticed this discrepancy you would not have been mean-spirited enough to drag my attention to it but would, if it had bothered you, have quietly eliminated your margarine and nuts and maybe chocolate. Right?

by the USDA. There certainly seems to be a growing band of people swearing blue-green murder that spirulina does matchless things for their minds and bodies. But it is probably too early for a clear verdict: spirulina is now "in," and so must be viewed with suspicion. My own desultory experimentation suggests that the stuff either does me good or is a splendid placebo; and, as in all such cases, it hardly seems to matter which is "true." Recommended daily dosage "if consuming regular meals": 3 grams, or 6 tablets.

But the really revolutionary claim made for spirulina is that it "can greatly reduce the quantity and quality of other food needs"—and can even form the sole solid constituent of a diet. The suggested daily requirement, "if consuming just liquids," is 30 grams. Now, a backpacking menu streamlined to water plus 60 500-mg. tablets a day, weight 1.07 ounces, opens up fragrant possibilities. But does it work? One New Waver I know says he thrives on such a diet, or something close to it— though it takes time for his body to adjust to the lack of bulk and to the need for only one bowel movement about every four days. I have heard other similar, unconfirmed stories. And one of my nutritional advisors tells me that during a period of extreme grief, when she stayed up day and night for a week and took frequent long walks, she lived entirely on water and 30 spirulina tablets a day and maintained high energy levels without any debilitation—though with some weight loss that may have been at least partly due to her emotional state. (She says spirulina is not suitable for everyone: her mother tried it during the same period and suffered marked allergic reactions.) Such reports seem at first glance to leave us with only four possible conclusions: the reports are false; the people involved have done themselves hidden, long-range harm; they metabolize in a bizarrely unfair way; or our current ideas about nutrition, bulk and calorie needs are a load of crap. But one backpacker I know offers a fifth possible explanation: While walking the most rugged section of the Appalachian Trail he subsisted for four days on water and spirulina powder (with a few fresh raspberries on the last and longest day, when he covered 32 miles). And he found that he walked with even greater gusto than on a regular diet. "At the time," he told me, "I thought spirulina was 'it!' But since then I've fasted for several days while walking hard and found myself with even higher energy levels. I've come to the conclusion that a great deal of the whole nutritional business is mental."

If that sounds deplorably unscientific to you, and you sort of rather go along with scientific thinking, remember that Konrad Lorenz, Nobel Prize-winning zoologist, said, "Truth, in science, can be defined as the working hypothesis best fitted to open the way to the next better one." So just hang around.

.   .   .

Any noncooking regimen, even short of nothing-but-spirulina-and-water, promises stunning advantages—and possible penalties.

The fundamental argument of noncookers is that an ounce of extra food provides far more calories for the body than does an ounce of fuel used to heat food. So far, so true. But if you do not cook you save much more than fuel weight. You need carry no stove or accessories, no pots, no utensils beyond a cup. Already we have eliminated over 4 pounds. But that is by no means the end of it: you can also get by with a far smaller tent, even in foul weather. (In snow, noncooking New Wavers say, you simply "eat" snow—letting body heat convert it to drink.) A tiny tent, or bivvy sack, will save maybe 2 or 3 pounds, compared with a bigger model. And if you carry your noncooking to the spirulina extreme you eliminate in food alone, for a week's trip, 14 pounds or so.

Not cooking saves time too. "It makes life so simple," says my practitioner informant. "On one recent trip I made a severe error: I forgot to take a book. And I repeatedly found that when I had done everything —taken all the pictures I wanted to take, washed myself, admired all the views—there was nothing to do. So I ended up walking all day." I suspect that most people find, like me, that on a normal backpacking day there is always enough, if not too much, to be done—and would revel in the richness of more spare time.

But it seems to me that noncooking may impose unacceptable burdens—even millstones. I mean more than the heavy load of deprivation laid on incurable fancy cookers or, even more onerously, on tea or coffee addicts. For I do not think we should write off the pure efficiency value —perhaps even survival value—of hot food. It could be dangerous to dismiss its effects as "psychological"—as if that were something utterly detached from "physiological." A thought, after all, "is" molecular movement—and as such can surely be affected by immediately available calories; furthermore, the nature of your thoughts in critical situations can radically influence your survival chances. And while it may be just possible to dismiss a hot breakfast drink as mere hedonism, I can only regard a hot dinner differently.*

Just before dinner, at the end of a long, hard day's walking, there often comes a moment when you suffer from something suspiciously like incipient hypothermia (page 574). All day you have been sweating freely.

* About that hot breakfast drink, though: A reader has sent me a neat calculation, based on drinking one cup (¼ liter) of tea or other hot beverage to bring him back to early-morning life. If the drink is at 80° C (the upper limit of tolerability) it provides, in cooling down to body temperature of 30° C, 12½ calories—enough for 7½ minutes of basal metabolism for the average person. And these calories are immediately available, surging through you, and therefore set you up to assimilate the main breakfast and get on with the day. As the reader writes: "This system does not make me fast or efficient in the morning. Nothing can. But it does simplify getting up."

As soon as you stop, you put on warm clothing. But for a few minutes, as the sweat dries, you feel not only on the verge of coldness but also mentally and physically sluggish. These symptoms are the classic early signs of hypothermia. I am not suggesting that in most such cases they are at all dangerous, or even serious, but I notice that in my case they often persist until a hot meal sends warmth coursing through me (see, for example, page 434). To overcome the sluggishness and prod me into preparing dinner, I often supply my body with quick energy in the form of a little sugar-rich food. And although that tends to help marginally, it is only after I get hot food inside me that I feel the internal radiators turn on. In other words, far below the danger level, your body may need hot food to get the furnace roaring. If hypothermia approaches the critical stage, of course, you may need hot food to keep the fires from falling below the point of no return—and flickering out (page 574). So a non-cooking regimen, it seems to me, might possibly prove highly inefficient, even dangerous: in critical situations you would have no practical way of providing hot food when the need began to crystallize in your already sluggish brain.

Now, please do not read these thoughts as blanket condemnation of noncooking—any more than the preceding list of advantages as a blanket recommendation. I am merely expressing cautious misgivings. Noncooking may turn out to be the Wave of the Future. I suggest, anyway, that it is possible, as so often happens in life, to benefit from the actions of extremists without stumbling into their snakepits. For al fresco eaters form a continuum, from the fanciest cookers to the spirulina Spartans. It has always been so. John Muir apparently used to subsist largely on bread. Teddy Roosevelt probably did not. And even down toward the austere end of the continuum you can ring almost infinite changes. Tibetans, I understand, favor a day-after-day menu that is soul-sustaining in both hot and cold weather, easy to carry and prepare, and surprisingly palatable: hot tea with butter and salt, mixed to a gruel with parched barley. (Note that this traditional menu meets almost all our current complicated criteria—yea, unto a caffeine fix.) But if you want to travel with a light and simple kitchen, regard all such models as no more than signposts. Devise a menu that suits and satisfies your own tastes. Keep modifying it too. For years, whenever conditions demanded or indicated, I carried only a "rock-bottom, tin-can kitchen" (page 278) designed to boil water but do little more. Under that regimen I sometimes subsisted, ad nauseam—breakfast, lunch and dinner—on meat bars, mitigated only by tea, trail snacks and fruit drink. I once ad-nauseamed it like that for ten days in some Arizona mountains and emerged fit and happy with lots of miles and no vomiting behind me—though I did cheat with one fancy rest-day lunch that tasted, I admit, transcendentally ambrosial. On other occasions I mitigated further with such thrilling variations as bacon bars, dry cereal and dried fruit. Today, because I know of no acceptable meat bar, I would substitute Bear Valley Pemmican—perhaps with soup for furnace-stoking dinner—and thereby cut the cooking even further. Or I might take Mountain House no-pot-needed packages and, though losing some simplicity and a point or two on my ounce/calorie rating, achieve a more varied diet. I repeat, though, that the important thing is to suit your own taste and temperament. Experiment. And keep experimenting. You are limited by little but your imagination.

In the last edition of this book I outlined the then-new Swedish system of dietary preparation for an endurance event: eating fat and protein almost exclusively for about three days to deplete glycogen stores and then, in the last three or four days before the event, adding large amounts of carbohydrate to the diet. At the time I expressed a natural and necessary skepticism, especially for such extended "events" as back-packing. And an advisor now says that a consensus seems to regard the system as valid, if at all, only for such relatively short-spurt activities as marathon running; as something that does not suit everybody even then; and as too often producing undesirable side effects. But remember Konrad Lorenz. Once again, if you're not happy with the way things seem to stand right now, just hang around.

WATER

You can if necessary do without food for days or even weeks and still live, but if you go very long without water you assuredly die. In really hot deserts the limit of survival without water may be barely forty-eight hours. And well before that your brain is likely to become so addled that there is a serious risk of committing some irrational act that will kill you.

Dangers of dehydration

Too few people recognize the insidious nature of such thirst-induced irrationality. It can swamp you, suddenly and irretrievably, without your being in the least aware of it.*

* The length of time a man can survive without water, or with very little, will clearly depend not only on his build, health and state of mind but also on how much exercise he

I described one such case in *The Man Who Walked Through Time*. In July 1959 a thirty-two-year-old priest and two teenage boys tried to follow an old trail down one side of Grand Canyon to the Colorado. They carried little or no water. More than halfway down, hot and tired and already very thirsty, the priest made the barely rational decision to climb back to the rim. Before long the trio lost their way. Next morning, desperately dehydrated, they tried to follow a wash back to the river. Soon they came to a sheer eighty-foot drop-off. The priest, apparently irrational by now, had all three take off their shoes and throw them to the bottom. Then he tried to climb down. A few feet, and he fell to his death. The boys soon found a passable route but one of them died on the way down to the river. The other was rescued by helicopter a week later, eight miles downstream.

I know only the bare outline of this story. But a few years ago I interviewed many times, and eventually wrote a magazine article about, two boys who were trapped in the Mojave Desert. This is not a walking

---

takes and on ambient temperature, humidity, wind and available shade. Still, the following table makes interesting reading:

WATER REQUIREMENTS

Maximum daily temperature (°F.) in shade	0	\multicolumn{6}{c}{Available water per man, U.S. quarts}

			1 qt	2 qts	4 qts	10 qts	20 qts
	Maximum daily temperature (°F.) in shade	0	1 qt	2 qts	4 qts	10 qts	20 qts
				Days of expected survival			
	120°	2	2	2	2.5	3	4.5
	110	3	3	3.5	4	5	7
NO WALKING AT ALL	100	5	5.5	6	7	9.5	13.5
	90	7	8	9	10.5	15	23
	80	9	10	11	13	19	29
	70	10	11	12	14	20.5	32
	60	10	11	12	14	21	32
	50	10	11	12	14.5	21	32

	Maximum daily temperature (°F.) in shade	0	1 qt	2 qts	4 qts	10 qts
			\multicolumn{5}{c}{Available water per man, U.S. quarts}	
				Days of expected survival		
	120°	1	2	2	2.5	3
WALKING AT NIGHT UNTIL EXHAUSTED AND RESTING THEREAFTER	110	2	2	2.5	3	3.5
	100	3	3.5	3.5	4.5	5.5
	90	5	5.5	5.5	6.5	8
	80	7	7.5	8	9.5	11.5
	70	7.5	8	9	10.5	13.5
	60	8	8.5	9	11	14
	50	8	8.5	9	11	14

© Reprinted from *Physiology of Man in the Desert*, by E. F. Adolph and Associates (Interscience Publishers, New York, 1947).

story, but it is the only case in which I know full details of the kind of irrationality that any dehydrated hiker could all too easily develop. The boys were Gary Beeman, eighteen, and Jim Twomey, sixteen. Their car bogged down near midnight in soft sand, 200 feet off a remote gravel side road. It was June. Daytime shade temperatures probably approached 120° F. Humidity was virtually zero. The only liquid foods in the car were two cans of soup and one of pineapple juice, plus two pints of water. By the end of the first day—during most of which the boys rested in the shade of some nearby rocks—they had finished all the liquid. That night, working feebly, they moved the car barely fifteen feet back toward the firm gravel.

The second day, back among the rocks, both boys suffered delirium. At sunset Jim Twomey staggered toward the car. Suddenly he sank to his knees, pitched forward and lay still. The older boy, Gary, saw him fall. In midafternoon he had staggered irrationally out from the shade of the rocks into blazing sunlight in order to "try to find some water," and had finally dug himself into the cool sand. Now he felt less lightheaded. He went over to his friend and bent over him. Jim's face was deathly pale. His mouth hung open. Dried mucus flecked his scaly white lips. Gary hurried to the car, searched feverishly through the inferno inside it and at last found a bottle of after-shave lotion. He wrenched off the top and put the bottle to his lips. The shock of what tasted like hot rubbing alcohol brought him up short. He had a brief, horrible comprehension of his unhinged state of mind. Afterward all he could think was, "We need a drink. We both need a drink."

Desperately he ran his eyes over the car. For a moment he considered letting air out of the tires and somehow capturing its coolness. Then he was thinking, "My God, the radiator!" He had always known that in the desert your radiator water could save you; yet for two days he had ignored it! Again he had that terrible momentary comprehension of his state of mind. Then he grabbed a saucepan, squirmed under the front bumper and unscrewed the drainage tap. A stream of rust-brown water poured down over the greasy, dust-encrusted sway bar and splashed into the saucepan. "That water," he told me later, "was the most wonderful sight I had ever seen."

After he had drunk a little, Gary found himself thinking more clearly. He went back and poured some water into Jim's open mouth. Quite quickly Jim revived. All at once Gary saw what should have been obvious all along: a way to run the car clear, using some old railroad ties they had found much earlier. He spent almost the whole night aligning the ties—five or six hours for a job that would normally have taken him twenty minutes. At sunrise he helped his half-conscious friend into the car and made what he knew—because they had now finished the radiator water—would have to be their last attempt, however it ended. Moments later, with wheels spinning madly and the bucking car threatening to stall at any second, they shot back onto the gravel road. Four hours later, after many sweltering halts for the now dry motor to cool, they hit a highway.

Since that day Gary has never driven into the desert without stocking up his car with at least 15 gallons of what he now calls "the most precious liquid in the world."*

Important: Note that I tell this story only to illustrate the quick onset and dangerous nature of thirst-induced irrationality. Today almost all cars come with coolant solutions containing ethylene glycol in their radiators, and ethylene glycol is deadly poisonous to man, even heavily diluted. Worse, the first symptoms resemble drunkenness or delirium, which in the desert could easily be misconstrued.

Conservation of body fluids

You can very easily, in your minute-by-minute behavior, take sensible steps to conserve your body's precious water. People brought up in hot climates often train themselves, early, to reduce losses on torrid days by keeping their mouths closed. Talking is reduced to the minimum. The moist membranes of the mouth certainly lose a lot of water if exposed to free air, and such precautions are well worth taking.

Theory and folklore suggest you wear clothes that cover almost all your skin and so reduce perspiration loss. But other factors come into it, and in practice I tend to do exactly the opposite (pages 427–8).

For recycling of body fluids in a solar still, see page 202.

For replacement of essential electrolytes lost through sweating, see page 177.

How much water to carry

When you're backpacking you can't play it as safe as Gary Beeman now does and carry 15 gallons of water (1 U.S. gallon weighs 8⅓ pounds); but in any kind of dry country you'll have to carry more than you would like to.

* When I asked Jim Twomey how he had felt when his friend came with the radiator water, he said, "Oh, I just wanted him to leave me alone. I was so tired. You know, I'm fairly sure I'd never have regained consciousness if Gary hadn't brought that water, and I guess it sounds a pretty horrible way to die. But it isn't. I wasn't suffering at all—just terribly tired. All I wanted to do was to lie down and go to sleep, quite peacefully, and never have to wake up again."

In the mountains you may not need to pack along any at all—though even in the mountains there are often long, hot stretches without a creek or lake or snowbank, and unless I am sure of a regular supply I tend to carry at least a cupful in a canteen. In deserts water becomes the most precious item in your pack—and often the heaviest. In the drier parts of Grand Canyon I left each widely spaced water source carrying at least 2 gallons. Together with the four canteens, that meant a 19¾-pound water load. At the start of several long dry stretches I carried a third gallon in a disposable plastic liquid-bleach bottle from a food cache. On such occasions I would walk for a couple of hours in the cool of evening, drink copiously at dinner and breakfast, then leave in the morning, fresh and fully hydrated, on a long and waterless stretch that was now two critical hours shorter than it had been.

The amount of water you need under specific conditions is something you must work out for yourself. As with food, requirements vary a great deal from man to man (though see page 189, footnote).*

For me, half a gallon is under normal conditions a comfortable ration for a dry night stop, provided I am sure of finding more by midmorning. In temperatures around 90°, and in near-zero desert humidity, a gallon once lasted me thirty-six hours, during which I walked a flat but rather soft-surfaced thirty miles or so with no appreciable discomfort, though with no washing or tooth-cleaning either. But I was steely fit at the time, and well acclimated; I would not dream of attempting that stretch "cold" with so little water.

I always lean toward safety. I can recall only three occasions on which I have been at all uncomfortably thirsty, even in the desert; and lack of water has never even threatened to become a real danger. It pays to remember, though, that only a hair's breadth divides safety from potential tragedy. If you are alone, one moment of carelessness or ill luck could send you stumbling across the threshold: a twisted ankle miles from water would probably be enough; certainly a broken leg or a rattle-snake bite. I try to make some kind of allowance for such possibilities, but in the end you have to rely mostly on caution and luck. Perhaps the two are not altogether unconnected. An ancient Persian proverb has it that "Fortune is infatuated with the efficient."

* Small, wiry men are generally regarded as better adapted to living in deserts than are big, muscular ones. In a sense this is true. As any solid increases in size, its volume is cubed every time its surface area is squared. So the bigger a man's body, the less surface area it has for each unit of volume; and the surface, or skin, is where we lose excess heat, mainly through perspiration. As usual, though, there are compensations—both ways. Although small men are able to keep their body temperature down more efficiently than are big men, this extra sweat efficiency means that they tend to drink more water for their size than big men do. And because a rough relationship exists in most cases between bodyweight and acceptable load (see page 32), big men can normally carry heavier weights—and therefore more water.

How often to drink

The old Spartan routine of drinking water at infrequent intervals, and rarely if ever between meals, is perhaps necessary for military formations: only that way can you satisfactorily impose group discipline. But for individuals the method is inefficient. For one thing, you tend to drink unnecessarily large quantities when at last you get the canteen to your lips. And although thirst may not become an actual physical discomfort, you often walk for hours with your mind blinkered by a kind of dehydrated scum that seals off any vivid appreciation of the world around you.

In well-watered country I take a drink, if I feel like it, at any convenient creek or lake. (At least, I used to. See Giardia, below.) Up high or in winter I sometimes suck snow or ice as I walk along. In deserts I drink a few sips of water at each hourly halt, swilling it around my mouth before swallowing. I am almost sure I use less water this way. I certainly know that the little-and-often system keeps washing the first traces of that blinkering scum away from the surface of my mind, and so rehones the edges of my appreciation. And appreciation, after all, is the reason I am walking.

Water sources

In assessing the purity of any water supply, the only safe rule is: "If in doubt, doubt." Rather suddenly, in the few years since the last edition of this book appeared, things have deteriorated so badly that in most places you should now maybe doubt any source except fresh rainpockets and springs (and, as we shall see, there are certain dangers even with springs). You can blame mankind, exploding toward disaster, or find some other scapegoat; but the sad fact remains that—as suggested in an excellent article in the May 1981 issue of *Audubon Magazine,* by Bert Newman—"the days of drinking directly from streams may be over." It is difficult, standing beside a clear, cold, rushing mountain torrent in the Appalachians, Rockies, Cascades or Sierra, to believe that such water is probably polluted. But the chances are, no matter how high you go, that it is. And the hazard now lurks there, too strong to ignore, almost everywhere in the U.S.—and, indeed, in the world.

The danger can stem from any one of many infectious organisms, but nine or ten of them (all except one transmitted by feces) account for most of the trouble. And in the U.S. the most common of these now seems to be a protozoan called Giardia lamblia. Giardia is most often passed from organism to organism in the form of a tiny oval cyst about

10 by 20 microns—though it may measure only 7 microns across. About 16,500 can fit on the head of a pin—to the exclusion of all angels in the vicinity. One stool from a moderately infected human can produce 300 million cysts—and the ingestion of as few as 10 or 20 of them can infect you. Once in the upper small intestine, the cysts hatch into active, wineskin-shaped trophozoites, then divide and multiply, and soon establish a ravenous colony.

Of the 16 million Americans who probably now have giardiasis (also known as "backpackers' disease"), many may be only carriers who remain perfectly healthy, showing no sign of the disease—yet can excrete cysts for months or even years. It remains unclear why some infected people get giardiasis symptoms while others do not. But the unlucky ones discover that the disease is no laughing matter. After an incubation period of from 7 to 14 days you suffer "a fulmination of diarrhea, cramps, visible bloating, weight loss, nasty burps, and anorexia [loss of appetite]." Get a bad case, and you may vomit too. As soon as possible, consult a doctor. In the backcountry, even more than "outside," the results can be serious. "Everything you eat promptly comes up or out," says one victim. In seven days his weight plummeted from 165 pounds to 115. And weakness and other symptoms may persist for months. All this stems, by the way, from an organism that, although long known to occur in humans, was until forty years ago thought to be harmless to them.

Unfortunately, humans are only the start of it. Other animals that are sufferers and carriers include several of our hangers-on—cattle, horses and dogs—that also travel the backcountry and are even less particular in their sanitation habits than the most undisciplined human. Also susceptible: rabbits, coyotes, deer—and, probably, beavers, who routinely defecate in creeks and therefore spread the disease like wildwater (hence the alternative name, "beaver fever"). The wildlife carriers make it seem overwhelmingly likely that once an area has become infested, Giardia will be there to stay.

Reasons for the recent spread of infestation remain obscure. Most likely culprit: man, in increasing numbers, with decreasing discipline. But livestock, especially horses, could be culpable. (Few dogs and no cattle visit such recently infested areas as Sequoia and Kings Canyon National Parks in the Sierra Nevada.) As with other imbalances in today's world, with its exploding human population, the root may be purely a matter of density. But, whatever the cause, the end result—and especially its probable permanence—is pretty damned sad.

For treating water suspected of harboring Giardia, see next section.

Even today most springs are safe—from Giardia and other contaminants. But mineral springs, especially in deserts, can be poisonous. One culprit is arsenic. What you do if you suspect an unposted bitter-tasting spring, I really don't know—though a marked lack of insect life would be good reason for doubting its safety. I would guess that if you're in danger of dying from thirst you drink deep; and that if you're not in danger you stand and ruminate for a few minutes, then walk on. Perhaps I should add that in out-of-the-way places I've come across some remarkably evil-looking springs, bubbling and steaming and reeking, and have discovered that the water was drunk regularly by some hardy local. But the only safe rule remains: "If in doubt, doubt."

Do not rely on maps, by the way, for information about springs. Even the excellent USGS topographical series often show springs that dry out each summer or have vanished altogether due to some subterranean change. Other springs may fail in extra-dry years. Rely only on recent reports from people you feel sure you can trust (page 486). If any doubts linger, carry enough water to take you not only as far as the hoped-for spring but also back to the last water source.

Sometimes, of course, snow will be your surest, or only, source of water (page 281).

Water purification

Consult the purity rule: "If in doubt, doubt," and either boil all suspect water or treat it chemically.

Ten minutes of boiling should make any water safe, though longer will be needed at high altitudes (for every thousand feet elevation gain, the temperature of boiling water drops about 2 degrees). But boiling consumes time and energy and fuel, and leaves you with a hot, unquenching drink.

For years chemical treatment in lieu of boiling meant chlorine-liberating Halazone tablets. But they have proven unstable and only marginally effective, and are now rarely obtainable and also costly (100-tablet bottle, 2 ounces [.48 ounce net]; about $4). Chlorine has given way to iodine—in tablet or crystal form. The most popular iodine tablets are Potable Aqua (2-inch-tall bottle of 50 tablets; 1 ounce [.2 ounce net]; $3.25). The tablets are dangerous if swallowed, and they must be kept dry (they lose one-third of their effectiveness if exposed to air for four days). So do not try to save weight by carrying them in a plastic bag; take the small bottle along—and always recap it tightly. Directions for use are explicit—and worth following in principle with any chemical purifier:

"Add 1 tablet to 1 quart or liter of water. Cap loosely to allow a little leakage. Wait 3 minutes.

"Shake thoroughly so that a little water leaks out and rinses the screw threads. Then tighten cap.

"Wait 10 minutes before drinking.

"If water is very cold or contains rotten leaves or is dirty and discolored, use 2 tablets. Wait 20 minutes before drinking."

The makers claim that Potable Aqua, used as directed, will make any water "bacteriologically suitable for drinking." But Giardia—a protozoan, and not a bacterium—may resist in cold or cloudy water. Even doubling dose and time exposure may not do the trick—though the Environmental Protection Agency rates it 85 percent safe (see also Pocket Purifier, below).

The Kahn-Visscher purification method with a saturated solution prepared from iodine crystals seems effective against Giardia. But danger lurks (iodine is poisonous in all but very small doses) and the method is rather complicated. So I will not describe it in full because it seems to be on the way out—superseded by the latest small filter systems. (For a full account of the Kahn-Visscher method, see an article by Frederick H. Kahn and Barbara R. Visscher in *The Western Journal of Medicine* [122, Jan./June 1975: 450–3], reprinted in *Backpacker* Magazine [#26, April/May 1978: 31 ff].)

Most current "water-purifying" filters are ineffective against Giardia.

The blue plastic Walbro Water Purifier (3½ ounces; $21) filters out most organisms and is surprisingly practical. You simply pour water into a filter-plus-iodine-element unit (which nestles for storage inside a capped cup) and collect it underneath in the cup or a canteen. The water flows through very quickly and is immediately ready to drink. The unit is guaranteed to produce at least 100 gallons of bacteria-free water (three 12-ounce glasses every day for a year). Muddy or silt-laden water must be allowed to stand long enough to clear (or, alternatively, strained through cheesecloth). Unfortunately, the iodine components, though effective for some organisms, will not kill all Giardia cysts; and as they can be as small as 7 microns across, the 20-micron filter will not block them—though it does remove almost all objectionable tastes, including that of iodine.

The 6-inch-long Super Straw Washer, filled with Dacron-wool and activated charcoal, is useful for sucking up sediment-rich and foul-tasting water "with nary a hint of foul taste or sticks and mud." But to make sure the water is safe you must treat it with Potable Aqua or some other purifying system—which rather takes the gleam out of the idea. (Straw and Potable Aqua, 2 ounces; $6.75.)

Other small suck-through devices offer more. The Pocket Purifier (¾ ounce; $13) embodies "space age resins and filters." The Environmental Protection Agency says it gives 80 percent protection against Giardia used alone, 98 percent if used with Potable Aqua.

But we will probably soon have filters specifically designed to eliminate Giardia. I have used a lightweight prototype devised by the staff at Sequoia-Kings Canyon National Parks HQ and found it reasonably convenient. Lighter, stronger versions now exist and commercial versions stand in the wings. Any light and fully effective model, free from all iodine-poisoning danger, that filtered fast enough to allow you to drink almost immediately after reaching any water would seem to reduce the Giardia hassle to about the lowest imaginable level. *(Later:* Test reports on some commercial filters, specifically made for backpacking, have begun to come in—and they look good. At least one model has pores small enough to filter out bacteria as well as Giardia. Warning! At present, not all filters advertised as giving protection against Giardia seem certain to do so. The crucial factor: a filter with pores smaller than 7 microns. Note that any such filter will need some kind of pressure system to ensure passsage of water at a practical rate.)

Water in an emergency

Cunning ideas are always being propounded about what to do if you run out of water. Typical examples are "Catch the rain in a tarp" and "Shake condensed fog off conifer trees" and "Dig in a damp, low-lying place." Then there are various crafty systems for distilling fresh water from the ocean. In an Armed Forces Research and Development publication I once ran across a description of what at first seemed a practical rig for sea-skirting backpackers: a series of foil sheets between which you heated salt water, either in the sun's rays or "by sitting on them." But right at the end came the killer: "With additional sheets, a survivor can obtain about one pint of water in 16 hours."

Unfortunately, the occasion on which you're really in desperate straits for water is pretty darned sure to come just when there is no rain, no fog, no damp place and no ocean (not to mention no sheets of special foil). In other words, in the desert, in summer.

For years the only advice I'd heard that sounded even vaguely practical was "Cut open a barrel cactus." An experienced friend of mine says he rather imagines you'd "extract just about enough moisture to make up for the sweat expended in slashing the damned thing open." But I find that the *Air Force Manual* (SIN 050-012-0071-0, obtainable from the Superintendent of Documents, U.S. Government Printing Office, Washington, DC 20402, for $9) exhorts you, in a desert fix, to "cut off top [of a barrel cactus], mash pulp, suck water through grass straw or mash the pulp in a cloth and squeeze directly into the mouth."

The Air Force Manual also gives details of the desert still I described in the second edition of this book.*

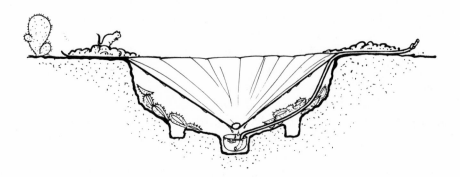

The beauty of the device is that it works best in the time and place you're most likely to need it: summer desert. The hotter the sun, the more water you get. And the water is as pure and clear as if it had been distilled in a laboratory. An Air Force medical colonel has called this still "the most significant breakthrough in survival technique since World War II"—and the colonel headed a team that experimented with the still for twenty-five days in the Arizona desert. Judging by the team's findings, which essentially confirmed those of the original researchers, there seems no reason why this still should not save your life, or mine, if either of us ever gets into water trouble while backpacking in the desert —provided we have a clear understanding of what to do.

The still's only essential components are two items we might seem reasonably likely to carry: a container to catch the water; and a 6-foot square of clear or almost clear plastic sheeting. Up to a point, the container is easy: cooking pot or cup or Svea stove cover or a plastic bag or

* Sources:

1. "Solar Distillation of Water from Soil and Plant Materials: A Simple Desert Survival Technique," by Ray D. Jackson and C. H. M. van Bavel. *Science,* 149, No. 3690 (September 17, 1965), pp. 1377–9.

2. Private correspondence with Dr. Ray D. Jackson of the U.S. Water Conservation Laboratory, Phoenix, AZ.

3. "Water, Water, Everywhere," by Frank James Clifford. *FAA Aviation News,* 5, No. 1 (May 1966), p. 10.

4. "Water, Water, Everywhere," by Joe Bailey. *The Airman,* 10, No. 8 (August 1966), pp. 24–5. (Less technical detail than above, but one or two additional findings.)

Articles on the still have appeared in many other places, including these: *The American Rifleman,* July 1970, p. 35; *Outdoor Life,* August 1965, p. 14; *U.S. Army Aviation Digest,* October 1965, p. 18; *The Flying Physician,* July 1966, p. 37.

even a small piece of plastic sheet or aluminum foil (page 211) shaped into a hole in the ground. But the container should be wide enough to catch all drops falling from the sheet—as a cup would not. And a metal container will get very hot and "boil off" some of its precious water. So a cooking pot will do but a plastic bowl or bucket (page 425) will do better. At first blush the 6-foot square of plastic sheet looks easy too: we should simply get used to taking a *clear* plastic groundsheet on desert trips, and carry a poncho as sun awning (page 331). But because plastic groundsheets are almost always polyethylene, a difficulty arises; as we shall see, though, there is a way out.

A desirable but not essential component for the still is a piece of flexible plastic tubing, 4 to 6 feet long (the kind sold for aquariums is fine). Hardly a likely thing to be in your pack, you say? For other reasons you might consider taking it, see page 208 and footnote on page 264.

Constructing the still sounds a simple enough job for even a weak and scared man, provided he has kept a modicum of his cool: Dig a hole about 40 inches wide and 20 inches deep. Dig the sides straight down at first, then taper them in to a central cavity (see illustration). Failing a toilet trowel (page 538) or a staff or stout stick, your bare hands will do the job, provided the soil is not too rocky. When the hole is finished put your container in its central cavity. If you have plastic tubing you should tape it inside the container so that one end lies very near the bottom. Lead the other end up out of the hole and seal it by knotting, or doubling and tying with nylon. Next, stretch the plastic sheet over the hole and anchor it around the edges with soil. Alternatively, you can dig a circular trench, about 4 inches deep, a few inches beyond the perimeter of the still, in which to stuff the edges of the plastic—and so obviate any problem with dirt sliding down the sheet into the pit. Next, push the sheet down in its center until it forms an inverted cone with sides 25 to 40 degrees from the horizontal. The plastic should run 2 to 4 inches above the soil and touch it *only* at the hole's rim. Place a small, smooth stone or other weight dead center to hold the conical shape and reduce wind flutter. Pile extra soil around the edge to hold the sheet firmly in place and block off *all* passage of air. In high winds, reinforce with rocks or other heavy articles. Leave the free end of the plastic tubing uncovered —and clean. Estimated construction time: 15 to 30 minutes.

This simple structure works on the same principle as a conventional still: solar energy passes through the clear plastic and heats the soil (or added plant material); water evaporates, condenses on the plastic (which is cooled by wind action), runs down to the point of the cone and drops into the container. It takes 1 to 2 hours for the trapped air to become saturated so that water condenses on the plastic and begins to drip into the container. With a plastic tube you can suck up water at any time;

without it you have to keep removing the container—and each time you do so you lose ½ to 1 hour's water production.

It is the apparently simple business of the water running down to the point of the cone that raises the first groundsheet difficulties. Plastic groundsheets are polyethylene, which is slick, especially when new, and therefore sheds many drops before they reach the cone's apex, thereby reducing yield by about half. Any used groundsheet will be scratched, and water will adhere rather better. And scouring the sheet's undersurface with sand might make a critical difference. (I don't suggest you do it ahead of time: just file the idea away in your mind for emergency use.) But there are other groundsheet difficulties. A sheet punctured in any way, even with small holes, will drastically reduce the still's yield. Possible remedy: patch with Rip-stop tape (page 511). Again, the thinner the sheet, the more efficient: 1 mil is ideal. But a 1-mil groundsheet is close to useless; mostly, they're at least 3 or 4 mil. Finally, any loss of transparency, such as accidental or deliberate scratching will further reduce the still's yield. In other words, a transparent groundsheet, somewhat scratched and with all holes patched, will do at a pinch. But a thin special plastic, such as Du Pont's Tedlar, will do far, far better. Unfortunately, Tedlar is twenty times as expensive as polyethylene and is not readily available to the public. I do not at present know where you can buy any. The solution is to buy and carry a kit of the currently elusive kind mentioned at the end of this section (page 203).

A sandy wash makes the best site for your still. Next best is a depression where rain would collect: months after a shower such places still retain more water than nearby high ground. The finer the soil, the better. Make every effort to site the still where it will get day-long sunlight.

After long droughts you may be able to collect only small amounts of water from even favorable soil; but—and it's a gigantic "but"—you can probably save the day by lining the sides of the hole, under the plastic, with vegetation *cut open so that its moist interior is exposed.* Cactus is best. Prickly pear and barrel cactus yield most; saguaro comes next, cholla a poor fourth. Creosote bush helps very little.*

The vegetation should not touch the plastic; it may flavor the water slightly. Small ledges made in the sides of the hole may make it easier to keep the vegetation in place.

Seawater or brackish water (as found in many desert lakes) can be purified by building the still where the soil is kept moist by the underlying water table. Or keep adding the polluted water—either into a

---

* If you make your still in Mexico and happen to use the maguey plant you might, I understand, end up imbibing almost straight tequila. What a way to go!

trough (see below) or by pouring it well down in the hole, not up near the rim, where condensing water could touch the soil and carry impurities down into your container. If the soil is badly contaminated on the rim (by strong alkaline deposits, say) your precious harvest of water may be fouled, so raise the plastic slightly with small rocks placed underneath it, all around the hole. With these precautions you can even—cozy thought—operate in a region made radioactive by fallout.

Slightly modified, the still will purify water polluted by almost anything *except* antifreeze from a car radiator. So your body wastes become recyclable. To make full use of polluted material, dig a trough halfway down the hole (see illustration), line it if possible with a plastic sheet and pour the material in.

Yield will depend on many factors, but it seems reasonable to expect at least a quart a day from a properly constructed still dug in desert sand containing some moisture or lined with cut cactus. And although there seems to be an upper production limit of about 3 quarts a day for such stills, that yield can in relatively moist soil or with a good vegetation lining be maintained for four or five days. After that, make a new still or replace the vegetation. These 40-by-20-inch stills are the optimum size: if you need more water—and have the necessary materials—make more stills rather than a bigger one. Given fleshy plants or polluted water, *two* stills should provide adequate drinking water for one person *for an indefinite period*.

If rain falls, your plastic cone will naturally capture it. It may capture other things, too. In the desert, water always attracts animals, and the Air Force colonel's team found that "many small rodents and snakes become trapped in the middle of the plastic"—unable to escape over its slick surface. If you're hungry these poor little bastards are obviously going to end up in your gut. (For thoughts on rattlesnake steak, see page 552.) And even if you don't feel hungry, remember that the animals contain precious fluids.

A word of warning: it occurs to me that the quoted yields of water were achieved by men practiced in the technique and operating with minds and bodies in good shape. Don't underestimate the possible effects of weakness and irrationality (page 189). But you can take care of the technique problem by personal experimentation. (If you experiment, make sure you fill the holes afterward.)

I am ashamed to say that I have yet to follow my own sage advice and give the rig a trial run. But the idea still sounds to me like a practical proposition. A reader who had her Sunday School class of five- to nine-year-olds build a still, guided only by my instructions in the earlier edition of this book, reports that the children constructed one, "completely on their own, in 1 hour 15 minutes. . . . And when the first drops of water began to collect and run down into the bucket, they jumped up and down yelling, 'It works! It works! WE DID IT!' "

For car and airplane users, it seems to me, the components should henceforth be standard emergency equipment, kept stowed aboard against a nonrainy day.

A complete kit for such a still that used to be sold by Harbor Scientific of California is unfortunately no longer available. But it may resurface.

Water caches

On both California and Grand Canyon walks I had to establish several water caches. Bottles, I discovered, kept the water clear and fresh. Whenever possible I buried them—as protection against the hoofs of inquisitive wild burros and the fingers of other thirsty, thieving or merely thoughtless mammals.*

Unburied bottles are liable to crack from extreme heat (if you leave them in the sun) or from extreme cold (wherever you put them, if temperatures fall low enough for the water to freeze solid). I worried a good deal about the freezing danger in Grand Canyon, but found the unburied bottles at both caches intact, in spite of night temperatures several degrees below freezing. The bigger the bottles you use, the less danger that they will freeze solid. One-gallon wine bottles, thoroughly washed, are good; 5-gallon bottles, though cumbersome, are better. Plastic bottles such as those used for liquid bleach or for distilled or spring water are lighter and perhaps stronger, but they leave me worrying about rodents.

---

* On the California walk, at the southern end of Death Valley, an amateur rockhound operating from a pickup truck kindly gave me a gallon bottle of good drinking water that he had "found under a pile of stones, back up in the hills." The water tasted far sweeter than the alkaline spring water I had camped beside. But it brought on a bad case of worries: I became highly conscious that for three days ahead I would be relying on water I had cached out as I drove south through the valley two months earlier, and I hoped no thoughtless, light-fingered rockhound had stumbled on any of my caches. Fortunately, all the caches were buried and camouflaged. I found each one safe.

I also found them without difficulty. People often ask me how you can be sure of finding a cache again. The safest way is to draw in your notebook a sketch map showing important features such as gullies and bushes and rocks, and to pace out and record a few measurements from obvious landmarks. And then to mark the exact spot with a big stone. I did all these things. But I never actually used the maps. Each time, memory took me directly to the right place. City people sometimes express amazement at such a "feat." But once you have lived for a while in any wilderness its landmarks stand out quite clearly. Even a moderately practiced eye will detect at least as much difference between two neighboring desert gullies as between two neighboring downtown streets.

Water left for even a few weeks in 5-gallon metal cans seems to take on a greenish tinge, apparently from algae, but can still be drunk with complete safety. And these 5-gallon cans are light and strong, and easily lashed to a packframe when caches have to be made on foot. Twice in Grand Canyon I used 5-gallon cans in which my food had been stored (page 543) to pack water a half-day ahead and so break a long waterless trek into two much safer segments.

Canteens

In buying canteens, take no chances. If you find one is leaking badly, miles from the nearest desert spring, it may well be about the last thing you ever find.

Metal canteens, which I used for years, are, for backpackers, essentially things of the past. Today's polyethylene bottles are far lighter and cheaper—and in many ways tougher.

Good polyethylene quart-size canteens weigh about 3½ ounces and cost about $3.50; aluminum equivalents cost and weigh about twice as much. The old, beloved, "Western round" steel canteens have virtually vanished. A modernized version, with felt cover and metal band around a polyethylene container, still comes out at 1 pound and $10 in the half-gallon size, 1½ pounds and $13 in the one-gallon. At these weights, experienced backpackers are unlikely to carry them.

On the score of toughness, metal naturally impresses you with greater immediate confidence. But on my Grand Canyon trip the felt covers of both my metal canteens developed gaping holes, and when the canteens came on sidetrips—slung from my belt by their convenient little spring clips—the bared aluminum banged against rocks and developed seep holes. I fixed the leaks with rubber air-mattress patches—but my confidence had been punctured too. The polyethylene canteens I also carried on that trip showed no sign of wear, and since that time I have used only plastic canteens. They have proved astonishingly tough. Last year, at a "dry camp" on a steep hillside, the full one-quart plastic canteen holding my entire overnight supply tumbled more than 100 vertical feet down a steep but nonrocky canyon. It went in big bounces, emitting a dull, heart-rending thud at each contact. But I found it, lying in a dry watercourse, safe and sound.

In all canteens, leaky stoppers can be a source of grief. In my old aluminum canteens the threads of both neck and stopper tended to wear; cross-threading became horribly easy; in the end the stoppers even threatened to flip off. The best new plastic stoppers, with large bungs held in place by separate screwcaps, seem immune to this infirmity. But some stoppers may eventually begin to leak a little. Padding with string—

much as you pad a sleeve fitting with asbestos string—may stop the leak, but in time the always-damp string apparently harbors bacteria and begins to reek. Inserts cut from automobile inner tubes work better. But the likeliest solution I've heard comes from a reader who suggests cutting liners or gaskets from the plastic lids of coffee cans—preferably colored plastic, so that if the gasket drops out it is easily found.

When new, and to a lesser degree after being stored for long periods, the polyethylene of the canteen tends to smell. It may even taint water. As with many things in life, time cures.

There is one feature of metal canteens that plastic cannot match. If metal canteens with felt jackets are wetted and put out in the sun, evaporation from the felt soon cools the water. You can rig a makeshift jacket for a plastic canteen with almost any article of wettable clothing, but because plastic is a poor conductor of heat the cooling system does not work very efficiently.

Most old metal canteens had good, solid spring clips for attaching to your belt—a valuable feature on packless sidetrips. I long ago rejected the traditional idea that in thirsty country you carried a canteen clipped outside your pack, readily available: thirsty country almost always means sunny country, and direct sunlight soon turns even cold spring water into a hot and unquenching brew. In thirsty country I carry my canteen near the top of the pack but insulated under a down or pile jacket. In any case, a canteen clipped outside your pack, especially if swinging loose, is pretty sure to be a poorly placed load (page 126). A few good plastic canteens now come with small spring clips, or at least with holes for attaching them; though I've yet to see one that looked strong past doubt. But you can carry a clipless quart-size canteen in one of the neat little woven-nylon bags by Sierra West (1 ounce; $6). A small stuff sack with its mouth rimmed by elastic instead of a drawcord, it has a strong belt loop stitched to one side. On sidetrips, or even when wearing your pack, you can slide the bag onto your belt and into it stuff a canteen— or anything else you please. The elastic holds the contents safely in place. Too safely, almost: removing the canteen for a quick drink can be a pain.

The best plastic canteen for sidetrips still seems to be the green, 1-quart Oasis—comparatively expensive but widely available—that has a stout metal slip-over-your-belt clip (and a screwtop that is, though imperfect, an improvement on the old, very shoddy one), (4½ ounces; $5). Oasis also make a flat, circular, plastic, quart-size model with a fabric cover and carrying strap (6 ounces; $9). It has, no doubt, certain advantages.

Any stopper attached to its canteen is virtually unlosable. A less obvious profit in this arrangement, but one I rate almost as high, is that the thong or chain attachment gives you something to hook finger or thumb through when you're carrying several canteens back from water source to camp or pack—a convenience you may learn to bless at least once a day. On such occasions you can interlink the stopper thongs of two or more canteens for even easier carriage. And if you ever carry canteens, full or empty, up at the very top of your pack, such an interlinkage will make just about sure they can't fall out.

A reader recommends a push/pull stopper from an empty plastic dish-detergent bottle: he fits one on "a poly bottle sold at liquor counters to hold a fifth of booze. . . . The push/pull cap threaded right on and has proved absolutely watertight. . . . Due to the lip-shape of the cap's tip I can get a drink one-handed by prying the nozzle up with my teeth. . . . The best part is the squirt stream of water, good for direct hits on mouth, neck, armpit, etc." See also page 208.

The catalogues feature many well-made canteens, and provided you go for the features that seem important to you and settle for nothing less than highest-quality materials, especially in the stopper threads, it probably does not matter much which you buy. Many people now use Nalgene bottles (page 216). The canteens I presently use are quart-size, octagonal models (illustration, right) by Mirro (3½ ounces, $3.50). Mirro also make pint, 1½-pint and 1½-quart sizes. Occasionally I still carry a plastic, clip-belt Oasis. Plastic Army canteens, and Taiwanese copies, tend to be heavy (5–8 ounces) but cheap (as little as $2).

Flattened canteens make tolerably comfortable pillows, especially if padded with clothing. In weather no worse than cool, the pillow routine also keeps the stopper from freezing (and for an infuriating minor frustration few things equal waking up thirsty in the middle of the night and finding yourself iced off from your drinking water). Simply putting the canteens on air mattress or foam pad may be enough to keep the stopper ice-free, but in really cold weather take one canteen to bed with you. If you think there is any danger at all of the others freezing solid make sure they are no more than half full. That way, they can hardly burst.

Unless weight is a real problem I mostly carry four one-quart canteens. Even when I do not expect to carry as much as a gallon for safety purposes I feel it's worth the extra freedom they give me, at 3½ ounces a shot: I can camp well away from water and, unless it's very hot, stay for twenty-four hours without a refill.

No matter how many large canteens I take, I now nearly always add an Evenflo baby-feeder bottle (half-pint capacity; 1 ounce, $.73). It does more than boost my carrying capacity. In hot weather, particularly if walking along a riverbank or lakeshore where the water is suspect, I often fill it at every halt, add a Potable Aqua tablet and slip it into a pack pocket (page 528). At the next halt I have, immediately available, just enough safe water to see me through another hot, dry hour. In the desert I have found such a bottle invaluable for collecting water from shallow rainpockets, and I've often been glad to have it for collecting water from other small sources. At a pinch, you can even use one for rescuing a little water from seeps that no ordinary canteen will even begin to tap; but for a better alternative, see page 216. Baby bottles are also convenient for short sidetrips; failing a canteen bag (page 205), one will slip into your pants pocket—though it can also slip out. These little bottles are tough too. Once, when mine held my last precious half-pint of water and I dropped it on a boulder, it bounced quite beautifully. Warning: The two-piece lid (for fitting baby's rubber nipple) is a mild nuisance. To hold it in one piece and so prevent the inner disk from dropping off every time you remove the lid, just slap a piece of Rip-stop tape on top (page 511). Renew it occasionally. The tape will allow the disk to turn a fraction when you replace the lid, and so jam into a watertight joint— provided you keep the rubber nipple in place. Know ye that without the inner disk—or the nipple—the damned thing will leak.

Collapsible water bags and bottles of various shapes and sizes (see most catalogues) take up little room in your pack and will fill you with gratitude as well as water if you want or need to camp far from the latter. The lightest bags are thin, single- or double-thickness polyethylene. But after a little use they tend to leak. Those with a nylon fabric outer shell to protect the double-thickness inner bladder seem much more reliable (typically, 2½ gallons; 3 ounces; $7.50). They have a handle too, as well as an efficient spigot that you can operate with one hand. Hung in the sun by its handle, the bag's dark fabric absorbs heat and provides hottish water for tea, cooking or a shower. Inflated with water or air, the bag makes a semi-serviceable pillow (it's not easy to get the softness just right). For a 1-ounce shower attachment, see page 494.

Possible canteen accessory: rubber or plastic or metal tubing

A "survivalist" reader writes that "a ¼-inch piece of brass tubing 8 inches long makes a good metal drinking straw. You can suck water drippage out of a rock fissure that normally you cannot get your lips at," or you can suck water drippage up with the straw and blow the mouthful of water into a canteen. You can buy the tubing at a hobby shop.

It occurs to me that rubber or plastic tubing would do the job almost as well; would be lighter, and less liable to damage; might even come in useful for siphoning into the canteen; and, most important of all, would mean—provided it was 3 feet long—that you had a highly desirable component for an emergency solar still (page 200) and for an "exhilarator" (page 264, footnote).

A reader volunteered yet another use for such tubing. "I'm very proud of my water support system," he writes. "I carry a baby bottle, like you do, in one of my upper pockets. Connected to the bottle is a yard of aquarium tubing. If I get thirsty while I'm hiking along, I don't have to stop. I just reach for my tubing." Early Winters offer a fancy version of this device: the Waterline ($9.95) consists of a 3-foot, double, surgical-grade tube (water comes out one tube, air goes in the other) with stopper that fits a wide-mouth Nalgene bottle (quart size, $2.95) and a flow-control clamp and clip for attaching to clothing.

KITCHEN UTENSILS

Keep your utensils as few and as simple as you can, consistent with your personal requirements of weight, comfort, convenience and obscure inner satisfaction. Naturally, no two backpackers are likely to make identical choices. I know one man-and-wife hiking team who never carry more than one cup and one spoon between them. At least, so they say. Other people like to pack everything along, including the kitchen sink. My current standard list reads:

	Lbs.	Oz.
Cooking pot		9
Stainless steel cup		3
Spoon		½
Swiss Army knife		3
Salt and pepper shaker		1
Sugar container		¾

	Lbs.	Oz.
Margarine container		1
Milk squirter		1
Bookmatches—7 per week		1
Waterproof matchsafe		1
Total	1	5¼

Ten years ago, when I wrote the last edition of this book, the total came to 2 pounds 7⅛ ounces. Most of the saving comes from discarding a second, large, nesting, 11-ounce pot; but lighter spoon, knife and sugar and margarine containers have pared away 6¾ ounces, and I've also discarded, mostly, a ⅛-ounce can opener.

As we shall see in the following pages, this standard list is far from immutable. Various items get added, subtracted or replaced, as conditions demand. For simple, depotted variations, see "Rock-bottom, tin-can kitchen," page 278.

Pots. Until recently, spun aluminum-alloy pots—light, strong and sub-exorbitant—were standard. But recently, in the slipstream of allegations that the lead in many aluminum-alloy pots could taint food and cause lead poisoning, there has been a swing to stainless steel—which distributes heat more evenly than aluminum and is said not to pit or to taint food. Some versions are surprisingly light. One popular nesting set, by Ever New, includes two pots with lids (⅔-quart and 1-quart capacities), fry pan and plastic cup, and weighs 1 pound 5 ounces ($20). For similar sets, consult catalogues.

I continue to use either one or, if conditions demand, both of my tried and trusted nesting Sigg spun-aluminum pots (1½- and 2½-quart capacities; 9 and 11 ounces: $18 and $20). (A 3½-quart size weighs 15 ounces, costs $22). Because of their price, these once-popular models have become difficult to find. But they are highly practical units: corners are rounded and easily cleaned; low profiles and broad bases promote rapid heating; lids double as plates or pans; bail handles lock firmly into upright positions; and even the smaller one, alone, is big enough for simple solo cooking—and, if in-pack space is a problem, to house the Svea. These pots are tough too. The smaller one, which for years traveled protected inside its mate but now more often comes solo, has a quarter of a century's fairly solid service under its lid yet stands unscathed. My original, larger one withstood a dozen years of brutal use (it once bounced 150 feet down a talus slope in Death Valley) and then had to be retired only because it got so dented that cleaning became difficult. Its replacement has, after its own dozen years, begun to mature—and even to usurp the niche in my affection once held by that old and honored friend.*

Some people complain of difficulty in lifting the lids of these Sigg pots. Nowadays I mostly use the lids inverted, even though they seal less tightly that way, because it is then simple to lift them by the rims, with your hand insulated by a bandanna or sock or whatever. Even if you use a lid right way up, you can still lift it easily with one end of your spoon, then hold it ajar and insert a tea bag or grasp and remove it with the other hand.

Among many other, much cheaper aluminum pots are the popular series by Mirro ($6 and up), and their cooksets for from 1 through 8 people (1 pound, $11.50, through 9 pounds 3 ounces, $58). See also the shiny 1-liter pot that comes with the Salewa stove (page 241). An interesting lightweight variant by Mountain Safety Research, with a blackened outer surface to "absorb heat rather than reflect it, like conventional pot surfaces," is no longer available; but I understand you can nigrify any pot with engine-block enamel.

Sigg now make two versions of their Tourist Cook Kits. One is designed for use with the Svea 123 stove, stripped of its windshield, the other with the Peak 1 stove. (For stoves, see page 229.) A set of 2½- and 3½-pint aluminum pots, with lid that doubles as fry pan, and also a windscreen, it nests compactly for packing, with the stove inside. It erects into a high-rise that encages the stove and seems to shield it effectively from wind. Said to be suitable for one, two or three people.

---

* The two original pots, which I bought for my Mexico-to-Oregon walk in 1958, are currently taking part in a pleasant, echoic, quarter-century celebration. They are retracing the route of that trip in the pack and hands of a man who, in that same summer of 1958, as a sixteen-year-old, used an identical set (also bought from the old Ski Hut but now, like the Ski Hut, a mere memory), on a long, solo canoe trip he made down Lake Champlain and the Richelieu River, deep into Canada, and then back to his home in Burlington, Vermont.

(Beware of Taiwanese equivalent, reported to contain dangerous levels of lead and copper.) (Cooksets only [no stoves]: for Svea, 1 pound 8 ounces; for Peak 1, 1 pound 4 ounces; each about $32.)

See also the alcohol-burning Optimus Model 81 Trapper stove and cookset, page 246.

A reader suggests an Ensolite "cozy" for keeping pots warm once the cooking has been done. A fire does the job for you, of course, but with a stove some coddling arrangement is often worthwhile in cold weather. I have used clothing, sand, even piled leaves.

For pots as washing machines, see page 425.

Fry pans. Second-generation Teflon pans, known in the U.S.-made version as Silverstone, are state-of-the-art. Mirro make 8- and 10-inch sizes with folding handles (12 and 14 ounces, $10 and $11). A "wunder-gauze" (page 260) makes frying, even on a stove, fairly simple. I used to carry a fry pan in trout country but now mostly get by with a few sheets of aluminum foil: I just wrap the gutted fish in foil, maybe add a little margarine, then bake on a small-stick fire.

Fancy cooking. Gourmets may wish to consider an aluminum Tote-Oven, heated from below by stove or campfire and from above by a small fire, hot coals or even Sterno (25 ounces, $18.95—or, with "donut" that permits baking with only a lower heat source, $27.95; Bendonn Company, 4920 Thomas Avenue South, Minneapolis, MN 55410). But a 1½-quart ring mold of the kind used for Jell-O (4 ounces, $8.50) will apparently enable you to bake bread, cake or pastry, and will also serve as a steamer.

Cups. The Sierra Club stainless-steel cup (the later, slightly enlarged version: capacity 10 fluid ounces; weight 3 ounces; domestic-made, $2.75; imported, $2) is one of those simple but gloriously successful devices that man occasionally invents. It is tough. It cleans easily. Its rim rarely burns your lips, even with the hottest food or drink—a feature that anyone who has suffered an aluminum cup will appreciate. The open-end steel-wire handle stays cool too, hooks over belt or bough or cord and snaps easily and securely onto a belt clip (page 522). (A reader writes: "Have you ever found an efficient way, or even an inefficient way, to stop the occasional intolerable rattle of Sierra cup in belt clip?" Another responds: "Yes. Just slip the cup into a worn but clean sock. Or even a dirty sock.")

An Illinois reader has made a simple but interesting modification to the Sierra Club cup handle. "The extra bend," he writes, "affords a secure grip and counterbalance that I have not found in any other cup. If you fill the cup with liquid you will get the full impact of its practicality." He sent me a modified cup and, by God, he's right! (Note: the bent handle tends to improve the cup's stability, at least on perfectly flat surfaces; but it will not fit the Nomad staff [page 81]).

Beware of cups that look like the Sierra Club version but cost half as much. They may be lip-burning aluminum abominations.

Unfortunately, the Sierra Club cup has in certain wilderness circles become a badge of conformity: you are not considered "in" if you do not sport one dangling from your belt. A dismal fate for a first-class article. But it is entirely possible, I assure you, to be a member of the very worthwhile Sierra Club and to carry one of their excellent cups and yet not qualify as what has been aptly called a cup-carrying member. The status symbol game hits a new high (or low) with Early Winters' brass, silver- or gold-plated Sierra Club cups (no weights revealed; $10, $20 and $35; engraved monogram or message extra).

For a reserve cup in case of loss or unexpected company, see cover of Svea stove (page 235). The cover is aluminum, though, and a guaranteed lip-scorcher. Ditto the MSR X-GK stove cover (page 232).

There are now several plastic competitors to the Sierra Club cup, some of them insulated. Mostly, they hold rather less, but are lighter and cheaper (average: 1 ounce, less than $1), are tough and cleanable, lack the Sierra Club cup's protruding and dirt-collecting lip, cannot burn your lips and are often measure-marked in 2-ounce (½-cup) increments (see illustration, page 216). (You can calibrate your Sierra Club cup by measuring in successive ¼-cups of water, marking the surface lines in pencil, then making dent marks on the inside of the cup with screwdriver and hammer while the cup rests on a wooden block.)

Plastic cups, being less heat-conductive than the Sierra Club cup, should in theory keep food hotter.*

---

* I once conducted a rather elegant experiment to clarify this point. Using a standard Sierra Club cup and a plastic one made by the now-defunct Palco organization, I several times filled both cups, side by side, with water of known temperature and then exposed the cups, still side by side, to cool environments of known temperature. Summary of results:

Unfortunately, the lightness and deepness of most plastic cups mean less stability (a real factor, this, and perhaps the main reason I continue, except when going ultralight, to carry a Sierra cup: I find that a plastic cup, when close to empty, tends to tip over if you rest a spoon in it). The smaller top area also means less convenience with the lumpy stews and even hamburgers that the Sierra cup handles with such surprising grace. And you cannot cook in a plastic cup—though a reader writes: "You can almost boil water in [one]. Heat stones in a fire. Drop them in the cup of water. Use greenstick tongs or chopsticks." Again, you cannot hang plastic cups, as presently made, onto a belt clip, though I understand it is possible to drill or burn a hole for this purpose in the usually rather small handle, fit a wire-ring, and attach a belt clip to it. Unmodified handles will not, unfortunately, hook over your belt with anything like the Sierra cup's security. Finally, gung-hoers complain that no plastic cup is in the same class as the inverted Sierra cup when it comes to digging handholds in snow slopes.

The collapsible, stainless-steel Bob Lane cup—now retitled the "fold-cup"—folds flat, fits in your shirt pocket, does not rattle and snaps open into a cone (capacity 4 fluid ounces, weight ½ ounce, $2 in the L. L. Bean catalogue). Unlike most telescopic folding models, it looks easy to keep clean. But one experienced user reports: "This otherwise fine gismo suffers from four incurable handicaps: one, it has no flat bottom, so cannot be put down; two, it has no handle, so hot liquids are a problem; three, no matter how old and properly worn in it may be, it still leaks a few drops at the long seam; and, four, under adverse jarring circumstances it can fold up all by itself."

Another reader says that he carries a plastic cup, but, because it will not clip onto his belt, supplements it with a Bob Lane. After all, he says, the pair weigh less together than one Sierra cup.

A crushable plastic Fold-A-Cup has now appeared in the catalogues,

Water at start	Cool environment	Minutes exposed	Water temps. °F. Sierra	Plastic
Boiling	Garden, 58° F., windless	15	120	126
		18	112	118
		20	109	115
122° F.	Freezer box, 15° F.	5	96	100
Boiling	Freezer box, 15° F.	10	120	126

I assume that any impartial observer would accept these figures, which were supported by lip-service tests, as clear demonstration (taking into account the time and temperature parameters probable in field use, and reducing all readings to two decimal places) that the plastic cup is, as a heat conserver, superior to the Sierra Club cup by a factor remarkably close, all expectations considered, to zero.

and looks mildly interesting—though I hear rumors that in cold weather it may resist folding with iron will (holds 7 fluid ounces; 3 inches diameter, 2 inches deep when folded; 1 ounce, $2).

Spoon. Any tough, light spoon will do. One from a clip-together knife-fork-and-spoon set will have two little protuberances that are not only ideal for hooking onto pot rims when you leave the spoon standing in one but also unbeatable for collecting dirt. Alternatively, you can bend over the top of any metal spoon so that it hooks over the pot rim rather than slipping down into the soup. Although you cannot do this with the new Lexan plastic soup spoons (⅓ ounce, $1.10), they are so light and efficient that I find I nowadays almost always choose to take one, rather than my old metal friend.

Metal spoons with protruding tabs on handles, for hooking on rim of pot, are now appearing (aluminum, 1½ ounces, $1.25; heat-resistant stainless steel, no weight given, $2).

Fork. Redundant.

Knife. After two decades of blind faithfulness to a 6-ounce sheath knife I have been philandering with the Swiss Army knives that are, understandably, backpacking standards.*

The two reputable makers of Swiss Army knives, Victorinox and Wenger, both offer lifetime guarantees. Avoid imitators. The range of available models is now so rich that you can not only be sure of finding one that meets all your requirements and whims but also have a ball making the selection. For two or three years I have very happily used a Victorinox Tinker (3 ounces, $17). In addition to a large and a small blade, it embodies an excellent pair of scissors, which I use a great deal, and slide-out tweezers and toothpick. It also grows a Phillips screwdriver, bottle-opener/screwdriver, can opener and reamer which I rarely if ever use. Last month I thought I had lost my Tinker and, being on a lightweight kick, I bought a 2¼-inch-long Victorinox Classic (1 ounce, $10.50) with one blade, scissors, tweezers and toothpick—and also a "manicure blade" that I may just, in some paranoid gram-paring moment, cut off.

The number of fixed-blade and lock-blade knives now on the market —most of them rather heavy—makes you wonder who buys them all. For those who really feel they need a big fixed blade, the all-metal Tekna Knife looks interesting (5 ounces with sheath; $35). Case now make a lock-blade pocket model, 2½ inches closed, that weighs only 1 ounce

* I note with sadness that the current wave of inflation has begun to transform "Swiss Army Knife" into "Swiss Army Officers' Knife." Does tomorrow hold the specter of galloping inflation and "Swiss Army Cavalry Officers' Knife" or even "Swiss Army Generals' knife"?

Last fall, when a Swiss tourist kindly gave me a ride from roadhead back to my car, he assured me that, as I had long suspected, such knives are not really even Swiss Army knives.

($19). And I see that Wenger embody a lock-blade in all their new Backpacker Swiss Army series (3 to 12 tools, $13–$40).

One reader reports that he tapes his sheath knife to his packframe, level with his right ear and immediately reachable.

Knife sharpener. Sharpen your knife at home. Standard for touching up in the field: a small Carborundum stone (3 inches, 1 ounce, $3.50). Alternatives: a miniature steel (a good one comes with a sheath designed for Swiss Army knives, but does not seem to be sold separately; another has diamonds set in the stainless steel and is said to be "great."); or one of the new folding ceramic crock stocks (1¼ ounces, $7), angled so that even we duffers can hone a knife correctly. Suggested New Wave substitute, which I've now adopted on ultralight trips: Carborundum sandpaper.

Salt and pepper shaker. Neatest current idea: plastic, perforated lids with strong snap-open covers that fit recycled 35-mm. plastic film cans (with cans, ¾ ounce a pair; $2—from many mountain shops or direct from Hall Brothers, Box 771, Morgan, UT 84050). For use with footpowder, see page 88.

Less widely sold now are variations on the more traditional plastic combination—divided down the center, either laterally or longitudinally—that holds both salt and pepper (about 1 ounce, $1).

Containers—for staples and goodies. Make sure all containers are easily distinguishable by sight and touch. Years ago I used to carry detergent powder and sugar in identical plastic boxes—and I can heartily unrecommend predawn cereal sleepily sweetened with detergent powder.

My reduced, 6-ounce weekly quota of sugar now travels in one of the little squared-off half-pint plastic bottles (¾-ounce, sort of free) in which you buy Fruit Stand and other fruit drinks; my margarine in a small, rounded Tupperware container 2¼ inches high, 3-inch diameter, that weighs 1 ounce. I no longer carry detergent powder (see page 488).

Some people carry food items, and even water, in wide-mouth plastic bottles of various sizes. A whole family of cousins, in various shapes and sizes, sprinkles the catalogues. But Nalgene bottles, made by the Nalge Company of New York, seem by far the most reliable. They come in 36 shapes and 17 sizes, rounded and squared, large- and small-mouthed, 1 fluid ounce to ½-gallon capacity, weighing ½ ounce to 9 ounces, costing $.69 to $4.50. They are strong, the lids don't leak and the plastic doesn't contaminate. A new entry: a package of nine small, pharmaceutical-size and -quality containers called Dispensalls (total weight 3 ounces; $7).

An alternative for margarine and also for such potential pack wreckers as jam, honey and peanut butter is a poly-squeeze tube, refillable by disengaging the end clip (now markedly and mercifully improved by a center pin in the clip, which really holds). You can carry exactly the amount you want in such a tube, and so escape the limitations of pre-packaged products. (Warning! Rumors persist that certain substances, such as mayonnaise, may cause these tubes to disintegrate.) I know one man who carries a squeeze tube in his packet as a "cup" for quick drinks from trailside sources. It is the only thing, he says, that's any use for small rock seeps: you press the open tube against the rock and it conforms to the rock's contours and collects virtually all the seepage. The untethered caps are easy to lose, though.

I'm told you can break eggs into squeeze tubes, or even doubled Ziploc bags, and halfway trust the yolks to be intact for morning fried eggs. Alternatively, buy yourself a hard plastic egg box, biovular through duodecimovular (½ ounce, $1.30, through 4½ ounces, $2). I used a biovular job with profit on a summer-long walk up England when

I could often drop into a farmhouse in the evening and buy a couple of eggs for breakfast. But if shells break in such containers you get egg on much more than your face.

Milk Squirter. I use one of those pliable, squeezable polyethylene containers in which honey and mustard are sometimes sold. For refilling with milk powder, unscrew main top. For making milk, remove only the little dunce-cap top and squirt powder down onto water, tea or coffee. Even in a raging gale you suffer virtually no loss. A simple but valuable device—and one that lasts. The Sue Bee honey container (12-ounce size) that I started with almost twenty years ago is still squirting strong. At least, I think it's still the same one.

Bookmatches, though useless in a high wind, are otherwise more convenient than wooden ones. I find a book a day more than enough.

A *waterproof matchsafe* holds about 20 large, wooden, strike-any-where matches for use in wind or wet.

For extra safety you can coat match heads with candle wax; but you *must* remove the wax before striking—and I find that even then they are difficult to ignite. Now available: Greenlite water-resistant matches, 47 to a water-resistant box (package of 12 boxes, 4 ounces; $.90); and high-altitude, windproof, water-resistant matches in wooden box (½ ounce, $.89). Coughlan also make both types. British Lifeboat Matches, chemically treated to burn in any wind, even when wet, come 25 to a sealed container (¾ ounce, $2.45). I'm always rather surprised at how rarely I use a matchsafe, but when I need one, I need it. And in practice I find I often carry two. (They are also safe and convenient places to keep needles and a little thread [page 512].)

My first-line matchsafe is the screw-tight metal kind (1 ounce, now $1.80). I've carried it for years, but at one time grew unhappy with both the difficulty of opening it and also the way the metal attachment loop can pull loose. If it weren't for the usefulness of this loop, which permits you to tie the matchsafe to your belt, or to an inflatable vest on river crossings (page 535), I would probably switch to a simpler plastic model (¾ ounce, $.75) that I often carry as back-up—even though the striking bar in the base is, at best, marginally effective. 120-size film cans are said to be useful makeshift matchsafes.

L. L. Bean now offer an interesting toy: a combination matchsafe, whistle and compass, 4¼ inches long, "large enough to hold a decent supply of matches and even a small candle" (1½ ounces, $6.25). At the opposite, frugal extreme is a reader's suggestion: "Through accident I discovered what has proven to be an airtight, light, buoyant and free matchsafe. Just take any square, 3-inch-high spice can of the type that bay leaves come in (not the ones with the shaker tops) and you'll find enough room for matches, needle and thread, safety pins or whatever.

You have to pry the lid off with a knife, coin or strong thumbnail (not advisable), but it's lighter than any other I've tried. And again, it's free."

A *can opener*—U.S. Army type—maybe worth carrying if you don't have a Swiss Army knife with one. Ordinary canned foods make hopelessly inefficient backpacking fare but you may need the opener for canned goodies that you include in cache or airdrop, or buy as a welcome change at a wayside store, or are given by some kind, heavy-toting, backcountry horseman. One end of the opener doubles as a screwdriver. It's not particularly effective. But as can openers these tiny instruments (⅛ ounce, $.90 for 2) are astonishingly efficient. The Ski Hut catalogue used to call them "one of the noblest products of the U.S. Army." A larger, tougher, British version embodies bottle opener and small emergency spoon (¾ ounce; $1.20 for 2).

Warning: These can openers are easily lost, especially in sand, so thread a small piece of red rag through the key-chain hole. On the rare occasions I now carry it, my opener goes into the office (page 506), wrapped in its own small plastic bag.

A *prospector's magnifying glass,* most often useful for examining rock samples and such sights as the horrifying head of a dragonfly, forms an emergency reserve for fire-lighting (page 265). For years I carried a metal-cased 10-power glass that weighed 2 ounces but have recently found a plastic-cased, 9-power substitute (¼ ounce, $1) intermittently available from The Nature Company stores in the San Francisco Bay area and from Audubon. An elephant treading on it might cause disruption, and the glass is no doubt of inferior quality. But I find it eminently practical as well as deliciously light. And its two swiveling lenses—4- and 5-power —give you added flexibility. Thread a thin nylon cord inside the end bar and you can hang it around your neck. Bausch and Lomb offer a sturdier, fancier version with three lenses—5, 10- and 20-power (.6 ounce; $12).

A reader recommends a detachable camera lens as both magnifier and emergency fire-starter. I rarely carry a full-size camera these days, but in an emergency I guess binoculars might do a fire job.

Other emergency fire-starters. For Flint Sticks—"the official Boy Scout firestarter"—see page 500. Palco's Metal Matches are no longer available. I have, when conditions seem apt, taken to carrying an alcohol-impregnated paste (page 257), such as Mautz Fire Ribbon. Coughlan's Magnesium Firestarter is also said to be good (2 ounces, $5.60). Readers' suggestions include "a Cricket butane lighter or cheaper facsimile (½-ounce, $.80–$1.50)" and "a five-minute railroad fuse [no weight or price given] that worked 1000 percent better than the 'Metal Match' my brother had when our canoe trip last February ended rather suddenly, in hail and rain and high winds and 45° temperatures, and we saved nothing but us and what we had in our pockets and what was attached to our life jackets."

Keeping utensils clean

I generally carry a single "paper" washrag (actually rayon or similar, sold as Miracloth, Wash 'n Dri, or the like) for wiping pots clean (maybe ½ ounce, around $.20). Several readers write that they always take scouring pads of various kinds (Chore Boy, Scotch Brite, Brillo or Dobie) which they swear will clean anything instantly, even in cold water. Two other readers' suggestions: "lined rubber gloves for washing cookware in icy water"; and preventing blackened pots and fry pans by soaping the underside, before cooking, with liquid or even bar soap, so that "the black gunk washes right off (a trick any well-bred Girl Scout knows like the back of her hand)."

For soaps and detergents, see page 488.

For notes on the actual practice of cleaning utensils, see "A sample day in the kitchen," page 274.

HEAT SOURCES
Fires

The campfire is one of man's most ancient traditions (indeed, you could define man as "the fire-lighting animal"), and even today a fire is to many people half the fun of camping. Understandably so. For cheer and warmth as well as for cooking—not to mention for drying out you and yours—there is nothing quite like it.

The warmth is not very efficient—you tend to be toasted on one side, iceberged on the other—but there's no doubt about the cheer. Beside your fire you live in a private, glowing little world. All around you, fire-shapes dance across rocks and bushes and tree trunks. A grasshopper that you have been watching as it basks on one verge, motionless, leaps without warning clear over the flames and out into the darkness. But most of the time you just sit and gaze into the caverns that form and crumble and then form again between the incandescent logs. You build fantastic worlds among those pulsating walls and arches and colonnades. No, not quite "build," for that is too active and definite a word. Rather, you let your mind slip away, free and unrestricted, roaming wide yet completely at rest, unconnected with your conscious self yet reporting back at some low, quiet, strangely decisive level. You sit, in other words, and dream. The East African has an almost limitless capacity for this masterly and delightful form of inactivity, and when his friends see him squatting there, lost, they understand and say in Swahili, poetically, "Anahota moto"—"He is dreaming the fire."

But there is another side to this shimmering coin. For many years now, in places it was both easy and reasonable to build campfires, I have almost always done without one. Perhaps laziness has a lot to do with it. But I am very aware that a fire cuts you off from the night. I do not mean only that it makes most night animals give your camp a wide berth. Within the fire's domain you exist in a special, private, personal, isolated world. It is only when you walk away and stand for a while as part of the silence and immensity beyond that you understand the restriction. And then you find that the silent, infinite, mysterious world that exists beyond the campfire is truer than the restricted world that exists around it—and that in the end it is more rewarding. I walk out into wilderness primarily, I think, to reestablish a sense of unity with the rest of the world, with the rock and the trees and the animals and the sky and its stars—though perhaps I mean only that when I return to the city a renewed sense of this affinity is, above all, what I bring back with me. Anyway, a campfire, by its very charms, disrupts my sense of inclusion.

But if I do not build a fire I erect no lasting barriers. After I have cooked my evening meal on the little stove I use instead, and have switched off the stove and registered the unfailing astonishment I experience at the noisiness of its hissing, I am alone in and with the night. I can hear, now, the magnified sounds of its silence: a field mouse thinly complaining; a dry leaf rustling; a wedge of wind sliding down the far slope of the valley. And I can look deep into the shadowy blackness or the starlit dimness or the moonlit clarity. Or, best of all, I can watch the moon lever itself up and flood the starlit dimness into landscape.

Always, over each of these separate mysteries, spreads the sky, total. And I, at the center—my center of it—am small and insignificant; but at the same time a part of it and therefore significant.

Then there are the ethical considerations.
A thousand charred forests bear black witness to the dangers of open

fires. These dangers are as old as the dry summer hills; but in recent years new imperatives have crowded in on us. They depend, as do so many things, on numbers. Twenty years ago popular wildernesses like the High Sierra were so lightly used that a backpacker could, within reason, light a safe, properly controlled cooking- and camp-fire every night with a clear conscience. No longer. And it is not only that round black fire-site pockmarks have in places become so common they rupture the sense of wilderness that people are presumably there to capture; or that too many fires—even small, safe fires—in such fragile places as meadows may seriously damage root systems. The fundamental and inescapable fact is that wood fires consume wood.

This slow consumption by humans does not at first seem to matter much. If you like tidy, parkland sort of country rather than genuine wilderness—which is rarely tidy, close up—then you may even like the result. I can do no more than differ with your aesthetic judgment. But dead and decaying wood is a component of the mechanism that has built what you find in the corner of the planet you have camped in. At moving margins—a meadow's edge, a forest's flank, the battlefront between soil and sand dune—it may be the most important component of all. It provides shade; holds soil and moisture; becomes home and food for plants and insects and even birds—and so sets off new chain reactions that soon employ more plants and insects and birds, then reptiles and mammals too. And eventually—dust to dust—it re-becomes soil. A new, richer, more productive soil. Reduce the wood available for decay, and you slow down this process. Reduce it a bit more, and you halt all progress. Reduce a bit more, and you begin to impoverish the corner of the planet you have camped in. Natural accretion is slow; it moves by the decade, the century, the millennium. But our depletion is rapid: man consumes by the year, the day, the hour, the minute. And when he can find no more dead wood to consume, he begins to cut green wood. . . .

And now I have a confession to make. To make with reluctance. My draft of this section ecologized along to considerably beyond this point. When it was written I sent copies of it, for a check on facts and arguments, to two qualified outdoorsmen friends—one a geography professor and the other a doctor of ecology who drives airliners for a living. To my surprise, both came up fighting. Each suggested, independently, that I had employed a common current ploy: using tenuous and questionable "ecological" arguments to justify what was really a gut feeling. On reflection, I pleaded guilty. Each of them then proceeded to demolish my "ecological" arguments with an expertise beyond my grasp. In particular, they zeroed in on my use of the word "impoverish." In some areas it might be applicable; but fire-lighting man might equally be said to stimulate growth by releasing the nutrients bound up in dead wood. More had to be learned about the chemistry of such burning. Again, in much prime backpacking country, decades of successful fire prevention had created such an accumulation of fuel in the form of choked bush that when the inevitable fire came at last it was, instead of a clean-up operation, a holocaust. Hence my "charred forests."

Both my friends then said at some length that to them campfires were, anyway, "a part of it all." They extolled the warm skills and traditions of woodcraft. They listed all the campfire pleasures I had listed. They added more. For groups, they said, the pleasures multiplied: there is nothing like a campfire to promote community spirit within a heterogeneous party. My "sense of inclusion" idea had some merit in bright moonlight; but "what about a dark night?" Anyway, you only had to move away from a fire to see the stars. And too damned often there was a "hair shirt" element in doing without a fire. Maybe a campfire was even one of man's "deep evolutionary needs." And so it went on.

Now, both my friends are honest men, and both readily admitted that they were no doubt doing exactly what I had done: justifying gut feelings with any "logic" that came to hand. But both remained adamant. They were very much attached to fires. They disagreed with me "one thousand percent." And they disagreed with terrible competence.

I am slightly intimidated but not, I find, convinced. I fail to detect the faintest tickle of a personal hair shirt. And I continue to feel that the building of campfires in much of today's wilderness is harming that wilderness. On further reflection, I think I may be talking less about genuine ecological damage than about fires' charring effect on the "natural," harmonious, nonhuman timbre of true wilderness—the quality I probably value above all. My opinion is no doubt based on gut feeling rather than logic. But I make no apologies for that. Rather the reverse. Few people accuse me of clear thinking but I like to consider that on occasion I can *feel* with some accuracy.

Finally, I call for support on another friend who has spent long months backpacking around the High Sierra. He is a man who dotes on wilderness cooking and drools over smoke-tanged steak. He sees stoves as "revolting, noisy, heavy little bastards." But he has reluctantly concluded that in heavily used backcountry all wood fires should be banned. Since the second edition of this book appeared, such a restriction has been imposed in many places at high-fire-risk times. And rightly so. But any broad, blanket ban would be a deplorable step in many complicated ways (see, for example, page 46), and I am not sure I would really approve; yet I might well come to regard it as the lesser of two looming evils.

All this is very sad. As I have said, there is nothing like a fire for warmth and cheer. In real cold and wet, drying you and yours can be a crucial matter. And let us not forget such soft delights as "dreaming the fire" (or of being choked by billows of smoke, or of watching red-hot sparks spit onto hapless sleeping bags). Fortunately, there are still places in which even a protectionist more rabid than I would condone campfires: below high-tide mark, for example, on a beach littered with logging debris, as so many Pacific beaches are littered. And there are occasional times and places, even now, when I light my own small campfire (see, for example, page 435).

When it comes to cooking fires, I find myself in the same minority position—for the same reasons (a properly handled stove poses no fire hazard), plus others that are perhaps simpler to explain.

Cooking outdoor food on an open fire is the obvious as well as traditional way. (For operating with one, see page 261.) But a quarter of a century ago I bought a small gas-burning stove for use in a fuelless mountain area above timberline, and the stove turned out to be so efficient that very soon I virtually gave up open-fire cooking.

For me, a stove wins on every count except weight. When selecting a campsite you no longer have to worry about fuel supply or to hunt for wood as soon as you stop—an important advantage when you want to push ahead until dark, and always a comfort in rattlesnake country. Instead you light up the stove (an operation that takes only a minute or so, even with the less convenient kinds, once you're competent), then leave the meal to cook by itself while you set up camp—another sharp gain, especially when you're flop-down tired. And heat control is almost as easy and instant and exact as on the gas stove back home. On a stove, too, the outside of your pot stays bright and clean. You won't write this off as a minor benefaction if you've ever discovered that the plastic bag sheathing your fire-blackened pots in the pack has sprung a leak next door to the sleeping bag; or if you have woken up one morning to find that you unsuspectingly went to sleep the night before with one hand soot-black from handling a cooking pot in the dark. A stove allows you greater freedom in choosing campsites too; you need not worry about having firewood available, or about that appallingly combustible layer of pine needles. When it rains or snows, there's the huge advantage of being able to cook "indoors." Also, no matter what the weather—and this is vital to me—a stove makes it possible to cook and eat all meals comfortably cocooned in a sleeping bag (page 270). For groups, though, a fire yields one important practical advantage: you can heat more than one pot at a time—especially if you carry a grill or grate, as many experienced backpackers do.

It is true, of course, that even a small cooking fire offers, in miniature, any campfire's glowing, pulsing mysteries. It is at once a relaxing and yet stimulating change from modern home life—including its own emasculated shadow, the suburban barbecue. Then there are the smells. And food cooked on it can pick up a delightful tang. But to my mind these attractions hardly begin to offset the practical and ethical drawbacks. And nowadays, except when cooking trout (page 211), I almost always rely on a stove.

Stoves

suitable for backpacking come in two species, each subdivided into two varieties:

Tank stoves hold liquid fuel in refillable tanks that are, with one or two exceptions, integral parts of the stove. Fuel is led from tank to burner jet by a wick that, abetted by a strainer, prevents dirt from reaching and clogging the nozzle. In heavier models a hand pump pressurizes the tank. In lightweights pressure comes initially from preheating, then is maintained by the stove's own warmth (though a detachable minipump can be used for initial pressurizing). Most tank stoves are specifically designed to burn either

(a) Gasoline (normally "white gas" or a brand-name equivalent) or

(b) Kerosene.

Kerosene stoves are mostly used in extreme cold, at high altitudes, or in countries where you cannot buy white gas.

Several new "multiple-fuel" stoves (pages 230–4) can burn both gasoline and kerosene, and even other concoctions, including alcohol.

Cartridge stoves are fueled by replaceable pressurized butane cartridges with either

(1) Vapor-feed—in which the fuel reaches the burner in gaseous form (and performance tapers off as pressure declines) or

(2) Liquid-feed—in which a wick feeds pressurized liquid fuel to the burner (and performance holds steady until the cartridge is empty).

Also available: alcohol-burning stoves; and a device that burns pine cones and other natural fuel, fiercely, in a draft generated by a battery-operated fan!

Tank stoves—mainly gasoline burners—have long been standard for backpackers. But cartridge stoves offer advantages that are eye-catching to the inexperienced. So it becomes necessary to summarize the evidence in the case of

Gasoline stoves vs. cartridge stoves.

Heating efficiency. Gasoline outperforms vapor-feed cartridges roughly two to one (for figures, see table, page 229). This apparent advantage is slightly reduced by the need to preheat gasoline stoves; but it is radically widened by the way vapor-feed cartridges lose efficiency as they empty, while gasoline stoves and liquid-feed cartridges burn at peak to the end. The best liquid-feed cartridges rival the performance of small gasoline stoves.

Cold radically reduces the efficiency of vapor-feed stoves, but high altitude means lower external air pressure and therefore makes them work better, and as it is usually cold up high, performance becomes a seesaw balancing act. The effects of cold and high altitude on gasoline and liquid-feed stoves are less acute—though far from negligible.

Wind has an extreme and usually underestimated adverse effect on the performance of all stoves. Generally speaking, gasoline stoves do better than cartridge models. For specifics see individual stoves, pages 230–40.

"But why all this fuss," I hear you mutter, "about what probably amounts to a couple of minutes' difference in boiling a quart of water?" The grisly fact is that when the wind is iceberging and you are tired and cramped as well as aching cold, and everything you do is difficult and so tends to get done inefficiently, then 2 or 3 minutes' difference registered under indoor test conditions may run to 10 minutes or 20—or even to the difference between boiling and not boiling: as the water nears boiling point, loss of heat from stove and pot to a hostile environment increases and in the end may balance that generated by the stove, so that the outfit hunkers down into a docile but immovable state of equilibrium, maddeningly shy of boiling. (This condition follows Boyle's First Law: "The heating efficiency of a gas [or cartridge] stove varies in direct proportion to the goddam ambient temperature." And it epitomizes, of course, Boyle's Second Law: "A watched pot never . . .") Even in cozy indoor tests such stalemates can occur when vapor-feed cartridges run low.

Heating efficiency forms by no means the only admissible evidence in this hotly contended case.

Reliability is even more critical. A stove that fails, miles and days from succor, can ruin a trip—and in winter could place you in real jeopardy. But this is a criterion not easily assessed. One stove expert writes: "Only many years of fooling with these little devils under many conditions will produce reliability information." The opinions I give here and under specific model listings (pages 230–50) are based on my own experience, heavily colored by the testimony of three men who have spent years repairing stoves in busy mountain shops.

Good gasoline models tend to be markedly more reliable than cartridge stoves. The latter have an intrinsically high Murphy coefficient—in matters that lie wholly outside your control. For one thing, some cartridges turn out to be as much as 20 percent short of fuel on delivery to the retailer. And if a cartridge blocks or otherwise malfunctions—as one occasionally will—you can find yourself heatless and without recourse. The coupling of cartridge and stove is also a rich source of torment.

Weight. Two figures apply: what you start with, and what you pack out empty. So to assess the relative weight merits of gasoline and cartridge stoves for any specific trip you must first estimate how much gasoline or how many cartridges you would need, given the maximum number of days you will be out and the expected conditions. Then you calculate starting weights and finishing weights and compare the averages. For a specific example, see table, page 250.

Convenience. Cartridges win, nolo contendere. This is what catches the inexperienced eye: instant heat whenever you want it. Cartridge stoves are also cleaner and less noisy. And in cool weather you can relight them briefly to heat chilled food—an unreasonable operation with any tank stove.

Beginners boggle at the imagined difficulties of preheating gasoline stoves, but once you achieve competence (page 254), it is in fact a minor chore. Mostly, anyway.

Safety. Gasoline stoves have safety valves designed to prevent their tanks from exploding. You hear and read lurid but apparently true stories of these valves sprouting jets of flaming vapor; but I know of no experienced user having such trouble. This is not, by God, to say that it can't happen; only that I'm suspicious of half-screwed-down filler caps and grossly overheated bowls.

For vital words on the danger of using automobile gasoline instead of white gas, see page 252.

Most cartridge stoves have positive cartridge-to-stove locking systems and, provided they are properly used, they seem very safe. I've heard of no accidents. In one model the cartridges connect more informally. For overheating dangers, see page 242.

Fuel availability. Gasoline stoves have the edge in the United States and Canada. Overseas, probably not. In many countries, kerosene tends to be more easily available. See opposite page.

Bleuet cartridges are sold worldwide. For details, and certain incompatibilities, see pages 243–4. For availability of other cartridges, see pages 241–5.

Cost. Initial outlay: most cartridge stoves are markedly cheaper, though the gap has recently begun to close. Running costs: cartridges now cost at least $2–$3 each, so even with white gas at $6 a gallon, gasoline stoves win, wallets down. For words of warning about economizing with auto gas, see page 252.

The litter problem. With gasoline stoves: nil. With cartridges: a

growing menace. EMPTY CARTRIDGES MUST BE PACKED OUT. That seems
no more than common sense, common decency. Yet many people either
do not care or are too dim-witted to comprehend that they degrade the
land, and themselves, when they toss empties away. Nickel refunds have
been tried—but, sadly, did not seem to catch on.

The verdict. If you feel you must be able to cook, yea unto boiling,
any place, any time, under the most blood-curdling or heavenward conditions, pronounce judgment in favor of gasoline. Or consider kerosene.

If you can be sure of benign conditions, place high value on convenience and cleanliness, do not demand particularly quick cooking, and
are not a litterlout, settle for a cartridge stove.

I find it highly relevant that many experienced backpackers, after
affairs with the seductive cartridge stoves, seem to return to the gasoline
fold—though they may, like me, continue to use cartridge stoves for
short trips when all suns shine.

Kerosene stoves, standard for backpacking before gasoline models replaced them, are now used mostly, though not entirely, in remote parts
of the world—where white gas is rare, kerosene common—and in very
cold weather and at high altitudes—where you almost have to use a tent.
Kerosene is safer than gas, especially in tents, because it will not ignite
readily if spilled. And it is so little affected by cold that you can set the
stove directly on snow. It also burns rather hotter than gas and is sometimes still cheaper. But it demands priming with some other fuel (solid
or paste primer, alcohol or gasoline). If spilled it leaves, unlike gasoline,
an oily residue. And it tends to burn with an odor—though there is now
a deodorized version (Jasco)—and to produce soot as well. It is, in other
words, not nearly as convenient as white gas, let alone cartridges. So few
purely kerosene stoves are still made. But multiple fuel stoves can be
easily converted, in the field, to burn kerosene—or several other less
refined fuels. And that capability can be a life-saver; see page 232.

A viable *alcohol stove* and a *fan-assisted natural-fuel-burning stove* mean
that you can now, on occasion, say "no" to all of the above.

Choosing your model or models

Getting someone to change his religion can be difficult, but the
task is often simple compared with that of getting him to change his
backpacking stove. So before you establish a stovial loyalty it is important
to try to achieve what we often find difficult with early religious loyalties
—bringing logic to bear. Note, by the way, that nothing in the Consti-
tution says you must stick with one stove. Different conditions may call

for different models. As we shall see, I habitually ring the changes on a team of three favorites and experiment with others.

Note that the only backpacking stoves worth considering used to come from Sweden but that they are now being challenged, and perhaps surpassed, by U.S.-made brands. And Japan is just entering the field.

In deciding which stove or stoves best suit your temperament and your kinds of walking, the first criterion is obviously that the stove heats well. For the second edition of this book I therefore went to considerable pains to prepare and present comparative figures for heating efficiency of the leading models. This time I can be briefer because

(a) Several other tables of figures for most stoves have now appeared in trustworthy places, and

(b) increased competition has not only eliminated stoves that do not burn hot enough but also effected a refinement in other features, so that high heating efficiency, while necessary, is no longer sufficient. In fact, it is not always the prime criterion.

The following table has evolved from those in earlier editions of this book, from others in the catalogues of REI and EMS and in *Backpacker* Magazine #16 (August 1976), plus the fruits of one or two recent personal experiments (annotated as such). I have restricted the table to stoves that are

(1) widely available, and

(2) already proven in adequate public field use, or that have evolved from stoves with such backgrounds.

The figures for emerging models, not yet fully tested, cannot be fairly compared with those given. Information on emerging models, and also on some older but not widely sold ones, appears in the text at the end of the section on each group of stoves (multi-fuel, gasoline, cartridge, alcohol).

It is important that you do not treat the information in the table as gospel. The fickleness of stoves remains one of the deeper mysteries of life. So every series of tests remains subject to the vagaries and variabilities of individual stoves (any stove may perform differently on successive burns), of fuels and cartridges, and of experimental conditions. But none of these things quite seems to explain why independent investigators, seeking only the truth, generate figures so disparate that you sometimes wonder if they all live on the same planet. Still, the disparities are a fact. I therefore rest confident that, in spite of the care I took with my original tests and with modifying and adding to them from other staunch sources, somebody somewhere will do similar tests, come up with wildly different answers and be able to revile me (as, in fact, someone did after the last edition appeared). It's rewarding to know that your work can bring so much happiness into the world.

PROVEN BACKPACKING STOVES: VITAL STATISTICS

> **WARNING! THESE DATA ARE FOR SHELTERED, SMILING CONDITIONS**
> They do not indicate how any stove will perform in the unkind field. And no figure
> should be assimilated, raw, without a check for maddening qualifications in foot-
> notes or text.

	Weight empty or w/o cartridges (Ounces)	Fuel capacity (Pints)	Burning time[a] (Minutes)	Boils quart water (Minutes)	Price
TANK STOVES					
Multifuel stoves					
MSR X-GK	15	1.0 (or 2.0)	120 (or 240)	3½	$80
Optimus 199 Ranger	32	.30	[b]	[b]	$60
Optimus 111 Hiker	60	.80	[b]	[b]	$90
Gasoline stoves[c]					
Optimus Svea 123R	18[d]	.35	60	6	$40
Optimus 99 Ranger	21	.30	60	8	$60
Optimus 8R	23	.30	60	7	$44
Coleman Peak I	32	.60	60 (210)[e]	3½	$37
Kerosene stove					
Optimus 00	24	1.00	150	5	$49
CARTRIDGE STOVES[c]					
Husch-Salewa Minigas	5[f] ⎫ 11	5¼[f]	120 (??)[f]	5 (?)	$24[f] ⎫
Husch cartridge (full/empty)	6/3 ⎭				$ 2.25 ⎭
Mini Mark II (Hank Roberts)	8 ⎫ 18	6¼	160	7	$30 ⎫
Cartridge (full/empty)	10/3 ⎭				$ 3.50 ⎭
Bleuet C206	16[g] ⎫ 26	8	60–220[h]	11[i]	$23.50[g] ⎫
Cartridge (full/empty)	10/3 ⎭				$ 2 ⎭
OTHER STOVES[c]					
ZZ Zip Ztove (w/pot)	15	—	—	6 (?)	$22

a. At continuous full flame. In the field, with much simmering, stoves will assuredly
burn longer.

b. No figures yet available that are confirmed, reliable and free from taint of bias.
Company-supplied boiling times (1 quart water at 70° F.), for both Optimus 111 and 199:
3½ minutes. Note: Their figures for their other stoves run 1 or 2 minutes faster than in my
table.

c. For news of others that have arrived too recently for inclusion in table—because their
performance, reliability and even safety are not yet proven—see text, pages 237 and 246.

d. The "naked" Svea—without cup and windscreen—weighs 12 ounces.

e. Figures are for full-blast and full simmer.

f. The stove alone actually weighs only 3 ounces, costs $18.50. But to make it a viable
backpacking unit you need two optional extras: windshield (1 ounce, $2.35) and folding
stabilizer base (1 ounce, $3.50). The stove can also be bought—and in my opinion should
be—with a neat little pot into which everything fits (see text, page 241). Figures are for

Multi-fuel stoves

Note: All multi-fuel and gasoline stoves cited in the table, except the two MSR models, have self-cleaning jets. When you turn the valve fully open a wire rises from inside and cleans the orifice.

In this connection, remember that stoves, and tank stoves in particular, are subject to one of the sadder laws of our universe: almost every time you gain something, you lose something else. If you make a stove more convenient—with a built-in cleaner, say, or a simmer setting— then you increase its complexity and therefore the chances that it will go wrong. In other words, there is a built-in trade-off of sorts between convenience and reliability.

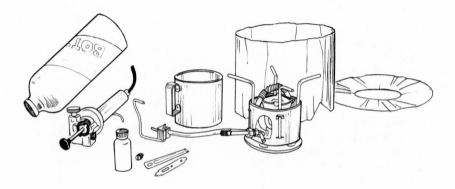

MSR X-GK

Made by Mountain Safety Research of Seattle. Burns white gas, leaded and unleaded automobile gas or aviation fuel; also, once you have made a simple switch of jets, kerosene, deodorized kerosene, Stoddard solvent, #1 diesel fuel, #1 stove oil and even, as I have learned, other

---

small-size Husch cartridge. No performance data available for larger sizes or for Primus 2203 (page 245).

g. Weight and price include optional but pretty damned necessary windshield (4 ounces, $3.50) and plastic stand (1½ ounces, free).

h. First figure is end of effective life (rather arbitrarily designated); second is when feeble flame finally dies.

i. Loss of efficiency as pressure drops (page 243) makes this figure subject to much disagreement.

j. Wouldn't life be barren without footnotes?

unfairly noxious concoctions. But note that "some auto fuels" can cause stoves to explode.

The radically designed MSR is probably the safest and most efficient stove around, and one of the most reliable. It's a tankless "tank" stove: you pump fuel directly into the burner from a spun aluminum Sigg or MSR bottle (page 252) and so save weight and increase safety and stability. The MSR is a veritable blowtorch (it was originally developed to melt snow quickly in high-altitude cold), and the effective if Rube-Goldberg-looking windscreen and heat reflector keep fuel efficiency high even under atrocious conditions. With gasoline you do not need matches: a built-in sparker ignites it. Well, mostly ignites it. Ten years' widespread use has proved the MSR's reliability and safety. (My stove-repairer advisors rated it a close second to Svea for reliability, and tops for safety.

As one of them said, "I've heard of MSRs blowing up—but there are people who'll catch water on fire.") If something does go wrong the MSR is almost always easy to repair, even in the field—especially if you carry the 1-ounce maintenance kit ($6). At first the stove's odd architecture suggests difficulty in assembling and operating. Yet, although erecting windscreen and reflector remains a mild fiddle even when you've grown accustomed to them (especially after repeated folding ages them into premature wrinkles), using the stove soon becomes very simple. True, you must take care not to screw the fuel knob too tight (or you may damage the plastic O-ring) and must keep the pump leather lubricated with oil or, at a pinch, saliva; but the very full instructions alert you to such matters. And I have found the stove's reputation for poor simmering to be somewhat overblown—certainly if you use a wundergauze (page 260). Warning: Make sure the thin metal tube that draws fuel out of the container is bent so that it touches the container's bottom side: otherwise the supply will fade long before the container empties. Even with the tube properly bent, a small but annoying residue always remains unusable. (*Later:* New models have a flexible plastic tube, and it deflects the problem.)

The MSR is now my choice for really tough conditions—and sometimes for not-so-tough conditions. On one relatively easy twelve-day trip a year or so ago, I soon became intensely grateful that I had chosen it. On the second day out I discovered that through a series of unlikely errors—which do little to soften my shame—my fuel bottle held not white gas but a mixture of regular, leaded automotive gas and SAE 30 oil, intended for a chain saw. By that second day the stove was repeatedly blocking. Yet when I switched to the K (for Kerosene) jet it once again functioned. I do not say it functioned at full roar. I had to keep cleaning the jet with the pricker provided, too. But I could cook, always. On the sixth day I reached my halfway food cache and found to my relief that the spare bottle of fuel indeed held white gas, and all I had to do was change back to the G (for Gasoline) jet and decoke the surge filter (which has been eliminated in later models). For the rest of the trip I had to clean out the jet occasionally; and the heat generated fell short of the stove's normal blowtorch level. I was back in something close to full business, though. And I doubt that any other stove would have seen me through so gastronomically unscathed. (Exceptions, just possibly: the new Optimus 111 or even 199, neither available at that time.) Afterward I had the stove cleaned and was told it needed very little attention. It now seems as good as new. Note that the MSR's jet cleaner is an important accessory. You will probably have to use it occasionally with almost any fuel except white gas.

The MSR's aluminum 1-ounce burner cover doubles as a not very good cup or water dipper. Possibly useful optional accessories include two kinds of stuff sack (fancy, 3½ ounces, $13; standard, 1½ ounces, $7), and a new spun-aluminum fuel bottle, similar to the Siggs but midway in capacity (22 fluid ounces or 1.4 pints, 4½ ounces, $5).

*Optimus 199.**

This is a new stove, and therefore unproven in long-term field use, but I include it in the table because it evolved directly from the 8R and 99, which have been roaring away for decades.

---

* Optimus, who long dominated the small-stove field, had in recent years slipped badly. But new management at both Swedish HQ and American subsidiary seems to have revivified technical development, distribution and service.

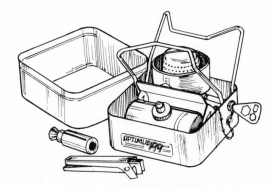

Optimus say that the 199 works on kerosene, white gas, any combination of these, or alcohol. (When switching from kerosene and/or white gas to alcohol, the tank must be dry.) The weight (32 ounces) includes minipump (page 257) and potholder as standard equipment; the cover doubles as a 1½-pint pot. The 199 has a new circular windshield that "hangs" from the edge of the burner.

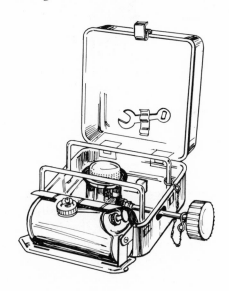

Optimus 111 Triple Fuel Hiker.

This "new" stove appears in the table because it too evolved directly from long-established models—the old 111 and 111B, which it has now replaced.

The new 111 is designed to burn the same fuels as the 199 (above). Current versions will not work well with diesel oil and the other cruder fuels that the MSR consumes, but it is possible that in the near future, with minor modification, it (and perhaps the 199) will do so. Although much heavier than the MSR it is less hassle to use and it stands among the most stable stoves. Unlike the old, roaring 111's, it burns relatively quietly. Its built-in pressure pump (which requires occasional oiling) made it for many years the standard for groups for high-altitude and uncivil temperatures, and the new fuel range may partly restore its position.

Gasoline stoves

(*Note:* The Svea and Optimus 8R and 99 have no hand pumps [though see page 257 for optional minipumps]; after priming, the stoves' heat maintains pressure.)

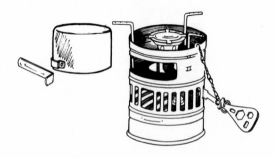

Svea 123R (by Optimus).

Rated by my advisors as probably the most reliable little stove ever made—even though the newer models with a built-in cleaning needle seem to be rather less reliable and are decidedly more touchy for flame adjustment than the older ones. (Note that it is still possible to special-order old-style vaporizers, with the built-in cleaning needle. The vaporizer tube [#2005] costs $17.90; but to complete the conversion you need several other parts, including burner cup and plate, as well as a separate cleaning needle, and Optimus advise me that the total cost comes perilously close to that for a new stove.)

Still, even with the new-style models there are still very few things to go wrong. And the stove is reasonably stable. I have tipped a pot off a Svea only once during the twenty-five years I have used it (and most of that time it was virtually the sole stove I used). The current model is still my trusted friend and favorite (see page 250). Its predecessors have roared sturdily away for me at over 14,000 feet and in temperatures around 10° F. And none has ever let me down.

Some people seem to find it difficult, going on impossible, to prime the Svea. But once you get used to a system that suits you (page 254) such complaints should fade away.

To me, a minor but very real bonus the Svea brings is its removable aluminum cover that doubles as pot or cup—hellishly hot on lips but a useful reserve in case of unexpected company or loss of regular cup. I occasionally carry the cup on sidetrips away from my pack and brew tea in it over a small wood fire. But its main use is as a cup stand (illustration, page 305). By rotating the open end a couple of times on any rough surface except rock I can dig it in enough to form a raised, level and stable platform. Even on rock you can experiment and soon find a firm base. Anyone who has watched precious tea or coffee spill from his tilted cup will understand the value of this instant table. In snow, where a hot cup quickly melts its own hole, I invert the cover and rest the cup in its hollow. The heat dissipates much more gradually, the food stays hot longer and the cover, kept cool, sinks into the snow only very slowly. To correct even that minor fault I put the stove's Ensolite pad (page 260) underneath once it is no longer needed for the stove. This cup stand may sound like the blatherings of a man blinded by personal loyalty to an old friend; but every time I use another stove I am re-amazed at the way I chafe at not having the Svea cover to put my cup on. In fact, I sometimes take it along.

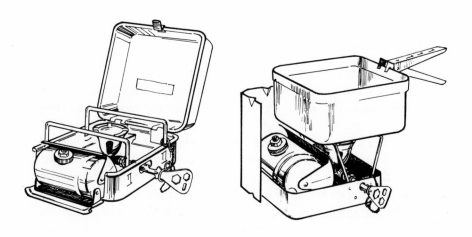

Optimus 8R and 99

The 8R, with blue hinge-lid steel casing, is an old and well-tried model. The 99 has the same working parts, but an aluminum case with separate windscreen and a lid that can double as 1½-pint pot.

Both models are very stable. And they are easier to prime than Sveas —either with an eyedropper or a minipump (page 257). Aficionados of the 8R claim that it also starts more easily than a Svea at high altitudes or in zero weather and call it "stronger and more reliable." I remain unconvinced. The first one I tested performed so poorly that I rushed out and bought another: it performed, marginally but consistently, rather worse. This report will raise (and has raised) a storm of swirling personal loyalties. I'm sorry. But the fact is that the 8R and 99 may, even before the advent of the 199, have been sinking slowly into extinction—as the third member of the old "lightweight four," the Optimus 80 (or Primus 71L), has already done. Note, though, that they remain appreciably lighter than the 199.

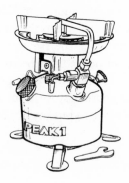

Coleman Peak I

At the moment more people are probably buying this stove than any other. But the buyers tend to be rather inexperienced backpackers, often those who mostly go on weekend trips. And the reasons seem fairly clear.

The Peak I is in many ways a very good stove. It burns hot. Its quadrant-divided windshield means that one-fourth of the burner will often stay alight when the rest is blown out—and will then relight the whole circle. In tests the stove rates high in fuel efficiency. It probably simmers better than any other. It has a large tank capacity, and the convex base means that you use the last drop of fuel. It has a pump, and in warm weather it is simple to light. It is at least reasonably reliable.

But starting the Peak I in any kind of cold weather can be a pain. I had minor trouble in a windless 42°. It is vital, I'm told, to follow starting instructions exactly, "with no jumping the gun on any step." But one experienced climber reports that on Mount Shasta "we had to soak the damned thing in gas before it would start." Priming with paste (page 257) helps, and some users advocate letting the stove run in the LIGHT position for at least 2 minutes rather than the 1 minute prescribed in the directions. Otherwise the flame may turn yellow and the stove flood with liquid gasoline. And simmering, though easy in shielded situations (such as in a Sigg Tourist, page 210), becomes problematical in even a 2- or 3-mile-an-hour wind. Simmering for an extended span can also lower the vaporizer tube's temperature so that the flame turns yellow and the stove eventually floods. (If the flame turns yellow, remove the pot and then switch back to HIGH until the tube reheats.) Because of such quirks the Peak I tends to be less fuel-efficient than tests suggest. As one of my advisors said, "There are a lot of little things about this stove that people need to know." To promote easy starting, for example, it pays to set the fuel valve to START for 15 to 30 seconds before shutting it off, to clear the vaporizer.

Although reasonably reliable, the Peak I seems less so than the Svea and other Optimus small stoves. And it is not easily repairable: to do anything, you need a Phillips screwdriver and small wrench; and the trouble usually lies in the valve system, which cannot be fixed in the field.

Finally, the Peak I seems too heavy for solo backpackers—though this judgment is softened by the big tank, which means that you may need no extra fuel for a typical one- or two-night weekend trip.

To summarize, then, the opinions of my expert advisors (supported by limited personal experience) suggest that the Peak I is a useful stove for three-season use by parties of two or more when failure would not be devastating, especially in warm weather and when ease of use looms large and ounce-paring does not.

Other gasoline stoves, omitted from my table on page 229 either because they are not yet fully field-tested in public use or because they are not widely available, include (see illustration overleaf):

MSR Firefly. Although bearing a superficial resemblance to the MSR X-GK (it also uses a Sigg or similar fuel bottle as its tank), and weighing the same (15 ounces without fuel bottle), it is somewhat simpler and costs much less ($40 against $60). Company claims 90-minute burn time, 3½-minute boil time. The Firefly is rated for four-season use and has an ingenious optional suspension system ($11.75) that keeps stove and bottle off snow. I have not yet used the stove, but reliable sources say that, once some initial problems have been overcome, it may make a very good three-season lightweight stove. The connecting tube between tank and burner is rubber or similar, not metal as in the X-GK, and, although short, raises questions of safety if it should ever burn through because of some accident. (*Later:* New models have a fireproof tube.)

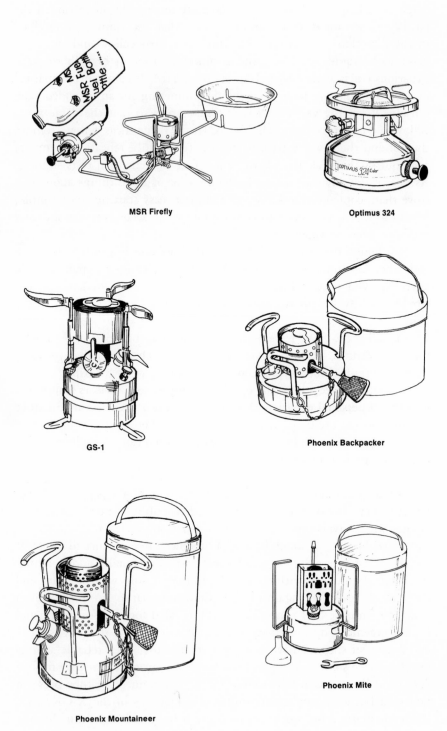

MSR Firefly

Optimus 324

GS-1

Phoenix Backpacker

Phoenix Mountaineer

Phoenix Mite

Optimus 324. An apparent attempt to make a smaller and lighter version of the popular Coleman Peak 1 (page 236). But a predecessor, the 323, had problems. For example, the windshield was, unlike the Peak I's, unidirectional; and the tank's concave base does not allow use of fuel left around its edges. Controls were also sited too close to the burner. A key-type control in the 324 corrects at least that problem, and the windshield looks better. The stove is built for convenience: it has pressure pump, lighter and simmer control. (Given statistics: 24½ ounces, .44-pint tank, burns 45 minutes, boils in 4. Typically retails at around $36.) Rated for four-season use. Like the Peak 1, the 324 aims at convenience, and it remains to be seen whether it is stalwart and reliable enough to make a fully viable unit—for four seasons or fewer.

GS-1 (in three models, A, B and C). This is an old U.S. Army standby, in use since at least the 1940's, and unchanged since 1950. It was produced in the forties by Aladdin and in the sixties by Coleman. Now made by State Machine Products of Dry Ridge, Kentucky, and only very recently released on the commercial market. The stove is said—by an Army manual, no less—to burn both white and automotive gas, including leaded (because the Army obviously needed that feature for field use, when white gas would not be available). But although the makers assure me that the stove has an extra filter system, doubt seems to persist about whether it will indeed work much if any better on leaded fuel than do the longtime backpacking standards. (See also note, page 252, re dangers of using automotive gasoline.) Still, this is a newcomer (to the open market) that may be worth considering. Time will tell.

The GS-1 (called the M1950 by the Army) has a built-in pump, three fold-out feet for stability, and what looks like an efficient windshield. The stove is 6⅝ inches tall and 4 inches in diameter, and weighs 21½ ounces. I have no tank-capacity figure, but burning time is said to be 3½ hours. Suggested retail price starts at $40 for the basic Model A. The three models are essentially the same, but the olive-drab A has a steel tank, nickel-plated inside and out; the B has a brass tank and nickel-plated windshield (and runs ½ ounce and $6 more); and the C has the nickel-plated windshield, and its nickel-plated steel tank is painted brown ($2 extra).

GS-1s have been available in Army/Navy Surplus stores since early 1983, are now being offered to mountain shops and will soon appear in general sporting goods stores. A cheaper model may appear later, for sale in general merchandise stores.

Austrian-made Phoebus stoves—rather crude but trouble-free workhorses—are no longer being distributed in North America, apparently because of exchange difficulties. But Precise International of New

York ("a leisure division of Esquire") distribute under the name Phoenix not only two stoves that they describe as "patterned after" the Phoebus 625 and 725 (and which certainly look like copies) but also a stove "patterned after"/copied from the Optimus 8R and 99. Also a tiny stove of flimsy construction that I have seen in a store but did not buy.

All these stoves are made in Taiwan. I can offer no opinion, first- or secondhand, about their performance, reliability, servicing or even safety. Company supplied data:

Phoenix Backpacker (resurrected Phoebus 725): Weighs 23 ounces. Tank capacity: .66 pint. Maximum burning time: over 90 minutes. Boils quart water in 8 minutes. No hand pump. Suggested retail price: $30.

Phoenix Mountaineer (shadow of Phoebus 625): 31 ounces; 1-pint tank; burns over three hours; boils quart water in 7 minutes; hand pump; suggested price, $36.

Phoenix Pathfinder (legitimate or illegitimate son of Optimus 8R and 99—structurally indistinguishable, and therefore not illustrated): 28 ounces; .30-pint tank; burns one hour; boils quart in 9 minutes; no hand pump; suggested price, $32.50.

Phoenix Mite: 10 ounces; .30-pint tank; burns one hour; boils its quart in 9 minutes; no hand pump; price, $16.

Kerosene stoves

Optimus 00

An old and efficient warhorse that collapses for packing but might still be mildly awkward—and smelly—unless you carry its 6-ounce tin box.

Optimus 96. Another old warhorse, not included in table because it is now available in the U.S. only on special order and at "a much higher price than the 00." At 21 ounces it weighs only 3 ounces less than the 00, yet has a tank of half the 00's capacity (½ pint) and is rated to boil its quart in 6–7 minutes (against 5 for the 00).

Cartridge stoves

Husch-Salewa Minigas Stove

Although this tiny butane stove is designed primarily for climbers bivouacking in precipitous places (clips will hold the special pot in place even if the rig is hung at an angle, as could happen on a cliff-face) and should not be considered for regular day-after-day backpacking use, it has its place in special circumstances. You can buy the stove with or without pot and extras. (Stove with optional extras [see table, page 229, footnote f] and small, 200 ml. cartridge, 9 ounces, $24; Mini-set complete, 17 ounces, $31. Pot, with handle and clips, 7 ounces, $7.)

In spite of its extreme lightness, the stove burns remarkably hot, and with windshield and stabilizing base becomes a practical rig, provided you remember that it remains appreciably less stable than the Pyramids. (Warning: Do not operate the stove with windshield on while using an oversize pot or piled rocks as screen: the resultant overheating may melt the epoxy-like substance that attaches the burner head.) Field trips have convinced me that the alleged 3-hour burning time is fantasy: with a standard 6-ounce cartridge I once boiled 2½ cups of water for dinner and again for breakfast, and managed three other 1-cup boilings, well spread out, before the fading flame finally became useless. But if reliability lives up to reports I've received, the stove could be a viable unit for day or overnight trips—and just possibly for weekends—under Spartan kitchen regimens. It could certainly make a back-up for a rock-bottom, tin-can kitchen (page 278). (*Note:* New, larger Husch cartridges (300 ml., 9 ounces, $3.35; 750 ml., 19 ounces, $5.90) may extend the Salewa's uses. You can also substitute threaded Primus 2203 or Coleman cartridges.)

The little 1-liter pot is excellent and its lid makes a good plate. The whole stove, complete with one small cartridge and all optional extras, fits neatly into the pot. Because a little gas escapes every time you thread the cartridge on or off, it pays to store the stove with cartridge attached. It will still fit in the pot if you remove base and pot supports.

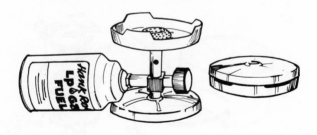

Hank Roberts Mini-Stove

(Formerly made by Gerry, then EFI and many others.) (Also accepts identical cartridges for Optimus 731, below.)

Years ago, when I first saw this stove packed up like a large but tinny yo-yo, it struck me as just the sort of damn clever, impractical little device I deplore. But it soon earned my respect. Assembling the stove and repacking the yo-yo turned out to be not the finicky business I'd feared but simplicity itself. Although cartridges tend to vary rather widely in performance, the stove heats very efficiently—and, being liquid-fed (page 224), does not lose power as a cartridge empties. Unlike the Bleuet (below), the Mini packs away very compactly—and cannot possibly turn on in your pack by accident.

Even with a pot on it the stove is temperamental during the first minute or so after lighting: it tends to flare or simply go out, and you have to watch the flame like an arsonist and adjust the flow to keep it alive. Even when the burner has warmed up the flame is far from impermeable to wind. Yet you must be careful how you shield it. Make sure the stove is sufficiently ventilated to prevent heat build-up. For as with all stoves, and cartridge stoves in particular, you must not encase it too efficiently, with stones or a windscreen or anything else. The cartridge must remain cool or even bloody cold to the touch. Check occasionally. If it feels hot, *turn the stove off at once.* The cartridge is in danger of exploding—and that can produce horrifying results.

The Mini's rubber cartridge valve is self-sealing. You moisten (usually with saliva) a smooth, protruding rod on the stove and slip it into the hole in the cartridge valve. The seating is not rigid, and the cartridge, which sits on its side, has a tendency to be forced outward by the taper of its top against the stove base. If it drops, performance can fall sharply. Cylinders removed from the stove occasionally fail to reseal. Remedies: first, slide back onto stove and remove again; if this cure fails, push matchstick or nail or similar into hole—though this could be dangerous. Although the whole valve ensemble still fills me with less than bounding confidence, time seems to have proved its effectiveness.

Given my general reservations about cartridge stoves' reliability (page 225), I would have to rate the Mini-Stove high. The most common failure is a clogging of the filter. Suggestion: carry a small tool for removing the nut at the base of the protruding rod that connects with the cartridge; or, better still, make sure that nut is never more than finger-tight.

Gaz C206 Bleuet

(Commonly called just "the Bleuet"; distributed in the U.S. by Wonder Corp.)

Vapor-fed. French. The first widely available butane stove. Reliability now amply proven. With plastic stand, quite stable. Pot supports good and wide. With metal windshield fitted, has fair wind resistance. You can now buy stoves and cartridges all over the world: I've even found them in small African village stores.

I will not reproduce here a page of rather involved figures from the last edition of this book, demonstrating the exact fall-off in performance when a Bleuet cartridge nears empty, and also if the stove is run continuously, without rests, so that the cartridge becomes cooled to a point of very low efficiency. But you should know that, as with all vapor-fed-cartridge stoves, this is a problem. Within these limitations, though, the Bleuet is a workhorse. Although it produces the least heat of all stoves I have tested, it can surprise you, especially up high. During a 24-hour stay in a hut at about 16,000 feet on Kilimanjaro, with temperatures around freezing, mine brewed me many cups of tea and all regulation meals. Admittedly, I seem to remember that it was pretty slow work. And my cartridges may have been filled with the butane/propane mix commonly found overseas rather than with the less efficient straight butane mandatory for safety reasons in the U.S. (The good reports from Everest years ago that did much to build the Bleuet's reputation were of butane/propane cartridges under higher pressure. Note that such cartridges are not necessarily compatible with U.S.-sold stoves.)

Cartridges are attached to the stove by a strong pressure system that is leakproof, *provided* you clean the indented portion of each new cylinder and the rubber cone against which it will seat. But you are specifically warned not to remove cartridges until empty. So if you have a half-empty one on the stove when you want to start a trip you either have to light it and let the cartridge burn empty or, alternatively, pack along an uncertain amount of fuel in an inefficient form, weightwise. And empty cartridges reek: you may get butane whiffs from your pack as you walk along. Remedy: seal exit hole with a piece of Rip-stop tape (page 511) or a plug of spiraled paper.

Bleuet now also produce the Globetrotter cookset, with a smaller version of the original stove and a smaller cartridge that nests inside two pots (1 pound 11 ounces, $36; cartridges, $2.25). But it rarely seems to appear in mountain shops, perhaps because of the relatively high cost of the small cartridge.

Other emerging or old-but-sparsely-available cartridge stoves are:

The Pack-In stove (by Ever New). This new Japanese-made lightweight (9 ounces without cartridge) is a cleverly designed little rig that takes any of the threaded cartridges by Husch, Primus and others. It comes with a convenient little holding sack. Though heavier than the Husch, it is much more stable. It assembles and lights easily and seems to heat well under placid conditions; but no wind blew on the few short trips I've used it. The tube connecting cartridge to burner is long and convenient—but made of rubber or similar, and could therefore burn, with possibly dire results (see Firefly, page 237). Like the Husch (page 241), it should be left attached to cartridges, to avoid gas loss at each disconnection. It will still fit into the Salewa pot if you detach the leg assembly and store outside the pot. No reliable performance figures seem to be available yet. But the stove retails for around $12, which these days is something.

Optimus 731 Mousetrap. Operates on Optimus cartridges identical to those labeled Hank Roberts, apparently with same heating efficiency as that stove. But reliability seems questionable, design flaws provoke operating difficulties, even danger, and it has not caught on. May possibly be replaced by another Optimus cartridge stove. (12 ounces without cartridge; $30. Cartridge, 10 ounces; $2.50.)

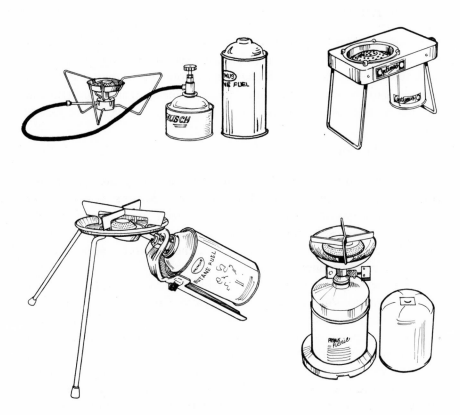

Primus Picnic (Primus products are still made in Sweden but are now distributed in the U.S. by Century Tool of Cherry Valley, Illinois). An apparently new stove, similar in essence to Bleuet, with same puncture insert system and butane cartridge (#2210) that looks much the same. 16 ounces without cartridge. No other particulars.

Primus Ranger Ministove. Vapor-fed, but with screw-on butane cartridges (#2203, 10 ounces, $2.50) that can be replaced before they are empty. In my old tests, outperformed the Bleuet by 10 to 20 percent in boiling tests. Fails to make current table because only sparsely available, perhaps because of precariously high stance, meager pot supports, poor protection from wind (though current models have an improved windshield)—and limited availability of cartridges (catch 2203). Note that cartridge fits Husch-Salewa stove (page 241). Weighs 18 ounces; 90- to 240-minute burn time (see footnote h, page 230); boils its quart in 10 to 15 minutes (footnote i); $24, without cartridge.

Alternate cartridge attachments

Lamps and heaters that attach to butane cartridges sometimes appear in stores but most of them are, at best, marginally practical for backpacking. For details, see page 453. Note that unswitchability of cartridges in the Bleuet, the most common, means that in practice you can hardly use it in conjunction with a stove.

Alcohol stoves

The normal fuel is "denatured alcohol" (or "methylated spirits")—ethyl (or booze) alcohol rendered poisonous by additives. It costs about $7 a gallon. It generates only about half as much heat as the same weight of gasoline or kerosene but is said to be "explosion proof and absolutely safe." If you cock a jaundiced eye on the energy future, note that it is not a petroleum product.

The new Optimus 199 and 111 triple-fuel stoves can be used with alcohol (provided you dry out the tank before switching from gasoline or kerosene); but most alcohol stoves are of an open, non-tank type. They offer one real bonus: they burn in absolute silence. None of the current models qualifies for the main table, but the

Optimus 81 Trapper may well do so after full field trials. It offers two important advantages over its predecessor, the 77A: the flame is easily and effectively adjustable with a lever at the base that controls an air-draft baffle; and because the fuel does not burn direct but in the air-draft that sucks fumes from a saturated wick, your pots are no longer blackened. So far I have tried the Trapper in the field only under benign conditions. But it looked good. Very good. It is certainly a vast improvement on the 77A, which I found reasonably effective in the field—though I did not favor it too strongly, because of the lack of any flame-adjustability and because of the way it copiously blackened pots. I am inclined to believe Optimus's claim that the Trapper burns "much hotter" than the old 77A, and that "the flame is more steady." Sparse field reports on the older version, at altitudes of up to 9000 feet and temperatures down to 10° below zero, suggested (though not unanimously) that such stoves are viable units even under wintry conditions. I have just interned the burner unit of the Trapper in my freezer for an hour and then, before it had time to warm up from its 26°, lit it first time with an ordinary bookmatch dropped into the wick funnel. It burned merrily.

The Trapper weighs 34 ounces—but in comparing it with other stoves remember that the figure includes 2 pots (each approximately 2 quarts), a lid/fry pan, windshield, fuel measure scoop and pourer, an

excellent potholder and a securing/and carrying strap. Company-supplied performance figures: burning time, with ½ pint of fuel, 45 minutes; boils its quart in 7 minutes. Retails at $50.

The *Trangia #25 and #27* (by Denali International of Waitsfield, Vermont) seem to be non-regulatable units that burn alcohol direct, and are therefore comparable to the old Optimus 77A. But I'm afraid I have yet to see them. They weigh 48 and 35 ounces respectively, come with fairly lavish cooksets, and retail at $56 and $52.

Precise International offer two small alcohol stoves, made in Hungary. Both apparently burn the fuel direct and are not regulatable. Company statistics for stoves alone (they come without cooksets):

Phoenix Lil' Hobo. 12½ ounces; tank capacity, .31 pint; burn time, 90 minutes; boil time, 13½ minutes; $11.

Phoenix Packrat ("totally collapsible, fits in pocket . . . perfect for that hot quickie drink or snack"): 5½ ounces; tank, .31 pint; burns 90 minutes; boils in 13½ minutes; $8.

Other stoves

Sterno (solid alcohol in a can) is a word that used to reverberate around the woods. Today it conjures up outdated pictures of cold, wet groups huddled hopefully around a small pot perched on a smaller can, waiting for water to boil. Waiting . . . and waiting . . . and waiting . . .

Two recent "stove" entries that I have not tried—the Esbit and Pocket Wing—look suspiciously like updated, but still low-tech, Sternos.

And now for something completely different:

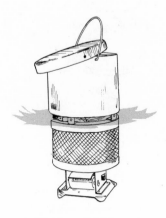

The ZZ Zip Ztove or Sierra.

Although this device looks like a Monty Python prop—great fun, but of questionable use—it works. It works, in fact, remarkably well.

Natural fuel, burned in the container, is "supercharged" by a tiny electric fan, powered by a C battery (one heavy-duty cell is said to last for 8 hours' cooking, or a 2-week trip). The fan blows preheated air (preheated, that is, by the fire itself) through holes near the base of the fuel container—and produces a fierce flame, astonishingly like that from a small gasoline stove, that under optimum conditions may jet out from under the pot. Heating efficiency is about the same as a small gasoline stove too. For statistics, see table, page 229.

The strength of the device lies in the fuel it uses: almost anything. Small twigs, of the kind often in virtually limitless supply, are perhaps the most convenient. But the Zip Ztove cheerfully consumes pine cones, charcoal (the hottest and cleanest fuel, and often available from other people's campfires) or even dry animal droppings. Once you have the fire going, even wet fuel burns. Tinder can be paper or some excellent little sticks of very light fuel called Zip Fires that light readily even after being submerged in water, have no odor and are nontoxic (18-stick pack, 10 chunks to a stick, 10½ ounces, $3.25). Mautz Fire Ribbon (page 257) works well too. You just light the tinder, wait about 30 seconds for the burner to warm up and preheat the air below (warm air speeds up combustion), then switch the fan on. Before you've had time to say "I don't believe it!" the first twigs or whatever are glowing and flames are shooting out from under the pot. You soon learn how much fuel you need for a specific task—and how easy it is to feed small twigs into the burner with the pot in place. Make sure you have plenty of reserve, though: relighting can be a real and needless hassle. For simmering or frying, just switch off the fan. To boost the heat again, switch it back on.

The optional 1-liter pot (8 ounces, $10) that for packing conveniently encases the complete stove, with blower unit nesting neatly inside its burner, performs reasonably well, but could be improved. An optional pan-handler is very good.

The Zip Ztove's advantages are obvious: You need carry no fuel, except perhaps a few Zip Fire chunks. It's the most economical of all stoves. And it's so close to omnivorous that at most campsites you can feel confident of collecting enough fuel for a meal almost instantly, even after dark. The makers claim that the stove "is practically unaffected by weather or altitude" and they're probably right. Finally, the stove burns almost silently (but check that the unit you buy does not, like my first, have a tight bearing in the motor that whines or rattles).

Life being life, there are, of course, disadvantages. Except perhaps with charcoal, you have to add fuel pretty often. Stability is no better than fair. And you are relying on a tiny electric motor that you cannot possibly fix—unless you're a little Leonardo—should Murphy enter therein. But reports suggest that failure is rare. The makers say the motors are those used in many cassette recorders and they rate odds against motor failure in the lifetime of any backpacker longer than 1000 to 1. To satisfy cynics like me, though, they now offer spare motors (1½ ounces, $3 plus $1.25 handling). Of course, you cannot use the stove above timberline—unless, for one-day ventures up there, you consider carrying twigs or relying on Zip Fires. And with any fuel but charcoal the pot gets pretty black. For heating efficiency, this is an advantage: "a hard black coating," say the makers, may "speed up cooking as much as 15 percent." But if, like me, you abhor black pots you may want to coat the exterior with vegetable oil or soap (page 219), carry "a small brush to brush off the loose soot" or simply use a small plastic bag to keep your hands clean when handling the pot—or picking charcoal out of somebody's old fire. At first I feared that the fire hazard would rule out the Zip Ztove in my normal in-sleeping-bag mode of cooking (page 270). These fears quickly evaporated: the stove seems to pose no more fire hazard than a gasoline or cartridge model.

After only short-trip trials in mostly amiable weather I can offer no resounding verdict. But it seems to me that under many conditions, and especially for fire-loving stove-haters, the Zip Ztove may turn out to be a rather surprising gem. I know two experienced backpackers who already regard it as about the greatest backpacking invention since feet.

My choices

Because I have had to test most of the little devils, I now own at least one each of most long-established and currently available stoves. But I find that in practice I mostly use only three.

For any kind of severe conditions I favor an MSR—because it burns like a blowtorch, even in the cold, up high and in winds, and because it is light and reliable and burns many fuels.

For general three-season backpacking I continue to use my Svea—because it is so reliable and because, although 3 ounces heavier than the MSR, it is, for me, several minutes a day lighter in fiddle time. (I mean, I could probably operate the thing in my sleep.) A pinch of sentiment too? Possibly.

For one- or two-day trips when weather seems sure to cooperate, and especially if I want to keep my hands clean, I sometimes overcome my general distrust of cartridge stoves and save a few ounces by taking along a Hank Roberts Mini-Stove.*

On the ultralightweight trips I am now beginning to make occasionally I find myself using the Hank Roberts, Husch-Salewa or Zip Ztove. And I shall continue to look for viable, ethereal alternatives.

Other considerations can, of course, outweigh weight. In pine-cone country, or when some other good fuel seems sure to be plentiful, I might well lean toward a Zip Ztove, especially if I continue to gain confidence in it.

---

* The arithmetic for comparing tank and cartridge stoves must take into account the packing out of empty cartridges (unless you expect to call in at a ranger station or some other place with garbage disposal; if so, then, in the table that follows, you can deduct 3 ounces for each empty cartridge). The exact sums depend, of course, on your personal cooking demands: the table (which considers three sample stoves, and is based on the table on page 229) assumes that for a week you need, like me, either three cartridges or a full Svea tank plus 1⅓ pints of white gas in a 3-ounce Sigg bottle; and that you also lack the courage/stupidity to rely on any one cartridge for a full 48 hours. Amend these parameters to fit your regimen.

	Day (1 tankful or cartridge)		*48-hr. Weekend* (⅔ pint of fuel or 2 cartridges)		*Week* (1⅔ pints of fuel or 3 cartridges)	
	Full (Oz.)	*Empty (Oz.)*	*Full (Oz.)*	*Empty (Oz.)*	*Full (Oz.)*	*Empty (Oz.)*
Svea	22	18	29	21	41	21
Hank Roberts Mini-Stove	18	11 (?)	28	20 (?)	38	17 (?)
Bleuet (with windscreen and stand)	30	23 (?)	40	30 (?)	50	29 (?)

OPERATING YOUR STOVE

Safety

Don't be afraid of any stove. But each time you touch one, exercise meticulous care in every little act. Your first failure to screw a filler plug or cartridge fully home could be your last.

Never have your face over a lit stove. The chances of a malfunction at such a time may be remote, but it would be devastating. Less obvious but more likely, and almost as dangerous, is the risk of the flame's igniting hair or beard.

Beware of big pots, especially with encircling windscreens. They can entrap so much heat that the cartridge or tank may explode. (In tank stoves the danger is especially great with leaded gasoline. It cannot arise with tube-connected stoves such as the MSR X-GK and Firefly or the Ever New Pack-In.)

Beware of sleeping bags near stoves. Nylon shells melt easily and are very difficult to extinguish. (I say only "Beware," not "Keep stoves away." As we shall see, I mostly cook with my stove close to my sleeping bag. But I take care.)

Stoves in tents: see page 283.

Convenience is the cartridge stoves' strong point, and with them you don't really have to learn much except how to put a match to a burner. It is almost—though not quite—like lighting a nonpilot stove back home. But for such things as must or should be done, see under each model, page 241 and onward. For "Protection from wind" and "Keeping cooked food warm," see pages 258 and 260.

Their convenience is undoubtedly the reason cartridge stoves consistently outsell small gasoline stoves. But the latter are really far better performers and, in the long run, less aching sources of grief. "At least 50 percent of the problems with gasoline stoves arise because people don't understand how to operate them," one experienced repairman told me. "And today's instructions are often worthless." In other words, to make a gasoline stove realize its potential you must know what you are doing—from the start.

Fuel

In cities, bulk white gas has become less and less easy to find. But most sports stores now stock gallon cans of Blazo, Coleman Appliance Fuel, Camplite or other similar equivalent—all distinctly more expensive than bulk white gas and maybe marginally more efficient. Before using fuel from a can that has stood for some time, always shake well and reduce the risks of trouble by pouring through a Coleman or similar filter. All these fuels deteriorate in storage. When I filled my new Svea with Camplite fuel that had been standing in the garage for God knows how many months or even years, tested boiling time for a quart of water rose from 5 or 5½ minutes to between 7 and 8.

Because Blazo and the others now sell for around $6 a gallon there is a temptation to use unleaded gas, at less than $1.50. Don't. Lead-free does not mean additive-free, and in time the stuff will assuredly clog the works. Worse, it increases the risk of a dangerous blow-out. If in an emergency you have to use automobile gasoline it is better, even with stoves designed for the job (MSR X-GK, GS-1), to buy low-octane grades: they contain fewest additives. Avoid leaded gas.

Overseas, you can rarely buy white gas. In Europe a relatively common replacement is naphtha—a first distillate of gasoline that's very efficient but highly volatile.

For kerosene, see page 227.

Fuel containers

The most popular containers, and the ones I use, are the cylindrical, spun-aluminum Sigg bottles, made in Switzerland (½ pint, 2 ounces, $4.50; 1 pint, 4 ounces, $4.75; 1 quart, 5 ounces, $4.95). Buy the bare aluminum, non-anodized kind: the more expensive, colored, anodized versions are needed only for corrosive liquids, such as booze (page 180). MSR now make an intermediate-size 1.4-pint (20-fluid-ounce) bottle (4 ounces, $4.95).

These aluminum bottles (see illustration opposite, and with stoves, pages 230, 231 and 238) are extraordinarily tough. My original Sigg, though battered like a pug, was still sound after a dozen years; but dents finally reduced its capacity so severely that I retired it, with honor. After another dozen years its replacement remains in good shape. You may have to replace a worn gasket every few years, but that's about all. If a stopper is hard to remove, apply overwhelming leverage by twisting a spoon or stick pushed through the stopper arch. It seems that "care should be taken" when using Sigg bottles as tanks with MSR stoves. MSR bottles are tested for the pressures involved with MSR stoves.

A full 1-pint bottle of white gas plus the starting tankful will just last me and my Svea or MSR a week, provided I exercise care. If snow or ice must be melted for water I carry two bottles or one large.

Filling the stove

For years I carried a tiny plastic or aluminum funnel (⅛ ounce, $.50) and poured directly into it from my Sigg bottle. But when the bottle was full I always spilled a little gas, no matter how carefully I poured. Once the level dropped, the difficulty vanished; but that wastage of precious fuel hurt. Then came the Candy, or Sigg, pouring cap (see illustration below, at extreme right), made from a standard Sigg plastic stopper. With a fingertip on a small hole drilled in the stopper you can control, very accurately, fuel flow from the short pouring tube. Variations on this cunning device have for years come from several makers (average, ½ ounce, $2.25) and they work like a dream. You simply tie the pourer to the solid stopper with a length of nylon cord and switch stoppers when you want to pour. Warning! Make sure you replace the solid stopper before returning the bottle to your pack. Painting the Candy cap wholly or partly red might help, I guess.

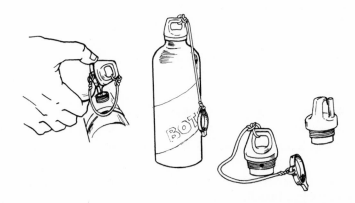

Some years ago Sigg introduced a modified stopper with holes of differing size drilled on opposite sides of the stopper, up near the top of the threads. The idea was that you unscrewed the stopper to the last thread and poured through the larger hole while controlling flow with your fingertip on the smaller. But the control hole remains so recessed that not even a half-grown Hobbit could get a fingertip on it; and the slack fitting of the almost-unscrewed stopper allows air to pass—and nullify the control effect. Result: gasoline dribbling miserably down the side of the bottle, and a loosened stopper liable to pop off. But the Otter Works (4911 E. Mercer Way, Mercer Island, WA 98040) have recently produced the Companion Pour Spout, a hollow, ⅒-ounce device ($1.39) that aligns with the new Sigg holes and similar ones on the MSR bottle and is then screwed tight. See illustration above. The Companion, made of red plastic to reduce loss risk, also works by finger- or thumb-tip control—satisfactorily, though less efficiently than the Candey. With some stoves, such as the Peak I, its lack of a markedly protruding spout can be a nuisance. Still, compared with the Candey, it saves ⁴⁄₁₀ ounce and about $.85 and is now sold in many mountain shops.

(*Later* [too late for illustration]: The new Fuel Faucet by Limelight replaces the stopper of any Sigg or MSR bottle and has a built-in, turnable top that you pivot into the pour position. You control fuel flow with fingertip on air hole. Then you "turn again to seal without a leak." Maybe. But I'll need convincing that it's safe. The arrangement sounds painfully susceptible to those rare but inevitable occasions when Murphy comes down like a wolf on the fold. Let's hope I'm just paranoid. At ½ ounce, $3.95, this could be a gem. The Super Pour Spout sold by REI looks identical.)

You may sometimes have difficulty unscrewing your stove's knurled filler cap. Failing pliers, try nylon cord: loop it around the knurled portion and jam (not tie) it tight, then pull. It works, I promise. Or can.

Priming (preheating)

Before lighting any gasoline stove you must prime it by preheating the generator. The theory is simple. First you fill the little bowl at the foot of the generator with fuel. (Although almost everyone uses the white gas that fuels the stove, because that saves carrying something else, you can—as we shall see [page 257]—use alcohol or a special paste.) You light the fuel in the bowl. When it has almost finished burning— thereby heating the generator and vaporizing some fuel—you open the stove valve. If you time it dead right the dying flame lights the jet. If not, you apply a match. And once the jet is alight its heat will maintain pressure for as long as there's fuel in the tank.

What causes dismay among beginners and ecstasies of disagreement among pundits is the apparently simple business of filling the bowl. The Svea's instructions tell you to open the valve slightly and then cradle the tank in the palms of your hands: they will warm the fuel and cause it to expand and emerge from the nozzle and run down the generator and fill the bowl. But the fact is that, except when temperatures are cool but not cold, you run into difficulties. At one extreme, the cold metal murders your hands. At the other, the gasoline is already so warm that the increase in temperature, if any, is too small to force out fuel, and you sit there for minutes on end, solemn and expectant as Aladdin, and nothing happens.

I rarely bother with the warm-hands routine. Sometimes I just put the stove in the sun or on a hot rock for a few moments and just sometimes it works. More often I light a fragment of paper under the bowl. Toilet paper does fine, but—in one of those old-womanish habits that seem so important in the wilderness, and are—I hoard in a pants ticket-pocket every discarded paper wrapper from tea bags and meat bars and mintcake and the like, and I reach for one automatically when I want to light the stove. For reasons still occluded from my comprehension, the "little pieces of paper" routine has stirred considerable merriment among reviewers, other writers and, for all I know, humans. But I assure you that the system works well, especially if you remember, as I almost never do, to open the valve when the stove has cooled after use, and so nullify the internal vacuum. Note, though, that I restrict the heating to little more than one tea-bag wrapper. I cannot endorse the recommendation of a reader who says: "Mountaineers discovered years ago that the only way to light [a gasoline stove] was to douse the whole thing with gas and then stand back and throw a match in. A stove lit in this manner will light 'first time every time.' " No doubt. But too much heat, especially underneath, can melt the solder securing the tank. All it takes is a pinhole: within seconds the whole stove can become Mount St. Helens.

Sometimes no heating is necessary: when temperature or altitude is much higher than on the last occasion you used the stove, especially if you refilled it then or remembered the devacuum business, the fuel often wells out as soon as you open the valve. But nine times out of ten (except with the Peak I—and sometimes with it too) you will have to prime. There are, as one correspondent insists, "a million ways to prime." The one you select will depend on chance and on your general character, specific prejudices and model of stove. My paper-burning method works well with a Svea, not quite so well with the old Optimus 80 (because you have to remove the stove from its can and then replace it) and is hardly possible with an 8R or 99. Alternative methods work better with these other stoves.

There are two currently sanctified alternatives—both promulgated in several readers' letters and also bruited about in other literature.

One is to carry a small plastic eyedropper. To prime stove, remove filler cap (automatically devacuuming tank), fill eyedropper with gas and transfer it to preheating bowl. Repeat if necessary until bowl is full, and preferably overflowing. Close filler cap firmly—and you're all set. This system works well with the old Optimus 80 (you need not remove the stove from its can), even better with an 8R or 99. And the eyedropper can travel in the can of either. If it has a white or bright red rubber bulb, or a piece of bright material attached, the danger of losing it is no doubt reduced. The dropper can travel inside a Svea's windshield; but because Svea lovers have to remove the windshield to get at the filler cap they may, like me, find paper-burning better. One reader recommends, instead of an eyedropper, a 2-inch length of plastic straw—white, so that it shows up in almost total darkness.

Describing the second method, a reader points out that "there is no rule that says you can't take off the cap and blow gently. Gas comes squirting out of the nozzle and into the bowl." He adds that he uses an 8R, which has "easy oral access," and admits that with a Svea or Optimus 80 "a little gas might dribble down onto your nose." Worse, it seems to me, is the damned nuisance of having to remove these stoves from windscreen or can and also the near-certainty that they will transfer to your lips and nose some of the soot they'll assuredly have accumulated from repeated priming. Still, the method seems to work well with the 8R. And, as the reader tartly reminded me, "it eliminates the messing around with lighting little bits of paper."

There are other, less publicized, priming tactics. A 75-year-old reader confides: "It took me two-thirds of a lifetime for this idea to hit me, so best I pass it on while yet there is time. . . . Next time you fill your Svea, screw the filler cap on, then unscrew the conical burner from the vaporizer stem, open the valve, put your mouth tight over the nipple (no bum cracks, pliz) and apply all the breath-pressure you can (it will be about 2½ lbs. p.s.i.) for about 20 secs. Close the valve before you relax the pressure or you'll get 'gassed.' Your stove now is pressurized. If you now opened the valve, fuel would shoot 8 inches high, so replace the burner. From here on proceed as heretofore. You will add the pressure due to heat to that you already have built up by breath and Svea will take off like a 747. You'll find this especially useful in cold weather."

Yet another reader writes: "Open the valve a few turns, then turn the stove upside-down and let it rest there a minute or two. . . . Holding the match or, as I use, a cigarette lighter under the nipple will cause the stove to light within a couple of seconds. Only a rapid return to uprightedness and closing the valve somewhat, and the stove is ready to go." So he says. I wish you better luck than I've had.

Finally, if you have just refilled the stove, then you can—given a suitable filler, such as a Sigg cap or, less conveniently, a Companion Pour Spout (both page 253)—pour direct from container into bowl. This method is inadvisable at other times not only because getting the container out of your pack would be a nuisance but also because there is a remote chance of fire or even explosion—not, obviously, when the stove is cold, but if, as can happen, the first priming was not fully effective and you decide to give the partly heated stove another dose. At such a moment you could, especially when weary at the end of a long day's walk, overlook a lingering spark. Or the heat could cause spontaneous combustion. If the flame flashed back into the container it could conceivably explode. And that is not a chance to take.

As an alternative, you can carry a small plastic container, proven leakproof, of priming fluid. Such a container comes with the MSR stove. A reader suggests the kind used for storing contact-lens solutions. The best priming fluid is alcohol: less flammable than white gas; if spilled, quickly evaporates without stain; but also, if it does catch fire when spilled, burns with an invisible flame and can therefore be dangerous. At some risk but a gain in simplicity you could carry white gas instead of alcohol. The best primer, especially under bad conditions (see page 433), is probably an alcohol-impregnated paste (Mautz Fire Ribbon, 6-ounce tube, $2; or Optimus Priming Paste, 2-ounce tube, $2.29). Both squeeze out like toothpaste. I used to carry my priming paste in a plastic film can, but after it popped open at 10,000 feet I switched to the smallest-size round Nalgene plastic bottle (page 216). A small dab of paste stroked onto the right part of any stove with a knife blade lights easily and burns in wind or rain with a safe, nonflaring flame. It's effective for starting the Zip Ztove too, or any emergency fire.

Today, of course, the trend is toward "natural," recyclable everything. One reader reports that a neighbor, a contractor, "insists he warms the tank of his Svea by urinating on it." "Migawd!" says this correspondent. "Now we gotta study the science of Thermodynamic Urination."

As you see, priming your gasoline or kerosene stove is a creative and almost limitless field.

Several years ago Optimus introduced a minipump (illustration, page 233) that would fit all their small tank stoves, and it looked as if the days of creative priming were over. But the pump turns out to be marginally useful, at best. The awkwardness of fitting it to the Svea (which you cannot do with the windshield in place) has meant that I have not even tried the device. On the Svea it sits so close to the burner as to be dangerous, and should be used only for starting, not operating. (You *can* remove it because you must replace the standard tank cap with a special threaded cap which you leave in place.) The same stricture applies to the old Model 80 and even, though to a far lesser degree, to the 8R and 99. If you ignore the over-heating danger, leave the pump on, and increase the pressure in the tank, you may get a bigger flame—though that increases fuel consumption—but it may burn so hot that it overloads the pressure in the tank and can even result in a blow-out of the safety valve or, worse, a tank explosion. One mountain shop reports seeing "six or more bulged tanks as a result of overpumping."

Protection from wind

Wind is a major difficulty in lighting a stove. A guttering warm-up flame does precious little warming up, and the stove will burn feebly, if at all. So make sure you shield it adequately. Cupped hands work reasonably well.

But wind remains a problem even when the stove is well alight. It drastically reduces the effective heat. And because this is something you cannot see, the only way you know about it is that after a while you find the wretched water still hasn't come to a boil. Most of us, I fancy, tend to become careless about protecting our stoves from wind. Every now and then I get a reminder. I once spent a night on a mountain in winds that I later learned had gusted to 50 miles an hour, and was forced to sleep in a sheltered rock crevice. At the back of the crevice I found a beautiful little grotto of a kitchen that might have been made for my Svea. Although the elevation was over 12,000 feet, the stove burned in that perfectly protected place with the healthiest and boomingest roar I have ever heard it make, as if overjoyed at being given this chance to defy the rage outside. And my dinner stew that night seemed to start bubbling and steaming much more quickly than usual.

Sometimes a gust of wind will blow a stove clean out, particularly before the burner ring becomes red hot, or when you lower the flame for simmering. At such times, and especially when you are relighting it, a match left across the burner helps keep a reluctant flame alive.

To shield your stove you can build a makeshift structure with pack, boots, clothing, spare pots or anything else you can lay hands on. (But take care not to overheat a cartridge stove [see page 242].) Or you can, as I often do, carry a

Windscreen.

This excellent little three-sided folding aluminum screen, designed for the Svea but usable with other equally squat stoves, has unfortunately vanished from the marketplace. But it may reappear. And any handyman should be able to generate one of his own. Be sure to include the 1-inch holes near the foot: otherwise your stove—tank or cartridge—may overheat and St. Helens on you (see page 255).

Unsung uses: folded flat under a gasoline stove when priming it in a high-fire-hazard place, to make sure no gasoline leaks down onto deck; as a level stand for cup or pot; and, in an emergency, as a sun reflector to air or land rescue team if no mirror available (pages 545–6 and 547).

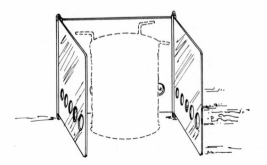

See also, if keen-eyed, illustration on page 278.

The MSR windscreen (illustrations, pages 230 and 231), which you can buy separately (2 ounces; $4) is so effective that it would probably cause most small stoves to overheat and perhaps explode unless modified with several additional cuts around the base or holes a little way up.

For taller stoves, such as the Bleuet, the only practical device I know comes in cloth, with aluminum stakes.

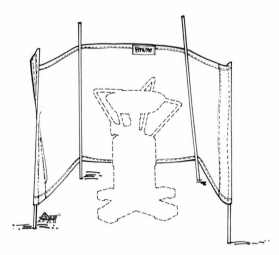

Though no longer commercially available, this seems like another easy target for handymen. Frankly, such a screen falls lamentably short of perfection. But it works fairly well provided the ground is soft enough to accept its stakes. The simplest way to keep its sides reasonably taut is to remove the two middle stakes from their sleeves, plant the outer pair firmly, leaving the screen slack, then force the screen outward as you plant the middle stakes.

Protection from cold feet

Snow (or very cold rock or earth) may cool a gasoline stove so severely that even after it has been burning well it will lose pressure and finally go out. Cartridge stoves can be similarly affected. If I foresee any such danger I carry a small square of Ensolite cut from a foam bed pad (page 336). One man I know uses the foam kidney pad from his day pack. At night, if you're sleeping on a plain, uncovered foam pad, you can put the stove on one corner of it.

Wire-and-asbestos wundergauze

Years ago a reader suggested that you could improve frying on almost any stove with one of those 6-inch-square wire gauzes with 4-inch diameter asbestos centers (1 ounce) that are used in chemistry labs to attenuate Bunsen-burner heat. It works like a charm. I carry mine rubber-banded into a small, strong plastic envelope (to keep the inevitable soot closeted), bagged in with a metal windscreen (page 259) to hold it flat. Reputedly, the wundergauze can double as a toaster—and also as heat pad for cup or pot. But there are better ways of

Keeping cooked food warm.

With a gasoline stove the chore can pose problems. You can't leave the stove on low indefinitely: fuel is too valuable. And relighting any stove that needs priming is next door to unthinkable. In cold or windy weather you can wrap the cooking pot in the sleeping bag or some other spare insulator, or can embosom it in dead leaves or some other natural insulant; or you can stand the pot on the small Ensolite stove pad shown above or on a corner of your sleeping pad. One reader has suggested a foam pot cozy.

When it is both desirable and reasonable to light a large campfire (not for cooking [page 262]), you can put the pot of cooked food beside it—close enough to keep warm, far enough away to keep clean. You have to keep reversing the pot so that half the food doesn't get cold, but you can do this very simply each time you pour or ladle out another cupful of food.

Maintenance

"Most trouble with backpacking stoves arises from stupidity or neglect," says one of my stove advisors. I guess stupidity ain't readily curable. But neglect is.

Any gasoline stove that lacks a built-in cleaning needle (MSR, Optimus 80) comes with a little wire pricker for cleaning the jet. Carry it, always. You won't need it often, but when you do you'll need it bad.

After a trip, don't leave your stove half full of fuel. It may separate out and gum up the works. But some experts advise leaving a little fuel in the tank to keep the wick damp. It pays to spray carburetor cleaner into the tank occasionally to clean things out. And always use filtered gasoline.

If you are the sort of person who repairs his own stove when it malfunctions, my advice is probably useless. But a reader reminds me that you can easily fix a leak around a fuel-adjusting shaft by packing with heavily waxed string of the kind used on water-pump seals.

Some of the big, quality mountain shops have stove repairers who know their business well. They can cure most woes. You can also buy replacement parts (the MSR comes with a repair kit) and do your own work. But any of the little gasoline stoves will eventually begin to show its age, and once it starts giving trouble no amount of replacing doubtful items such as generator or wick seems to work. The only remedy is to ditch it and buy a new one. Several people confirm this apparently illogical fact. I use my Sveas a fair amount, and five years seems to be about their life span. Specific troubles are not the only signs of aging. I have long suspected that heating efficiency eventually declines, and some years ago I checked my third Svea, already booked for retirement, against its new replacement: the new one boiled its quart in 5½ minutes; the old one took 7½.

Or was that my fourth Svea? I'm not sure. Rather surprisingly, I don't seem to generate a warm affection for individual stoves. But for Sveas as a tribe, yes. Very definitely. A reliable stove earns your gratitude times without number, at the most God-awful moments. Don't forget that. And if you're wondering whether 38 pages of print tell you a hell of a lot more about stoves than you wanted to know, ruminate afresh on the nature of that gratitude, and of its anguished opposite—and also on the pockmarking of wilderness by rampant woodcutters and by the scars of open fires.

OPERATING YOUR FIRE

Cooking fire

Nowadays I find that, except when stove fuel runs low or I brew tea on sidetrips away from my pack or I'm operating on a rock-bottom, tin-can menu (page 278), almost the only time I cook on an open fire is for frying fish or cooking them in aluminum foil (page 211). But I still light a fire occasionally, and so will other people, so we had better take a look around.

For frying, I find that the best hearth is a two- or three-stone affair with a shallow trough for the fire. The stones must be flat enough to form a stable rest for the pan, and deep enough to leave space for a sizable fire. Wind direction and strength dictate the angle of the trough. A light breeze blowing down its length keeps flame and glow healthy; a high wind is best blocked off by the side stones, perhaps with an assist from others.

On the rare occasions I use an open fire with my cooking pots—and the last was years ago—I usually make a two- or three-stone hearth. A useful alternative that makes it easier to build and replenish a sizable fire and to control its heat is a double-Y-stick-with-crossbar rig (though very few places remain in which you can ethically cut sticks for the job):

The two forked (or, more often, branched) sticks must be planted firmly, and far enough apart to be safe from burning. As a precaution I may splash them from time to time with water. The crossbar must be tolerably straight and either green or wet enough not to burn too readily.

If there is any hint of fire hazard I carefully seal off my fire, no matter which kind, with a circle of stones (page 266).

The hottest fire comes from small sticks; the best are those that burn fairly slowly and/or remain glowing for a long time. (See also "Rock-bottom, tin-can kitchen," page 280.)

Another satisfactory cooking method that I occasionally use, especially for frying, is to build a small extension to the stone ring around a big campfire. It's simple, then, to transfer a few glowing embers from the main fire, and to keep replenishing them.

If you build a fire in an untouched place, try to keep it small; then you can remove all, or almost all, traces when you leave. Pockmark sears, remember, are a major objection to open fires.

For fire precautions, see page 266.

Lighting a fire

An outdoorsman's ability to start a fire—anywhere, anytime—is the traditional criterion for judging his competence, and for years I accepted it in an unthinking, uncritical sort of way. But now, if I try to assess my own competence, I find it surprisingly difficult to award a grade. Perhaps that is just because I am not a prolific lighter of fires. But I suspect that the traditional criterion has outlived its validity.

Every modern outdoorsman should be able to light a fire, but the act is not, it seems to me, a particularly important or testing part of his life. There are exceptions, of course. In cold, wet country where you are always needing a fire for warmth or for drying out clothes, getting one alight quickly is both a testing and an important business. And doubly so in an emergency, without matches. But the generalization stands.

I certainly seem to have survived without undue discomfort on a meager and rather incoherent grab bag of fire-lighting rules that I've made up as I went along:

Carry plenty of matches, and *keep them dry.* (See waxed and also waterproof matches, page 217.) An old tip for helping keep a match alight in a stiff wind (it appears in the November 1915 issue of *Popular Mechanics*) is to cut and turn up the wood just above the striking material: the curled-up shavings will light easily and hold the flame.

What matters most in starting a fire is the kindling (once you've got a small but healthy fire going, almost anything will burn on it). Unless your kindling is very dry indeed and very small, use paper as a starter. If the whole place is dripping wet, look for big stuff that will be dry in the center and from which you can cut out slivers that are easily split and shaved into serviceable kindling (the dry side of a dead cedar is a good bet, and so are the dead and sheltered twigs at the foot of many conifers), but don't overlook sheltered rock crevices and hollow trees (mice or other small animals will often store small sticks there, and you can rob them with remarkably little guilt). If you anticipate real trouble in starting a fire (if, for example, you had just one hell of a time doing so last night), carry along some kindling from wood that you dried out on last night's hard-won fire; and don't just stuff it into your pack; wrap

it in a plastic bag and keep out the damp air. If necessary, do the same
with some fire-dried paper too; in really wet weather even paper can be
hard to light. Some people, when they expect bad conditions, take along
some kind of starter: candles (which are dual-purpose tools), heat tablets
or tubes of barbecue igniter paste. See also priming pastes, page 257.

If you need a fire to dry your gear out after a storm when every piece
of wood within miles is soaking wet, but you have a stove, the situation
demands precious little ingenuity—especially if your stove is an MSR
(see page 433).

The basic rules for the actual lighting of a fire are simple and fairly
obvious: Have plenty of wood ready in small, graduated sizes. Arrange
the sticks of kindling more or less upright, wigwamwise, so that the
flame will creep up them, preheating as it climbs. Keep the wigwam
small. Apply your match at the bottom. In the first critical moments,
carefully shield the flame from wind. If in doubt what to do with a just-
started fire that looks as though it may go out, leave it alone. If a fire
with plenty of hot coals under it happens to go out, put small sticks or
tinder on the coals, uprightish, and wait. Often the heat will recombust
them spontaneously. A mild blowing applied after a decent interval will
almost always convert them into a sudden small inferno.*

With these simple rules I seem to have got by without serious
trouble. Oddly enough, the only real difficulties I can recall have been in
the desert. Lighting a fire there is normally simple: you just break off a
few twigs of almost any growth, dead or alive, and it lights. But desert
plant life must, to survive, be adapted to absorb every drop of moisture.
And it does so alive or dead. One sharp shower of rain, and every plant
or fragment of plant you break off will feel like damp blotting paper. I
vividly remember one cold and windy evening in Grand Canyon when a
day of intermittent rain had ended with a snowstorm. At dusk I found a
shallow rock overhang that offered shelter from both wind and snow but
fell appreciably short of coziness. Tired and damp and cold after a long
day, I wanted a fire more than anything else. But every piece of wood I
could find under the thin blanket of snow was soggy, clean through. I
made a few abortive attempts at starting a fire with the driest wood, but

---

* "In the old *Outing* magazine of about 1898 or 1899," writes a reader who was fifteen
or sixteen at that time, "Stewart Edward White, one of the most experienced hunters and
campers, gave a lot of sound tips. I made one of his *Exhilarators*, and used it to start balky
fires successfully for many years. It's a little blowtorch, made from a piece of small brass
tubing, flattened out at one end, and the other inserted in a rubber tube about 3 feet long.
Blow through it to make balky wood burn or to expedite a blaze."

For reasons you might be carrying a piece of tubing, see p. 208.

even the scraps of paper from my pocket did little more than smolder. Because I was running desperately short of white gas I could not afford to use my stove as wood-drier. But eventually I found the fairly thick stem of a cactuslike century plant or agave and managed to whittle some shreds of dry kindling from its center. It lit first time, and I spent a cheerful and almost luxuriously warm evening.

It is only common sense to site a fire so that the smoke from it will blow away from your campsite—but it is also common sense to expect that the moment you light the fire the wind will reverse itself. Objective research would probably confirm the existence of something more statistically verifiable behind this expectation than the orneriness of inanimate objects: campfires tend to be lit around dusk, and winds tend to change direction at that time, particularly in mountain country.

Some people speak learnedly about the virtues of different firewoods. Frankly, I know almost none by name. But it does not seem to matter too much. It is no doubt more efficient to know at a glance the burning properties of each kind of wood you find; but you have only to heft a piece of dead wood to get a good idea of how it will burn. Generally speaking, light wood tends to catch easily and burn fast. Heavy wood will last well, though the heaviest may be the devil to get started, even in a roaring blaze.

I have never, thank God, had to produce a flame without matches. I have not even given the matter the thought it deserves. The magnifying glass that I carry primarily for other purposes (page 218) is always there as an emergency concentrator of sunlight onto paper or tinder, but I have never, in spite of intermittent good resolves, actually tried it out. See also "Flint Stick," page 500. A reader suggests that a detachable camera lens might do a better job. Ditto binoculars. But the uncomfortable fact is that the day on which you need a fire most desperately is likely to be wet and cold, and even a camera lens would then be about as useful as a station wagon in outer space. So would the time-honored recipe of "rubbing two Boy Scouts together."

In an emergency it is theoretically possible to do the trick with a piece of string or bootlace that you wrap around a rotator of a stick whose end is held in a depression in a slab of wood. The idea is to twirl the stick fast enough and long enough to create by friction enough heat to ignite some scraps of tinder dropped into the depression. Simple, primitive men certainly started fires this way; but I have an idea that we clever bastards might find it extraordinarily difficult.

To be honest, I'm singularly unimpressed by the woodsy fanatic who's rich in this kind of caveman lore, especially if he'll pass it all on at the drop of a snowflake. I always suspect that he'll turn out to be the sort of man who under actual field conditions can stop almost anywhere, any time, and have a pot of water on the very brink of boiling within 2 hours and 35 minutes—provided it isn't actually raining and he has plenty of matches. But maybe you'd be right to chalk my cynicism up to plain jealousy.*

Fire hazards

These days the way you guard and leave your fire (on those occasions you judge it reasonable to light one) may well be a more valid criterion for judging your outdoor competence than the way you start one. A deliberately apprehensive common sense is your best guide. But here are some general rules, based on those laid down by the Forest Service:

Never build a fire on deep litter, such as pine needles. It can smolder for days, then erupt into a catastrophic forest blaze.
Clear all inflammable organic material from an area appreciably bigger than your fire, scraping right down to bare earth. (This destructive suggestion is unacceptable in much of today's tramped-over wilderness; but the need for it as a safety measure is another reason for forgoing fires.)
Generally speaking, and where possible, build a ring of stones around your fire. It will contain the ash and considerably reduce the chances of spread.
Never leave a fire unattended.
Where a fire hazard exists, do not build a fire on a windy day.
Avoid wood that generates a lot of sparks. The sparks can start fires in surrounding vegetation—and your sleeping bag.
Above all, *don't just put your fire out—kill it, dead.* Stir the ashes, deep and thoroughly, even though the fire seems to have been out for hours. Then douse it with dirt and water. You can safely stop when it's so doused you could take a swim in it.

Oddly enough, you can forgo such precautions in most kinds of desert. The place is curiously immune to arson. I have only once seen an

---

* At least one reader shares my cynicism. She writes:

"A terribly procedure-conscious walker from Stanford once told me, 'One evening in the Sierras, I lighted a fire in a snowstorm WITH ONLY ONE MATCH!'

" 'Yes,' said his long-suffering wife. 'And it only took him an hour and twenty minutes to prepare it.'

"I call this sort of nonsense 'One-match Machismo.' "

extensive "burn" in treeless desert. Individual bushes may catch fire rather easily, but vegetation is so widely spaced (a necessary adaptation to acute moisture shortage) that the fire rarely spreads. The heat and dryness of deserts would seem sure to cause fires in mass-inflammable vegetation, so perhaps susceptible species have been selected out by the natural process of destruction by fire.

General fire precautions

Cultivate the habit of breaking all matches in two before you throw them away. The idea is not that half a match is much less dangerous than a whole one, but that the breaking makes you aware of the match and conscious of any lingering flame or heat. Bookmatches are rather difficult to break, but as I use mine only for fires or the stove I always put used matches into the former or under the latter.

The big match danger comes from smokers (with a seven-year non-smoking halo now tilted rakishly over my bald patch, I feel comfortably smug*). In some critical fire areas you are forbidden to carry cigarettes at certain times of year. In many forests you are not allowed to smoke while on the move, and can do so only on a site with at least 3-foot clearance all around—such as a bare rock or a broad trail. Increasingly, smoking is restricted to posted locations that have been specially cleared. Even there, make absolutely sure you put your cigarette stub OUT. Soak it in water; or pull it to shreds. If you doubt the necessity of following such irritating rules to the letter, make yourself go and see the corpse of a recently burned forest.

See also "Garbage," page 269.

THE KITCHEN IN ACTION
Packaging and packing

My kitchen travels, almost exclusively, in plastic bags. The most useful sizes are small ("sandwich"-size), medium (1-gallon capacity) and capacious (thick, pillow-size trash bags or the kind you can get from machines in some laundromats—or, best of all, the heavy, translucent kind in which your butcher maybe gets his offal). Before knotting small and medium-size bags with food in them, expel most of the air. And secure them as high as possible, so that bag and contents can adjust to

---

* It breaks my heart to recorrect that boast from the first edition—but I am now more than two years into my third Fifty-year Trial Abstention Plan.

external pressures and occupy the minimum and most convenient space. To avoid frustration, knot bags loosely. If bags are too full for knotting, secure with a rubber band. Ziploc plastic bags have their uses too.

For iron-seal plastic bags, less permeable than the standard polyethylene kind, see page 181.

Into the very small sandwich bags go herbs and spices, spare salt and bookmatches; also, if carried, can opener and stove-nozzle cleaner. Just about everything else goes into medium-size bags: dry cereal mixture (emptied from its heavy cardboard box); soup and gravy packages (they tend to split open); powdered milk packages (they split too, and you can picture, I'm sure, a faintly milk-coated kitchen on a rainy day); each day's dinner that is not a store-bought package but is instead my own make-up of grain or vegetables plus meat package or bar and perhaps sauce; the complete collection of very small bags containing herbs and spices; the various trail snacks that travel in my "nibble" pocket; trail snacks for the rest of the week; tea bags; fruit-drink mixes; and margarine container (always mildly greasy). Also, sometimes, the stove—though I now tend to use a stuff sack. The more rebellious items (cereal, soups, margarine, milk, chocolate) get double-bag protection. The blackened frying pan, if it comes along, slips inside two medium-large bags.

All the food, bagged and unbagged, is then divided between two pillow-size bags. Into one bag goes everything needed for the current day —plus, perhaps, an extra dinner, so that I have a choice. I try to keep the top of the milk squirter pointed in toward the center of the bag, so that it does not keep poking holes in the plastic. Into the other bag goes the balance of the week's rations. (If you put the whole lot into one bag you'll never be able to find what you want.) Because it is difficult to find pillow-size bags that are strong enough you may have to use doubled bags—at least for the much-handled day's-ration bag. Once a day I choose the morrow's menu and transfer the rations (page 274).

Into one of the pack's upper outside pockets (my "nibble pocket"— page 528) go the between-meals trail snacks (page 174) and one pemmican bar—so that if there's no time to stop for a regular lunch I need not unpack the main food. For easy recognition of pockets by color-coding, see page 125.

Into one of the lower side pockets go my baby-feeder water bottle (page 207, and illustration, page 206), a package of fruit-drink mix, and water-purifying tablets.

Large canteens travel in the main compartment—loaded back or front, high or low, haphazardly or meticulously, according to whether full or empty, needed next halt or next day, requiring or not requiring insulation from hot sun (page 205).

The nesting cooking pots, or the single pot, travel in a large plastic bag, folded around so that no residual water can escape. Well, not much, anyway. (Campmor now catalogue a waterproof nylon cook pot bag [14 by 15 inches, flat; no weight given; $3.]) My spoon and cup normally go inside the inner pot, though in well-watered country I often carry the cup ready for use on a belt clip (page 522). When space is tight the stove may, if it fits, travel inside the pot.

Garbage

In recent years the wilderness litter problem has reached grotesque proportions, and food wrappings are the most obvious—though not always most serious—source. No matter how carefully you select food that comes in burnable packages, you'll always find small items that can't be burned. And burying is no solution to litter: animals will soon smell the adhering food and dig it up. I stow all unburnable garbage (except tea-bags, which I dismember and broadcast in bushes) into doubled, medium-size plastic bags that travel, easily get-attable, in the cover-pocket of the pack. Into these bags go empty foil wrappers from freeze-dried foods, soups, meat products, milk and the like. Also used plastic bags, half-burned matches (usually) and, on the rare occasions I use them, cans. (Some people recommend burning cans before packing them out, to remove adhering food.) For those who smoke, add cigarette butts—especially if filter-tipped—to this list. I may fill several double-bagged garbage dumps, but the total weight rarely amounts to much. I've checked three times with standard menus. Recently, after 10 days in the mountains, my garbage totaled out at 12 ounces; another time, at the end of 7 desert days, at 9 ounces; and once, after another 7-day trip, at only 4 ounces. A few national-forest ranger stations now provide ingoing backpackers with plastic garbage bags (which tend to be unnecessarily huge).

For disposal of stove cartridges, see page 227.

I used to feel nothing but contempt for those who desecrate the countryside with litter. But I'm uncomfortably aware that once, in a mild alcoholic haze and pleasantly provocative company, I heaved an empty wine bottle out onto the virgin desert sand—and did it maliciously, with delight, with satisfaction. Like a good, rabid antilitter man, I retrieved the bottle later. But the memory is still there, and although I continue to look on litterlouts with contempt and loathing I can in my more charitable moments feel a twinge of understanding. But only in the more charitable moments.

For further sermons, see pages 320 and 587.

A SAMPLE DAY IN THE KITCHEN*

(Not to mention the bedroom, and most other departments too. Meticulously applicable only to those who operate on the Fletcher in-sleeping-bag culinary system; but embodying, I hope, suggestions useful to those who for good—or merely conservative—reasons persist in getting out of bed to cook.)

Something stirs inside you, and you half-open one eye. Stars and blackness, nothing more. You close the eye. But the something keeps on stirring, and after a moment you slide another inch toward consciousness and turn your head to the east and reopen the eye. It is there all right, a pale blue backing to the distant peaks. You sigh, pull up one arm inside the mummy bag and check that the luminous hands of your watch say five o'clock.

---

* There are several similarities here to an account in *The Man Who Walked Through Time* (pp. 19–24) of how I prepared an evening meal.

Because the pith of this sample day is method, not details of diet, I have allowed the simple dishes I described in the first edition to stand. And although I now tend to take one cooking pot rather than two, I have retained the older and rather easier bipottal system. Ditto, mostly, with clothing. The only serious amendment I might have made was to have you (traveling this sample day under the name Fletcher) respond to such a chilly morning by putting on hat or even balaclava very much earlier. You would probably, in fact, have been wearing the balaclava all night. These changes have been brought about by the passing of further years and residual hair.

Note that there are no bears in our chosen land.

There is one other thing. In the years since I wrote this section I have been increasingly impressed by the broad range of practices that exists among even highly experienced backpackers. The differences embrace almost every sector, but quite a few emerge in the ground covered in the next few pages.

Instead of taking a long lunch, as I tend to, and then walking in the cool of evening, most people, most days, seem to make lunch a biggish snack and to camp early and take their rest or recreation then.

Most people probably still do not eat dinner and breakfast while semi-cocooned in their sleeping bags, as I do—though I've had some warm letters from converts.

One reader reports a first-thing-in-the morning system that works well for him. At night he arranges everything for a quick getaway from camp. At first light he gets up without food, walks "for an hour or so until the sun comes up or I fully wake up," then has a leisurely breakfast. "This," he says, "breaks up the morning pretty good."

Then there was the very experienced backpacker who mentioned the other day that he never carried a bandanna. "But what do you use as a potholder, for example?" I asked. "A sock," he said. "Always have done."

And so it goes on. There's a huge range of viable variations. The important thing to remember is that none of them—well, almost none of them—is either "good" or "bad." If it suits you, it suits you.

After a decent interval you loosen the drawstrings of the mummy bag so that there is just enough room for you to slip on the shirt (which has been coiled around your shoulders all night, keeping the draft off) and the down jacket (which you have been lying on). Then, still half-cocooned in the mummy bag, you sit up, reach back into the pack (which is propped up against the staff, just behind your head) and take out your shorts (which are waiting on top of everything else) and the pillow-size bag containing the day's rations (which is just underneath the shorts). From the ticket pocket of the shorts you fumble out bookmatches and an empty Lipton tea-bag wrapper. You stuff the shorts down into the mummy bag to warm. Next you take the flashlight out of one of your boots (which are standing just off to the left of the sleeping pad or air mattress). Then you put the tea-bag wrapper down in the little patch you cleared for the stove last night (on the right side of the bed, because the wind was blowing from the left last night; and very close to the groundsheet so that you don't have to stretch). You set the tea-bag wrapper alight and hold the stove (which is the Svea) by its handle with the base of the bowl just above the burning paper. Soon you see in the beam of the flashlight that gasoline is welling up from the nozzle. You put the stove down on the tea-bag wrapper, snuffing out the flame. Gasoline seeps down the generator of the stove and into the little depression in the bowl that encircles the base of the generator. When the depression is full you close the stove valve and ignite the gasoline. When it has almost burned away you reopen the valve. If you time it dead right the last guttering flame ignites the jet. Otherwise you light it with another match. The stove roars healthily, almost waking you up.

You check that the roaring stove is standing firm, then reach out for the larger of the cooking pots (which you half-filled with water after dinner last night—because you know what you are like in the morning —and which spent the night back near the pack, off to one side, where no restless movement of your body could possibly knock it over). You put the pot on the stove, with its lid inverted. Next you put on your hat (which was hanging by its chin band from the top of the packframe) because you are now conscious enough to feel chilly on the back of your head where there used to be plenty of hair. Then you reach out for the smaller cooking pot (which is also back in safety beside the pack, and in which you last night put two ounces of dehydrated fruit cocktail and a shade more water than was necessary to reconstitute it). You remove the cup from inside this pot (it stayed clean there overnight) and put it ready on the stove-cover platform (which is still beside the stove, where you

---

So just bear in mind as you read the next few pages that all you are learning is what suits me.

used it for dinner last night). You leave the spoon in the pot (it too stayed clean and safe there overnight). You pour a little more water into the pot from a canteen, squirt in some milk powder (the squirter stood all night beside the pot), stir, and add about two ounces of cereal mix. Then you lean back against the pack, still warm and comfortable in the mummy bag (the hood tapes of which you retighten if necessary, just below your armpits) and begin to eat the fruit-and-cereal mixture. The pale blue band along the eastern horizon broadens.

Soon—without needing to use the flashlight now—you see steam jetting out from the pot on the stove. You remove the pot, lift the lid by its exposed rim (using a bandanna to insulate your hand), and swing-flip one tea bag inside. (You had put the tea bag ready on top of the pot at the same time as you took the cereal out of the day's-ration bag.) You leave the label hanging outside the pot so that later, when the tea is strong enough, you can lift the bag out. Then you turn off the stove. And suddenly the world is very quiet and very beautiful, and for the first time that morning you really look at the silhouetted peaks and at the shadows that are the valleys. You swirl the teapot a couple of times to suffuse the tea, take a few more mouthfuls of fruit-and-cereal, then pour a cupful of tea, squirt-add milk and perhaps spoon in a little sugar (the sugar container also spent the night beside the pots), and take the first luxurious sip. Warmth flows down your throat, spreads outward. Your brain responds. Still sluggishly, it takes another step toward full focus.

And so, sitting there at ease, leaning back against the pack, you eat breakfast. You eat it fairly fast today, because you have twenty miles to go and by eleven o'clock it will be hot. You pour a second cup of tea, and it helps too. Spoonful by spoonful, you eat the fruit-and-cereal. It tastes good. When it is finished you chew a stick of beef jerky. And all the time the world and the day are unfolding above and below and around you. The light eases from gray toward blue. The valleys begin to emerge from their shadow, the peaks to gain a third dimension. The night, you realize, has already slipped away.

Do not let the menu deceive you: there is no better kind of breakfast.

When the meal is over you wash up rather sketchily (there is plenty of water, but time presses). You rebag the food and utensils and stove and stow them away in the pack. The light moves on from blue toward pink. Still inside the mummy bag, you put on your shorts. And (because this is a day in a book) you time it just right. The sun moves majestically up from behind those distant peaks, exploding the blue and the pink into gold, at the very moment you need its warmth—at the very moment that the time arrives for you to pluck up your courage and forsake the mummy bag and put on socks and boots.* Ten minutes later you are walking. Another half-hour and you are wide awake.

(This is only a sample morning, of course—a not-too-cold morning on which you know there is a hot and fairly long day ahead. If the night had been really cold, or the dew so heavy that it soaked the mummy bag and everything else, you would probably have waited for the sun to make the world bearable or to dry out all that extra and unnecessary load of water. If, on the other hand, the day promised to be horribly long, or its noonday heat burningly hot, you would have set the something to stir inside you even earlier—probably suffering a restless night thereby, unless you are a more efficient alarm clock than I am or carry a mechanical one of some sort—and would have finished breakfast in time to start walking as soon as it was light enough to do so safely. By contrast, this might have been a rest day. Then you would simply have dozed until you got tired of dozing, and afterward made breakfast—or have woken yourself up first by diving into lake or river. But whatever the variations —unless you decided to catch fish for breakfast and succeeded—the basic food theme would have remained very much the same.)

You walk all morning, following a trail that twists along beside a pure, rushing mountain creek. Every hour you halt for ten minutes. At every halt you take the cup from the belt clip at your waist and dip it into the creek and drink as much of the sensuously cool water as you want. (Let us assume that this is one of those places in which you can still drink safely from creeks.) And at every halt—except perhaps the first, when breakfast is still adequately with you—you take one or more trail-snack bags out of the nibble pocket and munch a few delicacies. At each succeeding halt you tend to eat rather more; but without giving the matter much direct thought you ration against the hours ahead. In midmorning a stick of beef jerky helps replenish the protein supply. Later you boost the quickly available energy, and the fats too, with a piece of chocolate. At the last couple of halts you add candies to the menu.

Just after noon you stop for lunch. You choose the place carefully —almost more carefully than the site for a night camp, because you will spend more waking hours there. You most often organize the day with a long midday halt, not only because it means that you avoid walking through the worst of the heat but also because you have found noon a

---

* Such perfect timing is not, I find, restricted to sample days in books. One reader, whose sole mentor for his first backpack trip was apparently an earlier edition of this book, reports that on his first morning, at precisely the moment he was ready to emerge from his sleeping bag, the sun rose.

more comfortable and rewarding time than late evening to swim and wash and launder and doze and read and write notes and dream and mosey around looking at rocks and stones and fish and lizards and sand-flies and trees and panoramas and cloud shadows and all the other important things. A long lunch halt also means that you split the day's effort into two slabs, with a good long rest in between. Come to think of it, perhaps this after all is the really critical factor.

Anyway, you choose your lunch site carefully. You find a perfect place, in a shady hollow beside the creek, to prop up the pack and roll out the groundsheet and then the sleeping pad (and maybe, in cooler weather, even the mummy bag), and within three minutes of halting you have a setup virtually identical to the one you woke up in that morning.

The soup of the day is mushroom. The directions could hardly be simpler: "Empty the contents into 1 liter (4 measuring cups) of hot water and bring to the boil. Cover and simmer for 5–10 minutes." So you light the stove and boil as much water as you know from experience you need for soup (what *you* need, not necessarily 4 measuring cups). You stir in the soup powder, add a smidgen of thyme (after rubbing it lightly in the palm of your hand), lay the wundergauze over the stove's burner, replace the pot cover at a very slight tilt so that the simmering soup will not boil over, reduce the heat as far as it will go (a mildly delicate business) and then lie back and stretch out, tiredly but luxuriously. After five minutes you add a dollop of margarine to the soup, stir, and pour out the first cupful. You leave the rest simmering. When you pour the second cup you turn off the stove and put the pot in the warmest place around—a patch of dry, sandy soil that happens to lie in a shaft of sunlight. Within half an hour of halting you have finished the soup and dropped off into a catnap.

When you wake up you wash all pots and utensils—thoroughly now, because there is time as well as water. You do so well away from the creek, to avoid polluting it. You use sand as a scourer, grass or Miracloth as a cleaning cloth, biodegradable detergent as detergent and the creek for rinsing. (If the pots had looked very dirty and you had been "out" for a long time, or if an upset stomach had made you suspicious about cleanliness, you might—if there was fuel to spare—have put spoon and cup into the small pot, and the small pot and some water into the big pot, and boil-sterilized the whole caboosh. Or, more probably, you would combine this operation with making tea later.)

Next you do a couple of chores that you have made more or less automatic action after lunch so that you will not overlook them. You decide on the menu for the next twenty-four hours and make the necessary transfers from bulk-ration bag to current-day's bag—including the refilling from the bagged reserve of the containers of milk (an everyday chore) and salt (once, in midweek). You also replenish the nibble pocket with trail snacks. If necessary you put a new book of matches in a ticket pocket of your shorts or long pants or in a side pocket of your jacket. (You carry a book in each.)

Finally, you refill the stove.

(Naturally, it does not matter much what time of day you choose to do these chores. In winter, for example, when the days are short, you'll probably just snatch a quick lunch or succession of snacks and will do the reapportionment and refilling during the early hours of the long, long darkness. But on each trip you try to get into the habit of doing the chores at about the same time each day, because you know that otherwise you may find yourself fumbling down into the pack for the bulk-food bag in the middle of a meal, and at the same moment hear the dying bleat of an almost empty stove.)

For the next two or three or four or even five hours you either do some of the many make-and-mend chores that always keep piling up (washing, laundering, writing notes and so on), or you mosey around and attend to those important matters that you came for (rocks, lizards, cloud shadows), or you simply sit and contemplate. Or you devote the time to a combination of all these things. But eventually, when you know you ought to be walking again within half an hour, you brew up a sizable pot of tea (this particular day, remember, you too are walking on a British passport). And because there are still four hours to darkness and night camp and dinner, you chew a sampling of trail snacks or perhaps serve yourself some cold cereal. Then you pack everything away, hoist up the pack, and start walking—leaving behind as the only signs of occupation a rectangle of crushed grass that will recover within hours and, where the stove stood, a tiny circle that you manage to conceal anyway by pulling the grass stems together. These are the only signs you leave at any of your campsites, day or overnight.

You find yourself walking in desert now (a shade miraculously, it's true, but it suits our book purposes better to have it happen that way), and it is very hot. Because you expect to find no more water until you come to a spring about noon the following day, you have filled all six quart canteens you brought with you. Now you go easy on the water. You still drink as well as munch at every hourly halt. And you drink enough. But only just enough. Enough, that is, to take the edge off any emerging hint of thirst. At the first couple of halts this blunting process calls for only a very small sip or two. Later you need a little more. Always, before you swallow the precious liquid, you swirl it around your mouth to wash away the dryness and the scum. And sometimes you hold it in your mouth as long as possible so that it seeps bit by bit down your throat and gives long, delicious minutes of thirst-quenching sensation.

One canteen must always be nonfumble available at halts but, because direct sunlight would quickly turn its water tepid, you put it inside the pack—on top, but insulated by your jacket.

With an hour to go to darkness, and a promise already there of the coolness that will come when the sun drops behind the parched, encircling hills, you begin to feel tired—not so much muscle-weary as plain running out of energy. So at the hourly halt you pour some water into either your cup or the lid of one cooking pot, squirt-add milk and pour in some cereal mixture. (Looked at objectively, this cereal snack has always seemed a highly inefficient business. It ought to be enough to take a booster bonus from the nibble pocket. But on the few long, hard days that such tiredness hits you, the cereal snack seems to work better.)

At this final precamp halt you empty into the inner cooking pot the dehydrated beans and mixed vegetables that are on the day's dinner menu (if they are the old, recalcitrant kind that need pre-soaking or prolonged cooking) and add salt and just enough water to reconstitute them. (Presoaked like this, they cook in ten minutes rather than half an hour.) You know from experience how much water to add. It is surprisingly little: barely enough to cover them. You add as little as possible, to reduce the danger of spillage, and from now on, when you take the pack off, you are careful to keep it upright.

You walk until it is too dark to go on (keeping a canny rattlesnake-watch during the last hour, because this is their time of day—see page 552). You camp in any convenient place that is level enough, though it is a kitchen advantage, stovewise, to have adequate shelter from desert winds (usually *down* canyons at night).

Dinner is the main meal of the day but it is very simple to prepare. It has to be. You are tired now. And because the rising sun will be coercing you on your way again in less than eight hours you don't want to waste time. So as soon as you halt you roll out the groundsheet and pad and sleeping bag and sit thankfully down and set up the kitchen just as you did last night and at lunchtime, except that because of a hump in the ground and a gentle but growing crosswind you find it expedient to put everything on the other side of the bed. Even before you take off your boots you empty the already soft vegetables out of the small pot into the big one, scraping the stickily reluctant scraps out with the spoon and swirling the small pot clean with the water you're going to need to cook the meal anyway. You add a little or a lot of water, according to whether you fancy tonight's stew in the form of a near-soup or an off-putty goo. (Only experience will teach you how much water achieves what consistency. For painless experience, start with near-soups that won't burn, and then work down toward goo. Your methods are rough-and-ready, so you will from time to time add the pleasures of surprise to those of variety.) You light the stove (using the flashlight to check when the gasoline wells up) and put the big pot on it, uncovered. Then you crumble one meat bar onto the vegetables and sprinkle in about one-fifth of a package of oxtail soup and a couple of shakes of pepper and a healthy dose of hand-rubbed oregano. You stir and cover. Next you take off your boots and put them within easy reach, on the opposite side of the bed from the kitchen, and put your socks in one of the boots with the sweaty lower portions hanging outside to dry. Then, if you feel they need it, you anoint your feet with rubbing alcohol, taking care to keep it well away from the stove. (If you are using an air mattress or inflatable pad, you inflate it at this stage: you never leave that breath-demanding chore until after dinner.)

At this point steam issues from the stew pot. You reduce the heat to dead-low or thereabouts (taking care not to turn the stove off in the process), lay the wundergauze across the burner, stir the compound a couple of times, inhale appreciatively and replace the cover. While dinner simmers toward fruition you empty two ounces of dehydrated peaches and a little water into the small cooking pot and put it ready for break-fast, up alongside the pack, out of harm's way. Then you jot down a few thoughts in your notebook, stir the stew and sample it, find the beans are not quite soft yet. So you study the map and worry a bit about the morning's route, put map and pen and pencil and eyeglasses and ther-mometer into the second bedside boot, take off your shorts and slide halfway down into the mummy bag out of the rapidly rising wind, and stir the stew again and find all ready. You pour-and-spoon out a cupful, leaving the balance on the stove because the wind is distinctly cool now. And then, leaning comfortably back against the pack and watching the sky and the black peaks meld, you eat, cupful by cupful, your dinner. You finish it—just. Then you spoon-scrape out every last possible frag-ment and polish-clean the pot and cup and spoon with your Miracloth or, failing that, a piece of toilet paper. If you use toilet paper you put it under the stove so that you can burn it in the morning. Then you put the cup and spoon into the breakfast-readied small pot, pour the morning tea water into the big pot, set the big pot alongside the small one and the sugar and milk containers alongside them both, put the current day's-ration bag into the pack (where it is moderately safe from mice and their night allies) and your shorts on top of it, lean one canteen against the boots so that you can reach out and grasp it during the night without doing more than loosen the mummy-bag drawstring, zipper and drawstring yourself into the bag, wind your watch, belch once, remind yourself what time you want the something inside you to stir in the morning, and go to sleep.*

THE KITCHEN IN ACTION UNDER
SPECIAL CONDITIONS

Rock-bottom, tin-can kitchen

Over the years I have several times met conditions that demanded and also permitted a radically simplified kitchen. The demands concerned weight: I wanted or needed to pare every eliminable ounce, down beyond

---

* The elapsed time between halting and going to sleep will obviously vary with many factors, including how eager you are to get to sleep. It is difficult to give meaningful average times. You just don't measure such things very often. The only time I remember doing so was under conditions markedly similar to those of our sample evening. I was in no particular hurry, but I did not dally. And I happened to notice as I wound my watch that it was exactly forty minutes since I had halted.

my normal comfort requirements. The permission concerned fires: in the country I would be walking through it had to be easy and ethical and preferably legal to build very small open fires any place I camped.

In one case I wanted to walk for ten days along a desert mountain range that offered no possibility of replenishing food stocks but every chance that I would at times need to carry 2 gallons of water. Faced with the prospect of a house that would put 25 pounds of food and 16 pounds of water on my back before I even began to install the standard furnishings, I cast around for ways to cut the load. Careful inquiries about the mountains revealed, as I had expected, that the country I would be walking through abounded with small sticks, presented no fire hazard at

that time of year and was so little traveled that small fire scars would probably heal before being seen by human eyes. I therefore opted for a rock-bottom, tin-can kitchen. I cast out my cooking pots and stove, and also the two gasoline containers (one of them half full) required for ten days' stove-cooking. That saved me 4½ pounds. As sole cooking utensil I took an ordinary medium-size, one-pound-of-fruit tin can with its top removed and a wire handle threaded through two holes punched with a nail near the carefully tamped-down rim. Total weight: 2 ounces. The simplified menu (page 188) meant a saving of about 1½ ounces a day, or a pound for the ten days; and the simpler packaging meant a further saving of at least half a pound. Total saving: 6 pounds—which feels like a hell of a lot, I assure you, when it means around 54 pounds on your back instead of 60. Anyway, it turned out to be a rewarding, unback-breaking ten days, and I did not regret my decision.

Another time, conditions were different. I was planning one of my sudden, periodic, spur-of-the-moment, two- or three-day therapeutic disappearances into some local hills in which you are always, like it or not, going uphill or down. Mostly, I'm content to take it easy in there. But on that occasion I for some reason felt within me the urge to walk fast and, compared with the normal Fletcher-amble, furiously. So to keep my load down I again opted for my tin-can kitchen. And again it worked: I indeed walked fast and far and furious, reveling in the light load, and emerged amply restored. (Note: Both these trips took place before the days of ultralight New Wave gear, but our wider current options do not undermine the general principle.)

The fire for a rock-bottom, tin-can kitchen should be small and concentrated, so that when you have covered your traces Sherlock Holmes would be hard put to discover you had passed that way. You want fast, short-lived heat, so you use only very small sticks. And to make full use of their heat you build them up around the sides of the can.

A Wisconsin reader writes that he sometimes gives "a new twist" to the rock-bottom, tin-can kitchen by taking along a "stove" for firewood—made from a one-pound tin can:

Clearly, any tin-can kitchen can be modified back toward "normalcy" in various ways to meet different conditions or wants. Obvious candidates for heat sources with minimum weight include the Salewa stove (page 241) and the Zip Ztove (page 248), with or without their pots, and even the Mini-Stove (page 242).

High altitude

At sea level, water boils at 100° C. But the boiling point falls 1° C. for every rise of 1000 feet. At 5000 feet: 95°. At 10,000: 90°. At 15,000: 85°. (These figures are for pure water under average barometric pressures. When the water contains salt or other impurities the boiling point rises slightly. Marked weather changes may raise or lower it.)

As most outdoor cooking depends on the boiling point of water, food therefore takes longer to cook at high altitudes than at sea level. With my simple menus, and at the maximum elevations I normally reach (little over 14,000 feet), I pay almost no attention to the differences. I just sample and go by the taste. But with more complicated dishes you should probably work out some kind of graduated compensation. The only time I ever noted any figures was at 14,246 feet. There, an egg boiled for ten minutes turned out to be still slightly underdone. It would be difficult, I imagine, to find a more superbly useless item of information.

For the vagaries of appetite at high altitude, see page 154; of stoves, page 225.

In snow

For keeping canteens de-iced, see page 206; for insulation of stove tank and also pots with Ensolite pad, page 260; and for use of inverted stove cover as cup platform, page 235. But the big problem in snow—or, rather, the big labor—is water.

Even in midwinter you can, in clear weather and while the sun is high, often find little runnels of water on rock surfaces or at sharp drop-offs in the snow. And a few places that drip slowly but steadily will enable you, given time, to collect all the water you need by putting pots and pot lids and cups and canteens under the drips. Or you may be able to spread out a groundsheet or poncho or both, anywhere but on the snow, and scatter snow on it for the sun to melt. Sometimes you'll find a creek appearing intermittently at small openings, far down in deep drifts, and a cooking pot lowered on a nylon cord will land you all the water you need. Where such creeks are common, some backpackers carry tin cans with baling-wire handles. See also the LL Engineering staff cup attachment, page 81.

Traveling up high in summer or fall, you may sometimes have to melt snow for water (though you naturally stand a good chance of finding the liquid form). The winter's snow will by then have compacted, and a potful of it may produce as much as a half-potful of water. Under these amiable conditions you need adopt no tight melting techniques. Just pack snow into a pot, heat and pour the water into your canteens.

But in winter, in powdery snow, you must apply a little more thought. The object is to produce a reasonable volume of water with the least possible expenditure of time, fuel, energy and fret. From limited experience I have evolved this procedure for tent camping:*

Before you crawl inside the tent, pile up a heap of snow just outside the entrance and within easy reach of your lying position inside (and on the opposite side from that on which the zipper opening has just jammed halfway). Stamp the pile of snow down to a reasonably compact consis-

---

* Though note caveat on stoves in tents, page 283.

tency. When you are safely inside and have the stove set up, reach out and, using your cup as a scoop, fill both cooking pots with the compacted snow and also build tall piles on both inverted pot lids. (If you are carrying a toilet trowel [page 538] scoop with that. Because of its everyday role you'll probably have to overcome a natural revulsion—but a little thought will convince you that there's no reason the trowel should be contaminated.) Tamp the snow in the big pot firmly down. Light the stove and heat the big pot. Wait until water appears at the surface of the snow—which will by that time have shrunk almost to the bottom of the pot—and then begin to add spoonfuls of snow from the small pot. (You wait for the water to appear because once it has a chance to permeate the new snow it conducts heat far more efficiently than the dry crystals do.)

Continue spooning in more snow. Keep matches ready for immediate use, because water tends to condense on the outside of the pot and drip down, and it may occasionally douse the flame. Replenish the lids from the snow pile outside the tent. When the pot is almost half full of water, stop adding snow. Just before the last snowbergs disappear, pour all the water except about an inch depth into the small and now empty pot. Quickly replace the big pot on the stove and refill with snow from the waiting lids. Replenish lids, rather feverishly, from the outside dump. At a convenient pause in the rush, pour the water with tremendous care from the small pot into a canteen. Leave small particles in bottom of pot. Restopper canteen and place on your foam pad. (By transferring the water from big pot to small you reduce fuel wastage, keep the big pot hot, introduce a double-sedimentation process for removal of inevitable dirt particles, obviate the pouring hazard of floating snowbergs [if one or two flop down into the small pot, wait until they dissolve before filling the canteen] and also give yourself a more sharply curved and therefore better-pouring vessel with which to transfer water into the canteen.) Continue adding snow to big pot. When half full, transfer again. Continue ad nauseam.

Do not expect to do much all this time except melt snow. For one thing, you will find yourself fully occupied. For another, you can bet your bottom layer of clothing that if you take your mind off the stove and pot for more than ten seconds straight you are, in those cramped quarters, going to swing a careless arm and send the whole caboodle flying.

This kind of snow-melting is a long and tedious business. The time needed to produce a given volume of water varies with, among other things, the consistency of the snow and the efficiency of your stove and technique. As a guide on the first attempt, allow twice as long as seems reasonable. Then double this allowance. And don't be so naïve as to imagine you'll really do that well.

In a tent (especially, but not necessarily, in snow)

Every time you convert your tent into a kitchen, two dangers lurk. Today the dangers are so well recognized that some experienced back-packers now try, when using a tent, to eat uncooked food as often as possible. But, as I have suggested (page 187), that may not always be desirable or even safe. And you must sometimes melt snow for water. When weather permits, you should certainly cook outside the tent. But weather does not always permit. At such times the only practical solution is to be achingly and constantly aware of the dangers and to exercise great care. But that exercising is easier said than done: the one time you really need a tent is in bad weather, up high, and under such conditions your brain is liable to be working at about 10 percent of normal capacity. That, I am sure, is how many of the worst kitchen-in-tent accidents occur.

The first danger is fire. In the cramped confines of a tent you are hardly likely to be absent-minded enough, no matter what the altitude, to drop a still-glowing match. But any stove—gasoline, kerosene or cartridge—being lit in low temperatures is apt to flare into a sudden oversize flame that can quickly engulf a tent. The instructions for MSR stoves go so far as to warn "Gasoline (appliance fuel) is hazardous: do not light any stove in a tent or indoors." But bitter cold and/or ferocious wind or even lashing rain (though see page 433) may make it impossible to do the job outside. If you absolutely must do it inside, be ready at any moment to hurl a flaming stove out into the quenching elements. As you may have to batten down tight while lighting the stove, in order to cut wind disturbance to the minimum, you cannot always leave a zipper or drawstring undone. But at least you can be mentally ready, somewhere in the recesses of your mind, to pull them open at the first sign of trouble. I'm not sure that's enough; but under certain conditions you really don't have much choice.

An even more serious danger, and one more likely to occur, is carbon-monoxide poisoning.

Unless you ensure adequate ventilation, a burning stove can very quickly consume almost all the free oxygen in your battened-down little world. And a stove burning in a confined space that lacks a free oxygen supply will give off carbon monoxide.

It is important to understand the distinction between asphyxiation (lack of oxygen; presence of too much carbon dioxide) and carbon-monoxide poisoning. If you are starved of oxygen, your breathing will in time fill the space around you with carbon dioxide, and you will usually be warned of the danger of asphyxiation—even awakened from sleep—

by being made to gasp for breath (page 314—though also page 327). But carbon monoxide is a colorless, odorless, highly poisonous gas—the gas that occasionally kills people in enclosed garages. It does not warn you of danger by making you gasp for breath. And it does not extinguish or even dim a flame.

Carbon-monoxide poisoning is no mere theoretical hazard for campers—especially in snow, which can very effectively cut off all ventilation. Down the years there have been many tragedies and near-tragedies. Vilhjalmur Stefansson, in his book *Unsolved Mysteries of the Arctic* (1938), gives some graphic examples. The gas almost killed Willem Barents and his entire polar party when they holed up in a snow-encased cabin on Novaya Zemlya in the winter of 1596 and tried to keep themselves warm with "sea-coles which we had brought out of the ship." Stefansson himself was lucky to escape in 1911 when his four-man party found an old Eskimo snow-house, sealed the doorway too tight and began cooking on a kerosene-burning stove. A kerosene-burning heater almost killed a man on the first Byrd Antarctic expedition of 1938, when a blizzard partially blocked the flue pipe. Stefansson maintains that the two men of the ill-fated Andrée arctic balloon party of 1897, whose bodies were not found until 1930, probably died from carbon-monoxide poisoning: a kerosene-burning Primus stove stood between their bodies, and there seems every reason to believe that their tent may have been partly covered by drifting snow.

Only a few years ago two young men apparently died from carbon-monoxide poisoning while camping in the Inyo National Forest of California. It seems almost certain that, in unexpectedly cold weather, they battened down their impermeable plastic-tube tent (page 322) and for warmth left their Sterno stove (canned heat) burning when they went to sleep. They never woke up.

Now, I do not want to make you afraid of cooking in a confined space. But I do want to make you keenly aware of the dangers. It is vital to remember that, as becomes clear from the accounts of survivors from near-tragedies, you get no warning of carbon-monoxide poisoning beyond, perhaps, "a slight feeling of pressure on the temples, a little bit as if from an elastic band or cap." Unconsciousness may follow within seconds. Unless someone else recognizes the danger in time and lets in fresh air before he succumbs himself, you die.

The necessary precautions are simple. When you are cooking in a tent or other enclosed space, especially in snow, always make sure that you have adequate airflow. In a high wind, that is hardly likely to be a problem. But if snow is falling, keep checking that the air vents do not become blocked, and keep clearing away drifted snow, so that the entrance is never in danger of being completely buried (see also page 314).

Bedroom

"No doubt about it, Ed, you're the best-equipped
backpacker in the business."

THE ROOF

Under most conditions the best roof for your bedroom is the sky. This
common-sensible arrangement saves weight, time, energy and money. It
also keeps you in intimate contact with the world you are presumably
walking through in order to come into intimate contact with.

That world often mounts to its most sublime moments of beauty at
the fringes of darkness; and the important thing, I find, is not just to see
such beauty but to see it happen—to watch the slow and almost imperceptible transitions of shine and shadow, form and shapelessness. You

cannot see such events by peering out occasionally from under a roof.
Certainly you cannot lie under a roof and let yourself become a part of
them, so that their meanings, or whatever it is that is important about
them, move deep inside you. You must be out under the sky.

For me, the supreme place to watch beauty happen is a mountaintop.

I shall never forget a calm and cloudless autumn night when I
camped roofless and free, yet warm and comfortable, on the very summit
of Mount Shasta, in northern California. Shasta is an isolated volcanic
pyramid that rises 10,000 feet from a broken plain. Its apex stands
14,162 feet above sea level. From this apex, as the sun eased downward,
I watched the huge shadow of the pyramid begin to move out across the
humps and bubukles of the darkening plain. At first the shadow was
squat and blunt. And its color was the color of the blue-gray plain, only
darker. As the sun sank lower, the shadow reached slowly out toward the
horizon until it seemed to cover half the eastward plain. Its color
deepened. The pyramid grew taller, narrower. At last its slender apex
touched the gray and hazy horizon. There, for a long and perfect moment, the huge shape halted; lay passive on the plain. Its color deepened
to a luminous, sumptuous, majestic royal blue. Then the light went out.
The shadow faded. Night took over the gray but still humped and
bubukled plain. And slowly, as the western sky darkened, the shapeless
shadows moved deeper into everything and smoothed the plain into a
blackboard. Soon a few small lights bloomed out of the dusk. But the
real happenings were over, and after a while I went to sleep, high above
the stage and yet a part of it.*

But you do not have to climb a 14,000-foot peak in order to sleep
above and yet in the night. Sometimes, when I feel the need for a new
perspective on my tight little urban life, I go—often late at night—to
the place in which I wrote the opening chapter of this book. I heave my
pack into the car, drive for an hour and park the car on a dirt road that
winds steeply through a stretch of still-untrampled ranch country, now
set aside as a public park. An hour later, aided by a flashlight and the
pleasurable excitements of change and darkness, I climb up onto the flat,
grassy summit of an isolated and "unimproved" hill. This little tableland

* Important safety note: mountain peaks, although superb, are treacherous. Some, like
Shasta, are so big they make their own weather—and it can change within minutes. So if
you are going to camp on a peak you must know what you are doing. Shasta, I understand,
has killed a fair number of people; and before I decided to camp on its peak I made sure that
(a) the weather pattern was stable in a way it rarely is in that part of the world; (b) I had a
tent ready, should the weather change; and (c) a tentative evacuation-to-lower-elevations plan
was always lurking ready at the back of my mind.

stands almost 1700 feet above sea level, and from it I can see the sprawling blaze of lights that now rings San Francisco Bay. I can watch tiny
headlights creeping in and out of this web, like unsuspecting fireflies,
along the freeways that link it, eastward, with the black and mysterious
continent. And when I have rolled out my mummy bag and cocooned
myself inside it against the cold wind sweeping in from the Pacific, I can
sometimes see as well, quite effortlessly, in the moments before I fall
asleep, both a time when the shores of the Bay were as black as the rest
of the continent and a time when the eastward view from this hill will
blaze almost as brightly and beautifully and senselessly as the present
thin ring around the blackness that is the Bay. I should find it almost
pointless to camp on that hill in a tent.

But there is more to rooflessness than panoramas. Some worlds only
come alive after dark, and my memory often cheers me with warm little
cameos it would not hold if I always roofed myself off from the night.
Deep in Grand Canyon, inches from my eyes, floodlit by flashlight, a
pair of quick, clean little deer mice scamper with thistledown delicacy
along slender willow shoots. On a Cornish hillside, with the Atlantic
pounding away at the cliffs below, the shadowy shape of a fox ambles
unconcernedly out of and then back into the darkness. On the flank of a
California mountain, in sharp moonlight, a raccoon emerges from behind
a bush, stops short and peers through its mask at my cocooned figure,
then performs a long and comically exaggerated mime of indecision
before turning away and, still not altogether sure it has made the right
choice, sea-rolling back behind the bush.

Without a roof you wake directly into the new day. Sometimes I
open my eyes in the morning to see a rabbit bobbing and nibbling its
way through breakfast. Once I woke at dawn to find, ten feet from my
head, a doe browsing among dew-covered ferns. Near the start of my
California walk, camped beside a levee that protected some rich farmland
that had been created from desert by irrigation with Colorado River
water, I woke in a pale early light to find myself looking into the rather
surprised eye of a desert road runner that stood on top of the levee, as
still and striking as a national emblem. There was a light frost in my
little hollow, and I lay warm and snug in my bag, only eyes and nose
exposed, and watched the bird. It watched me back. After a while I
heard a noise off to the left. The road runner came to life and retreated
over the levee. The noise increased. Suddenly, sunshine streamed over
the dike. Soon a tractor pulled up, twenty feet from my bedroom, beyond
some low bushes. A large and cheerful and voluminously wrapped black
man got down and swung his arms for warmth and made an adjustment
to the motor. Then, seeing me for the first time, he grinned hugely and

enviously and said, "Well, *you* look warm enough. That's one of us, anyways."

Yet, in spite of the obvious advantages of rooflessness, most people seem to assume that camping means sleeping in

TENTS.

In this connection I always recall the instinctive remark of a young lady whose forte was indoor rather than outdoor sports, but who was for a time the very close friend of an experienced outdoorsman. One close and friendly evening she lifted the sheet above them both with the tips of her pink toes so that it formed a neat little pup tent and exclaimed, "Look! Camping out!"*

It amazes me, though, that most practicing backpackers also seem to regard a tent as obligatory, even in fair and stable weather. One experienced mountain-shop manager recently told me, "People want to be in an enclosure. They seem to need the psychological 'safety' of four walls—even if part of the enclosure is only netting."

There are, of course, certain conditions under which a tent becomes desirable or even essential.

Very cold weather is one of them—the kind of weather in which you need to retain every possible calorie that your body generates. But in calm weather such conditions occur only when the temperature falls really low. That night I camped on the peak of Mount Shasta, the thermometer read 9° F. at sunrise. Yet, with nothing for a bedroom except an Ensolite pad and a good sleeping bag, I slept warm and snug. But that night was dead calm. In almost any kind of wind, even when the temperature is up around freezing, you need walled shelter: all but the warmest sleeping bags, unprotected, lose too much heat (though a Gore-Tex shell helps). In a high wind you may also find it virtually impossible to cook food or do any other partway-out-of-the-bag chore. A cave may be the best hideout, but in most places good caves are rare. When you're on the move a tent is, unfortunately, the only dependable solution.

You also need a tent in any appreciable snowfall—if you want to be sure of reasonable comfort. And if it is also very cold a tent may be necessary for survival—though a snow cave (page 328) may be just as good.

It is my personal opinion—not very widely shared—that you rarely need a tent in rain. There are, as we shall see, lighter alternatives. When rain is heavy and prolonged and wind-driven, though, a tent may be the

---

* No, come to think of it, it was a friendly afternoon.

best answer (but see page 430 for a nontent that worked). And if mosquitoes or other insects routinely mount mass-formation attacks—as they often do during northern Canadian summers, for example—then a tent may be the only way to retain your sanity. To this end you can now choose among several small tents with walls mostly of netting.

Unless you are an eager and habitually diurnal lover, privacy is no reason for taking a tent. You may need one overnight at a crowded roadhead campsite; but, if once you start backpacking you persist in camping in crowded places, don't worry about a tent, consult a psychiatrist.

On the other hand, a tent may well be worth packing along if you are going to set up a semipermanent camp and move out from it each day—for fishing, hunting, climbing or whatever. It is convenient then to be able to leave your gear unpacked and ready for use but still protected. Protected, that is, from any weather that may blow up, and also from most animals. Naturally, no tent will keep out every kind of animal. Ants can usually find a way in. So, less certainly, can mice. But a properly battened-down tent with a sewn-in floor will keep out most middle-size creatures that can be a daytime nuisance: birds (especially jays, which are sometimes called "camp robbers") and such inquisitive mammals as chipmunks and squirrels and, worst of all, pack rats. Fortunately, most of the big mammals—deer, coyote, bobcat, cougar— seem to steer well clear of anything that smells of man. There are two dire exceptions. One is light-fingered man—a breed that is, I sadly understand, becoming more widespread in backpacking habitats; the other is man-habituated bear—also becoming less rare. See page 566.

Outside North America the animal situation may be rather different. In parts of East Africa, for example, it is unwise, on account of lions and hyenas, to sleep in the open on your own. You do not need much protection: almost anything that completely surrounds you seems to keep the predators off (a mosquito net is probably, though not quite certainly, enough). But it is important that you be completely surrounded. Lions, in particular, have been known to wander in through the open doors of tents. During a six-month East African safari, when I spent much of the time watching wild game and camping out alone, I soon gained confidence in the protection afforded by my two-man A-frame tent (page 296). It had a zipper door at one end, a tunnel door at the other. By closing the lower halves of both entrances and fully closing their mosquito-net coverings, and by leaving a small mosquito-netted air vent above the tunnel door open, I maintained adequate ventilation. And the lions and hyenas that often circled around camp at night never bothered me.

Kinds of tents

In the last decade, catalogues and mountain shops have sprouted whole villages of new tents. But the initially confusing array can conveniently be categorized two ways: by function and by structure.

"4-season" models are all-weather units, designed to withstand the heaviest snow and rain and the fiercest winds. "3-season" tents (a category that covers most modern backpacking tents) should see you through the worst that spring, summer or fall can produce but will not assure protection from a deep-winter onslaught. The sturdiest of them might do so at a pinch; but some of the ultralightweights are really for late spring through early fall, or for mild climates. These are sometimes labeled "2-season." "1-season" (a term you never see) might be used to describe what were once known as "forest" or "family" tents—flimsy and often floorless jobs, usually A-frame, that are fine for benign car camping. You still see a few of them in general sporting-goods stores (but not in mountain shops) and some of them are reasonably inexpensive (which backpacking tents no longer are, ever).

But note that "season" categorizing depends a great deal on the driver. An experienced, resourceful mountaineer caught with his precautions down in an early blizzard would probably survive with the lightest 3-season tent or even a sketchy nontent shelter. Indeed, he might enjoy a passing comfortable rest. But an inexperienced, panicky, uninventive, fumble-fisted summer camper caught in a three-hour thunderstorm could, even if equipped with the latest 4-season wonder, soon get God-awful wet and decline into misery and hypothermia. So learn your onions.

Another form of functional categorizing is body count. The labels "1-man," "2-man," "6-man" seem self-explanatory. But they demand close and cynical scrutiny. Tentmakers naturally rate their models according to the greatest number of human bodies that can be laid out, corpse-like, on the floor. Smallish bodies too. But a tent that will accommodate x corpses will not accommodate x breathing individuals. Not through many rainy nights, anyway, let alone a week-long blizzard.

It is my opinion, probably shared by most experienced solo backpackers, that for comfort, even for efficiency, someone on his own needs what the catalogues call a "2-man tent." A snowstorm once kept me more or less confined in a 2-man A-frame tent for four straight days; I was warm and tolerably comfortable and could cook and do all necessary chores without hazard. I would not have liked to spend those four days cooped up in a small, coffinlike 1-man tent I owned at the time.

With two or more people, lack of space takes even greater toll. Pack any catalogue-given number of normally stable personalities into a tent for a protracted spell and you can rest pretty damned sure that some emotional fur (or perhaps I mean down) will eventually fly. Extra roominess for the same floor space will help. A tent in which you can actually stand up and move around helps even more. But in the end the only effective response, almost always, is to lower the catalogue quota. Remember, too, that backpackers carry packs. And they need to cook. So when you body-calibrate any tent for use in bad weather make allowance for accommodating your pack and having it get-attable, and also for cooking, either in the tent itself (for dangers, see page ooo) or, better, in a vestibule. Tents that make allowance for such matters in their body counts are sometimes called "2-man plus," "3-man plus," etc.

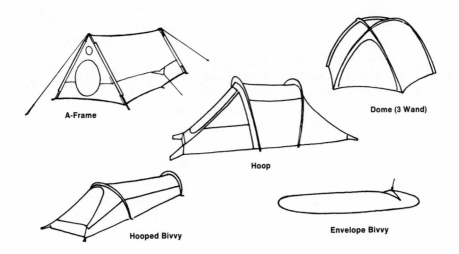

A-Frame

Hoop

Dome (3 Wand)

Hooped Bivvy

Envelope Bivvy

Current structural categories embrace:

1. Traditional A-*frames;*

2. *Hoop tents*—sometimes called tunnel or wand tents (in which one, two or even more non-intersecting, flexible, curved wands support the fabric);

3. *Domes* (in which two or more intersecting hoops form a more or less inflexible, geodesic-type skeleton);

4. *Hybrids* that embody features from two or more of the above (illustrations, page 306);

5. Occasional *off-beat shapes* (often subject to derision at first; but remember that all new designs stem from such mutations) (illustrations, page 306);

6. A subspecies for soloists known as *bivvy sacks* or *bivvy shelters* that can be: (a) plain, unsupported envelopes (sometimes called "body bags"); (b) shrunken, simplified hoop tents.

Certain other less basic structural features sometimes serve to categorize tents:

Unusual floor plan (hexagonal, octagonal, etc.); and

Method of ensuring waterproofness:

a) A single wall (or occasionally a double wall) of impermeable fabric (now usually Gore-Tex); or

b) the more traditional inner wall of breathable, permeable fabric protected by an impermeable fly sheet, which may be:

i) separate or

ii) integral.

Don't let this mess of categories daunt you. Labels embodying most or even all of them turn out to be virtually self-explanatory. There should now be little doubt in your mind about the basic nature of the tent under discussion if someone specifies "a 2-man, 4-season A-frame with separate fly" or "a 3-man plus, 3-season Gore-Tex hoop tent" or even "a 6-man, 3-season octagonal dome with integral fly."

Virtually all backpacking tents other than Gore-Tex models (page 303) are still made with some form of woven nylon taffeta; but the current high-thread-count versions are likely to be 1.5 ounces, rather than 1.9 ounces as they were a few years ago, yet are stronger as well as lighter. (Rip-stop is a taffeta with the weave reinforced every quarter-inch or less by thicker threads, clearly visible, that indeed stop most rips but can cause puckers across strained cloth. Other taffeta variants: Nyl-silk and Luscious.) Most tent canopies are left untreated and can therefore breathe. Fly sheets are urethane-coated and impermeable. Similar but heavier fabric is used—because the coatings suffer heavier abrasion—for the "bathtubs" that form most floors and lower sidewalls. But 2.2-ounce is now standard, as against 2.6-ounce a few years back.

Single-needle stitching—a single line of stitches covered with bias tape—suffices for bathtubs, where the enemy is abrasion, not wind force. But some of the best makers regard it as a no-no for walls, where the fabric is lighter and under stress from wind. There double-needle stitching—a double line of stitches—renders the seams stronger than the fabric itself. It also forms "shed seams"—constructed like shingles, so that gravity carries water down and away. For maintenance of seams, see page 315.

Green or pale blue fabric—for main walls and fly sheet—means a soft light inside your tent in bright sunlight, and an inconspicuous camp (easier on everyone in heavily used backcountry), but can produce a cold and depressing ambiance in dim light. Orange or yellow fabric keeps the interior from getting too dark and oppressive in snowstorms and the like, stands out well in case of search-and-rescue (yellow is said to be best in dull weather, orange in sunlight) and catches the customer's eye in the store, but it can generate near-psychedelic effects in glare. Currently popular: white, cream and tan.

Poles

may form the costliest single element in a tent (often 30 percent, sometimes 40 percent of the price).

The straight, rigid poles of A-frames are still hollow aluminum tubes, about ⅜-inch diameter. But curved, flexible poles can be made from aluminum of smaller diameter or from fiberglass, solid or hollow. Perhaps 80 percent of poles are currently aluminum, which is 30 percent more expensive and getting costlier. Aluminum poles are 20 percent lighter than old-style fiberglass poles but weigh the same as the latest versions. Fiberglass tends to be less stiff but will take a sharper bend without breaking, and its splintering and ferrule problems seem to have been largely overcome. Aluminum can be weakened by prolonged exposure to salty sea air; fiberglass by high-altitude ultraviolet light. Take your pick.

Most poles—except, of course, solid fiberglass versions—are now shock-corded together. Don't underestimate the gain. Shock cords can so control undisciplined pole sections, especially the long wands common in domes, that the sheer hell of pitching your tent in a gale or downpour or both becomes mitigated to a mere nightmare.

Poles are the most easily damaged part of a tent, especially during pitching or striking. Particularly vulnerable: the floppy wands, up to 15 feet long, that support some domes. So it may pay to carry one or two small aluminum sleeves, available from some tentmakers, to slip over and reinforce near-breaks. But the best hollow fiberglass wands are now spun with a combination of linear and circumferential threads, and short damaged sections can often be bandaged back into working shape with duct tape or fiberglass strapping tape.

When carrying curved poles in your pack, pad them with soft gear or protect them with something strong and rigid. You can do the same with straight poles or can lash them, very securely, to the sideframe of most external-frame packs or carry them, preferably in tent-pole bags, flush with the sides of internal-frame packs. Some such packs now come with pockets near the bottom to make things easier and safer.

Before assessing the factors to consider in selecting a tent we must examine certain facts and theories.

Tents derive their strength from a balancing act between compression members (poles) and tension members (fabric, guy lines). The straight, rigid poles of A-frames are extremely strong when compressed along their length, and in well-designed tents most of the tension is applied in that direction. The flexible wands of hoop tents and domes are, on their own, floppy and weak. But if tension is applied evenly around their curve they become laterally very strong. Such tension can come from fabric stretched in an unbroken surface across the semicircle of an end wall (though any door or window or other break radically reduces the effect); or it can come from fabric stretched tightly and evenly over the outside of the poles. Such tension comes most often and most purely from a fly sheet. These factors, and many more—such as the "bias" in all fabrics which makes them stretchier one way than the other —are carefully balanced by today's tent designers, who often use computers to achieve optimum systems. Even for us users, understanding some of the implications offers practical advantages. It is certainly worth knowing, for example, that in most modern tents the fly provides much of the strength. In hoops and domes it can account for 85–90 percent. And even in A-frames the fly helps. So in high winds, whether or not you need a fly for protection, rig it—firmly.

In recent years many tents have appeared with integral flies: they are sewn in as part of the main structure and cannot be separated. Clearly, this makes erecting the tent simpler. In rain it vastly improves your chances of getting the damned thing up without the main walls being soaked. But the arrangement also imposes debits. You cannot use either the inner tent or the fly alone (page 316). Drying out after a storm is painfully slow. And repair can be a pain. But by far the most serious drawback is that it seems impossible to make an integral fly that will not touch the main tent wall in wind-driven rain or heavy snow. And once the two surfaces touch, water begins to percolate through the porous inner wall. For this reason I remain convinced that the only practical fly is a separate one, designed to stand well clear of the inner wall. Most— but by no means all—tentmakers now seem to agree.

Separation of fly and wall is vital, too, in circumventing condensation. But here we enter a murky and controversial area of theory. The basic facts are clear enough. The humidity in an enclosed tent can become very high. Your body contributes a little by sweating and a lot through breathing. Average exhalation amounts in cupfuls are sometimes quoted, but it is important to remember that people vary enormously (page 304). Wet clothing or other gear often boosts the water-vapor content, and so can such easily overlooked sources as moisture dragged in as you enter, water spilled from a canteen or small leaks in walls or floor. And cooking inside—especially with an uncovered pot—may send it rocketing. You can, and probably should, take reasonable precautions to reduce output from all these sources—preferably without ceasing to breathe. But under certain conditions of humid or cold air (for cold air can hold less water vapor than warm) the air inside the tent may still reach saturation point. And then, just as dew forms when the night air reaches dew point, moisture will begin to collect on the highest parts of the roof (because hot air rises and is cooled by the cold fabric). The surest way to prevent or at least ameliorate such condensation is to create a steady inflow of cool air at a low point in the tent and a steady outflow of warm, saturated air from one or more high points. This effect can be achieved in an A-frame with a small, closable, net-covered vent near the top of one or both vertical end walls. Such a solution is less easily attained in most hoop tents because of the sloping walls, and it becomes very difficult in domes. In both, condensation therefore tends to present a more serious problem.

Now, it has long been tentmaking gospel that condensation can also be reduced by ensuring plenty of circulation between tent wall and fly: water vapor escapes through the porous wall and moving outside air carries it away. But this is where murk and controversy now swirl. Voices are heard in tentland maintaining that little or no water vapor escapes through the tent wall and that condensation can best be fought by reducing the temperature difference between the inner and outer sides of the wall (because it is the cooling of the hot, rising air that precipitates moisture). Therefore, far from striving to ensure good circulation between tent and fly, you should try to create air pockets which will hold warmer air against the outside of the wall. In domes, for example, the air-holding capacity of the sleeves that suspend tent from poles should not be mitigated by perforation or other methods—as has been the recent tendency—but should be increased by all possible means. My own hunch, based on very little but guesswork, is that this view will in the end not prevail. But it may. You should certainly know that it exists.

SELECTING A TENT

First, obviously, you must decide how many people you will be housing. Then, if you are wise, and especially if you will need the tent for cooking or holing up in during bad weather (and if you don't need that, I suggest maybe you don't need a tent), you look only at those catalogue-calibrated for one more person than you expect. Next you decide whether you need a 4- or 3-season tent or even a lesser breed. And then you begin to weigh the pluses and minuses of each major kind of tent.

There is, of course, no single "best" kind: you must choose the one that seems most suitable for you and yours under each set or amalgam of expected conditions. Among the nubs you heft—in your own personal order of importance—are weight, degree of protection from rain and from snow, stability in wind, reliability (resistance to damage), difficulty of erection in fair weather and foulest, ease of access in ditto, roominess, cost, freedom from condensation problems and whether guyed, guyless or fully free-standing.

Traditional A-frames

A decade ago most backpacking tents were A-frames. No more. A-frames tend to be rather heavier than equivalent hoop tents and domes, and their sloping sidewalls mean that they offer less roominess for the same floor space. So they have become "old hat." But don't let that fool you. In a gale-whipped rainstorm the best of them are at least as easy to erect as most hoops or domes. They generate fewer condensation problems. And they tend to cost less than more fashionably shaped equivalents. Above all, they afford the surest protection against tempestuous snow, rain and wind. And they are the most reliable design. (One acid test: stores that rent tents report far less damage to A-frames than to any other kind.) So they remain popular for expeditions as well as in such weatherbeaten places as Alaska. And if I were planning a macho trip I would still opt for an A-frame.

I still own a Sierra Designs 2-man Glacier—recently discontinued —which has seen me safely through Sierra snowstorms, a three-week Alaska trip that turned damp and many tropical storms in East African game country. I therefore trust it. But if I expected really appalling weather ("The hell with weight and cost, I want protection") I might invest in the model I still regard as the acme of A-frame design (though I frankly have not yet field-tested one): the 2-man Trailwise Fitzroy III (headroom 51 inches; zippered triangular door at one end, spacious tunnel at other [promising a good crawl]; 8 pounds 5 ounces; $300. Optional ridgepole now available for God-awful, blasting conditions [3 ounces; $6.75]).*

The prime design aim in the Fitzroy was maximum space for minimum size of main panel—to reduce sag and its attendant horrors. The A-frame poles were therefore placed a little in from the ends, and the

---

* Both the Fitzroy's entrances are, as in almost all tents we shall consider, backed by zippable mosquito-net screens. And its panels, like those of virtually all modern backpacking tents with any pretension to quality, come with "catenary cut." The phrase stems from the Latin *catena* ("chain"). It refers to the curve caused by gravity in any chain or cord suspended freely between two fixed points not in the same vertical plane. A piece of fabric curves or sags in the same way. So the edges of fabric for tent panels are cut in curves that will, when the tensions of the erected tent are applied, compensate as accurately as possible for the tendency to sag. The tent therefore remains taut and does not collect water or flap unduly in wind (the key to stability). Catenary cut reduces, though never altogether prevents, the sagging caused by a heavy snowfall.

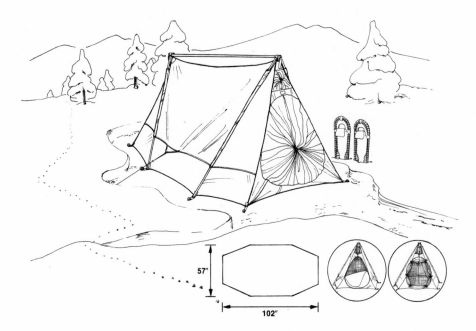

whole tent outboard of them tapered somewhat. The result hits its prime
target and several more. Above all, you need no guy lines (except under
extreme wind conditions, when end guys may be advisable); you peg
only the tent's four corners. The poles, pulled into slight tension by the
fabric, hold the structure firm, and the stakes that secure the corners do
what little else is needed, with the fabric acting as guy lines.*

Other than the Glacier and the Fitzroy, current catalogues feature
only a scattering of the once-dominant A-frames (notably tents by Eureka, North Face, and EMS [their free-standing, 3-season Tabernac has a
ridgepole]). The swing to other designs began a decade ago with the
growing popularity of

Hoop tents.

Because of their curved side walls, hoop tents offered more space for
a given floor area and could be built lighter. Most models were easier to

---

* All traditional tents were guyed—often cobwebbed down with eight or ten guy lines
that were hell to put out in a storm, delighted in pulling loose and would trip you at the
drop of a flashlight. But many modern tents of various shapes, even those not fully free-
standing, are guyless, or close to it. "Most backpackers like that," says one. "They're afraid
of guy lines." Guyless tents certainly tend to be easier to pitch and also demand less flat or
near-flat space. This is both a practical and a mercantile advantage (page 301).

Note that all tents illustrated in this chapter are shown without fly sheets, in order to
reveal details. Please do not write and say, "No fly—in snow country?"

erect than all but the best A-frames. And although they at first looked fragile and most were in fact less sturdy than good A-frames, so that few were genuine 4-season units, they proved remarkably strong. One disadvantage: their curved wands—fiberglass or thin, flexible aluminum—remain more liable to damage, especially during erection or dismantling, than the thicker, rigid A-frame poles (page 296).

Among the earliest and most innovative hoop tents were the Warmlite series by Stephenson, now of New Hampshire. The current line offers three sizes and many variations, with everything still designed for lightness—from anodized aluminum poles to impermeable, polymer-coated, 1.2-ounce Rip-stop nylon walls (single or double; no traditional fly). As with all Warmlite products, the design is ingenious, if not always superbly practical, and the workmanship excellent. The tents seem to

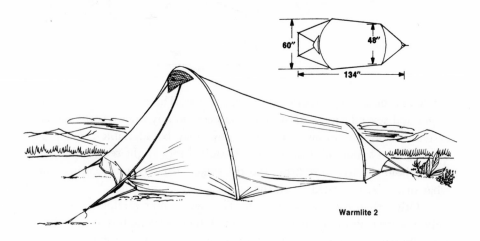

Warmlite 2

attract a small, enthusiastic group of true-believing users, but many people, including me, doubt their ability to stand up to severe weather, especially heavy rain, or to even reasonably careful everyday use. But you can't ignore a 2-man tent that weighs less than 3 pounds. And I still consider using my old 2-man, double-walled version occasionally when weight looms big and lousy weather small—that is, mostly, when I really don't need a tent. (Double-wall current models, without fancy options: 2-man, 2 pounds 15 ounces, $270; 3-man, 3 pounds 15 ounces, $355; 5-man, 5 pounds 12 ounces, $460.)

The big boom in hoop tents came when Moss Tent Works produced their Conestoga-wagon-like Eave series.

Although very floppy ("flexible tension"), Eave tents do indeed seem, as claimed, to roll with the wind's punches and so escape damage. For a time they came close to being the standard for "serious" backpacking. And they remain popular. (2-man Eave II, 6 pounds, $280; 3-man Eave III, 6¼ pounds, $315.)

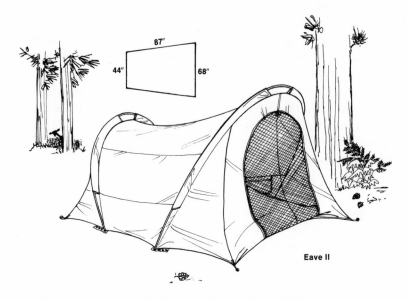

Eave II

But recently, after a flirtation with domes (below), fashion seems to be swooping on lighter hoop tents, aptly described as "personal shelters," which are exemplifed by the Sierra West L.I.T.E. series. (Three reputed 2-man units: Gimme Shelter, 3 pounds 4 ounces, $150; Skylite, 4 pounds 2 ounces, $198; Litehouse, 4 pounds 12 ounces, $248. [Plus two new additions for which no prices are currently available: Skylite II, 4 pounds 2 ounces; and Daystar, 4 pounds 7 ounces.] And one 3-man tent:

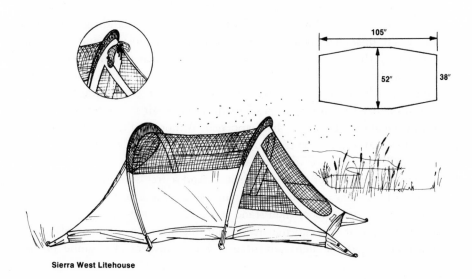

Sierra West Litehouse

Trilite, 6 pounds 2 ounces, $325.) Other makers, notably JanSport, Eureka, North Face, Sierra Designs, Trailwise and Black Ice, offer models in the same general class.

The great advantage of such tents is, of course, their weight. But they could best be described as "2-season" (the very honest JanSport rating). In fact, the Sierra West series comes in net-wall as well as solid-wall versions: the netting gives greater ventilation and a view of stars and scenery but also, I fear, greater risk of rain-in, not to mention spindrift snow-in, even with the attached flies pulled down. And the steeply sloping entrances inherent in the design seem to demand Houdini expertise for dry ingress in a storm. (Any tent with a sloping door clearly suffers this drawback: and once you get rain into the bathtub you have . . . a bathtub.)

Domes

are essentially hoop tents rendered remarkably rigid by single or multiple crossings of the hoops. This rigidity makes the best of them good 4-season tents. But the attractive and roomy structure complicates condensation-fighting ventilation (page 295). And domes tend to be difficult to erect under vile conditions ("Practically impossible after a little wine," says one practitioner): much threading of long, fragile wands through sleeves (though JanSport has introduced a helpful color-coding system), and an inevitable stage at which you have the thing half up but still flapping. (For an exception, see the Sphinx, page 302.) Most domes are entirely free-standing, and salesmen make a lot of this feature: "You can pick it up and move to another place without taking it down," they say. But that seems more a sales- than a tent-pitch. After all, how often do you really want to move house? Furthermore, a free-standing tent tends to be left unstaked, held down by only the gear inside, and a sudden wind may then pick it up and waft it away. Such unscheduled flights occasionally occur. It is true, though, that if the unmanned hang-glider lands in a lake, its rigid structure proves a huge advantage: it may amphibianize the glider into a sailplane and deposit it, contents still dry, on the far shore. This, too, has happened. A more real if minor advantage of a free-standing tent is that you can erect it and set it to one side, ready for quick use in case of rain, and then sleep or rest nearby with an unobstructed view of scenery or stars. And a free-standing tent is certainly easy to dry: you just pick it up, shake the grossest moisture and crud out the open door, then stand it on end or hang it, floor facing the morning sun (if you can marshal a morning sun). In other words, such tents offer genuine field advantages; but I suspect that some of the bouncy sales talk may stem from advantages they offer in the mountain shop. There, as in the mountains (and as with all guyless models), they take up far less valuable ground space. What's more, they can be hung, leaned and generally flung around in delightfully eye-catching poses. And I think we should all, when buying, maybe try, as a precautionary measure, to bear that morsel of information in mind.

JanSport pioneered large, practical dome tents. Later The North Face almost dominated the market with their VE series (VE = Vector Equilibrium, the Bucky Fuller geodesic design concept). (Current 2-man, 4-season VE 24, with four poles, zipper- and sleeve-doors, and fly: 43 square feet floor space, 9 pounds 8 ounces, $340.)

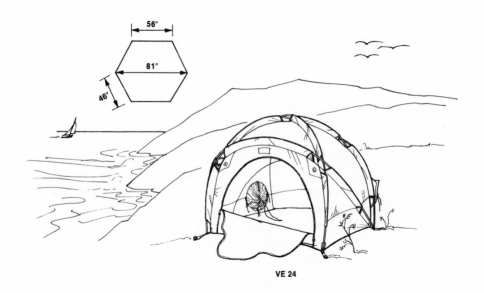

VE 24

Many domes tend toward high profiles—opting for headroom rather than wind-shedding strength. An exception: the attractive 2-man Great Arc Dome by Trailwise (8 pounds 6 ounces, $390) that crouches and looks very sturdy. Other good domes come from Sierra Designs, Early Winters, Caribou, Eastern Mountain Sports, Wilderness Experience, Eureka and Black Ice.

I have little experience with dome tents, and none in really bad weather. But they are certainly popular. The mountain shops—and the mountains too—now teem with eye-pleasing, practical models, many of them small, reasonably lightweight 3-season versions. In spite of the recent fashion drift toward lightweight "personal shelters" (page 299), they have clearly come to stay.

An interesting recent dome innovation is the Sierra Designs 2-man, 3- or 4-season Sphinx (5 pounds 9 ounces; Sphinx I with fiberglass poles, $258; Sphinx II with aluminum poles that pack shorter, $280).

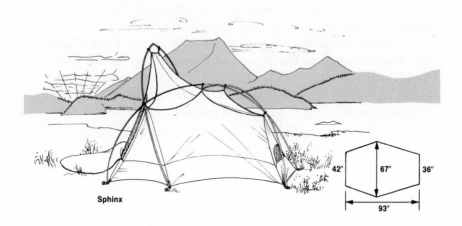

Sphinx

42"   67"   36"

93"

The tent's high profile worries me a little (though the designer claims it is aerodynamically very strong). But the notion of using clips instead of sleeves to attach tent to poles strikes me as seminal. It clearly improves circulation between tent and fly (but see page 295 for a view that decries such "improvement"). More important, the clips make erection, even in a gale, relatively simple: you raise the poles, which have almost no wind resistance, with the tent flat on the ground, and then, while standing up, you quickly clip the tent into place. (The Sphinx has won the last two industry-wide pitching contests. It went up in one minute three seconds, including a thirty-yard dash.) At first glance the points at which the clip tabs are stitched to the fabric seams look like an obvious weakness. But Sierra Designs say that the stitching goes through six layers of fabric and the poles will break before fabric or stitching. If they are right, then the Sphinx (and the larger, similarly constructed Domicile) could herald a new line of domical evolution. One critic says, "The clip tongue itself is weak, and if it breaks . . ." But last year I used the Sphinx on a week's late-fall Sierra trip up to 10,000 feet and, although untested by heavy snow or high winds, it shrugged off torrential rain and light snow without a murmur. I suffered no condensation problems, and the easy erection was a pleasure. But a feature that worried me was the shallow dip below the apex: it collected a little snow during a flurry, and in heavy snowfall might prove disastrous. So perhaps the Sphinx is, as critics suggest, a 3-, not 4-season, tent.

Later: I have just learned of a new and interesting series of domes— unfortunately not in time to illustrate them or give them any but brief mention. These tents' fabrics and aluminum poles, though high quality, are unexceptional. But the fabric is attached to the pole structure at strategic points by ingenious two-part flexible-plastic "grip clips," said to "hold our canopies tautly without any stress on stitching or seams." (They also furnish convenient internal suspension points for clotheslines, lanterns, ditty bags—and an optional insulating/frost liner.) The pole structures consist of one or more triangular strut systems that peak into strong Lexan "spider hubs." Once tension is released, the poles slip easily out of these hubs without removal from their sleeves. Erection is therefore simple and quick. I have yet to use one of these tents, but they have low profiles and feel sturdy and resilient. The makers, Shelter Systems of California, are headed by a co-founder of Sierra Designs and by a long-time tent designer who pioneered geodesic domes for The North Face. At present, Shelter Systems produce three backpack models: the guyed, single-triangle, 2-man Critter, 4 pounds 6 ounces, $170; the free-standing, double-triangle, 2-man Orbit, 6 pounds 14 ounces, $285; and the larger, multiple-triangle, 3- or 4-man Wilderness 3, $335. All models are rated 4-season—and look as though they may well prove to be so.

At present, controversy swirls around

Gore-Tex tents

like a mountain storm.*

"Gore-Tex is the greatest!" thunder the boosters. Because a single layer acts as both breathable inner wall and rain-impermeable fly, they say (see main discussion of Gore-Tex properties, page 405), the pole structure can be simpler yet stronger and the tent will provide more usable space for any given weight. And it will be not only simpler to erect but also dry-pitchable in a downpour, which no separate-fly tent can be.

"Gore-Tex tents simply don't work," rumble the detractors. The stuff may be fine for garments, when it's close to sweaty skin and the vapor pressure inside is still high enough for vapor to be forced through the fabric; but in any tent except maybe a small bivouac the fabric is simply too far away. Result: vicious condensation. Besides, Gore-Tex tents are wickedly expensive—and not all that much lighter.

* I have let "Gore-Tex" stand here because when I drafted this section it was the only waterproof-but-breathable material available. But now Klimate may begin challenging it (see page 407). Evolution II—another laminate, though polypropylene-based—is heavier, apparently suitable only for family-style tents, and, if applicable to backpacking at all, is still some years down the trail. Other suitable fabrics may appear, of course, perhaps waterproof by construction rather than by coating or lamination.

Boosters flash back: "Gore-Tex breathes just as well as most materials, so a well-designed Gore-Tex tent is as condensation-free as any other. It all depends how well you make it."

The detractors' reply tends to be unprintable.

This argument rages against a legal-mercantile background. Seven states (California, Louisiana, Massachusetts, Michigan, Minnesota, New Jersey and New York), encompassing one-third of the U.S. population, have passed laws that prohibit the manufacture *or* sale within their boundaries of tents not treated with certain prescribed flame-retardants. Other states are in the process of following suit. The laws apply only to tents. They apparently stem from old statistics that showed a significant number of deaths from tent burnings—mainly of children using gas lanterns or open fires, and almost all in the once-popular canvas tents. Makers of such tents lobbied effectively to have the laws apply to *all* tent materials. Years of research at last produced for nylon taffeta a treatment that strengthens rather than weakens the fabric and does not make it heavier—though it certainly jacks up costs. But all known legal treatments ruin Gore-Tex's properties, and neither that hurdle nor the laws seem likely to change. Although it is perfectly legal to place out-of-state mail orders, the economic effect is very real. At least four manufacturers presently sell Gore-Tex tents: Early Winters and REI of Washington State and Marmot Mountain Works and Bibler Tents of Colorado. But they praise Gore-Tex tents to the weeping skies. In other words, they are the boosters. And the detractors—surprise!—are the stymied makers and retailers in the seven proscribing states. "Oh, we could easily have Gore-Tex tents made elsewhere and shipped to customers by mail," say some of these. "We just don't believe they work, that's all." But after listening to more than my fair share of such verbiage I seem to detect an odor of ground axes pervading the air—on both sides.

Yet I note that independent users also tend toward extremes. I met one man, apparently lacking a blunt ax in his pack, who professed tenderness going on love for a Gore-Tex tent in which he had lived for a year under all manner of conditions, from Sierra snow to Alaska rain. Other users vividly curse the way condensation forms on the walls of their Gore-Tex tents (though see page 310). At least a partial explanation may be that, as with all tents, occupants as well as weather play a big role in condensation. An experienced backpacker with the metabolism of a 180-pound shrew once shared a Gore-Tex tent on Mount Shasta with a companion equipped with a more humanoid system. The copious sweater awoke during the night to find ice thick on his half of the tent and his sleeping bag soggy from the drips: his companion's domain remained bone dry. My lone trial—a one-night stand with a Marmot Twilight (3 pounds 10 ounces; $290)—generated only a little untroublesome condensation; but conditions, though cold (20° F.), posed no severe test. For the moment, I'd have to say that we need more time, more collective experience, before we can know whether lightning has indeed struck.

Meanwhile:

"This is the future!" flash the Gore-Tex boosters.

"Their market's already fading," crackle the detractors.

Bivouac sacks,

for soloists only, evolved from old-style sleeping-bag covers—which never proved really acceptable because they either failed to breathe or let the rain in or both. Came Gore-Tex. And with it came, first, simple envelopes with entrance-and-breathe holes of various designs. Some people loved them—and still do. But, perhaps because the envelopes tended to induce claustrophobia (and also because they slumped unattractively on the salesroom floor, like body bags), they soon grew small hoops, top and often bottom, that held them clear of your sleeping bag.

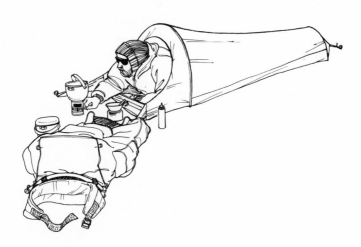

Bivvies by no means please all soloists, but they seem to have collected fewer and less vehement detractors than Gore-Tex tents. The reason? Either that the bivvy's walls remain closer to your body than a tent's and therefore the Gore-Tex works better—in part, perhaps, because you cannot accommodate your soaking-wet pack or even much other gear within the restricted space; because you cannot possibly cook inside; and also because in many models your mouth lies close to the main vent and breath vapor readily escapes. Or, on the other hand, because bivvies are, in one of the fine and featherbrained distinctions beloved by law, not "tents," and therefore stymie neither makers nor retailers in seven of these United (sic) States.

I have yet to try a bivvy, except on a salesroom floor—where, battened down in an envelope, I felt a most unusual moment of claustrophobia. But I'd guess that for certain Spartan soloists with low or medium metabolic rates they would, under certain conditions, fit like a glove.

Many makers now offer bivvies. Among the most popular envelopes: Blue Puma's Bear Necessity (1 pound 6 ounces, $130) and Early Winters' Sleep Inn (1 pound 2 ounces, $85). Among fully hooped versions: the Sierra West Bivvy Sack (2 pounds 8 ounces, $135) that is essentially the midget in their line of "personal shelters" (page 299). The popular Marmot Burrow (1 pound 15 ounces, $155) is really an envelope with a small hoop to raise the fabric at the head opening.

Do-it-yourself tents

Modern light tents are complicated affairs. But Frostline still meet you halfway with kits for a 3-man-plus hoop tent, the Trailridge II (11 pounds 5 ounces; kit, $220), and a 2-man-plus modified A-frame, the Kodiak (7 pounds 11 ounces; kit, $129). But one advisor warns, "Sewing a tent is a bitch."

Hybrids and off-beats

Searchlight

Flashlight

Solus

Mushroom

Some tents, especially small ones, are variations on standard structures. An A-hoop, for example, has mildly curved side poles with a flat or gently curved top member. A few models, such as the Sierra Designs Searchlight, even use one type of support at the door, another at the foot.

Among off-beats, the superlight Sierra Designs 2-man, 3-season Flashlight has trapezoid-shaped pole structure and is 44 inches high at its head-end peak (3 pounds 9 ounces, $160). And the 1- or 2-man, 3-season Solus by Moss, with main walls of netting and a roll-down fly, has a single aluminum pole arched end-to-end (3 pounds 10 ounces, $165).

Eureka's "4-season" Mushrooms are really lightened versions of an old standard, with near-vertical walls and umbrella roof (2-man, 7-by-7-feet floor, 8 pounds 4 ounces, $270; 4-man, 8-by-8-feet floor, 11 pounds 2 ounces, $300).

A new off-beat tent that has just come to my notice and house is an interesting throwback—or simplification. It lacks all the current "essentials": fancy pole system, windows, even a floor. In fact, the Chouinard Pyramid (2 pounds 8 ounces complete with poles, pegs and stuff sack; $109.50) is not so much a tent, really, as a rainfly with centerpole.

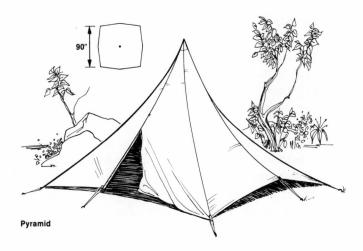

90"

Pyramid

The Pyramid is useless as protection against mosquitoes but seems to do 'most everything else. It works well, I'm told, in snow: you build a snow wall around the foot, or maybe dig down a little ways, and use the tent essentially as roof. (Note that a light butt plate—a 7-inch square of masonite, say—will prevent disastrous pole subsidence.) The catenary-cut panels of 1.5-ounce waterproof coated ripstop will spill snow and high winds (it has been used up to 20,000 feet) and also torrential rain. This last quality, and also the lightness, surprising roominess and simplicity of erection—you just stake out the four corners, then inject the telescoping, shock-corded aluminum pole—have apparently begun to make the Pyramid popular among backpackers, especially ultralighters, and cyclists. It will sleep four, is luxurious for two, palatial for one; and you can "stand two bikes up inside, against the centerpole, and still have room to sleep on the sides." You can also adjust the telescopic pole so that the tent's hem is raised ten inches high, for ventilation and head-room, or hugs the ground, to hold the elements at bay. I have yet to pitch my Pyramid anywhere but in the garden; but, although I'm mildly dubious about the rather large open area you need, and accept that "just stake out the four corners" is a touch less easy to achieve with first-time accuracy than it sounds, I look forward to becoming a live ringer for a dead pharaoh.

Tent pegs

Plain round Duraluminum pegs are probably the best for most normal purposes (typically, 7 inches, 1 ounce, $.40). An alternative: light steel twisted skewers, rated "worthless" by one of my advisors (package of 8: 5 ounces, $1.75). Angled or rounded (half-tube) alumi-num pegs that nest to save space will hold better in loose soils but do more damage to fragile soil cover—and weigh 1½ ounces each and cost $.85. Lexan plastic angled or I-beam pegs, though bulkier, are very strong (1 ounce, 9-inch, $.50; 12-inch, $.60). I often use them for one or two primary guys, even with non-tents (pages 316–30).

Note that some tentmakers include pegs in published weights, others do not.

If a campsite is too soft to hold your pegs firm (sand) or too hard for you to drive them in (yes, rock), and if the wind is not too strong (if it is, try to go someplace else), tie the guy lines to the middle of the pegs, lay them flat and block them from sliding toward the tent with heavy rocks. For this job, strong sticks are even better than pegs: their greater friction reduces the chances of slippage. Either method works better than trying to tie guy lines directly onto all but ideally shaped stones. But it is often easier and safer to loop your guy lines around the lowest branches of a bush. Or you can tie a loop of nylon cord to the bush and thread the guy line through it so that you can more easily adjust the guy. Another alternative: crampons (page 85). For yet another, see Fabric Tent Anchor, page 312. Same page for snow pegs—and alternatives.

Guy-line tighteners

Nylon or aluminum tighteners, once standard on backpacking tents, have almost vanished. Instead you tie knots—thereby saving weight and money and reducing the danger of both snarled guy lines and abraded tent fabric.

The knot said to be best is some kind of tautline hitch, which you can slide easily with two hands but which holds in a wind. I normally use the amateurish-looking figure-of-eight-and-slip-knot, which is simple enough even for me and seems to hold fine.

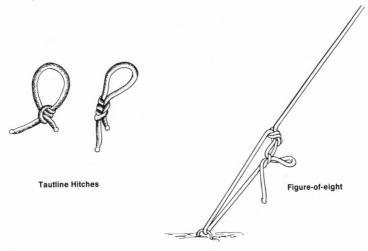

Tautline Hitches

Figure-of-eight

See also guy-line shock absorber in illustration, page 312.

Cookholes

A cookhole is a 30-inch semicircular, nylon-zippered flap on the floor of the tent. Years ago I found the device admirable, not only for cooking (to keep food scraps and condensed water off the floor) and for garbage disposal (just sweep snow and debris into it—see page 314) but also for indoor sanitation (though to perform you need to be half-sibling to a contortionist). The cookhole is perhaps better on the left side of the tent: if you are right-handed, you probably find it easiest to cook lying on your left side, using your right arm for most of the work. Many experienced people regard cookholes as abominations that not only reduce a tent's strength, especially in high winds, but also provide ingress for snow and water. Certainly, few current tents have cookholes—or

Frost liners.

In temperatures well below freezing, moisture from breath and body may coat your tent wall with ice crystals. I've had it happen as high as 20° F. One response is a detachable liner, usually of light cotton or some similarly absorbent material, that can be taken out and shaken, and will also absorb the moisture should the crystals melt. That's the theory. In practice any inadvertent shaking—especially when taking it out—is liable to prompt an ice shower onto you and yours; and the first sun's rays may melt the crystals and start an internal drip storm. These sad realities, plus the trend to lighter tents, may account for the virtual disappearance of frost liners.

Marmot Mountain Works claim that the Nexus with which they laminate the underside of the Gore-Tex used in their tents has a paper-toweling effect that acts as a condensation absorber and built-in frost liner. "Interesting stuff," admits a competitor.

TENTS IN ACTION

Pitching a tent in a high wind

Every tent has its own stratagems for driving you to the brink of lunacy when you try to erect it in a high wind. But there are standard defensive measures with which you can counter. Before you unroll the tent itself and allow the wind to breathe berserk life into its billowing folds, have all the support weapons ready and waiting—poles, pegs and an assortment of articles from pack or nature that are heavy enough to help hold down the wind-filled tent and yet smooth enough not to tear it. Then drive in the first peg partway. For obvious reasons, wind- and door-wise, this peg should be the one for the center guy line of the foot end of the tent—or, in guyless tents, for one of the corners at the foot end. In guyed tents, if possible, hook the line over the peg before you unfold the tent. Drive the peg fully home, so that the line cannot by any devilish means flap free. Then take a deep breath and unfold the tent. Unfold it slowly, close to the ground, and onto each foot or so of unfolding fabric put one or more of the heavy, smooth articles. Their size and nature will depend on wind strength and campsite: sometimes all you can use is the full pack; big stones, when available, are godsends, but they must be smooth. Failing adequate heavy support weapons, sprawl yourself over the whistling, flapping bedlam. Slowly, painfully, drive in the pegs that hold down the edges of the stretched-out floor. If no stones are handy, drive in the pegs with your heels. Unless you've attempted this maneuver from the prone position in a thirty-mile-an-hour wind—brother, you haven't lived.

The sequence in which you tackle pole-erection and the securing of the other guy lines will depend on the structure of your tent and the vagaries of your temperament, but in general you fix the windward end first and you try to keep everything flat on the ground until you are ready to lift the fabric quickly into a taut, unflappable position. You can't possibly accomplish such an act but you might as well aim for it. Once you've come anywhere close your troubles are almost over. But if you get the tent up within double the time you figured on, count yourself a candidate for the Tent of Fame.

Once the tent is up you should check several times that no pegs are threatening to pull out. And because even the tautest tent will flap in a very high wind, you may have to tighten the lines occasionally. End-to-end stability is the most vital factor, and it pays to place the head-end peg so that the adjustment knot or line-tightener comes close to the apex of the tent and you can adjust it by simply reaching out from inside. If necessary, shorten the line by tying in a sheepshank.

Drainage moats

It was long the practice—and a wise one too—to dig a small ditch or moat around your tent even when there was little danger of heavy rain: if the rain came you diverted all invading surface water. Tents without floors almost demanded such precautions. And in a real deluge even the best floored tents can, unless moated, begin to ship water through a cookhole, the foot of a zippered entrance or a worn sector of the waterproof floor and lower wall; and once the flood begins there is Noahscape.

But times have changed. A single large party of well-meaning but unaware people who assume they are being good woodsmen by meticulously moating each tent in their little village can turn a beautiful campsite, almost overnight, into a scarred eyesore. In today's heavily used backcountry such a place rarely gets, as it used to, a year or so's rest. And the disruption to the delicate drainage and soil-binding relationships of a fragile place may turn it within a few years into a rutted, eroded mess. "Ah," you say, "but I always travel alone." Maybe. But one moat-minded person camping in a place every day of the month (which is the kind of usage many backcountry campsites now suffer) is little different from thirty such people camping there for one night: although the damage will at first be confined to a smaller area, it will be locally more severe—and will soon force campers farther and farther afield. The result is the same.

So we must desist. What a man does in one of those fortunately rare cases when no amount of good site-choosing and tent-pitching can save him from the flood must be left to his own terribly human conscience. My guess is that, like me, he would reluctantly dig as small a moat as possible and fill it carefully when he strikes camp. But the routine digging of tent moats, though a perfectly reasonable practice when backpackers were few and farflung, is in today's congested wilderness no more acceptable than digging a septic tank for your downtown office.

Pitching a tent in snow

In hard snow the only vital difference from pitching a tent elsewhere (unless you have to level a site) lies in the pegs. Ordinary round tent pegs are useless in snow. Special angle pegs (1¾ ounces each, $.75) are surprisingly efficient. Once you've driven them in, in fact, the only difficulty tends to be getting them out when you strike camp. The best extractor is the point of an ice axe. It is also a highly efficient tool for making holes in tent fabric.

Alternatives to snow pegs include "deadman" snow anchors—light alloy or fiberglass disks or slabs, usually about 6 or 8 inches across, with holes for tying in the guy line (or, better still, for tying in a loop of heavier cord through which you thread your guy line). You bury the anchor and stamp the snow firm on top of it, or maybe slide it in sideways. You dig it out with shovel, ice axe, ski, snowshoe or whatever your ingenuity devises. Early Winters offer an aluminum-alloy deadman, 6 by 8 inches, that weighs only 4 ounces, costs $5. They also have a triangular 1½-ounce Fabric Tent Anchor (12-inch sides, 3 web loops; set of 2, $7) that you can fold over, fill with snow and bury. (Other uses: on rock or hardpan, loop to tent and pile rocks on fabric; in soft dirt, drive stakes in two corners for twice the holding power.) Even more efficient are snow-filled stuff sacks (5 by 7 inches, 4 ounces, $3.50) carried specially for the job—perhaps with a small "bunjy" cord as shock absorber on the guy line attached to it. An alternative: a *one-piece* rubber shock loop—not the untrustworthy kind crimped together with a metal clamp. Rigged like this

the line gains elasticity in a wind, and if the bunjy cord or shock loop should break it will do so when the line is almost fully extended and can take the load without sudden strain. Either of these devices can, of course, be used on any guy line, in or out of snow.

A stick makes a serviceable snow anchor. It need be no more than a foot long and as thick as your little finger—with a loop tied to its center.

Bury it in a small trench, dug at right angles to the tension. A real advantage: you need not retrieve it.

In case of lost pegs or "deadmen" or substitutes, snowshoes or skis or ski poles or ice axes make good emergency replacements. Some people even use them regularly and so reduce their load—though that means, of course, that they probably can't move far from the tent without collapsing it.

In soft snow it is essential that before you attempt to pitch a tent you stamp out the site. Do the job before you take anything out of your pack, and make sure you know beforehand how many paces or boot lengths you need for length and for width, allowing room for you to move around outside the tent during the pitching operation. Stamp out narrow extensions for any guy lines, and a broad one around the entrance (illustration, page 296). In bad weather this stamped-down entrance area will reduce the risk of drifting snow blocking all ventilation (pages 283–4 and 314–15). In good weather you'll find it invaluable as a place you can probably stand up in without snowshoes or skis. A little alleyway extension as a john is a worthwhile refinement.

The tent in action in snow

In snow camping, your tent is your castle. Outside, the world howls, white and hostile. Inside, you create a little domain of your own —cramped, imperfectly dry, and frigid by town-indoor standards; but livable and surprisingly snug. Of course, you have to work to keep it that way. Above all, you have to work at keeping things reasonably dry. Primarily, that means keeping the snow out. Some tents, notably by Caribou, have extra-long tunnels to make this task easier. But with or without such a tunnel, brush all the snow you can off clothing and person before you crawl inside. Stamp as much as you can off your boots too. And do not wear them all the way in: swivel around before they come more than an inch or two over the threshold, take them off (less easily done than written) and immediately slip your feet down into the sleeping bag. Legs and body probably go into the bag too. (If you're covered with snowflakes or melted snow you must obviously brush off or dry or remove your outer layer before getting into the bag.) Then bang the boots together and get most of the remaining snow off them. In good weather hold the boots outside for this operation. In vile weather bang the snow onto something waterproof laid out just inside the entrance and empty it outside when you get a chance. A cookhole (page 309) makes it very simple to dispose of such snow as collects on the waterproof floor, and you can relax some of these precautions. But you still have to be careful not to get sleeping bag or clothing wet.

Boot-desnowing is not the only reason for having a waterproof mat of some kind just inside the entrance (I use the large tough plastic bag that wraps my cooking pots—see page 269). This doormat collects most of the snow that inevitably comes with you when you crawl in, and also the smaller but by no means negligible amounts that dribble in whenever you have a small opening for ventilation. It also serves as an interim garbage can for all the foreign matter you'd just as soon didn't lie around inside: gas spilled when you're refilling the stove; water spilled when you're filling canteens after melting snow; food fragments; even, if you're feeling house-proud, the inevitable stray feathers from sleeping bag and down clothing. At convenient intervals you empty all this debris outside —or into the cookhole if you have one. Some people carry a small sponge for regular snow- and debris-cleaning. ("Otherwise," one of them says, "your friends use your socks.")

A waterproof mat also acts as a doormat when the weather is good enough for you to put on your boots outside: you tread on it in stockinged feet while you put on the boots. You can also stand on it in stockinged feet, just outside, when you have to answer the liquid calls of nature. The right kind of gloves make good short-service slippers, but the ideal is a pair of down or maybe pile booties (page 416). For more on sanitation, see page 538.

For techniques and precautions when cooking in a tent, see page 283 and maybe 281.

The most vital precaution of all when camping in snow is to keep the tent from getting buried. You can buy lightweight aluminum shovels (page 328) to carry along for the job—and, of course, for clearing tent sites, digging snow caves (also page 328) or even clearing a route. But a snowshoe is a very efficient tool for keeping your tent unburied. In extremely heavy snow it may become necessary, if the snow keeps falling for a day or two, to take down your tent, raise the platform by shoveling in snow and stamping it flat, and then repitch the tent. Failure to guard against burial could prove fatal.

In mid-July 1958 a party of four climbers camped in stormy weather on an exposed Alaskan ridge at about 11,500 feet. They had two 2-man tents: a Gerry model made of permeable material and with two entrances, and an impermeable Army mountain tent with only a sleeve entrance. On the second stormbound night a very heavy fall of snow formed a 10-inch-thick windslab over the tents so quickly that none of the climbers appreciated the danger before morning. Around 6:00 A.M. one of the men in the Army tent woke, breathing rapidly, and realized that the air was foul. Unable to find knife, boots or gloves in the semicollapsed tent, he just managed to dig his way out through the clinging folds of the

sleeve entrance, barehanded, then had to slide back inside to rest and
warm up. (The outside temperature was around − 10°.) Suddenly he and
his companion found themselves gasping for breath. The first man immediately started out the entrance again but was unable to free himself
from the door, stopped digging to rest—and lost consciousness. Around
8:30 A.M. one of the men in the Gerry tent dug free and saw him lying
halfway out of the entrance, with evidence of frostbite. Carried into the
Gerry tent, he soon recovered consciousness. His companion was found,
still inside the Army tent, motionless and not breathing. Four to five
hours' artificial respiration failed to revive him. He had died, of course,
from asphyxiation (lack of oxygen, presence of carbon dioxide) due to the
tent's being buried.

Extremely bad snow conditions caused this accident, but contributory factors included the impermeable tent fabric, the clinging nature of
the only exit, and a guying system that failed to preserve adequate
internal air space. (For a full report and analysis, see "Accidents in
American Mountaineering," Twelfth Annual Report of the Safety Committee of the American Alpine Club, 1959, pages 22−4). The story is a
vivid object lesson in how alert you must remain—under conditions
horribly conducive to weariness and boredom—when there is any danger
of your tent's being buried by snow.

For more on blocked ventilation, see page 284.

Care of tents

Damp does not harm nylon tents the way it did old-style canvas-
and-rope models. In the field you do not have to keep loosening and
tightening the lines to meet humidity changes. And once the weather
swings around on your side the tent dries out very quickly. But mildew
can still form, and if you arrive home with a wet nylon tent you should
dry it out. The simplest way is to erect it on the lawn, wash it if necessary
with the garden hose and just leave it to dry. If you have to do the job
indoors, hang the tent by its normal suspension points. Some makers
recommend washing nylon tents after use in a tumbler-type—not agita-
tor-type—washing machine, with mild detergent, then drying them in
a spin drier. (To avoid grisly tangles, remove all guy lines.) Other makers
cry, "Never!" There seems to be general agreement that any coated
fabric, and especially old ones, may peel like sunburn if washed with
certain detergents (Ivory Flakes are fine, but Ivory Snow is not); and that
coated fabrics should be kept out of driers.

Cost prohibits waterproofing of tent seams in the factory. So all
seams—or at least fly-sheet and bathtub seams—must be sealed before

first use, and periodically thereafter. Because of the folding that occurs every time the tent is packed and because of general deterioration with time, almost any seam may need rewaterproofing after the equivalent of three months' constant use. Some tentmakers provide seam sealant with new tents or bivvies. For sealing Gore-Tex seams, see page 406.

NONTENTS

Your roof need not be a tent, of course. The several alternatives are all lighter than tents and easier to erect. All perform more efficiently as cool retreats in hot weather. And all are much cheaper. On the other hand, all are useless for protection against insects. None can approach the efficiency of a tent in blocking out a really high wind or in conserving warmth (though it is often overlooked that all of them, except in a very high wind, reduce the rate at which warm air from your body can escape, and so increase your warmth at night to a surprising degree). Although some of them repel the average rainstorm as well as most tents do, or even better, nothing rivals a good tent *with* fly sheet for protection from prolonged rain, whether it is a heavy downpour or a swirling, penetrating mountain drizzle.

You choose your roof, then, to suit expected conditions.

A fly sheet alone

You can use a standard fly sheet or have a special one made. Twenty years ago, during a four-month walk up England through the soggy maw of what the British sportingly call summer, I relied entirely on a simple unit that I had made up from untreated nylon fabric. It worked fine. And I hope to experiment soon with an updated version developed from a modified fly.

Catalogues intermittently feature large coated-nylon tarps, multi-grommeted and often with double tapes attached at various points. Unfortunately, they tend to be both heavy and expensive. (Range: 1½ to 4 pounds, $23 to $48.)

Note that the Chouinard Pyramid tent (page 307) is essentially a fancied-up fly sheet.

Plastic sheet with Visklamp attachment

This cunning and convenient though unlikely-looking rig is strong, light and very cheap. The plastic sheet is smooth, white, translucent

.004-inch polyethylene, known as Visqueen, that is absolutely water-tight and a great deal tougher than it looks. (Make sure, though, that you buy good-quality sheeting. One sample that I tried soon began to tear. And check that the material is translucent, not semitransparent, or it will make a scurvy sun awning.)

For years Visqueen sheeting and Visklamps have been difficult to find. But Liberty Organization of California now distribute them, and they should be more generally available in mountain shops. Sizes and weights vary, year to year, but current figures are: 5 by 8 feet, around 1 pound, $5; 7 by 10, 1½ pounds, $6; and 8 by 10, 1¾ pounds, $6.50. You can probably save money if you special-order 100-foot rolls. For normal solo use I favor the formerly available 8-by-9 size, but if really wet weather looms I may take the 9-by-12, which is entirely adequate for two (complete with 8 Visklamps and 6 strong pegs, about 2¾ pounds).

The sheets are plain, without grommets or attachments of any kind. You secure them with the improbable little two-part devices called Vis-klamps (¾ ounce and $.40 each).

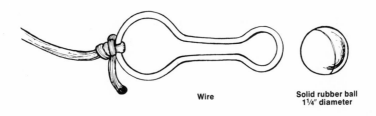

Wire

Solid rubber ball
1¼" diameter

A Visklamp is extremely easy to use. At whatever point you want to attach a guy line, you simply wrap the rubber ball in the sheet and twist a couple of times so that the ball and the plastic envelope around it form an isolated isthmus. Then you pass the enveloped ball through the larger metal loop and slide the twisted neck of the isthmus down the narrow connecting channel until the ball is held in the smaller loop. Attach a nylon cord to the larger loop, and you have a guy line that will take remarkable strain. For easy adjustment, run the guy line back from tent peg or substitute and thread through the Visklamp. Pull downward, using the Visklamp loop as a pulley. When the guy is tight, knot the free end at the Visklamp. You can then readjust the tension on any line without leaving your shelter.

The great advantage of this system is its flexibility. You can build an orthodox, tentlike bedroom:

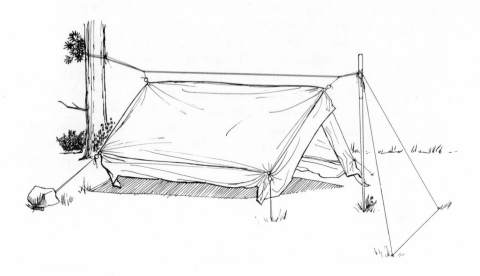

or a sort of eccentric rotunda (though you have to be careful about the angles, or you end up with almost no roof—only folds):

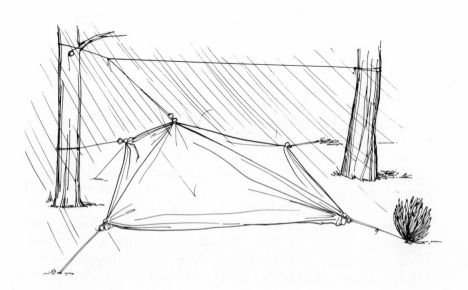

or a useful lunchtime shelter in wind-driven drizzle:

For further ideas, see variations on the poncho theme, pages 323–8.

An advantage of this rig is that you can, by moving one or two Visklamps, very simply make a major readjustment to meet new conditions of wind or rain. And in most setups you can, while still in bed, slip one Visklamp loose and lift the roof aside for cooking or working or for looking around, and can immediately replace it if rain threatens or you want more warmth. Carrying this idea further, you can put up your shelter because you think it may rain or get cold enough to make you grateful for the roof's assistance, and can then remove one or more of the rubber balls (filing them in a pocket or some other instantly reachable place) and so enjoy all the freedoms of rooflessness and yet know that if it rains, even in the middle of the night, you can get the roof over your head in about ten drops flat. I often rig such a ready-roof. In fact, it may be the prime reason I continue, despite raucous laughter from serious, haughty backpackers, to use my Visklamp shelter more than any other.

If you have not used this prophylactic system and rain catches you unawares you can as an emergency measure simply spread the sheet over yourself. One recent summer, caught in a fierce and prolonged mountain thunderstorm that struck with about three minutes' warning just as I camped at dusk, I was even able to cook dinner under the quickly spread sheet. That night the storm cleared within a couple of hours, but even for sleeping you can wrap the sheet loosely around everything in a makeshift cocoon—taking care to leave an opening at your head for ventilation. (For details, drawing and dangers, see pages 326 and 327.) This wraparound system, by the way, will help you keep warm, rain or no rain. Do not wrap yourself too tightly or your sweat may condense on the impermeable sheet and soak the sleeping bag.

I normally carry eight Visklamps and six aluminum tent pegs for this setup, but in really cramped and awkward corners a couple extra of each can make all the difference. If you lose a Visklamp just tie the nylon directly around the twisted isthmus below the rubber ball. The 4-mil polyethylene sheeting is tough enough to stand up to this makeshift arrangement. Once or twice, when I needed more attachment points than I had Visklamps, I have just twisted up a tumor of plastic and tied the nylon directly to its neck. A reader recommends using a small rock or even a ball of dirt.

One summer, when a desert afternoon wind was blustering across the plateau on which I'd camped, it repeatedly tore the sheeting at a Visklamp. So, although that has been my polyethylene's only failure, I would certainly not trust this rig in a full-scale mountain gale. But I almost always take it on summer trips of a week or so when there seems a chance of heavy rain. For its remarkable success in a wild November storm, see page 430. On short trips the wear factor can hardly become serious, but I am not sure I would rely on the plastic for a really long trip when I could not replace it.

Because the sheeting is white it does not make your den dark and dismal, even in oppressive weather. And because it is translucent-going-on-opaque it makes an excellent sun awning.

Visqueen is versatile stuff. It's exactly what you need for waterproofing your pack contents on major river crossings (pages 532 and 535). And if you have to swim across a river on a packless sidetrip you can wrap all your clothes and gear in the sheet, tie it with cord and have yourself a buoyant, watertight bundle that you can push or pull along (page 531). In any kind of terrain not covered by snow, the sheeting also makes a first-class marker for airdrops (page 546).

The use of Visqueen sheeting involves an important matter of principle that applies even more stringently to other items but which we had better examine before we go any further:

The ethics of using disposable plastic equipment.

Although matters are mercifully a little less horrendous than they were a few years ago it is still a sad fact that, in some of the more heavily

used backcountry, certain popular campsites—whole meadows, even entire above-timber rock basins—have been transformed into garbage
dumps by discarded plastic groundsheets, tarps and tube tents.

The causes of this defilement seem clear: an exponential increase in
the number of human visitors; the inability of uneducated newcomers to
grasp the gulf that yawns between behavior acceptable in a human society
still sick with the no-deposit-no-return syndrome and behavior acceptable in an essentially nonhuman society with its fragile economics totally
dependent on recycling; and the cheapness, lightness, efficiency and wide
availability of plastic sheeting molded to many backpacking uses. The
remedies are less clear. One possibility is to limit, forcibly, the number
of human visitors. This highly undesirable step has already been taken in
many places (page 45). Another alternative is enlightenment of the uneducated (such as I am attempting now, I guess) or a more general attempt
—which seems to be in hand, thank God—to eradicate the no-deposit-
no-return mentality. Another approach would be to remove the plastic
offenders from the marketplace. Several firms have, to their eternal
credit, made the attempt. Horrified by the results of their legitimate
business, they at first tried charging refundable deposits for disposable
plastic items; and when that scheme proved ineffective they ignored
profits and stopped selling plastic groundsheets, tarps and tube tents.
(The old Ski Hut refused to do so to the end.) I applaud, long and loud.
But I am not hopeful. It seems unlikely that all outdoor-equipment
suppliers can be persuaded to follow this public-spirited lead. And as
long as the offenders are for sale the only people likely to refuse to buy
them are precisely those people least likely to strew them around. Besides, even if all outdoor-equipment suppliers embargoed plastic-sheet-
ing articles, the raw sheeting would still be available—and bought.
(Retailers who continue to sell plastic items such as tube tents [page 322]
point out, accurately, that much of the backcountry litter consists of
empty stove cartridges and shredded packs—and that no one stops offering these items.)

In the end, only backpackers can stop the plastic defecation. So for
all of us the question arises, "What should I, personally, do about it?"
Should we stop using such vastly useful articles—you and I, who would
never by God dream of ditching a plastic groundsheet or anything else
in a wild place? (I mean, after all, would we?) The sacrifice would
without doubt generate a cozy holier-than-thou feeling—which is always
rewarding, and the reason self-denial remains so improbably but perennially popular.*

---

* For years I have sporadically packed out some of the trash other people left behind.
Although finding the act rewarding (that is, it made me feel good), I have always suffered

For me, the question also arises, "Should I remove all reference to the offending items from this book?" Such a course would certainly ensure that cozy glow of holiness; but I doubt its effectiveness. So for the time being I shall, a shade unhappily, continue to use certain plastic items; and I shall let my plastic paragraphs stand. But I remain in a state of some confusion.

The trouble is, I think, that the situation in those sad campsites and out in those desecrated meadows and rock basins is simply another manifestation of the current general human malaise: imbalance with the rest of the world. And the only way to correct that imbalance lies through a broad change of heart and actions. (See, for example, *Muddling Toward Frugality* [page 504, this book]; also *The Third Wave* by Alvin Toffler [Bantam Books, 1981].)

One of the worst sources of plastic litter has been the

Tube tent.

The standard form of this popular device is a tube of inexpensive polyethylene, usually 3.5 mil or lighter, about 9 feet long and 8 to 10 feet in circumference. The tube can be quickly strung up on any ridge line. The weight of your gear and body—perhaps with an assist from smooth stones—anchors the floor. Some models have grommets at each

---

from the bitter and inhibiting knowledge that it was an insignificant drop in a gigantic bucket. Now a Texas reader offers an excellent idea: "No one person can clean up all that plastic and other gunk that has been left in the mountains. But there are a lot of civilized backpackers. If—in the later stages of every trip, when we aren't carrying so much and won't have to carry it so far—we all picked up at least one piece of abandoned plastic and schlepped it out with our own trash it would make one hell of a damn dent in the wilderness trash accumulation. Doing so gives a tremendous 'holier-than-thou' rush. In other words, schlepping somebody else's garbage on one's back for twenty miles, just to help save the wilderness, would appeal to all 'holier-than-thou' junkies. And it might soon become as trendy and aware to have a recovered abandoned groundsheet in one's pack as to have a Sierra Club cup on one's belt—and to casually mention it when you stop to chat with other walkers. . . . Can't you imagine a whole new leitmotif in casual conversation? Trash machismo!: 'Yeah, I carried thirty pounds of abandoned groundcloths down Mount Whitney in a January blizzard. Roughest descent I ever had. Published a note in *Mountaineering Gazette!*' . . . Seriously, though, and exaggeration aside, perhaps it should become a sign of conservation awareness to pack out more trash than you generated yourself. And while very few people would do this as isolated individuals (feeling that it would not make enough difference) they might do so if they knew they were part of a large group, all doing it. If, for example, it began to be urged in print by one or more of the authors they consider to have earned some attention, Mr. Fletcher, sir."

Gladly. Delightedly.

end for drawing the openings more or less closed. The lightest—and flimsiest—may weigh only 10 ounces, cost $6.

Tyros tend to see tube tents as a wonderful idea; experienced back-packers, to steer clear. In rain the open ends are almost sure to let in some water—which will collect in puddles on the impermeable floor. If you batten down the ends to keep rain out, fierce condensation on the impermeable walls may in time produce as many puddles. And if the ridge line sags beware of the suffocation hazard, and of carbon-monoxide poisoning (page 284). Also, hail or even high winds can shred the thin plastic. That is why so many get left behind, particularly up high.

When certain states passed fire-retardant laws for tents (page 304), tube tents for a time faded away. But now they have eluded the law's embrace by assuming the names "tube shelters" or even "tube ground-sheets." The fact remains, of course, that a tube by any other name will burn as bright.

When the rain threat is minor I often rely for an emergency roof on my

Poncho or groundsheet.

Most heavy ponchos have grommets along their edges and it is a simple matter to string them up with nylon cord. Lightweight ponchos often lack grommets, but I have up to six or eight specially inserted. To build your roof you can string a ridge rope between trees and make an orthodox tentlike bedroom or you can attach the poncho by its corners to surrounding bushes and branches or to sticks held in position by stones. In heavy or driving rain you can stay surprisingly dry if you keep the roof so low that there is only just room for you underneath. I have on occasion carried one Visklamp as a roof-lifter for the poncho: with the low-level, battened-down roof, it makes life much more comfortable.

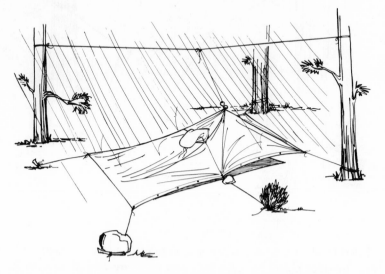

If you suspend the roof by the poncho's hood cord you do not risk damaging the fabric with the Visklamp but you put the roof's high point in the wrong place and probably get some rain in through the hood opening.

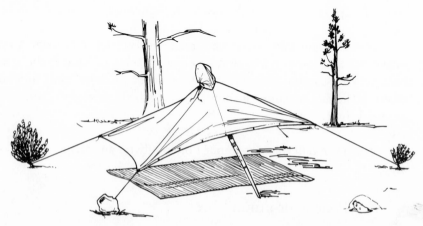

Under milder conditions you can use your staff either as an external upright or as an inside prop to force the roof pleasantly high above your head and also to keep it taut, so that rain does not collect in sagging hollows. When you use the staff this way, pad it at the top with something soft so that it will not cut the poncho.

The poncho rig is especially useful in open desert, when you may find yourself in desperate need of an awning at midday halts. The difference between the sun-scorched ground and the little coffin-shaped patch of shade under your poncho will seem like the difference between hell and . . . well, something a comfortable half-hitch short of hell. (See figures for desert ground temperatures, page 88, footnote.) The awning will certainly make a critical difference to your sense of well-being and therefore to what you are capable of doing in the cool of evening. Under certain conditions it could even spell the difference between life and death.

On desert afternoons a strong wind often blows for hour after hour. When it does, the continuous flapping of the poncho makes a hideous din, always threatens to tear grommets loose and sometimes does. One way of reducing both noise and strain is to secure only three corners of the poncho to fixed points and to tie a large rock on the downwind corner with a cord of such length that the stone will just rest on the ground under normal conditions, but will lift, and so ease the strain, when the poncho billows under an especially strong gust.

A grommeted *groundsheet* can make as effective a rain roof as a poncho. As it is usually bigger it will when new make an even better one —but groundsheets rarely stay unpunctured for very long.

Economy-size groundsheets (which in our peculiar modern tongue are distinctly large ones) can be folded so that they act both in their normal role and at the same time as an angled wall that will protect you from driven rain (and from a cold wind, dry or rain-bearing). You can hold the angled edge down with full canteens or other heavy equipment, with your staff (anchored by large stones) or with smooth stones alone.

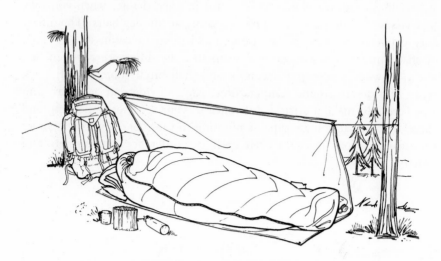

As awnings, clear plastic groundsheets are, of course, comprehensively useless—and translucent colored ones only a shade better.

Whether you choose to use groundsheet or poncho as your emergency rain roof depends on conditions. If you can race an approaching storm you will probably be wise to consider rigging your capacious groundsheet over a dry piece of ground and doing without anything under your mattress. Then you'll be able to wear the poncho when necessary. Try to resist the temptation to use it as a groundsheet; it will certainly develop holes. If the ground is already wet you will need the groundsheet as a floor, and the poncho goes up as roof.

Finally there is the problem of what to do about a roof when you go to sleep in the open, confident that no rain will fall, and wake up later to the pitter-patter of tiny raindrops or the clammy drift of drizzle. One solution is to unwrap your groundsheet (which, if it's big enough, is doubled under you) and cover yourself with the open side to leeward. If the weather gets worse you can quickly improve this makeshift cocoon by lacing the open side with nylon cord threaded through the grommets, if any (you get only mildly wet in the process). Another solution is to use the poncho in the same way, laced or unlaced. (If I harbor any doubts at all about the weather I go to sleep with the poncho ready, close at hand.) Better still is a combination of groundsheet and poncho: the groundsheet as main cocoon, the poncho wrapped like an elephant's foot around the bottom of your sleeping bag, which otherwise persists, steadfastly, in pushing out into the open. Provided the rain is not too heavy, such a makeshift shelter can keep your sleeping bag surprisingly dry, and yourself totally so. (One good friend of mine, an experienced backpacker, holds with ferocity to the childiotic notion that if he erects any rain shelter more complicated than a poncho-groundsheet cocoon he is pandering to his weaker instincts.) Gore-Tex-covered sleeping bags may mean that, except for your head, you need take no precautions against mist or very light rain (page 346).

The extent of the action you take when surprised by rain during the night depends on your sleepy estimate of the probable heaviness of the rain. If you think it is going to come down but good it pays to make the hard decision early and get up and rig poncho or groundsheet into an adequate roof. Of course, any man with an ounce of sense will rig a roof whenever there's a hint of doubt about the weather. I have at last learned to rig a ready-roof (page 319) at such times—with poncho or groundsheet if necessary. Well, I've more or less learned.

The cocoon bedroom in all its variants is also a useful makeshift measure in unexpected light snow. Even in dry weather it gives you a surprising degree of extra warmth, particularly in high winds. Remember, though, that unless there is adequate ventilation your sweat will condense and soak the sleeping bag. An unventilated cocoon—or a tarp or groundsheet just spread over your sleeping bag—can be dangerous. In early April 1961 a co-ed from the University of New Hampshire camped beside the parking lot of a New England ski resort. She had considerable winter camping experience. The weather had been warm and there was melt water on the packed snow. It rained during the night. Then the weather cleared and the temperature fell. Presumably to keep the rain off, the girl had covered her sleeping bag with an impermeable plastic tarp. In the morning she was found dead. It was presumed that she had suffocated, for the edges of the tarp were frozen to the ground ice and she had been sealed in. The carbon dioxide that would normally have awakened her by making her struggle for breath may have been absorbed by the moisture collected under the tarp. Lesson: always leave plenty of ventilation at your head, especially if there is any danger of the tarp's being frozen to the ground.

Snow caves (and trenches)

A few experienced winter backpackers habitually travel without tents; for shelter, they dig snow caves. The trade-off is weight for time: you save several pounds; but you must camp early enough, and with enough energy left in you, to allow for from one to three hours of hard digging to make your cave—although, as we shall see, it is sometimes possible to get by with far less work. On balance, then, digging a cave may not make sense if you expect to move every day but may be eminently worthwhile if you expect to use it for several successive nights. Knowing how to go about the job, at least in principle, is certainly a useful hedge against an emergency.

Frankly, I have never dug a snow cave. But once, in a Sierra Nevada winter storm that brought four feet of snow yet left temperatures up around 25° F., I found a U.S. Air Force survival-training group dug in, apparently without sleeping bags, on a steep ridge. As far as I could make out (when I stumbled on them, visibility was down to about ten yards), they seemed reasonably comfortable. They certainly sounded cheerful.

I talked recently to an experienced cave-digger. "If you know how to use it," he said, "snow can be your friend." Apart from know-how, all you need to build a snow cave is plenty of time, good waterproof clothing—preferably including rain chaps, because most of the digging will be done on your knees—and lots of snow. The snow should be somewhat consolidated; otherwise there is a danger of the roof's falling in. The best site is a wind-packed drift or gentle slope but at a pinch you can build almost anywhere there is enough depth, even on the flat. You dig a small entrance, level or sloping up (easier to dig), then hollow out a chamber just big enough for however many people are in your party. The excavated snow can be banked up into a windbreaking wall, just outside the entrance.

The best tool for digging is one of the lightweight aluminum shovels made for the job (about 1¼ pounds; light-duty, all-aluminum, $6.50; heavy-duty, wooden-handled, $20). Good models come from Alpine Research, Witco and MSR. In hard, crusted snow you may also need a snow saw (12 ounces, $13). Emergency substitutes for digging: snowshoe, spare ski tip, cooking pot, a thick stick or, as a last and unrecommended resort, hands (preferably protected by waterproof gloves).

Inside the cave a raised platform for sleeping on puts you up where the temperature is highest, makes a convenient seating place and keeps you and yours out of the watery run-off that tends to collect on the floor. Because snow is an excellent insulator (it holds small air pockets, just as down does) the temperature in the cave, fueled by your body and cooking stove and maybe a candle or two, will often be above freezing. So roof and even walls may develop a coating of ice that appreciably strengthens the structure—and also drips. A domed interior not only makes the strongest roof but also encourages moisture to run down the walls instead of dripping maliciously onto you or your sleeping bag. But any cave tends to be a humid place, and a Gore-Tex-covered or synthetic-filled bag will assuredly perform better than a traditional taffeta-covered down model. You must, of course, have a groundsheet (or, better still, a space blanket [page 585]) and also a foam pad or some other good insulation under the bag. Into the walls of the cave, at convenient places, you cut little alcoves for cooking stove, candles and anything else you fancy. Properly positioned, they can make the cave not just a convenient refuge but an attractive, even beguiling, little temporary home.

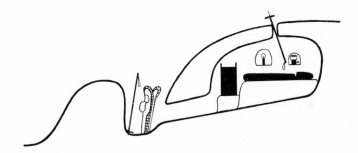

Roof thickness can vary from as little as two inches in well-consolidated snow to as much as three feet in new snow or the wetter kind commonly found in the East. The smaller the cave, the stronger the roof. The danger of collapse is apparently not great—though you are at first likely to feel nervous on that score as you lie looking up at the blank snow just above your head, especially if you are the body farthest from the entrance. A sensible precaution: always sleep with your shovel or other digging instrument at your side. Real danger of roof collapse can come from passing bears or people (mark the site carefully, especially in flat terrain) or from rain. Ventilation can be controlled, at least to some extent, by leaving the entrance open or partway open (a block of cut snow acts as door) and by cutting or poking a hole in the roof. Some people recommend leaving a ski pole or stick in the hole so that in case of heavy snowfall it can be kept open by jiggling from the inside. Others maintain that snow then falls into the cave, usually all over your bag.

The time needed to dig a good cave will vary with site, snow conditions and, above all, the expertise of the digger or diggers. With luck and experience, two men (changing places: inside and shoveling to the entrance; outside and removing the shoveled snow) may get the job done inside two hours. But a solo digger, making his smaller residence, may finish in an hour. And shortcuts sometimes present themselves. A hummock in the snow may indicate a sapling curved and weighed down by the snow, and beneath it may lurk an almost ready-made cave; if you're on your own you may with care and imagination be able to complete a cozy little nest within twenty minutes.

If you lack the time, energy, know-how or inclination to construct a cave you can maybe get by with a trench. You simply dig a "foxhole" two or three feet deep and just big enough for your sleeping bag not to touch the walls (but also as small as possible, to conserve body heat). Pile the excavated snow into an encircling wall. Then lay skis or snowshoes or tree branches across the open trench and cover them with a tarp or space blanket or whatever you have available. Secure it with snow. The result, says my informant, can be an astonishingly effective shelter, especially as protection against wind—though it's not really viable in stormy weather.

GROUNDSHEETS

Under benign conditions it is entirely possible to operate without a groundsheet. But I find that I never do. You need one in most places to keep out the damp, in even more places to reduce wear and tear on such fragile items as pad or mattress and sleeping bag, and just about everywhere as a general keep-clean-and-keep-from-losing-things area for the gear you take out of your pack. A slippery groundsheet also forms a natural defense zone against ants and ticks and scorpions and their brethren. In addition, remember the groundsheet-as-roof-and-walls-or-even-cocoon (pages 323–8).

When your load problem is acute and the chances of rain slight (a combination that applied on my Grand Canyon trip) you can carry a light poncho that doubles as groundsheet. A groundsheet does highly abrasive duty, so do not expect the dual-purpose article to last very long as a waterproof poncho. In Grand Canyon mine, sure enough, didn't. But all the rain and snow fell near the start, just as I had expected, and the arrangement worked out fine.

For a long trip on which you cannot get equipment replaced you need a strong, though still lightweight, groundsheet. Coated nylon remains the best bet. But it is expensive. Typical 1.9-ounce-fabric groundsheets (reinforced with eight brass-plated grommets, so that they can double as tarps) run $33 in the 7-by-9-foot size (1 pound 6 ounces) and $45 in the 9-by-11 (2 pounds 2 ounces).

On all but the longest trips I have for years used ordinary 4-mil painters'-cloth plastic sheeting, available by the yard at builders'-supply stores (from 6- to 12-foot widths, $.36 to $.72 a foot). You can cut it to the exact size you want for any given trip. Mostly, you use it single and small (say, 3 by 7½ feet). But if you are going light on overhead protection and therefore may need something to pull over your bag you cut your cloth accordingly.

Color matters little, unless you may want the sheet to double as an awning (page 326). I find I almost always use black: it is the only kind in my local store.

Plastic groundsheets are waterproof—when unpunctured. But because they often get punctured and torn they form a considerable part of the plastic desecration of wilderness by uneducated oafs (see, *please,* pages 320–2). Each of us must make up his own mind about his personal response to this messy problem.

MATTRESSES

When you are young and eager and tough, and the weather is not too perishingly cold, you do without a mattress. I did so all through the six months of my California walk (except for the first few days when, to cushion the shock of changing from soft city life, I carried a cheap plastic air mattress that I didn't expect to last long, and which didn't). I soon got used to sleeping with my mummy bag directly on all kinds of hard ground, but I often padded the bag inside with a sweater or other clothes. On that trip temperatures rarely fell more than a degree or two below freezing, though on one occasion I slept on stones at 25° F. (That night I had a floored tent and a few sheets of newspaper, which make a very useful emergency insulator.)

But failing to use some kind of insulation under your sleeping bag (unless it's a foam bag) is, in all but consistently hot weather, grossly inefficient: your weight so compresses the down or synthetic directly beneath you that its air-holding and warmth-conserving property is cut almost to zero. And even when cold is no problem you are liable to find that if you have grown used to an ordinary bed the change to unpadded-bag-on-the-ground ruins your sleep for at least a few nights. This reduces both your efficiency and enjoyment, and the saving in weight just isn't worth it—unless you can be sure of finding soft, dry sand for a bed. Then all you need is a couple of wriggles to dig shallow depressions for shoulders and rump, and you've got yourself a comfortable sleep.

The traditional woodsman and Boy Scout routine was to build a mattress from natural materials: soft and pliable bough tips, or moss or thick grass. On the California walk I did for a while use branches from desert creosote bushes. But in today's heavily traveled camping areas the cutting of plant life is not merely illegal but downright immoral—an atrocity committed only by the sort of feeble-minded citizen who scatters empty beer cans along our roadsides. Besides, the method is inefficient. Even when you can find suitable materials, you waste time in preparing a bed. And the bed is rarely as warm or comfortable as any of the modern lightweight pads or mattresses.

For perhaps twenty years the standard equipment under almost all conditions was an air mattress. Then, for perhaps a decade, foam pads ruled.*

An air mattress amplifies the efficiency of your sleeping bag by keeping a cushion of air between it and the ground. The air can circulate within the tubes, though, and therefore passes heat by convection from warm body to cold ground—and especially to snow. But an air mattress also neutralizes the sharpest stones, supports your body luxuriously at all the right places, converts into an easy chair and will if necessary float you and your pack across a river (pages 531–7). It also gets punctures.

Still air trapped in small enough chambers—less than quarter-inch diameter—forms an excellent barrier to heat transfer. Foam pads hold the air in just such small chambers and therefore insulate far better than air mattresses. They also tend to be lighter and cheaper—and puncture-immune. But they are bulkier, and most of them are far less comfortable except on snow or sand or a deep pile of leaves or other soft underlayer. In addition, they make inferior chairs, and will help you precious little on river crossings. On balance, though, they proved better than air mattresses and superseded them for general backpacking, especially in cold places. For years no one in his right mind has carried an air mattress for snow work.

By now, thanks to Cascade Designs of Seattle, you can, under almost all conditions, have the best of both worlds.

It is very rare for a new piece of backpacking equipment to sweep aside, almost overnight, all the oldies. But Cascade Designs' Therm-a-Rest mattress has virtually pulled it off. The Therm-a-Rest is at least as comfortable as an air mattress and insulates better than most pads. The idea is simple: an open-cell foam pad (1½ inches thick in the regular

---

* Note that, in spite of fire-retardants, all foams—and also many nylon fabrics as used in sleeping bags and other equipment—present serious fire hazards. I don't say they'll burst into flames at the drop of a match. But they'll burn. And foams may give off toxic gases. I'm not sure what you can do about it, beyond exercising reasonable care. But I feel I must sound this warning.

models, 1 inch in the new lightweight version) that is covered with a tough, waterproof, airtight nylon twill cover bonded to the foam (200-denier oxford fabric in regulars, 70-denier taffeta in the lightweight). A metal screw-valve at one corner enables you to control the air pressure in the foam's spaces. To deflate for packing you roll the mattress on a flat surface or your thighs, then close the valve. The mattress remains rolled and is reasonably compact. To inflate you simply open the valve: the mattress will slowly unroll, and within a few minutes—the time needed to erect a tent, say—it is ready for use. You can simply close the valve or you can—as I almost always do—blow more air in and then close the valve. Inflated that way, the mattress is more comfortable as well as a more efficient insulator. Rather to my surprise, I find that the harder it's inflated, the more comfortable it is. But you can experiment and then minister to your personal druthers.

Like most mattresses, the Therm-a-Rest is slippery. Your sleeping bag tends to slide off it. I've heard of, but not yet tried, two simple ameliorations: with barge cement, bond a couple of strips of 2-inch Velcro pile across the mattress (for another use of such strips, see page 334); or make up a lightweight, fairly tight-fitting cloth envelope (with hole for valve access). But Cascade Designs now sell a non-sticky aerosol spray (Slip Fix, $4) that I find indeed reduces slipperiness very appreciably. (It is also said to improve the grip on gloves and canoe paddles and to be "good for tennis and racquet ball strings.")

A wet mattress dries quickly when left standing on its side with both surfaces exposed to the air. At home, to avoid mildew inside and out, store it unrolled, flat, and with the valve open. Punctures occur only rarely (full instructions for repair come with each mattress, and there is now a repair kit [1 ounce, $3] said to be good); and even a punctured Therm-a-Rest is still a serviceable open-cell foam pad (for open- and closed-cell pads, see pages 336–7). Faulty valves can be replaced fairly simply (spares, $1.50). But it is my experience, widely shared, that if you treat your Therm-a-Rest with anything less than brutality it will give good service. It is very well made and the makers stand sturdily behind their product—even, sometimes, beyond the two-year warranty.

Naturally, all this joy does not come cheap—in ounces or dollars. The regular hip-length size (1½ by 19 by 48 inches), which I have long used, weighs 1 pound 8 ounces and costs $36.50; the full-length size (1½ by 20 by 72 inches), necessary in snow (though see below), is 2 pounds 5 ounces and $48.50. But an overwhelming majority of experienced backpackers clearly accept the expense. You can get fitted nylon stuff sacks (1 ounce, $6), but I've not found the need for one.

A new hip-length Ultra Lite Therm-a-Rest is the same length and breadth as the regular, weighs 7 ounces less, folds appreciably smaller—

and costs $39. I find the reduction in comfort surprisingly small. In bitter weather you might suffer appreciable insulation loss, I guess. But for ultralight travel the new model is a little gem. A full-length version lurks.

A hip-length Therm-a-Rest (or air mattress or foam pad) supports your butt, shoulders and possibly head; in cold weather you keep your feet off the ground with spare clothing or your pack or whatever else you can lay hands on. The extra weight (and cost) of a full-length model may be worth it if your body demands full comfort for a good night's sleep, and also in bitterly cold weather. For snow work, most people go the full hog. On a recent high trip in late fall I saved weight, bulk and dollars by cutting a 20-by-28-inch piece of closed-cell foam from an Aerolite pad (4 ounces), cementing matching halves of a 2-inch Velcro strip to one end of it and to the foot of my hip-length regular Therm-a-Rest, and conjoining them. It worked fine on that trip, and again on a week's spring snowshoeing over deep snow.

A pair of Therm-a-Rests (or of other foam pads) can be conjoined for bilateral sleeping by encircling each with a "couple kit": a pair of ¾-inch bands that interlink (1¼ ounces; $4.50). Variations obviously abound.

Naturally, not everyone will want a Therm-a-Rest. Some people are, for good, bad or indifferent reasons, wedded to conventional air mattresses or foam pads. Both can be lighter and less bulky, not to mention cheaper. And cost may be a crucial factor, especially if you backpack only rarely. Again, an air mattress makes a better chair than either a Therm-a-Rest or a pad. You may also choose to take along an air mattress, not necessarily a lightweight one, for overnight camping at roadhead—perhaps with a foam pad on top of it for sybaritic luxury. For other considerations, see "Traditional air mattresses," below.

I suspect that a Therm-a-Rest might even fill the special role of air mattress as flotation device for you or your pack (pages 531–7)—though if you ever got water in that open-cell foam . . .

Later: Evolution pads on. Sierra West will soon introduce an egg-crate-patterned, open-cell, non-inflatable foam pad, designed by Chet Russell of Texas, that is the same weight as a regular Therm-a-Rest but, they claim, markedly more comfortable. A waterproof cover on bottom and sides reaches around partway on top to meet a lighter, breathable fabric so that the pad, when rolled and held tight by Velcro strips, becomes virtually waterproof.

Traditional air mattresses have almost, but not quite, disappeared from mountain shops. But I still use one occasionally when I judge the night will not be cold enough to make sub-sleeping-bag insulation a major problem and weight, or even just comfort, might be; when I think

I might need it for a river crossing; when bulk poses a load problem; or if I want to spend a lot of time sitting and reading or writing, and like hell fancy the idea of an easy chair (page 336).

If you decide you want an air mattress for some reason, avoid at all costs—unless you want it only for a night or two—one of the cheap, thin, plastic jobs. They puncture and tear almost without provocation, and often don't get the chance to do either before a seam pulls open. Coated nylon does better.

The most popular air mattress now readily available is the Blue Wing by Air Lift of Berkeley, California. A compartmentalized Rip-stop nylon cover, zippered at one end, houses nine separate plastic tubes, each with a valve. Each mattress comes with stuff sack, patch tape and a spare tube. A punctured tube can be quickly replaced, and even a second or third puncture does not leave you unsupported. These mattresses are very light and compact, and I still use an earlier model with satisfaction—though other people report a high incidence of punctures. There is certainly a hassle element in having to inflate—and, worse still, deflate—through nine separate valves; on the other hand, you can inflate the outer tubes hard, the inner ones progressively softer, and so reduce the danger, inherent in all air mattresses, of rolling off while you sleep. (Hip-length Blue Wing-42; 20 by 42 inches, 11 ounces, $38; full-length, 22-by-72-inch model, 21 ounces, $47; spare tubes, $2.50 and $3. ⅛-inch insulation pad, 22 by 72 inches, 10 ounces, $4. Velcro tape set for conjoining mattresses, $3.) At least one similar design has now hit the market.

As far as the punctures go, all you have to do is keep a wary eye open for thorns, carry a repair outfit (2 ounces, $4) and practice periodic prophylactic prayer. Traditionally, such outfits seem to include a wild selection of patches but nothing like enough adhesive. Consider carrying an extra tube of rubber solution—or two complementary tubes of epoxy, which will repair not only your air mattress but everything from sunglasses through boot soles to packbag and even aluminum packframe. But beware of crushed tubes! And keep the two tubes securely separated.

Inflating an air mattress—any air mattress—is easy, but not quite as easy as it sounds. For sleeping, the mattress should be fairly soft. (Therm-a-Rests are a different matter; see page 333.) Inexperienced campers tend to blow their mattresses up far too tight, spend a night or two bobbing around like corks on a rough sea, then give up the great outdoors for good. The trick is to inflate the mattress just hard enough to keep every segment of you off the ground—and no harder. The easiest way to achieve this end is to blow the mattress up considerably harder than it will finally need to be, wait for the hot air from your lungs to cool and therefore contract, lie on your side on the mattress and press down unnaturally hard with your hip, and slowly let air out of the valve until your hip just touches the ground. Then close the valve. The mattress will now be firm enough to hold your hip clear of the ground when you're lying naturally but soft enough to accept your body into its bosom rather than to send you bobbing around or rolling off to one side. And because the protruding portions of your body compress the air, the mattress will support the parts that need support: knees, neck and small of back. If your mattress has a pillow section as a separate compartment inflate it rather hard. Again, overinflate and, when you lie down, reduce the pressure to what feels right.

Rather to my surprise, I long ago came to the conclusion that if I carry an air mattress then a separately inflatable pillow section is worth having. It certainly makes for a more comfortable bed. And it also means that you carry along, without extra weight, an excellent easy chair. For the chair, reverse the inflation routine for the bed: blow the main section up hard but leave the pillow soft. Then reverse the mattress too, propping the main section up against your pack as a backrest and laying the pillow flat as a seat. You can hardly make the backrest too firm. The best way to get the pillow right is once more to overinflate and then to fine-adjust with your butt in position. You may possibly classify a wilderness easy chair as rampant hedonism—until you have sampled the difference between eating the evening meal with and without a comfortable backrest or have spent an afternoon leaning against a gnarled tree trunk while you tried to read or write. The difficulty these days is finding a lightweight air mattress with a pillow section. For more on pillows, see page 363.

Closed-cell foam pads have impermeable surfaces and trap tiny air pockets almost permanently. They therefore insulate extremely well and are mostly waterproof. But they compress very little and, although thin (3/16 through 1/2 inch), are bulky to pack. When a pad is new, indentations quickly disappear; but with age it becomes, like people, less resilient. And severe cold makes some foam stiff and brittle. The thinness and incompressibility mean that closed-cell pads do not cushion you well; but comfort can be increased—at considerable cost in weight and bulk—by laminating sheets together. Pads come in various hip- or full-length sizes, or in sheets you can cut to suit.

Most early closed-cell pads were Ensolite. It has been improved and joined by others, and we now have a spectrum of pads in a wide range of sizes, weights, costs and resistance to cold and abrasion. A few current spectrum points: gray or beige or black Ensolite (flexible down to −30° F.; 3/8 by 21 by 42 inches, 9 ounces, $7.50; 1/2 by 28 by 72 inches, 2 pounds 8 ounces, $15); Regalite (does not crack until −90° F.; 3/8 by 20 by 59 inches, 10 ounces, $18.50); several similar, differently colored foams, such as Aerolite; and white Volarfoam (lightweight, excellent insulant, flexible to $-50°$ F., but not abrasion-resistant in prolonged use; ½ by 25 by 60 inches, 1 pound 1 ounce, $12). Others exist. More will assuredly follow—and wax and wane with the passing moons.

Open-cell foam pads compress easily and are therefore more comfortable than Ensolite and its cousins. But to achieve the same insulation they must be about three times as thick (normal range, 1½ to 2½ inches). So they are bulkier, heavier and more expensive. The bulkiness is more apparent than real: stuffed hard into a packbag, they compress halfway well. Open foam's underside is often corrugated, in "egg-box" or zigzag form, to increase comfort with minimum additional weight.

Because the open-cell structure soaks up water, the pads mostly come with covers—coated waterproof nylon underneath, cotton/Dacron on top to reduce slipperiness and permit perspiration to dissipate. A pleated pocket at the head of the cover may offer holding space for whatever pillow you choose to inject (page 363). Before the advent of the Therm-a-Rest, I used a Sierra Designs version of such a pad for years under most conditions except snow and found it as warm and trouble-free as Ensolite and almost as comfortable as an air mattress. (Typical current models: 1½ by 20 by 48 inches, 1 pound 8 ounces, $18; 2 by 22 by 72 inches, 3 pounds 3 ounces, $25.) A Georgia reader suggests a cheap, do-it-yourself covered pad: open-cell foam, 25½ inches wide, 1 or 1½ inches thick, with two industrial-strength plastic garbage bags slipped over opposite ends, joined amidships with duct tape, and punctured at one end (for air escape and easier packing) with slits placed at ½-inch intervals.

Down-filled air mat (DAM). This unlikely device by Stephenson is an attempt, like Therm-a-Rest's, to combine the sink-in comfort of an air mattress with the much greater insulation of small, trapped air pockets. A box-baffled, urethane-coated nylon shell, fitted with an air valve, is filled with goose down, as in a sleeping bag or jacket. The great gain compared with a Therm-a-Rest is reduced bulk for packing. But in case of a puncture you lose the back-up of a conventional foam pad. And because your breath would soon soak the down you must inflate the DAM with a short plastic tube attached to a special sleeping-bag stuff sack that acts as pump. In addition, because DAMs are made in special conformations to fit specific Stephenson sleeping bags, they are damned expensive: $80 plus. Average weight, with "pump": 1¼ pounds.

HAMMOCKS

A reader writes from Liberia that he often uses his Army hammock from Vietnam for backpacking, "with no regrets . . . only a few reservations." Now, most people shy away from the idea of sleeping in a hammock, especially after a long day with a heavy load. I certainly do. But you may not. And I guess a light hammock can be useful as a bed if you want to keep cool (air all around you) in a place as hot as Liberia; if the ground, every place, is soaking wet; if you're petrified beyond sleep by the thought of rattlesnakes or scorpions or other things that might go chomp in the night; if the local ground insects are a ravenously hungry host; or if you're an old-style sailor, landlubbering but pining. Other suggested uses: for slinging food and gear from trees, high above the ground, as protection against flood, bears and other invaders; for rest, not sleep, at a base camp; and, with poles, as an emergency stretcher.

My Liberian correspondent's hammock seems to be of some solid fabric: he does not like or trust "the net-type sold for packers." But sold they are—or at least offered: knotless synthetic-mesh jobs described as rolling into "a pocket sized ball" and damn nearly doing so (main body 32 by 72 inches; 8 ounces; $7). Also sometimes seen: a Mayan Indian design, "made of miles of 100% pure cotton lace, hand woven and hand tied . . . so big and strong it'll sleep three adults. . . . Easy to care for, will last and last" (10 by 11 feet; 3¼ pounds; $58).

SLEEPING BAGS

For good reasons, we will consider the fundamentals of warmth retention in the "Clothes Closet," not here. See "The prime purpose of clothes," page 377 and "The fundamentals of insulation," page 384. If you can't be bothered to check those pages, at least remember that sleeping bags, like clothes, are not to "keep the cold out," as the old saying goes, but to conserve heat from the only available source—you; also that (although the distinction is less important than with clothes) the bag is not meant to make you as warm as possible, but to maintain "thermal equilibrium" —a state in which your heat production roughly balances your heat loss.

Because the first sleeping bags clearly evolved from the idea of stitching two blankets together they took the rectangular form of a bed. But most backpacking bags are now mummy bags—designed for human forms rather than for small upright pianos.

A few people say they feel uncomfortably confined in mummy bags. Claustrophobics may certainly face difficulties; but if you have given mummies a fair trial and just cannot get used to any real or imagined constriction you do not necessarily have to put up with the inefficiencies of the old rectangular piano-envelope. Although most backpacking bags are now distinctly form-fitting (in spite of a recent trend away from

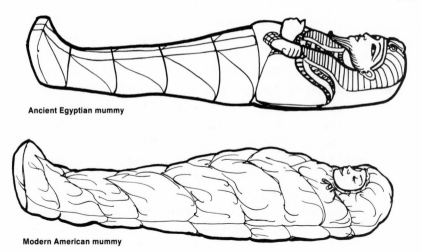

Ancient Egyptian mummy

Modern American mummy

extreme sheathing), the catalogues still offer a continuum ranging from slim through mesomorphic to downright obese—some of these are tapered but unshaped—as well as old-style rectangular. Take your well-pondered pick. But remember that each size up means marginally greater weight and bulk. And, worse, that your body has to warm, all night long, a marginally greater volume of contained air.

Some outdoor lovers complain that mummy bags do not leave enough room for maneuver. Opportunists may face a problem here (though a local Don Juan advises: "You'd be surprised what has been achieved. As in all games, desire is very important"). Those who plan their amatory operations in advance should note that it is now possible to order most mummy-bag models with zippers on opposite sides so that they will join convivially together. And any two bags with zippers of the same kind and length will conjoin—though the hoods will face opposite ways. See also double mummy bags, page 360.

A battened-down mummy bag is a very efficient heat-conserver. Old-style rectangular envelopes gave your head no protection at all, tended to leave your shoulders exposed too and let a great deal of precious body heat escape through the bag's wide mouth. A mummy eliminates all these faults. When you pull on the drawstrings of the hood, the fabric curls around your crown and not only protects head and shoulders but also bottles the body heat. On a really cold night you pull on the drawstrings until the opening contracts to a small hole around nose and mouth. If, like me, you prefer to sleep naked because you wake feeling fresher you may sometimes find cold air seeping down through the hole and moving uncomfortably around bare shoulders. All you need do is wrap a shirt loosely around your neck (though see "Collars," page 347). But this arrangement often holds the warm air in so well that you soon find you are too hot. To reduce the inside temperature (whether you are using a neck wrap or not) simply slacken the hood tapes a little. That will make a lot of difference: your head dissipates heat more quickly than any other part of the body (page 347). (You will not question this statement if you are balding fast into coot country: you'll probably, like me, have taken to wearing a balaclava at night.) In warm weather you can leave the tapes undrawn so that the mouth of the bag remains as open as in old-style envelopes. In hot weather you can go two steps further—if you have the right kind of bag. A mummy bag designed for use only in cold weather (that is, for polar exploration, high-altitude mountaineering and winter hunting) may have no zipper openings. But although an uninterrupted shell is the lightest possible design and also conserves heat the most efficiently, such a bag is now very rare. It may do its special job well but it lacks versatility. In anything but chilly weather you are liable to find yourself sweating even though the mouth of the bag is open—with no alternative except getting partly or wholly out (see page 355). A zipper opening solves the problem, and nearly all bags now come with 72-inch side zippers. The modification is not pure gain. To prevent air passage through the closed zipper it has to be faced inside with a down-filled draft flap, or the zipper zone has to be blocked with a broad extension of the main wall that snugs in tight when you close the zipper. Or there may be two full-length zippers. But even a single zipper and its flap add several ounces to the weight of a bag, and, no matter how good the blocking device there is bound to be a slight loss in heat-conserving efficiency; but if you expect to operate at times in temperatures much above freezing then the very great gain in versatility is well worth such minor drawbacks. A few mummy bags have zippers that open all the way around the foot so that you can ventilate your feet as well as the rest of you—and can also convert the fully opened bag into a flat though markedly tapered down cover, very useful for warm nights in the bush and cold ones back home in bed. But I understand they do not zip together efficiently around the foot. Almost all bags now have two-way zippers: you can operate the zipper from both top and bottom, and by opening it partway at shins as well as shoulders you gain a valuable aid—in the almost nightly game of adjusting your bed to suit different and changing air temperatures (pages 373–4).

Of the major sleeping-bag components—fill, shells and liners—

The fill

is what matters most. It must hold within itself as many pockets of air as possible, to act as an insulant between the warmed inner and cold outer air, and for backpacking purposes the best material is that which does this job most efficiently for the least weight. But there are subsidiary considerations: compactibility (the packed bag should not be too bulky); fluffability (the fill must quickly expand to its open, air-trapping state after being tightly packed); efficiency when wet; even, for a few people, possible allergic effects.

Traditional down-filled bags still dominate the high-quality field. But synthetic-filled bags, which have for years been nipping at their drawstrings, continue to make technical advances, and it is just possible that they are on the brink of pulling level. Among high-quality bagmakers, a few (Bugaboo and Blue Puma) still stick exclusively with down. But most of the big producers (including The North Face, Sierra Designs, Trailwise, Wilderness Experience, Eddie Bauer, REI, Kelty, Camp 7 and JanSport) have added synthetic lines. And a few small, first-class specialists (such as Moonstone Mountaineering of California and Bristlecone Mountaineering of Ohio) use only synthetic fills.

Down is still the most efficient fill, warmth for weight. Compressed for packing, it is markedly less bulky than any known synthetic fill. It also fluffs back to its open, air-trapping state more quickly and totally. When not compressed it free-flows, almost like a liquid, so that it continuously and evenly fills, in a way no current synthetic will, a space that is always changing shape—as is a compartment in a sleeping bag. In addition, a good down-filled bag should, with real care, last 10 to 15 years, against 3 to 6 years for current synthetics. On the other hand, down is useless when wet (synthetics retain at least some insulating property, and often most of it); once wet, it is difficult-going-on-impossible to dry in the field (synthetics dry much more readily); and over a long period of continual use, as in an expedition, dirt and repeated dampness tend to reduce its loft and therefore its efficiency (though see Gore-Tex shells, page 346). Down, unlike synthetics, can also generate allergies in rare individuals. It demands rather more care in maintenance. And high-quality down is now murderously expensive (about $30 a pound, wholesale, against $3 or $4 for the best current synthetics).

It is generally accepted that the best down comes from geese (mostly from China). Much learned discourse used to occur in catalogues and mountain shops—and to some extent still does—about the virtues of white versus gray goose down (probable ultimate verdict: the difference is either nil or very little), the adulteration of down with fluff (by law, "down" must be at least 70 percent *down*), and even the occasional perfidious sale of mere duck down under a "goose" label (all new bags must bear a sewn-in label showing government specifications of the fill —though classification varies from state to state, with New York and California the most rigorous). For some years, though, a generally accepted qualitative measure has been dampening this ongoing discourse. "Fill power" is not, thank God, yet another political rallying bleat: it shows the number of cubic inches an ounce of uncompressed down will occupy. (The scale is not used for synthetics.) The best bag- and garment-makers use down with a fill power of 550, 600 or even 700, and somewhere in the blurb about their gear they will give the figure. Or should. Note that costs rise sharply with fill power. If a good bag containing 2 pounds of 600-fill-power down costs $200, an identical one with 700-fill-power will be around $275.

Synthetic fills with fancy names and low prices have been around for years. For backpacking, I would not touch them with a walking staff. But the latest versions are a different kettle of fuzz.

Current trade names do not matter too much: they'll likely be gone tomorrow. But it's worth knowing that there are three main kinds of fill presently in use and that at least one novel form lurks in the wings:

1. Long, continuous-filament fibers that cling together and are used in thick, cohesive sheets or batts—usually in 5-, 8- or 10-ounce layers (rated by weight per square yard). A 5-ounce layer, uncompressed, is about one inch thick. Current dominant: PolarGuard.

2. Much shorter, noncontinuous-filament fibers (2¼–2½ inches) that can be used either in cohesive batts, much like the long-fibered layers, or in a more amorphous form. Current trade names: Hollofil II, Hollowbond and Quallofil.

3. Even-shorter-fibered forms that can be blown into separate baffled compartments of the shell, as down is blown. Names still being juggled.

All three forms are now being "lubricated" by spraying with silicone or other liquids to reduce the "boardlike" feeling and make them feel more silky, more downlike.

I've heard that there already exists in a Japanese test tube a synthetic constructed rather like a down pod, with ribbonlike fibers twisted around a central point. In a bag it is said to feel remarkably like down. Some reports put it on the market in a year or so. Maybe.

These proven and rumored advances suggest that we may now be not far away from a synthetic that warms and wears as efficiently as down, perhaps in a form that can also be blown into compartments. If so, it will revolutionize the sleeping-bag and down-garment field. As the R&D man for one leading maker told me recently: "If and when we get the right synthetic it will destroy down—because of its price, because it stays warmer when wet and because it will be easier to take care of." The owner of a firm that specializes in down-filled bags says he has seen fill that was half down, half Hollofil, and found himself "impressed."

Thinsulate, a thin-fibered polyolefin/polyester synthetic insulation very popular in certain kinds of clothing (page 384), does not now seem suitable for sleeping bags. Ditto pile and its allies (page 379). And foam bags seem to have faded away (page 359).

Two variations on the normal method of using fill have recently enjoyed considerable vogue. Both appear mainly if not solely in down-filled bags.

One is simply to put 60 percent of the fill on top, 40 percent below —instead of the normal 50/50 division. Assuming a good insulating pad underneath, that makes theoretical sense: most of the heat you lose presumably escapes upward. But it seems to me that unless you tend not to move at all during the night, or always move the bag around with you when you do so (and some people apparently train themselves to do just that, even in mummy bags), then the "top" of the bag is by no means always on top. Most people lie at least part of the time on one side, and curled, so the underfilled portion tends to pull tight along your back— the most vulnerable area. That kicks a colander in the theory; but the fact is that many, perhaps most, down bags are now filled 60/40. Some, for mountaineering, even go 70/30 near the foot.

The second variation is to modify a shell so that fill can be moved around, top to bottom. This is achieved by omitting side-block baffles —the line of baffles that runs down the side of the bag opposite the zipper and keeps down from traveling, top to bottom, along transverse tubes (see below). The idea is that in cold weather you shift down from bottom to top; in warm weather, vice versa. Satisfied users tell me it works, even when done in the dark. Frankly, I remain apprehensive of cold spots. But many bagmakers now produce at least one model, usually a lightweight, built this way.

The shell

Down demands one kind of internal construction; synthetics, quite another.

Down tends to move away from the points of greatest wear, notably from under your butt and shoulders (where it will be compressed and not very effective anyway) and also from the high point above your body (where, because heat rises, good insulation is vital). To minimize fill's movement the shell is therefore divided into a series of self-contained tubes that keep the down from moving very far (see above). Because of a general tendency for down to migrate from the head toward the foot of a bag, transverse tubes work far better than longitudinal.

If tubes are made by simply stitching through the inner and outer walls of the shell you are left unprotected at the stitch-through points. If some form of batting is inserted at these points (a simple and cheap system) there is some improvement. But not much. And except for one or two ultralight models (see page 358), all down sleeping bags now embody tube systems in which the tube walls—known as baffles—are constructed on one of three box systems:

slanting

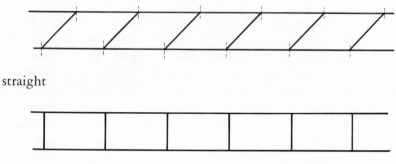

straight

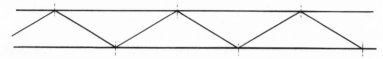

or, very occasionally, "V"—also known as "overlapping tubes."

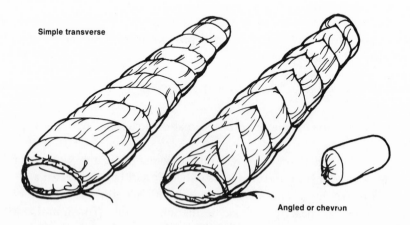

Most tubes run straight across the bag, but Trailwise have long used an angled or chevron system.

Simple transverse

Angled or chevron

The theory is that down tends to cling to baffle walls and that the greater length of wall inherent in the chevron system means a greater tendency for the down to be held in place, especially at the important apex (when the bag is elevated by your body). Most competitors predictably dismiss the idea as poppycock, but one or two grudgingly admit its possible value. JanSport use a baffle system known as "body contour," the theory of which eludes me. Competitors deride this one almost in unison. But no one knocks baffles in general. A popular saying runs, "You're only as warm as your baffle system."

With blown-in synthetic fills, construction may be similar to that in down bags—though the fibers do not flow as liquidly as down but tend to cling to themselves and therefore require smaller tubes.

Long-fibered, continuous-filament synthetics, such as PolarGuard, need no tubes. A single layer or combination of layers encircles the bag, with extra at the foot. Most such bags have quilt lines that look like baffle tube seams, but in at least some cases they seem to be largely cosmetic: people are used to transversely sewn bags, say the makers, and demand "the down look." Actually, the quilting of the synthetic to the shell increases costs and may slightly reduce insulation efficiency— though it can be argued that a floppy, unsecured shell would be a nuisance, especially on the inside. The important thing with such bags is "edge stabilization," which simply means that the layers (or at least the outer layers) are sewn securely to the shell along their edges. Other- wise they tend to pull away and leave an insulation-ruining gap, and the insulation ends up twisting on itself.

Edge stabilization is equally important with shorter-fibered synthet- ics, such as Quallofil, when they are used in batted layers. With such fills, quilting over the main surface is usually necessary—even when, as often happens, the batts have a lightweight scrim attached to one side to hold the material together structurally.

To conserve weight and reduce the volume of trapped air that must be kept warm, the best mummy bags are now made widest at the shoulders and narrowest at the ankles, then flare out again to accommo- date the feet. Until recently, "differential cut" was almost gospel among bagmakers, especially for close-fitting bags: they cut inner shells smaller than outer, reputedly creating a "thermos" effect, permitting fill to "loft" freely (page 352) and keeping protruding knees and elbows from pushing tight against the outer shell and so losing virtually all insula- tion. But some revisionist makers now dismiss the "thermos" effect as applicable only to rigid bodies, and claim that inner and outer shells of the same size not only reduce costs but actually work better: the slack inner shell folds itself warmly around your body. Infighting between opposing factions can wax passionate. The people at Bugaboo Mountain- eering, who use both systems in their bags, say that "in all honesty, we feel the difference is almost academic." A main-line maker who read that comment said, "Hmm, thank heaven for academics!"

With one exception, materials used in sleeping-bag shells have changed little in the past decade. Woven nylon taffeta in some form remains the standard. Most common are Rip-stop (page 511), Tenaya and new variants seductively labeled Nylsilk, Snowsilk and Luscious. Luscious, the best grade, with high thread-count, is indeed soft and kinda sexy. Some shell interiors are now Trinyl (27 percent cotton, 46 percent nylon, 27 percent Dacron), which, though rather heavy, is said to be rot-resistant yet to wick moisture like cotton, and feel like it too.

The one dramatically new shell material is Gore-Tex—used on the outside of the bag. (For a full survey of Gore-Tex, see page 405.) In this case the material's important property is not its waterproofness. Because of the seams, Gore-Tex bags are, though water-resistant, not waterproof: they'll probably withstand a light shower, drizzle or fog, or some dripping from condensation on a tent's roof, and that, of course, is a big gain —but they should not be expected to withstand a steady rain, let alone a downpour. (Gore-Tex bags could, in theory, be made waterproof— except for the head hole—by applying seam sealant. But few people would be willing to desecrate their beautiful new $300 sleeping bags by applying the necessary half-inch-wide band of sealant along each seam so that the bags looked as if snails had crawled all over them. Besides, you cannot effectively seal seams on which the stitching is hidden [see tuck stitching, below].) A sealed bag, furthermore, would be unstuffable. On the other hand, Gore-Tex is not only waterproof but also virtually windproof. It therefore greatly increases a bag's warmth (most nylon taffeta blocks little wind). Although controversy still rages over whether Gore-Tex on the outer shell is too far from the body to breathe properly (see pages 304 and 407), some recent scoffers in the trade are now believers. Many makers are now using Gore-Tex outer shells in at least some of their bags. Such shells certainly seem likely to prove popular with expeditions, when the gradual reduction of down's efficiency by repeated dampness is often a problem (page 341). It seems to me they will also make the drying-out of wet or damp bags in the field even more difficult: wind will be unable to pass through a hung bag. Gore-Tex shells add a great deal to the cost of a bag. But they actually reduce the weight, though by an almost negligible amount. Only time will tell whether they have come to stay. After trying out a Gore-Tex shelled mummy by Western Mountaineering (the Narrowlite, 3 pounds, $350), which I used for a week in soggy weather up to 10,000 feet, I must reclassify myself as at least a tentative believer.

A few makers now tuck-stitch shell seams: the fabric is tucked inside before stitching. So although you can see the seam lines (which occur wherever panels join or meet baffles), the stitches are hidden—and therefore protected from snagging zippers, cracked toenails and other destroyers. Tuck-stitching increases costs. But Sierra Designs report that its adoption reduced their stitching repairs in bags from one a week to about one a year.

Shell accessories

Built-in collars that fit across the sleeper's chest and so reduce draft through the head opening are becoming more popular. They can be down-filled appendages or plain fabric. And while they may possibly reduce somewhat the bag's flexibility in wide ranges of temperatures they undoubtedly help keep you warmer in real cold. Warmer, certainly, than any makeshift measures (page 339).

Zippers on bags are now almost all nylon—either toothed or coil type—and large enough for you to pull snagged fabric free. The best coil zippers are self-healing: if the teeth pull apart, you can zip down and back up and lo! you're in business again (for a limited number of times, anyway). Many bag zippers now seem to be coil-tooth hybrids. Whatever its "genes," make sure the zipper is high-quality. Any failure is sure to be infuriating, likely to be uncomfortable and might even prove fatal.

A sleeping-bag zipper slider should have a pull tab inside as well as out.

For two-way and around-the-foot zippers, see page 340; for conjoining two bags, page 339.

Hoods that encapsulate your head when drawn tight form an integral part of most modern mummy-bag shells. They are important: the human animal, with two of its major evolutionary features (brain and expressive face) housed in its head, naturally serves that member with a hugely complex blood-supply system. The capillaries often travel near the surface and are therefore subject to rapid cooling (the head, like a computer, requires a more or less constant temperature—which usually means it needs cooling). The old "facts"—that at 40° F. it may, if unprotected, lose up to half your heat production, at 5° up to three-quarters—have been challenged; but there can be no doubt that it is the body's prime heat-loss area. And perhaps too little attention has been paid to this problem in sleeping bags. Certainly, all hoods are not created equal, or even equal enough. But several makers, including Sierra Designs (beginning with their Cloud series) and Down Home (who even offer a "floating hood" that moves with you when you roll over within the bag and sleep on your side or stomach), have recently advanced the art a worthwhile notch.

The *drawstrings* that pull the hood around your face and hold it there (page 339) used to be—and sometimes still are—plain cord or tape that you tie in a simple quick-release knot. But drawstrings now often come equipped with spring-loaded plastic toggles or other secure but quickly adjustable devices. Sometimes there are two such devices, one at each free end of the cord or tape, near the top of the zipper; but many bags now have a single toggle in the center of the hood on the opposite side from the zipper, so that you can adjust the hood with a single device instead of the two and need not loosen the drawstring if you want to open the top of the zipper (to cool off a little or to emerge briefly in the middle of the night to urinate). This arrangement means that the drawstring ends are anchored near the zipper top, one on each side, and when you tighten the hood you place strain on the zipper and may pull it open. The bag should therefore have a snap or Velcro fastener to take the strain and also keep the draft edge closed. (Velcro is easier to open and close than a snap but can, I hear, grab long hair or even beards.) One designer suggests that perhaps you really need two fasteners, each pulling at a slightly different angle.

Vapor-barrier linings (VBLs)

have been around for years. But although embraced fanatically by a few they have not caught on. It is possible that they may now, in modified form, be on the brink of more general acceptance.

For the theory behind VBLs, and some discussion of the practice, see pages 387–90. I have good reasons for attacking the matter there, in the "Clothes Closet," rather than here; but understanding the theory so that you can practice properly is a major component of VBL usage, so I'm afraid you will have to read most of pages 387 and 388 if you are to grasp the meat of what follows.

Both theory and practice are simpler with sleeping bags than with clothes, because in a bag you lie more or less still and your metabolic rate changes only very slowly (though the practice is complicated by your being mostly unaware of temperature changes, and the need to adjust, until cold or heat wakes you up). But even with VBL sleeping bags you must understand what you are playing with—which is something very different from a conventional breathing-shell bag.

More than a decade ago I tried a VBL bag by Warmlite, a pioneer in the field, on a five-day test up to 12,000 feet and down to a windless 16° F. In a tent, wearing little or no clothing, I found that I was far too hot, soon began to sweat and simply could not adjust the rather complicated bag to an all-around comfort level. Now, the real trouble may have been the bag's built-in foam pad. I normally lie first on one side, then on the other, moving the whole bag with me and thereby keeping any opened zipper to my front; but the built-in pad could not move with me and the opened zipper was, in one of my lying positions, bound to run close and cold to my curved back. (A reader recently wrote that he had a similar unsatisfactory experience, and also thinks the trouble is the built-in pad.) I had further minor difficulties too (though the makers assured me with heat that I had misused the bag). In the years since I have met many people who have tried VBL bags and found them wanting. The reasons could lie in extraneous matters like that built-in pad or such personal idiosyncrasies as high metabolic rates. But I suspect that in many cases the bags were simply used in temperatures too high for the system. The maker of perhaps the best current VBLs recently told me that he felt they were really not for use above 35° F. The difficulty is, of course, that many nights may begin much warmer than that but end up much colder. And one night may be much warmer, the next much colder, especially in the mountains. Bags with built-in VBLs are simply not versatile enough for such very common conditions.

The way to achieve versatility is fortunately simple: a removable VBL. I have recently taken to carrying one on all but the most guaranteed-warm trips. I'm convinced that it extends the low end of any bag's comfort level by at least ten degrees and probably by twenty.

The price in weight and bulk is small; in money, very reasonable. I use a simple, coated-Rip-stop half-sac by Moonstone of California that weighs 4.7 ounces, takes up about as much room as a pair of jockey shorts and costs $18. True, I normally also carrying a matching VB shirt (6 ounces, $35—see page 388) and use it with the half-sac; but the shirt performs major daytime functions—and other warm torso clothing would often be enough in conjunction with the half-sac. By taking a bag that's a tad on the light side for a given trip (or even several tads) and regarding the VBL as a reserve for cold occasions I can save considerable weight and bulk. And if temperatures drop markedly during the night I simply slip into the VBL, which I have put ready, inside the bag. My Moonstone half-sac extends up to my upper chest and is held there by an elastic "waistband." Provided I wear polypropylene underwear (page 378) I experience little or no damp or clammy feeling—and none of the uncomfortable wrapping around legs and torso that some people report with full-length liners. I find the half-sac particularly useful with a very light bag (page 358).

But with removable liners we are beginning to move over from traditional, more-or-less-one-purpose sleeping bags into

Sleeping systems.

The idea is hardly new. One early approach was Warmlite's "solo-triple" bag that I described in the last edition (with two zipper-off topsides of different thicknesses that can be used alternatively or together

—giving a solo sleeper three bags in one). Camp 7 have for some years been offering a lightweight synthetic-fill bag (current version: Pioneer II, Hollobond-fill, total weight 2 pounds 5 ounces, $70) that can be used alone as a summer bag (rated to 40° F.) but is designed to fit as an outer shell around any of Camp 7's main line of down bags—boosting their warmth and also protecting the down from external moisture. A removable VBL (6 ounces, $27) can greatly increase the cellar range of either bag or of both together. Down Home of Oregon offer a Modular Sleeping System that features an ultralightweight down bag (Zephyr, 1 pound 11 ounces, $179), rated to 30° F. for use alone, that functions as a liner, with tie-ins, to any of their superbly designed and made Bird Series of down bags (off-the-peg or custom-made; mid-range Dipper, rated to −5° F., 3 pounds 12 ounces, $431). The system embraces not only VBLs but also Gore-Tex shells and optional built-in foam pads. The full system is so efficient that Down Home have discontinued their expedition bag. Bigger, less specialized makers have begun to play with the rudiments of similar systems, and may soon opt for them fortissimo.

The ingredients are certainly at hand, if not yet fully proven: increasingly efficient synthetic fills, Gore-Tex shells and VBLs—not to mention the pile sleeping shell (2 pounds 5 ounces, $61) now made by Patagonia for use alone on warm nights or as a sleeping-bag liner. Sleeping systems could soon become not merely the fashion but the eminently sensible standard.

In other words, the beds in our bedroom, after appearing for some years to hunker down in an array of gorgeous, beautifully designed down bags refined close to perfection, seem to be on the move—to the glowing benefit of all backpackers and co-movers. Yippee!

A material now beginning to appear in sleeping bags is *Texolite.* An entirely flexible laminate, only 1/32 inch thick, Texolite—a space-program spin-off—consists of two very thin aluminized polyethlene sheets pierced with a pattern of holes to give some breathability and sandwiched between three layers of fine polyethylene mesh that deaden annoying rustle, help cut conductive heat loss and increase strength (though doubts have been expressed about the material's durability, especially after two or three washings, and about its tendency, once wet, to stay that way). Texolite's prime stated purpose is to block radiant heat loss (page 385). But in spite of the holes it is virtually a vapor barrier, and when used as a whole liner that function may in practice be more important. When a fixed VB would be out of place—that is, in most bags, which must be comfortable in warm weather as well as cold—the breathability could surely be improved with little loss in radiant heat blockage by markedly increasing the size and/or number of holes—yea, to the point of collapse.

The resultant material would be to current Texolite as fishnet underwear is to wool: a lot of holes joined together by fabric rather than a fabric embodying a lot of holes. I guess the already suspect strength factor could prove an insuperable difficulty. But at least one leading bagmaker agrees that the idea seems worth pursuing.

Orcothane is another radiant-heat-blocking material. An aluminized Mylar sheeting that can be covered with a hard, protective film, it is not designed to breathe and seems most promising used in staggered strips inside a bag's shell so that it will block radiant heat but not act as a VB. It is said to be one-quarter the weight of Texolite and much stronger— though doubts have been voiced about its washability. I'm told it also emits a distinct rustle—"like windblown leaves"—whenever you move. A similar Mylar sheeting: *Kodalite.*

Texolite seems certain to get a fair trial: a number of makers are already using it, either as a liner or midway through sleeping-bag shells. North Face are experimenting with Orcothane and Wilderness Experience are Kodaliting.

If any of these materials—or a successor—finally proves out, then the prospect opens up of lightweight bags with a minimum of down or synthetic main insulation, and perhaps with Gore-Tex shells, that will work over a wide range of temperatures, with a remarkably low cellar. More yippee!

Costs

Any good sleeping bag is now a damnably expensive item. But the range is large—from $125 for a reasonably serviceable 2- or 3-season, synthetic-filled semi-mummy to almost $600 for the best of Down Home's sophisticated, superbly crafted, custom-made models. Mostly— surprise!—you get what you pay for, and you must make your own decisions about what you can afford. I'm aware that backpackers who use their equipment only once or twice a year may not feel justified, in view of other responsibilities, in spending the sums now demanded for really good bags. (Do-it-yourself Frostline kits cut the cost appreciably— though see page 21.) The current prices may curdle your financial blood; but remember that when you take a sleeping bag out of your pack as night falls on a frigid, windswept mountain you understand without having to think about it that dollars are meaningless frivolities.

Choosing a bag that will suit your purposes

The usual criterion for gauging the efficiency of a sleeping bag is the lowest temperature at which it can be used with comfort. "This bag is excellent for use down to 25° F.," the catalogue may proclaim. Such generalizations have their uses. Beginners need guidelines. But there is a serious danger that people may accept the figures uncritically. Many factors other than temperature are involved, and a wide variation in one or more of them can throw out the whole works. Still, the general rule is sometimes promulgated: "For summer use, with temperatures above freezing—2 pounds of high-quality down; for temperatures down to 0° F.—3 pounds." (For most synthetics, increase weights about 50 percent.) For more on fills, see pages 340–3. For construction and other shell desiderata, see pages 343–8. You can check the construction of most blow-filled bags light enough for backpacking by simply holding the shell up to a strong light.

One way sometimes recommended for checking the probable efficiency of both fill and construction is to measure what is called "free loft." Unroll the bag on a flat surface and shake its edges with a gentle fluffing action that allows air to become entrapped in the fill. Then measure the height of the bag at its midsection. The amount of loft depends on both the quality of the fill and the efficiency of the shell construction (see differential cut, page 345). Unfortunately, different makers seem to measure loft in different ways; but it seems reasonable to assume that, as is claimed, a relationship exists between free loft and heat-retaining efficiency. What the exact relationship is I have no idea.

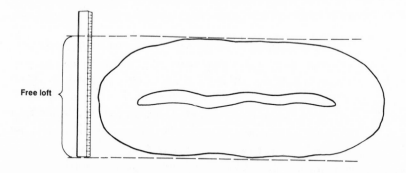

Free loft

It is important to remember that temperature tolerance figures for sleeping bags are now generally based on the assumption that you sleep in a tent with good insulation under you. A bag that keeps you comfortably warm at 32° F. on a full-length foam pad will obviously not begin to do so if you roll it out on bare ground. And the same kind of difference exists between different roofs—tent, sky or intermediate. The temperature inside a tent may run 10° or 20° higher than outside. Again, much depends on what clothes, if any, you choose to sleep in. My solution to all this is always to carry a pad (or, occasionally, an air mattress) and to take a sleeping bag, perhaps with a separate VB liner, that I judge will keep me warm under normal conditions for the time and place if I sleep without clothes or roof (except in snow), and will just about do so under the worst recorded conditions if I wear every garment in my pack and protect the bag with every form of shelter I am carrying—whether a simple poncho or a Visklamp-and-polyethylene roof or a tent. Nowadays I seem to guess about right. I cannot remember a night in the past twenty years when I have slept in a sleeping bag and been uncomfortably cold. Now, it may be that I am a little overcautious. "When it comes to sleeping bags," one store owner told me recently, "most people overbuy —and then sweat their arses off." But in a modern, full-length-zipper bag it is easy enough to stay cool. And for an example of how "overcaution," at least in support items, can pay off when it really matters, see pages 428–35.

One major difficulty with temperature ratings for sleeping bags is that the relationship between air temperature and what the human body feels is a remarkably tenuous one.

First, weather is much more than just temperature. Above all there is wind. A bag that keeps you snugly warm in the open on a calm 10° F. night may be frigidly inadequate at 32° in a 30-mile-an-hour wind. See, importantly, "windchill table," page 575—though Gore-Tex shells may be taking the edge off the wind problem. Humidity comes into it too. Dry air is a poor conductor of heat, damp air a good one. So in wet weather the air pockets held in the fill of your sleeping bag insulate less efficiently than in dry. This is no idle theorizing. Using equipment that has proved entirely adequate in dry weather at freezing and below, you may find yourself decidedly cool in a temperature of 40° after heavy rain has saturated the atmosphere, even though your bag remains dry. It is even possible for a drop in temperature to make you feel warmer. At 34°, with the air full of water vapor, the weather may seem rawly cold. When the temperature falls a few degrees and the moisture that has been ruining the insulation freezes, you'll probably feel much cozier.

But the most variable factor of all is the individual.

Some people "sleep cold," others "hot." The theory—no more—is that the bigger you are and the more generally active, the warmer you tend to sleep. After camping under various conditions with other people using similar equipment you will probably get a fair idea of your own rating. Or you can tap indoor experience: do bedmates regard you as iceberg or hot-water bottle? (This is a purely thermal rating, of course— nothing to do with the factor involved in that libelous dig, "Which would you rather have—an English lover or a hot-water bottle?")

Remember, too, that no individual is a neat, predictable, laboratory-conditioned guinea pig. At different times he may react very differently to similar conditions. Tiredness, emotional state and fullness of stomach certainly come into it: someone who sleeps snugly in a given bag at zero when he is rested, secure and well fed is unlikely to do so if he is exhausted, worried stiff about a sick companion and has not eaten since morning. (Don't overlook the eating business. After a good meal your high blood sugar—available for heat production—will mean you sleep much warmer than on an empty or half-empty stomach. So if you tend to dine early consider a sugar-rich snack just before you go to sleep.) Again, personal variations may be simply a matter of not being used to the cold or the heat or the elevation or whatever prime stress the situation imposes. Our bodies need time to adapt to radically changed conditions. Two or three days' acclimation may be plenty; but if the change is too abrupt those two or three days can be distressing.

The solution is to get used to a new environment gradually. One word for this process is "training." In Europe during World War II we often used to sleep in the open or in slit trenches in subfreezing weather with nothing over our distinctly temperate-country clothing except a thin antigas cape. I don't say we liked it. And I don't say we slept very well. But we slept. We were young, we were fit—and we got used to it (mainly, perhaps, because we had to). By the time I made the California walk I was a dozen years less young; but after a month of walking I was probably just as fit. Yet I remember a night in Death Valley, when I had no sleeping bag, that might make you wonder if I were the same person. That warm desert night I put on all the clothing I had—which was certainly as warm as, if not warmer than, British battle dress. Then I wrapped my poncho around me and curled up in a little gully. I had just finished a 20-mile day, and I promptly fell asleep. But before long I came half awake and tried to pull the poncho more closely around me. There was no wind; nothing that could even be called a breeze. But cool night air was moving slowly and steadily across the desert's surface. Like the tide advancing across mudflats, it penetrated every corner. It passed over me. It passed around me. It passed underneath me. Soon it seemed to be passing through me as well. Minute by minute it sucked my warmth away. No matter how closely I cuddled to the gully wall, the cold bit deeper and deeper. For shapeless hours I fought the sleep battle. Occasionally I dozed. More often I lay three-quarters awake, telling myself I was half asleep. By two o'clock the dozes had become unreal memories. And at 3:30 I got up, packed my bag and headed north into the darkness.*

Later I learned that the temperature that night never fell below 58°. This is admittedly an official reading, taken 5 feet off the ground; but a

---

* From *The Thousand-Mile Summer*, p. 86.

thermometer lying beside my bed just before I left would probably have registered about the same. Now, 58° is a very mild temperature. But the reason I felt so bitterly cold is simple: I wasn't used to it. I had been walking through deserts for more than a month, in day temperatures that had risen to a peak of 105°. Recent nights had been warm too, and the day I entered Death Valley the minimum temperature had been 80°. But what mattered most was that all this time I had been sleeping in a highly efficient 2½-pounds-of-goose-down mummy bag. Then, two days earlier—wanting to cut my load, and feeling I did not need a bag in night temperatures that seemed likely to fall no lower than 80°—I had given it to two Death Valley rangers who checked my arrival at a spring at the south end of the valley. I arranged to collect the bag when I passed through a ranger station a couple of weeks later. But that same night an unexpected storm sent temperatures plunging. The next night I found myself curling up in that miserable little gully with no protection except my clothes and poncho—and, what was even more important, with my body unprepared for the shock of sleeping in what seemed reasonably warm conditions. (Note, though [pages 575 and 576], that two-thirds of maximum windchill effect occurs when the wind is blowing at only 2 miles an hour.)

Acclimation can also work the other way. One September I spent a week walking along a mountain crest that rarely fell below 12,000 feet and rose at one point to 14,000. In clear autumnal weather the panoramas and the wind were both breathtaking. On the third night my route took me down off the crest for the only time all week, and I camped in a sidecanyon at 10,000 feet. At dusk my bedside thermometer read a bare degree or two below freezing. Because I was trying out a very efficient experimental mummy bag that had been designed for Alaskan mountaineering (it had 3 pounds of down and no side zipper) I did not bother about shelter, except to camp just below some bushes. The bushes, I felt sure, would blunt the almost inevitable down-canyon wind. To my surprise, no wind blew. Soon I was far too hot to sleep. I slipped into my wool shirt and a very thick, hooded, down parka, then eased up partway out of the sleeping bag and pulled on longjohns and pants. With the sleeping bag pulled loosely up around my midriff and a pair of big leather gauntlets to protect my hands, I immediately fell asleep.

I woke at dawn, glowingly warm, to find the thermometer registering 22°. But what really surprised me was that during the night one glove had come off and my bare hand, lying unprotected on the grass, felt perfectly warm. The circulation in my hands had always been rather poor in cold weather, and I would not have believed it possible for one of them to feel pleasantly warm at 22°—even with the rest of my body glowing and the air very dry. The point is, I think, that I had been up in cold, windy country for two days. I very much doubt if the hand would have felt so warm under identical conditions on the night I left the car.

I hope this long discussion has not led you to believe that temperature ratings have no value as a means of expressing a sleeping bag's efficiency. I repeat: they're useful guidelines. But if uncritically accepted as absolute statements they can be dangerously misleading. Bear that danger steadily in mind when you are making your choice. And ponder ponderously. Buying a sleeping bag is a serious business. If you make a mistake you will have many long, slow, purgatorial hours in which to repent.

These days the mountain shops tempt us with serried ranks of gorgeous, gossamer, butterfly-colored sleeping bags—gleaming, curvaceous works of art that almost demand to be stroked. Faced with such an array and the need to choose one among all those superb creations, it is often difficult to know where to begin.

In easing toward a decision you will probably—after weighing the general and sometimes subjective elements I've outlined—move on to a relatively objective survey of shell materials, including Gore-Tex outers and VBLs. (You will, of course, buy only a bag that fits you: one so short that your feet press against its end will prove a very expensive mistake.) But in the end the elimination process may boil down, economics aside, to deciding which minor variants seem to offer some advantage. If you like a bag to turn with you as you roll over (which I do, so that a partially opened zipper stays in position along my front, where my natural curl will hold it at a distance, rather than close and cold along my back) then a slender, form-fitting mummy will probably suit you best. But if you prefer—or rather think you prefer—being able to turn over in a more or less stationary bag, then consider ampler envelopes—the barrelsome daddies or even unabashed biggies—or at least avoid those contoured to fit your feet. Next, cast a critical eye on all hoods. Then examine in the beam of your druthers such accessories as drawstrings and built-in collars. And look closely at zippers and the draft flaps or block baffles inside them. See if the base of the flap is sewn right through and might create cold spots. Check that the flap (or baffle) lies snug along the zipper line. If in any doubt on this score (and maybe even if not) take the bag into a strong light, put your head inside and see whether, with the bag in the kind of position it will assume when full of you, any gaps show. If they do, take the bag back to a dark corner and leave it there.

In the end, though, your decision may rest on your assessment of workmanship.

Meticulous workmanship is the key to toughness and long life in any first-rate backpacking bag, stripped as it must be of every unnecessary gram. It is no assembly-line product. To ensure high quality, at least one maker has each bag "constructed by a single seamstress who is personally responsible for that bag." In the finished bag almost the only outward and visible sign of this inward and invisible pride and expertise is the stitching. Check it carefully. Check it most of all in difficult places, and those that will undergo most strain—such as around the top of the zipper. But I suspect that most backpackers are as poorly qualified to judge the quality of workmanship as I am. (Note that, in spite of earnest consultation with manufacturers, I have not—except for the words on tuck stitching [page 346]—found it possible to describe just how you should rate stitching.) In the end the safest way is probably to check reputation. Don't just shop around; check around. Pay some attention to good reports, great attention to bad ones. Finally, you may even want, if you can, to try out the model you favor by borrowing or renting one.

Makes and models

The comforting thing about the present plethora of gorgeous sleeping bags is that it has become difficult to go diabolically wrong. Fierce competition and the high costs of both materials and labor—which virtually force anyone entering the market to aim for a quality product —mean that there are few if any crummy bags around. You won't find them in reputable mountain shops or specialist catalogues—and probably not even in general sports stores.

But the sheer loft of numbers makes it impossible to list, let alone recommend, even the toughest and thistledownest of the super-efficient calorie trappers. So I shall make no attempt—beyond those hints I have already dropped with some care—to name names. Instead I shall describe in detail a bag I have used for eight years under almost all conditions short of the coldest. It is the second of the same model that I have bought, and both have done me proud. I do not want to suggest that this bag is the very best of the whole magnificent bunch, but I know it is a good one and I know it inside out and therefore feel I can use it as a guide to the features you might care to look for.

The bag is a Trailwise Slimline—a beautifully made, close-fitting mummy with Tenaya nylon shell (taffeta, not Rip-stop) differentially cut and chevron-baffled. The current equivalent version of my bag is an overfilled regular size—for people up to 5 feet 10 inches (1 pound 14 ounces of 600-fill-power goose down; total weight 3 pounds 9½ ounces; 9½-inch loft; rated to −10° F.; $300. Standard fill: 6 ounces and $40 less). The bag also comes in large size—for people up to 6 feet 2 inches (standard fill: 3 pounds 7 ounces, $280. Overfill: 6 ounces and $35 more). Colors: blue or red. All current Slimlines have 70-inch double zippers that can be fitted on left or right side and will couple with a mate. The draft flaps work. Drawstrings pull the hoods around your head to any degree of enwrapment including everything-except-the-nose. On my bag the drawstring has leather toggles designed to hold the hood at its chosen position; but they tend to slide, and in any kind of battened-down hood mode I tie a slip knot. Current bags come with positive-locking plastic toggles, which are an improvement.

I have for years taken my Slimline confidently on all trips on which it seemed from weather records that the temperature (here I go already!) was almost certain to go no lower than about 15° F. and was unlikely to fall more than a few degrees below freezing. In hot weather the bag zips almost completely open, leaving only my feet enveloped, and I can spread it over me, partly or completely, and adjust during the night (page 374). I find that when it is battened down I can sleep naked in it down to about freezing with total comfort. And it has several times proved itself in temperatures rather lower than I bargained for. Not long ago, making an exit south from Lower Grand Canyon in November, I camped without tent or tarp on a high plateau. At dawn the thermometer registered 13° F. but I remained comfortably warm. Mind you, no wind blew, and I not only wore every item of clothing I had with me but was able to spread over my air mattress (which I had taken in preference to a pad because of possible Colorado crossings) a well-insulated Neoprene wet suit (taken for the same reason). On another occasion I slept warmly in my Slimline, roofed only by stars, at 10,000 feet on a windless night when the temperature fell to 11° F. Although I wore a wool shirt and down jacket and long whipcord pants and down booties (page 416), I was also carrying a pair of down pants and a large plastic sheet, but used neither. So I'd have to say that I have been, in every respect, entirely satisfied with my Slimline.

I have recently bought a supplement and occasional substitute: an ultralightweight down mummy, the Bear Cub, by Blue Puma. My regular size, for people to 6 feet 1 inch, comes with 15 ounces of 600-fill-power down, has a 3-to-3½-inch loft, is rated to 35° F., and weighs only 1 pound 12 ounces. That weight is achieved by stark simplification. The bag even dispenses with baffles: it is sewn through, like a down jacket—just the way I said no self-respecting modern bag was sewn. Yet the bag works. I have yet to use it in its supplemental role—fitted inside the Slimline for bitter-weather bravadoing. But as a load-cutting substitute in nonbitter weather it has already proved its worth. On the few trips I've taken it I have backed it up with my Moonstone VBL half-sac (page 349). The combination has yet to face really bad conditions but has worked well in damp, windy, around-freezing weather and also throughout a windless, 18° F. night, in a tent, with the bag pulled up only waist-high but my torso cocooned in polypro vest, pile jacket and balaclava, all enveloped in a Gore-Tex jacket.

Note that by buying the Bear Cub and VBL half-sac I have, almost without planning it, converted my Slimline into a sleeping system. And the evolution has occurred, I now see, in a simple and pragmatically selective way that anyone can match without prohibitive outlay and often without discarding a tried and trusted old sleeping partner.

Foam bags

A decade ago sleeping bags made from two shaped sheets of compressible open-cell polyethylene foam seemed to hold promise for backpacking. I guess they still do. But their glint has tarnished, to say the least.

The great advantage of a foam bag is that you can sleep comfortably in it over a broad temperature range ("From zero to 70° F.," say supporters. "Nonsense!" say detractors). Foam is also windproof, non-allergenic, reasonably cheap and light and durable, reputedly fireproof (when correctly treated) and extremely resilient (it springs back almost instantly from compression to full loft). It loses little of its insulating properties when wet, and even if thoroughly soaked can easily be squeezed out and restored to usable condition. What's more, as long as it remains undamaged, with the few necessary joinings intact, it provides completely even insulation, with none of the thin, cold spots that clumped down can cause, for example. And with a foam bag you need no mattress. But the bags are bulky. Very bulky. They are stiff too: rather than fold cozily around your body, the way most bags do, they stand aloof, coffinlike. This property is at first disconcerting; but it can be overcome, and even offers certain advantages. Finally, remember that most foams, *if* they burn, give off toxic fumes.

My limited experience with a model by Ocaté supports some of the claims made for foam bags. There is certainly something in the contention that you can use them comfortably in fairly high temperatures. One night it was 60° F. when I lay down, dog-tired—and 62° when I resurfaced after eleven hours' pretty sound sleep. All night the bag was zippered at least halfway, but I felt only very slightly too warm. And I sleep hot: similarly zippered in even a very light down bag, I would under such conditions have sweated blood. On a later trip I semideliberately allowed parts of the bag to get mildly wet during a night of light drizzle and a brief spell of heavier rain. With the temperature never lower than 50° F., I felt warm if rather soggy. Next afternoon, when the skies cleared, the bag partially dried. But it remained moist, and the second night I slept in a heavy down jacket and wool pants (page 402), partly in the bag, with a space blanket (page 585) between me and the damp underside of the bag. By dawn the temperature had fallen to 28° F., but I remained just about pleasantly warm, even though by morning the pants felt pretty damp.

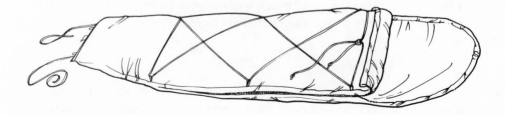

My Ocaté bag has adjustable criss-cross nylon cords that, when tightened, pull the foam semicozily around your body. I found that I soon came to ignore the residual coffinlike feeling of the still somewhat standoffish foam. And the standoffishness may contribute to the bag's broad comfort range: if you leave the neck wide open your every small movement, perhaps even your chest movement in breathing, helps drive out air in a sort of bellows action that ensures good ventilation. This action more or less ceases, of course, when you want to conserve heat and pull the head flap around you in a normal mummy configuration.

But although I often throw the Ocaté into the trunk of my car when I'm traveling, and (because of the way it continues to work when wet) would seriously consider it for a whitewater boat trip, I have not taken it backpacking for a long, long time. I am not alone. The R&D man for one of the leading and most innovative equipment makers wrote me that during his "foam-bag period, in early 1972, I spent several nights miserably cold before I junked the idea." Today most people seem to have junked it too. You see virtually no foam bags in either stores or mountains.

As far as I know, CosyQuip of New Mexico, successors to Ocaté, still make foam bags. I have written several letters requesting information but I might as well have mailed them to Mars.

Double mummy bags

are lighter, less bulky and cheaper than two individually used bags—and reputedly warmer too. But perhaps because almost all good single bags can now be zipped together (page 339), few makers produce double mummies. One that does: Western Mountaineering of California.

Children's sleeping bags

These bags are usually made of cheaper materials than full-size ones, are more simply constructed, and filled with synthetics rather than down, no doubt on the reasonable assumption that if you are going to invest in a high-quality bag you are not going to buy something your children will grow out of within a year or two. But price is not the only reason synthetic fills are more popular than down: synthetics can be repeatedly rinsed and washed; with down you can, particularly during the diaper years, land in big trouble.

Lower-quality children's bags apparently sell very well. One possible reason is that children tend to sleep warmer than adults. In theory they should sleep colder: their smaller bodies, with a wider surface-to-volume ratio, should lose heat faster. But to balance this factor their metabolism tends to operate at a higher rate. What happens in practice is a matter of opinion, but a limited poll I conducted among friends tended to support the opinion of one mother of five children ranging from four to thirteen years old, whose family seemed to spend half its young life camping or cabining in the mountains. "Yes," said this seasoned troop leader, "I'd say there may well be something to the sleeping-warmer business—certainly when the kids are young and covered in puppy fat. I've found our four-year-old almost out of his bag on quite cold nights, still fast asleep. Once children start beanstalking up into their teens, though, it's rather different. It could easily be that at that stringy stage they tend to sleep somewhat colder than adults."

There now seem to be few bags specifically made for children—though I'm told that Bristlecone make a good one, and REI offer the PolarGuard-fill Little Tohama II for people up to 4 feet 11 inches tall (2¾ pounds, $90). (Frostline, who used to make a cunning small bag with add-on sections "for the growing years," have discontinued it.) One answer is to take the initial step in building a sleeping system (page 349) by buying a lightweight adult bag that will later serve not only as a hot-weather bag but also as an inner component for colder use. An adult footsack (used later with a down jacket or similar warm upper-body clothing) might serve the same triple purposes. Western Mountaineering of California make a child's bag/elephant's foot that encases those up to 4 feet 6 inches (rated to 0° F., 18 ounces of down, total weight 2 pounds, $160; with Gore-Tex shell, $195). Parents can help justify the expense by reminding themselves that they are buying something that might come in useful later on—for both generations.

The footsack, or elephant's foot

Essentially, a footsack is the bottom half of a slim mummy bag with a drawstring at the top. Good models are cut higher in the rear than in front—to protect the sensitive small of your back when you are lying down and also to keep it covered in the pull-apart sitting position. A footsack is designed as an emergency bag for use with a good down jacket or other garment (on occasions when you do not plan to sleep out but just might have to) or as a straight substitute for a bag (when you really have to cut down the weight and think you can trust the weather). Don't forget that you need warm gloves with this rig—unless, like one friend of mine, you can sleep comfortably all night with hands deep inside the bag in a fig-leaf position. Footsacks are presently hard to find, but see the Western Mountaineering model, above.

SUBSTITUTES AND SUPPLEMENTS FOR SLEEPING BAGS

Convertible down pants/footsack

Because It's There of Washington State make down pants that zip the full length of each leg and have foot extensions that snap up inside when not in use. You can zip the legs together and join the foot extensions to them with a Velcro strip and so form a reputedly draft-free footsack (2 pounds, $145).

Cagoule-and-footsack bivouac

The knee-length parka or cagoule (page 413) is designed for use as a bivouac—either alone (when you draw your knees up inside it) or with a companion footsack. The idea is presumably to use the combination when nights are really warm, but there are few climates I would trust. As an emergency bivouac the rig sounds ideal. But "emergency bivouac" means sleeping out when you do not expect to—and therefore are unlikely to be carrying equipment for the job. Besides, a modern VBL shirt and pants or half-sac (page 349) do the same job better. Still, it is possible to imagine certain situations in which a cagoule-and-footsack rig might be worth packing along. Anyway, the world would be poorer without it. It is one of those intriguing items that make catalogue browsing the dreamy, time-wasting, utterly delightful pursuit it is.

Packbag as emergency footsack

See page 149.

Pillows

Some people do not mind sleeping without a pillow; others even prefer it that way. Unless I am too tired to notice I find it disconcerting not to have one. Minor back trouble sometimes forces me to carry a specially shaped foam pillow (my "security pillow"), but mostly I still make do with older, more orthodox devices. For me, an air mattress with pillow (page 336) is ideal. With a Therm-a-Rest or foam pad I normally just roll up my long pants or down jacket or another garment and stuff it (or them) under my head. If you push the gatment partway into a stuff sack you can fine-adjust pillow size to meet your need of the moment. Sometimes I bolster the clothing with a plastic canteen or the day's-ration food bag. If the night is cold enough to make me wear all the clothes I have brought, I may use a canteen alone. This arrangement helps keep the canteen unfrozen; and because I am sure to be wearing my balaclava helmet and perhaps a hooded parka as well, it is tolerably comfortable. Or I may pad the canteen with the packbag or ration bag —making sure that soft food such as cereal is directly under my head. You can, of course, buy a separate, inflatable pillow (4 ounces; $6); or, much more cheaply, an ordinary Ziploc bag. REI offer a Hollofil II–stuffed pillow (12 by 12 inches; 5 ounces; $4.95).

On sand or other loose soil the simplest and most comfortable pillow is a roughly banked-up guillotine block. No matter how much you want a soft pillow, there are precious few places left in which it is justifiable to use bough tips or moss or any natural material. Occasionally, manna falls. One reader reports that when, as a member of a large party, he was the bearer of an inflatable plastic arm splint, he found it made "a luxurious pillow."

Knee pillows

If you have any kind of back trouble (not exactly rare in *homo backpackerens*) you may find that when sitting up in your bag or lying on your back you need some kind of knee support. Anything from a down or pile jacket through food bags to the half-empty pack can be pressed into service, either inside or outside the bag. This knee pillow must be so arranged that when you turn over onto one side your knees can circumnavigate it with next to no assist from your conscious mind.

Stuff sacks

Years ago I used to stuff my sleeping bag loose into the pack or even tie it unprotected onto the outside. But eventually I became, like most people, a convert to stuff sacks. They are normally cylindrical affairs with drawcord closures, and they protect your bag—and down clothing and other items too—from unnecessary wear and tear and also from rain. If you're at all worried about the bag's getting wet, line or envelop its stuff sack with a large plastic bag filched from almost any other use (page 521).

Most stuff sacks are made of waterproofed woven nylon. (Typical range: 7 inches diameter by 18 inches long, 1¼ ounces, $5.50; through 11 inches diameter by 21 inches long, 3¼ ounces, $6.25.)

Lowe make a Telecompressor stuff sack with four buckled straps that run almost the length of the sack and can be cinched down. Uncompressed, the sack houses the bulkiest sleeping bag (though extended use can take the life out of PolarGuard). Compressed, it snugly protects one of almost any size. And you can cinch the straps differentially, to bend the package into a shape that conforms to your packing (or pillow) requirements. At 10 ounces and $17 (large size), it's an idea an equipment nut may not be able to resist. Ditto a sack by Early Winters that doubles as fanny pack. And others by Sierra West and Slumberjack.

Note that coated-nylon stuff sacks are the simplest backpacking item to make—ideal for feeling your way into the do-it-yourself field.

The small-stuff-sack fallacy

Manufacturers tend to make stuff sacks for sleeping bags and other items as small as possible, if not smaller. Apart from saving material and a scrittage of weight, and convincing customers that the stuffed product is small and neat and probably light, the only advantage I can discern is a possible increase in waterproofness due to skin-tightness when packed. That may be a gain for those who carry sleeping bags outside their packs. For others it is offset with acres to spare by two weighty debits.

First, you do not, as might be imagined, save space. A tightly packed stuff sack tends to sit stalwartly and nonconformingly in its corner of a pack, and unless you have soft, yielding articles to stuff around it you leave wasted space at its peripheries.

Second, and more important, there's the stuffing difficulty. A bag of such a size that you can just about cram in your sleeping bag or down jacket or whatever with no more than a minor struggle in store or living room at a windless 70° F., when you are fresh and fed, may seem beguilingly efficient. In a gale, at 20° F., when you're hungry and weary and in a hurry, it transmutes into a monster.

I always try to buy a stuff sack big enough to take its load with room to spare, leaving it soft, malleable, odd-corner-fitting—and easily stuffable.

Carrying your sleeping bag: strapped on frame or stuffed inside packbag?

Washable liners (not VBLs)

A feasible though fussy and rather heavy way to keep the inside of your bag clean, and therefore less often in need of washing or cleaning (see below), is to use a liner. It adds some warmth and, if you dislike the feel of modern sleeping bag interiors, some comfort. Teton Enterprises of Arizona (Appendix II) make a Light Sky-liner that opens to mid-thigh, with Velcro closures (65/35 Kodel/cotton, 8 ounces, $14.95).

CARE OF SLEEPING BAGS

Any sleeping bag should be aired after use. Just open the bag and leave it spread out, preferably up off the ground. With nylon-shell bags, which tend to pick up body odors, two or three days is not too long. Outdoor airing, especially in sunshine, seems best. Purists will warn you that sunlight is nylon's archenemy. Technically, they may be right. But life is too bloody short.

It is best not to store a bag for long periods compressed in its stuff sack: if you do, the fill—especially synthetics but also resilient down—will tend to retain its cramped conformation and will therefore lose at least some of its insulating power. So lay the bag out flat, hang in a closet or roll loosely.

Normally, cleaning should amount to no more than sponging the shell, inside and out, with a mild soap (not detergent) and tepid water. Rinse, then dry thoroughly. If a bag becomes so soiled that it demands more stringent measures, that presents no problem if it has synthetic fill: you simply wash it. (Do *not* dry-clean it.) But take care with the drying: PolarGuard, for example, suffers irreversible damage at 140° F. (Note that car trunks can easily reach 140° F.)

Down demands greater cleaning care. You can take the bag to reputable launderers, accustomed to down clothing, and have them wash it in soap or mild detergent and then tumble dry; but you can save a lot of money by doing the job yourself. There are now several soaps made especially for the job, including Fluffy Down Soap (a package that washes one sleeping bag or two jackets, $2.50) and Down Suds (1 ounce per washing: 4-ounce plastic bottle, $3.50). With such soaps you can do a good job in a bathtub with tepid water. But don't use too much soap. And rinse carefully. Do not manhandle the bag: soaked, it is so heavy that its own weight can tear the internal baffles. Be prepared for a tedious drying job. One manufacturer recommends letting the bag drip dry for a couple of hours (in a chaise longue, say, or a hammock) or even spin-drying it in a top-loader, then putting it in a commercial drier at a laundromat "for several hours (when it feels dry, give it another hour)." Set drier to FLUFF or SYNTHETIC cycle: otherwise you can melt nylon and fuse zippers. Don't let a bag lie in a drier once it has stopped. Some experts recommend throwing a pair of sneakers in with the bag: "they will help pound clogged down apart, and the rubber/nylon combination generates the static electricity needed to loft the down fully." Counter-experts judge the sneakers to do more harm than good, and warn that they are especially likely to damage old bags.

A few people—even some soapmakers—say that with the right soaps you can safely use tumble washers (but not top-loaders).

An alternative (for down bags, not synthetics) is dry-cleaning. The experts' advice on dry-cleaning or not dry-cleaning your bag seems to change about as often as skirt lengths. So I shall stick with my first-edition advice (though there does seem to be a tendency for more and more makers to recommend dry-cleaning at reputable cleaners).

Ever since one favorite old bag of mine lost a great deal of its virtue after two or three widely spaced visits to the cleaners I have been inclined to avoid commercial cleaning. But so that I should not pass on pure hunch I made careful inquiries before writing this section. The manager of one dry-cleaning plant, who owns both down and synthetic sleeping bags (the latter for car camping), advised me that only dry-cleaning will do a really satisfactory job on badly soiled shells. Some synthetic fills, he said, remain unaffected by cleaning. And no harm comes to down if the solvents used are petroleum-based and are not chlorinated hydrocarbons (which, though excellent for most jobs, are just too efficient at removing greases and therefore remove essential oils from the down). It seems that only small cleaning firms use chlorinated-hydrocarbon solvents; the process is too expensive for big plants. So have your bag cleaned, if at all, at a big plant. But make local inquiries first; a good mountain shop should know which local cleaners do a restrained but effective job on sleeping bags. And there are now outfits on both coasts that specialize in cleaning down products. I hear excellent reports of The Down Depot in San Francisco (allow two weeks for cleaning). San Diego has both Gregory Mountain Products and the A16 Backpackers Laundry and Rental Service. *The New York Times* recommends Leon Greenman's Down East Outdoor Service Center (four to five days). You can send bags, by mail or UPS, to all these firms. For addresses, see Appendix II.

One reason it is sometimes advisable to have a bag cleaned is that in time the down begins to mat. Clumps of it coagulate, and large areas in each baffle tube are left empty. Dry-cleaning certainly seems to redistribute the down effectively. But the plant manager I have quoted (and he can hardly be accused of commercial bias in this opinion) maintained that the redistribution was purely the result of mechanical tumbling in the drier. In other words, the way to redistribute the down in your bag, especially if it has been soaked, is to put it in the tumble drier at low heat—back home or at a laundromat.

Warning: almost any kind of patch that's taped or glued on will come off a bag during dry-cleaning, and fill will escape. So if your bag has been patched, try to avoid having it cleaned unless the patches are sewn on.

Repairing

Like it or not, small cuts and burns happen. Adhesive repair tape (page 511) is the remedy. It used to be that the adhesive was enough on its own, but this no longer seems to be so. Certainly not for permanent patches. My opinion, based on many years' patching of one ancient cotton-covered bag, is apparently not purely attributable to crabbed age: I recently forced one experienced salesman to admit that, owing to the slipperiness of the new materials, the stuff really does not adhere the way it used to. The solution: sew permanent patches around all their edges.

Pensioning off

There comes a time—no matter how much cleaning or tumble-drying or self-deceiving you do—when a patched and trusted old bag is no longer sure to give you a warm sleep within its temperature range. There is only one remedy. But it is always a sad moment when another old friend bites the Goodwill.

CHOOSING AND PREPARING A BEDROOM

Level bedsites

There are few simpler ways of ensuring a bad night's sleep than choosing a bed that slopes. If the slope is sideways you spend the night in a thinly conscious hassle with gravity; and you wake, tired and aching, to find yourself still pressing fiercely on the downslope with arms and knees and a battery of assistant muscles. If the slope runs from feet to head you don't go to sleep at all. No matter how gentle the incline (and it is sure to be gentle, or you would never have overlooked it) you discover the horrible truth the moment you lie down. The feeling that all the blood is going to rush to your head is so disturbing that after a few feeble attempts at telling yourself that it's all imagination you gruntle up and switch head and feet.

If you can't possibly avoid a sloping bed you should sleep with your feet downhill. That way, if the slope is not too severe, you spend a passably comfortable night: you may come half awake occasionally to find yourself a yard and a half downhill from pillow and groundsheet, and have to do an undignified wriggle back uphill; but you wake with nothing worse than mildly aching leg muscles.

Do everything you can, then, to organize a level bed. I routinely check by lying full length on the bare ground (or on a groundsheet if it's wet), adjusting to the most comfortable position, and then lying still long enough to make sure my head is not too blood-collecting low. If you have to camp on generally sloping ground then try to do so on a trail or just above a tree or in some other place where there is a ready-made level platform. Or go to considerable pains to make a platform. Often you can find a place with soil loose enough to kick away with your heels. You can always do so on talus. But in heavily used country you must these days accept a bedsite that needs leveling only if the construction work will do no damage to the ground and can be completely repaired before you leave. Sand, talus and a deep leaf-carpet qualify. Grass like hell does not: leveling it means removing the roots and therefore killing it. And unless you sleep in a bureaucratically consecrated campsite where the ground is likely to be scraped or worn bare you should try to leave no sign—beyond a rectangle of crushed vegetation if you *have* to crush any—that you slept there. Leave, that is, no more trace than a bear, or even a deer.

Improving a bedsite

When I lie down to check the levelness of a bedsite I naturally discover any bumps, rocks and other body-prodders. I quickly banish the worst offenders. And if I'm sleeping on a thin, closed-cell foam pad (which nowadays is rarely) I may work with bare hands or a stick or even my toilet trowel (page 538) until the place is reasonably smooth. With a thick foam pad, a Therm-a-Rest or an air mattress, I need take far less care.

But, provided the country and the under-bed material permit, it often makes sense to contour a bedsite to fit your form—certainly if there'll be no cushion between bag and ground; probably with a closed-cell pad; possibly even with a more voluptuous mattress. The idea is to emulate a waterbed by digging or merely boot-scratching a shallow depression for your shoulders and a rather deeper one for your butt. Excavated material builds a pillow, or raises the legs a trifle. Determine your needs by trowel and error.

Choice of under-bed material

Grass is one of the poorer choices for a bedsite. Except when very long, it cushions you precious little; and even aside from the unacceptable scarring (opposite page), it is difficult to contour to fit your form. An air mattress or thick foam pad takes the sting out of loose gravel or talus, and they are far easier to contour. Bare earth is often as easy, and appreciably softer. Sand rates higher still. A deep carpet of leaves, and especially of pine needles, offers the ultimate luxury in warmth and comfort—and sometimes a monumental fire hazard. Leaves should never be chosen if you intend to light a fire. Even with a stove you must clear a hearth to bare soil—and still exercise meticulous care.

Shelter from wind

The level-bed business is so important that when I camp at nightfall and expect to move on again first thing in the morning it is often the only campsite feature I worry about. In fair weather, that is. But when the wind rises to gale force or feels like a disembodied iceberg then shelter from wind supplants level ground as the one thing you absolutely must have.

Unless you have both a tent and confidence that you can erect it in the teeth of the gale, go to great pains to find natural shelter. I tend to do so anyway. It's much simpler, and often warmer. A clump of trees or bushes will deflect the full fury of any wind. And even in exposed places, quite minor irregularities, if themselves total windbreaks, make remarkably good refuges. I have spent comfortable nights, well sheltered from icy gales, in the troughs of shallow gullies, behind low walls, even tucked in close to a cattle trough. But the best hideout of all is an overhanging rockledge. (A full-fledged cave protects you better, of course; but caves tend to be both rare and unappetizing.) Even a very shallow ledge, provided it's on the lee side of a hill or rockpile, can be a snug place. The rock retains much of its daytime warmth, and after one comfortable night in such a sanctuary you understand why cold-blooded rattlesnakes like to live among rocks. The floor of the ledge is rarely as level as you would like it to be but there are often small rocks lying around for a rough construction job. Such construction can rarely be justified in heavily used country. Even less can the still-general practice of camping in an unprotected place and then collecting boulders and building a wall or, sometimes, an embryo cabin.

Remember, by the way, that winds often die at dusk, then revive from a different quarter. Desert winds fairly consistently blow up canyons by day, down them (and cold) at night. The night downwind is also common on mountains in generally calm weather.

Shelter from rain

Rockledges make good shelters from rain too—and caves are even better. But beware of shallow caves in thunderstorms (page 581). Hollow tree trunks are traditional wilderness shelters but, to be honest, I have never tried one. In rain I just tend to put up whatever roof I've brought along. Naturally, I choose the most sheltered site I can find.

Shelter from snow

In heavy and prolonged snowstorms an obvious campsite in the lee of a cliff or steep rise may prove dangerous: drifting snow could bury your tent while you sleep. At least, so they say. Such a site may also be prone to avalanches. Before you venture out into any depth of snow in any country that is not flat or close to it, make damned sure you ascertain from a genuine avalanche authority that it is safe to do so. If not, stay at home. For more on avalanches, see page 580.

For snow caves and trenches, see page 328.

Cold bedrooms

Meadows, especially when cradled in hollows, often collect cold, damp air. They're delightful places to camp, though, and—provided human usage is light (page 311)—should not necessarily be avoided. A hillock or rockslab a few feet above the meadow itself is often enough to ward off the worst of the cold, improve the view—and spare the fragile grass.

Riverbanks also tend to be damp and therefore cold places—and to provide richly rewarding campsites. But see page 539.

Siting your bedroom to catch—or avoid—the morning sun

It can occasionally be important that your bed should catch the first rays of morning sunshine. Sometimes only the sun's warmth will make a bitter world habitable. Sometimes you go to sleep without a roof—

because you are tired or lazy or just because you like it that way—
expecting heavy dew during the night but knowing that morning sunshine will quickly dry it off and save you packing along pounds of water.
Or it may be that a tent needs drying. And on days on which you are
planning not to move camp, or to move late, it is always more pleasant
to start the day in sunshine. At least, almost always. In deserts, in
summer, you will want to avoid the sun. And some people prefer to
avoid it, especially if they want to sleep late, in all but icebergial
weather.

Anyway, whatever your reason for wanting to know where the sun
will rise, the solution is simple: on the first day of the trip—or before
you start, if you can remember it—measure with your compass the exact
bearing on which the sun rises over a flat horizon. Pencil the bearing on
the back of the compass. Then, at any night camp, all you have to do is
take out the compass, sight along the correct bearing, make due allowance for close or distant heightening of the horizon, and site your camp
in the right place. With a little experience you can prophesy accurately
enough to make use of even narrow gaps in trees.

But perhaps you know you'll forget to take a sunrise bearing before
you start, and are afraid there will be no sun on the first day. If you
delight in dabbling with tortuous theory and have a copy of *Practical
Boating: Inland and Offshore—Power and Sail* by W. S. Kals (Doubleday,
1969, now out of print) you're still in good shape: on page 121 you'll
find a table showing the true bearing of the sun at sunrise, at various
latitudes.

Minor factors in choosing a campsite

Your criteria for a good campsite will vary a lot with the kind of
country, your expected length of stay and your personal preferences. For
the first day or two of a trip, especially in strange country, you may find
yourself—as I did during *The Thousand-Mile Summer*—circling around a
promising area like a dog stirred by ancestral memories. But before long
you are once more recognizing a good site at a glance: not only a flat
bedsite with reasonable protection from wind but also (if you want a fire)
plenty of firewood and (where there's water) a bathroom.

Don't underrate the importance of a good bathroom. There is a
yawning gap between a camp with running bedside water (where you can
without effort scoop out drinking water, wash, wash up and wash your
feet) and a place in which you have to crash through tangled undergrowth
and yards of sucking swamp to reach a tepid outpuddle of a river. By
comparison, the difference between hotel rooms with and without a
private bath is so much fiddle-faddle. Naturally, I'm speaking now of

large lakes or rivers in genuinely remote places. In most of today's teeming wildernesses it's rarely possible to make your choices with so little consideration for fellow-travelers (page 425).

You earn, by the way, an oddly satisfying bonus if you succeed in choosing a memorable camp from the map—as you can sometimes do once you grow used to a certain kind of country. If you play the percentages and hunches and get everything right—level bed, shelter from wind, firewood, water, morning sunshine, pleasing surroundings, even (and this is what makes a camp truly memorable) the stimulation or mystery or magic that can come from an isthmus of woodland or an oddly shaped hillock or a quietly gurgling backwater—if you get all these right you experience the same slightly surprised pleasure as from finding that your checkbook total tallies with the bank statement.

Dry camps

I was astonished to read in a magazine not long ago an article about the "new" practice of dry camping—that is, of carrying enough water, for a short or long distance, to enable you to choose a campsite independent of any water source. Under a wide range of conditions—from deserts to almost any place there is no regulation that you must camp in a bureaucratically consecrated campsite—I have for years carried enough canteens to give me such freedom. I may fill up at a creek and carry the necessary extra load only half a mile. Or I may lug it much farther. Sometimes this is purely a making-mileage ploy (page 193). But often it is not. And when it is not I almost always find that the extra convenience or shelter or privacy or beauty of the campsite I am freed to select makes the effort well worthwhile. I would guess that these days, except in well-watered high mountains, at least 50 percent of my campsites, and probably more, are half a mile from my water source.

THE BEDROOM IN ACTION

We examined most details of how the bedroom operates in our "SAMPLE DAY IN THE KITCHEN" (pages 270–3 and 276–8). More appears under "A SAMPLE DAY IN THE RAIN" (pages 428–35). And for modifications under various kinds of roof, see their separate subheadings in this chapter. But several points remain unmade:

Keeping tabs on the flashlight

After dark you must always know exactly where the flashlight is. Otherwise, chaos. My flashlight spends the night in an easy-to-feel position in one bedside boot. And I used to have a rule that when it was in intermittent use, such as before and during dinner, I never let go my grasp on it without putting it in the pocket designated for the night (*which* pocket depended on what I was wearing). This rule was so strict that I rarely broke it more than three or four times a night.

Nowadays the rule has been superseded: I virtually always have the flashlight tied to a large loop of nylon cord that slips over my head.

For more on flashlights, including head-strap models, see pages 437–46.

For candle lanterns and even fancier illumination, see pages 453–4 and 455.

Fluffing up the sleeping bag

Although I am told that many people fail to do so, it seems only common sense that before you get into bed at night you should always shake the sleeping bag by the edges and so fluff up the down or even synthetic fill and suffuse it with the air pockets that actually keep you warm. At this point in the first edition of this book I wrote: "One of these nights I must try it out." I'm happy to report that the act of writing that sentence prodded me into doing the job fairly regularly. It's good to know, firsthand, that the book has taught somebody something.

Adjusting to suit the night

With experience (and I guess there's no other way) you can usually gauge pretty accurately how much clothing, if any, you will need to wear in your sleeping bag. Or, in warmer weather, how tightly you need pull the hood drawstrings, and whether you should unzip the bag partway. But you will never get so good that you always hit the nail dead center.

In general, be a pessimist: if in doubt, wear that extra layer of clothing, and pull the drawstrings tight. Sleeping too hot is uncomfortable; but sleeping cold is murder. In any case, the night will usually, though not always, get progressively colder (the coldest time typically comes either at dawn or, even more often, in the last few minutes before sunrise).

There is another and even more important reason that you do better by deliberately looking on the bleak side: boosting insulation is a major operation, reducing it a very simple one. When you wake up uncomfortably hot (and you will do so occasionally unless you consistently under-insulate, and then God help you) all you need do is slacken off the drawstrings. At least, that usually lets out enough heat, especially if you flap the bag in a bellows effect a couple of times to introduce some cold air. If you find that to establish the right balance you have to slacken the drawstrings until there is a gaping hole around your head you will probably discover that the upper part of your body gets too cold and the lower part stays too hot. If you are wearing heavy clothes, take off one layer. (A minor disadvantage of a close-fitting bag like the Slimline is that putting on or taking off socks and pants "indoors" is a struggle. But it can be done. At least, taking them off can.) If you wake to find yourself too hot when you're wearing few or no clothes (which will mean that outside air temperatures are not too barbarously low) feel for the inside tab of the zipper and slide it partway or all the way down. A two-way zipper, now becoming almost standard, allows you to open up a breathing hole at your calves as well. Once again, only experience will tell you how far to go, and also how to tuck the opening under you, or to wriggle it around on top, or away from the wind, or whatever else achieves the balance you want. If you unzip you may well have to rezip as the night grows colder, and/or to tighten the drawstrings; but you soon learn to do so without coming more than about one-eighth awake.

On really hot nights the only comfortable way to use the bag may be as a cover—fully unzipped and just spread out loosely over your body. At such times it may be most comfortable to wear a shirt to keep your shoulders warm and to tuck your feet partway into the foot of the bag. A little to my surprise, I find myself sleeping this way more and more often on windless nights when the temperature is over about 40° F. One advantage of using the bag instead of wearing a couple of layers of clothing is that as the night grows colder (which it mostly will) you can compensate, without coming even one-eighth awake, by pulling the edges of the outspread bag a little more firmly around you.

Dealing with a full bladder at night

See page 541.

Getting to sleep

An experienced outdoorsman once suggested that I include in this chapter "the ritual of getting to sleep in a bag," and as he was my editor I decided that I had better attempt the task. In an earlier edition I wrote that my technique was to lie down, close my eyes and go to sleep. That's still true, mostly. But if I experience any difficulty—as I understand some people regularly do—I now quieten myself with Selective Awareness (page 99), and soon slip down and away.

Clothes Closet

The best dress for walking is nakedness. But our sad though fascinating world rarely generates the right mix of weather and privacy for such freedom, and even when it does the Utopia never seems to last for very long. So you always, dammit, have to worry about clothes.*

The most sensible way to set about deciding what clothing to take on a trip and what to leave behind is to consult weather statistics (page 36) and your own experience and so arrive at an estimate of the most miserable conditions of temperature, wind, exposure, humidity and precipitation that you can reasonably expect to suffer. The worst conditions recorded in, say, twenty years. Then all you have to do is judge what you need to take to keep you warm under daytime conditions when you are wearing everything and doing something or at least are only sitting down and doing nothing for short intervals. If you hit this target around about center you can feel reasonably sure that at night, with shelter and sleeping bags selected to match, you will sleep tolerably warm under the bitterest conditions possible if you wrap yourself up in every stitch of available clothing that remains dry. During the day, if you stop doing anything for any length of time and begin to feel cold, or even to think that you might soon feel cold, then—provided your clothes and the weather are dry enough—you simply pupate inside the sleeping bag.

This kind of calculation involves not so much a precise balancing of conditions and clothing as an exercise in extrapolating from experience. But it works. I do not remember being seriously cold at any time in the last twenty years for more than the few minutes it took me to do something about the problem. And although I have never operated in bitter

---

* The executive director of an Eastern Trail Conference delights me by reporting that he has walked "over 1000 miles of the Appalachian Trail wearing shoes and socks and a pack."

cold—never below zero, in fact—people who do so fairly often seem to apply much the same methods of choice and the same techniques.

This general approach works irrespective of the kind of clothing you wear.

Fifty years ago mountaineers scaled formidable peaks—even challenged Everest—wearing tweed shooting jackets. Five years ago most backpackers wore modified forms of their everyday informal wardrobe. (Down jackets, which transformed outdoor wear two decades ago, had already become part of that wardrobe. So had windbreakers.) But new synthetics, and older fibers put to new uses, have now seeded

A revolution in the clothes closet—

a renovation more radical than that assailing any other sector of backpacking equipment.

The new elements are polypropylene underwear, fiber-pile clothing and Gore-Tex shells. These three basic ingredients and their variations, alone or with addenda, can constitute a layered system for backpacking in all non-extreme temperatures and in almost any kind of rain you can nightmare up. For the moment, I shall speak of a simple, idealized system—though one of its advantages is that it can be modified to meet the demands of widely differing conditions as well as those of tradition, habit and idiosyncrasy.

The new three-layer system

offers solid advantages. Its constituent items are lighter, sometimes more durable and generally less expensive than traditional equivalents. Properly used, they are more flexible. Above all, they work far better than traditional garments when they become wet, either from sweat or from rain that has penetrated the "waterproof" shell. Finally, each item, raw or slightly modified, can become—as the down jacket and windbreaker quickly did—a standard part of everyday town wardrobes.

The seeds of the clothing revolution, planted years ago and cultivated by the New Wave (page 26), are now bustin' out all over; and while it is just possible that the garden will fail to flourish, I doubt it. A burgeoning band of backpackers, particularly in such aqueous places as the Pacific Northwest, are already dedicated converts. For an occasion on which I found it excellent, see page 435.

In addition to the new three-layer system there is the older but only recently popular vapor-barrier system—which can be used as an extension of the three-layer system. We will examine it in due course.

Before attempting to compare traditional clothing with the new systems we must take a closer look at the newcomers. But first it might be wise to review

The prime purpose of clothes.

For the moment, we will ignore protection from rain and sun and also such ancillary matters as beautification and conventional decency (a.k.a. prudery), and will consider only warmth. And warmth only in a simple sense. For the different kinds of heat loss and heat barriers, see page 384.

Two basic and obvious facts are sometimes overlooked by beginner backpackers. First, when you put on clothes for warmth you are not "keeping the cold out," as the old saying has it; you are conserving heat from the only available source—you. Second, you normally wear clothes not to make you as warm as possible but to maintain "thermal equilibrium"—that is, a state in which your heat production roughly balances your heat loss and you remain within your comfort range whether you are sitting still, being active enough to sweat like crazy or, most demanding of all, sitting still after sweating.

To achieve thermal equilibrium under changing conditions your wardrobe must be versatile. Gross adjustments can sometimes be made by putting on or taking off layers in response to the weather and what you are doing. But that is often foully inconvenient or even impractical, especially in cold or wet. So you aim for as broad a range as possible over which each item or combination of items will maintain you in comfort. Generally speaking, this is best achieved by clothing that will trap dry, still air and therefore insulate you but will also, when you are being active, allow water vapor from your sweat to pass through and escape. Your sweat can then do its job of cooling you by extracting from your body the latent heat needed for water to turn to vapor. But if the clothing absorbs some of the moisture and therefore remains damp when you cease your activity and stop sweating—as wool does to some extent, and cotton markedly—then the absorbed water will not only reduce the clothing's ability to hold dry air and so impair its insulative value but will also continue to draw from your body the latent heat needed to turn it into vapor. Result: you suffer from "after-exercise chill." Experiments at the U.S. Army Research Institute of Environmental Medicine showed that "with an absorptive textile [wool-nylon] the after-exercise chill is large and persists for about two hours but with a non-absorptive type [fiberpile] it is negligible."

This efficiency in circumventing after-exercise chill is a big reason for the growing popularity of the new three-layer clothing system.

Most of the fabrics used in the system have only recently achieved widespread success, at least in the backpacking field, and it seems certain that, as almost always happens during the early success stage of any evolutionary process, things will continue to develop fast. By the time this book appears some of the current buzz-word trade names may have melted away. Perhaps a fiber or two will have been superseded. So in trying to describe what is happening I shall bear in mind that we are living through the rapidly shifting arc of an ongoing continuum. Rather than simply name names, I will try to describe those properties that fit the new fibers and fabrics so snugly into the backpacker's clothes closet. With luck, you will then be able to penetrate beyond outdated trade names and understand the functions of replacement equivalents.

The strata of the present three-layer system are:
1. Polypropylene underwear
2. Pile garment(s)
3. Wind- and water-proof outer shell.

Polypropylene underwear

Strictly speaking, "polypropylene"—now often known as "polypro" —is one fiber in the larger group of "polyolefins"—sometimes called just "olefins"; but for our purposes all these terms are interchangeable. The very durable fiber—derived from propylene and ethylene gases—is the lightest and least expensive of the synthetic fabric fibers. It also has the lowest "moisture regain": it will absorb only .1 percent of its weight in moisture. It therefore wicks moisture away from the skin very rapidly by capillary action. (Please don't ask me to explain "therefore": the molecular processes remain unclear to me and, as far as I can determine, to everyone else.) The fiber's non-absorbency also means that polypro fabric dries out very quickly. One booster told me that "if you put a polypro undershirt in a bucket, then swing it twice over your head and put it on, within a minute it will be bone dry and you will be warm." I have just carried out the experiment (purely for you, oh buster, bustress) and I have to report that in spite of modifying the prescription to a sextupular waving and subsequently encasing myself in a pile jacket I am now, five minutes later, back at the typewriter, agreeably warm but clammily short of dry. So our booster traffics in hyperbole. It is probably true, though, that if you fall profoundly into the drink a polypro undergarment will dry out faster and more comfortably than anything else now known. Of course, the stuff is not perfect. It melts at 385° F. and therefore cannot be ironed. If put in a drier at high heat it may shrink, skulkingly. And some users report that "it's hard to get the smell of sweat out of the stuff. If you've worn it for ten days you may need to wash it twice—with a lemon-scented soap." More serious is the comfort quotient: the simple, extruded, monofilament fabric, though acceptable to most people in low temperatures, tends to feel itchy as things warm up. To me, a change seems to come around 50° F. But the fabric is improving rapidly. Spun-yarn versions, especially if brushed to give a nap on the inner surface, promise even greater relief. For more on comfort, see page 391.

Polypropylene seems to wick best when made thin. And thin undergarments are both extremely light and reasonably priced. Long-sleeved undershirts and longjohns both average around 4 ounces and $17. Popular current brands include Odlo, Patagonia, Allen-A, Lifa and Helly-Hansen. Patagonia make a thicker, "expeditionary" weight that is warmer, though slower-drying. Scandinavian Knitters make fishnet underwear (page 393) in polypro and also in 80/20 polypro/wool.

Polypro underwear can be worn much as fishnet: to keep you warm when you are cold or, if fully ventilated, to keep you cool when hot. It works well as a warmth retainer under not only pile but also any traditional wear and even alone under a waterproof shell (page 389). For most people, it is indispensable with vapor-barrier clothing (page 388). And I have worn it with success at night in both normal sleeping bags and a vapor-barrier lining.

Until recently, polypropylene was not made into thick, insulating fabrics. For one thing, the fiber tends to become entangled in the machines necessary for that operation. Worse, the fiber strands are rather limp, and thick fabric therefore tends to be "dead"—to mat down and lose loft. But 100-percent-polypro outer garments are now surfacing. I have tried a set of long pants and jacket by Royal Robbins, and it seems good. One leading garmentmaker is currently testing a clothing system with no insulators except three layers of polypro—underwear, heavy turtleneck and an additional sweater—in an attempt to determine whether the polypro will wick away all sweat rapidly, clear out to the air, and provide enough insulation for warmth.

In the normal three-layer system most convective insulation comes from

Pile garments.

For backpacking, such garments are mostly made of polyesters: the fiber is stiff and springy (in technical jargon, "has a high modulus") and therefore holds the fabric in a lofted position that effectively traps dead air, the prime insulant.

The word "pile" demands some definitions. It is often used, generically, as I have so far used it, to encompass a group of fabrics that includes "fleece" and "bunting" as well as a different end-product known specifically as "pile." All three fabrics are made from the same base—a rather thin, dense knit that looks like terry cloth. First, this base passes through a "napping" machine: a series of rollers with very sharp wire wrapped around them (hooked and straight wire alternating). The wire picks out and rakes up the loops on one side of the "terry cloth." The result is a fluffier but still fairly dense fabric: "fleece." Fleece napped on both sides is called "bunting." (Polarfleece and most other backpacking fleeces are buntings.) To make "pile" you subject single-sided fleece to further processes. A "napper" machine with very sharp, straight-wire "brushes" frees and combs out the fleece's entangled surface. Next, the heated cylinders of a "polishing or ironing" machine make the fibers stand erect—and stay that way. Finally, a "shear" machine cuts off wild and uneven fiber. The resultant "pile" is a very open fabric, five times as thick as the terry-clothic base. At present all piles used in backpacking garments are single-sided and about half an inch thick.*

Piles and fleeces have been around for decades (in carpets, warm-up suits and teddy bears, for example), but only a few years ago were they introduced as backpacking clothes—by Yvon Chouinard, founder of Patagonia (the outdoor-clothing makers in California, not the sheep-raising region in Argentina). At first Chouinard and others used only pile—in the narrower sense of a one-sided, sheared fabric. It filled the bill admirably. The durable fabric makes rugged clothes with a life span still undetermined. Because of its resilience you suffer no cold patches at such pressure points as elbows or knees. The fiber's high conductivity means that when you put on a pile jacket you experience an immediate sense of warmth—"like slipping into a bed with flannel sheets," says one aficionado. (For less positive words on the quality of its warmth, see page 391.) Polyester wicks almost as efficiently as polypropylene (and Monsanto are said to be trying to increase its wickability), so the open-structured fabric dries out very quickly. If it gets soaking wet you can take it off and wring it out, and even while your body heat is drying it out the stiff, springy fibers retain their loft and you remain at least

---

* Different piles—such as Borglite (made with hollow, modified Hollofil fibers and 15 percent lighter than regular piles)—may undergo variations on these processes. But that does not alter the basic distinctions between fleece, bunting and pile.

I am indebted to Malden Mills of Massachusetts for the information on fabrics, and to the 3M Company of Minnesota for basic facts about fibers.

My informant at 3M suggested that "in turning to pile as an insulant we have in a sense circled back to beginnings. Long, long ago, men wore animal furs, and furs are essentially natural piles." More accurately, of course, piles are synthetic furs. But it's a nice thought.

reasonably warm. ("You only need one experience with a wet down jacket," a certain mountaineer told me, "and you'll convert to pile.")

In other words, pile may be less efficient, weight for warmth, than new, dry down, but unlike down it is always functioning at or close to optimum. That's why it has already caught on among boaters and especially kayakers, among fishermen (it does not compress to uselessness under waders) and now among backpackers—notably those who haunt soggy places. Pile also dries quickly, of course, after washing. And you can wash it easily—and repeatedly, to the point where down would simply give up—without causing harm. That makes it perfect for kids: if they wallow in dirt you just throw the jacket in the washer; and if they roll in the snow it will, I'm told, "be dry before you go brush it off."

Few pile jackets presently come with hoods (though Sierra Designs have just introduced one). Because head and neck account for a high percentage of human heat loss (page 347), I at first opposed the omission; but I've now learned the value of a separate pile balaclava (page 418) and understand.

Polyester pile (and fleece) has a rather high "fiber friction," and you may experience some difficulty in slipping your arms down the sleeves, especially if you're wearing a chamois shirt. This is an old difficulty with other fibers: hence satin linings in formal suits. Nylon pile offers less friction than does polyester pile and retains its shape rather better (all piles stretch somewhat with use and then tend to fit better), and at least one pile jacket (page 383) now has a polyester trunk but nylon sleeves. Its makers say it "drapes" better, stretches more (allowing freer arm movement) and is hard enough to resist "pilling" (see next page) without a stiff protective coating. But nylon pile is a somewhat less efficient insulator than polyester. So is acrylic pile, which accounts for perhaps 80 percent of the overall pile market. Efforts are being made to render acrylic pile more efficient by chemical applications, and it seems that we may yet see it in backpacking garments.

Piles, though they're improving fast, fall short of perfection. They compress very little and therefore tend to take up a lot of room in your pack. Because of their open texture, most of them give very little protection from wind. And the pile's lack of elasticity means that at present almost all jackets must have ribbed cotton/nylon cuffs and waistbands to prevent warm air from bellowing out. The trouble with this arrangement, which makers are striving to improve—with polypro knit cuffs, for example—is that the ribbings suck water from the pile and dry very slowly. They are the only reason you would ever need to put a pile garment in a drier. And driers—especially large commercial ones—can raise problems. At 350° F. polyesters "cook": colors change, and so does the very nature of the fiber's membranes. So if you must use a drier, stick with the LOW or DELICATE setting. Beyond that, you really have to "blow it" to damage pile.

Pile is hardly fashion-plate stuff. At present it comes only in blue or gray or, occasionally, tan and "berry"—though that may change tomorrow. And because pile garments are worn with the "roughed up" surface inside, to hold air better, the unattractive unbrushed surface is what the world sees. What's more, wear and washing tend to make the surface "pill" or generate little balls of fluff. To reduce pilling, the outsides of some piles are now resinated—but that makes them "boardy." All in all, no one would accuse pile of beauty. Some would call it plain ugly. And that is where fleece comes in.

Double-sided fleece, or bunting, is good-looking stuff. (Recent improvements have markedly reduced the pilling that it, too, used to suffer.) And because general-use "soft goods" now loom large in the turnover of most mountain shops there is a tendency for makers and retailers to recommend fleece jackets as good garments for both town and backcountry. Up to a point, they are right. Fleece would indeed do both jobs. But it will not do as good a backpacking job as pile: the material is denser and therefore a less efficient insulator, ounce for ounce; and while it wards off the wind rather better (not a crucial factor, as we shall see) its density means it breathes less well and therefore has a narrower range of use. Worse still, dual-purpose garments tend to be designed with one and a half eyes on fashion and therefore to be heavier, more expensive and less functional than they should be for the backcountry.*

Fortunately, pile jackets, being unlovely, tend to be pretty functional. Good models come from Patagonia, Wilderness Experience, Sierra Designs and a growing number of other places. Mine, by Mark Pack

---

* Fashion is always fighting function. And the bruises show, all the time, on all kinds of garments.

It is backpackers and climbers, presumably interested only in function, who "legitimize" the garments. They are the ones the ads feature, stalwarting on Everest. But the ads are often aimed at the general public—and the general public wants something that can be worn in town, even out to an informal dinner. Add the soft-goods orientation of today's mountain shops and it's easy to see why pile and down jackets come "styled" and hoodless, why Gore-Tex jackets sprout unnecessary, percolative pockets . . . and so on down many lines.

One designer recently told me, "Frankly, it's years since there's been a down jacket on the market that was really made for backpackers." And the current trend with fleeces is to reduce their pilling (a purely cosmetic flaw) by shifting to tighter knits with less nap—a trend that fights, head-on, the functional demand for maximum insulation.

No wonder retailers report a stream of hardcore backpackers and climbers who complain, "Why is there now so much goddam stuff that's fashion-oriented?" But then, it always was a sad, sad world. Let's have a drink.

Works of California, has a Borglite trunk and Antron nylon sleeves (page 381) and—for use with vapor-barrier gear—armpit zippers (page 388) (1 pound 6 ounces, $62.50). I've used it a good deal, now: in fair weather; in wet conditions around freezing (page 435); and also at night, as part of unsleeping-bagged torso-covering at 18° F. (page 359); and I am more than satisfied. The armpit zippers work well, and have proved invaluable. The nylon knit wristbands dry rather slowly, but the makers are working on that.

Because pile (and even fleece) jackets do a sievelike job of warding off wind you must if you use one also carry an

Outer shell.

The shell acts as both windbreaker and rainjacket. At present it is usually made of Gore-Tex. We will discuss Gore-Tex and its alternatives later (page 405). For the moment, all that needs saying is that the shell should be roomy and hooded and have a full-length front zipper and, probably, armpit zippers—often called "pit zips." For the pros and cons of pit zips, see page 410.

A few further notes on the three-layer system:

As promised, I have delineated a simple, idealized system. It will often prove adequate in that form. But it is wide and pleasantly open to modification. If you like to wear a cotton T-shirt when moving in warm weather you are free to do so with no more penalty than an extra three or four ounces. But remember to take off the sweaty T-shirt before you bundle up in "the system"; otherwise the wet cotton will nullify the wicking warmth of underwear and pile. If habit or tradition dictates a wool shirt or even a thin down vest, well, that's fine too. I still often take a thin wool shirt for halts, and even around camp. But once again you must guard against damp wool fouling up the wicking system. In bitterly cold weather you can, of course, add compatible layers to the system over your pile jacket: a sleeveless pile vest (pretty damned bulky) and/or a wool or polypro turtleneck sweater (normally made for some reason without zippers or with only a short one at the neck, but hopefully coming out with full-length zippers for greater versatility).

I have deliberately concentrated so far on upper-body protection. Under normal backpacking conditions your prime consideration should be head and trunk: if they are warm and reasonably dry, you'll likely be comfortable—as long as you keep moving, anyway. Old-style clothing —even shorts—will take care of your legs. But really low temperatures may demand full three-layer leg protection, either somewhat modified or including pile pants, even though they're still very bulky. The new polypropylene pile pants look promising. And Gore-Tex pants (page 414) are pretty well proven.

As addenda to the system or even possibly as replacement items, there lurk in the wings several new "hi-tech" materials. *Thinsulate* is an aery, white, cottonlike batting, usually about half an inch thick, that makes an excellent insulant inside a shell of taffeta or similar light material. Strands of polyesters form the backbone of its structure, and they hold very, very fine microfibers of polypropylene that create an immense number of small air pockets. The air apparently clings to the microfibers in such a way as to provoke reports of "deader air" and "blowing to hell the notion that greater warmth demands greater loft." Thinsulate breathes. But it neither drapes nor compresses well. And although it has already proved popular among fashion-conscious skiers who welcome the lack of bulk, it has yet to find a secure niche among backpackers. Reasons given vary from "they avoid it because it doesn't look 'lofty' " to "it's heavy . . . and styled too often into unsuitable garments." *Supersilk* is crushed and processed real silk. It may turn out to offer advantages. But it promises to be almost as expensive as down. *Texolite* (page 350) may possibly find clothing uses.

In order to understand how the new materials work we had better pause for a look at

The fundamentals of insulation.

The ideal insulator for clothing has to meet demands different from those made on an insulator for sleeping bags (wherein the sleeper maintains a roughly constant metabolic rate). The clothing insulator must be able to cope with radical metabolic changes: when the encasee is sitting still it must, as in a sleeping bag, retain all possible heat; but when he is active it must draw the heat off, or at least allow it to escape.

The achievement of these already conflicting tasks is further befouled by the existence of four different kinds of heat loss, and therefore four kinds of heat barrier. The percentage of loss by each route, far from being constant, varies according to the channels open at the time.

Convective heat loss—the most common form—occurs when air (or, occasionally, water), after contact or near-contact with the body's surface, moves away and carries heat with it. Under normal conditions, convection accounts for the highest percentage of the body's heat loss, and most heat barriers are therefore convective: they encapsulate the body in a layer of dead air, an excellent insulator. Convective heat loss is measured by the R factor, familiar to anyone interested in insulating his home.

We have seen how pile, enveloped if necessary by a windproof shell, acts as a convective barrier. Down or synthetic substitutes such as PolarGuard or Hollofil work the same way. Ditto Thinsulate, wool, et al.

Well-designed convective barriers are flexible: when you sit down and button up they keep most of the warmth in; as you become more active your increased body heat tends to drive warmed air out through the porous material; and before things get unpleasantly hot you begin to unbutton or unzip.

Evaporative loss comes from the conversion of moisture on your skin into vapor: the latent heat required to bring about this change is drawn from your body. That is why we sweat: it is the body's mechanism for shucking excess heat. And it's a very efficient method—the one we use in refrigerators and air-conditioners.

But sometimes—as when we sit down after heavy exercise in sweat-soaked clothing—evaporative loss becomes undesirable and uncomfortable, even dangerous. See "After-exercise chill," page 377.

Fortunately, efficient modern wickers such as polypropylene virtually prevent evaporative heat loss—by removing moisture from the skin before it vaporizes. (For the wickers' role in preventing loss from insensible sweating, see "Vapor barrier clothing," page 386.)

Conductive heat loss occurs when heat passes directly from the body into a stationary medium (air, water, fabric) that is in contact with it and at a lower temperature. Conductive loss is generally minor. But if you fall in a cold lake you will lose heat almost wholly by conduction to the water surrounding you (though some will be convected away by moving water), almost none by radiant heat and absolutely none by evaporative heat. In very cold water the conductive loss may be so rapid that you soon die.

Radiant heat loss occurs without warming of the air through which the heat passes: transfer occurs only to solid objects. The sun heats the earth and other planets by radiation: sunlight does not warm the air directly, only by heating the soil or other solid ground objects, which in turn warm the air by convection. That's why the air is much hotter one inch above sunlit soil than it is five feet, or five thousand feet, higher.

Radiant heat loss from the human body is usually minor. But when other channels are closed that can change, radically. If a naked man stands still in a room at the same temperature as his body, two-thirds of his heat loss may be by radiation. But in practical backpacking situations, radiant heat loss tends to occur not directly from the skin but from the fabric next to it: the body heats the fabric by other channels and then, if the next layer offers direct pathways, the fabric radiates heat outward. (Direct pathways may exist, though: hold a batt of PolarGuard up to the light and you can see through its holes.)

Radiant heat loss is prevented by reflective barriers: they turn the heat back toward the body. Texolite and Orcothane work that way. And that's fine in sleeping bags, because you want to conserve such small amounts of heat as you are generating. But it's the opposite of ideal in clothing: when you are sitting still and in the greatest need of heat conservation you are generating very little and the reflective barrier has no useful work to do; but when you are active and producing a lot of surplus heat and the problem is to dissipate it, then reflective barriers work hard, turning back toward the body heat that is not wanted there —except perhaps in the most intensely cold weather.

And that, thank God, is all we really need to know about the theory of insulation.

Vapor-barrier clothing,

though it has been on the minimarket for decades, only recently began to achieve popularity. A distinctly patchy popularity. It still divides the backpacking fraternity (sic) into five discrete but hardly discreet camps: True Believers (TBs), who view it as the Holy Grail and are always seeking a pulpit; those who loathe it with such venom that at mere mention of its name they Throw Hands Up In Horror (THUIHs); those who regard it as a valuable system in extreme cold but otherwise more nuisance than it's worth; those who use it in extreme cold and also, sparingly, under temperate conditions; and finally—still in the heavy majority, I suspect—those who have not yet fully grasped what the hell the whole thing is about.

Until recently I was—based on the sketchiest of early experience with a VB sleeping-bag liner (page 348)—second cousin to a THUIH. (Note that TBs maintain, perhaps with some truth, that most THUIHs have tried the system only once, misused it, and remained bitten and shy.) But recently—at least in part because I felt I had to give the damned stuff a fair trial if I was to write this chapter (greater love hath no reporter)—I have been experimenting. And a little to my surprise I am now, though by no means a TB, totally estranged from the THUIH family. My still rather inadequate experience, bolstered by considerable reading and discussion, suggests that VB clothing, though no general panacea, is valuable for most people in temperatures below 20° F. and useful in much higher temperatures for those who have learned to operate it and are willing to fuss with frequent fine-tuning of the ventilation. And its extreme lightness, relative cheapness and flexibility when properly used certainly make it a good three-season back-up system for unexpected cold. Used with a half-sac, it can also allow you to cut down drastically on the weight of your sleeping bag. But it's important to remember that idiosyncrasies may play a role: a few people apparently eager to use VBs seem unable to tolerate, even in cold weather, a real or imagined sense of sweatiness or enclosure; others find that their bodies take time to adapt to the system. Yet my prime TB-guru wears his VB shirt with joyous bravado, backpacking and civilianizing, in temperatures up to 50° F.

Two things seem clear: if you're going to operate satisfactorily with VBs you must understand the theory behind the system; and you must put in some practice so that you can almost without conscious thought make the frequent adjustments necessary in all but bitterly cold weather.

To understand how VBs work you must hold clear in your mind the differences between two kinds of sweat our bodies produce. First, there is the normal, obvious moisture that sweat glands secrete when we get too hot. Its purpose: to cool the body by removing unwanted heat through evaporation (page 385). This is known as "sensible sweat"—because we can easily become aware of, or sense, it. But we are never really aware of "insensible sweat"—a continuous small seepage of moisture out onto the surface of the skin that occurs independently of internal or external temperatures and continues when we are at rest. (Rate of moisture loss is heavily influenced by relative humidity: cold, dry conditions can boost it to remarkable levels.) The mechanism's apparent purpose: to keep skin moist so that it will not crack or chap.

It is this insensible sweat that VBs are designed to conserve. Worn next to or at least close to your skin, they keep it moist and comfortable by creating a warm, high-humidity envelope—thereby discouraging or even halting the production of insensible sweat. Because there is little or no evaporation from that envelope, evaporative heat loss virtually ceases. You also prevent water loss—and so can avoid the dangerous dehydration common in extreme cold at high altitudes. And you save calories you would otherwise expend in producing sweat and in achieving evaporative loss. In addition, you avert the sweat-dampening of outer insulating layers.

Provided you keep moving and the world is not too damned cold you may not need any insulation outside the VB. But the moment you sit down or even stand still the convectional and conductive heat loss from the surface of the nylon-fabric VB is likely to become apparent. Even at about freezing you'll immediately feel cold. So you block the convectional and conductive heat loss with a layer of insulation. The best, by far, is pile. If there is wind you will need a Gore-Tex or similar outer shell to hold dead air in place within the open-textured pile. It sounds odd, I know, having two somewhat impervious shells; but it is necessary. And I assure you it works.

The difficulty with VBs, of course, is sensible sweating. If the outside temperature or your activity level gets too high you begin to sweat and quickly create an overheated, saturated air envelope. Unless you remove insulation or increase ventilation you are soon wallowing in moisture. But repeatedly removing insulation and then replacing it is not practical when you're wearing a pack. And the normal ventilation adjustments at neck and sleeves may not be enough with VB clothing. Hence armpit zippers—or "pit zips" (page 410). For the arrangement to work, of course, all garments you wear, except underclothing, must have matching pit zips. That may sound like a hassle. And some people rate pit zips more trouble than they're worth. But one TB I know says that unless all garments have matching pit zips he'll almost guarantee any new user will dislike the VB system. I think he's right too.

Frequent fine-tuning of the ventilation is an integral part of the system. And it's not just a matter of responding to each change in activity level or slope of ground or strength of sun or wind. You must try to keep ahead of the game. Don't wait until you're halfway stewed or refrigerated. That's inefficient as well as damnably uncomfortable. Instead, try to anticipate the effects of a strenuous rock-scramble or steepening hill or sun-blanketing wedge of cloud. That way you'll keep your cool—and warmth. It's like taking frequent sips of water to prevent thirst rather than waiting until you're parched. You may need a couple of days' usage to get accustomed to the fine-tuning, but it soon becomes almost second-nature. So say the experts, anyway. And my still limited experience suggests they're right. But then, I belong to the keep-adjusting-your-clothing school of walking (page 427). Members of the put-it-on-and-keep-it-on faction will no doubt shudder at the prospect of such perpetual fuddy-duddying.

The basic VB garment is a simple lightweight shirt made of coated synthetic fabric. Mine, by Moonstone of California, is thin nylon taffeta, silver-gray. It has raglan sleeves for free arm movement, 18-inch pit zips, Velcro-tabbed cuffs and full-length zipper backed by a flap; also a waistline hem through which you can thread a pull-tight cord in case you do not tuck the shirt inside your pants. It weighs just 6 ounces (large size) and costs $35.

A few TBs apparently feel comfortable wearing such shirts next to their skin. But most people—unless they sport a mat of gorilla hair—find that uncomfortable going on unbearable. Before I started experimenting my TB guru said, "Promise me you'll wear polypro underwear, at least at the start. Otherwise you may never get past day one." Those who find polypro itchy, at least in its monofilament form (page 379), can try wool fishnet underwear (page 393). It does a similar though less efficient job. But avoid cotton in any form: it holds enough water, tight against your skin, to chill you and so undo the whole system.

In anything but bitter weather your legs are probably best protected by traditional rather than VB garments. But VB pants seem to work below about 20° F. and may prove life-savers below zero. My own guru also likes them for sleeping in, with a light sleeping bag, even in summer. He prefers it to a half-sac (page 349) because he can "motor around in it." VB pants by Moonstone, the only current makers, weigh 7 ounces and cost $42 (as against 4.7 ounces and $18 for the half-sac). Preferred underwear: polypro longjohns.

For VB liners on feet, see page 69; on hands, page 416.

Because your metabolism remains almost stable while you sleep, and this makes things much easier for the inexperienced, it may pay to start by trying VBs at night. In daytime, even more than at night, the way your body feels inside VB clothing will obviously exert a profound effect on whether you continue to use it; and the way the body feels can vary a lot, person to person. So if you want to explore VB possibilities without serious financial outlay you may want to experiment at first with cheap disposable substitutes such as plastic trash bags, suitably tailored and ventilated. They could give you a line on how the system will suit you. But remember the need, in a real VB jacket, for pit zips.

It is important to understand the order in which, as you feel the need for more clothing, you should add another item of a combined three-layer-and-VB clothing system. (The order in which you need them, that is; not the order in which they end up on your body.) First, in warm weather, only polypro underwear. Next, in mild coolness or any wind or rain, the Gore-Tex or similar shell. Then, if you are still cold (or expect to be, because you have, for example, stopped walking), the pile jacket —worn *under* the shell, of course. Only if this combination leaves you less warm than you want to be will you normally don your VB shirt— between underwear and pile jacket. (These principles for torso protection also apply in general to lower-body protection, though less rigidly, especially if you wear shorts.) In many cases the VB shirt will go on only when you stop walking. Then it should go on immediately, before you begin to chill.

"If used as outlined above," says an expert maker-user, "the addition of a vapor barrier (in most instances) will provide more additional warmth with less weight and bulk than any other clothing item— though several good snorts on a bottle of Jack Daniel's is probably competitive. The exception is in cold conditions where the relative humidity is high. High levels of relative humidity reduce the body's need to secrete insensible perspiration, thereby negating the major benefits of using a VB."

Remember, though, that it is entirely possible to use a VB shirt alone or over polypro underwear. Many people do so—not only in rain (when the shirt doubles as raingear) but also in fair but cool weather. My limited experiments in this mode have certainly worked well, though it seems to me that you almost always need a pile jacket on top as soon as you stop walking, to block heavy conductive heat loss.

Will the new clothing systems—three-layer and VB—make traditional backpacking wear obsolete tomorrow?

I doubt it. For one thing, we are creatures of habit. Beyond that, we rightly tend to favor things we have learned to trust. At present the new systems are still used mainly by an avant-garde—and leaders usually run about five years ahead of their pack. Then there are economics: someone with a good, expensive, traditional backpacking wardrobe is unlikely to rush out and buy a radically new one just because he hears or reads that it works rather better; and many people who backpack only occasionally will no doubt continue to make do with the most suitable of their everyday informal garments (though some of the new stuff is already becoming "everyday"). I'm also willing to bet my bottom layer that many converts will still take along shirts or other old-favorite garments for use when the weather smiles.

Even when we move from such human vagaries to more objective matters of merit, the future looks far from pre-ordained. Although the new synthetic-based systems can produce some aces, they by no means hold all the cards. To summarize:

Weight: Generally, the news have it. A simple three-layer-system outfit will, as one winter-experienced user put it, "weigh half as much as the equivalent from 1975." Theoretically, down remains the most efficient insulator, but see page 341 for what tends to happen in practice.

In both old and new camps there remains room for ponderous weight reduction. And it may be coming. Most backpacking garments have been overbuilt. See, especially, down jackets, page 397; but the same applies, pianissimo, to pile jackets—and, recrescendo, to Gore-Tex shells. But there now seems to be a move by at least some makers to produce simpler, lighter and less expensive versions that will be entirely adequate for most backpacking.

Durability: The current synthetics come close to being indestructible —though nothing yet made seems more durable than the very best wool fibers.

Ease of care: This round to the synthetics too. No contest.

Performance when wet—from rain or sweat: this is the new system's ace of spades. See pages 376, 377, 378 and 380.

Bulk: Underwear and shells: a stand-off between old and new. But pile jackets will not compress, so they occupy far more pack space than easily compressed down or wool.

Cost: Polypropylene underwear tends to be marginally more expensive than other kinds—but a polypro undervest costs far less than the fishnet ditto and thin wool shirt that it replaces. And a good pile jacket is half the price of a down equivalent. True, Gore-Tex shells may cost three times as much as nonbreathable coated versions—but they have almost become standard for traditional as well as new-system wardrobes. On balance, I guess the new beats the old, financially, by a TKO.

Comfort range: The breathability and non-absorbency of pile and polypro mean that they can keep you "in thermal equilibrium" under a wide range of temperatures and activities. (And it's worth noting that more backpackers are now operating in early spring and again in very late fall, when the summer hordes have hibernated back into cities. Also that the new clothing works fine for skiing.) VB systems, even when constantly adjusted, seem to pose difficulties for many people in the temperate weather that houses most backpacking. Traditional wardrobes stand somewhere between these extremes.

Comfort against skin. Polypropylene underwear tends to itch, and this is a big deal for some people, especially in warm weather. But things may be improving: one factor in next-to-skin comfort is the number of points of contact (others seem to be softness and, perhaps, absorbency), and synthetic-fiber researchers are worrying at the problem (page 379). Pile, worn next to the skin, can also tickle. And although coarse wool also irritates some people, cotton is, when dry, always comfortable. So here the oldies win, hands down—except on the skins of those who are allergic to them. Here, synthetics rule triumphant. The oldies win again in a related yet separate category that I call

Quality of warmth. Both VB and three-layer systems, though they can keep you comfortably warm and may even at times make you too hot, never seem to generate the "toastiness" that you often experience, even sitting still, when wearing a wool or cotton shirt and down jacket. Almost anyone who has tried both new and old systems will know about the difference. I recently confirmed it by ringing the changes on all three systems within a few minutes one windless evening when the thermometer registered 32° F. Yet I have never seen the difference mentioned in print, let alone described. The closest I can come is to say that "plastic warmth" rarely if ever seems to move beyond a mere absence of coldness, while "old-fashioned warmth" can and commonly does become a positive, glowing radiance—a luxurious sense of well-being, a sensual pleasure.

It's interesting, I find, that at least some textile researchers recognize the difference. But although they like hell want to understand what goes on, so that they can do something about it with improved synthetics, the causes remain unknown. Naturally, the researchers will not admit, officially, that old-fashioned warmth is necessarily "better" than plastic warmth. And I guess it *could* turn out that the latter is more calorie-efficient or something. Still, sensual pleasure is sensual pleasure. And you presumably go backpacking for pleasure. But pleasure can be measured in many ways, and one of them—as TBs always remind you— is by the lightness of your load.

So the future remains sweetly uncertain. At a guess, traditional clothing based on cotton and wool and on down or synthetic fills will refuse to fade away, especially in dry, temperate places. But the new systems seem likely to make heavy inroads, especially where backpackers can sometimes expect bitter cold or prolonged rain. And they'll prove irresistible to congenital equipment freaks. As for your personal choice, you will as usual have to balance the conflicting claims of old and new— then judge which works best for you, and when. To balance, that is, likelihood of getting wet against quality of warmth, to weigh the claims of versatility (with or without a VB system), and to heft your own standards of weight, cost and perhaps bulk. I only hope you now know enough to go out and make up your own cotton- or polyester-pickin' mind.

Foam clothing, which a few years ago showed some promise, at least for extreme cold, seems to have faded away. Compare page 359.

A few general considerations:

For most people, choice of clothing is largely a matter of selecting each individual garment carefully for warmth in relation to weight, for toughness in wear, for versatility in use, for performance when wet and, in rainwear, for water resistance. Also, I suspect, in response to those obscure promptings, probably esthetic, that lurk, shadowy and often unsensed, behind most of our apparently logical choices.

On purely practical grounds, it pays to choose clothes that are dark but bright. Dark, so that they will not advertise the inevitable dirt. And bright (especially red), because you can hardly walk away from camp and leave gaudy garments lying on the ground or hanging up to dry; because if you are brave enough to go out and walk during the hunting season, a plain-as-a-pikestaff exterior may save your life; because in case of accident, worn or waved clothing may attract rescuers' attention; and because a small splash of red or orange can crystallize an otherwise amorphous color photograph.

But it has been suggested, with reason, that if backpackers chose inconspicuous clothes (and packs and shelters) it would reduce the visual impact of man on today's semicrowded wilderness. A set of outer garments in some obscurantist shade of brown or green or gray is certainly worth having for those occasions when you don't want to be seen: fishing, photographing game, keeping out of people's way, trespassing.

The distaff wardrobe

I'm afraid I can offer only a few snippets of comment and advice. For full, firsthand information, see one of the books for women backpackers (page 25). Also page 419 for keeping your loved ones warm.

Two recent minor helpfulnesses: Helly-Hansen now make polypropylene underwear with more spacious upperworks for women. And jog-bras that control breast bounce have become popular among backpackers.

Fabric-makers recognize that although most women like nylon underwear, men will not touch it. This seems to suggest that different perceptions of comfort may affect backpacking choices—though I'd guess that self-images, on both sides, may in fact weigh more heavily than physical comfort.

An item of advice from an experienced subcommittee that I coopted for the first edition seems worth repeating. She found that by taking along one attractive garment ("something that makes me feel good") she helped sustain her beleaguered sense of femininity.

It is now time, I guess, for us to rummage through

THE CLOTHES CLOSET, GARMENT BY GARMENT,

taking a look at the old along with the new. But our inspection must be quick: in this edition of the closet, space is now limited.

Underclothing

Polypropylene underwear (page 378) works well not only with three-layer and VB systems but also with traditional clothes (see, for example, page 432), and it may in time replace older alternatives for almost all next-to-the-skin uses.

Meanwhile, though, many people still prefer fishnet underwear. These rather unlikely-looking garments are a lot of big holes tied together with string. At least, the original models were.*

---

* During World War II, I was for a time with a British unit that had been issued true fishnet vests as special mountaineering equipment. Eventually the unit was converted to cliff-assault duty and moved to a Cornish fishing village. Our string vests astonished the fishermen and their wives. For several years they had, as experienced netmakers, been producing these strange devices for the war effort, in great secrecy, but they had never been able to guess

In today's fishnet underwear the string has been replaced by soft knitted cotton (which, used alone, retains too much moisture) or wool or polyester or, more likely, some combination thereof. And polypropylene "stringies" have now appeared. But the holes are much the same—about ⅜ inch in diameter. And the holes are the important thing: they are what keep you warm when you want to keep warm and cool when you want to keep cool. To keep warm you button up all outer clothing and close neck and wrist openings. The holes of the fishnet weave then hold air in place close to your skin, and your body heat soon warms this air.

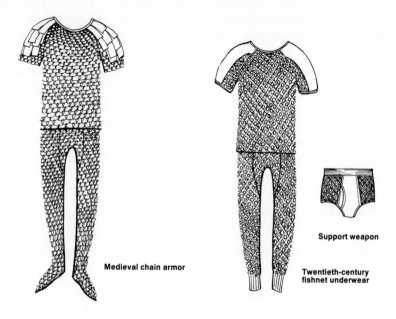

Medieval chain armor

Support weapon

Twentieth-century
fishnet underwear

To cool off, you simply loosen the neck opening of your outer garments and allow warm air to escape. Loosening wrist openings speeds up the process. If you get too hot you unbutton jacket and shirt and allow all hot air to be replaced by cold. When you are unbuttoned like this, air circulates freely, and then a string vest is far cooler than conventional underwear. To get full two-way benefit, wear outer clothing that unbuttons completely down the front and carry a scarf so that you can block off the passage of air at your neck. The best fishnet vests for backpacking are those with solid shoulders that eliminate the chafing and even blisters that bas-relief fishnet can generate under the pressure of packstraps (though that pressure should, with a well-adjusted modern pack, really be minor). Such vests average about 4 ounces, $17.

---

what the peculiarly shaped nets were used for. No one, when sober, had seriously entertained the notion that they might be some kind of clothing.

Traditional underwear will undoubtedly remain popular. Cotton, though worse than useless when wet, is very comfortable. And various wool or wool-plus-something combinations, such as Duofold and Stil-Tops, are especially good for sitting around in the cold.

Nether underwear echoes the uppers' pattern. Polypro longjohns are excellent for both backpacking (pages 432 and 436) and cold-weather town use. Fishnet shorts and even longs are good too. And some traditionalists still swear by wool or Duofold or Still-Long longjohns.

Mostly, I still wear ordinary cotton jockey briefs (people who find the tight fit causes itching and even rawness may prefer the boxer type). But the way the cotton retains moisture displeases me and I'm looking around for replacements. At the moment, Baggies (page 401) without underwear are beginning to look good. And always, if the weather is at all warm, I tend, the moment I've escaped from civilization, to dispense with underpants, no matter what pants I'm wearing. This brings me into closer conformity with the Second Law of Thermodynamic Walking: "Give your balls some air." *

In considering the clothes layer next above underwear, let us start with

Torso housings.

For pile jackets, see page 379; for addenda to the three-layer system —T-shirts, wool shirts, pile vests and turtleneck sweaters—page 383; for VB clothing, page 386.

Shirts. Among traditional fabrics, wool or wool-plus-something is best. True, some people complain of wool's itchiness. But there are wools and wools. Angora is the softest and most comfortable—and most expensive. Some wool garments now have the inner surface brushed, and that helps too. Then there is "virgin wool"—which does not really promise an unmolested ewe but means that the wool came from an animal that had never been shorn before and was therefore equipped with soft "baby hair." ("New wool" is merely that which has never been used before.)

In cold weather, when not using the three-layer system, I like thick wool shirts, such as Woolrich or Pendleton. In summer, even with the new system, I often carry one of the relatively thin Viyellas (55 percent wool, 45 percent cotton), but they have become scarce as well as tragicomically expensive ($50). For some years I used the popular Chamois shirts—made with a 100-percent-cotton cloth that looks and feels a little like chamois leather (around $18). They are durable, warm, sweat-absorbing and easy to wash, and they get softer with each washing. But

* The first law, of course, reads, "Walk is heat and heat is walk."

then I learned that, being cotton, they become useless when wet, and now I take mine only when I'm confident there's little chance of heavy rain.

Some people sensibly take a spare shirt—often a light sweat shirt —to replace the perspiration-soaked regular shirt at the end of each day. For me, a sweaty shirt rarely presents a problem: except in cold weather I tend to walk stripped to the waist. But when I stop I want something comfortably warm to slip on. That is why I favor wool shirts. Otherwise my only criteria are that the shirt shall unbutton all the way down the front, have at least one breast pocket (preferably with button-down flap), not weigh too much and be either a bright color-photography red or some soft camouflage color. But everyone has his own shirt preferences. One friend of mine will use only those with zippered rather than buttoned fronts. His specialties are blue jobs made for railroad workers (Hickory, Big Mac, or Lee), but the zippers reach only halfway down the front, and for me that's hopeless. Recently, on a clear-sky spring snowshoe trip up high I wore a light cotton shirt for protection against sun.

Sweaters. In cold weather one or more thin sweaters between shirt and traditional overclothing can make a lot of difference. On the presumably sound assumption that many thin layers work better than one thick one (because they hold air between them and also afford greater flexibility), I suppose I should take along my old cashmere sweater—peppered with holes but still beautiful—more often than I do. (For an occasion I was grateful I did so, see page 432.) Weight for warmth, there is said to be nothing to match a cashmere—except, of course, for

Quilted clothing (down- or synthetic-filled)

When Western man woke up a few decades ago to the idea of taking a feather out of the birds' book and making down-filled clothing as well as sleeping bags (the Chinese apparently tumbled to the idea long ago), the result was so much more effective than anything he had used before that it revolutionized polar and high-altitude exploration. Men could operate with safety and even comfort where they once had to battle simply to exist. Even in kinder environments they quickly accepted the breakthrough with gratitude.

Then, a few years ago, synthetics began to challenge down as quilt filling—at least in part because the cost of down rocketed ruinously (page 341). As with sleeping bags, synthetic fills have steadily gained ground and will no doubt continue to do so. Although still less efficient insulants than down, warmth for weight, and less able to bounce back to full loft after many compressions, they remain markedly cheaper as well as non-allergenic—and, most important, they become far less fatally impaired when wet. For a time PolarGuard led. Now it's Hollofil or Quallofil. Others, capable of being blown into baffled garments even more easily, seem on the way (see page 342). But synthetic-fill quilted clothing is now, with the advent of pile, fading. Once again, "quilted clothing" mostly means "down-filled."

Down clothing is a special case of torso housing (not to mention leg and extremities housing) because it is not really compatible with the new systems and therefore has to stand in unabashed opposition; because it has come to epitomize backwoods clothing and also old-fashioned warmth (page 391); and because a good, unimpaired down garment is still the warmest for weight by a significant margin.

Down's weakness lies in the word "unimpaired." A down jacket dampened by rain or heavy sweat loses appreciable virtue; soaked, it becomes almost useless—and is the very devil to dry. Grime can also reduce efficiency. So, eventually, can wear and tear and repeated washing. And washing a down garment is a pain in the tub (page 365). All these drawbacks also apply, in varying degrees, to synthetic-filled garments. Yet, although the much cheaper pile is better on all these counts, quilted garments' advantages (including their much greater compressibility) will surely keep them around.

Unfortunately, down jackets have suffered the same Detroit syndrome as other backpacking garments: they've undergone creeping growth. Virtually all of them have for years been made for polar or mountain expeditions or for working on the Alaska pipeline or, almost as bad, for fashion-conscious urban users. So from a backpacker's point of view they've been overbuilt and overstuffed. For three-season backpacking you rarely need a bulging, Michelin-man, expedition-type jacket. And a light Rip-stop or taffeta shell will save almost half a pound over a more fashionable one of 65/35 cloth that's designed to resist showers in town but is unnecessary for backpacking, when you will be carrying raingear of some kind. Nor do you really need the rash of pockets beloved by town users, or heavy two-way zippers.

Two decades ago I carried on my length-of-Grand-Canyon trip a simple, hoodless jacket that weighed just 1 pound 1 ounce, and although snow fell during the first two weeks I do not remember that I was ever cold. For years such stripped-down models have been almost unobtainable—though you could sometimes find sleeveless, lightweight "vests" that weighed around ¾ pound. Fortunately, there now seem to be signs, as with other garments, of a return to lighter, more genuinely serviceable down jackets. Sierra West, for example, make the Snow Goose jacket at

15 ounces and $103. For all but bitter cold, a properly designed jacket of around that weight should be adequate.*

Over-engineering aside, quilted garments seem, like sleeping bags, to have attained a design plateau of excellence. Fine jackets now come from virtually all the established bagmakers (page 341), and again there is generally little to choose between them. If you select from a reputable catalogue or store a model that seems to meet your requirements of the moment, and examine its workmanship as for sleeping bags (page 356), you're unlikely to go far wrong. But it might pay to check certain details.

Strive for a single rather than two-way zip—and not only because of lightness and expense. In a warm store you may be able to align double sliders fairly easily, but in the field—always in a storm and often in fair weather, even in daylight and when you're not wearing gloves—the damned things generate wills of their own. And rarely if ever, except perhaps in town, do you need or even want to ventilate by unzipping from the waist. But when I tried to get a single zip put on a jacket being made for me by an experienced manufacturer he said he had none of the right length in stock because the overwhelming demand was for double zips on down jackets.

When pervestigating a new jacket don't overlook closure arrangements at wrists (Velcro or snap fasteners are fine) and waist. (Avoid models without a drawstring or at least a hem through which you can thread one: because you can't trap warm air inside, the jacket loses half its effectiveness.) Pockets are convenient, but they should add a minimum of weight and not reduce warmth. Above all, I would suggest—though by no means everybody would—that you buy a jacket with a hood (see heat loss from head, page 347). Snap-detachable hoods are probably the most common. But I have nightmares of mine being whisked away over a cliff in a storm, and I much prefer the safe, built-in kind. When not in use it hangs harmlessly out of the way, and if you're worried about sartorial elegance back home you simply tuck it inside. I'm told that it's no big deal to sew on a detachable hood without loss of insulation.

Prices for down jackets are now back-breaking. A simple sleeveless

---

* After consigning to paper all this wisdom about what I thought I thought, and still think I sort of think, it surprised me to discern, after a minimum of introspection, that in practice I most often choose, from among the several down jackets I have somehow acquired, a doughty Michelin-man model that weighs almost 2¼ pounds. Deep rumination unearths only the plea that I'm probably establishing a sensible safety margin (and for one occasion on which I was certainly thankful I did so, see pages 428–35). All this adds up, I guess, to a lesson in the folly of reading books that purport to instruct you in the game, art, science, sanity, idiocy or what-have-you of backpacking.

vest often runs around $75; a good general-duty sleeved and hooded jacket, perhaps $150; a bulbous expedition-type "parka," over $250.

Because labor forms such a high proportion of the cost, do-it-your-self, ready-to-sew jacket kits by Frostline are much cheaper: some simple vests as little as $17 (Hollofil II) or $30 (down); hooded mediumweight down jackets at $77; "expedition" jacket, $107. Unfortunately, the Frostline catalogue gives no weights for finished products. For words of warning on sewing, see page 21.

For quilted pants, see page 403; for booties, page 416; and for balaclavas, page 417. I once saw, somewhere, a mildly delectable report about a down tie (¾-inch loft for three-season wear; blue, with green stuff sac).

Leg housings

To most backpackers, pants still mean things that come down to your ankles. But in recent years there seems to have been a sensible drift toward

Shorts. I have long been a wholeheartedly bigoted devotee—so much so that I often find myself wearing shorts until the temperature drops into the low thirties or the wind develops a really keen cutting edge. At least once I have arrived at a 14,000-foot peak in shorts. But I hasten to add that there are not too many places and days you can do such things in comfort. A few years ago I wore shorts up 5000 feet of snow, on a cloudless April day of icy winds, to the 12,000-foot rim of Fujiyama—and paid for my stupidity for the rest of the week every time I tried to force red, raw legs into the steaming hot baths that are the only form of ablution in Japanese inns, and which *noblesse* apparently obliges you to refrain from tempering with cold water. But I remain an unrepentant shorts man.*

I have for years preferred my shorts to be brown, or some other color that hides the dirt, and to have a built-in waistband, reasonably adjustable so that it can conform to a midriff that, like many people's, fluctuates in response to prolonged packing of heavy weights and to such other variables as food, love life and tennis. I also liked my shorts to have pockets that are strong, numerous and tailored to my fancies (preferably

---

* Shorts may at times even help reap you rich and unexpected rewards. Once, at a busy Tennessee trailhead, as I sat on a tree stump lacing my boots, preparing for a walk up onto the Appalachian Trail with a companion—a New Yorker born in Venezuela—I noticed a group of tourists eyeing me. I was wearing ordinary corduroy hiking shorts, chamois shirt and beard. One of the tourists edged toward my companion and asked, in a hushed, almost awed voice, "Is he *really* a Tennessee hillbilly?"

two hip pockets, two side pockets and two ticket pockets at the waist-band, front—one for bookmatches and the other for fire- or stove-prim-ing scraps of paper [page 255]). In theory, I maintain these preferences; in practice, as we shall see, I seem to be retreating from them.

Shorts allow much more efficient ventilation than long pants do. And I long ago reached the point at which I feel, or imagine I feel, dragged down by the restrictiveness of long pants. Fortunately, real cold seems to override the sensation. But several times I have started out on bitter mornings in longs and have realized later, after the day had warmed up, that I was making meager progress simply because I was still wearing them. A change to shorts has usually been enough to get me moving well again.

Really pesky insects might, I guess, drive even me to give up shorts for a while. See page 491.

Recently I seem to have been moving toward lighter and lighter materials for my shorts, and I guess you could say I'm now in a state of evolutionary uncertainty. For years I regarded corduroy as best. And maybe I still do. Corduroy is warm and absorbent, washes well and wears prodigiously—provided it's good quality. The quality depends on both the sturdiness of the backing and the way the cotton plush is run through it: typically, each strand of plush is attached in a simple V; but superior stuff is double-threaded in a W. Many people, I'm told, look at cords and dismiss them as "too hot"; but, provided leg openings are wide, preferably to the decency limit, I find them plenty cool. They're also tough (in the backcountry you always use unpadded chairs, often granite-rough) and wind-resistant, and provide the sort of padding I find com-forting if not essential under the hipbelts of most heavily loaded packs, at least during the first few days of a trip. Still, there's no denying that they are the devil to dry out, even from sweat.

For several years I have worn a pair of the excellent Clark's Crag-hoppers corduroy shorts (mine, 1 pound 3 ounces; but the newest 32-inch waist size, apparently 13 ounces) that used to be fairly widely sold in the U.S. but are now, due to financial fluctuations, mostly obtainable only direct from the makers: Craghoppers, Bradford Road, Birstall, Bat-ley WF17 9DH, West Yorkshire, U.K. (About $30 plus shipping. Moleskin versions, 2 ounces less, $3 more.) Lighter cord shorts now come from American makers. Royal Robbins offer some with beltless waistband and elastic side panels (10½ ounces, $29). I have tried out, with satisfaction, a pair of corduroy Blue Spruce Jammers (see Appendix II, Colorado) (my 36-inch-waist pair, 12 ounces, $32). Jammer shorts (and also longs)—now made only to order, custom-fitted—have no but-tons, zippers, hooks or snaps, only Velcro fastenings, broadly adjustable. They come in regular and women's cuts. The latest makers' figures:

shorts, 5 to 10 ounces, $27 to $32; longs, 14 to 30 ounces, $32 to $42. The corduroy is 84/16 cotton/polyester. Poplin versions (65/35 polyester/cotton) are lighter, less expensive. I have also tried, with about equal satisfaction, some tough, good-looking stretch drill shorts by Sportif (62/35/5 polyester/cotton/spandex, 13 ounces, $26). And I have recently been wearing a pair of Baggies by Patagonia that represent a sort of rugbyized version of the "in" thing for the current avant-garde backpacker: pocketed lightweight running shorts with built-in liner (liner 100 percent nylon, outers 41/38/21 nylon/polyester/cotton; size 36-inch waist, 6 ounces, $23.50). The great advantage of such synthetic-fabric shorts, beyond their lightness, is the speed with which they dry. Even after crossing a river you simply wade out the far side, shake your fanny, then mince on down the trail. At least, so "they" say. And I liked the idea of that—though applied to rain and sweat rather than rivers. I have yet to give the Baggies any really tough test, but they felt great during a week-long snowshoe trip to 10,000 feet in deep snow but brilliant sunshine, with a 58-pound pack, and again on several shorter trips, mostly with ultralight loads. So far I have had no difficulty with two areas of concern: wear and discomfort from sitting on the backcountry's unpadded chairs; and lack of padding against hipbelt bruising with a heavy pack (though this last may be almost entirely due to the excellence of my new Gregory hipbelt [page 138]). So, provisionally, I'm Baggie-sold. I'll be interested to see what kind of shorts I'm favoring a year from now.

For protecting shorts in rain, see "Colin's kilt," page 414. I have several times thought of carrying this idea a step further, following Thermodynamic writ (page 395) and Scottish precedent, and wearing a kilt of suitable material in lieu of shorts. But almost all women backpackers seem to spurn skirts, which after all amount to the same thing, so I guess hidden disadvantages lurk.

There are, of course, times when you may want to switch from shorts to longs. And catalogues occasionally feature shorts cunningly convertible to longs with zippers or studs or even Velcro strips. But I'm told they never sell.

A pair of Gore-Tex or similar breathing rainpants (page 414) or even rain chaps (same page) do a good job of converting shorts instantly to viable leg housings for semicold conditions, particularly if you also put on polypropylene longjohns.

Long pants are still probably more popular than shorts among backpackers. And even if you prefer shorts you almost always need a pair of longs in your pack for cold-day or -evening use.

Ordinary jeans still seem to outnumber every other kind: being cotton, they are very comfortable, breathe well and are reasonably light

—but are useless when wet and difficult to dry. In wet, wool is better, though rather too hot for general use. And now new options exist.

I presently find myself in a state of even greater evolutionary uncertainty with long pants than with shorts.

Except in low desert in high summer, I have for years almost always carried a pair of stout wool-blend whipcord longs, forest-ranger style (1 pound 10 ounces, around $50). I rarely seem to use them, even on cool evenings, and from time to time wonder just why I carry the extra weight; but occasionally I'm thankful I do (see, for example, page 432). A functionally similar but much cheaper alternative: Army surplus pants, often available at REI and other places (45 percent wool, 55 percent polyester, 1 pound 5 ounces, $5; all wool, $8; zippers reported questionable, but you can replace with good ones or Velcro strip). Other traditional-type alternatives: Jammers (above) and climbing knickers, tight-fitting below the knees. A California reader raves about surplus U.S. Air Force tropical-combat trousers: "lightweight Rip-stop poplin, baggy, have drawstrings at ankle [for] prickly or buggy country . . . belt loops but also adjustable straps . . . and [at least seven] capacious, flapped and buttoned pockets"; no weight given; $4 in 1976 from a Philadelphia Army-Navy surplus store. I am told that pants with instep straps are good in extreme cold. But all such long pants, made of traditional fabrics, are now being challenged by the new—and not so new—synthetics, and I find myself wanting to try at least a cross-section of them.

Long versions of Baggies (above) sound interesting. Then some people swear by full-zip nylon running longs. Such thin-shelled pants seem primarily for use in place of shorts—though many experienced backpackers maintain that, used with polypropylene longjohns and a waterproof shell, they are all-weather stuff. It seems to me that, given the new fabrics, we should by now have something eminently suitable for cool-weather use—something to replace the wool whipcords I still carry, and weighing less and drying out more quickly. Although pile is the obvious candidate, current pile pants are thick and appallingly bulky, and in wind, not to mention rain, you need an overshell of Gore-Tex or something similar—and waterproof pants suffer serious, unwaterproofing abrasion if worn too often. If I can find a fairly thin pair of pile pants I shall probably try them, though bunting, being less bulky and more wind-resistant, may work better. I'm hoping for other alternatives (see, for example, polypro pants, page 379). Meanwhile, I mostly soldier on—or ranger on—with my wool whipcords.

Pile pants, though not yet carried by many backpackers, do seem to be replacing down pants for use when sitting around in the cold or for walking in the really bitter—primarily because of their far better performance when wet. They could also, I guess, be used, as down pants are by some people, in conjunction with a down jacket, in lieu of a sleeping bag. I still carry down pants in extreme cold. Full-length side-zippers make it possible, even easy, to put them on and take them off without removing boots, and also to adjust ventilation.

See also "Windwear," page 415. And, for VB pants, page 389.

Belt—or suspenders

If possible, buy pants with built-in waistbands and avoid a belt. This is not only a question of weight; any belt is uncomfortable under the waistbelt of your pack. When you go off on packless sidetrips and, lacking a belt bag (page 101), need something around your waist to which you can attach a poncho-wrapped lunch and a cup and camera tripod and so on, simply use a few turns of nylon cord (page 518).

Broad suspenders have now achieved some vogue. They clearly overcome any packbelt pressure problem, eliminate waist constriction and increase midriff ventilation. But their real attraction may be an "in" funkiness.

Leg protectors

If you wear shorts you may find that in certain kinds of country, especially desert, you need something to stop your bare and vulnerable lower legs from being savaged by scrub, thorn brush and cacti. The best protection I've come across is a pair of Ace or Champ bandages (that I always carry anyway; see page 525), wrapped puttee fashion from boots to just below the knees.

Gaiters

See page 69.

RAINWEAR

The pitch of your concern about rainwear will vary according to the places you walk. In southeast Alaska or the Pacific Northwest or, to a lesser degree, New England, the problem looms large and almost perpetually; in desert it does no more than peek occasionally. But all of us have to worry, sometime, about how to avoid getting wet when it rains. And nowadays our rainwear can and should triple as windwear and outer-warmth shell.

Even regarded only as rainwear, no single garment is "best" for all conditions. In fact, there is probably no final and satisfactory response to prolonged heavy rain except getting the hell out of it. But when you're backpacking you can't always shelter. So you have to make the best of trying to reconcile apparent irreconcilables: the need to cocoon yourself against getting soaked by external wetness; and the sometimes equally pressing need to ventilate so that you don't get soaked in your own perspiration. That is why rainwear has long been the least efficient part of a backpacker's clothes closet, perhaps of all his equipment. Today it retains—along with boots, maybe—that dubious pennant. But in the last few years we've come a long way, babies.

The efficiency of any rain garment depends on:

1. Its fabric;
2. Its nature, design and workmanship;
3. The way you use it.

Fabrics

Backpackers and others have long sought the Holy Grail: a fabric that is waterproof but breathes. (Fabric is waterproof, says a U.S.-government ukase, when it keeps out water under a pressure of 40 pounds per square inch—though heavy wind-driven rain seems ignorant of this ruling [not to mention another that stipulates "25 pounds"]. Fabric breathes, I guess, if you can use it to cocoon yourself against rain in warm weather when walking uphill with a pack and still not get rained on by your own perspiration even if you are, like me, one of the sweaters of the half-century.)

For the last couple of decades most backpacking rainwear has been made of woven nylon (or sometimes cotton) waterproofed with an inner liquid coating—usually of polyurethane ("urethane-coated"). Such fabrics are light, inexpensive and flexible and will last several years provided they're dried after use and not overheated. New, improved, nonbreathing fabrics include Quarpel and Water Loc—said to be very waterproof, strong, light, washable and dry-cleanable. Some alternative and less common coatings offer advantages but are heavier: polyvinyl chloride (PVC; "vinyl-coated"), acrylic nitrile and neoprene. Most coated fabrics are reasonably waterproof or better, at least when new. But none breathes worth a damn.

Fine-weave cotton fabrics impregnated with various cunning concoctions tend to breathe appreciably better, but they rarely keep the rain out for very long.

Plastic (vinyl) garments have always looked good to beginners—mainly because they are cheap and seem totally waterproof. But the stuff tears at the sound of a harsh word (so much so that you almost never see zippers on it, or even drawstrings). And cold weather makes it so brittle that it may crack along folds. It therefore tends to get discarded in the backcountry—and has become a hideous source of litter. Beyond all that, it breathes like a corpse.

For many years these were the only choices open to backpackers. But dreams of the Holy Grail persisted. All through the 1960s new miracle fabrics burst regularly on the scene claiming Grailhood—and consistently biting the mud because in the field, as opposed to the lab, they leaked, failed to breathe or did both.

Then, in 1976, came Gore-Tex.

The heart of Gore-Tex is a thin, white, stretchy, microporous membrane that looks like condom material but was originally developed for surgery, to graft arteries. It's a very light, pliable form of Teflon—a petrochemical polymer called polytetrafluorethylene or PTFE. (Gore-Tex and the new, similar Klimate are often known collectively as PTFE laminates.) This membrane has, say its makers, 9 billion pores per square inch, each of them "20,000 times smaller than a drop of water (which makes it waterproof) but 700 times larger than a molecule of water vapor —allowing the material to 'breathe.' " (Waterproof rating: around 100 pounds per square inch.) Gore-Tex consists of this membrane or film bonded to one or two layers of protective fabric. Some Gore-Tex rainwear is made of a two-layer laminate: the PTFE film and an outer fabric of nylon taffeta or Taslan. Normally, it is then used with a nylon lining to protect the membrane. Two-layer laminates are supple and drape well, and the lining gives the garment-maker something to which he can attach accessories—storm skirts (page 409), drawstrings and inside pockets—without external, potentially leaky seams. Three-layer laminates incorporate an inner layer of nylon tricot and are normally used without linings. In both two- and three-layer laminates the outer fabric can run from 1.1-ounce nylon taffeta to 3-ounce Taslan. The lighter fabrics save ounces and are cooler (or less warm) but abrade more easily. Heavy Taslan, though it may make the fabric stiff and "boardy," wears better and is warmer (or hotter).

Gore-Tex is windproof as well as waterproof and, as we shall see (page 415), this greatly extends its usefulness.

When it appeared, Gore-Tex was duly proclaimed the Holy Grail. But reports soon began to trickle, then flood, in of leakage through the fabric, not just seams. What had happened, it eventually emerged, was that Gore-Tex's surface readily became contaminated in such a way that water droplets in contact with it lost their surface tension and their round, beady shape and broke down into smaller particles that could pass through the membrane's pores. The culprit might be poor laundering or spilled food or plain, earthy dirt; but the most common, almost impossible to avoid, was ordinary human body oils.

W. L. Gore, the makers, hurried back to their lab drawing board and in 1978 marketed a "second-generation" Gore-Tex that they claimed was "incapable of being contaminated" and therefore remained waterproof yet still breathed like the earlier versions. Some voices claim that the new Gore-Tex breathes less well than the old. And a few still question its noncontaminability. (One trip leader advises his charges against Gore-Tex for trips over fourteen days because, he says, the stuff is likely to leak by the end of that period. But he mostly leads teenagers, who rarely look after their clothing well—and Gore-Tex demands at least reasonable care. He may also, like many others, still be smarting from first-generation failures.) But it now seems safe—well, almost safe—to say that these are just voices in the metaphorical wilderness. The jury on second-generation Gore-Tex is in: it may not be quite the Holy Grail but it's the holiest we've got so far and, hell, this is an imperfect world. Retailers certainly report that returns have dropped off to a trickle or even very occasional drops. Gore claim that there are "virtually no returns at all." And they have "developed a policy of replacing any first-generation jackets with the . . . second-generation product."

The current consensus seems to be that you must take care of your Gore-Tex garments. Keep them clean. Avoid hot driers. And eschew dry-cleaning, which may transmute your Holy Grail into base and worthless metal. Gore's new washing instructions are certainly simple: "Machine wash in powder detergent. Drip or tumble dry. No other treatments are ever necessary and contamination will not be a problem." (*Later:* REI now offer a special, biodegradable "Gore-Tex Soap"—Revive —said to clean the stuff without affecting its properties or leaving a residue [4-fluid-ounce bottle, $3.25].)

For a time Gore-Tex garments suffered, as does a lot of rainwear, from seam leakage. Applying the necessary two coats of seam sealant was too labor-expensive a task to be done in the factory, and users often evaded or botched it. Then Gore came up with a machine for garment-makers that welds a ⅞-inch-wide tape onto sewn seams with hot air and pressure. The tape—itself a laminate of Gore-Tex film between tricot knit fabric and a hot melt adhesive—seems to do the job. But the method of application leaves a central channel that acts as a gutter down which small amounts of water wick or dribble. That doesn't matter provided the tape continues unbroken down to the hem of the garment. But it doesn't always do so. It may end at the waist, for example— because tape tends to pucker the Teflon waistband. (Gore maintain that the tape-channel problem has now been overcome.)

Factory-sealed garments, now distinguished by gold hang-tags, are certainly a marked improvement. The seam-sealing machines are expensive, though, and some small makers cannot afford them. But I hear whispers of a new and simpler sealing method. Meanwhile, don't forget that even factory seam-sealing, though good, is not perfect. The machines need good drivers. So check all tapes for wrinkles or imperfectly sealed edges. Factory seam-sealing appreciably increases costs, so to economize you can buy unsealed garments and double-coat all seams by hand with Gore's Steamstuff (2-ounce tube, $3). (Note that all seams, in any fabric, are best hand-sealed from the outside, to prevent wicking through the stitches [it seems that even "self-sealing thread" doesn't really self-seal, especially in Gore-Tex]. As with sleeping bags [page 346], the operation makes a garment look as if snails have crawled all over it. And no hand-sealing seems as effective as the factory job with tape.)

Gore-Tex, remember, is not perfect. The means by which it achieves breathability demand that outgoing moisture be in vapor form: once it condenses it can no more pass out than rain can come in. So as the fabric is moved farther away from your warm skin you suffer a logarithmic loss of breathability. Gore-Tex clothing should therefore hug you reasonably closely. (Note that the theoretical logarithmic loss in breathability raises questions about Gore-Tex tents—except form-fitting bivvies—and even Gore-Tex-shelled sleeping bags.) In addition, Gore-Tex—like virtually all "waterproof" fabrics except the heaviest yachting stuff, which is hardly practical for backpacking—may still plain leak in the very heaviest rain, especially if you are bent over and the fabric is stretched across your shoulders. Ditto if you push through wet snow. But there's no doubt about its popularity. Although it remains hideously expensive—two or even three times as much as nonbreathable, urethane-coated fabrics—some retailers find it now outsells the latter three to one.

The high price reflects not only expensive oil-based raw materials and involved production methods but also long years of R&D and heavy launching advertising. But competitors may force the price down. Another PTFE laminate, Klimate, has been on the market for some time, sort of: Gore repeatedly hit its makers with patent-infringement suits that repulsed the challenge; but in late 1982 a court found in favor of Klimate, and I guess they may soon be goring Gore.

Other competitors do not offer serious backpacking challenges. For Evolution II, see page 303, footnote. Storm Shed—a 65/35 cotton/polyester blend, silicon-impregnated and with a thin inner coating—is water-repellent, but its makers carefully avoid calling it waterproof (it does not meet U.S. requirements). No Sweat—formerly Bukflex—is a polyurethane film bonded to a knit polyester liner that no longer seems to challenge Gore-Tex seriously. The new, Japanese-made Entrant, another polyurethane-coated fabric, remains unproven.

A totally different approach by Patagonia produced foamback rain-gear: waterproofed fabric with a very thin foam lining that collected your sweat and let it drain harmlessly down and away. To work properly it had, unlike Gore-Tex, to stand well clear of your body, and Patagonia used it in a sleeved and hooded cape that I found eminently satisfactory one long day's fly fishing in Alaska drizzle, and again during pick-and-shovel work in Pacific Coast mountains: I detected no condensation. But worn under a heavy pack, with waistbelt and yoke exerting pressure, results might not be so good, especially during hard hiking. In any case, Patagonia have now halted production—perhaps because Gore-Tex has swept the market.

The future? A knowledgeable insider murmurs something about "waterproof materials by construction rather than by coating or lamination." We shall see.

Design and workmanship in raingear

Design features can be as important as the fabric.

Seams are the Achilles' heel of most rainwear. So the fewer seams, the better, and those that are essential should if possible (which it often isn't) avoid such vulnerable, rain-pelted places as shoulders and upper back. For seam-sealing Gore-Tex, see page 406. The hand-sealing wisdom on that page applies to all fabrics.

Zippers also leak. Check and if necessary hand-seal all attendant seams. Full-length parka zippers (page 410) should have storm flaps. Some makers maintain that they're more likely to work if the flaps are secured by Velcro tape rather than snaps. But an interesting alternative that has passed all tests to date appears in my current Gore-Tex parka (page 411): the zipper folds around to form a flap and is protected from heavy rain when a line of snaps, with the male components two inches from the zipper, is closed.

The short neck zip on anoraks (page 410) is sometimes backed by a V-shaped piece of fabric that allows some neck ventilation but looks like a great drip-catcher and I'm told is.

A two-way zip on a jacket may occasionally make ventilation easier, but I doubt that it's worth the drawbacks (page 398). Nylon zippers jam less in icy weather than metal ones.

For pit zips, see parkas (page 410).

Hoods. To me, a hoodless rain garment is an idiocy. Yet some people prefer big hats and high collars. Certainly, hoods can pose problems. Because it seems impossible to make them seamless, they always have leak potential. They also tend to make ventilation difficult. So in light, warm rain without wind it may indeed be better to leave the hood down and wear a hat. But in wind-driven rain a hood is to my mind the only decent protection. As wind-protector and warmth-provider for the most vital part of your body (page 347), nothing compares with it. It should, of course, be big enough for you to wear at least one and maybe two balaclavas underneath. And it must be designed to pull flush around your face and so keep rain from driving in and dripping down your neck. A good system is an internal storm flap, pulled tight by the drawstring: the best allow you to pull the collar in tight under your chin, so that rain does not drip down your neck, or alternatively to leave it standing tall, up to your nose, as protection against wind. A small, flexible peak also helps shed rain. The more protection you get, though, the less vision you're likely to have. On balance, give me the protection. A wide field of view, though certainly pleasing, is not vital in backpacking, the way it is in cycling.

Sleeves in rainwear must be full-cut (raglan type) for free arm movement and longer than in other garments, so that they will not slide up when you extend your arms. The extra length also means that most of the time you can keep your hands protected inside them. Although you must be able to close off the wrists in cold or driving rain you must also be able to ventilate, and the best answer seems to be a simple Velcro-secured strap.

Hems, drawstrings and storm skirts. Rainwear should always be cut fairly long, because even the best-designed models will pull up a little if you raise your arms. And whether you like it or not, a certain amount of rain is going to get in under the hem. A drawstring there helps, especially in keeping you warm (when that is what you want). More common, perhaps, is a drawstring at the waist, to allow more freedom of movement. A viable variation that reduces seam and wear difficulties at that crucial circumference is a storm skirt—a ring of fabric, usually nylon, elastic-hemmed and closable with snaps. When you're not wearing a pack—the belt of which does the job, anyway—it insulates your upper body and keeps snow out yet lets the garment stand clear.

Pockets on rainwear are rarely waterproof. And they add not only weight and cost but also more seams and potential leaks. Yet although you often can't get your hands into them when you're wearing a pack, they're undeniably useful at times—and people seem to demand them. Pockets with Velcro-secured flaps are probably best. Long jackets with waist-level drawstrings or storm skirts may have low side-entry pockets without seams sewn through to the outside: such water as may possibly breach even a baffled opening will mingle more or less harmlessly (provided you don't expect to keep the contents dry) with that inevitable quotient coming up from the hem.

Kinds of rainwear

Remember in choosing any rain garment that it must be big enough to fit with something to spare over the thickest clothing you ever expect to wear with it. Restrictive rainwear is not only uncomfortable: it's likely to increase condensation.

The most obvious torso housing is some kind of *jacket*. It permits free movement yet protects you fully. And because fabric is kept to a minimum it's likely to be light. Old-style, coated-fabric jackets were a snare: you tended to soak in sweat. But Gore-Tex et al. have changed that.

There are two kinds of jacket: parkas and anoraks. "Parka" is an Aleutian word originally meaning "a fur jacket or heavy, long woolen shirt, often lined with pile or fleece, with attached hood." "Anorak" is the Greenland Eskimo name for a similar hooded garment, though it may be made of leather or cloth. But time has worked on language. Today a parka is a hooded jacket of almost any material with a full-length opening, usually zippered, down the front. An anorak is a similar garment without a front opening other than a short neck zipper. This zipper makes it possible to put an anorak on and take it off and also provides some ventilation. But although the garment's simple barrel structure makes it highly efficient as protection against both wind and rain, ventilation can be a problem. And if you've ever stood on a mountain ridge in a howling gale and tried to battle your way up into an anorak, especially one a shade small for you, or if you've taken a soaking-wet one off in order to shed a layer of clothing and then tried to reinject yourself without irrigating everything, you'll understand why parkas are more popular.

The parka's full-length front zipper, no matter how well protected against rain (page 408), is always a potential leak line. But it makes ventilation adjustment much easier. And putting on and taking off, even in rain, are relatively painless. On balance, I vote for parkas every time.

And now, with the difference between anoraks and parkas understood, we can consider both garments together, simply as jackets.

Urethane-coated and other highly waterproof but nonbreathing jackets are still available, but if you do much walking in them in any but very cold weather you're likely to wallow in sweat. So most jackets are now made of Gore-Tex or one of the other breathable fabrics.

The question of whether such jackets should have underarm zippers (pit zips) provides one of today's minor backpacking battlegrounds. "If the stuff breathes, why?" says one camp. "The wretched things always leak, too." The opposition replies: "Under certain conditions you need to vent, and the armpits are the place to do it. With VB clothing, pit zips are a 'must' anyway" (page 388). Limited but growing experience leads me to agree with those who say that the "small loss of sleeve integrity" that occurs in heavy rain (I can vouch for such leakage) is worth the gain in temperature flexibility—certainly with VBs and maybe without. Note that flaps may help reduce the leakage. And also that, with the three-layer system, polypro underwear and pile jacket mean that rain invading down a sleeve matters very little: it is quickly wicked out and expelled. But in deciding pro or con pit zips you must strike your own balance. Make sure, though, that if you vote "yes" the pit zips extend only a short way down your torso: you'll be much happier sacrificing your arms to the rain than your ribs.

Current backpacking rainjackets, like other garments, tend to be overbuilt. But lighter jackets, designed for backpackers—more sparingly constructed, often with lighter laminated fabrics—are now appearing. Sierra West make a good series. Remember, though, that lighter fabrics mean some loss in warmth and appreciable loss in abrasion resistance.

Many Gore-Tex jackets are now appearing with some inner insulant such as down, Quallofil, Thinsulate or Kodalite. They're often fine for general town winter use. But they're not really versatile enough for backpacking: you can't ring the changes necessary for a wide range of weather and activity.

Gore-Tex and other rainjackets now throng the mountain shops as thick as Fourth of July backpackers in Yosemite. Choose carefully among them, examining features you think important. My present jacket is an unlined, three-layer parka by Sierra Designs that comes down to within 5 inches of my knees. A pair of side-entry pockets, just above the hem, have no seams sewn through to the outside; fold-back flaps screen the entries. The internal, nylon-fabric storm skirt at the waist is elastic-hemmed and closes with a single snap. The full-length zipper is two-way (dammit) and folds over for protection (page 408). The sleeves are full-cut and extra long, with Velcro closure straps. The light, unprotected pit zips extend 10 inches down the arm but only 4½ inches down the torso. The hood has a small peak and a toggle-controlled drawstring that runs through a small internal storm flap and can pull the collar tight under my chin in rain or leave it standing tall in wind. The jacket did me proud on its first real test (page 428) and has continued to do so (page 435, for example). This model weighs 1 pound 4 ounces and costs $135 —about the current average for high-quality jackets. (Frostline have a kit at $80.)

Ponchos remain popular and offer advantages, especially on trips with low rain risk.

A poncho is a waterproof sheet, 4 feet by 7 feet or a little bigger, with a head hole and hood in the middle. In good backpacking ponchos the hole is placed somewhat off center and the longer rear section covers your pack. At least, that's the theory; but if a wind is blowing don't expect too much overlap from theory into practice. Most hoods can be tightened flush around your face with a drawstring, but the rest of the sheet hangs down like a shroud and in a high wind attains a will of its own—though snap fasteners on the edges allow you to make rudimentary sleeves that may help keep the shroud from flapping too wildly. Some heavier models have a drawstring at the waist that not only cuts down the flappage but also holds in warmth—too efficiently on occasion. A length of nylon cord around your waist will do the job almost as well, though its rubbing may damage the waterproofing.

Ponchos are simple and therefore relatively light and inexpensive. They are also, except for the hood, seamless. And they are the only garments you can wear over your pack. This means you always achieve good ventilation (often, far too much) and so avoid the worst condensation problems. They're therefore still made of coated fabrics. (Note that, worn under or without a pack, ponchos can very definitely cause condensation.)

Ponchos are clearly not ultra-efficient rain-defeating devices. Some experienced backpackers rate them tormenting futilities. But they give you a certain leeway. You can wrap yourself up reasonably well against most rain, provided it doesn't last all day—and accept that you'll sweat a bit. Or you can leave matters loose and allow a little rain in but know that at least your body will get some air. A poncho is also one of the most versatile garments around. Those snap fasteners along its edges help, and so do the grommets sometimes put in at each corner. (I always have at least one other grommet—and probably three or four—inserted along each long side; the short sides rarely have a wide enough hem to take even a small grommet.) With these simple fittings, a poncho can be much more than a waterproof garment. It can be a windbreaker—especially useful when a thin down jacket is the only warm garment you have with you. As we have seen (pages 323–8), the grommets allow you to turn it into a wild assortment of roofs and side walls and cocoons that will ward off snow, rain, wind or sun. With two ponchos snapped together by their fasteners you can build a big ridge-backed shelter. Under certain conditions (pages 326 and 330), you may be forced to use your poncho as a groundsheet; but in such cases do not expect it to remain waterproof for long. On packless sidetrips or on short walks from home or car, a bundled poncho secured around your waist with nylon cord makes a useful belt bag (page 101) for lunch and oddments, especially convenient if there is danger of rain. Cunningly molded to the landscape, it can form a washbasin (page 426). Finally, it will help waterproof your pack contents during a river crossing (page 532) or make a floating bundle of your clothes and other necessaries if you're crossing without a pack (that is, will act in lieu of a white plastic sheet, page 531).

Poncho materials include heavy-duty rubberized fabrics, urethane-coated nylon and other synthetic fabrics, and thin plastic (vinyl). Rubberized fabrics are very strong but too heavy for most modern backpackers. Urethane-coated woven-nylon fabrics are very light and are becoming progressively stronger and closer to waterproof, though not all of them stay waterproof for long. Plastic ponchos are hot and eminently tearable but have short-term, shallow-pocket uses—and a horrifying litter potential.

Weights run from around 2½ pounds for a rubberized poncho down to as little as 10 ounces for a nylon or plastic one. A tough, coated-nylon poncho may cost as much as $35, though a less fancy and less durable one may run only $18. The plastic horrors sell, unfortunately, for as little as $3.

Cagoules are full-cut, knee-length, sleeved capes with hoods. (The word is French and originally meant "a monk's cloak" or "penitent's cowl.")

Cagoules (around 19 ounces; $70) are made primarily for climbers, who often have to make emergency bivouacs: you can if necessary draw your knees up inside the long "skirt" and seal yourself off by pulling tight on a drawstring that runs around the hem. If you carry a companion footsack-and-carrying-bag of the same urethane-coated nylon fabric you are in even better shape. See page 362 for ruminations on the practicality of cagoules as bivouacs for backpackers.

As day garments, cagoules are good at keeping rain out, heat and sweat in.

Capes. For an interesting foamback model, currently not being made, see page 408.

For protecting your legs,

Rainpants are now a thoroughly viable proposition—because Gore-Tex makes them breathable. I have a pair in the L.I.T.E. series by Sierra West, with 14-inch zippers at the cuffs so that you can pull them on over lightweight boots (9 ounces, $85). Such lightweight pants must be babied a bit, of course. They won't stand up—or, rather, sit down—to many granite boulders or even other, less abrasive, chairs. One man I know who has a pair wears Patagonia Baggie shorts (page 401) over them. Taslan- rather than taffeta-covered Gore-Tex may help—at a price in ounces and dollars. Somewhat heavier Gore-Tex pants are now widely available, up to about 1 pound and down to $60.

Rainpants should be reasonably full-length. But provided you carry gaiters (page 69) they need not reach down, clumsily, over your boot tops.

You can also get—and probably get pretty damned sweat-soaked in —urethane-coated nylon pants. A supercoated, zippered pair by REI that "resists water pressure up to 120 pounds": 10 ounces, $35. Helly-Hansen make Taslan lightweights: 6¾ ounces, $30.

Overalls or bibs are rainpants that extend up to the chest and midback and have built-in "suspenders" to hold them up. They clearly protect you better than anything else—but if you hike far in them, except in extreme cold, they're likely to cook and sweat-soak you. So very few backpackers use them. REI sometimes offer a lightweight model at 1 pound 2 ounces, $96.

Rain chaps, because they cover legs but not butt and environs, permit better ventilation than pants and are lighter and cheaper (typical urethane-coated 6-ounce pair, $15; yet a Frostline kit, for some reason, $16). Although some weigh only 4 ounces, so light a pair may not withstand much abrasion. Heavier, tougher models exist too.

Chaps are definitely worth considering if your rainshell is long enough to protect your thighs and you fear prolonged rain or expect to slog for hours through sodden scrub (for a specific case, see page 436).

You may, especially if you wear shorts, like to replace or augment rain chaps with a device that has been called

Colin's kilt—a.k.a. Everyman's Wonderful Waterproof Trash-bag Skirt (4 ounces, $.50). To make it you take a plastic trash bag, preferably 4-mil, and with a knife convert it to the subspecies profundissimus (i.e., bottomless). Then you step into the tube and tuck it inside your shorts top or secure it around your waist with nylon cord or what pleases you. If your rainshell is even halfway adequate the kilt will extend its protection to the bottom of your shorts. If it's not raining but you're walking through wet brush or long grass you probably won't need the shell, and the kilt is a gem: that's what I originally devised it for. You hold the kilt in place with the pack's hipbelt and raise or lower your hemline according to your warmth requirements, length of shorts, heaviness of rain, windiness of wind and surliness of underbrush. The kilt can be invaluable when used with chaps if windblown rain threatens to breach an incipient gap between chaps and shell or poncho. For specific occasions on which I have used the kilt, see pages 429, 435 and 436.

If you carry trash bags for other uses (page 521) you can, of course, create a kilt instanter and anywhere. But evolution may sweep us beyond trash bags. If some enterprising body wants to design a stronger and less tearable kilt of coated nylon or something . . . well, I've not yet patented my brainchild.

Umbrellas. You may occasionally see pictures of—or even meet—backpackers carrying umbrellas. Umbrellas' huge advantage is that they banish all the overheating problems. And they can, if there's not too much wind, protect your pack as well as you. But because they're almost useless, going on a menace, in high winds or middling brush or branches you more or less have to carry some more traditional rainwear as well, and that rather wipes the shine off them.

WINDWEAR

The advent of Gore-Tex rainjackets means that traditional anoraks and parkas—no more than mildly water-resistant, and primarily used as windbreakers—have become virtually obsolete. Now you need carry only one Gore-Tex garment for both rain and wind protection—and warmth as well. But there are, I guess, certain dry conditions under which the older-type, non-waterproof jackets might still prove useful. And in cool, breezy weather, if you expect to do some climbing or even scrambling, it might be worth considering ultralight jackets and perhaps pants that allow almost total freedom, breathe well, afford some protection against light rain and, although not 100 percent windproof, block you off pretty well. REI offer a slip-on jacket made of Triblend—26 percent cotton, 48 percent polyester, 26 percent nylon—at 8 ounces, $30. Royal Robbins make a similar jacket with matching pants ($36 and $50). I've tried the pants (8½ ounces), and see them as useful and abrasion-resistant alternatives to Gore-Tex versions under certain dryish, windy conditions.

EXTREMITIES AND ANCILLARIES

Gloves

Some hardy souls lighten their loads by going without gloves, even in spring and fall. But except in really warm weather I always take along a pair of light woolen gloves or mitts (about 2 ounces, $4). Mitts—in which all four fingers cohabit and only the thumb lives alone—are warmer than equivalent gloves but leave you fumble-fisted for any but the simplest tasks. A best-of-both-worlds compromise: Multi-mitts by Royal Robbins—fingerless wool gloves inside wool mitts, with a slot in the mitts, near the wrist, so that you can curl your gloved hand into a fist, slip it out through the slot, Velcro the mitt back onto your wrist and do intricate tasks in semi-comfort (5 ounces, $23). Polypropylene gloves, though they keep your hands warm even when wet and also dry out faster than wool, are otherwise no warmer, apparently wear less well and certainly cost three times as much ($13).

For rather colder weather I have a pair of pile-lined mitts with taffeta shell (Polar Mitts by Helly-Hansen, 4 ounces, $14). They seem excellent—though I've yet to get them wet.

Standard leather or canvas/leather work gloves may be worth taking for such heavy chores as digging or wood-gathering. They're also useful in mild winds and cold. I rarely carry them, but some backpackers always do—for fire-lighting, cooking and protection against sunburn and insects.

For really severe cold, down mitts—useless when wet—have been pretty much replaced by pile versions. And Gore-Tex shells are beginning to appear on cold-weather mitts and gloves. The verdict is not yet in on whether the increased breathability is worth the cost and intricacy.

No matter what cold-weather gloves you choose you will in bitter cold probably need inners—to afford some protection when you must take off the outer gloves for a task that demands dexterity, and also to wick moisture away. Polypropylene now seems the best bet on the second count, and reasonably adequate on the first. For brutal cold, when touching metal can be horrendous and even dangerous, there are "silver liners" (the Kombi XR 30 liner, 41.4 percent polypropylene, with metallic, "space age thread" interwoven "to reflect body heat"; 1½ ounces, $4).

Plastic bags as makeshift VB liners are said to work.

Booties

I have for years used down booties. Once they kept my feet totally warm—perhaps even a shade hot—in a Slimline bag, unprotected, at

11° F. (page 358). On Kilimanjaro, when the temperature hardly fell below freezing but murkily miserable weather and the thin air at 16,000 feet made it seem colder, they kept my feet comfortable in a similar lightweight bag. Such booties—with light nylon shell and thick waterproof nylon sole padded with ¼-inch Ensolite—are also excellent for brief excursions from your tent out into the snow (page 314), provided the snow is cold and dry. Many makes and models (average: 8 ounces; $37).

As far as I know, every foam-soled down bootie comes equipped with a resident little devil whose sole aim in life is to slide the foam off to one side of your foot, where it becomes comprehensively useless. Some models incorporate elastic inserts at the heels, intended to exorcise these devils. Intended.

Because down booties are very hard to keep dry, PolarGuard-filled versions are tending to replace them.

The even newer pile booties ought to be better still. But they don't look warm and apparently don't sell—perhaps in part because they have not yet appeared with foam soles. Wait.

Electric socks, yet,

are presumably for the winter hiker who has everything, including chronically cold feet. Each sock—a blend of wool, acrylic and nylon—is warmed by a D-size battery (alkaline E95 recommended) fastened to the calf band (Lectra-Sox by Timely Products Corp., 210 Eliot Street, P.O. Box C, Fairfield, CT 06430; 1 pound, $18).

Stuff sacks

are worth considering for many clothing items, from down jackets to booties. I use them, mostly. For smaller garments, ordinary plastic bags sometimes suffice. Sierra West now make lightweight nylon stuff sacks in three sizes, and I find my large size (8 by 14 inches; 1 ounce; $8) good for use with New Wave gear. Occasionally you see nylon net bags, very light, also said to be useful for drying things in sun or wind. For more on stuff sacks, and the small-sack fallacy, see pages 363–4.

Hoods and balaclava helmets

Never underestimate the importance of covering your head in cold weather. The head is the body's radiator (see page 347). Hence the old adage, "If you want to keep your feet warm, put your hat on."

Because time has reduced my natural head covering to a joke, I always carry at least one balaclava, for use at night. In any kind of cold I carry three: a silk one for nontickling wear next to the skin ($1\frac{1}{2}$ ounces, $9); an Orlon one for general use, particularly at night ($2\frac{1}{2}$ ounces, $7); and, recently, a pile hood or balaclava that I've used on only one trip but am already halfway in love with. This hood, by Patagonia, extends down onto the shoulders and has a drawstring for snugging around the face (one size fits all, $3\frac{1}{2}$ ounces, $14.50). You can also roll it up to make a hat. Being pile, it demands a shell to ward off wind. But it absorbs only 2 percent of its weight in water, compared with wool's 50 percent. For notes on it in action in miserable conditions, when it proved itself as a heat regulator, see, once again, pages 435 and 436.

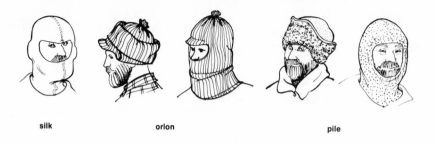

silk   orlon   pile

Some balaclavas come with small peaks to help shed rain. Adventure 16 make a pile "Bomber Hat" with Gore-Tex shell and semistiff brim ($3\frac{1}{2}$ ounces; $17.50).

Wool balaclavas (around 4 ounces; $7.50) are much more popular than Orlon ones, but some people find that both wool and Orlon tickle and, like me, they wear silk underneath. Research among several experienced backpackers has elicited three distinct positions on the question of the relative value of wool and Orlon when wet: Orlon is not good when wet; it is better than wool; there's precious little difference. I am, uh, inclined to agree.

Ultralight polypropylene balaclavas (1 ounce; $11) have now appeared, and may challenge silk. They come in mediumweight too. Both, particularly in spun as opposed to extruded fabric, are said to be non-itchy. And of course they wick like crazy. A model by Patagonia has stretch tape around the eyes so that when you wear it in the face-mask mode your breath does not escape upward and fog goggles or glasses.

Face masks

These entrancing, horrifying protectors against blood-curdling wind come in down (unknown ounces, $15), nylon-lined Gore-Tex (also unknown ounces, $7.75), leather (2 ounces, $13.75), and even plastic (in which, I'm told, you look like an Imperial Storm Trooper from *Star Wars*). Essentially for skiers, whose motion generates the wind, masks may very occasionally be necessary or at least comforting for backpackers, but they're more popular among bank robbers.

Scarves

The human neck is no doubt necessary, but it is a hell of a thing to keep warm. And it creates a weak point in almost any clothing system. Even in warm weather I always carry a small (2-ounce) wool or Orlon scarf to block off the escape of precious warm air from the main reservoir that clothing has created around my body. Unless you have tried it you will have difficulty believing how much difference this small detail can make, especially when your clothing is on the light side. In particular, a string vest unsupported by a scarf is only half-effective.

Sport or jog bras

See page 393.

"Keep your loved ones warm"

Now offered: down cups for breasts and for genitals.

Swimsuits

When there's a chance of a swim you may, unless you're reasonably sure of privacy, like to take along a thin nylon swimsuit. On one trip that involved repeated river crossings with my pack (page 535) in rough water and hot weather, I wore mine every time, so that in the unlikely event of being separated from the pack I would at least have some protection from the sun (2½ ounces, around $6; Ocean Speed by Ocean Pool Supply Company, 17 Stepar Place, Huntington Station, NY 11746).

If you wear Baggies or other running-type shorts (page 401) they can double as swimsuit. So can underpants.

Bandannas

A large cotton bandanna or handkerchief, preferably bright-colored and therefore not easily lost, is your wardrobe's maid-of-all-work. It performs as potholder, napkin, dishcloth, washcloth, towel, emergency headgear, wet inside-the-hat cooling pad in hot weather, Lawrence-of-

Arabia neck protector (especially cooling if damp), hand pad for snow-peg-as-trowel (page 539), snooze mask and even fig leaf (page 428).

Traditional "cowboy kerchief" cotton bandannas or curlicue-pattern equivalents weigh about 2 ounces and come in 24-inch ($1.50) and 27-inch ($2) squares. And you can now "rub your nose in knowledge" with Trailhead bandannas (same size and weight) in assorted colors and imprinted with nose-encyclopedias concerning butterflies, clouds, shells, knots, whales, animal tracks, birds of prey and shore birds; there's even a "Trailhead game." But the butterflies et al. are not free: $4.25 each. Variations: a map of Yosemite and a backgammon board.

Wash bandannas frequently. They soon dry if tied on pack.

Hats

Hikers wear about as many different kinds of headgear as you'll see in a fully fashioned Easter parade. But the valid practical criteria are lightness, protection afforded from heat, ventilation quotient and ability to stand up to brutal treatment. (I pay little attention to rain resistance: I rely on parka or poncho hood. But not everyone agrees. See page 408.) Beyond such practical matters, suit your fancy—though should you be thin on top but still able to enjoy the finer things of life it is desirable that the hat be of such a nature that if it becomes dislodged during totally engrossing delights under a hot, hot desert sun it is easy, without any interruption at all, for her to reach up, if she really loves you, and replace it.

On occasion, you must be able to arrange things so that the hat will stay on your head in a half-hurricane. The only way you can do so is with a chin strap. If the hat you like doesn't have one (and it probably won't) all you have to do is punch a hole in the brim on either side, close to the crown, then grommet the holes or have a shoemaker do the job, and thread through the grommets a suitable length of braided nylon cord. (Red cord dirties less objectionably than white and also helps color photography.) When not in use the chin strap goes up into the crown: you soon get used to flicking it up without thought as you put the hat on. Or, sometimes, you can tuck it into the hatband.

Some people like caps with visors—which certainly have some worth in snow. And cycling caps are light and cool, and work in fair weather.

Down the years I have, for no clearly discernible reason, run through a mild fashion parade of hats, from felt Half Stetsons through minifacsimiles to an ordinary U.S. Army surplus fatigue hat. All did their job well. But they took a continuous beating: they not only got soaked and trampled on but spent long hours stuffed inside the pack or slung by their chin straps from the packframe or clipped onto the belt-clip-on-cord-from-top-of-packframe that was primarily there for my camera (page 473). Each lasted several years but eventually became so limp or frayed, especially around the crown, that finally I was forced to pension it off. I can never bring myself to throw such old friends away, and several of them lie on a shelf in my gear closet. Every now and again my eye lights on them and my face up.

Although I'm aware that light-colored hats reflect the heat better I note that all mine have been brown or gray or blue—no doubt because I liked the look of them and because I knew they wouldn't show the dirt. About the only other feature they've shared is a crown high enough to leave air space between bald pate and murderous sunshine. For more on that, see page 423.

Recently I've fined down to a simple, fashion-free hat by Sportif that stands up clear of my dome and is mildly brimmed, tough, eminently packable, cool and ultralight (2½ ounces, $6).

And that's how things go in backpack hatting: it's a strictly free-lance field, and you buy what and where you want. But outdoor catalogues brim with suggestions—felt and now Gore-Tex crushers, crew hats and assorted nondescripts. Early Winters have offered some beauties —the Panama Crusher, "made of real Ecuadorian grasses . . . one size only . . . but easily shrunk or stretched to fit . . . and folds for storage in a pocket or purse" (2 ounces, $12.50); Hatfield Gore-Tex peaked caps ("the real McCoy," four colors; 2 ounces, $7.45); and, for mosquito relief, a "genuine French Foreign Legion Jungle Hat," complete with khaki crown, elastic headband and a cotton veil with neck drawstrings and "metal forms" to hold it clear of your face (3½ ounces, $3.95). (Sierra West have a net that fits over any hat and can be worn at night in the sleeping bag [1 ounce, $1.50].)

Many readers have written recommending their favorite hats with passion, eloquence and illustrations. Among them, Suede Hiking Hat ("necessary to lay it in front of a buffalo stampede to make it wearable, but then it can't be beat") and a Portuguese army cap ("purchased in Mozambique . . . rather nifty . . . but do not fail to waterproof these cotton hats with Scotchgard and have them shrink on you every time it rains hard. . . . The neck flap offers good insect and thorn protection (such as needed when you canoe through rose bushes)."

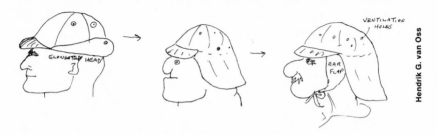

A long-peaked version of this gem now appears under the name Up-Downer in several catalogues, including REI and EMS (3 ounces, $7).

One reader drew my attention to a hat described in *Inventions Necessity Was Not the Mother Of,* by S. V. Jones (Quadrangle/New York Times Book Company, 1973, $6.95, but now out of print) and invented by Harold W. Dahly of Chicago. Mr. Dahly's 1967 patent (#3,353,191) "describes a solar cell that generates current to run the motor. To regulate the speed of the fan or shut it off entirely, a cover can be swung over the cell. Air is admitted through holes in the side of the crown and is circulated for the comfort of the wearer. "It is well known," says Mr. Dahly, "that cooling the top of the head will have a cooling effect on the entire person."

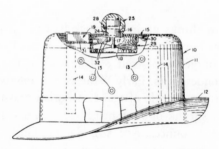

Another reader eulogizes the ultimate in nonhats: the shaved head ("never overheated . . . there is something sinfully fantastic about sitting on a mountain with the air literally whistling around your ears: great, great feeling").

Shaved head or no, the way you wear the crown of your hat in hot weather can be critical. From force of city habit we tend to indent the top "stylishly." But doing so in hot weather radically reduces the vital air-insulation barrier between the top of your head and the sun's rays. The thing to do is to push the crown out to its rounded maximum.

A rounded crown hardly helps you to look intelligent, but if appearance counts enough to force you to stay with a dented crown you had better confine your walking to the financial district.

Some sober and reliable people classify as pure myth the tradition that you need a hat in hot, sunny weather. But I know that if I go without a hat in any kind of hot sun I very soon feel dizzy. Or, at the least, I imagine I feel dizzy—and the two states are indistinguishable. So to me, in summer desert, a hat is no joking matter.

On my California walk, when I rested for a day at the southern end of Death Valley, the temperature was 105° F. in the extremely rare shade. During the morning of that day I climbed up into some stark hills to photograph the gray trough that was the valley—the trough I would within twenty-four hours be walking through. All morning a strong west wind had been blowing. As I climbed, the wind increased. But the heat lost none of its intensity. By the time I reached the first summit ridge, the wind had risen to a half-gale. On the ridge I stopped to take a photograph, and used my hat to shield the camera lens from the sun. Afterward, in a careless moment, I forgot to slip the chin strap back under my chin. Before I could lift a hand, the wind had snatched the hat away and sent it soaring upward.

Suddenly the sun was battering down on my head like a bludgeon.

I cannot have stood there looking at the flying hat for more than two or three seconds. But I do not think I shall ever forget my feeling of helplessness as the twirling brown shape grew smaller and smaller. I stood still, watching it twist up and away into the hard blue sky.

Then the hat dived behind one of the fantastically colored ridges that stretched back and back as far as I could see.

Its disappearance snapped the spell. I broke into a run. As I ran I remembered how, only a couple of weeks before, a wise old desert rat had shown me a magazine picture of a corpse sprawled beside a bicycle out in the Mojave Desert. "No hat—not surprised," the old-timer had said. I raced on over bare rock. A makeshift hat in Death Valley? I might go days without seeing anyone. And I knew that I could hunt for hours among those endless ridges without finding the hat. I scrambled onto a chocolate-brown crest. And there, its strap neatly looped over a spike of rock, lay the hat.

I picked it up, chin-strapped it firmly onto my head and walked slowly back down the hill. Now the danger had passed I felt thankful that the desert had reminded me how fine a line divides safety from tragedy—and how easily a moment of carelessness can send you stumbling across it.*

Necessity being the mom of invention, you find that if you lose your hat you soon devise something as substitute. The only time I've lost mine was on a seventeen-day trip in Lower Grand Canyon, when temperatures ran over 100° F. just about every day. My bandanna had been acting as a wet-pad cooling system inside the hat and was lost with it. For a couple of days I used jockey shorts, then managed to lose them too. Because I was following the Colorado River and had to cross it from time to time I was carrying a life vest (page 533), and I devised a method of folding it, lightly inflated, and lashing it with nylon cord into such a conformation that, with its web belt under my chin, it would stay on

* From *The Thousand-Mile Summer*, pp. 82–3.

top of my head. This unlikely rig, immersed every hour in the river, and with the wet swimsuit stuffed into its hollow center, turned out to be just about the coolest hat I've ever worn, even if not the most becoming. I had to hold my head fairly upright to keep it on, but that was probably good for my posture or something.

CARE OF CLOTHING

In the field

In civilized temperatures I generally try to wash most of my clothes at least once a week.* This works out well because I find—and I think most people find—that about once a week you need a day's more or less complete rest from walking.

Whatever soap or detergent you choose it must, today, be biodegradable. The stuff you use for kitchen and personal purposes (page 488) will probably do fine for most clothes. For wool articles, see "Care of socks," page 76.

The time has passed, just about everywhere in the world, for washing clothes directly in a river or lake. Suds persist, and with our numbers now up to 4½ billion and wanderlust epidemic, the chances are simply too great that someone a little way downstream will soon be drinking that same water. Besides, with today's heavy usage the accumulation spells undoubted pollution. (Exceptions: huge rivers, maybe; and genuinely remote country.)

The simplest solution: use your cook pot or pots. But you can also buy cheap, light buckets and bowls in plastic or waxed fabric:

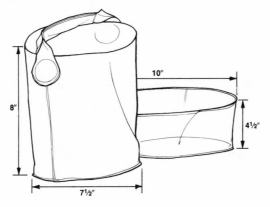

* In really cold weather you simply don't do any washing of clothes—or of yourself; which means that when you get back to civilization that first hot shower is not only sheer heaven but highly necessary.

You scoop up water in the bucket and wash clothes (and yourself) in the bowl. Dirty water can safely be ditched 50 feet back from the river or lake: it will filter clean as it seeps down through the soil. A plastic bucket-and-bowl set by Sierra West weighs 9 ounces, costs $10, takes up almost no room in your pack, and is much more efficient than it looks —though the bowl walls tend to fold unexpectedly and disastrously inward. Turning the bowl inside out improves stability—and also kills fungus and algae that may invade if it's left damp. The waxed-canvas French-made IT bowls (2 ounces) occasionally found in U.S. stores, do not crumple so easily. But they sometimes leak. Failing bucket and bowl, you can improvise a bowl from any impermeable fabric—poncho, groundsheet, fly sheet, awning—by laying it in a natural hollow, by scooping a hollow out of sand or soil that will not be damaged, or by arranging stones or wood as under-rim supports. Fill from canteens.

To dry clothes, string them out on bushes or a nylon line. I'm indebted to a New York reader who apparently carries a light nylon line for what she calls her "twist-and-shove," which she maintains is simpler than it looks and has become a one-minute-or-so part of her evening camp routine. You loop the line around whatever two aids you can find —with the center of the line at one of them—twist tightly, then shove the clothes into two or more twist-loops.*

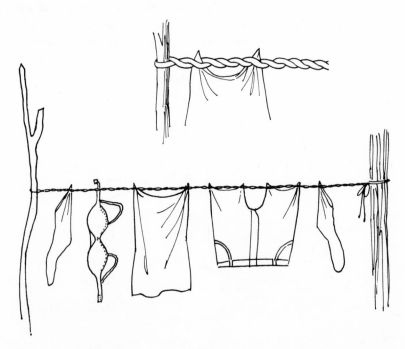

---

* A reader of this paragraph in the second edition: "I used this clothesline and it was a great success. Who says book learnin' ain't scalded no hogs?"

For shirts, if you're fussy about looks, it's easy to make a clothes hanger out of a piece of stick and some nylon line. For socks, see page 76.

In wet weather the only way to dry out clothes is often a fire (see page 435). But sometimes you're reduced to using the cooking stove inside your tent—if there's enough fuel. A tent with a clothesline attachment—grommeted tabs at each end of the ridge for joining with nylon cord—may allow damp clothes to dry from a combination of stove and body heat. For final drying, take clothes to bed with you.

At home

Treat most articles of clothing like their everyday counterparts. For down-filled clothing, see sleeping bags, page 365. For Gore-Tex, see page 406. For polypropylene, page 379. For pile, page 381.

THE WARDROBE IN ACTION

Sartorially, hikers can be subdivided into two distinct breeds: the put-it-on-and-keep-it-on school and the keep-adjusting-your-clothing-all-day-long-so-that-you're-always-comfortable faction.

You undoubtedly save several minutes a day if you put on at the start what you judge is about right and can then stick it out hour after hour without discomfort. But I belong, unreservedly, to the fussy, thermally responsive faction. With every variation of effort and environment I button and unbutton, unzipper and rezipper, peel and restore and then peel again. I find that in any but frigid weather it takes barely a mile of walking and a side glance of sunshine to strip me down to hat, shorts, socks and boots. That, I find, is the way to walk. With air playing freely over your skin you feel twice as fresh as you did with a shirt on. And although you may lose precious body liquids more quickly this way, experience has convinced me that you walk so much more comfortably that you more than make up for any loss. At least, I do. Besides, I enjoy myself more.

On those rare but by no means unknown occasions when you are traveling beside a river or lake in very hot, low-humidity weather, you have a cooling system ready for use. On my 17-day trip in lower Grand Canyon, when I hiked day after day beside the Colorado River, I learned to utilize this system to the full. I found that I could keep walking comfortably, even through the heat of the day, if at the end of each halt I dived into the river wearing my drill shorts and Dacron-wool shirt. For almost the whole of the next hour the continuous evaporation from the rapidly drying clothes surrounded my body with a pleasantly cool "micro-climate." For the highly efficient hat I used, purely by accident, see page 424.

Occasionally on that trip, because of a cut on one leg that I wanted to keep dry, I just soaked the clothes in the river. At other times, when the heat was not too ferocious, I simply draped the dripping-wet shirt around my neck and kept resoaking it with barely a check in my stride by dropping it in the river and in one easy movement pushing it under and lifting it up with the tip of my walking staff.

It is not often that you meet the right and necessary combination of weather and privacy and so can carry the keep-adjusting-your-clothing-all-day-long-so-that-you're-always-comfortable system to its logical conclusion. The first time I did so for any length of time was on my long Grand Canyon journey. Of course, I exercised due care for a few days with the previously shielded sectors of my anatomy. In particular, I pressed the bandanna into service as a fig leaf. But soon I was walking almost all day long with nothing above my ankles except a hat.*

Now, nakedness is a delightful condition, and by walking naked you gain far more than coolness. You feel an unexpected sense of freedom from restraint. An uplifting and almost delirious sense of simplicity. In this new simplicity you soon find that you have become, in a new and surer sense, an integral part of the simple, complex world you are walking through. And then you are really walking.

In assembling your clothes closet for any trip you probably tend to carry, if you are wise, just a little more than common sense indicates. This overlay will, when things go wrong, leave you some margin of safety. It may take many years—and more than just unexpected cold— for events to confirm your wisdom; but you can bet your bottom layer that in due course the dice will fall appropriately. Consider

A sample day in the rain—

a Murphy-ridden day, anything but normal yet rich in precept; a day during which you do some big things wrong, thereby placing harsh and unreasonable demands on the clothes closet (and several other departments) but during which you sort of make up for that by also doing a

---

* Warning! Not everyone can take such liberties with his skin in hot sun. And most people need a lotion (p. 492), at least at first.

few things right; a day that might be subtitled "How to Get Yourself into a Wet Hole—and Out of It."*

You are taking a two-week trip through coastal mountains. It is November. You are, among other things, trying out several new equipment items.

You have spent most of the day walking along a 4000-foot ridge in weather that has evolved, very slowly, from calm and clear through wispy fog, mist, heavy mist, drizzle and heavy drizzle into steady, windblown rain. Because the temperature has throughout this evolution held at an amiable 54° F. you began the day stripped to socks, boots and a pair of corduroy shorts. (In accordance with the Second Law of Thermodynamic Walking [page 395], you wore no underpants.) As the weather deteriorated you responded only by slipping on your trash-bag kilt (page 414) and a brand-new, second-generation Gore-Tex jacket—the first you have ever tried. Initially, you wore the jacket over your bare torso. In spite of your 50-pound pack and one hour-long spell of cross-country travel across steep, rough terrain, you felt, to your surprise and pleasure, no condensation discomfort. You did not even feel hot. Eventually, in fact, on top of an open ridge, you buffered the jacket against the rising wind with an equally untested polypropylene undervest. And after that, as long as you kept moving, you stayed just on the warm side of cool—which is how it ought to be. The only trouble has come from the pit zips. They leaked. Now, as you push on along the ridge, both your forearms are damp. But otherwise you seem to be totally dry.

---

* I like to think of myself as a competent operator, so you can hardly expect me to admit that what follows is a drop-by-drop account of what happened to me on one damp and recent occasion.

"I wonder if Colin Fletcher ever has days like this?"

Around two o'clock you reach the trail that will take you eastward, down off the ridge. You are glad. The wind has risen beyond playfulness. The rain is now slanting down in deeper earnest.

Off the crest, sure enough, things are appreciably calmer.

A little before three o'clock you reach the first running water. You have been traveling since 7:30, and with only two hours of daylight left and the rain now gaining even greater momentum—though the wind is still mercifully tamed, down here at 3000 feet—you decide to camp.

You go through the routine slowly, carefully: you suspect that this may be more than an overnight camp. By the time you have chosen a flat site that will not be swamped, no matter how much rain falls, that will be partially sheltered from almost any wind and that also looks safe from terminal compression by any of the dead trees burned in a big fire a few years ago and now crashing down in every storm, you feel a little less robustly warm. Not cold yet; not even cool. But barely warm. You eat some gorp and a couple of candies and they help stoke you up a bit.

During your reconnaissance you left your pack in the lee of a tree, sheltered from the worst of the rain. Now, as deftly as possible, you slacken the flap, slip the groundsheet out from its position just under the flap and drape it, half unfolded, over the pack. From under this protective overlay you fumble out your four quart canteens, fill them at the nearby creek and stand them beside the pack, ready.

At this point you run the attributes of the chosen campsite over in your mind again; and eventually you decide that the lee of the next tree offers even greater attractions. You move the pack over to the new site and fumble out from under the groundsheet your 12-by-15-foot plastic Visqueen tarp (page 316) and its attendant plastic bag holding eight Visklamps and six lightweight pegs. By the time you have Visklamped the tarp into a defensive, battened-down configuration and have double-checked each stone-assisted peg, the rain is bloody well pouring down. Naturally, you have not yet attempted to put on any extra clothing under your Gore-Tex jacket: that would surely soggy everything. So by now, although you are still not cold, barely even cool, you are brinking. And you know that the next few minutes are the ones that count.

When the tarp was part erected you put the pack in under it, up at the head, leaning against the tree. Now you follow it in. And just inside, up in the corner that you have predesignated the "wet or decompression chamber," you take off your dripping jacket and kilt, fold them and stash them up in the farthest corner of the wet chamber, just clear of occasional ricochets from the lashing rain. (You have pegged the tarp so that its sides mostly reach down to ground level, but you built that corner a little higher, for access and stove-lighting.) As you take off kilt and jacket you do your best to keep their insides dry, but in the gloom and damp it is difficult to tell just how successful you have been. You would like to have postponed the stripping off of outer garments, to conserve body heat, but you know that if you did so you would drip water onto everything as you unpacked. The shock of taking off the Gore-Tex jacket was substantial but bearable. As far as you can tell, your polypropylene vest is, except for the forearms, still dry.

By now the worst of the wetness has drained off both pack and covering groundsheet. But only the worst. You shake the sub-worst off the groundsheet, unfold it and spread it out, wet side down. The "up" side seems remarkably dry. Carefully, in spite of your eagerness to get extra clothes on, you begin to unpack. You do so with some trepidation.

Among the new equipment you are testing is the pack. This is, in fact, the first time you have used an internal-frame model on a trip. You have always been careful to carry your sleeping bag inside a stout stuff sack in the very heart of your single-bloody-great-sack of a packbag, but this time you have been forced—because the configuration of the I-frame pack demands it—to stuff the sleeping bag into the bottom section of the packbag, cramming it deep into both corners so that they wrap around your hips (page 139). When you asked about the danger of the bag's getting wet in rain you were assured that it rarely happens (the "rarely" hardly comforted you), and that if a deluge threatened you should wrap the sleeping bag in one plastic trash bag and maybe line the main sack with another. You duly brought along two big black 4-mil trash bags. But that morning, because the weather was so calm and clear and because you were in a hurry to get moving, you had not thought to press them into use. Later the storm had evolved so insidiously that by the time you were sure that was indeed what you had on your hands it was too late to encapsulate the sleeping bag or line the packbag without getting everything unholy wet. Or so you had judged at the time. Now you are less sure about your decisions. And you are worrying like hell.

As soon as you begin to pull the sleeping bag out you know your worries are justified. In the failing light you can see (and also feel, though your cold and still-damp fingers are for the moment pretty poor sensors) that there are large wet patches. When you finally pull the foot of the bag free you find that part wholly wet, going on soggy. You take your flashlight from a side pocket. Its beam confirms the diagnosis, in spades —and by chance also illuminates a patch of your bare thigh. It is goose-pimpled—and all at once you realize that for the first time you are cold. Not dangerously cold. Not yet. But the objectively warm air—52° F. when you checked just before pitching the tarp—is, subjectively, now a world removed from warm. You know that the objective temperature does not have to be very low for hypothermia to set in: exhaustion and wetness are the big deals. Though certainly not exhausted, you are by now undeniably a little tired. And it is beginning to look far from sure that you will have dry bedclothes.

Forewarned, you continue unpacking. It is neither a surprise nor a disaster to find that your undershorts and wool shirt, traveling in the pocket-on-the-flap, are only one step short of water-logged, but the discovery adds a certain edge to the unpacking of the main sack. That edge sharpens when you find your Therm-a-Rest pad patchily damp. You unroll and inflate it, then cover it with the two dry plastic trash bags. The kingpin comes out next: your favorite down jacket—the thick, heavy one you had almost decided to leave behind this trip, in favor of a lighter model. (You have yet to buy a pile jacket.) The jacket's stuff sack is far from dry; but although the jacket itself has absorbed some moisture it seems largely unscathed, and you feel sure that, thanks to its thickness, such moisture as there is will stay clear of your inner garments and will soon be driven off by body heat. Next you pull out the cashmere sweater you rarely carry but put in at the last moment; enclosed in a plastic bag, it turns out to be bone-dry. Thankfully, you slip on over the polypropylene vest first the sweater, then the down jacket. You flip up the jacket hood, pull hood- and hem-drawstrings tight. At once you know you have stopped the worst of the heat loss. Even your forearms feel warm.

Next from the pack come your long, wool-whipcord pants. They weigh 1 pound 10 ounces. Down the years you have lugged them many a mile yet rarely used them, and lately you have seriously considered replacing them with something lighter if less protective. The pants, you discover, are essentially anhydrous. So are the new, untried polypropylene longjohns, also protected in a plastic bag.

All this time you have held your feet off to one side of the ground-sheet. Now at last you take off your boots and socks—both wringing wet, in spite of gaiters—and put them near the side of the tarp. Hurriedly, you more or less dry your feet with the less-soaked parts of your shirt, then slip off the damp corduroy shorts (damp, probably, from sweat and general high humidity) and pull on the polypropylene long-johns and whipcord pants. The change is immediate, astonishing, delectable. Only your feet are cold now—going on icy. But two minutes after encasing them in a dry set of woolen under- and over-socks you know you have turned that corner too.

For years you have carried a small space blanket (2 ounces, page 585), and although you have never used it for anything of importance you have always felt that someday it might prove its worth. You take it out of the plastic bag in which it travels, unfold it and wrap it around the lower part of your body, clear up to your down jacket. The cocoon effect is immediate and beautiful. For the first time you feel almost sure you will spend a reasonably comfortable night. After all, you sleep like a hot-water bottle—and have grateful bedmates to vouch for it.

The discovery that your silk balaclava (page 418) is distinctly wet does little to dampen your good cheer—which is immediately fueled again, anyway, by the discovery that the thicker Orlon balaclava is wholly dry. Your scarf too. And wool gloves. You slip them all on, refit the jacket hood. Then, feeling the warmth beginning to spread outward from your core into all sectors of your body, you restoke the fires by eating a couple of candies and spirulina tablets. After that you sit for a moment and rest, recalling with pleasure how you fought off the idea that carrying two balaclavas was unnecessary, and how you chose rather heavier, long-wristed wool gloves over a lighter pair. You smile to yourself, confident that once you get a good hot meal in your gut you will positively glow.

It is while you are sitting there, beginning to plan the meal, that you remember the canteens. They are standing at the foot of the tree you originally chose as a campsite. They are standing, that is, all of thirty feet from your snug little temporary home. And outside, now, the rain is lashing down in sheets.

It does not take you long to reject the wrenching prospect of stripping off all those layers of wonderful, dry, heat-conserving clothes. Instead you unwrap the space blanket (which is bad enough) and pull on your coated-nylon chaps—unused to date, and still dry. Next you take off both pairs of socks (which is horrible) and slip your feet into camp-shoes. Then you ease up into the "wet corner" and arrange the Gore-Tex jacket over head and shoulders (finding to your joy that you apparently did a fair job of keeping the inside of the jacket dry when you took it off). You take a deep breath. Then you crawl out into the lashing rain and crouch-shamble toward the canteens. Seconds later you are crawling back in. When you strip off jacket and chaps you find that, as far as you can tell, nothing underneath has gotten wet. Within a minute or two you have your socks back on and your midriff rewrapped in space blanket, and you can feel the furnace working again. The brief spurt of exercise actually seems to have helped.

From that point on, the storm became a rather pleasant, restful interlude.

You cook a tasty Weepak Turkey Tetrazzini dinner (preheating the stove outside the tarp with fire paste [page 257]—grateful for your decision to bring the MSR stove, because it means you can, by igniting the paste "indoors" and quickly shoving the burner outside but keeping tank and controls inside, avoid both getting hands or wrists wet and also almost all danger of setting the tarp alight while the stove does its initial flaring). Sure enough, hot food stokes your fires. Soon warmth is coursing through you.

The warmth quickly dries off the worst of the dampness from the Therm-a-Rest pad. You remove the two plastic trash bags that were covering it and use one of them as a footsack. This enables you to shift the space blanket upward so that it more efficiently encases your crucial midsection. When you reinforce your socks with a back-up set (that you almost decided not to bring) you find that in combination with the footsack they make you feel almost too hot. By now the upper part of the sleeping bag has begun to dry out a little, and you drape it loosely over your lower body. The trash-bag footsack and space-blanket cummerbund will protect pants and jacket from the bag's dampness, and the bag will help keep more warmth in as well as tend to dry itself out. By this time you are almost too dozy to check that the outside temperature still stands —as it will, day and night, throughout the storm—at 52°. Before long you feel yourself drifting warmly and contentedly down into unconsciousness.

You wake in daylight, after a long, log- and toast-like sleep, to find the rain, if anything, even heavier, the wind gone steadily crazy. And you spend the entire day lying there, remarkably cozy in your small, white, double-slanting refuge. All day the wind howls and the rain cascades down. But it is Friday the thirteenth, so you know everything will be fine.

For a change, you brought no reading matter on this trip, yet you never, all through that day of immobility, even flirt with inaction, let alone boredom. As often happens, it is curiously difficult, looking back, to pin down just what you found to do, beyond doze occasionally. When the wind rose to gale force and the tarp began to flap rather dangerously, you certainly had to rebatten down. That meant swiveling around and crawling to the foot of the house to deal with the final two Visklamp guys; but you were able to complete even that operation without consigning anything but your hands to the perils of the storm (see Visklamp tightening, page 317). Several times, after things that came boomp out of the day had boomped onto the tarp (they were probably pine cones), you detected pinpricks and small slits that needed patching with Ripstop tape. Soon you had a gay little galaxy of red stars pulsating overhead like a celestial Moscow parade. You also had to make ongoing checks that nothing important was getting wet—from condensation, slight galaxy leakage or ricochets from the unfriendly outside world. In addition, there were the usual food-sorting chores. But otherwise—as far as you could remember later—you spent the time drifting into pleasant reveries, farting and, once, exchanging world views with an orange-tinted, comfort-loving salamander that you found hunkered down among your snacks. Yet by nightfall, when you look back, that hardly seems a full day's work. The stubborn fact remains, though, that you have not even had time to finish catching up with your notes. Odd.

By that second night your body heat has dried out the sleeping bag enough for you to push your feet, still cocooned in their trash bag, inside its foot. And that not only makes you so warm that eventually you have to take off one set of socks but also helps dry the sleeping bag even further.

Next morning you awake to calm: no rain; no wind. You emerge. Above the canopy of washed and silent trees slides a hint of watery sunlight. Within half an hour you have a fire going and are beginning to dry things out. (Once again you are thankful you brought the MSR stove —and plenty of white gas: you use the stove to torch sodden wood into reluctant flame, while keeping the gas bottle a safe distance from flames and heat.)

By midafternoon you have dried everything out, sort of, and are on your way again, singing.

Back home, four days later, you learn that a weather station on the next ridge over from your cozy little refuge—less than 7 miles away—registered 11.7 inches of rain from the storm, and that even down at sea level the winds reached 71 mph.

The three-layer system in action in rain and snow

My experience with the system remains sketchy, but two recent days taught me a lot, and maybe their lessons and encouragements are worth passing along.

Late October in the High Sierra. I am camped at 10,000 feet and ready to head down. At 9:30 A.M., as I leave, it is 34° F. and raining lightly. No wind. I wear polypropylene vest, pile jacket, Gore-Tex shell, jockey and Jammer corduroy shorts and plastic trash-bag kilt (styled longish). Headgear: lightweight Sportif hat under pulled-up shell hood. Short gaiters, Easy Hiker boots. I walk all day, descending steadily. It rains most of the time, though never heavily. There is little or no wind. Temperatures rise to 40° but no higher. With pit zips mostly open when walking (but closed at most halts, and especially at the half-hour lunch, when I put on the pile balaclava—and possibly wool gloves [notes and memory are fuzzy]) and front zip occasionally opened, I am very comfortable. Intermittent slight coolness of hands no doubt stems from water-absorbing knit-nylon wristbands of pile jacket. I camp at 5 P.M. at about 7500 feet. As soon as the Sphinx tent is up I slide into my sleeping bag (removing wet and lower garments first). Not until after dinner do I need to put on my VB shirt, under the pile jacket. At no time, all day, have I been either too hot or too cold.

Next day the sun shines briefly. I stay put and dry out all gear. When mist envelops the camp I add only pile jacket to jockey and Jammer shorts, and am entirely comfortable. Later the pile balaclava wards off intimations of coolness.

Next morning, after a night of heavy rain, the tent alcove is a lake. Dawn temperature: 36°. During breakfast the rain becomes hail. By 9:30, when I leave, snow has been falling for over an hour and the temperature is 28°. I wear the same torso gear as before (plus silk and Orlon balaclavas and, at first, the pile one too). I replace shorts with polypropylene longjohns, wool whipcord pants and rain chaps, and seal off a potential gap between them and shell with the kilt. Short gaiters again. I walk until midafternoon, descending about 1000 feet, in light snow that slowly turns to sleet and, eventually, rain. Wind variable but never strong. The temperature creeps up from 28° to 34°—which is a miserable range, particularly in such sogginess. But except for my feet, which at halts tend toward coolness and even coldness (the boots have never really dried out from two days earlier, and all day I am walking through slushy snow), I manage, adjusting pit zips and taking off the pile balaclava and then putting it back on at halts, to stay snugly comfortable. I find that the balaclava does a magnificent control job, and mostly comes off once I have been walking for a few minutes after a halt. At roadhead, before hitching a ride back to my car, which is out at a place kept plowed in case of snow, I take off shell, kilt and chaps and put on VB shirt under the pile jacket. At the car I probably (though notes and memory again fuzz) take off boots and socks and replace them with dry footwear. Two or three hours later, down in the foothills, the only dress change I make before dining in a restaurant with friends is to take off the pile jacket and replace the mildly damp wool-whipcord pants with a pair of old warm-up pants. Also, possibly, to change my boots at last. Everything else is totally dry and I am still snugly comfortable. In the restaurant I open VB-shirt pit zips and front zip (and, because I have been up in the mountains for a week, seat my friends upwind). I am fairly sure that if I had been wearing old-style clothing that day of snow, sleet, rain, sweat, hitch-hiking and then driving it would, long before dinnertime, have been a miserable instead of a rousing experience.

Furniture and Appliances

No matter how grimly you pare away at the half-ounces you always seem to burden your house with an astonishing clutter of furniture and appliances. At least, I do. Each item, of course, is a necessary aid to some necessary activity. For example, there is the vital matter of

SEEING.

To lighten your darkness you almost always need to carry a small, lightweight

Flashlight,

and you now have a wild and plastic selection to choose from: a flock of hand-held models and a growing number of practical headlamps.

Hand-held flashlights have in recent years evolved dramatically, but in spite of strides in the right direction there is still, in my opinion, no light wholly satisfactory for backpacking.

The old, angular plastic Mallory, no longer made by them, is still preferred by many people over its successor. And copies of the old model, with innards slightly improved, are now on the market, though not always easy to find (empty, 1½ ounces; with two alkaline AA batteries, 3 ounces; comes complete with two ordinary AA cells at $3). Copies have appeared under various names, and some, though not all, are less tough than the original. The big and compelling edge the old model holds over the new is its larger reflector: it therefore throws a more powerful and concentrated central beam, far better for trail-following. There are other advantages, too. Its roll switch can, unlike its successor's, be securely taped in the OFF position (page 446). You can wedge a spare bulb behind its reflector. And a ridge near the bottom of the case provides a good biting grip if you want to hold the light in your mouth to leave your hands free. But the old model's innards are finickier than in the new (both sets of innards are easily get-attable for drying, cleaning or repair —though fixing their fragile components can be a hell of a game). In the old model a little screw that holds the halves of the case together can drive you down on hands and knees, peering and cursing, if you have to change batteries after dark (though a dab of Duco cement will hold the female part in place). Unfortunately, there is no ready-made attachment for a nylon neck-loop. Neither model claims to be in any way waterproof but both of them can, like all flashlights, be galoshed against heavy rain by a Ziploc or other strong plastic bag.

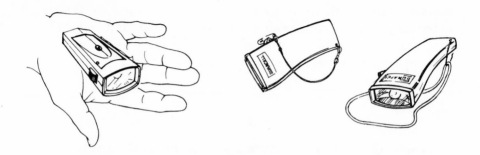

In spite of the new competitors, the Mallory Duracell Compact 805 probably remains—partly because of its price—the most popular back-packing flashlight (empty, 1 ounce; with two AA alkaline batteries, 2½ ounces; $3). It provides a less effective beam than the old model (see above) but in spite of more delicate lineaments it seems about as strong. (Note: neither model is Tarzan-tough and when either reaches that stage of decrepitude, undetectable by the eye, at which you have to press on some part of the case in order to keep the light steady, the time has come to discard it.)

The 805 is certainly convenient. To change batteries you pry the halves of the case apart by inserting the wilderness equivalent of a coin (your spoon handle, for example) into a small recess and twisting; there is no screw to fall out (though once the batteries are removed it is possible for the bulb to decant spontaneously). A small hole in one corner of the case will take a loop of very thin nylon cord or dental floss that will in turn hold a length of standard nylon cord as neck-loop, and the small loop will during repairs or battery change hold the case's two halves together and unlosable. The curved case, unlike the symmetrical earlier model's, allows for rapid determination of which side the switch is on— no matter how dark the night or bleary the mind. Unfortunately, the small tipping switch, though now somewhat stronger than in early versions, cannot be securely taped in the OFF position.*

A recent and very real bonus with the new Mallory: you can now buy a Headlite Holder—a simple plastic clip on a stretch-fabric headband (1 ounce, $4)—that converts the light into a headlamp (though the side mounting means mild shadow trouble). Similar adaptors for other hand-held lights (including the Durabeam, below) are now beginning to appear.

A new two-AA-battery light—which I have yet to use, but of which I hear good preliminary reports—is the Durabeam Compact by Duracell (3 ounces, including batteries; $4). It is said to throw "a 250-foot-beam."

Most of the interesting challengers to these lightweight lights seem to have been developed for scuba diving and foisted off on backpackers as a merchandising afterthought. They are cunning, elegant and rugged. But the diving advantages of extra-bright beams for murky depths and resistance to God knows how many feet of water are passing useless for us and often generate unhappy side effects (fast battery drainage; unnecessary weight). Field use reveals other serious drawbacks—notably in the rotary switches.

The Tekna-Lite II is small, light, simple and black-belt tough (empty, with #222 bulb, 1½ ounces, $9; with two AA alkaline batteries, said to give "four hours operation," 3½ ounces). Waterproofness (to 2000 feet, yet) and simplicity have been achieved by replacing the traditional switch with a head that screws down for ON, partway up for OFF. But such a switch is not very practical for backpacking, when you need to conserve battery life by dousing the light whenever possible. With a brand new Tekna-Lite II and warm hands you can, in an unstressed store scene, turn the light off and on with one hand. Maybe. If you're an experienced puppeteer. But with use the flashlight develops slightly

---

* Letters I have written to Mallory on this subject have generated the usual response: silence. But one man I know holds the switch down with a strong, fat rubber band. And an Oregon reader suggests another solution (see illustration): "Burn or drill a small hole through the switch, near the case, when the switch is in the 'off' position. Place a small safety pin through the hole to lock the switch in the 'off' position. Secure safety pin to a light cord lanyard which passes through hole in corner of flashlight. This arrangement not only prevents accidental discharge but also allows pinning light to shirt front to serve purposes of a long lanyard looped around the neck."

worn and soiled threads and the bulb's base tends to oxidize and the head must be turned rather farther to douse the light completely; and then, even when you're not cold or tired, you definitely need two hands— unless you hold the head in your mouth and turn the body with one hand. In practice, all this is a perishing nuisance. An even more serious drawback is that, although the diffused light is fine for lighting a tent and a convex lens molded into the bulb gives a spotlight up to 2 feet, there is no reflector and therefore no concentrated beam of the kind needed for trail-following and some other tasks. An alternative and now more common head, similar to that on the Microlite (see illustration), seems to improve the beam a little—but to reduce tent-lighting efficiency. In early models the bulb tended to work loose and leave you lightless without warning, but I found that a sliver of pencil eraser jammed down beside the bulb base held it firm. Later models, which apparently do not suffer from that fault, sport small strap-fittings on the case so that you can secure the light to your wrist. Coincidentally, these fittings bring one-handed operation within the outer limits of feasibility —if you hold the light by the head and move the strap-fittings with finger or thumb. All Tekna models have a lanyard hole big enough to accept standard nylon cord.

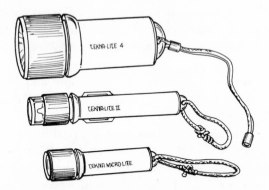

I have yet to try the tiny new Tekna Micro-Lite that works on a single AA lithium cell (page 448) and krypton bulb (1.4 ounces, $16 complete with bulb and cell; spare bulb, $7; cell, $6), but I hear reports of a good beam and 4–5-hour life. The bulkier Tekna-Lite 4 floats and is said to operate for one and one-half hours on four AA alkaline cells and PR#13 bulb (5 ounces, $20). Both have head-rotary-switches, similar to the Tekna II's.

The Moonlight by Early Winters (empty, with three spare bulbs cradled in base, 3½ ounces; with one Lithium C cell, 5 ounces, $24.50;

lithium cell alone, $12.50) comes with both potential and bugs. (The bugs remain in lights now appearing under different names but that seem unchanged except for colored, opaque casings.)

First, the good news. The transparent Lexan case, with no separate lens, looks and feels as tough as it's made out to be ("it will survive a fall from a mountain top . . . you can beat it with a hammer or run it down with a Mack truck . . . if it ever breaks we'll repair or replace it without charge"). It is waterproof. And although its single Lithium C cell is expensive it has twice the voltage of an alkaline and reputedly gives "10 hours of light with a guaranteed shelf life of 10 years . . . [and] will work down to −65 degrees." (For more on lithium cells, see page 448.) For space lighting you can hang the Moonlight by its neck lanyard or stand it on its base, recessing the lanyard in the notches provided. And its reflector has a nonradioactive band that "by day stores the sun's energy [and] by night glows softly to make [it] easy to find in your tent, pack, or by your bed."

Now the bad news. Although the Moonlight does a good job of space lighting its small reflector produces a poorly concentrated beam. That's bad enough. But the maxi-glitch lies in the switch. Like the Tekna-Lites', it is a rotary type—though in the base, not head; but plug and flange are so recessed that even with warm, ungloved hands, turning it becomes a major chore. And one-handed operation is out of the question. It seems a shame that such a well-made and otherwise practical tool should be sunk by such a bummer.

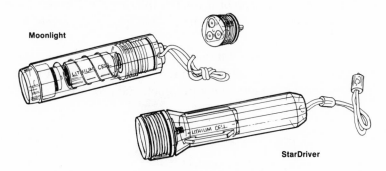

Moonlight

StarDriver

Fortunately, Early Winters recognized the bugs and have sought to unbum things. The result is the StarDriver (empty, 4 ounces, with krypton bulb and lanyard, 4 ounces, $19.95; C-size batteries—2 alkaline, $2.85; 2 rechargeable nickel-cadmium, $12.95; 1 lithium plus blank, $12.95; spare krypton bulb, $9.50; optional headband, $5).

The StarDriver should be an improvement on the Moonlight. Made of the same tough Lexan, it lacks the spare-bulb storage and luminous band but has a much improved reflector and, therefore, beam. With its three alternative battery arrangements, it is—at a small cost in weight —much more versatile (though see page 450 for warning words re rechargeable batteries). Above all, the rotary switch is built into the head, not recessed in the tail. This arrangement is far better. But it is not, to my taste, good enough. After semi-extensive tests I still find the rotary switch a pain. Worse still, I have already had lithium batteries die on me twice, many hours before they "ought" to have done so. One failure occurred at the very start of a week-long trip. Now, I must make it clear that I'm uncertain whether the fault lay in flashlight, battery or me. It could be that I failed to unscrew the switch far enough to prevent accidental switching-on when the light was not in use. There may, just conceivably, be a bug in the flashlight. Or another dissatisfied user may be right when he says that present performance figures for lithium cells reflect "a gross overestimate of life-spans." I simply do not know, yet, where the trouble lies. But I'm currently walking scared—and disappointed.

I refuse to accept, though, that the recent sunburst in backpacking flashlights has climaxed. I'm damned if I see why, living beneath a sky studded with satellites, we should not have a small, lightweight flashlight as tough and versatile as the StarDriver (preferably, like the Moonlight, with a luminous band and storage space for at least one bulb) that can operate satisfactorily on something lighter than two C cells and is equipped with a switch that's instantly and one-handedly operable under all backpacking conditions—even if that means it's nonrotary and therefore may not remain waterproof if you're exploring the *Titanic.*

All candidates for this Immaculate Concept unfortunately flunk in at least one category.

The Kel-Lite 2-C cell (empty, 7 ounces, $24; with 2 alkaline cells, 10 ounces) is made of anodized aluminum alloy, has a Lexan lens and a standard thumb switch said to be waterproof, and produces a good beam.

Kel-Lite

It's beautifully made, as it should be at that price, and rugged. After several years' intermittent general use, mine still looks and works like new. Although it lacks a lanyard attachment, making one should not be a gigantic task. I understand that it cannot, for some reason, be used with lithium cells. And it is certainly on the heavy side. But I still carry it backpacking on occasion.

The newer, similar 2-C cell Mag-Lites (empty, 15 ounces, $20) focus from spotlight to full flood with a turn of the head. But for me their weight just about sinks them. (They will apparently not take lithium batteries either.)

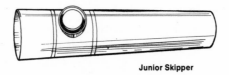

Junior Skipper

Another candidate: The Eveready Junior Skipper, sometimes labeled Junior Floating Flashlight. It is inexpensive, little more than half the weight of the Kel-Lite equivalent, and widely available, even in supermarkets (empty, 4 ounces, $3.59). And it has a waterproof on-off pushbutton switch that's guaranteed for 10 years. Its red plastic waterproof case is bulky and lacks a lanyard fitting but seems very strong. The beam is good. You can apparently use it with lithium batteries. A few undemanding trials have left me surprisingly if tentatively impressed.

I find that I now own no less than seven reasonably viable handheld backpacking flashlights. I seem to select one for a specific trip according to weight pressures, danger of downpours or river dunkings, probable need for space- or trail-lighting and, no doubt, whim of the moment. But I continue to wait, and pray, for the Immaculate Concept.

Whole galaxies of other hand-held flashlights float around the marketplace, of course: bigger and heavier scuba-diving lights and Kel-Lites and similar, and also many small, light, marginally strong or ineffably fragile traditional flashlights of the kind that crowd hardware and drug stores and should, for our purposes, be left there. Some backpacking catalogues even offer minifluorescent lights. Then there is something called a Flex-Flash that is sure to attract gadget bugs but is, I'm told on good authority, as susceptible to Murphy as it looks. There are also scores of penlights with replaceable batteries, apparently convenient but often as frail and evanescent as flowers.

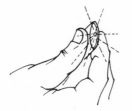 

The little ultrasimplified, disposable flashlights that go by such names as Gloworm, Globug or Lightning Bug have their uses as back-ups or even, perhaps, as short summer-trip mainstays. Each is just a pair of very small carbon-zinc batteries, really, with a small bulb attached (½ ounce, $2.50). Such lights are switched on by simultaneous pressure on both sides of the case and are said to last for "about two hours of steady use." The obvious risk of accidental switching on in pack or pocket demands an antidote that so far eludes me.

There is no such difficulty with another variation on the same theme: throwaway clip-on penlights, such as the Clip-lite (Wonder Corporation; 1 ounce, $1.39) and Penlite (Ray-O-Vac; 1 ounce, $2.29). A plastic sleeve slides up to block the effect of the combined clip and switch. Batteries are standard carbon zinc. Continuous-use life is rated at 45 minutes. I was carrying a Clip-lite as back-up when my Starlight-with-lithium-battery failed on the first night of a recent week-long snowshoe trip. Used sparingly (the late-May nights were not too long), it filled the vacated niche well, showed little or no sign of dimming and still sits beside my bed at home for emergency use. I am beginning to wonder whether two or even three such little gems—which seem to be reasonably water-resistant—may not be the best current answer for certain backpacking situations. The doubtful elements, of course, are strength of beam (even at its virgin-brightest it may not be potent enough to light your way down any but the simplest trail) and its lifespan in prolonged trail-following use.

Interesting and economical alternatives to battery-powered flashlights are the dynamo lights that I remember as popular in Holland during World War II: you squeeze a handle slowly and rhythmically and generate a steady light. I have just bought a Japanese-made Hi-Dyna (5¾ by 1½ by ⅔ inches, 8½ ounces, $14.50). Dropping it in water apparently does no damage, the handle locks away for packing and a spare bulb sits tucked in behind the reflector. The device is far from ultralight, but remember you need carry no spare batteries. And although I don't dote on the whirring noise it makes, and am underwhelmed at the thought of having to keep squeezing it for all camp chores, I purr at the prospect of surefire all-night emergency trail-illumination on demand, no matter how cold the air.

Many backpackers—and especially snow campers—favor headlamps over hand-held models, even though they tend to be heavier. You always have both hands free—for erecting a tent, cooking and every other chore or delight. (Along this line a Rhode Island reader recommends, for setting up camp after dark, taping your hand-held flashlight to your knife and sticking it in a tree.)

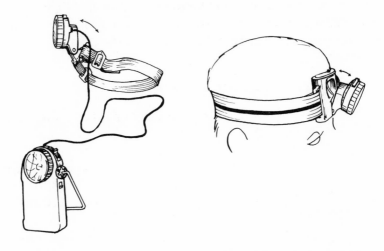

Headlamps come in two conformations: those with the whole unit, including batteries, up on the headstrap—thereby eliminating troublesome cords but putting a lot of weight on the head and sometimes inducing headaches, especially if you walk at night; and those with only a light bulb-and-lens unit on the headstrap and a separate battery unit, often with a built-in additional light, that can clip on clothing, travel in a pocket or even stand alone—thereby necessitating a cord but holding headaches at bay and also keeping the batteries warm (often an important matter with all but lithium cells, as anyone who has dropped a flashlight in snow will attest).

Some years ago I tried a headlamp that kept malfunctioning, and I have since steered clear of such units. But many current models seem proven. Their number is now so large and the specifications change so fast that after several efforts at compiling a useful list I have decided to say only that good lightweight models (5 to 9 ounces, empty) come from Eveready, Mountain Safety Research, Panasonic, Hitachi and Toshiba (about $15–$25). Batteries may be AA, C or D size, and they are now often single lithium cells. Heavier versions, for such special tasks as search-and-rescue, abound.

For another kind of "flashlight" that can just possibly be used for trail illumination, see the Cyalume, page 455.

Stowing the flashlight

Naturally, you must always know exactly where your flashlight is. During the day mine used to go into the inside pocket of the pack, where it was reasonably well protected and tolerably accessible. But my present pack has no inside pocket, and for some years the flashlight has traveled without damage in an upper outside pocket, padded by scarf or balaclava.

For use and storage at night, see pages 372–3.

Accidental battery drainage

This by no means minor mishap should not occur with flashlights that have rotary switches, provided you take care to unscrew them far enough—though that is a major proviso (see page 442). But it is all too likely to happen in your pack when something presses against other kinds of switch. Preventative measures depend on the kind of flashlight you use. With orthodox cylinder-shape, end-loader models such as Kel-Lite, you simply reverse the lower battery. You soon come to do it automatically every morning. Restoring the flashlight to working condition is something you most often do at dusk or after dark, but again it's all very simple. You just unscrew the base, shake out the bottom battery, replace it right way up and screw the base back on. In wet weather you can do the job in a few seconds with the flashlight held out of rain and therefore out of sight under your poncho. Ditto, though a little differently and more carefully, with head-loaders like the Junior Skipper.

With the old Mallory, such an operation is complicated, and rough on the mechanism; but, fortunately, all you need do is put a piece of adhesive tape over the large-surfaced roll switch. With the tape in place the switch cannot turn. At night, park the tape on a flat side of the flashlight. In the morning, replace it on the switch. A 2-inch length of the 1-inch tape from my first-aid kit does the job perfectly and lasts through a two-week trip.

For the new Mallory, see page 439, footnote.

Batteries

Until recently we could choose only between standard carbon-zinc cells (with their boosted "heavy duty" versions) and alkaline cells (a.k.a.

"energizers"). But now there are also lithium cells, which we must consider in detail, and rechargeable nickel-cadmium cells, which we need only glance at.

Standard carbon-zinc cells are entirely adequate for intermittent use. But if the light has to be kept switched on for long periods—as can happen in an emergency or through miscalculation or even by design, early and late in a long day—then the battery quickly loses energy and the light soon dims to a useless glow. Heavy-duty cells may last up to twice as long under such continuous-drain service. And alkaline cells are far more efficient. According to the makers they may give "up to ten times" more service. For normal field use, this table gives a fair idea of what to expect with today's cells.

WEIGHTS, CONTINUOUS-SERVICE LIVES, AND COSTS FOR
PAIRS OF VARIOUS FLASHLIGHT BATTERIES*

Size	AA	C	D
Name	Penlight	¾ size	Regular
Diameter	$\frac{9}{16}$ inch	$1\frac{1}{32}$ inch	$1\frac{11}{32}$ inch
Bulb	PR4 or #222	PR4 or #233	PR2 or #14
Standard	1.0 oz. 1 hr. $1	2.8 oz. 2 hrs. $.90	6 oz. 2 hrs. $.90
Heavy-duty	1.2 oz. 2 hrs. $1.20	3.0 oz. 6 hrs. $1.60	6.2 oz. 6½ hrs. $1.60
Alkaline	1.6 oz. 4½ hrs. $2.05	4.4 oz. 13 hrs. $2.65	9 oz. 15 hrs. $2.65

For continuous-service use, then, alkaline batteries are by far the most efficient, ounce for hour—though their sudden final blackouts are a minor disadvantage.

Service-life figures for the kind of intermittent use a flashlight gets

---

* Eveready–Union Carbide kindly supplied the facts and figures on which I have based this table and the paragraphs of text that follow.

Tests I conducted some years ago generally confirmed the AA figures.

As cut-off point for "continuous-service life" I tried to determine, as well as I could in my garden, when I would no longer be able to find the way down a reasonably clear trail by flashlight alone. If anything, I tended to underestimate service life. And Union Carbide now agree that, given the low end-point voltage I found acceptable, my figures are correct.

During my trials, temperatures averaged 66° F. The tests were for continuous life: batteries were switched on and left on, with no rest periods. I did not warm the flashlights by holding them in the palm of my hand. Standard batteries soon dropped off peak performance and lost strength gradually, to the useful point and beyond. The alkaline batteries held close to their peak for about 3 hours, and after 4½ hours were still giving enough light to read this print by. Then, quite suddenly, they blacked out.

Tested again after 11 hours—with no heating or other coercion—the standard batteries lasted about 5 minutes with a rather poor light, the alkaline for rather more than ½ hour. Tested four days later, the standards again lasted about 5 minutes (though more faintly than before), the alkalines for about 20 minutes.

in camp are so subject to imponderables that they would be close to meaningless. But it seems that in the larger cell sizes alkaline batteries might deliver two to three times the service of their standard equivalents. In the AA size you could expect much larger advantages from alkaline batteries—perhaps seven or eight times.

I find myself in some doubt about how to report on lithium batteries. The paragraphs that follow were written before I ran into problems (page 442)—and found that other people had, too. These problems may or may not stem from the lithium cells themselves. On balance, it would seem that the best I can do is to let the supposedly factual material stand, but to sound words of warning.

Lithium batteries are very light and extremely efficient, operate almost without retrenchment in extreme temperatures—and suffer from some drawbacks.

One lithium cell (2.7 volts) replaces two standards or alkalines (1.35 volts) and cuts the weight by about half (AA cell, .5 ounce; C size, 1.5 ounces; D size, 2.8 ounces; dummy C or D cells for flashlights that also use two standard or alkaline cells, .1 ounce). I have not included lithium cells in the table on page 447 because they require special bulbs (often giving brighter light—see page 451), and because such plain figures do not show that the increased output of lithiums is sustained for far longer. This table, by Mountain Safety Research, for certain combinations of cells and bulbs, makes clearer comparisons.

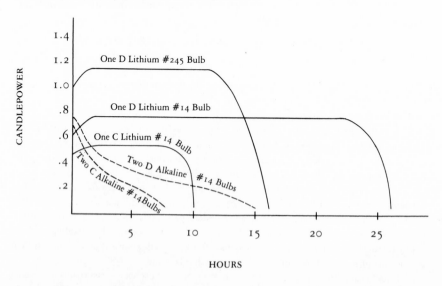

I have not yet been able to obtain reliable data for lithium AA cells, but they seem to offer similar if somewhat less striking advantages.

In cold weather these advantages soar. See following table, based on one supplied by Power Conversion Inc., makers of Eternacell lithium batteries:

Characteristic	Carbon Zinc	Alkaline	Eternacell® Lithium
Low Temperature Percent of (70° F.) Capacity			
+20° F.	5%	15%	96%
−20° F.	0%	3%	85%
−40° F.	0%	0%	60%
* Shelf Life Storage Temp.			
(70° F.)	1–2 yrs.	1–2 yrs.	10 yrs.†
(130° F.)	1.5 mos.	2 mos.	8 yrs.†
Watt-Hrs. per pound	19.5	26	125

* Time in years or months that a cell will provide a minimum of 75% of its initial capacity at room temperature.
† Projected.

Lithium cells continue to function (no figures given) even at −65° F.

Note the comparative shelf lives. With lithiums you run far less risk of buying a cell of diminished capacity, and for most practical purposes you can stop worrying about how long you keep spares.

The clearly visible drawbacks of lithium cells—none very damning —are cost, availability, need for special bulbs and restrictions against carrying in aircraft.

At first glance the prices of lithium cells look exorbitant: AA, $6; C, $13; D, $18.50. But when you compare with a pair of equivalent alkalines, allow for the longer life and then dub in the savings in weight for both original and spares and also the huge temperature tolerance, the difference narrows or vanishes. (Even in summer temperatures, for example, the theoretical energy-to-weight advantage of a lithium D cell over a pair of alkalines is 5:1; over standards, 6:1. For Cs and AAs the ratio is closer but still highly significant.)

At present lithium cells are not widely available. But good mountain shops now tend to stock them, and you can presently get AAs from REI and Cs from Early Winters. To my surprise, scuba-diving stores do not seem to have heard of them. At a guess, the supply situation will improve.

Rumors have circulated that lithium cells are dangerously liable to explosion. This seems to be untrue. They are approved for military use "in exigent nonfail situations." It is true, though, that in extreme heat (over 225° F.) or under prolonged shorting there may be a small leakage of sulfur-dioxide gas. In the open air this is mere inconvenience; at worst, a minor and temporary smell. But it is no doubt the reason lithium cells cannot currently be shipped outside the forty-eight contiguous states, and why *it is illegal to carry or ship them in any aircraft.*

To summarize: In theory, lithium cells offer overwhelming advantages for use in below-freezing weather and considerable savings in weight, hassle, and reserve demands—in almost any situation where cost is not paramount. Yet public acceptance has been limited. The reason may lie, as I have suggested, in a possible dissonance between theory and practice. Wait, and ye shall learn.

Rechargeable nickel-cadmium cells, which cost about the same as lithiums and can be recharged at any household outlet, are clearly economical in money terms. But they are heavy and they need frequent recharging. With the high-intensity krypton bulb used in the Star-Driver, two C-size nickel-cadmiums are said to last 3–4 hours, compared with 5 hours for two alkaline cells and 7 hours for one lithium. Except perhaps for friendly overnight summer jaunts they therefore seem marginal for backpacking.

Bulbs

Any pair of standard or alkaline AA, C or D cells generates close to 3 volts. So does a single lithium equivalent. Any "3-volt" bulb will therefore work with them, after a fashion. But for even halfway satisfactory results you must match batteries with the right bulbs.

There are two series of flashlight bulbs: those identified by a number prefixed by "PR" have smooth, flanged bases; those identified by a plain number have screw bases. General Electric advise me that "the better flashlights normally use the prefocused PR types." Battery matchings for pairs of standard or alkaline cells or for single lithiums:

AA: PR4 or #222
 C: PR4 or #233 (#243 gives less light, longer battery life)
 D: PR2 or #14 (PR9 and #245 give less light, longer battery life)

Makers' figures for bulb life-spans range from 5 hours (#222) through 10 hours (PR4, #233, #243) to 15 hours (#245); but I would guess that in fact they mostly last a lot longer. Costs average $1 or less per bulb.

Halogen (krypton-filled) bulbs, now being used in some flashlights designed for lithium cells, are compatible with other batteries. They certainly liberate loads of lumens. They're rated to last 20 hours, but they seem to drain batteries faster than standard bulbs. They are also damnably expensive ($7–$9.50). And they come with bases that will not fit most flashlights.

Always carry at least one spare bulb; I normally carry two or more. Some flashlights have places for storing spares (see, for example, pages 437 and 440—and illustration page 441), but mostly mine travel in a 35-mm. film can marked "Odds and Ends" (page 522).

Candle lanterns

When nights are long, and particularly if I expect to do evening reading or note-taking, I sometimes carry a candle lantern. It will illuminate a decent-sized tent pretty well and a small tarp shelter even better, especially if the tarp is white. You get enough light to write by, just about enough to read by if you have big print and good eyes, and more than enough to cook and housekeep by, even if you go roofless, provided you hang the lantern high so that household goods do not cast too many concealing shadows. Theoretically, candle lanterns present a fire hazard, so I take care. For roofless camping the danger is nillish, and even out in the open the best candle lanterns generate a surprisingly practical light and will withstand a certain amount of wind.

For years I used an aluminum, French-made, cylindrical model (3¾ ounces), no longer available. Now I have a somewhat similar U.S.-made version by Kamp-Zeek that's heavier but tougher, simpler and at least as efficient (5½ ounces, $14). The spring designed to push the candle up as it burns and so keep the flame in the middle of the Pyrex globe (which is protected for packing by revolving the outer case) seems to work better than in the French version. You can suspend the lantern by tying a nylon cord to the 4-inch hanging bail without fear of burning the cord—and with an auxiliary sideways-pulling cord, and perhaps some such convenient handle as a staff (page 80), can adjust the 180-degree sector of light so that it illuminates what you want to see while the blanked-off sector shields your eyes from bedazzlement. You can leave the 4-holed top battened down (as shown) in winds or thread the bail through two holes and raise the top, thereby holding the bail more securely. The enclosed foot of the lantern, unlike its open predecessor, collects rather than distributes hot tallow.

Pink, slow-burning stearene candles for these lanterns drip far less wax than the ordinary household "plumber's" kind. French stearene candles are still sometimes available at $.59 for 4; but they burn only 2

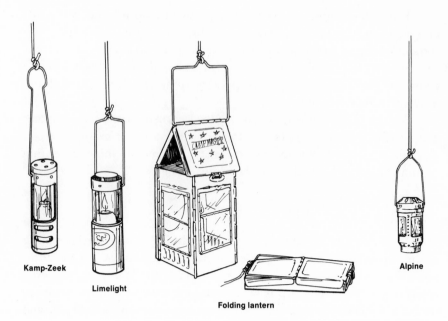

Kamp-Zeek

Limelight

Folding lantern

Alpine

hours, and domestic equivalents that burn for 4 hours are a better buy at
$.79 for 4. But note that the lantern takes only half a candle, and
therefore burns, even in theory, for no more than 2 hours (and actual
mileage will probably be lower). You can replace a candle at night, while
the wax is still hot and malleable, without too much grief—given a
flashlight and reasonable familiarity with the device—though a pair of
asbestos hands would help. You can replace a candle in daylight, even
when the wax is cold and hard and intractable—given a stout twig to
depress the candle platform, a wax-cleaning instrument such as the nail
file on a small Swiss Army knife, plus a good deal of determination and
patience.

I have just bought, but not yet used operationally, a neat little
lantern by Limelight Productions (5 ounces, $15) that, for carrying,
telescopes down to 4 inches (against 6½ inches extended, as shown; 10
inches with bail). Though built a tad less robustly than the Kamp-Zeek,
it hints at transcendence. Above all, its candle (1½ ounces; 3 for $1.79)
is quite a different cylinder of wax: 1¼ inches in diameter and 3 inches
tall, it does not need cutting, and it reputedly burns for 9 hours. A cut-
away slot lets you see how much candle remains. And replacement promises to be easier. Limelight even make little protective carrying sacks
(pile, leather or fancy leather; no weights or prices available). Lanterns
that look identical are sold by Early Winters and REI under their own
labels. (*Later:* One brief field test has pretty well convinced me that
earlier models can't hold a candle to this excellent little lantern.)

I also own a folding model with mica windows (7 ounces, $16), but have pensioned it off because, like most experienced backpackers, I find it overcunning and Murphy-ridden.

A small, simple, cylindrical model that's made in Taiwan and sometimes called the Alpine (3 ounces, $4) uses a special flat, 1½-inch-diameter candle with metal casing (1 ounce, $.55). It is cheap, popular —and poor. I'm told that it becomes hot enough to burn through nylon cord used to hang it, and that if bumped it spills wax every time.

White-gas and cartridge lanterns

These big, heavy, fragile lanterns are hardly normal backpacking ware, but in dead of winter they lengthen an otherwise very short day and also generate a wonderful amount of heat. On short-haul, permanent-camp trips at any time of year I guess they become feasible, even desirable. They certainly have uses at roadhead camps (also known, sort of soixante-neuf, as trailhead camps). But remember that in backcountry a lantern screens you off from the night even more drastically than does a fire (page 220). And that although it does not roar the way a stove does, the damned thing hisses all the time, right there by your bloody earhole.

The most popular lantern is probably the white-gas-burning Coleman Peak 1, with a base similar to that on the stove (page 236) (9½ inches tall, 8-ounce fuel capacity, 1 pound 14 ounces, $34; red plastic protective case, 11 ounces, $10). It burns for 3 hours with 125 candlepower—"like a floodlight," says one backpacker I know. "It'll blast all your neighbors out of the backcountry." Spare mantles ($1 a pair) are smaller than for regular Coleman lanterns and not always easy to find (the big ones will do at a pinch). Like all pressure-lantern mantles, they're very fragile for backpacking. Recent reports have alleged that the mantles emit dangerous radioactive material on burn-off; but Coleman assure me that, although their mantles indeed contain a small amount of thorium, users "receive at least 50,000 times more radiation due to natural radiation and about 20,000 times more radiation from radium dial watches during a normal year. The average individual dose due to *eating* a mantle is only 1% of the environmental annual dose." The company also say that independent physicists and the U.S. Nuclear Regulatory Commission have both concluded that normal use of mantles presents no radioactive hazard.

Mantles seem even more difficult to find for the two lanterns, distributed in the U.S. by Wonder, that use Bleuet (or Gaz Eco) butane cartridges: the lightweight Eco (30 candlepower, 7½ inches tall, lantern alone 12 ounces, $30; small cartridge, 5 ounces, $2); and the larger

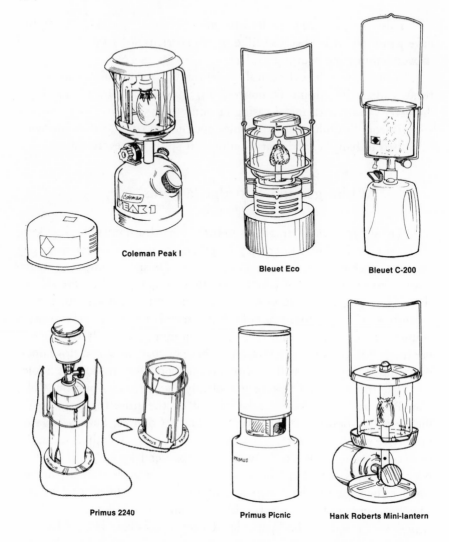

Coleman Peak I

Bleuet Eco

Bleuet C-200

Primus 2240

Primus Picnic

Hank Roberts Mini-lantern

C-200 (80 candlepower, 10 inches tall, lantern alone 1 pound 5 ounces, $38; large, standard cartridge, 9 ounces, $2.75).

The one pressure lantern that had possibilities for regular backpacking—at least with loads not heavy enough to make every ounce a penance —is still made but seems very sparsely available (Century Primus 2240, lantern alone 9 ounces; burns 7 hours on 11-ounce #2203 cartridge; folds down into stout, compact, 5½-inch plastic case). I suspect that it is being slowly replaced by the Primus Picnic (20 ounces, $35), which operates on the same #2210 butane cartridge as the Picnic stove (page 245).

A newcomer: a lantern attachment (19 ounces, $32) that fits onto the Hank Roberts Mini-Stove (page 242).

Lightstick

The Cyalume Lightstick (1 ounce, $1.80) is a nontoxic, nonflammable, waterproof and windproof device that you "switch on" by just bending and shaking the plastic case and thereby mixing two chemicals. Unfortunately, you can't switch the thing off. But its surprisingly bright greenish-yellow light, said to last 8 to 10 hours at around 70–80° F., really does so. And it continues to glow for very much longer. In higher temperatures it shines brighter but fades sooner. Colder: the reverse. I have no comparative figures. The light is said not to attract bugs and does not seem to.

The Cyalume lights a tent adequately and even lets you read smallish print—though because the all-around light, left unshielded, contracts your eye pupils it is advisable to block off the light directed toward your eyes with finger, hand, stick, shoe or some other handy and opaque item. In some ways the Cyalume outperforms a candle lantern: it cannot set a tent or anything else on fire; knocking it over won't put it out; neither will wind or rain; and you can hold it in your mouth. A new high-intensity version is said to glow much brighter for 30 minutes and be "perfect for setting up camp and fixing dinner" (also 1 ounce, $1.80). A new twin-pack has one of each kind (no price yet available).

If, after balancing weight and cost, you decide to take Cyalumes, make sure you pack out all spent sticks.

Although its nonswitchoffability rules the regular Cyalume out for general "flashlight" use, I find to my surprise that it will light your way down a faint trail that you know well, and would certainly do so on a well-defined trail. But you must use the stick properly. Tie or tape it to the end of a staff or stick and push it ahead of you like a mine detector. It is essential that, to eliminate the pupil-contracting glare, you hold staff or stick at the right, blocking angle.

Sunglasses and goggles

Dark glasses are a comfort and convenience just about anywhere, almost indispensable in deserts, totally so in snow or at high altitudes.

If you find your eyes bothered by glare in low, snow-free country, any sunglasses that are optically true should nip the trouble, even in deserts. (Notes: Blue eyes tend to be more affected than brown. And you can check the optics of sunglasses by looking at reflections of straight lines—such as fluorescent store lights—in the concave surfaces: if the lines curve near the outer edges of the lenses there is distortion.) Polaroid glasses protect eyes and also let you look through the surface glare of water—often a big advantage in fishing. Sunglasses come in various tints, and choosing between them is often a matter of personal psychological preference rather than optical efficiency: some people like the world rose- or blue-gray-tinted, others rebel.

If you wear eyeglasses all or some of the time, prescription sunglasses will do the best job. But clip-ons or a large pair that fit over your normal glasses will do, and they certainly make good spares. (Other useful spares: the flimsy, frameless plastic affairs that oculists give you to protect your eyes after dilation; for permanence, patch with Rip-stop tape at the bends.) Once you've graduated to bifocals, clip-ons or big overglasses are the only practical answer if you want to read a map or indeed to see anything close up. I like clip-ons (though they are fragile and must be protected when not in use) because I can just flip them up when I walk from sunlight into shade—a surprisingly valuable bonus. You can sometimes get ordinary sunglasses big enough to wear over your prescription pair.

At high altitude—above about 6000 feet, say—and especially in snow, your eyes, of no matter what hue, need protection from ultraviolet and infrared rays. Ultraviolets are the "tanning" rays: the skin recovers from their effects, but your retinas may not. Infrareds can also cause permanent retinal damage but, long before that, may produce fatigue and, eventually, excruciatingly painful "snow blindness"—which may not develop until hours after you've come in out of the sun. So up high, where the earth's atmosphere filters out far less of these rays than lower down, you need protection from both UV and IR. Glass of any kind filters out UV, but you need special darkened glasses to deal with the IR. Plastic clip-ons or overglasses which filter neither may do more harm than good: they allow your pupils to open up and admit more light to the retinas. Plastic-over-plastic guards against neither UV nor IR; plastic-over-glass at least eliminates UV.

In snow, even low down, and especially in sun, your eyes are about as much at hazard as at high altitudes. For treatment of snow blindness, see page 496.

The standard high-altitude sunglasses have for some years been those made by Vuarnet. The glass lenses are so tempered that even if broken they shatter into harmless round blobs, not lacerating shards. And the cadmium-coated lenses have green zones at top and bottom to filter glare from sky and underfoot snow, and an amber zone amidships. They work well in both sunglare and flat light. Frames are so pliable and tough that you can tie a knot in the temple and let it spring back to normal. Average weight: around 2 ounces. Cost range: $50 to $70 plus. The excellent Vuarnets have perhaps become something of a fad, especially among skiers, but many viable alternatives are now cheaper or lighter or offer other advantages. The spectrum is too broad to detail here, but the names include Ray-Ban (by Bausch and Lomb, with G15 lenses the most popular), Royal Ski Optics, All-Weather Ski Optics, Phonet, Bouchet, Julbo, Galibier and Bolle. Catalogues—especially REI's and EMS's—teem with others. Those with plastic lenses (treated to remove all or most UV as well as IR light) are lighter and less liable to fog but need greater care to prevent scratching.

Adjustable elastic restraining straps (.1 ounce, $1.50) will hold glasses in place no matter what you do. Jeepers Kreepers Peeper Keepers (³/₁₆ ounce, $2) are thin elasticized cords that will do the same if knotted, and if left unknotted hold glasses on your chest when not in use. Croakies (¼ ounce, $4) do a similar job and are said to keep your glasses floating in water.

Some high-altitude and snow sunglasses come with leather side-guards for additional protection, and guards can be fitted to most glasses. Removable ones are best—to reduce misting problems in hot, humid weather. (*Note:* Sideguards are now illegal for driving in California and some other states—and tickets have been issued.)

Goggles are primarily for skiers and mountain climbers, but you sometimes need them for backpacking, up high or in winter. There's a wide selection, ranging from simple Soft Sides (2 ounces, $4.50), which I mostly find adequate, to bigger and fancier models, including those by Jones and also Smith, who keep up with them (average weight, 4 ounces; price range, $20–$35). Such goggles leave room for prescription glasses inside, have breathable, hypersoft foam top and bottom, and offer rose- or lilac-tinted lenses that both protect eyes from glare and increase con-trasts in flat light.

Goggles, though highly protective, inherently tend to cause fog-ging as your sweat condenses on cold, poorly ventilated lenses. Various forms of ventilation combat the problem. Breathable foam padding seems the most likely to succeed in driving snow: any other system that lets in enough air also lets in snow. But some models now incorporate inner lens coatings that absorb moisture and spread it around. Others fight the fight with double lenses. One Smith model, the Turbo, comes with a built-in fan, driven by a transistor battery, that you intermittently switch on for a few seconds to dispel the fog (8 ounces; $75). No kidding. Of course, you can apply antimist preparations to untreated goggle lenses, and you may sometimes need to do so with sunglasses, especially if they have sideguards, or even with ordinary eyeglasses. Current liquid preparations that come in small plastic phials (around 1 ounce) include Sight Savers, available in most drug stores ($1 plus), and See Spray by Amway ($4). EMS offer Fog Away, a 1-ounce antifogging stick ($2.50). A makeshift substitute: wetted soap. Apply a thin film to goggles or glasses and rub into invisibility. The effect lasts a surprisingly long time.

Lacking sunglasses or goggles, you can make mild glare more penetrable by rubbing charcoal on lower eyesockets—as football players know. In an emergency, in snow, you may be able to ward off snow blindness by shielding your eyes with almost any opaque material that has cross-slits or a small hole cut into it. Possibilities: cardboard from the "office" (page 506), Rip-stop tape (page 511), cover from a paperback book, part of a map or food wrapper.

Your seeing—of all kinds—can be greatly amplified by

Binoculars.

I am always astonished that so few hikers carry them. It is not merely that a pair of binoculars can be extremely useful—that by leap-frogging your eyes out far ahead and disclosing the curve of a creek or the impassability of a rockwall they can save you hours of wasted effort; or that they might even act as an emergency fire-starter (page 265). They are the key to many unexpected and therefore doubly delightful bonuses.

They lift you up so close to a planing hawk that you feel you could reach out and straighten a misplaced wing feather. They convert a small low-flying plane from an impersonal outline into a solid construction of panels and colors and markings, even of pilot and passengers with faces and lives of their own. They transform a deer on the far rim of a sunlit meadow from a motionless silhouette into a warm, breathing individual —alert, quivering, suspicious.

You can focus most binoculars down close too—sometimes onto one of those unimportant, utterly fascinating little cameos that you are apt to stumble on when you are in the right place and the right mood, with no stupidly important things to occupy your time and attention. You can even move over into the insect world. Early one fall, on the slopes of a desert mountain, I sat idly watching with my naked eye as a clapper-rattle grasshopper made a series of noisy, stunted airborne journeys. In flight, with its wings beating furiously, it looked like a small and ungainly green butterfly. After one flight the creature landed near the edge of a gravel road 8 feet in front of me, and rested. Squatting there beside a tiny tuft of grass, it was just a small, dark smudge, barely visible. I screwed my binocular focus adjustment fully out. The grasshopper crystallized into view: huge, green-armored and apparently wingless, its front end tapering into the kind of chinless and no-brow head that to the human mind spells vacuity. Above the head towered a gigantic forest of grass blades. After a while the grasshopper moved. It advanced, bent-stilt leg slowly following bent-stilt leg, until it came to a small blade of grass on the edge of the forest. Dreamily it reached out with one foreleg, pressed down on the blade, manipulated it, inserted the tip into its mouth and clamped tight. Slowly it sidled around until its body and the grass blade formed a single straight line. And then, still unutterably dreamily, it proceeded to devour the grass blade as if it were a huge horizontal strand of spaghetti. It ate very slowly, moving forward from time to time with an almost imperceptible shuffle of its bent-stilt legs. All at once, when the blade of grass was about three-quarters gone, the grasshopper relinquished its grip and the truncated blade sprang back into place on the edge of the forest. The grasshopper moved jerkily away, skirting the enormous and overhanging green forest, traversing a tract of sun-beaten sand, then lumbering out over huge boulders of gravel. Suddenly, for no apparent reason, it launched once more into clapper-rattle flight and rocketed noisily and forever out of my vivid binocular world.

If you are going to carry binoculars as a matter of habit when you go walking, be sure to get the right kind. They must be light. They must be tough enough to stand up to being banged around. And they must not tire your eyes, even when used for long periods.

In choosing a pair of glasses, people tend to consider only magnification (indicated by the first of the two numbers stamped on the casing —the 7 in the average-power 7 × 35, for example). But powerful lenses magnify not only what you see but also the inevitable "jump" imparted by your hands. So, unless you can steady the glasses on something, magnification beyond a certain power—about 7 or 8 for most people— does not necessarily allow you to see more clearly. Generally speaking too, the greater the magnification, the narrower your field of view.

Again, if powerful glasses are not to darken what you see, they must have objective lenses (the lenses at the far, non-eye end) that are big enough to let in adequate light. The second of the two numbers on the casing—the 35 in the 7 × 35—gives the diameter of the objective lenses in millimeters, and for daylight use there is no advantage to having that second figure more than five times as big as the first: except at night, the average human eye cannot use the extra light that bigger lenses let in. And big lenses mean cumbersome glasses that are too heavy for ordinary use. Once the first thrill of ownership has worn off, they generally get left at home—ask anyone who has invested in a pair of those impressive-looking naval-type binoculars.

New lens coatings and other technical advances mean that good-quality glasses with a magnification/objective lens ratio as low as 1:2½ —as in 8 × 20s, for example—now admit enough light for perfect sunlight viewing and reasonable results in overcast or even twilight. And a 1:4 ratio can now give good definition in starlight.

On some binoculars a knurled wheel on the center post focuses both lenses, and any eye difference (except for very marked variation in long- or short-sightedness) is corrected with the right eyepiece. In other models each eyepiece focuses independently. Both systems have advantages. For quick refocusing at any range, you need center focus. Individual-focus glasses, more simply constructed, will stand up to rougher use but are now relatively rare.

Standard binoculars have cupped eyepieces that cut peripheral glare and also compel you to locate your eye pupils the right distance from the lens. But if you wear eyeglasses they force your pupils too far away and you suffer a severely restricted field of view. Models made for eyeglass wearers are now generally distinguished by the letter B—as in 8×32B —and have as eyepieces rubber cups that in the extended position perform the normal non-eyeglass functions but can be folded down so that with eyeglasses your pupils move in correctly close. The rubber also cushions eyeglass lenses. Such cups are an advantage to anyone who ever wears sunglasses and a boon to those who often operate in snow or high altitudes and need sunglasses or goggles for long spells.

All binoculars used to be "porro-prism": the prism system bent the light onto a new path during its passage through the glasses, so objective lenses were always wider apart than eye (or exit) lenses. But modern "roof-prism" binoculars route the light straight through and are smaller and lighter as well as more robust (though they lose some three-dimensional effect). This system has led to the appearance in recent years of fully viable miniature binoculars that weigh between a quarter and half a pound and have brought joy to backpackingdom.

Within that group—and outside it—a wide selection now beckons. To decide what best suits you, balance your requirements, or priorities, in weight, magnification, field of view, toughness, waterproofness and cost. Weight is something only you can rate. A high magnification—7 or 8, or even 10 if you have a rocklike hand—is best for route-finding: you can decipher more distant details. But given a certain size (and weight) of instrument then the larger the magnification, the narrower the field of view. Field of view is measured—and often marked on the binoculars—either as an angle (say $7°$) or as the width of view at 1000 yards (say 336 feet). And the wider the field of view, the easier it is to pick up a fleeting target such as a bird or deer. So for such tasks 6-power may be best. Backpacking demands toughness, and, generally speaking, the more you pay, the sturdier you get. "Armored" models, with rubberized housings, designed for Calibans, tend to be heavy and expensive, but Early Winters offer an 8×21 at $7\frac{1}{2}$ ounces and $118. Others now appear daily. There are also special models of high-impact plastic.

If moisture gets inside binoculars it may cause fogging that only the factory can remove, so unless you're always prepared to stow your binoculars away in any kind of rain, get a pair reputably described as at least "watertight." That should see you through minor drizzle, and maybe more. (Even high humidity may get moisture into cheaper models.) And if you want to operate fearlessly in downpours you should buy a pair with a reputable name that is designated "waterproof." If you pay a lot, it probably will be. The very best shockproof German models now run close to $1000 in large sizes, around $400 in miniatures. But you can get comparable Japanese-made miniatures, such as Pentax, Nikon, Minolta, Bushnell and Jason, with good optics and reasonable toughness, that are "more than $200 lighter." Some models now have broad central platforms under which the barrels fold for protection and compactness; they leave me uneasy about retaining the all-important exactly parallel adjustment, without which the image, and your eyes, will suffer. Below $100, quality tends to fall off sharply, but if you are willing to baby your binoculars and put up with less-than-perfect optics you can still find something viable in that range, provided you shop around and outdoubt Thomas.*

Monoculars are half (or, to be more exact, rather less than half) a pair of binoculars. They therefore save ounces and dollars and are easier to carry when not in use. But they are less easy to hold steady—and demand the abnormal and therefore probably strainful business of looking through one eye. Still, some people with two eyes seem to get along fine with them. Be warned, though, that others do not. Roof-prism systems mean that monoculars can now be straight and compact and robust. Most binocular-makers, up and down the scale, offer them. A good midrange model is the Pentax 7 × 21 (complete with close-up lens and 22-power microscope stand, 4½ ounces, $85; monocular alone, 3¼ ounces), and Zeiss make an exquisite little 8 × 20 (1½ ounces, yet, and only $180). With some ingenuity it should be possible to mate a monocular with almost any single-lens reflex camera, and perhaps with others, to make a passable telephoto lens—though you will probably not achieve consistent results.

Buying secondhand binoculars (or monoculars) is always a risk—unless you know exactly what you are doing. Even new ones should be bought only from reputable dealers who really understand their wares. New or old, make sure you test several pairs outside the store, in sunlight and shadow. Better still, insist on a cast-iron money-back guarantee in case you are not satisfied after, say, three days' trial: misaligned or un-

* For consistency, all prices I have quoted here and in the next 7 pages, for both binoculars and cameras, are "list." But list prices in this field are a chimera. Almost anywhere, anytime, you can buy "name" instruments at 30 or 40 percent below list (except that Leitz and Zeiss units tend to be more like 20 percent off). This is known as merchandising. In other fields, similar behavior is labeled bullshit, stupidity or deceit.

suitable binoculars can cause eyestrain, and they will probably, like too heavy models, soon get left at home. (Despite this good-store-only advice, I'm told that if you know precisely what you want and have a trusting nature the best buys now come from certain New York mail-order houses.)

Five years ago I grew tired of replacing good mid-price-range binoculars every couple of years (because I treated them so roughly), and in an expansive, expensive moment I invested in a pair of Leitz 8 × 32B Trinovids, at that time the newest (but nonminiature) roof-prism glasses available (18 ounces; now inflated to $987). They are beautifully made, optically superb and waterproof—and tough enough for near-Calibans (they carry a lifetime-of-owner warranty). They've done me proud. But the best binoculars for general backpacking use are now probably good roof-prism miniatures, 8 × 20 or 7 × 18. There are plenty around, up and down the scale. If I were to buy a pair today, in another spendthrift mood, I would probably go for Leitz or Zeiss 8 × 20s (as little as 4½ ounces independent focus, 6 ounces center focus, but as much as $400). I might lose a little durability (though the miniatures carry a 10-year warranty). I would certainly see less well in poor light and at night— but not, I suspect, 12 ounces or $600 less well.

To get the most out of your binoculars you must learn to use them automatically, almost without thought. First, set the barrels at the widest angle that gives you a circular field of view. Note the reading on the small center dial. Next, focus. Do not shut one eye while you do so: you may alter the normal muscle positions of the open eye. Instead, keep both eyes open, cover the right exit lens with one hand and move the focus adjustment on the center post (or on the left eyepiece in individual-focus models) until a selected object is as sharp as you can make it. Shift your hand to the left exit lens and, still with both eyes open, move the adjustment on the right eyepiece (or on the center post in some models) until the *same* selected object is again sharp. Then look through both eyepieces at once: the object should still be critically sharp. With center-focus binoculars, memorize the reading on the right eyepiece adjustment: it will be correct for your eyes at any distance. It is also convenient if you can memorize the long-distance reading on the center-post adjustment (or, in individual-focus models, on each eyepiece).

Some people tend to screw their eyes up just because they're looking through an unfamiliar instrument. Naturally, their eye muscles soon tire. But if the binoculars' two barrels are properly aligned anyone can, with practice, look through them for protracted periods without strain. After all, seamen and birdwatchers do, hours at a stretch. And there is never any reason for saying, "Oh, but my eyes are too old for binoculars." Given proper eyeglasses, age need make no difference.

Some people experience difficulty at first in getting what they want into the field of view. One way is to fix your eyes on the target and simply bring the glasses into position. Another method is to draw your eyes back a few inches and align the center bar on the target; then, without moving the instrument, shift your eyes to the eyepieces. The target should be dead center in your field of view.

Once you are so used to your binoculars that you use them without a thought for technique you will probably find yourself taking them along whenever you go walking. And they will always be opening up new possibilities. I still have a couple of unfulfilled wishes on my conscious waiting list. One day, for example, I'd like to look from a respectful distance straight into the eye of an ill-humored rattlesnake. For a long time I thought I also wanted to examine a nearby rainbow's end. Then, some years ago, I looked out of my bedroom window one morning soon after sunrise and saw a rainbow curving down into the foot of the hills opposite my house, barely half a mile away. I immediately turned and began hurrying for my binoculars. But halfway to the bedroom door I stopped. Faced with the impending reality, I knew that if I went ahead and looked, as I had so long thought I intended, I would find . . . nothing. So I turned and went back to the window, my dream intact. Well, almost intact.

Carrying binoculars

Back when binoculars were heavy, neck-wearying things, I used to sling mine over the projecting tubular top of one side of my E-frame, and keep them from falling too far if they bounced off by clipping them (with a belt clip, page 522) onto a length of nylon cord that was tied to a ring bolt on the frame. I even rigged a bump pad (page 145) to reduce noise and damage when the binoculars bumped against the frame. But my present binoculars are so light that even I, who fought this solution for years, commonly carry them slung around my neck. Mostly, I pass the carrying strap under one arm so that the glasses stay close to my chest but can still be lifted easily to eye level (illustration, page 144).

For those who still do not like plain neck-slinging, readers have suggested various cunning devices, including an open binocular case sewn to one of the pack's shoulder straps and a metal clip, fixed to the binoculars' "camera mount," that slips into a pocket sewn to the shoulder strap. But there are now various commercially made nylon-strap-and-buckle shoulder harnesses that take most of the strain off the neck and hold binoculars (or camera) snugly against the body yet ready for instant use. Best known is probably the Kuban Hitch (6 ounces, $10.50). Perhaps even better is the Harneasy (formerly Valstrap) (3 ounces, $9.95) by Necksaver Inc. of California (Appendix II), who make a full line of harnesses and accessories for both binoculars and cameras.

For close-up seeing of such wonders as flower stamens or bug eyes it is possible to use your binoculars in reverse: you look through the objective lens and hold the exit lens very close to the subject. But although magnification is good you get curvature distortion all around the perimeter, and I nearly always take along a ¼-ounce prospector's magnifying glass (page 218) for this job—and for others too.

RECORDING YOUR MARVEL

Nowadays most of us tend to accept that we are failing in some kind of duty if we do not record our outdoor doings on film. Chalk up another victory to advertising.

But you can fight back. And there are good, joy-filled reasons for doing so.

I have described in other books some of the less obvious and more dubious delights you can achieve with a camera.

Photography of any pretension at all eats up time at a rate that is rarely grasped by people who do no more than take snapshots of friends. And wilderness photography, even without interchangeable lenses, has its own special time-consuming idiosyncrasies. It is not just that exasperation and loving care have to fight their usual battles—first against each other, then as allies against form-balance, shadows, depth of focus, fluctuating light, parallax problems and a wobbly tripod. You also have to cope with the irresistible beckonings of more and yet more brilliant wild flowers every time you move forward for a shot of an especially magnificent display; with the flimsy psyches of lizards; with the pathologically antisocial attitude of bighorn sheep; and with a 50-pound pack that has to come off for almost every shot and then, by God, has to go back on again.

Now, this kind of in-fighting has its merits. Up to a point it can be instructive, diverting and satisfying. Up to a point.

Not until my Grand Canyon walk did I grasp, by sheer accident, that one of the great bonuses walking has to offer is

The delight of nonphotography.

The accident that opened my eyes happened one gusty Grand Canyon afternoon when my tripod and only camera blew over and the camera gave up the ghost. At first, when I discovered that its shutter refused to function, I simmered with frustration. I knew it would be at least a week before I could get word out that I urgently needed a replacement camera —a week in which I would walk through a spectacular, rarely visited landscape that I would almost certainly never visit again. It promised to be a bitter week. But within an hour I discovered that I had escaped from something I never quite knew existed: the tyranny of film. Photography, I suddenly understood, is not really compatible with contemplation. Its details are too insistent. They are always buzzing around your mind, clouding the fine focus of appreciation. You rarely realize this painful fact at the time, and you cannot do much about it even if you do. But that day in Grand Canyon, after the camera had broken, I found myself savoring in a new way everything around me. Instead of stopping briefly to photograph and forget, I stood and stared, fixing truer images on the emulsion of memory. And the week, set free, became a carnival.

I learned my lesson. These days I rarely take a camera. And if I want my walking to be, above all, carefree and therapeutic, I make sure I leave it at home—or at least carry only a roll or two of film. I find that, by and large, it works. Liberated, I have more time to stand and stare.

A Wisconsin reader suggests a less drastic antidote. "A viewfinder is restricting," he writes, "but I always take a *long* look at a view sans camera after I take a picture."

Now, there are certainly times when all of us, despite the delights of nonphotography, want to carry back home a thin facsimile of the marvel we have discovered; to record, that is, the highlights of a trip— not to mention the lowlights and some midlights. As a writer, I often employ a camera as notebook. Occasionally I need photographs for books or articles, and then I cannot use film smaller than 35 mm. So in practice I never do. And although it is possible to save weight—or was once possible—by using a camera that takes 110 film, the 60-percent reduction means serious loss of quality.

Nowadays, though, you can have it both ways: you can choose 35-mm. film and still meet classic backpacking criteria: equipment that is light, compact, light, simple, light, tough and light.

Cameras and accessories

For three years now, when I have felt the need for a camera of some sort on a trip, I have mostly taken only an Olympus XA (7.9 ounces, 1¼ by 2½ by 4 inches, listed at $250; illustration, page 470).

Do not let the XA's size deceive you. It is no toy. Its wide-angle (35-mm.) lens is better than that in my 10-year-old Pentax. Its shutter speeds run from 1 second to 1/500, apertures from f2.8 to f22. And exposure is automatic: as soon as you slide the clamshell lens cover aside a light sensor triggers operation of the built-in light meter. A needle to one side of the viewfinder indicates shutter-speed setting—which you control by altering the fingertip-accessible aperture-setting lever. The shutter release is also electronically operated and is therefore almost silent and causes virtually no camera movement; and it cannot release until the clamshell comes fully open. The wide-angle lens gives a depth of field from infinity to 4 feet (at f5.6). But the little camera has a rangefinder for close-ups (minimum 2.8 feet), a backlighting compensator (1½ stops) and a self-timer (important, especially if you walk alone; see page 469). Also—though I've never yet taken it backpacking—a tiny but efficient flash attachment (3 ounces, $50).*

Although the XA is not waterproof it's more weatherproof than most cameras. And it's tough. Mine withstood a month's hard traveling and minimum care in China, including one drop from waist height onto hard mud (the back flew open, but no damage done except to a couple of film frames) and one 100-foot tumble down a steep forest slope, with a brusque bounce-termination against a tree bole (damage: nil). Fortunately, the camera took this last ride encased in a little leather accessory pouch (1½ ounces) that zips over it like a womb and slips onto a belt or packstrap.

They may tell you in a store, as they did me, that there's no override for the XA's automatic exposure. Disbelieve them. About my tenth shot with the new camera I faced an interesting problem. In thick forest a narrow shaft of sunlight transfixed a single tiger lily, leaving all backgrounds virtually black. Even as close up as I could focus (2.8 feet), the frame included much black background, and I knew the automatic exposure would give me a woefully over-exposed flower. I therefore compared the reading at that range with the one shown when I moved the camera in almost touching the bright yellow petals so that they filled the frame. The difference was 2 stops. I therefore moved the ASA setting from 64 to a little over 200. And I must have done something right, because as I focused the flower a glorious Monarch butterfly landed on it. I got two shots—one perfectly framed and both perfectly exposed.

With the XA you naturally lose some flexibility: you cannot change lenses or even fit filters. But it's possible and perhaps wise to view these constraints as gains in simplicity. (For my attempt at complexity, see binophotography, page 472.)

---

* Failing a flash, a space blanket (page 585) makes an excellent reflector to fill out shadows, especially around human figures and faces, even in self-portraits. Just drape the blanket over a shrub, silver side out, so that it reflects the sunlight. Folded to about 1 by 3 feet it can help you catch much detail on the front of a flower close-up when you're using backlighting—one of the most effective ways to photograph flowers. If you want to "warm up" the colors you can even try the blanket's gold side.

Several other ultralight cameras do roughly the same job as the XA. The XA II is a simplified, Instamatic version of it with "zone" focusing that weighs the same but lists $90 lower. The Minox 35GT is 1 ounce lighter than the XA but $130 heavier, has a fold-in front that seems more damageable than the XA's clamshell, lacks a self-timer and is, I'm told, liable to light-flare if the sun is at the wrong angle—unless you shoot upside down, with the fold-out section as shield. Still, some people love it. Other more or less comparable models: Snappy 50 and Snappy 20 by Canon, Kosina CX-2 and Mamiya U. The heavier Rollei 35SE is no longer being made.

Ultralightweight and inexpensive Instamatics or simple rangefinder 110-film cameras that are reasonably rugged have long been common (6–10 ounces, $30–$200). And Pentax now offer a single-lens-reflex (SLR), apparently with a good lens—the Auto 110 (6 ounces, $166). It sounds interesting for weight-conscious backpackers willing to go smaller than 35 mm.

On rare occasions—when I know I'll want to photograph large animals, or professional demands include telephoto shots—I may still feel the need for a more flexible 35-mm. camera than the XA. For ten years that has meant my Pentax Spotmatic (2 pounds 6 ounces with case; 150-mm. telephoto lens, 11 ounces). It has done me proud. But it is now showing its age and technology has traipsed on, and the time nears when I'll need a replacement. I would once again get an SLR. And candidates swarm. They include newer Pentaxes under 15 ounces and over $400 and, at around the same weight and price, the Olympus OM1. For the less weight-conscious, add such heavier old favorites as Nikon, Canon, Minolta and Leica.

Rangefinder cameras lack some of the flexibility and ease in use that SLRs offer, but they tend to be lighter, smaller, cheaper and perhaps more rugged. Most leading makers offer good models. And the Fujica HD-S (15 ounces, complete with built-in flash, $240) has a resin/fiberglass case and is designed to withstand "surf, sand, rocks or rain . . . even volcanic ash. If it gets dirty, just rinse it in fresh water." Another "bombproof" model, in 110 size, is the Minolta Weathermatic-XA that's waterproof (underwater, to 15 feet) with a fixed 1/200 shutter speed and three-position exposure control (12½ ounces, $160). Specialist underwater cameras, though rugged, tend to be not only expensive but also too big and heavy for backpacking.

Ancillary photographic equipment should be as light and simple as your needs permit.

Special lenses. Most popular—and a virtual necessity for animal photography—are telephoto lenses. But they're heavy. My 11-ounce Pentax 150-mm. is a bantam of the breed.

Small, lightweight magnifying lenses called "converters" are a tempting alternative. I have two- and three-power converters (4½ and 6½ ounces, with cases) and have achieved occasional spectacular successes with them. But they make focusing a highly critical operation, severely cut available light and—worst of all—rarely give crisp definition. They certainly demand a high-quality lens in the camera. Some people swear by them; others, at. So it would be wise to approach them with suspicion as well as hope.

For another alternative to telephoto lenses, see binophotography, page 472.

Wide-angle lenses are particularly good for scenery. You can, of course, choose to take only a wide-angle, instead of a standard, lens. But my prime photographic advisor warmly recommends for general backpacking—because you may often want to take close-ups of flowers or other attractions—a "macro-lens" that will focus much closer than a standard (generally, down to 9 inches). Macro-lenses are more expensive than standard lenses, but slightly lighter. And they're now available for lighter 35-mm. SLRs such as Pentax and Olympus (Pentax 50 mm., 5.8 ounces, $255; Olympus 50 mm., 7.1 ounces, $300).

Unfortunately, most special lenses are not only heavy—and also cumbersome, fragile and expensive—they're dangerous. The danger lies in temptation. Once you start carrying them it is fiendishly difficult to avoid becoming involved, far too often, in physical juggling and technical expertise. In other words, spare lenses feed the maggot inherent in all photography (page 464), and I'm by no means convinced that, for the wilderness walker, they do not sometimes get in the way of the very best pictures. If you stick to one lens you will never have to stop and debate whether to fiddle about with a wide-angle or telephoto lens and will therefore always be ready to slip the camera off your packframe and capture, before the opportunity is lost, that superb but fleeting moment when a shaft of sunlight breaks through the storm clouds and arches a double rainbow across a somber mountain tarn; or ready to freeze for the future a pale but still evocative glimmer of the poetry that halts your breath when you look up the rocky trail and see once again the always new and wonderful and calming and cooling magic of sunset on fiery desert hills.

Close-up attachments can be used with any lens, including a macro. When I take my Pentax I often carry two screw-on glass affairs, two-power and three-power, that can be used separately or in tandem, are no bigger than filters, and together weigh 2 ounces. (A set of 3 currently costs $30–$40.) Some professionals prefer "extension tubes" that screw in behind the lens and "reduce minimum and maximum focusing distances"—but are also heavier and more expensive and hassle-ridden.

Filters. I keep a skylight (or UV) filter more or less permanently on the lens of my Pentax. But if you are determined to stay with one filter a polarizing filter may be better, at least with SLR cameras. Rotated to mesh with the angle of sunlight, it cuts reflection and intensifies all colors—and also lets you photograph fish or rocks beneath a reflecting stream surface. It's unsuitable for use in snow, though: reflections from crystal faces provide the beauty of snow scenes.

A *cable release* is useful for any long-exposure shot in which the camera must be kept still. My 8-inch cable weighs ½ ounce. Like all the accessories I've so far mentioned, it is not only unnecessary with my Olympus XA but plain useless.

Lens tissue and camel's-hair cleaning brush. I habitually carry both—in the inevitable plastic bag. A few virtually weightless sheets of tissue are for *gentle* cleaning of lenses, on binoculars as well as cameras. The brush dusts off the camera's guts at almost every film change and also *gently* removes tissue specks from lenses. Rubber, balloon-handled brushes (½ ounce, $2) do the job best, by blowing as well as tickling clean; but metal, lipstick-type models (¾ ounce; $2.50) keep themselves dustfree.

Tripod. You more or less have to carry a tripod—or usable substitute —if you walk alone: continuous shots of scenery without a human figure grow horribly monotonous. And it is amazing what you can learn to do in the way of running and positioning yourself in the 10 seconds that elapse between pressing the self-timer and the shutter's action.

From time to time, lightweight tripods weighing around 1 pound appear in catalogues and advertisements—then fade away. I used to buy 14-ounce models with telescopic legs that would last awhile before developing palsy, but the lightest I've found in recent years is a 1¼-pound job that's pretty solid but tends to get hefted in the hand and then left at home. Little tripods with legs less than a foot long are pretty useless for backpacking: you too often need something that will hold your camera clear of tall grass or even shrubs.

Check that the feet of any tripod you buy have large rubber toes, not just little pimples of rubber that quickly wear out and leave you with metal tips that slip on any rocky surface.

As a substitute camera stand, any walking staff forms a rough but very ready monopod. The metal, two-piece Nomad staff (page 81) can even be rigged into a tripod (see illustration, next page). A stray fallen branch, conveniently found at the desired site and if necessary trimmed at its thin end, fits into one of the holes in the staff's handle top. Into one of the other holes fits the optional pike, brought especially for the occasion and now screwed into the staff's foot (from which the rubber tip has been removed). The optional ball-joint camera mount screws into the fitting on the staff head, and the camera onto it. The rig works, I promise you—at home. Whether it is practical in the field no doubt depends on your foresight, degree of need, determination, and serendipity concerning branches.

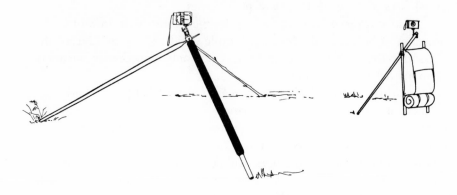

Years ago I bought a light-alloy clamp (4 ounces) that purported to be a tripod substitute. It clamped to "anything" and even had a detachable screw for use in wood; and a ball-and-socket screw attachment meant you could attach the camera at any angle. I carried this crafty device for months, if not years. But taking a good photograph involves positioning the camera in exactly the place and at exactly the height you want—and at that magic spot there is never, ever, any place, anything within yards or even miles to which you can by any means short of levitation attach that besotted clamp. It is a long time since I carried it. I see that variations now exist including some (5¼ and 11 ounces) with "collapsible tripod legs." Uh-huh . . . A reader suggests, perhaps with sagacity, that you could use one of these little darlings on a staff lashed to a packframe with rubber bands or nylon cord. See illustration above.

Film. It pays, I think, to get accustomed to one kind of film, so that you use it with very little thought. Few people now buy black-and-white film to record their colorful backpacking marvels. Color film is just about as cheap (if you'll permit that word).

Today there is precious little disagreement about the best color film for general backpacking. Kodachrome 64 (ASA 64) is plenty fast enough for almost all purposes, gives good density and color, can be found virtually everywhere and undergoes standard processing all over the world (though it may be a marginal advantage to have film processed in the country in which it was made). I often shoot it, as do many pros, at ASA 80 or 100, for greater color saturation and a little extra speed.*

Kodachrome film is extremely stable. Once developed, it lasts without fading for about 100 years, as against 50 for Ektachrome (those are official data: at least one pro believes the true figures are closer to 70 and 6 years). These figures assume proper storage, away from direct light and extreme heat. Refrigeration, while it helps, is unnecessary. But all unprocessed film and, even more so, exposed-but-not-yet-processed film is sensitive to high temperatures, especially when humidity also runs high. Even weak sunshine can soon raise the temperature in an outside pocket of your pack well above the possibly critical 75° F. mark, so in anything but really cool weather, take precautions. Replace exposed film in a can without delay. Wrap all film cans in a plastic bag or even in one of those insulated ice-cream bags that stores provide. Except in really cool weather, keep this bag deep in the center of the main section of your packbag, where the temperature changes less than anywhere else in the house. And get film processed as soon as possible. For protecting the film in your camera, see page 473.

I have no figures on the comparative stability, before or after processing, of other viable films. But I have used Agfachrome with pleasure: it is now the same speed as Kodachrome 64 and slightly cheaper and, though perhaps a touch grainier, has a whiter white and warmer colors. Overseas, where it may be called Agfacolor, there is sometimes the advantage that you can get it developed locally and quickly, though the quality of the work is not always entirely dependable. I understand that the new Kodacolor VR, for prints (ASA 100, 200, 400 and 1000), is excellent—as are both Fujichrome for slides and Fujicolor for prints (both ASA 100 and 400; slightly more expensive than Kodachrome). The

---

* While you tend to lose quality with higher-speed films (see below), it's worth remembering that the greatest source of unhappiness among non-expert photographers is fuzziness in their pictures—and that this is almost always due to camera movement. So shoot at the highest speed consistent with depth-of-field requirements. With a standard lens and normal hands, 1/125 second is certainly safe—though you can often go slower. If you doubt the accuracy of your shutter speeds you can have them checked for about $5 at a good camera store.

Note that using speeds of 1/125 to 1/500 or even 1/1000 second will in most outdoor lighting and with ASA 100 film mean lens settings can be kept between f5.6 and 8. Many people do not know, as I did not until recently, that the sharpest setting on any lens is 2 to 3 stops down from wide open—and with an f2.8 lens that means optimal sharpness at between f5.6 and 8.

Remember, by the way, that if your light meter Murphies out on you—or you don't have one—the printed instructions that come with every roll of Kodak film, showing exposures for varying light conditions, are a first-class guide. In emergencies even pros have been known to rely on them.

"new" 5247 film (really a longtime movie film), available only from RGB Lab, Los Angeles, and The Seattle Film Works, Seattle (ASA 100, but can be forced to 200, 320 or even 400), though at present much cheaper than Kodachrome, is a negative; your slides therefore suffer some inevitable loss of quality. And I understand that prints present certain problems.

Binophotography

Earlier editions of this book described at some length how to use binoculars as telephoto lenses; but for various reasons—including the design of modern binoculars, which makes them difficult or impossible to clamp in front of a camera—I have decided against devoting much space to it this time. But I cannot totally ignore what remains an intriguing subprospect.

Binophotography results are never quite as sharp as with a telephoto lens. And the technique is fussy. But it works. Although it works best with an SLR camera—you look directly through camera and binocular lenses and see exactly what you photograph—you can with practice, patience, determination and luck get by even with a rangefinder camera. My Grand Canyon trip was the first on which I tried binophotography in the field, and in the course of it I managed to capture presentable color bino shots of deer, wild horses, wild burros, beaver and a bighorn sheep. The shots of wild horses and the bighorn sheep were taken with a rangefinder camera—and the bighorn shot was good enough to appear (along with the burro shot, taken with an SLR) as a black-and-white in the hardback edition of the book about that trip.

For the rudiments of the technique, see the first or second edition of this book (probably still nestling in your local library). For further details, see a little paperback, *Binoculars and Scopes and Their Uses in Photography* by Robert and Else Reichert, 1961 (or a later edition, titled *Binoculars and Scopes: How to Choose, Use and Photograph Through Them*). The book seems to be out of print, but maybe your library can help again.

Because the rewards per ounce sparkled, I tried binophotography with my little Olympus XA and Leitz Trinovid binoculars; but I must report, sadly, that the difficulties have scuttled me.

Unregenerate gadget freaks intrigued with the binophotography idea should maybe know that Tasco offer a single instrument, the Bino-Cam, that embodies both 7 × 20 binoculars and a 110-film camera with 100-mm. lens—equal to a 200-mm. lens on a 35-mm. camera (19½ ounces, 5½ by 4 by 2½ inches, $200; 150-mm. lens, $70).

Care of camera

Keep lenses clean, but don't be fanatic about it. Even a coating of dust will only reduce contrasts, not cause specks on pictures. But clean the inside of your camera at every, or almost every, change of roll. That will help protect the most intimate works from murderous dust and sand, and also, with luck, from film chips—which can mostly be avoided if you don't try to force along that last frame of film when there's any resistance to turning the film-winder. Other camera enemies: vibration and moisture. Carrying the camera slung from your pack, the way I sometimes still do (below), is asking for trouble, "they" say. I've never had any problem—but I know from harsh experience that dropping a camera can be fatal to it. So check all carrying straps and other devices hawkishly. A good camera will likely shrug off a little light rain, but don't push your luck. If it rains heavily squirrel the camera away inside your pack—or, if you still want to use it, maybe cover it with a strong plastic bag, such as a Ziploc, and operate the controls through the plastic. Leave the lens uncovered, of course; and for prolonged protection tape the bag's mouth around the lens fitting or, better still, a filter ring. Ditto for use near a waterfall or, even more carefully, when there's any danger of corroding sea spray.

In extreme cold you may not only have to wear silk or other thin undergloves (page 416) so that your skin won't stick to the camera but also need to cover certain metal parts with cloth tape of some kind to protect your forehead. Taking a camera from extreme cold into humid warmth—into a tent, for example—may cause condensation on the lenses. Antidote: time.

Carrying a camera

Remember that there is film in your camera. If you stuff it into the side pocket of a dark-colored pack direct sunlight may raise the temperature beyond danger point, even in temperate weather. Slinging the camera from neck or packframe reduces that risk, especially if you use a light-colored, mildly insulative case. With an E-Frame pack and old-style, larger cameras I used to hang mine over the projecting top of the frame and protect it against long falls with a belt-clip-and-cord arrangement identical to that for my binoculars, on the other side (page 463). For shoulder harnesses, see page 463, too.

Special protective camera-carrying cases are now sprouting in both backpacking and photographic stores. Typically, they are Cordura-covered and foam-padded, waterproof or close to it, shock-absorbing and somewhat insulative (maybe 4 ounces, around $25–$30 but up to $60). Some come with both neck- and waist-straps. Others are hipbelt creations. This is such an exploding field that Hines-Snowbridge have stopped making backpacks and concentrated on their Atan line of cases for cameras and accessories. Competitors include Lowe Pro, Mark Pack Works, Tamrac, Foto 1, Tenba, Tough Traveler and Shutterpack.

ROUTE-FINDING

To nurture the holiday spirit on a minor trip into unfamiliar country I often go without

Maps.

Or I may take only rudimentary ones (page 476). In part, this stratagem works: it injects into each day a steady stream of that titillating element, the unexpected. But sometimes I find that traveling without a map becomes so inefficient that it diminishes my freedom rather than amplifies it. And when it is important that you get to the right place at more or less the right time, maps become indispensable. They're also a help in deciding what places you most want to see.

But maps are not merely for route-finding. They can radically influence many facets of your outdoor life. They act as aids not only to keeping going and to accurate estimating (page 95) but in water logistics, foot comfort, warmth and choice of campsites. Without a map to tell you where to find the next water—even though not always with certainty— you are liable to labor along under an unnecessary canteen load or to walk for long, half-lived hours with your awareness clogged by the gray scum of thirst. If your feet are beginning to get sore a map may help you ward off real trouble by avoiding a route that involves a long, steady, downhill, blister-inducing trek. On a day lacerated by icy winds you can with luck and a map select trails that slink along in comparative coziness under the lee of a steep ridge. And with practice you can choose good campsites, hours or even days ahead—and in doing so may even collect one of walking's unexpected and delightful little bonuses (page 372).

In the United States the only maps that really convey much detailed information of the kind useful to a walker are the U.S. Geological Survey topographical series. These maps come in various sizes and scales, though the standards are either 15-minute quadrangles (covering 15 minutes of both latitude and longitude; scale, 1:62,500, or roughly 1 inch to 1 mile; contour interval usually 80 feet) and 7½-minute quadrangles (scale:

1:24,000; contour interval usually 40 feet). Both kinds of "quad" are so detailed that you sometimes feel they would be adequate to guide you on a prowl around on hands and knees. But don't be misled: although the contours rarely prove inaccurate, trails all too often do—and sometimes badly so. There are hints that 15-minute quads may be phased out. That might possibly reduce eyestrain a fraction; it would certainly quadruple not only your weight of mappage but also the already fiendishly high chances that such vital fulcra as trailheads and peaks will nestle neatly at the convergence of four sheets.

A selection of local quads is often available in mountain shops and certain bookstores at around $2.25 each—the same price as direct from any USGS map office.

For broad-scale planning there is a 1:250,000 series (almost 4 miles to an inch, $3.60).

The central distribution agency for maps covering areas east of the Mississippi River is: Distribution Section, USGS, Washington, DC 20242. For maps west of the Mississippi: Distribution Section, USGS, Federal Center, Denver, CO 80225. For Alaska: USGS, 301 First Avenue, Fairbanks, AK 99701.

There are subsidiary map distribution offices in Dallas, TX; Salt Lake City, UT; Spokane, WA; Menlo Park, San Francisco and Los Angeles, CA; and Anchorage and Juneau, AK.

Any map office or distribution center will supply you, free, with an index map of your state or area. This map enables you to find the name of the quad or quads that cover the slice of country you are interested in. It also lists places within the state from which you can buy USGS topo maps.

In most big cities you can find out from the local USGS office (check in phone book) where to buy topo maps. Even if the office does not sell them itself, the staff will know the local retail outlets.

The Hubbard Company's "3D" raised relief topo maps in a 1:250,000 series and also for certain National Parks are now increasingly available in mountain shops and elsewhere. USGS topo maps for parts of the Sierra Nevada, clearly and accurately overprinted with trails (and also with an index of place names, identifiable on the map by a grid system), are published by Wilderness Press and available in some California mountain shops. Hikers Region Maps for the Catskills, Hudson Highlands and half a dozen other northeastern locales come from Walking News (Appendix II, New York).

The Canadian equivalent of the USGS maps is the National Topographical Series, scale 1:50,000 (1¼ inches to 1 mile). Larger-scale maps for planning include both a 1:250,000 and 1:500,000 series. For these maps, for information about their distribution, and for index maps, write: Canada Map Office, Department of Energy, Mines and Resources, 615 Booth Street, Ottawa, Ontario, Canada, KIA OE9.

U.S. Forest Service maps generally show roads, rivers and trails but little else. It's often worth picking one up from a ranger station to check that the trail details shown on a USGS topo map are accurate and up-to-date. And I sometimes use one on a minor trip when I want to know roughly where I'm going but also want to conserve that titillating element of the unexpected.

Another way to achieve that end is to take along only an ordinary road map of the kind you can buy at any gas station. Between roads these maps are mainly blank space. At most they offer some rather speculative hachuring—a light shading that indicates the slope and direction of hill and valley. With such a map you can easily set yourself the vague sort of target that seems necessary to almost any kind of walk. (As someone has said, "Every journey must have a soul.") You just find a big, blank space that intrigues you, drive to the edge of it, park the car and walk in and find out what's there. Such an expedition can take an hour, an afternoon, a weekend or a week. With a little experience, local knowledge and luck you may be able to burst clear not only of roads but of the last vestiges of any kind of trail.*

Occasionally, if I expect much rain or drizzle, I'll carry the map I'm currently using in a Ziploc plastic bag that travels in my "yoke office"

---

* Do not underestimate the importance of such a bursting free. There is a cardinal rule of travel, all too often overlooked, that I call *The Law of Inverse Appreciation*.

It states: "The less there is between you and the environment, the more you appreciate that environment."

Every walker knows, even if he has not thought very much about it, the law's most obvious application: the bigger and more efficient your means of transportation, the more severely you become divorced from the reality through which you are traveling. A man learns a thousand times more about the sea from the *Kon Tiki* than from the *Queen Mary;* euphorically more about space at the end of a cord than from inside a capsule. On land you remain in closer touch with the countryside in a slow-moving old open touring car than in an air-conditioned, tinted-glass-window, 80-miles-an-hour-and-never-notice-it behemoth. And you come in closer touch on a horse than in any car; in closer touch on foot than on any horse.

But the law has a second and less obvious application: your appreciation varies not only according to what you travel *in* but also according to what you travel *over*. Drive along a freeway in any kind of car and you are in almost zero contact with the country beyond the concrete. Turn off onto a minor highway and you move a notch closer. A narrow country road is better still. When you bump slowly along a jeep trail you begin at last to sense those vital details that turn mere landscape into living countryside. And a few years ago, on the East African savanna—where it was at that time not considered destructive to drive cross-country over the pale grasslands—I discovered an extending corollary to my law: "The farther you move away from any impediment to appreciation, the better it is."

It is less obvious but totally true that these secondary discrepancies persist when you are traveling on foot. Any blacktop road holds the scrollwork of the country at arm's length: the (page 144) and not only protects the map from moisture and dirt and general wear and tear but also seems to collect from time to time a pencil, a book of matches, camera lens tissue and even (in heavy rain) my notebook. Simple plastic map cases with zipper closures keep appearing in catalogues (1 ½ ounces; $2). Fancier ones too (2 ½ ounces; $10).

You used to be able to buy transparent plastic sheeting, adhesive on one side, with removable backing, that was designed to "protect maps against damage from water or wear." I tried it once, and it worked. But it seems to have vanished from stores and catalogues—probably because we now have a better maptrap. Stormproof is a liquid that impregnates and protects paper. I can confirm from field tests that, as promised, it dries quickly and is then invisible, and that it does not stiffen the paper, which can still be rolled or folded. Penciled notations can be easily erased; permanent ones made with waterproof ink. An advisor reports that "it held my maps together even through an 18-day canoe expedition in the Arctic, and I only brushed a coat on one side of my maps (instructions recommend impregnating both sides). It completely penetrates into the paper, giving it a bit more body and a smoother, more durable surface. The paper folds without cracking and does not shred or pull apart when the weather is damp." A half-pint of Stormproof weighs 9 ounces (so it's hardly for carrying in the pack), costs $4 and impregnates 50 square feet of paper, or about seven topo quads. Map Wrap sounds like a similar preparation (4-ounce can, with brush, $3.85; treats 4 to 6 maps).

Mostly, though, I just fold the untreated map that I am using rather loosely and stuff it into my shirt pocket or the "yoke office." The practice often strikes me as dangerously slapdash, but the spring of the loosely folded map seems to hold it in place. I can remember only one occasion on which I lost a map, and that was when I needed just one small corner of a large map and had cut it down to postcard size, so that there was none of the usual fold-pressure to hold it in my pocket. Some

---

road itself keeps stalking along on stilts or grubbing about in a trough, and your feet tread on harsh and sterile pavement. Turn off onto a dusty jeep trail and the detail moves closer. A foot trail is better still—and a barely discernible one far better than a trampled wilderness thoroughfare. But you do not really break free until you step off the trail and walk through waving grass or woodland undergrowth or across rock or smooth sand or (most perfect of all, in some ways) over virgin snow. Now you can read all the details, down to the finest print. They differ, of course, in each domain. Drifting snow crystals have barely begun to blur the four-footed signature of the marten that padded past this lodgepole pine. Or a long-legged lizard scurries for cover, kicking up little spurts of sand as it corners around a bush. Or wet, glistening granite supports an intricate mosaic of purple lichen. Or you stand in long, pale grass and watch the wave patterns of the wind until, quite suddenly, you feel seasick. And always, in snow or sand or rock or seascape grass, there is, as far as you can see in any direction, no sign of man.

That, I believe, is being in touch with the world.

of the fancier new yoke-offices, and especially the Gregory (page 144), have good, protective, transparent, flip-open flaps for maps.

I tend, especially if carrying many maps, to cut off their margins and also any areas that I know for sure I will not need, even for locating an escape route in an emergency. The actual weight saving may not amount to much, but with a really heavy load I find insupportable the knowledge that I'm carrying even one unnecessary dram.

Maps can, as I have said, furnish many bonuses that have nothing to do with efficiency. All you need to contribute is competence in using them and a certain quirky curiosity. At least, I think that is all I contribute, and I know I collect the bonuses. Map reading is one of the few arts I have been fairly competent at ever since I was a child—no doubt because I was fascinated from the start by wriggling blue rivers and amoeboid blue lakes and rhombic green woods and, above all, by the harmony and mystery of patterned red contour lines. These fascinations have never withered. I would not like to say for sure that I ever walked 20 miles simply because I wanted to see the three-dimensional reality represented on my map by a dragon's-head peninsula or a perfect horse-shoe river bend or an improbably vermiform labyrinth of contours. It is certainly many years since I did such a thing openly. For now that I am a man I have carefully put away such childish motives. In self-defense, I dig up more momentous reasons.

I am aware that, for many people, a map holds neither meaning nor mystery. I can only hope, compassionately, that the rest of their existence is not equally poverty-stricken.

Map measurer

A map measurer is a cunning little instrument with a tiny wheel that can follow any route, no matter how snaky, and which registers on its circular dial with many scales the mileage represented by the distance the wheel has rolled. Remember, though, that—except along absolutely straight roads or trails (come to think of it, who ever heard of an absolutely straight trail?)—your feet always slog a great deal farther than the wheel indicates (page 43). Still, a measurer can be a useful guide. I occasionally use mine for planning, but have never carried it in the pack (1 ounce, $10). It is of the old, round, metal kind. Odd-shaped plastic jobs have now begun to appear.

Trail guides

Trail guides have now become immensely popular. They line a shelf or two in every mountain shop, a column or three in most catalogues. And they continue to burgeon.

Their success is understandable. Armed with a trail guide you can plan a trip sensibly and logically, leaving very little to chance. You can strike camp each morning with a clear, numbered and verbalized picture of what the day will unfold: its mileages, gradients, difficulties, rewards. You can rest confident that you need not miss a single important geological, botanical or historical landmark. You will even know where to look for beauty.

My intellectual recognition of trail guides' usefulness prompted a mildly informative paragraph on them in the first edition of this book. After all, I told myself, the guides clearly met a need—or at least gave people what they thought they wanted. And some of them seemed excellent productions. But I'm sorry now that, in an attempt to be tolerant and "reasonable," I corked my true feelings. And I'm damned if I'll pussyfoot around any longer.

I loathe trail guides, strong and sour from the bottom of my gut. They gnaw at the taproots of what I judge wilderness walking (or any kind of sane walking) to be all about. The whole idea, surely, is to cast off the coordinates of civilization. You want to "get away from it all." And, less consciously perhaps, you want to "get back to it all." To get back to old roots, that is, and renew them. So once you have sprung yourself free from roadhead the heart of traveling ceases to be the civilized one of getting from A to B: it becomes finding out what lies between. Finding out, mark you. Not confirming mere intellectual lessons, strung out along a numbered and verbalized white line. Certainly not piling up sweaty records, mile and minute, for retail to the less stalwart. Simply finding out. Simply.

The very nature of the trail-guide beast cuts clear across this grain: the "sensible" subordination of doubt and chance; the mile-by-mile scheduling and checking; the rule of the written word. It is all inapplicable, stupid. It walls off, before you have even begun, the values you came so far to retrieve.

As I said, my aversion is a gut reaction, and I am weightily aware that my attitude gapes with inconsistencies. After all, I recommend meticulous planning. I carry maps. Again, how come a writer rails against the rule of the written word? Above all, how come the writer of this how-to book—even though he has admitted misgivings (footnote, page 16)—inveighs against written instruction? And do we not depend, all of us, every moment we are "out," on such stiff, technological cushions as aluminum packframes and polyurethane pads and gasoline-burning stoves? I admit these impeachments. Yet almost all the carefulnesses I recommend impinge only on ourselves and on the little worlds we carry on our backs. They do not blight the broader world we are traveling through. And if you use the props wisely they need not curdle your appreciation of that world. Given time to break free from accustomed channels of thought, you can establish new coordinates and so move on to discovery, wonder and illumination. But trail guides—these sensible, convenient, efficient tools—impose the old, straight-line, "civilized" coordinates, and so hold you at arm's length from the new, wilderness grid of meaning. It is, as I say, stupid. It is hardly surprising, though. One of our common stupidities is applying the criteria and then the tools of one realm to the exploration and exploitation of another. (See, specifically, top of page 589.)

Trail guides also do an altogether different damage. They bring people in by the goddam horde. If I learn a once-attractive place has been trail-guided, I sadly stay away. Most horrible of all are the now-mushrooming guides to the fragile desert. The disease has even spread to ski touring. An experienced backpacker and ski tourer once said to me, "Crazy! And you know what it'll lead to? It's the old business of the cow that wandered through the bush, and the man who followed it, and then other men—and before long the engineer was following too, putting his road in." Exactly. And trail guides are engineers working on your thoughts. You know what happens when engineers lay their hands on a river and channelize it: they make it safer, easier to control, and thereby more convenient, more efficient. They also kill it.

After this little tirade—which has already made me feel a good deal better—I shall no doubt be berated as quirky, going on cranky. It will hardly be the first time. And I remain unrepentant. I'm damned if I will, this edition, recommend any guidebooks for the blind. All you've got to do if you want one, unfortunately, is browse in a catalogue or mountain shop. And bad luck to you.*

I never walk far without

A compass.

Yet I can remember using mine only once for its primary emergency task: showing me which way to go when I'm unable to decide on or maintain direction by any other means. On that occasion I woke up one

---

* I have actively sought criticism of and counter-arguments to this section. On the whole I am pleasantly surprised. For example, the two friends who rose up in arms against my open-fires denunciation (p. 221) both endorsed this one. "It rests in my gut warmly and well," wrote one of them. "At this time, when the regulatory agencies—Park Service, Forest Service, etc.—are progressing rapidly towards a requirement of designated campsites and rigid itineraries, the philosophy you present here and in the section on maps very much needs equal time."

A request for counter-arguments to a leading publisher of trail guides—before this section was written—unfortunately elicited only points that to me seem either to apply to

morning in broken hill country to find that a dense fog had settled down overnight, cutting visibility to about 15 feet. I needed to get back to the car that day, I had no map and there was no general slope to the ground to show me which way to go—only a confusion of huge, rocky outcrops. And I could detect nothing that might help me hold whichever line I chose to take—not the slightest breeze, and no hint through the gray fog of where the sun lay. Fortunately I knew that only a couple of miles to the north a road ran roughly east and west. So after breakfast I struck due north by the compass. Every hundred yards or so I had to change direction as another huge, black outcrop of rock loomed up out of the fog. Under such conditions I doubt if I could have held any kind of

---

backpacking books rather than trail guides ("guides raise the level of hikers' ecological awareness . . . help develop a reverence for the wilderness . . . help in the fight to defend the land") or to cling blindly to the straight-line, man-world coordinates ("guides help hikers enjoy the country more by acquainting them with the flora, the fauna, the geology, the history, etc., of the places they go . . . help the Park and Forest Service get their messages to users of their lands by listing rules and regulations"). Another argument was: ". . . guides spread out hikers . . . help prevent the ruination of the best-known places by all these new people."

But another author of trail guides made a cogent point. "I spent a great deal of deliberating time before writing the first guide," he wrote. "I ultimately concluded the choice lay between the North Cascades being logged, mined and otherwise resource-extracted vs. being used or, if you will, overused recreationally. . . . It seems that most of our current decisions involve choosing the lesser of two evils rather than choosing between black and white. . . . In my opinion, only enough people who are aware of an area have the political clout to keep it reasonably safeguarded."

On the other hand, Michael Parfit, writing in *The New York Times Magazine* in 1976, described guidebooks as "fine for daydreams, but destructive of mood and mystery in the manner of fluorescent tubes hung in catacombs. This way, ladies; please mind the abyss."

Readers' opinions on this section in the second edition have varied.

One—who violently opposed my views on hunting (page 515)—supported me. He compared a dedicated trail-guide user to "the poor soul who can only look at the woods through his camera viewfinder."

A Texan admitted equivocality: he recognized that trail guides could "help keep novices out of trouble."

An Easterner protested that trail guides perform a necessary function in such places as the Appalachians, where trails mostly follow crests and water is rare and secretive. Maybe. But surely a map would do the job at least as well? And a map, though undeniably based on man-world coordinates, can be a wonderful and tickling thing.

Two friends suggested—with reason, I think—that a trail guide is a boon to a family on its first trail trip. But "perhaps Daddy could use the suggestion that he keep his burden of information under his own hat so as not to diminish the joys of exploration and discovery for the small fry."

Finally, a stern but valued critic wrote: "It seems to me here that you fall into a particular trap: you're confusing the elements of a how-to book with your own idiosyncratic way of dealing with the world." Sure.

course without the compass. But in little more than an hour I stepped onto the road.

Because of such possibilities I would feel dangerously naked without my compass. But the only purpose I use it for at all often is siting a night camp so that it will catch—or avoid—the earliest sun (page 370). It also serves, once in a while, to check my map orientation if I have not been following the detail closely enough. And I once made a pace-and-compass march out across the featureless salt flats of Death Valley to the genuinely lowest point in the Western Hemisphere. (For a pace-and-compass march you calculate from a map the magnetic bearing and the distance from starting place to invisible target. You follow this bearing —either by repeatedly checking your compass or by selecting a distant point on the bearing and homing on it; and after working out how many of your paces, across that kind of terrain, will take you to the target, you count each pace taken until that number is reached. Carefully calculated and executed, it is a surprisingly accurate method, day or night.)

For years I carried a 4½-ounce, aluminum-alloy U.S. Marine Corps compass. But during a recent weight-paring putsch I perceived the overload and invested $10.50 in a liquid-dampened Silva Huntsman that weighs in at just ¾ ounce. The Huntsman is a little black folding slab, 1⁹⁄₁₆ by 2¼ by ⁵⁄₁₆ inches, that looks like a toy but does all the things I'm likely to ask a compass to do. A newer version, the Landmark, has a sighting mirror. Both pin to your shirt; or you can carry them, as I have done, on a short, fine nylon cord that attaches, when you think you may need to check the compass frequently, to a shirt buttonhole or some other convenient point.

Compasses have radically improved in recent years, and stores and catalogues now glitter with constellations of them, basic through fancy, featherweight through ponderous. Many of those most suitable for general backpacking are plastic and at first glance look flimsy; but they turn out to be remarkably rugged. Range: ½–4 ounces, $4.50–$70—or even, for a Brunton International Pocket Transit, 9 ounces and $150. Silva of Sweden have for years made most of the backpacking compasses, but Brunton of Wyoming, long the standard in more complicated equipment, have now entered the field and are challenging strongly. Suunto of Finland are another quality competitor. For a sort of "toy" compass combined with whistle and matchsafe, see page 217.

Make sure you get a compass that's tough; it may lie around in your pack for months or even years, but when a testing time comes it must be functioning perfectly. And choose a model designed to perform the fanciest function you expect to use it for.

Most people, I think, want a compass only for unfancy functions. Those functions are very simple. For the basic emergency use of holding a given line, just see where the needle or north arrow points, then walk in the direction you have decided is the one to take. Base your decision about direction on the map, knowledge of the country, intuition, guesswork or desperation, in that order of preference; but stick with it. At night or in fog you must keep checking the compass, and hold dead on line (at night, if your compass has no printed-on luminosity, don't hold a flashlight too close: its magnetic field can deflect the needle). In good visibility a quicker and much more accurate method is to pick out a distant and distinctive point that lies on the required line, put your compass away and head for the distant point. Provided there is no danger of your losing track of the point you can detour as widely and as often as you like.

If you want to move in a given compass "direction" ("due north," say, or "south-southeast"), it is important to remember that "true north" and "compass north" are not the same. The difference is known as magnetic declination. Because the magnetic north pole presently lies among the Canadian Arctic Islands, about 1000 miles below the true north pole (it moves, slowly), the declination is different in different places. Along the West Coast of the United States, for example, it is now 15–20 degrees east (that is, the compass needle points well east, or right, of true north). Along the East Coast it is 15–20 degrees west. (The farther north you go, the greater the declination.) The declination for an area is normally given on good maps. A diagram at the foot of all USGS 7½-minute topos shows the declination at the map's center in the year of publication, and the USGS publish an isogenic chart showing current declinations, nationwide. The USGS Branch of Electromagnetism and Geomagnetism will also answer questions about precise calculations for specific places (Ms. Jill Caldwell, USGS (E&G), P.O. Box 25046, Stop 964, Federal Center, Denver, CO 80225. Phone: 303-234-5505).

For most rough-and-ready purposes, though, all you need is a round figure for magnetic declination, and the direction of error. But make sure you get the direction of error firmly in your mind. I sometimes pencil the magnetic declination for a given area on the back of my compass before a trip, as well as the bearing of sunrise (page 371).

For fancier uses—for which you will need to work out your individual compass error—consult one of the little paperback how-to books on the subject. For years the standard was *Be Expert with Map and Compass,* by Bjorn Kjellstrom (new, enlarged edition published by Charles Scribner's, Binghamton, N.Y., 214 pages, 10 ounces, $8.95), but it has been nudged, or perhaps shouldered aside, by newcomers, including *You'll Never Get Lost Again* by Robert R. Singleton (Winchester Press, Tulsa, OK, 1979, 118 pages, $9.95 hardcover, $6.95 paperback), *Orienteering* by Hans Bengtsson and George Atkinson (Stephen Greene Press, Brattleboro, VT, 224 pages, $9.95), and *Step in the Right Direction* by Don Geary (Stackpole Books, Harrisburg, PA, 1980, 224 pages, $9.95 paperback.) Orienteering, the now-popular sport of blundering accurately around the countryside with compass and legs, has nothing to do with backpacking, of course; but if you can orienteer effectively you certainly shouldn't get lost too often while backpacking.

Altimeters

Some people regard altimeters as navigational aids: in theory they advise you of your elevation, and at times that could be a vast help in pinpointing your position. The trouble is that the altimeter is also a barometer, and therefore a weather indicator; so when the air pressure changes your apparent elevation will also change. Good altimeters compensate for temperature changes, and that can help dampen such errors. But good altimeters are expensive. The best are by Thommen of Switzerland (4 ounces, $135). Good ones come from Gischard of West Germany (3½ ounces, $56). At least one Japanese model weighs only 2½ ounces and costs $16 and it no doubt makes a beguiling infuriator—plus dubious weather-forecasting aid. For the average backpacker, as opposed to the dyed-in-the-snowstorm mountain climber, perhaps that's all any altimeter is. But don't downplay the beguiling part (cf. thermometers, page 509). And if you really want to prove my warnings wrong consult *The Sportsman's Altimeter/Barometer: A Where, When and Weather Guide* by William J. Peet II, Peet Bros., NJ, 36 pages, 2 ounces, $1.50).

I suppose I should have a lot more to say about route-finding. But, beyond map reading, it is mostly common sense, and I am not very conscious of any particular techniques. Once or twice I have become aware that I was not where I thought I was because the sun hung in the wrong place or the wind blew from the wrong direction, so I suppose I must take some cognizance of such direction checks. Otherwise, route-finding is largely a matter of obeying that sturdy old adage, "Never lose elevation unnecessarily," and of getting to know the idiosyncrasies of the country you are in—the pattern its ridges tend to follow, or the way its southern slopes tend to be covered with impassable scrub, or the tendency of its northern slopes to drop away in unclimbable cliffs.

Failing your compass, you can check your bearings on a clear night by the North Star (Polaris). Pick it out by projecting the line formed by the two stars that constitute the outer lip of the Big Dipper's bowl. Project it for about five times the distance between those stars, then look a touch to the left. If you can't recognize the Big Dipper, go home. Unless, that is, you can recognize Cassiopeia. Cassiopeia is the group of five stars that sits on the opposite side of Polaris from the Big Dipper and forms an M when above it or the figure 3 or the letters W or Greek Σ (Sigma) in other positions. A line drawn at right angles to the base of the M, from its right corner, points almost directly at Polaris.

For more—much more than route-finding—see such books as *How to Read the Night Sky* by W. S. Kals (Doubleday, 1974, 155 pages, hardback, 13 ounces, $4.95) and—recommended by a Massachusetts reader—*The Stars: A New Way to See Them* by H. A. Rey (Houghton Mifflin, hardcover, 1967 [3rd edition], $11.95; paperback, 1976, $7.95). Another approach is through Phillips' Planisphere: you revolve two plastic disks to match time and date and come up with a plan of the night sky for there and then (10-inch diameter, 2¼ ounces, $8; Minisphere, 5-inch diameter, ⅝ ounce, $5).

Provided you know the time, the sun's position will give you a rough, common-sense bearing.*

With experience you will in unfamiliar country come to note without much thought the landmarks and the general lay of the land that will enable you to backtrack, should that become necessary; but I occasionally stop at points that may cause confusion—such as a junction of several valleys, or a watershed with diverging drainage systems—and look back in order to memorize the way I have come. This is certainly a worthwhile precaution at any unposted trail junction.

In certain kinds of country the question of scale can become crucial to route-finding. Among the repetitive rock patterns of Grand Canyon I at first found that it was often impossible to tell from a distance, even through binoculars, whether a sheer rockface was an inconsequential 3 or an unclimbable 30 feet high. But eventually I realized that the agaves or century plants that grew almost everywhere were a consistent 3 or 4 feet high, and from then on I used them as gauges.

In some kinds of country, particularly desert, game trails can be a tremendous help in route-finding. Decide by map, eye and cogitation what seems to you the best cross-country route. Then canvass it for game trails. Look first from a distance, through binoculars. It's often easier to spot them that way than close up. If you have no luck, search carefully at constricted places such as canyon narrows, breaks in wash walls, isth-

---

* "Yes, Aunt Josephine, the sun rises in the east. Well, kind of in the east. In summertime, if you're well north of the Equator, it'll actually rise quite a ways north of east. And in the winter, quite a ways south of east. In flat country, anyway. But at noon— standard time, not daylight saving—it's always due south. Unless, of course, it's overhead. No, that isn't very helpful, is it? And if you're in the Southern Hemisphere it'll naturally be due north at noon. . . . Yes, Auntie, unless it's overhead. . . . And yes, you're right again, it always sets in the west. Well, kind of in the west. In summertime, if you're well south of the . . ."

muses between lakes. In burro-traveled desert this search can be the most important thing you do all day. Once you hit a trail, latch onto it: route-finding apart, it is likely to afford far easier going than cross-country. But keep firmly and continually and questioningly in mind that the animals may or may not be going the same place you are.

Wild burros are first-class trailmakers. So are elk, I'm told. Wild horses are good; deer, fair; independent-minded bighorn sheep, next door to useless. The burros and horses and, to a lesser extent, the deer make excellent instructors. If you follow their trails and think, you'll soon turn from a tyro at route-finding in their particular kind of country into a quick and confident expert.

Game trails tend to fade out, of course. They are especially liable to do so in wooded or scrub country at the edges of meadows or other open places—where groups break from single file and spread out to feed. Trails may also vanish unexpectedly on steep sidehills—perhaps because the animals, rather than create a human-type switchback, have taken short individual routes more or less directly up (or possibly down) the slope and then re-formed in single file at a different level. So that is often where to look. (I am indebted to an article by Sam Curtis in *Backpacker* Magazine #23 for drawing my attention to these patterns of fading game trails.)

The advent of internal-frame packs, which lack the vegetation-snagging projections of E-frames, has made game trails more feasible routes for humans who are not contortionists.

Local human knowledge can also be an invaluable aid to route-finding, or at least to finding the most convenient route. But local humans are not always crystal-pure sources of information, and if you are going to travel in strange country you must command a certain proficiency in the art of sifting fact from embroidery. The only reliable informant is the person who both knows what he is talking about and is not afraid to admit he doesn't know everything. You don't meet such people every day. The surest way of finding out if you have just met one is to ask questions to which you know the answers.

As I approached Death Valley on my summer-long California walk I passed through Baker, at that time a very small populated road junction of the gasoline age. While I was there, one self-satisfied little man fixed me with beady eyes. "What's that?" he said. "Going through Death Valley? Huh, your feet must be stronger than your head. It'll be a hundred and ten up there by now. And climbing every day. I spent years right in the Valley, all summer too, so I know. I'm a real Desert Rat, I can tell you, a real Desert Rat."

"Oh, what sort of temperatures do they get on the floor of the Valley?" I asked—and waited.

I knew the Death Valley temperature position accurately. All-time high is a questionable 134° F., set in July 1913, that for many years held the world record. Later and more dependable readings have never risen above 127°. Most years the limit is 124° or 125°.

The Baker Rat pounced on my bait. "Summer temperatures in the Valley?" he squeaked. "Well, I can't quote exact figures, but it gets hot, believe me. Here in Baker we have summer highs of a hundred and twenty-five or thirty. And sometimes"—he turned to his wife—"some- times we run to a hundred thirty-five, don't we?"

"Oh, not very often, dear."

"No, not too often. But it happens. And you can add a good twenty degrees for the Valley. So you'd best get ready to sweat a bit, my lad."

I did not bother to ask the Baker Rat any of the other questions I had on my mind.*

A friend of mine who is a connoisseur of human foibles was de- lighted when I reported this conversation. "Now, there's a beautiful example of the dedicated weather-exaggerater at work," he said. "The real artist often uses that ploy—provoking something that seems close to dissent from one of his in-group so as to thicken the background."

It is not always so easy to winnow worthless information. Often you have to fall back on mere confirmation of details from several sources. But this technique can backfire. One afternoon more than twenty years ago I was wandering in leisurely fashion across the Coast Range in central California, aiming broadly for the Pacific, when I emerged from forest into ranchland and almost at once met the rancher—a pleasant-faced man wearing a ten-gallon hat and a red shirt and driving a green pickup truck. We chatted cordially for some time, discussing how far it was down to the ocean and what the best routes were. An hour later, far down the hill, I came to a cattle chute. A tall, baldheaded man wearing blue overalls was inoculating a herd of heifers. When he had finished he turned and walked toward me. Partly as an opening pleasantry, partly to confirm the figures and routes that the rancher in the green pickup had given me, I said, "Say, can you tell me how far it is down to the sea?" The man stopped and looked at me closely. Then, to my astonishment, he turned on his heel and walked back toward the chute. After a while I wandered away, wondering, through a belt of trees. Suddenly, beyond a small outbuilding, I almost walked into the green pickup. On its seat sat a familiar-looking ten-gallon hat.

Even now, all these years later, I still feel embarrassed whenever I remember that rancher.

---

* If this little scene seems familiar, maybe you've read *The Thousand-Mile Summer* (p. 77).

KEEPING YOURSELF CLEAN AND COMFORTABLE

Toilet gear

forms a highly personal department that every individual will stock differently, and which he will vary to meet varying conditions.

My list expands and contracts within rather wide limits, mostly in response to how crippling the load looks like being, but also according to whether I expect to touch civilization at all. The full selection includes:

Soap. I mostly use Trak, a biodegradable all-purpose cleanser that its makers anoint with the subtitle "Soapless Supersoap." The stuff comes in 1-ounce and 3.2-ounce tubes—designed to last one person, for all uses, 2 weeks and 6 weeks respectively ($1.40 and $2.95). It is said to have 2½ times the cleansing power of ordinary soap, and to lather and rinse equally well in any water—cold, hard or even salt. It is recommended not only for washing all parts of the body (its pH conforms to that of human skin) and for shaving and shampooing but also for washing cuts and bruises and removing makeup and as a—wait for it—"mustache deodorant." Also, of course, for washing both dishes and clothes (including white kid gloves). Although I can't claim to have assayed this whole spectrum, it seems to work. And to work well. For $4 you can buy a 3-ounce backpacking size, plastic pouched Mini-Trak Kit that includes a 1-ounce tube of Trak, a small vial of excellent dentifrice (see opposite page), a folding toothbrush and a plastic-reinforced all-purpose paper towel. You can buy these kits—and also the separate components—from certain stores or direct by mail (minimum order $5) from Freeman Industries (see Appendix II, New York).

My one small objection to Trak is that it comes in an opaque white plastic tube: though it's easy to see if left lying around, you have to judge how much is left by the uncertain squeeze-and-watch method.

There is now a wealth of "biodegradables" around—though precious little agreement on just how rapidly biodegradable even the best of them are. The safest attitude seems to be, "It takes maybe three weeks for them to break down, so *never* wash anything directly in or into a lake or stream, especially in cold mountain waters unable to sustain the necessary bacteria. Pour the dirty water onto soil, preferably deep and sun-warmed." Among Trak's competitors—many of which avoid the no-see-through tube problem but often come in unbackpackerly sizes—are Bio-Suds, Mountain Suds, Camp Suds and Paket, not to mention Sutter's original All-Purpose Camp Soap and Dr. Bronner's Supermild Mint Pure Castile Peppermint (and Eucalyptus) Soaps. But everyone has his or her own favorite. I know of one man who swears by Ivo—an Ivory Bar cut in half ("It's cheap, it floats and it's 99.44 percent biodegradable").

Washcloth, towel. I haven't carried either for years. If the weather is too cool or the privacy too porous to let the sun do the drying after ablutions or a swim I use a shirt or some other garment. Parents say cloth diapers are good. And one serious though not solemn backpacker assures me he always carries four 36-by-36-inch squares of cheesecloth (about 2 ounces, $1.80) that dry very quickly and not only serve as washcloth, towel and mosquito netting but can also be pressed into service, he maintains, as sling, headband, bandage, coffee- or water-strainer, handkerchief, makeshift jock, sanitary napkin, other napkin, gag or wedding veil.

Tooth toiletry. I now use a simple child's toothbrush, about ¼ ounce, that travels in a small plastic bag along with dentifrice and maybe a very small, ¼-ounce dental-floss caddy (see also page 520). I'm told the business end of an electric toothbrush is good. Zealots recommend cutting off part of any brush handle and boring holes in it, to cut weight to "about .1 ounce." One of these days I guess I must stir myself to zealotry. As cleanser I used to use salt—and somehow rarely cleaned my teeth. Since discovering Trak dentifrice (⅓-ounce and 1-ounce plastic vials, $.85 and $1.75), I find to my surprise that I actually enjoy the operation and therefore do it more often. (I even prefer the stuff for ordinary traveling.) Trak dentifrice can also be used to brush or soak dentures. It's a mouthwash too. Some people favor sample-size toothpaste tubes, from dentist or supermarket.

Deodorant, comb (or even a plastic Gemco "pocket hairbrush," often sold by barbers, that slips over one finger and works fine [¼ ounce, $.89]). Taken if the social standards of a trip demand it. That is, damned rarely.

Toilet roll. A roll, mark you, not one of those interleaved packs that in a high wind explode like bombs. Deftly remove the deadweight cardboard liner from the roll—and learn that it's then easier to unfurl from the inside. For use, see, at some length, pages 538–40. I understand that some people, when they know that washing is going to be a problem, take along a few pads of Tucks—a medication-impregnated toilet paper.

Scissors. Now on my Swiss Army knife (page 214). You can buy neat, folding scissors (1 ounce, $4) that cut well (though less well than a standard pair—which you can protect in the moleskin package in the "office") (see "Mirror," next page).

Razors. It is more than a quarter-century since I used one of these barbarous instruments, but I remain aware that they still exist and that some people actually carry them in their packs. EMS offer a Swiss-made electric one (5 ounces without required D battery or vinyl case, $14).

. . .

Items classifiable as "toilet gear" but discussed elsewhere:

Mirror. I used to carry one, for signaling rather than primping (see page 499). If your hand falls on the mirror a few washless days out and, by reflex action, you look into it, you may be in for a shock. It can travel conveniently in the package of moleskins, between the pads, and protect the curved points of nonfolding scissors (previous page).

Footpowder and rubbing alcohol. See pages 87–8.

Washing yourself is your business—except when it comes to polluting the water. For factors to consider—and a solution in inhabited country—see "Care of clothing," page 425.

Occasionally you get sensuously delightful washing surprises. I particularly like to remember finding, a couple of hundred feet below the peak of Mount Shasta, at 14,000 feet, a bubbling hot spring. The sulfurous water smelled vile. But it was very hot. And, although the sun already hung low, the air felt astonishingly warm for that elevation. So I filled both my cooking pots with snow and immersed them in the spring, which bubbles out of the ground over a fairly large area. I waited until the snow had become hot water. Then I stripped off and poured both potfuls over my head. It was a lusciously hedonistic rite.

I learned later that John Muir, the Scot who around the turn of the century did so much for the conservation of wild California, was apparently saved by this spring when caught up there in a blizzard. By lying on the hot earth and moving his body from time to time, Muir was able to keep himself comfortably warm. Well, safely warm, anyway.

There are several additional items, not strictly speaking toilet gear, that you'll often need in order to keep comfortable:

Fly dope. With luck you won't often have to use it, but once you have suffered helplessly from mosquitoes or their like you'll rarely travel without it. New and possibly better formulas appear regularly. The present batch all depend on some stuff that languishes under the name N, N-diethyl-meta-toluamide but is mercifully called, for reasons hidden from me, DEET. This goody fouls up the mammal-homing mechanism of insects (which incites them to move toward greater concentrations of carbon dioxide) by kidding them that instead of finding more carbon dioxide as they move closer to skin which exudes it, they are finding less.

Muskol is perhaps the best-known current brand. It contains 100 percent active ingredients, of which 95 percent is DEET (2-fluid-ounce phial, 3 ounces, $5.50; 1.06-fluid-ounce phial, 1½ ounces, $4.45). Repel 100 is essentially the same and claims to "protect for 8–10 hours" (1-fluid-ounce phial, 1½ ounces, $3.75). Standard Repel contains 52.25 percent DEET and "protects for 4–6 hours" (2-fluid-ounce phial, 3 ounces, $3.45). Jungle Juice has 71.25 percent of the stuff (2 fluid ounces, 3 ounces, $1.29).

The severity of the insect problem varies from person to person—some seem to suffer far worse attacks than others—and also from year to year, month to month and region to region. (Moisture and warmth are certainly relevant factors.) In the Sierra Nevada, for example, even in a bad year, summer mosquitoes are about the only serious pest. But in northern-tier states and Canada you're also likely to face, any summer, such barely carnate devils as the tiny "no-see-ums," sometimes also called "punkies" (either term appears to be generic, meaning anything that is very small and flies and bites, including gnats and sandflies and other species). There seems little doubt that for all these tormentors, in the worst locales and times, the most effective dope is that with the greatest concentration of DEET. So I play safe and go with the strong stuff. But the others are often cheaper, and you may want to use them in less pesky places and seasons.

Muskol—and no doubt the others—are said to give protection against ticks. My experience suggests that this is probably true. Some protection, anyway.

Though I've never experienced trouble I understand that prolonged use of insect repellent can irritate the skin. In such cases, if the insects become unbearable and applying dope to clothing doesn't work, it may be necessary to wear long pants, gloves and a face net. Nets come either attached to hats or alone (page 422). Consider multipurpose cheesecloth too (page 489). With any netting, use a broad-brimmed hat to hold the net clear of your face; otherwise the little bastards will bite through it.

Rumors persist that thiamine, a B Vitamin, in your blood tends to repel mosquitoes. And Skeeter Tabs, with slow-release thiamine, are made expressly for that purpose (30-tablet bottle, $4.70; 70-tablet bottle, $7.50). I cannot confirm or confute the theory. Doctors tend to pooh-pooh it.

A Pennsylvania reader writes that "the mosquito coils you can get at drive-in theaters" are light and work well in tents or even under tarps.

Another Pennsylvania reader reports that he always carries a fly whisk—a habit he picked up in Swaziland. "These remarkable devices, simultaneously invented in Africa, South America, Polynesia and Australia, will ward off any nasty insect that approaches within reach, with the possible exception of wasps, which get annoyed by your whipping at them. A whisk can be used with practically no conscious thought and even less energy by simply flicking it gently and fairly constantly around your head, or wherever. It also serves as a moderately efficient broom with which to sweep out a tent—and as a conversation piece. You may get a few comments about the pleasures of little old men in certain establishments, but these can be ignored. My present whisk, which I bought in Ethiopia, is made of horsetail hairs, braided and glued into a twisted wire handle whose end will fit over your finger. It should be rather easy to make.''

Suntan lotion. Indispensable for those who sunburn easily, recommended for those who rather think they don't. The mountains are always full of people who did not realize how quickly skin burns at high altitudes, where there is less atmosphere to screen off the sun's ultraviolet rays. Don't underestimate the effects of such sunburn. A severely peeled nose can be painful. A raw red back or shoulders can bring the whole outfit to a screeching halt. Ditto habitually shod feet exposed too long around sun-drenched camps. And even if you have not partly or wholly stripped off but like to walk in shorts, sunburn can more or less incapacitate you (see the story of a fool on Fujiyama, page 399). If your skin happens to be going-on-black, by the way, don't imagine you're immune.

Up high, almost everyone needs some kind of skin protection, especially in windy weather, and under such conditions many popular brands are ineffective: they simply do not block the additional ultraviolet rays you take. And the result can be not only short-term painful burning but premature aging of the skin and even, in the long run, serious skin cancer.

Most good current sun-screens tell you—in fact, blare at you—their Sun Protection Factor (SPF). An SPF of 4 means that it will take four times as much sun to burn you as when unprotected, and so on up the scale. The denomination—commonly 4, 8 or 15—is often incorporated in the lotion's name. A 15 rating is said to give everyone total sunscreening at all altitudes. You choose your lotion according to how high you expect to go, the degree of tanning you want and the sensitivity of your skin ("ultra sun-sensitive—SPF 15; burns easily—8; burns moderately—4"). The best lotions are creamy but nongreasy and do not wash off easily with sweating or even swimming. But make sure you cover *all* exposed skin: otherwise you may end up painfully piebald. Generally speaking—surprise!—the more expensive lotions do the best job.

Among current favorites: Eclipse 6, 10 and 15 (4-fluid-ounce plastic bottles, 4¾ ounces, around $4.25, according to SPF; also 1-ounce size, $1.35) and PreSun, similarly packed and priced. Eclipse 6 also comes in stick form, for protection of both lips and small skin areas (.15 ounce, $1.35). And Piz-Buin put out a stick of sun-screen (SPF 6) with a small capsule of lip salve on top (1 ounce, $3).

Some people get rashes from certain suntan lotions, so try any brand out before depending on it in the back of beyond.

After severe exposure to sun, ordinary drugstore Lubriderm Lotion is good (5-fluid-ounce plastic bottle, $2.50); but there is also, specifically, Sun and Ski Proof Outdoor Skin Protector (2-ounce tube, $4) by GK Laboratories, Londonderry Plaza, Londonderry, VT 05148.

Note that you can buy all the above in sizable, economical quantities and transfer the relatively minuscule amounts you may need into small Nalgene bottles (page 216). But if you do so, label the bottle.

Lip salve. Some people need it in cold and windy or hot and dry weather. Just about everyone needs it for prolonged living above 12,000 feet. Again, well-known drugstore brands are often ineffective under bad conditions. Recommended: Blistex, Carmax and Labusan (all in small tubes, less than an ounce and a dollar); and a Lip Moisturizer by GK Laboratories (see above) that comes in a neat little wooden box (1 ounce, $2). For combined sun-screens and lip salves, see Piz-Buin, above.

Hand lotion. For winter weather and, especially, places where the water is heavily alkaline. On the first half of the Grand Canyon trip my hands began to get raw from frequent use of Colorado water and I was thankful to be able to get a tube of lotion at the halfway mark. Ignore jibes about effeminacy. I once heard a modern-day pioneer who ranched beside an almost untouched stretch of the Colorado River, and was about as masculine a man as you'll find anywhere, say to his wife as he pulled off his boots at the end of a long day, "Better throw over the hand lotion, honey. Had my arms in that damned river half the afternoon."

Lubriderm Cream lubes my derma (small tubes no longer available; 4-ounce tubes, $5.45). I'm told Eusidrene is good too.

Cold protection. Certain creams (no current details available) are said to be surprisingly helpful in retaining body warmth when spread on exposed skin, hands and feet. Fire-Feet is an herbal vaso-dilator, recommended primarily for feet (1½ ounces and $9 for at least 28 applications).

Heaters

We effete, equipment-bombarded backpackers now face temptation —which I frankly find fairly easy to resist—from two distinct kinds of heater.

Optimus sell two sizes of small "catalytic" pocket hand- and body-warmers that burn up to 24 hours and are temperature-adjustable (2 ounces, $9.45; 4 ounces and hotter, $10.45). Both burn white gas (or lighter fluid or catalytic heater fuel) with *no* flame. They work in any position and are said to light anywhere with a match in less than 15 seconds (and indeed will—for an arson major still in practice). They're windproof and use precious little gas. Excellent for hunters and winter fishermen, they might justifiably intrigue winter backpackers who suffer from chronically cold extremities. In really bitter weather, one of them in each glove, or strategically sited elsewhere, could protect you from frostbite or worse. And one or even two of them in a sleeping bag might bring joy to a cold sleeper—and the very stuff of life to someone suffering from hypothermia (page 574). Optimus make a body- or "kidney"-belt that holds two warmers around the waist.

Non-adjustable warmers by other makers (they look like copies of old Optimus models) apparently weigh and cost only 2½ ounces, $2.50.

Intriguing but relatively heavy alternatives (relatively heavy, that is, for anything beyond one-day trips) are new, Japanese-made Shake and Warm Bags (almost 4 ounces, $1.50). You break an interior barrier and shake the contents so that two chemicals commingle, and within 10 minutes they attain maximum output—a moderate, steady warmth that lasts for 20 to 24 hours. If you want to stop the process you simply fold the bag in half—and the reaction stops. They seem a possible luxury for winter camping and a genuine temptation for someone who gets cold fingers in summer and is venturing out for the first time into winter profundissimus. I'm told the bags hold iron filings, salt, sawdust and "a bit of something else" that is no doubt a catalyst, and that the heat comes from rapid oxidation; that is, from rusting.

Space heaters that work off cartridges (Primus, Bleuet and Hank Roberts) exist, but strike me as very marginally practical.

Basic comfort

In wet or cold, a piece of scrap Ensolite or similar (page 336), 12 or 18 inches square, makes a good instant seat.

Shower baths

You can now buy shower assemblies—plastic tubes and small shower head—for water bags (page 207) (1 ounce, $5), and they may make solar-heated backcountry showers a practical proposition. The rather more elaborate but still simple SunShowers (2½-gallon capacity, 12 ounces, $18—not for potable water) are hardly worth packing in, except perhaps to short-haul, semipermanent camps; but they can be soul-and-body-balming when you get back to roadhead, I assure you— and on your veranda at home too, given enough privacy or a policy of charging entertainment tax. I've just used mine in an effort to stimulate me toward liquid prose for this paragraph.

MEETING EMERGENCIES

First aid

The contents of any individual's personal first-aid kit will depend on terrain, length of trip and—most of all—his outlook.

My kit, which these days seems to vary very little, includes:

1 roll 1- or 1½-inch adhesive tape (either cloth tape, with metal outer cover discarded to save weight, or thin, ultralight plastic tape—which I've now carried for years without using or really evaluating; paper tape that "breathes" is now available too)

1 roll 3-inch gauze (or gauze compresses)

A dozen Band-Aids

½-ounce tube Bacitracin or similar antibiotic ointment, such as Spectrocin (replace at expiration date, stamped on crimp of tube)

6 headache tablets (you may need more at high elevations): aspirins or allies

12 Tylenol-codeine tablets (see next page)

12 broad-spectrum antibiotic tablets, such as Tetracycline (see next page)

2 segments chocolate laxative (sometimes needed at the beginning of a trip, to combat radically altered routine and diet)—though I haven't used them in years (some people like to take a paregoric for combatting diarrhea, or to use multi-purpose pills such as codeine and Lomotil)

3 or 4 needles (for removing thorns, breaking blisters, etc.; kept with matches in waterproof matchsafe; see also pages 217 and 512).

Scissors—now on Swiss Army knife (page 214)

Because of a severe allergic reaction to a bug bite some years ago, I nowadays carry a small 2-ounce insect-sting treatment kit (page 563).

Items that a medical advisor says might be added:

1 packet Steri-Strips for skin gashes, in lieu of butterfly bandages, so that suturing becomes unnecessary

Throat lozenges, to quell coughing fits (may mean undisturbed and
   healing sleep)
Benedril, a prescription drug with dual use as allergy suppressant
   (insect bites and others) and also as sedative for good night's rest
   under certain circumstances
A 4-inch wraparound elasticized bandage (see page 525)
Ophthalmic drops or ointment, based on cortisone or a cousin, such
   as Decadron (they afford dramatic relief for sun blindness).

My kit travels in doubled Ziploc bags, averages around 4 or 5
ounces.

The broad-spectrum antibiotic tablets are in case of general infection
from an injury, or from some illness such as pneumonia. Also for bubonic
plague. When you get a prescription make sure your doctor puts you
wise to the pitfalls of usage. Check for allergy too. And take care you
replace at expiration date: time-expired Tetracycline tablets can, as with
many antibiotics, cause serious lung inflammation that may even prove
fatal.

Tylenol-codeine produces fewer side effects, particularly on the
stomach, than straight codeine. It is far safer than morphine and almost
as good for killing pain—and so lets you continue to operate with, for
example, a badly twisted knee. It also helps fight diarrhea. Again, check
for pitfalls in usage when getting a prescription. Do not, for example,
use with alcohol. And take care—once you make it "out"—in driving:
drowsiness can occur. Tylenol reaches its expiration date in one year, but
if kept cool and dry should remain effective for twice that long.

Because your drug requirements may be idiosyncratic, consult your
doctor before setting up your first-aid kit. If you have any particular
worries—if, for example, you are going up high for the first time—
consider talking to the nearest member of the American Alpine Club
medical committee (listed in the AAC *Journal,* which is probably available at your local library or Sierra Club chapter HQ). Memories being
what they mostly are, write down any sage advice for later reference
under stress.

In a party, individual first-aid kits are normally supplemented, but
not replaced, by a group kit. Contents will vary widely with size of party,
terrain, length of trip and philosophy of leader. Candidates include:

Inflatable vinyl air splints (now almost standard; weights and prices
   vary riotously; for use as pillows, see page 363)
Anti-venin kit (page 558)
Oral thermometer

Some rather fancier drugs, such as morphine and Dexedrine, that are reasonably safe when given with a competent outsider watching the patient's reactions

Articles that might be pressed into service as makeshift stretchers include tents—especially envelope bivvy sacks (page 305)—hammocks (page 338), ponchos (page 411) and their allies, and space blankets (page 585).

An experienced, first-aid-trained trip leader recently echoed my uninformed gut opinion of the average prepackaged first-aid kit for backpackers: "Mostly a bunch of garbage you'll never use." But the choice is now wide enough to satisfy a hypochondriacs' union, and some are apparently good, or goodish. Study the catalogues. Johnson & Johnson make several kits, from expedition to day's-jaunt-personal. So do Alpine Aid of California and Alpine Map of Colorado (Päk-aids), who both offer a good range, some tailored for backpackers. Yak Works offer Medi-Paks for individuals and leaders. A relatively recent addition: three kits—pocket through expedition—prepared by outdoorsman Dr. William Forgey and available from his Indiana Camp Supply (Appendix II). Their catalogue also lists individual items from which you can make up your own comprehensive kit.

An advisor suggests: "Don't take anything in your first-aid kit that you don't know how to use. If you're sitting bleeding you're in no shape to figure out how to use some unfamiliar item; you'd likely be better off using something that you do understand, fast, even if it's not quite as good. And much the same applies if someone else is hurt."

One partial solution to this knowledge dilemma is to carry some lightweight instructions. You may not look at them for years on end but in an emergency, when you find you simply don't know the correct response to the situation, they could save your life. Any Red Cross chapter office (in the United States, see under American Red Cross in phone book) will be pleased to supply you, free, with a useful advice sheet, "First Aid at a Glance." It is printed on both sides, weighs almost nothing, and gives some clear, basic information. My "office" (page 506) always holds one of these sheets, and also a compact little 2-ounce, 60-page booklet called *Mountaineering Medicine—A Wilderness Medical Guide* by Dr. Fred T. Darvill, Jr., an experienced outdoorsman. (Wilderness Press, Berkeley, CA, 10th updated edition, 1983, $2.95. Most royalty income is used to promote the rescue activities of the Skagit Mountain Rescue Unit or to educate the public about mountain safety practices.) This booklet is kept continually up to date and has sold over 115,000 copies. It gives practical advice on everything from "altitude sickness" through "fish hooks, removal of" to "ticks." I try to do a refresher read of my copy, under a tree somewhere, about once a year. I said "try." A somewhat similar booklet, apparently, is the *Emergency Survival Handbook* by the American Outdoor Safety League (in zip-up plastic pouch, 2 ounces, $2.95). A rather larger handbook, very well reviewed, is *Mountaineering First Aid;* a revised, third edition is due early in 1984 and will probably cost $4.95 from The Mountaineers, Seattle (see Appendix III).

The Mountaineers also publish what has long been the standard larger textbook: *Medicine for Mountaineering,* a comprehensive medical manual that goes far beyond first aid, edited by James A. Wilkerson, M.D. (2nd edition, 1975, 368 pages, 14 ounces, $7.95). It is often recommended for leaders of backpacking parties. An alternative: *Wilderness Medicine* by Dr. William Forgey (1st edition, 1979, 124 pages, 6 ounces, paperback $5.95, from his Indiana Camp Supply [see above]). *Advanced First Aid and Emergency Care* by the American Red Cross (Doubleday, 2nd edition, 1979, 318 pages, 13 ounces, $4.75) is a less advanced book, not specifically for backpackers but well suited to general self-instruction by laymen.

For hypothermia and its treatment, see page 574; for mountain sickness, page 577.

For first aid to people struck by lightning, see page 582.

For treatment of snakebite, see page 556; of rashes from poison oak, ivy and sumac, page 572.

For those who worry, with or without good reason, about dental catastrophe in the backcountry, at least two kits are now available: the comprehensive OR Dent-Aide kit (12 ounces, 5 by 7 by 2½ inches, $20, complete with 55-page booklet, from Dental Aide Products, P.O. Box 1164, Rahway, NJ 07065); and the simpler Dental Emergency Kit from Early Winters (less than 4 ounces, 1½-by-6-inch cylindrical roll, $10).

Finally, remember that as a good backpacker you can improvise in first aid too. I once read a hiking pamphlet that recommended meat tenderizer (unseasoned), dissolved in water, as a painkiller for insect bites. I'm sure you'll value this brainstorm; after all, who ever heard of a backpacker worth his salt who did not carry, every trip, a plentiful supply of meat tenderizer (unseasoned)?

Don't forget that when there is no one around to appraise your condition objectively, from the outside, it can be difficult to judge whether you need something more drastic than first aid.

I once tackled a doctor friend on the subject.

"Would it be true to say," I asked, "that one kind of disease arises when you have many species of germs or other organisms living in or on a body in a state of mutual balance and equilibrium, and then some quite slight change occurs and one species gains the upper hand and before long becomes, by its sheer weight of numbers, a danger to the parent body?"

"Yes, I think that's a fair description of a certain kind of disease."

"Well, if you had a planetary body with many species living on it in a state of mutual balance and equilibrium, and then some slight change occurred in the head properties of one species and it gained the upper hand so that by its sheer weight of numbers it became a danger to the planet—not to mention to itself, of course—would you not call that condition a disease of a certain . . .?"

"Oh my God, I take the Fifth Amendment."

Signaling mirror

I used to carry an ordinary 3-by-3¾-inch metal mirror, the kind you can pick up in any variety store (1 ounce) (see also page 490). In an emergency it could attract the attention of people on the ground or in the air by reflecting sunlight. But the crystal of my current watch reflects so well that I've sloughed off the mirror. A compass with a sighting mirror would also do the job. And makeshift substitutes include almost anything that will shine: aluminum foil, a metal windscreen (page 259), even sunglasses. You can buy special signaling mirrors with sighting holes, but most are unnecessarily heavy. For details of use in rescues or airdrops, see pages 545–6 and 547.

Smoke bomb or flare

I always have a bomb down in the bottom of my pack, for signaling in an emergency (page 586). Most bombs emit dense clouds of red or orange smoke that show up magnificently, even from the air (see use in airdrops, page 547). Current standard bombs: the Skymark 30 and 60 (which I carry), that burn, respectively, for 30 and 60 seconds, and float (1½ ounces, $4.85, and 2 ounces, $6.50, by Survival Systems Incorporated of California).

The same company makes flares for night use ("soar to 400 feet, burn for 7 seconds, visible for 20 miles"; 20,000 candlepower, waterproof, float; 1 ounce, $14 for 3). One mountain shop reports, "We sell more around 4th July than at any other time."

Strobe flasher

Hardly a regular backpacking item, but if you yearn for some long-lasting visual emergency signal, especially ground-to-air, know ye that various models have over recent years seeped into the catalogues. And they're getting lighter and cheaper. Current best is maybe the Tekna Mini-Strobe T3000 (250,000 peak lumens per flash, works 8–10 hours at 40–60 flashes per minute, claimed visible to 15 miles; 3.8 ounces with AA mercury cell, $60). The Tekna-Lite Survival II is basically a Tekna II flashlight (page 439) that works either as a flashlight or, with a different bulb, as thermal flasher (visible to 2 miles, flashes continuously for 24 hours on one pair of AA batteries; 3 ounces, $12.65).

Whistle, etc.

"A must for safety in the mountains," say some catalogues. Nowadays I always carry one (½ ounce, about $1). A possible bear warning, certainly. For combined whistle-matchsafe-compass, see page 217.

Both plastic and metal whistles work fine—if the balls are also plastic or metal. But avoid those with cork balls. A reader whose canoe overturned says his "was never the same again." He also suggests carrying, instead of an emergency whistle, a flageolet or penny or tin whistle: "My Generation D model ($4 in 1979) is lightweight, compact and indestructible. It makes pretty tunes at sunset, and when I play high D they hear me in County Down." Yes, that's the trouble. It all sounds wonderfully Arcadian. But other people, well short of County Down, may be "out there" for peace and quiet, free from *all* works of man. Even a poorly played whistle, half a mile upwind, is less aggravating than a totebike; but if you're in the wrong mood . . .

An alternative rescue device is a Shriek Alarm—a finger-pressure, spring-loaded little device, really designed for protection against muggings on city streets, that's shaped like a big lipstick (1 by 6 inches), weighs 1 ounce, and "when pressed emits a loud shriek" ($3.75; from Whistlestop, 605 Carmel Avenue, Albany, CA 94706).

Flint stick

For emergency fire-lighting. Flint-stick kits in some form seem to go in and out of production. Consult catalogues. A current model has a magnesium booster (3 ounces, $5.50; refill tinder tabs, $2 for 6 pieces) and claims to "light even when wet . . . virtually windproof." See page

265 for some alternatives (prospector's magnifying glass, camera lens, binoculars) and page 219 for others.

Emergency fishing tackle

The only living off the land that I normally do is fishing, and in almost any country I carry a tiny survival kit that weighs about ¼ ounce and contains:

    1 spool (60 feet) 6-pound nylon
    Half-dozen hooks, assorted sizes
    Half-dozen lead shot
    Half-dozen trout flies

The whole kit wraps into a small, tough, polyethylene bag and travels, almost unnoticed, in the "office" (page 506).

Such a kit can augment and vary a dehydrated diet, and might even help keep you alive.

In Grand Canyon I took along a 35-mm. film can of salmon eggs. They worked well. Using my staff as rod I caught many small catfish and one carp of about 1½ pounds. Small fish of any kind demand considerable cooking effort for rather little substance, but bigger fish are rewarding. Carp need only be laid on hot embers, as their thick skins act as aluminum foil. I often take along a little aluminum foil for less obliging species, such as trout.

For more elaborate fishing tackle, see "Enjoying extra-perambulatory activities" (page 513).

Rope

In really rough country, when there are two or more of you, a rope can be worth carrying as a safety measure. You need at least two people for a belay (that is, for tying yourself to rock or tree so that should your partner fall you can hold him with the rope)—or for a rescue. Alone, you'll rarely find much use for a rope, unless you expect to rappel down a cliff (that is, to pass the rope around your body in such a way that you can lower yourself at any desired speed by controlling with one hand the friction the rope creates on your body as you descend).

The only time I have carried a rope was in Grand Canyon. I knew that for weeks on end I would be walking 2000 or 3000 feet above the river, with my way down to it barred by a series of sheer cliffs. But there were places where most of the cliffs had eroded nearly through, and it seemed to me that in dire emergency a rope might just allow me to rappel down an otherwise impassable barrier to the life-saving water of the river. On short rappels I might be able to retrieve the rope for reuse by doubling it and pulling it down after me through some form of loop. (Rather than carry the orthodox carabiner—or metal spring loop—for this unlikely eventuality, I decided to rely on a multiple loop of nylon cord, or perhaps a convenient tree. On long rappels I would have to use the rope single and leave it behind.) After much balancing of usefulness against weight, I took a 100-foot length of ¼-inch laid nylon rope, about 1900 pounds test (1 pound 14 ounces).

No dire water emergency arose. But once, reconnoitering a tricky route, I found a rather steep 10-foot rockface that I knew I could get down but did not feel sure I could reclimb should the way ahead prove impassable. So I fastened the rope to a convenient rock pillar and hand-lined down. The route proved impassable all right, and I duly and thankfully handlined back up again.

I also used the rope several times to lower the pack down pitches I could manage quite confidently unladen but didn't fancy tackling with a pack. Nylon cord (page 518) will do this job, but rope is easier on the hands and waist or shoulders, which should be used for braking. Rope also gives you a better chance of pulling a pack up—though once you have tried this game with a 60-pound external-frame pack and seen how adept the frame ends are at grabbing the rock, you will go to some lengths to avoid a replay.

Currently, there are three kinds of rope suitable for such light-duty work. A cheap, utility, twisted polypropylene, 5⁄16 inch, at $.15 a foot, will bear a 1900-pound stress, stretch very little, and float. A braided nylon, ⅜ inch, at $.30 a foot, will bear 3700-pound stress but will stretch 11 percent. A Perlon rope (twisted core with braided sheath), 8 mm. (about 5⁄16 inch), at $.49 a foot, will bear a 3300-pound stress and stretch only 4 percent. Note that the average life of even a well-cared-for rope is two to three years. After that, it's liable to be unsafe for crucial tasks.

Guns

I was appalled to see in a magazine recently a serious two-sided discussion on "Packing Iron" ("Should Backpackers Carry Handguns?"). The case in favor, by a writer from the National Rifle Association, quoted specious arguments and statistics to suggest that we need to protect ourselves from co-members of the species. It even called guns "good in snake-infested territory" (any informed and balanced person knows that if you really want to kill a snake the safest and surest way is with a stick). The case against gun-toting, made by the National Parks and Conservation Association, advanced many of the good and obvious arguments: if someone wants to shoot you, then by the time you've got your gun out you're probably already shot; reaching for a gun is the surest way to turn threat into shooting; the terrible certainty of accidents from plain mishandling, especially by the inexperienced; the tragic danger, bordering on certainty, that some scared individual, imagining himself threatened at night by "a marauding animal," will kill a hiker. The case closed with the sensible comment that "the small benefits of carrying a gun are far outweighed by the negatives." Among the negatives it listed "increased hostility." And that, it seems to me, is the crux. The whole spirit of backpacking would be defiled. Perhaps I should add that this is no ivory-tower judgment. I once carried a handgun in Alaskan grizzly country (see page 564). During World War II I spent six years of my young life being trained to use and then using small arms for lethal purposes.

I can't help feeling that "Packing Iron" was published less because of the need for airing a genuine public controversy than because of the smell of a magazine-selling article. Unfortunately, the publicity probably increased the chances of widespread gun-toting. I therefore hesitated to broach the subject here. But I guess the damage has been done. And on balance, I decided, it is probably better for me to say my piece.

Happy cynics can, of course, rejoice. They no doubt see in this latest madness another straw in the chilly wind of Industrial Devolution, another hint of impending anarchy.

IMPROVING THE MIND

Reading matter

For me, the book should be light in weight and not too leaden in content. If your natural-history knowledge is as piebald as mine, one of those little identification books on trees or reptiles or mammals or such would seem a good choice. For bird books, see page 516; for night-sky books, page 485. Generally, I find myself taking books that are relevant to some aspect of my journey but which do not deal too closely with the detail around me. On the six-month California walk I browsed slowly through a five-book paperback Mentor series on philosophy (the books were mailed ahead singly to post offices along the route). In Grand Canyon I extracted many seminal thoughts from a paperback, now apparently out of print, that dealt discursively rather than didactically with present geological knowledge. Poetry is good too: wilderness can open new windows into old lines.

Everybody has his own reading druthers, of course, and there's huge variation. One man I know took the complete "works" of Sherlock

Holmes on a month-long trek. Another dismisses any book in the wilderness as an intrusion, almost on a par with a Walkman radio-cassette player. "I'm out there to see things," he says, "not to do something I can do at home." But if you decide to take a book an apt choice might be somebody else's view of where we stand today. If you have walked properly, with your eyes open, sometimes breaking free from the confines of your own species' normal thoughtways and standing halfway outside them, then you should be in a ripe mood to consider the astonishing human bubble. Two possibilities among many are *An Inquiry into the Human Prospect* by Robert L. Heilbroner (W. W. Norton, revised edition, 1980, paperback, 191 pages, 7¾ ounces, $3.95) and *Muddling Toward Frugality* by Warren Johnson—a rather more "optimistic" view (Shambhala Publications, distributed by Random House; also available through the Sierra Club; paperback, 252 pages, 6.2 ounces, $3.95). A third, rather different, candidate might be *Global 2000: A Report to the President* (but apparently not read by the incumbent) (1980; 47 pages; 4 ounces with cover removed; $5 from the Superintendent of Documents, Government Printing Office, Washington, DC 20402). The chances are good that you will glean from such sources many ideas that you might when in civilization reject, out of fear—though you may discover that they are only confirmation of something you had already learned aesthetically from the green world and had accepted, utterly, with everything except your intellect. You may even find yourself sitting on a mountaintop and pondering the question: "Would it be better for the world as a whole if the human species gets itself back in hand or if it lets itself burn out?" Should you find such ruminations "pessimistic," remember that they represent no radical innovation in human thought. Even men of science have for some time been riding this road. And, at their moments, Arnold, Eliot, Picasso, Mahler and other Travellers have long ago knocked on this same moonlit door. But never the least stir made most of us Listeners.

Lightweight games,

which you can now buy in mountain shops and specialty stores or by mail, provide an alternative to books for tentbound times or plain relaxation. Lightest are the Passport series by Invicta Games, currently appearing in a few catalogues: chess, checkers, backgammon, dominoes, Chinese checkers, Mastermind and Reversi (pieces stick to boards; 4 × 6¾ inches closed, 1½ ounces; $4 each game or $20 for all six). A more widely sold series features roll-up boards and tuck-in pieces: chess, checkers and backgammon (average 5½ ounces, $9 each) and also Pocket Scrabble and Parcheesi (each 6 ounces, $4) and a folding cribbage board

(2.6 ounces, $6.50). Specifically instructive but heavier—really for home use—are the Yotta Know series (separate games for mammals, birds, waterfowl) in which you throw dice and collect identification cards (1¾ pounds, $10). Early Winters currently offer Austrian playing cards (2 decks, each only 1¼ by 1¾ inches, in plastic case, 1½ ounces, $4).

For outside use, consider flexible Frisbees, a.k.a. Flipper Fliers (3 to 5 ounces, $2.50–$6.50) and Hacky Sacks—2-inch-diameter leather-covered balls filled with polyethylene beads (1½ ounces, $7.50) that you try to keep in the air with feet and thighs. For loners up to at least quintets. "Improve your reflexes and coordination," says the blurb. "Emphasis is on total body control and foot dexterity." "A great warm-up for climbing," says one happy hacker.

My personal preferences? I've never tried any of the whole assembly. But in a public-spirited search for a game demanding only pencil and paper—and a mirror or a mirror-imagination—I have come up with Colinvert (patent not pending): you strive to find words with meaningful mirror-images. Using suitably chaste characters, I have already generated "mom," "wow," "oxo," "bog/pod," and "mud/bum" but am beginning to glimpse the awful truth that the permutations frankly fall short of those inherent in chess. Is the game worth the dandle? Of course. At the termination of your labors you can rest tolerably confident that you've done nothing to increase the risk of war, rape, taxes or death, or to diminish the joys of walking, daydreaming, nose-picking or making love.

Notebook

If you intend to take notes of some sort on a trip but have not yet tried it, I sound a warning: time is the trouble (table, page 44). Note-writing always seems to be among the activities that get consistently crowded out. I used to assume that this was a personal inefficiency, but I gather it's an occupational hazard among geologists, naturalists and others committed to wilderness note-taking. I offer no solution other than determination. Don't kid yourself, as I used to, that you will just jot down a word or two for each thought, more or less as you go, and will spend each evening—or long midday halt—expanding it. The expansion rarely happens. Certainly not if you're having to push at all hard, physically. The best I've been able to do is to jot down as much as I can in my notebook *at the time* and then attack the fuller and more discursive stuff as opportunity offers. Mostly, that means on rest days.

I generally use a plastic-covered, spiral-backed, looseleaf notebook of the kind you can buy almost anywhere. It fits conveniently into shirt pocket or "yoke office" (page 144), and one 60-page, 37-cent book (1½ ounces) lasts at least a week. The spirals should be at the top rather than the side so that they do not catch in pocket or office. To make it easy to open the notebook at the current pages I slip rubber bands over both front and rear covers, halfway down, and slide each page under its band as I finish using it.

Waterproof pads now exist that "won't wrinkle, spot or fall apart even if soaked . . . [and will] always take a line from any pencil or pen" (one 64-page version, 3 by 4⅝ inches, 2 ounces, $2).

Sheet paper

Waterproof sheets for field notes also exist—under such fancy names as Waterloo (weight and price uncertain). See also do-it-yourself Storm-proof, page 477.

I sometimes take onionskin paper for fuller notes than my notebook can absorb—and back it with a rectangle of stiff cardboard, to which I secure the paper, top and bottom, with rubber bands. The cardboard can be bent or cut in half. Paper doubles as reserve TP.

Pens and pencils

Ballpoint pens, with refills. The press-in-to-reveal-point kind are instantly and one-handedly ready, and have no tops to be lost. But a topped, nonrefillable, half-length size (3½ inches), now common in drugstores, weighs barely ¼ ounce and costs only $.50. A Space Pen, reputedly developed for the moon program, has a nitrogen-pressurized cartridge that "writes in any position and under virtually any conditions . . . underwater, on grease at 400° or minus 50°" (1 ounce, $8; refills, $3.50).

I carry several pencils—two of them with pocket clips (preferably the spring-loaded kind that you open up with a fingertip as you clip or unclip the pencil to or from the "yoke office"). Spares go in main "office." Don't sharpen pencils too fine, they'll only break. And sharp points can savage you. Both pens and pencils should be a bright, conspicuous color.

The Office

I used to carry a specially made 12-by-16-inch envelope of coated nylon fabric, zippered at the top (4 ounces). But nowadays—partly, perhaps, because the envelope grew old and tired but also on general dram-paring principles—I tend to substitute doubled Ziploc bags, or sometimes a pair of such sets, to enclose the many items that need to be kept flat or otherwise protected and also small items of the kind that just ache to get lost: sheet paper for notes (often with cardboard back, as above), spare pens and pencils, paperback book, wilderness permit, first-aid handbook, stove-nozzle cleaner, Rip-stop patching material, moleskins with mirror and scissors (if carried), spare flashlight batteries, miniature can-opener, rubber bands, maps not in use, car key, dime (for phone), spare sunglasses and survival fishing tackle.

FIGURING

It would seem reasonable to suppose that you can escape from the man-world more easily if you walk out into wilderness without a

Watch.

But the stratagem may backfire. Without a watch (as can happen if you go without maps), you may find yourself operating so inefficiently that ways and means begin to obscure the things that matter. It is not simply a question of knowing the time of day (provided the sun shines, you can gauge that kind of time accurately enough—though in dank or snow-clogged weather or in country so precipitous that the sun sets soon after noon, even that may prove a problem): you have lost the sharp instrument that keeps prodding you forward. That is what I find, anyway, because if time and distance are important I often mark on my map (page 95) the time I stop for each halt—or at least note the time mentally. Without a watch, too, I cannot work out times and distances for the way ahead. And that, for me, means a loss rather than a gain in freedom. Some people find the precise opposite. But the fact remains that after a single week-long trip without a watch I went back to wearing one and have never rewavered.

Even without a watch, by the way, you can figure out the time at night, roughly—if you know what you are doing, which few of us do—by watching the position of the star Kochab, which circles the nearby North Star counterclockwise once every twenty-four hours.

If you decide to take a watch, choose one with a quartz "movement"; it is far less liable to damage than the old kind that really did move. Even with quartz, though, it is probably a good thing if the watch bears the words "waterproof and shock resistant" or some other encouraging legend. And check before you go on a trip that the crystal, or glass, is in first-class condition. Also that the strap (assuming you wear a wristwatch) is not only in good repair but of a suitable kind. Leather is all right, though sweat may rot both leather and stitching. I don't really like metal straps, but my present watch has one and I get by. I used to wear woven-nylon straps and found them excellent: they do not rot; it takes years for them to show any appreciable wear; and although they tend to reek of sweat, they can be easily washed and dried. Old-style plastic straps were useless: in the backcountry, even more quickly than at home, sunlight and cold and wear would cause dangerous cracks. But some new, mostly black plastic straps seem ideal; they absorb nothing and do not crack even under severe cold.

These are the kinds of strap that come on what seem the best current wristwatches for backpacking: small, light, accurate, waterproof, quartz models such as those by Casio. They are available in various grades of waterproofness and fanciness, mostly equipped with alarms and often with a phalanx of crafty meterings, temporal and otherwise. The fanciest models calculate everything except your income tax. The near-simplest weigh ¾ ounce, are water-resistant to 165 feet and cost as little as $15, and intrepid backcountrymen who own them report glowingly.

Unless you own some such marvel (and perhaps even then), it is always worth protecting your watch when you have to swim across a river, or feel that you may fall in—such as when you wade deep or venture out on a narrow log. Doubled plastic bags, knotted, should do the job. Another safe method, I'm told, is to tie your watch into a condom. For swimming across a river with a pack, my watch goes into the well-protected sanctum sanctorum (page 532).

The matter of an alarm is less simple than it sounds. I have yet to find a wristwatch alarm that would always awaken me when my arm was buried deep in a sleeping bag—and I am not alone. Such ploys as holding it against my largely unhaired cranium, inside a balaclava, can unravel through simple slippage. Of course, some people wake up at the merest bleep. Those of us who do not, and who occasionally feel the need for an alarm—such as on those days we want to wake unconscionably early, long before sunrise—may find it prudent to take the course I have adopted: carrying on such occasions a small, separate, rowdy alarm clock that's persistent. Mine is a cheap Timex quartz—$12, as far as I remember—that weighs 3 ounces but bleeps at you piercingly for half an hour, if necessary, until manually suppressed. Some alarms nudge you if you don't respond: their volume progressively increases.

A cruder kind of time-figuring is almost always essential:

Keeping check on the days.

Even if you have no vital commitments to meet in the outside world, you should before leaving roadhead give somebody a time and a date beyond which it can be assumed that, if you have not shown up, you are in trouble (page 524). Or you may have arranged an airdrop, or a meeting with packers or other walkers. In any of these cases a mistake in the day can cost you dearly. And the mistake is remarkably easy to make.

I always prepare a table on a page near the end of my notebook (not the last page, because it may pull out). I block out the days and leave room for writing in the name, actual or fancied, of the place at which I camp each night. This detail, I find, is the one that my mind distinguishes most clearly in identifying the days. Without my calendar table I would often—perhaps most often—not know for sure what day it was. The table also makes it much easier to figure out, days ahead, whether I really need to hurry or can afford to amble luxuriously along.

Having a watch that reports day and date has not made me forgo the calendar-table habit. But then, I'm a cautious s.o.b.

Pedometer

Theoretically, this instrument is a valuable item (2 ounces; $10–$16). But although I own one I've never got past the finicky job of trying to calibrate it to my normal stride. Perhaps that's because I question how useful such calibration would be over any but smooth, level ground— and because I regard wilderness mileage figures as being, in most cases, singularly meaningless (page 43).

Thermometer

It is many years now since I began taking a thermometer on walks, and I still have no reasoned explanation of why it makes such a beguiling toy. I have to admit, I suppose, that it is primarily a toy. It has taught me any number of intriguing facts: the remarkably tenuous relationship that exists between air temperature and what the human body feels (page 353); the astonishingly hot surfaces your boots often have to walk on and can sometimes avoid (page 88); and the actual temperature of a river I had to swim in (the body is a miserable judge here too, and the temperature can be critical if you have to swim far [page 537]). But the sort of information my thermometer has given me has more often been interesting than practical.

One February I took a three-day hike along Point Reyes National Seashore, just north of San Francisco. On the last day a cold, damp wind blew in from offshore fog banks. At lunchtime I sheltered from the wind in a little hollow on the edge of the sand dunes bordering the beach. Down in the hollow, the wind barely rustled the thin, tough blades of beach grass. And the sun's reflected warmth beat up genially from pale sand. After a few minutes I felt sweat beginning to trickle down my face. Idly, I checked the temperature in the shady depths of the densest grass: 64°. Then I moved the thermometer out into the sun, on open sand. The mercury finally stopped at 112°.

For no clear or logical reason I have for years checked and noted temperature readings: in shade and sun; in the air, on and below the surface; above, on and below different neighboring surfaces; in rivers and hot springs. Once I found myself delighted by the singularly useless information that it was still 55° in my boots half an hour after I had taken them off, when the ground temperature had already fallen close to freezing.

I suppose I gradually gain from such readings, in an untidy and diffuse sort of way, some new and rather tangential understandings of how our fascinating world works, but I doubt that this is really why I go on with the measuring and figuring. Mostly, I think, it's just that I enjoy my thermometer. And although I play with it less nowadays I never think of leaving it behind. It clips into my "yoke office," alongside pen and pencil.

It is an ordinary mercury thermometer by Taylor that comes in a metal, pencil-size case (⅜ by 6¼ inches) with a strong pocket clip and a carrying ring at the top. Range: −30° F. to 120° F. (which is really too low if you want to play) (1½ ounces; $9; refills, $4.75). These thermometers are reasonably tough; but I assure you that they'll break if you drop them far enough. I guess I go through about one a year. Some equivalents now come with plastic cases and red-liquid fill. But beware! The plastic may bend a little—and the glass won't.

Practical hints: Try to calibrate a new thermometer against a reliable and preferably official one. For a quick "shade" reading when there is no shade, twirl the thermometer around on the end of a length of string or nylon cord that you leave knotted to the carrying loop; but check the knot first (see knots, nylon cord, page 520). In hot weather be careful where you leave the thermometer; in the sun, surface temperatures can easily exceed 130° F., and much beyond that you may find yourself with an empty glass stem and a blob of freelance mercury.

Also available: an ambient and minimum liquid thermometer by Taylor that tells you how cold it got during the night (½ ounce, $12). But you have to lay the thing down flat for the minimum registration to work, and in spite of the bright yellow plastic case it is abominably easy to tread on. I did so with mine, first time out—and haven't gone to the well again.

You can now get tiny plastic thermometers, hangable "from pack or parka" (1 ounce, $2.50). I know nothing of their accuracy or toughness.

A nonliquid thermometer that looks very durable and is said to be reasonably accurate: a plastic-housed, bimetallic dial model that rotates into an attached leather case (range − 50° F. to 130° F., about 1 ounce, $6). And REI sell a fancier model (same range, 1½ ounces, $22.50) with 2¾-inch dial that records the day's high and low as well as ambient temperatures in both Fahrenheit and Celsius.

A reader writes: "You can save weight by buying a skin divers' watch-band thermometer. You wear it on your watch band. Pressure-proofed, and about the size of a nickel, it is within 2 degrees of true temperature and costs about $5." Maybe; but in air, what about the effect of my sweaty little wrist?

Of course, real cognoscenti scorn thermometers. They calculate ambient temperature instantly by counting the number of times any neighboring cricket chirps in 14 seconds, then adding their age next birthday.

Windmeter

Under certain conditions, especially in winter, knowing the wind-speed might be useful as well as interesting. The Dwyer Wind Gauge registers up to 66 mph (2 ounces, $10). And Taylor's Wind Chill and Speed Meter records windchill factors "at a glance" (6 ounces, plus 1.2-ounce case, $18; case, $5).

Altimeter

See page 484.

MENDING

Most good mountain shops repair gear and a few outfits specialize in such work, including Mountain Mend of Colorado (Appendix II). But you'll often want or need to do your own repairs. At home you can, if you like, attack such jobs as replacing zippers, Velcro fittings and grommets (special grommet kits for amateurs are made by Lord and Hodge Inc., P.O. Box 737, Middletown, CT 06457.

If you're wise you'll always have a few emergency repair items in your pack:

Tape

Rolls of adhesive repair tape now come in six colors and three fabrics —Rip-stop, taffeta and 60/40 (Kenyon K-Tape, 2 by 18 inches, ¼ ounce, $2). The difference in fabrics is essentially cosmetic: to match the garment or whatever. With all of them, you simply peel off the protective paper from its adhesive side and press the fabric in place. No heating, no nothing. And it sticks—though I'm convinced it sticks less well than it used to (page 367). Repairs seem to withstand a certain amount of washing but not dry-cleaning. To make a patch permanent, sew around its edges. I always carry a length of Rip-stop tape in my office (page 506) —up to 2 feet, according to the length of the trip. Unexpected uses include repairing the split lens of a pair of snow goggles, binding the splintering end of my staff (page 80) and stopping the reek of butane gas from the empty cartridge of a Bleuet stove by simply sealing off the hole (page 244).

Some people prefer stronger, if heavier, duct tape. And maybe they're right.

Needles and thread

For reinstating buttons and repairing anything from tent tabs to "yoke office." (Needles also puncture blisters. See page 90.) Three or four of them travel in my matchsafe (page 217). Short lengths of strong thread are threaded through three or four of these needles and are wrapped around them like pythons. A longer reserve of thread, wrapped around a small piece of paper, goes into the "odds and ends" can (page 522).

An Alaskan reader suggests "glovers' needles," with #7 a good starter size. Glovers' needles have flattened point-ends, and Eskimos apparently use them for skin-sewing.

Speedy Stitcher

A Speedy Stitcher Sewing Awl is essentially for groups—but might just (at about 3 ounces, $4.50) be worthwhile on long trips for individuals of suitable bent. The strong wooden handle houses a replaceable bobbin of waxed nylon thread and two interchangeable needles—straight and curved (both #8)—that have eyes near their points and enable you to make a machinelike lockstitch even in heavy pack fabric. Extravagantly praised by apparently sane and experienced users.

Spare parts for pack

Every pack has certain small attachments whose loss or damage could disrupt a trip. When using my Trailwise pack I carry in the "Odds and Ends" can (page 522) at least one spare end-button for the frame (page 115) and three of the aluminum eyebolts that hold packbag to frame (also page 115). Into a separate small plastic bag goes a spare set of the buckles, with bars and split rings, that attach the yoke to the foot of the packframe. Frankly, I've never had to use any item except end-buttons.

Makeshift repairs

One experienced backpacker I know says he would not hump his pack a mile without a few safety pins for emergency repairs to anything from shirt to doggy pack.

Occasionally, for such unexpected tasks as tying on a wrenched-off zipper tab, I've used nylon fishing line (page 501). Adhesive medical tape (page 495) and moleskins (pages 89 and 77) can also be useful.

For epoxy, see "Air mattress," page 335.

For "Dental floss," see page 520.

ENJOYING EXTRAPERAMBULATORY ACTIVITIES

For many people, perhaps for most, a walk is rarely a self-fulfilling operation, whether it lasts an hour or a summer. Alone, with an agreeable companion, or in a group, they walk as a means to some such specific end as hunting, fishing, photography, birdwatching, sex or geology.

Generally speaking, I regard the equipment for such activities as outside the scope of this book. There are two exceptions.

Fishing

An orthodox 2- or 3-piece rod is a perishing nuisance on a backpack trip. (I am thinking primarily of trout fishing, because that is what you usually find in the wilder areas still left for backpacking. And I am thinking above all of fly fishing, because in most remote areas that is the way to get the most pleasure from your fishing—and sometimes to catch the most trout. But what I have to say applies to most kinds of rods.)

If you lash an orthodox rod to an E-frame upright—the best place for it—the risk of damage is high, though a dowel or stick rubber-banded to the uncased rod may help. If you tote along an aluminum rod case, the wretched thing tends to get in the way, especially if you use an I-frame pack. When fishing is your overriding object, the inconvenience may be worth it; but if fishing is really an excuse for escape, and even more if it is just a possible bonus, the solution lies in a portmanteau rod —4- or even 6-piece.

The difficulty with this kind of rod is always its action: the perfect rod is a 1-piecer, and every metal ferrule marks another step down from perfection. Each ferrule also used to add critically to the weight, but new alloys have pretty well solved that problem. On this count, even some cheaper fiberglass rods now score high. And the very best dispense with metal ferrules: fiberglass fits into hollowed fiberglass. The results are featherweight wands with smooth, lively actions.

Many portmanteau rods, some of them ferruleless, now appear in outdoor catalogues. Among the best known are those by Fenwick. Among the least expensive is a 6-piece, ferruleless, fiberglass model by Daiwa, with reversible handle for fly fishing or spinning, that weighs 5 ounces (case 1½ ounces), costs $42.50 and is said to be good.

With an E-frame pack I carry my 4-piece, 7½-foot ferruleless fly rod custom-made by The Winston Rod Company, formerly of San Francisco, now of Twin Bridges, Montana (2 feet, disassembled; 3 ounces; cloth cover, 2 ounces; aluminum case, 7 ounces) fitting snugly down one side of the packbag, close beside the packframe. It mostly travels in the cloth cover and has never come to any harm. When using an I-frame pack I'll probably carry the protective aluminum case.

The rest of my backpack fly-fishing tackle fits into a small leather reel bag: the reel itself, six spools of nylon (2-, 3-, 4-, 6-, 8- and 10-pound test), a small can of flies, line grease and fly flotant. Total: 11 ounces.

Anyone with enough wit to resist the widespread fallacy that you go fishing mainly in order to catch fish will understand that spinning is a barbarous way to catch trout. But I have to admit that there are places, such as certain high mountain lakes, where fly fishing may often be useless. And there are times, of course, when you'll want to fish purely for food. For such occasions I have once or twice carried a little closed-faced abomination of a spinning reel (9 ounces) that takes most of the pleasure out of fishing but does not demand a large butt ring on the rod and can therefore be used with a fly rod. Into the abomination's little bag went some lead shot and weights, a few lures and bait hooks and a bobber.

There are times when fly fishing is plainly impossible. (Often, for example, when the fish are not trout.) So I have a 4-piece, 4-ounce, 6-foot spinning rod that breaks down to 20 inches. It was made to my specifications nearly thirty years ago from a hollow-glass blank that I selected from stock. My other spinning tackle is standard.

You can fish purely for fun—and get it—with emergency tackle (page 501) and a light switch cut from the riverbank—if cutting it seems acceptable in that place.

I'm aware that many people condemn fishing as a barbarous pursuit, lumpable with hunting. Seen from the outside, it may be—especially if the view includes close-ups of those pitiless (or, more likely, unthinking) rodmen who wrench their catch off the hook and leave it to gasp to death by inches. Even intellectually, though, I think it is possible to unlump fishing from hunting. Fish, for example, have simple nervous systems that do not seem to register pain as we mammals know it: I once hooked a small brook trout, brought it in almost to my feet before it came off the hook, and watched it swim back a few yards to its original position, then take my fly again within a minute or so. But hunters shoot birds or fellow mammals, with fellow nervous systems: a shot rabbit that just makes it back down its burrow, shattered leg gushing blood, is hardly likely to come back, like my brook trout, for another sample. Again, provided you wet your hands first and then work gently, you can, especially when fly fishing, return without harming it almost any fish you do not want for food. (Dry hands remove protective slime and leave a fish vulnerable to disease.) But you cannot by any known means set free a doe once it is lying there with its eyeball hanging and brains spattered—even if you had thought it was a buck, or if your natural hot hunter's blood has drained away and left only chill once you stand over your twitching victim. Furthermore, I see a fly rod as a delicate wand, a gun as an instrument of war. Here we may be closing on the nub. In the end, I think the difference is aesthetic. I find fishing a gentle and artistic pastime that calms me. And I see hunting otherwise. (I speak only of hunting as a sport. I have no quarrel with hunting *purely* for food, as a necessity. I would do it anytime.)

A Wisconsin reader who hunts has written in response to the above, disagreeingly but agreeably. He asserts that hunters as a whole are "a group of dedicated, aware conservationists" but readily admits they are "severely plagued by slobs in their ranks." He also claims, with considerable reason, that we have in many cases caused overpopulation—as with deer—and that "it is therefore the responsibility of man, who threw the monkey wrench in, to correct the situation by removing nature's intentional excesses." He sounds a sincere and likable guy. And in recent years I've become increasingly aware that certain men whom I like and respect, men whose knowledge of and even veneration for wildlife is at least as great as mine, find hunting a satisfying and natural pursuit

consonant with their veneration. Furthermore, I often feel more comfortable in the company of men who I know are hunters—even though I
deplore what they do in that role—than I do in the company of many
"ecologically aware individuals" who share my concerns but who never
for one moment, by God, let you forget that they are the Chosen De-
fenders of the Earth. It is all very difficult—yet another instance of the
not easily digested fact that you can like a man but dislike what he does.
And vice versa.

Birdwatching

For the first forty-four years of my life I thought of birdwatchers,
when I thought of them at all, as a frustrated and ineffectual bunch of
fuddy-duddies, almost certainly sex-starved, who funneled their energies
into an amiable but pointless pursuit. My competence in their field was
naturally close to zero. ("Naturally," because the firmest and most comfortable base from which to make sweeping judgments about any group
of people is total ignorance.) But a few years ago, on a return visit to
East Africa, I bought an identification book of the astonishingly prodigal
birdlife of that astonishingly prodigal land. And at once I began to
understand about birdwatching. It was not merely that birds, really
looked at, turn out to be startlingly beautiful, nor even that individual
birds, like individual humans, engage in funny, solemn, bitchy, pomp-
ous, brave, ludicrous, sexy, revolting and tender acts; after my first real
attempt to identify individuals from the book, I wrote excitedly: "Fascinating. Not just collecting species. This business makes you see."
Within days I was a full-fledged convert, always eager to try out the new
plumage by reaching for my birdbook.*

My conversion stuck (though it was maimed, and has never totally
recovered, when someone broke into my car and stole, among other
things, my American birdbook with its records of ten years' sightings).
And I long ago learned that, from a practical backpacking point of view,
a convert to birdwatching will find that if he did not take binoculars
before he will certainly do so now; that he will have even more difficulty
than before in not stopping and staring when he should be pounding
along; and that, everywhere for a while, and in new country forever after,
he will at least consider carrying a birdbook. The U.S. "standards" are
two books by Roger Tory Peterson, published by Houghton Mifflin: *A
Field Guide to the Birds: A Completely New Guide to All the Birds of Eastern
and Central North America* (1980; hardbound, 1 pound 2 ounces, $15;
paperback, 1 pound, $9.95) and *A Field Guide to Western Birds* (1972,

* Echo trouble, you say? Maybe. See *The Winds of Mara,* p. 190.

hardbound, 1 pound 1½ ounces, $12.95; clothbound, 1 pound even, $8.95). Some people prefer the *Audubon Society Field Guides to North American Birds:* 2 volumes—Western and Eastern Regions (Alfred A. Knopf, 1977, clothbound, 1 pound 3½ ounces, $12). There are other birdbooks, of course. *Birds of North America* by Chandler S. Robbins et al. (Golden Press, clothback, 13 ounces, $7.95) has range maps that I described in the last edition of this book as "excellent" but which I'm told could more accurately be designated "colorful."

The Audubon Society sell a strong denim "pelican pouch" that takes two birdbooks (6 ounces, $9.95). And Cutter Field Products of Olympic Valley, California, several years ago sent me a neat, simple, open-strap "book-tote," specifically for birdbooks, that strapped to belt or whatever (1½ ounces), but they seem to have gone out of business. Two readers have suggested simple open-top bags or pockets, stitched to clothing or hanging from neck-straps, possibly with extra room for protecting binoculars. But, however you carry your birdbook, it may pay, if it's green like the hardback Peterson, to stick a strip of bright red Rip-stop tape around at least half its cover so that it will, if lost, stand out from surrounding vegetation. I learned this lesson several years ago, the hard way. At 4:00 P.M. one day I discovered that my Peterson had slipped from its makeshift, nylon-cord sling somewhere in the course of a long, rough traverse across a desert slope; at 2:00 P.M. the following day, after many sweaty retraverses, I found the book lying in the open, green and inconspicuous, in a place I had already passed at least four times. Note that I not only learned about putting red Rip-stop on green books but also confirmed yet again that ancient proverb: "A birdbook in the hand is worth twenty-two hours in the bush."

Boating

and backpacking seem mutually exclusive—unless you classify canoe portaging as backpacking. You simply can't carry a boat in your pack. At least, you couldn't. But small, vinyl, inflatable, raftlike boats have now drifted into view. REI sell a 2-man Backpacker by Sevylor (15-gauge vinyl, 330-pound capacity, 6 pounds 6 ounces, $30). With oarlocks, light plastic paddles and foot pump, the outfit totals around 9 pounds. There's also a 3-man version (20-gauge vinyl, 600-pound capacity, 13 pounds, $50). And Sea Eagle make little 1-man boats that weigh 15–18 pounds. But I suggest that these are essentially toys. And, in backcountry, dangerous toys. Any wind could quickly blow them just where you didn't want to go. Even given exquisite care, their durability must be suspect. And if they let you down suddenly in a mountain lake or river the cold water would give you about five minutes' survival time.

I mention them for two reasons. People may see them and should be cautioned. And it is just possible to envision a situation in which a single, short, unhazardous water barrier, blocking off seductive terrain, might justify humping one along.

The remaining furniture and appliances can best be departmentalized:

ALWAYS-COMING-IN-USEFUL-AND-IN-FACT QUITE-INDISPENSABLE DEPARTMENT

Nylon cord

Braided nylon cord, sometimes still called "parachute cord" (⅛-inch diameter, 550-pound breaking strain, normally white but may now be yellow), is to a backpacker what adhesive tape is to a doctor: an indispensable maid-of-all-work. I always carry four or five hanks, in lengths from 2 to about 15 feet; and occasionally a half or whole 100-foot hank (6 ounces, $4). Braided red utility cord costs and weighs about the same but takes only half the stress. Gold ³⁄₃₂ cord has a looser weave and is less durable (100 feet: 5 ounces; $4). Finer cord saves a gram or two but tangles without provocation.

No matter what lengths and thicknesses you find it best to carry, remember that cut nylon cord always frays at the ends. To prevent fraying simply fuse the ends into unravelable blobs by holding them briefly in the flame of match or stove. Hanks of all sizes can travel, easily available, in an outside pocket of your pack.

Among their proven uses·

1. Rigging tents and allied shelters (pages 316–28)
2. Clotheslines
3. Fish stringers
4. Measuring lengths of fish and snakes, for later conversion to figures (mark with a knot)
5. Tying socks to pack for drying (page 76)
6. Securing binoculars and camera—or, alternatively, hat—to pack by clip spring, so that if dislodged they cannot fall far (pages 463 and 473)
7. Belt for pants (page 403) or for flapping poncho in high wind (page 325)
8. Lowering pack down difficult places (page 502) or even pulling it up (Don't try to pull hand over hand; bend knees, pass cord belay-fashion around upper rump, straighten legs, take in slack and repeat and repeat and repeat. . . .)

9. Replacement binocular strap
10. Chin band for hat (page 420)
11. Lashing tent poles to packframe (page 293)
12. When there's no wire, hanging cooking pots over a fire, from a tree, for melting snow for water. (This way you can build up a really big fire and keep warm at the same time. You do so, of course, in the uneasy knowledge that the cord may burn; but in practice it doesn't seem to.)
13. Wrapping around camera-case screw fitting, pulling, and so unjamming the screw for film-changing
14. Ditto with a jammed stove stopper (page 254)
15. On packless sidetrips, tying poncho into lunch bundle (food, photo accessories, compass, etc.) and securing around waist (page 412)
16. Makeshift loop sling for birdbook (page 517)
17. On river crossings:
    (a) Lashing air mattress to pack (page 535)
    (b) Lashing plastic sheet into virtually watertight bundle for protection of valuables, either as sanctum sanctorum of pack (page 532) or as lone floating bundle to be pushed ahead or towed on packless crossings (page 531), and
    (c) Towing walking staff along behind
18. Attaching flashlight to self at night with loop around neck (page 438). (For securing nylon to unholed flashlight, see "Dental floss" [page 520].)
19. Replacing frayed gaiter underpinnings
20. Spare bootlaces
21. Lifting water from well in cooking pot—or from deep-cut creek (especially in snow)

Among uses I've had in mind for years but have still not had occasion to try:

1. Double or tripled or quadrupled, as "carabiner-type" loop for ensuring that doubled climbing rope used for rappeling (or roping down) can be recovered from below (page 502)
2. As main rope for roping down low cliff (in extreme emergency only, as cord might be weakened to danger point by knotting at top and by possible wear, and would in any case be viciously uncomfortable even if used doubled or quadrupled)
3. In river work, for pulling yourself back up against slow-to-medium river current—in case you find it necessary to float a short way past a blind headland to see if a safe land route lies ahead around dangerous rapids

Most ordinary knots in nylon eventually slip. The only safe knot I know—and it is less difficult to tie and less bulky than it looks—is the fisherman's blood knot:

For permanent knots, burn-fuse all ends.*

Several readers have extolled the virtues of waxed nylon

Dental floss.

Acclaimed uses include: "most everything that nylon cord can be used for plus fishing line"; attaching line guides to fishing rods; binding around-the-neck nylon-cord loop to flashlight that lacks convenient hole (page 438); sewing thread; and toothbrush-eliminating dental care.

The only cavil: "low resistance to abrasion."

Most easily carried, primarily for teeth, in very small, ¼-ounce plastic caddy or wrapped around a card or in one of the larger tubes (1 ounce, $.69) that it comes in—and which make good homes for needles. To prevent slippage, burn-fuse knot ends.

Rubber bands

For all-round usefulness, rubber bands rank second only to nylon cord. Their most vital function in my regimen is as weak and nonrestrictive garters for my turned-down socks, to keep stones and dirt out of the boots. Other uses: resealing opened food packages; closing food bags that are too full to be knotted at the neck; battening down the moleskin package with its added contents (page 490); holding onionskin paper (for notes) to its rectangle of stiffening cardboard; and keeping notebook instantly openable at the current pages, front and rear (page 506).

---

* I considered adding a section on knots for all backpacking uses but finally rejected the idea. It seems safe to say that people are either fascinated or turned off by knots. If you're fascinated and haven't read the classic *Ropes, Knots and Slings for Climbers* by Walt Wheelock (La Siesta Press, Glendale, CA, 36 pages, 2¼ ounces, $1.50—updated 1967 by Royal Robbins), maybe you ought to.

Rubber bands have a habit of breaking and also of getting lost, and I recommend that if you use an E-frame pack and it has protruding arms you wrap around them as many bands as you think you need ready for immediate use. Then add the same number again. Then put into a small plastic bag about ten times as many as are on your packframe and put this reserve safely away inside the pack. Mine go into my "office" (page 506).

Plastic bags

I sometimes wonder what backpackers used as the interior walls of their houses before the days of plastic freezer bags. I use ordinary freezer, Ziploc and sandwich bags, in various sizes, not only for almost every food item (page 268), but also, copiously and often double thickness, for wrapping many other things: camp moccasins, clothes (especially in wet weather), dirty socks, cooking pots, frying pan, book, rubber bands, matches, toilet gear, first-aid kit, film, camera accessories, toilet paper, spare flashlight cells, can opener, stove-nozzle cleaner, signal flare, fishing tackle, certain spare pack attachments, Visklamps and rubber balls for plastic shelter, car key and unburnable garbage. Also, sometimes, as a wallet, and even as a stove container bag. I always take along a few spare bags. Standard marine sample bags give extra-strong protection for special articles. But the ultimate baggie is the Phoenix Waterproof Storage Bag (three sizes), made of soft, durable vinyl with roll-flap closure, nickel-plated brass fasteners, and even a bleed valve; sometimes available —at a price—from L. L. Bean.

For details of bag sizes and uses, and hints on packing, see pages 267–9. Ziploc bags can double as pillows (page 268). And household trash bags can serve not only as food bags (page 123), pack liners (page 364), sleeping-bag protectors, foam-pad covers (page 337) and kilt (page 414) but also as a poncho (with arm and neck holes cut) and even bivouac bag and emergency shelter.

Gear-storage bags for canoeing and whitewater boating, made of 20-mil vinyl, are heavy (22 by 41 inches, 1 pound 14 ounces, $8.37) but just might fill a specialist niche (Voyageur's, P.O. Box 409, Gardner, KS 66030).

35-mm. film cans

The old screw-top metal film cans made excellent containers. The new clip-on-top plastic versions look distrustable and are: I recently had one pop open in my pack at around 10,000 feet and spread Mautz Firepaste thin but wide. I also hear reports of squashings under pressure.

But once they're purged of chemicals I guess they are acceptable in moderation, down low. Their blackness makes them eminently losable, but a red encircling tape helps. Among items I've housed in the old metal kind: salt tablets, salmon eggs for bait, and coconut oil for lube jobs on hair and beard and even boots, not to mention for cooking. And one still sometimes acts as an "odds-and-ends can," which holds spare plastic end-buttons and three aluminum eyebolts for Trailwise pack-frame; two spare flashlight bulbs (if there's no place for them in flash-light); and some strong button thread wound around a small piece of paper. I now use the newer plastic cans for water-purifying and Vitamin C tablets. For other, more critical functions, I find small Nalgene bottles (page 216) much safer.*

Film cans for 120 film are said to make useful makeshift matchsafes.

Belt clips

Swivel-mounted snap hooks (1 ounce; $1.75) on small woven nylon loops are useful for carrying certain items suspended from either your belt or the built-in waistband of your pants: a cup, in good drinking country (page 211); occasionally, your hat; the camera tripod or other light equipment on packless sidetrips.

If you use a belt clip while carrying the pack (for a cup, say), make sure you pass its belt *inside* the clip; otherwise the belt's pressure may force the clip open. After a little while you find yourself flipping the cup outside automatically every time you put the pack on.

For many years I used two belt clips on safety lines for binoculars and camera (pages 463 and 473).

Check your belt clips occasionally. The springs eventually lose their youth and sometimes vanish, no doubt after breaking.

LINKS-WITH-CIVILIZATION DEPARTMENT

Generally, the last thing you want to do out in wild country is to carry any item that helps maintain a link with civilization. But there are

---

* I was amused—well, sort of—to hear from an Ann Arbor, Michigan, law firm that they quoted this paragraph (in its first-edition form) in the Great Film Can Marijuana Case. Police stopped a student for a minor traffic offense, saw a 35-mm. film can on the floor of his car, asked to be given it, duly were, opened it, found marijuana. One legal point at issue was the right to "search": if the object was in plain view and "an obvious instrumentality of crime," then search was legal. The police contended that 35-mm. film cans were standard stash points for counterculture marijuana and therefore suspicious. Defendant quoted this paragraph to establish legitimacy of such cans as containers for objects other than film or weed. Case dismissed. Hm.

exceptions. For example, it is sometimes more convenient and even cheaper to fly rather than drive to and from your chosen wilderness. And then you have to carry, all the way, some kind of suitable lightweight

Wallet.

The simplest and lightest is a small plastic bag. If that dissatisfies you, look in stores or catalogues for the now-popular Cordura versions. Into your choice you may want to put, according to the needs of the moment, some form of identification (driver's license is best, in case you need to drive), fishing license and fire permit. Also some money (although it's the most useless commodity imaginable once you're actually out in the wilderness). Consider both ready cash and traveler's checks, and perhaps one or two bank checks as reserve. A credit card may be worthwhile too: I once used mine to pay in advance for a short charter flight that put me down on a remote dirt road, and also for an airdrop of food that was to follow a week later.

A little cash may be worth taking along even when you are coming back to your car: late one fall, after a week in the mountains that ended with a fast, steep, 10,000-foot descent, I emerged with very sore feet onto a road 50 miles from my car, quickly hitched a ride in the right direction, and managed to persuade my benefactor that it was worth $5 for him to drive me several miles up a steep mountain road to where my car was parked.

Nowadays I always carry a dime—in my "wallet" or taped to the cardboard stiffener of my "office" (page 506) or to my first-aid booklet (page 497): few things are more frustrating than to emerge into man-country at last with a message heavy on your chest and find yourself at a remote telephone booth, dimeless and therefore mute.

Car key

The obvious place to leave your car key is at the car—taped or magnet-attached to some secret corner of it, or simply hidden close by. But I once came back from a winter mountain trip and found the rear bumper of my car, with the key craftily magnet-attached inside it, buried under a 10-foot snowdrift. Fortunately, a freak of the wind had left a convenient alley along one side of the car and I was able to get at the key without too much difficulty. But since then I find, rather to my surprise, that, at least on short trips, I tend to avoid vague worries about snow and torrential rain and landslides and thieves (human and other) by packing a key along with me, even though there is always one at the car, secreted away but attainable. Cached or carried, the key gets wrapped in the inevitable plastic bag.

Radio

Believe it or not, I am regularly asked, "But don't you carry a transistor radio . . . for company . . . or so that you can keep in touch . . . or anyway for weather?" You're allowed one guess. Well, you could be wrong. A miniature AM radio (around 8 ounces, $7) will, unless you're badly screened in a valley and sometimes even then, give you at least one station from which you can cull a weather forecast—though it may be filtered through the personality of a disc jockey; and a couple of times, on short trips when storms threatened, I've taken mine along. The practice is, of course, a booby trap. You may find you have trailed in just those outside-world cultural ties that you rather thought you wanted to shuck off. I remember once, a first night out, listening raptly to a key game during the dream season of the San Francisco Forty-niners.

To eliminate such cultural temptations, and also disc jockeys, and to get better weather forecasts, you can take along one of those small sets (as little as 6 ounces, $13) that receive broadcasts from the widespread NOAA network (page 36). The only question is whether you'll be able to receive signals in the country you're penetrating, particularly in deep valleys. I hear conflicting reports.

Nowadays it is becoming almost un-abnormal to see a backpacker striding along clamped between the earphones of a Walkman or equivalent. Such biworld perambulators inflict no hardship on others. But see page 504 for an opinion—not mine—on taking even simpler divertissements into wilderness. I go at least partway along. After all, one of the joys of wilderness walking is that when you return to civilization after your interlude of voluntary abstention everything seems better, from Beethoven to sex.

Dangling link with civilization: letting some responsible person know where you're going and when you'll be back *

This act should be automatic—before you walk out into any kind of country, whether for a few hours or for several weeks. It is not merely a question of your own safety. If you do not return, people will eventually

* What's that you say? "Wouldn't this section sit more comfortably on page 50?" Maybe. But it finally settled in this surely reasonable niche for reasons of the arcane kind known only to editors, designers and authors. If you don't fully comprehend, rest thankful.

come out to look for you; and if they have nothing to go on except the place your car was parked and perhaps the vague recollections of someone you happened to chat with, they will waste a great deal of time searching in useless places. And they may expose themselves to unnecessary dangers —on the ground and in the air.

In busy national or state parks and forests your permit is hardly enough. Its aim is control. And rangers cannot keep tabs on everyone who comes out. So, everywhere, cast about until you find someone who strikes you as thoroughly reliable (page 486). Your life may depend on his reliability. If you travel solo it would be wise to make some such registration. A little to my surprise, I find I almost always do.

It is probably sensible, at least in some cases, to leave a map marked with your proposed route—if you have a route. And even if you are going in simply to wander and have no idea where you'll end up, state a date and hour by which you will return—or will emerge elsewhere and immediately check back by phone. Let it be clearly understood that if you have not reported back by the time specified, then you are in trouble. In fixing the deadline, allow yourself a little leeway. And once you've fixed it, make hell-and-high-water sure you meet it. I repeat: make hell-and-high-water sure you meet it.

STRICTLY-PERSONAL-BUT-YOU'LL-PROBABLY-HAVE-YOUR-OWN DEPARTMENT

Everyone, I imagine, has one or two little personal items that go along. They'll vary according to individual interests and frailties. Two very experienced friends of mine always carry small pliers. And see cheese-cloth, page 489. In addition to items I've already mentioned, such as office and prospector's magnifying glass, my list includes spare eyeglasses (sometimes) and (always) one or two wraparound elasticized bandages— either Ace or the more convenient Velcro-fastened Champ. The bandages are primarily for a troublesome knee and for emergency use in case of a sprained ankle but they have seen most use in thornbush and cactus country, wrapped puttee fashion around my bare and vulnerable lower legs (page 403).

Housekeeping and
Other Matters

ORGANIZING THE PACK

Every backpacker eventually works out his own way of stowing gear into a pack, and it will probably be the one that best suits his equipment and techniques. But beginners may find some usable guidelines in the solutions that I have evolved. Although many of these solutions have appeared in earlier chapters it seems worthwhile to mention them here, more neatly gathered together. I have now swung toward I-frame packs for most uses but, while the switch does impose some packing modifications, it remains essentially irrelevant. My E-frame arrangements, taken together with new ones now mentioned elsewhere in the text, should suggest alternatives for a wide range of bags. What I'm trying to do, remember, is only to offer hints that may help beginners drift in the right direction: to provide guidelines, that is, not perpetuate idiosyncrasies.

The best way to stow your gear into your pack is to pursue, all the time, a reasonable compromise between convenience and efficient weight distribution.

For the main considerations in weight distribution in E-frame packs —loading high and close to the back—see page 125. For the more precise requirements with I-frames, see page 130.

Common sense and a lick or two of experience will soon teach you the necessary refinements: after some angular item such as the stove has gouged into your back a couple of times you'll make sure, almost without thinking, that flat or soft articles pad the forward surface of the packbag's main compartment; and once you've put both the full canteens that you're carrying on the same side of the bag and found that the load then rides like a one-armed gorilla you're unlikely to repeat the mistake.

If you use a compartmented packbag your ideas on where things should go will clearly differ from those of a bloody-great-sack addict like me. But as my experience is almost entirely sackish, and because on the rare occasions I've used compartmented bags I found that the general principles held good, I'll speak purely from experience.

The most convenient way to stow gear varies from trip to trip, from day to day, from morning to evening. Obviously, the things you'll want first at the next halt should go in last. So the groundsheet will normally travel on top. In dry country, so will one canteen—though in sunny weather it should be covered with a down jacket or some other insulator (page 205). And the balance-of-the-week's ration bag, the signal flare, reserve or empty canteens and refills for a cartridge stove should—on the score of sheer convenience—languish down in the basement. Otherwise, the important thing is not where each item goes but that you always know where it is.

There will be variations, of course. If rain threatens, your raingear must be on top and perhaps even sticking out, ready to be plucked into use. On cold evenings, have your heavy clothing ready to put on even before you start to make camp. If it looks as though you are going to have a long, torrid midday halt, make sure you don't have to dig down to the bottom of the packbag for plastic sheet or poncho before you can rig up an awning. But all this is just plain common sense.

I always pad the forward side of my packbag with the office, and sometimes with camp moccasins (soles facing out). In one forward corner of the main sack, fitting snugly against the packframe, go the gasoline container and usually, on top of it, the stove. If I'm carrying a second gasoline container and/or a portmanteau fishing rod, they fit into the opposite and similar corner.

There are few other firm rules for the main sack. Cooking pots and the food-for-the-day bag normally go side by side on the same level (because when I want one, I want the other), and they almost always ride high up. If space poses a problem a few small, allied and relatively unharmable objects may travel inside the inner cooking pot, along with or in lieu of cup and spoon. Candidates include sugar and margarine containers, salt-and-pepper shaker—and even, if bulk poses a problem, my stove in its stuff sack. Otherwise, the packing arrangements depend largely on what items I expect to need next—given, of course, that I try to pack heavy articles close to the packframe (see, again, pages 126 and 130).

Many smaller items in my pack—particularly in the kitchen— travel in plastic bags. See page 267. For stuff sacks, see pages 363 and 417 and—for the small-stuff-sack fallacy—page 364. Some people house almost everything in these light and convenient little bags; their packs become stuff-sack condominiums.

For the various sleeping-bag carrying systems, see pages 120 and 129.

My present E-frame bag, like most I've used, has five outside pockets: two on each side and one amidships aft (see illustration, page 124). Both it and my present I-frame pack have big flap pockets in lieu of the one amidships. In both bags, side pockets are color-coded—see page 125 —so that I can readily distinguish one side from the other, no matter which way the pack is facing.

The central or amidships pocket (flap pocket in the I-frame) is the easiest to get at, and into it go toilet paper and trowel, hanks of nylon cord and the current plastic bag of unburnable garbage. Also, sometimes, spare clean socks and even damp or dirty socks (in plastic bag) when for some reason such as rain or grabbing thorns it is inadvisable to leave them airing on the outside of the pack. From time to time this pocket also houses items that seem likely to be wanted in a hurry: gaiters, rain chaps, camera-lens tissue and close-up attachments.

The upper starboard pocket (outer starboard in the I-frame) is the "nibble pocket"—the most often used of all. Into it go the foods I nibble at almost every halt (page 174). The emergency meat or pemmican bar lives there too, at the bottom, so that if I have a replacement in the bag and I want one for a quick, no-cook lunch, I need not unpack the main food.

The lower (or outer) starboard pocket holds footpowder and rubbing alcohol (page 87), the small plastic baby-bottle canteen (page 207), one package of fruit-drink mix and the water-purifying tablets. Also, on occasion, fly dope and suntan lotion and, to prevent crushing in the main house, booze bottle.

The upper port pocket used to be my photography room, but as I rarely carry a camera nowadays (beyond the little Olympus XA that tends to get slipped in wherever there happens to be room) that pocket has been taken over—just as a spare room often is, back home—by a variety of junk: gloves and scarf and balaclavas, for example, which conveniently pad the flashlight (often protected inside a small Ziploc bag), soap tube and hand lotion.

The lower port pocket is for other miscellaneous items that must be get-attable in a hurry or are too small and losable to travel in the main sack: first-aid kit, compass, magnifying glass, whistle, knife (when not attached to pants), matchsafes, smoke bomb, odds-and-ends can and spare pack fittings.

Tent poles, when carried, are lashed to an E-frame upright (page 293) or to the side of an I-frame bag, between two pockets. Some I-frames now have an open side-pocket at the foot of each side, with grommeted drainage hole, to hold the low ends of tent poles and other long objects (page 140). A wet tent that would soak everything in the main house gets lashed onto the opposite side from the poles.

The only radical changes in organizing the pack come at

RIVER CROSSINGS.

Crossing small creeks is mostly a simple matter, and raises no problems. You can often make it across dry-shod, on the tops of boulders that are clear of the water or slightly awash. A staff to aid balance is often a godsend. If you are wearing normal old-style boots with no tread on the insteps you must make every effort to avoid the natural tendency of beginners, uncertain of their balance, to plant the instep of the boots on the curving summit of each boulder. New-style boots with treaded insteps make the need for such avoidance less obvious; but I still believe the ball of the foot is, in most cases, the part to plant—because it keeps you more delicately on balance.

Sometimes, of course, failing a natural log bridge or steppingstones, you have to take off your boots and wade. At least, I do. Some people keep their boots on, but I mistrust the effect on boots and feet. Or perhaps I just mean that I abhor the idea of squelching along afterward. On easy crossings, carry your boots, with socks pushed inside. Knot the laces together and twist them around one wrist. On deeper crossings, hang the lace-linked boots on the pack. In really difficult places it's safer to stuff them inside the packbag. Sometimes you can wade in bare feet, with safety and reasonable comfort, but if your camp shoes have good-grip soles and also dry out quickly (page 78) you'll often be glad to protect your feet in them.

A friend once suggested a method he uses regularly for fast and rocky rivers: take off socks, replace boots, wade river with well-protected feet, replace socks and go on your happy and reputedly unsquelching way. Somehow, I've yet to try it out. I unfancy wet boots. If you are fishing and have waders, the problem vanishes. A possible lightweight substitute: large plastic trash bags loosely tied over each leg.

Provided you choose the right places you can wade surprisingly large rivers. (Fast rivers, that is, where the depth and character vary; slow, channeled rivers are normally unwadable.) It often pays to make an extensive reconnaissance along the bank in order to select a good crossing point. In extreme cases you may even need to detour for a mile or more. Generally, the safest places are the widest and, up to a point, the fastest. Most promising of all, provided the water is shallow enough and not too fierce, tend to be the fanned-out tails of wide pools. Boulders or large stones, protruding or submerged, in fairly shallow water may also indicate a good crossing place: they break the full force of racing water, and you can ease across the most dangerous places on little mounds of stone and gravel that have been deposited by the slack water behind each boulder. But always, before you start across, pick out in detail, with coldly cynical eyes, a route that looks tolerably safe—all the way. Try to choose a route with any questionable steps early, not over where you would, if turned back, have to recross most of the river. And avoid getting into any position you can't retreat from.

Experience is by far the most important aid to safe wading (I wish I had a lot more), but there are a few simple rules. Use a staff—particularly with a heavy pack. (It turns you, even more crucially than on dry land, from an insecure biped into a confident triped.) In fast current the safest route for walking, other things being equal, is one that angles down and across the current. The faster and deeper the water, the more sharply downstream you should angle. The next-best attack is up and across. Most hazardous of all—because the current can most easily sweep you off balance—is a directly-across route.

Unless you are afraid of being swept off your feet (and in that case you'd almost certainly do better to find a deep, slow section and swim across), wading does not call for any change in the way you pack. But before you start across you should certainly undo your waistbelt. Always. The pack (at least until it fills with water) is much more buoyant than your body and should you fall in it will, if held in place by the belt, force you under. It is easy enough to wriggle out of a shoulder yoke, particularly if it's slung over only one shoulder. At least, I have always liked to imagine so—and a reader's letter confirms my faith. She and her husband were wading a turbulent stream in Maine—waistbelts undone and hanging free—when she lost her bare footing and was swept downstream. She quickly squirmed free of the harness and within 50 feet, still hanging onto the pack, grabbed a boulder and pulled herself to safety. Afterward she realized that having her waistbelt undone had been "a great thing."

The only other precaution I sometimes take when wading, and then only at difficult crossings, is to unhitch camera and binoculars from the packframe and put them inside the pack.

But if you have to swim a river you must reorganize the pack's contents.*

---

* I have been taken to task for not warning you that my swimming lessons mostly apply to large desert rivers. Fast mountain rivers are generally too cold for this kind of thing. The warnings were there all right in the first edition, at the end of this section. But this time I'll play safe and inject a reference to it here at the start: please read with care the last paragraph of this section, page 537.

The first time I tried swimming with a pack was on my Grand Canyon journey, in 1963. Because of the new Glen Canyon Dam, 100 miles upriver, the Colorado was then running at only 1200 cubic feet per second—far below its normal low-water level. Even for someone who, like me, is a poor and nervous swimmer, it seemed comparatively easy to swim across a slow, deep stretch with little danger of being swept down over the next rapids. I adopted the technique developed by the one man who had been able to help me with much information about hiking in remote parts of the Canyon. He was a math professor at Arizona State College in Flagstaff. He was also, his wife said, "like a seal in the water." And he had found that by lying across his air mattress with the pack slung over one shoulder, half floating, he could, even at high water, dog-paddle across the Colorado—which is the third-longest river in the United States and is muscled accordingly. I tried his method out on several same-side detours, when sheer cliffs blocked my way, and by degrees I gained confidence in it.*

The air mattress made a good raft. Inflated not too firmly, it formed a reassuring V when I lay with my chest across it. I used it first on a packless reconnaissance. Remembering how during World War II we had crossed rivers by wrapping all our gear in waterproof anti-gas capes and making bundles that floated so well we could just hang on to them and kick our way forward, I wrapped the few clothes and stores I needed in a white plastic sheet (page 316) and lashed it firmly with nylon cord. It floated well. I found that by wrapping a loose end of cord around one arm I could tow it along beside me and dog-paddle fairly freely.

With the pack, dog-paddling turned out to be a little more restricted but still reasonably effective. The pack, slung over my left shoulder and half-floating, tended at first to keel over. But I soon found that I could hold it steady by light pressure on the lower and upper ends of the packframe with buttocks and bald patch. It sounds awkward but worked fine.

My staff floated along behind at the end of 3 feet of nylon cord tied to the packframe. Everything else went into the pack. I had waterproofed the seams of the packbag rather hurriedly, and I found that water still

* My professorial informant, after reading the first edition of this book, wrote: "I never intended to let the pack hang from one shoulder, floating in the water. This happened only by accident on two or three occasions, when I was upset. Intentionally, I have only two positions on the air mattress: crosswise—as you used your shortie—when in rough water; and lengthwise under me in calm water. If I switch positions before reaching the waves, I am reasonably sure of keeping the pack in position."

I'm glad, though, that I got it wrong. The prof specializes in two- and three-day trips, carrying relatively light packs. I found my heavy burden an impossible shoulder-load when I was waterborne. But you might like to try a light pack that way.

seeped through. So into the bottom of the bag went bulky and buoyant articles that water could not damage: canteens, cooking pots and white-gas container. Things better kept dry went in next, wrapped in the white plastic sheet. Items that just had to stay dry went on top, in what I thought of as the sanctum sanctorum: camera and accessories, flashlight and spare batteries, binoculars, watch, writing materials and toilet paper. I tied each of these items into a plastic bag, rolled them all inside the sleeping bag and stuffed it into the big, tough plastic bag that usually went around the cooking pots. Then I wrapped the lot in my poncho. Before strapping the packbag shut I tied the ends of the poncho *outside* the white plastic sheet with nylon cord. (On one trial run the pack had keeled over and water had run down inside the plastic sheet, though the sanctum had remained inviolate.) On the one complete river crossing that I had to make, nothing got even damp.

This system, or some variation of it, should prove adequate for crossing almost any river that is warm enough, provided you do not have to go through heavy rapids. I am more than half-scared of water and a very poor swimmer, and if I can succeed with it almost anyone can. The great practical advantage of this method is that you do not have to carry any special equipment. All you need is an air mattress, a poncho and a plastic sheet or a groundsheet.

The method, by the way, turns out to be less than brand-new. A Washington State reader has shared this depiction of troops crossing a river on inflated skins—from an Assyrian relief of about 800 B.C.

Heavy rapids present a different problem. In May 1966 I took a two-week hike-and-swim trip down 70 miles of the Colorado, in Lower Grand Canyon. Although many people had run the Colorado by boat it seemed that everyone had until then had the sense to avoid attempting this very enclosed stretch on foot; but I knew from boatmen's reports that even if the route proved possible I would almost certainly have to make several river crossings. I also knew that, with the reservoir now part-filled behind Glen Canyon Dam, the river was racing down at an average of about 16,000 cubic feet per second—more than twelve times its volume on my 1963 trip. That meant I would almost certainly be carried far downstream each time I attempted a crossing. Even the calmer stretches would be swirling, whirlpooled horrors, and I would probably be carried through at least some minor rapids. Under such conditions I wasn't willing to risk the lying-across-an-air-mattress technique, and I evolved a new method, more suitable for a timid swimmer.

Just before the trip I bought an inflatable life vest (by Stebco—no longer available). It was made of bright yellow rubberized cotton fabric, with a valve for inflation by mouth and also a small metal cartridge that in an emergency filled the vest with carbon dioxide the instant you pulled

a toggled cord. The vest yoked comfortably around the neck so that when you floated on your back your mouth was held clear of the water. When I tried it out in a side creek as soon as I reached the Colorado I found that I could also swim very comfortably in the normal position. From the start I felt safe and confident.

I had already decided that rather than lie across the air mattress I would this time rely solely on the life vest to keep me afloat—partly because I was afraid the vest's metal cartridge or its securing wire might puncture the mattress, but even more because I did not fancy my chances of staying on the mattress in swirling water. (A young fellow crossing the Colorado on a trip with my math-professor friend had been swept off his mattress by a whirlpool and had drowned.) I decided that in fast water the trick would be to make the pack buoyant in its own right, and just pull or push it along with me.

The coated nylon fabric of the packbag was fully waterproof but, although I had applied seam sealant, water still seeped in. So I decided to try to keep the pack as upright as I could in the water and stow the really vital gear, well protected, up near the top. First, for extra buoyancy high up, I put one empty plastic quart-size canteen in each of the upper side pockets. Into the bottom of the bag as ballast went the two cooking pots and two ½-gallon canteens, all filled with water. Next I lined the remaining space in the main sack with my transparent polyethylene groundsheet and left the unused portion hanging outside. Like all groundsheets, mine had developed many small holes, but I figured it would ward off the worst of any water that might seep in from the upper seams or under the flap, and that what little did get through would collect harmlessly in the bottom of the pack. The items that water couldn't damage (page 532) went in first. Next, those preferably kept

dry. Then I made the sanctum sanctorum. Into the white plastic sheet (because rain was unlikely, I carried no poncho this trip) went all the things that just had to stay dry (as on page 532). Most of them were additionally protected inside an assortment of plastic bags. I lashed the white bundle firmly with nylon cord, put it on top of everything else, then folded over the unused portion of the groundsheet that was still hanging outside and carefully tucked it in between the main portion of the groundsheet and the packbag itself. I knotted down the pack flap, tight. Then I partially inflated my air mattress and lashed it securely with nylon cord to the upper half of the pack, taking care to keep it central. Finally, I took the 4-foot agave-stem walking staff that I had cut at the start of the trip (page 83) and wedged it down into the cross-webbing of the packframe, close beside one upright.

I held the pack upright in the water for several minutes, forcing it down so that water seeped in and filled the bottom 7 or 8 inches—thereby helping, I hoped, to keep the pack upright. Then I slid down into the river beside it. With my left hand I grasped the lowest cross-rung of the packframe and pulled downward. Provided I maintained a slight downward pressure (see illustration) the pack floated fairly upright, though tending to lean away from me, and I was free to swim in any position with one arm and both legs.

In addition to the inflatable vest I wore my ultralightweight nylon swimming trunks (page 419). I'd brought them because at the start, at the side creek in which I practiced, there was a possibility of meeting people. But I found that I actually wore the trunks on all crossings, so that I would have at least some protection from the sun if I became separated from the pack. And so that I could still light a fire in that unlikely event, I tied the waterproof matchsafe (page 217) onto the vest.

The whole rig worked magnificently. I made four crossings. The white plastic sheet hardly ever got damp, even on the outside, and the sanctum remained bone dry, every time. So, mostly, did all other items stowed near the top of the pack. Because I could swim freely, I always got across the river reasonably fast. Each time I could have landed within half a mile of my launch site; but twice I allowed myself to be carried a little farther down to good landing places. (And as I floated down the calmer stretches on my back, with both feet resting on the packframe in front of me—my mind and body utterly relaxed, and an integral part of the huge, silent, flowing river—I found that I had discovered a new and serene and superbly included way of experiencing the Grand Canyon of the Colorado.)

I also made two same-side river detours around impassable cliffs. And one of these detours was the high point of the trip.

For the first 50 feet of the rapid I had to go through, the racing water battered on its left flank into a jagged rockwall. I knew that the one thing I absolutely had to do was to keep an eye on this rockwall and make sure that if I swung close I fended off in time with arm or pack or legs. From the bank, the steep waves in the heart of the rapid didn't look too terrifying: not more than 3 or 4 feet high at the most. But throughout the double eternity during which I swirled and wallowed through those waves—able to think of nothing except "Is it safe to grab a breath now, before I go in under that next one?"—I knew vividly and for sure that not one of them was less than 57½ feet high. And all I saw of the rockwall was a couple of split-second glimpses—like a near-subliminal inner-thought flash from a movie.

I missed the rockwall, though—through no effort of mine—and came safely through the rapid. A belch or two in midriver cleared the soggy feeling that came from the few mouthfuls of Colorado that I had shipped; and once I got into calmer water and had time to take a look at the pack it seemed serenely shipshape. (In the rapid, frankly, I hadn't even known that I was still hanging on to it.)

The only problem now, in the fast water below the rapid, was getting back to the bank. It took me a full mile to do so.

At first I had to stay in midriver to avoid protruding rocks at the edge of another and only slightly less tumultuous rapid. Then, after I'd worked my way close to the bank, I was swept out again by tailwash from a big, barely submerged boulder. Almost at once I saw a smooth, sinister gray wave ahead, rising up out of the middle of the river. I knew at once what it was. Furiously, I swam toward the bank. A few strokes and I looked downstream once more. The wave was five times closer now, ten times bigger. And I knew I could not avoid it. Just in time, I got into position with the pack held off to one side and my legs out in front of me, high in the water and slightly bent. Then I was rising up, sickeningly, onto the crest of the wave. And then I was plummeting down. As I fell, my feet brushed, very gently, over the smooth, hard surface of the hidden boulder. Then a white turmoil engulfed me. But almost instantly my head was out in the air again and I was floating along in calmer water. For a moment or two the pack looked rather waterlogged; but long before I made landfall, a couple of hundred yards downstream, it was once more floating high. When I unpacked I found the contents even drier than on some of the earlier and calmer crossings.

After those rapids and that boulder, I feel I can say that my fast-water river-crossing technique works.

That trip was something of a special case, but it taught me a useful lesson: if you have to swim a river, and have no air mattress and no inflatable vest, rig your pack somewhat after the manner I did. It will float buoyantly, and vital items will travel safely in the sanctum sanctorum. (I'm fairly sure my air mattress did not "float" the pack, but only helped hold it upright at stressful moments.) Pull down on the bottom crossbar of the frame and swim alongside or in front or behind (in swirling water you'll do all three within seconds). A fair swimmer would have no difficulty, I imagine, in any reasonably unbroken water. And if, like me, you are a weak swimmer you could almost certainly keep yourself afloat and moving across the current by just hanging on to the pack and kicking. But if it's at all possible, try out unproven variations like this beforehand—preferably well ahead of time; or, failing that, in calm, safe water before the main attempt.

A reader suggests that for short emergency swims "a pair of tough (3 mil) plastic bags, blown up and tied or secured with rubber bands or nylon string, are very handy" for pack or person.

For crossing any but the widest rivers, parties of hikers have it easier than a man on his own—provided they are carrying enough rope or cord. Only one man need swim across under his own power. The others, after paying out a cord or rope attached to his body, can be pulled across by him. At least, I guess so.

Don't forget that water temperature can be treacherous in river crossings. Even when you're wading, cold water can numb your feet and legs to danger point with astonishing speed. And no one can swim for long in liquid ice—cannot even live in it for very long. Yet your body will work efficiently for a considerable time in 50° water. During my 1963 Grand Canyon journey the Colorado River temperature was around 60°. On the 1966 trip it averaged about 57°, and although the water always felt perishing cold when I first got into it (which was hardly surprising, with shade temperatures rising each day to over 100°, and precious little shade anywhere) I was never once, even on the longest swim, at all conscious of being cold.

SANITATION

(*Note:* Except for the paragraph on trowels, this section stands much as I wrote it fifteen years ago. But it is now twenty times as important: our burgeoning numbers have had hideous impact. See, sadly and specifically, "Giardiasis," page 194. The ignorance of some newcomers about how to operate in wilderness has made a sad, self-righteous mockery of my words about the respect normally accorded the earth by those who undertake demanding journeys, but I'll let the words stand, as a goad.)

Sanitation is not a pleasant topic, but every camper must for the sake of others consider it openly, with his mind unblurred by prudery.

At one extreme there is the situation in which permanent johns have been built. Always use them. If they exist, it means that the human population, at least at certain times of year, is too dense for any other healthy solution. (The National Park Service calculates that 500 people using a leach-line-system permanent john will pollute a place no more than one person leaving untreated feces, even buried.)

A big party camping in any kind of country, no matter how wild, automatically imposes a dense population on a limited area. They should always dig deep latrine holes and, if possible, carry lime or some similar disinfectant that will counteract odor, keep flies away and hasten decomposition. And they must fill holes carefully before leaving.

A party of two or three in a remote area—and even more certainly a man on his own—must make simpler arrangements. But with proper "cat sanitation" and due care and consideration in choice of sites, no problem need arise.

Cat sanitation means doing what a cat does, though more efficiently: digging a hole and covering up the feces afterward. But it must be a hole, not a mere scratch. Make it at least 4 or 5 inches deep, and preferably 6 or 8. But do not dig down below topsoil into inert-looking earth where insects and decomposing bacteria will be unable to work properly. In some soils you can dig easily enough with your boots or a stick. I used to carry my sheath knife along whenever I went looking for a cat-john site, and used it if necessary for digging. Then I came across one of the plastic toilet trowels (10 inches long, 2 ounces, $1) that now appear in many catalogues. At first I was merely amused. But I found that the trowel digs quickly and well and means you can cat-sanitate effectively in almost any soil. Now I always pack it along. Because these little trowels remind as well as dig, I'm tempted to suggest they be made obligatory equipment for everyone who backpacks into a national park or forest. I resist the temptation, though—not only because (human nature being what it is, thank God) any such ordinance would drive many worthy people in precisely the undesired direction but also because blanket decrees are foreign to whatever it is a man goes out into wilderness to seek, and bureaucratic decrees are worst of all because they tend to accumulate and perpetuate and harden when they're administered, as they so often are, by people who revel in enforcing petty ukases. Anyway, a rule that's impossible to enforce is a bad rule. And this one has been tried: a young reader of eighty-nine has drawn my attention to Deuteronomy 23, verse 13 (see Appendix IV, page 635).

Your kosher plastic paddle can come in useful, by the way, when you have to melt snow for water (page 282). Conversely, a 10-inch, angled aluminum snow-peg (page 312) makes a fair toilet trowel: for digging in hard soil, pad it at the top with your ubiquitous bandanna.*

In the double plastic bags that hold my roll of toilet paper lives a book of matches. I tear one match off ready beforehand and leave it protruding from the book, so that I need handle the book very little; and unless there is a severe fire hazard, when I have finished I burn all the used paper. The flames not only destroy the paper but char the feces and discourage flies. Afterward I carefully refill the hole. Unless the water situation is critical I have soap and an opened canteen waiting in camp for immediate hand-washing.

A hardy friend of mine suggests as substitutes for paper "soft grass, ferns and broad leaves, and even the tip of firs, redwoods, etc."

In choosing a john site, remember above all that you must be able to dig. Rock is not acceptable. Rock is not acceptable. Rock is not acceptable. I am driven to reiteration by the revolting memory of a beautiful rock-girt creek in California, a long hour from roadhead but heavily fished and traveled. And that raises the only other absolute rule: always go at least 50 feet, and preferably 500, from any watercourse, even if currently dry. Soil filters; but it demands time and space. The

---

* A Forest Service regulation apparently demands that every overnight visitor carry a big, heavy, Army-type entrenching tool. But the rule never seems to be enforced. No doubt the Service understand that it would be a joke among today's weight-conscious backpackers.

rest is largely a matter of considering other people. Wherever possible select tucked-away places that no one is likely to use for any purpose. But do not appropriate a place so neatly tucked away that someone may want to camp there. A little thoughtful common sense will be an adequate guide.

All other things being equal, choose a john with a view.

In deep snow there is unfortunately nothing you can do except dig a hole, burn the paper, cover the hole and afterward refuse to think about what will happen come hot weather. There is not much you can do, either, about having to expose your fundamentals to the elements. Actually, even in temperatures well below freezing, it turns out to be a surprisingly undistressing business for the brief interval necessary, especially if you have a tent to crawl back into. Obviously, blizzard conditions and biting cold may make the world outside your tent unlivable, even for brief intervals, but a cookhole in the tent floor (page 309) would solve this problem. For footwear when scrambling out of a tent in snow, see page 314.

It is horrifying how many people, even under conditions in which cat sanitation is easy, fail to observe the simple, basic rules. Failure to bury feces is not only barbaric; it is a danger to others. Flies are everywhere. And the barbarism is compounded by thoughtless choice of sites. I still remember the disgust I felt when, late one rainy mountain evening several years ago, I found at last what looked like an ideal campsite under a small overhanging rockface—and then saw, dead center, a cluster of filthy toilet paper and a naked human turd.

That rockledge was in a fairly remote area. The problem can be magnified when previously remote countryside is opened up to people unfit to use it. Power boats now cruise far and wide over Lake Powell, behind the Colorado's Glen Canyon Dam, and the boats' occupants are able to visit with almost no effort many ancient and fascinating Indian cliff dwellings. Before the dam was built these dwellings could be reached only by extensive foot or fast-water journeys. Now, people who undertake such demanding journeys have usually (though not always) learned, through close contact with the earth, to treat it with respect— and power boats do not bring you in close contact with the earth. I hear that most of the cliff dwellings near Lake Powell have now been used as toilets.

Urination is a much less serious matter. But dense and undisciplined human populations can eventually create a smell, and although this problem normally arises only in camping areas so crowded that you might as well be on Main Street, it can also do so with locally concentrated use, especially in hot weather and when the ground is impervious to liquids. During my first Grand Canyon journey I camped on one open rockledge for four days. As the days passed, the temperature rose. On the fourth day, with the thermometer reaching 80° in the shade—and 120° in my unshaded camp—I several times detected whiffs of a stale odor that made me suspect I was near the lair of a large animal. I was actually hunting around for the lair when I realized that only one large animal was living on that rockledge.

But urination is usually no more than a minor inconvenience—even for those who, like me, must have been in the back row when bladders were given out. An obvious precaution is to cut down on drinking at night. No tea for me, thank you, with dinner. Yet I rarely manage to get through a night undisturbed. Fortunately, it is surprising how little you get chilled when you stand up for a few moments on quite cold nights, even naked. I go no farther than the foot of my sleeping bag, and just aim at the night (hence the "animal lair" at that rocky Grand Canyon campsite). A distaff reader has written asking if I have any useful advice for her on this subject. Regretfully, I can offer only commiseration.* And a man wrote reminding me of the Eskimo who "reaches for his urinal and without leaving the bag captures another increment for tomorrow's emptying ceremony." I duly bought a wide-mouthed plastic bottle and have used it with total success, kneeling up, in a tent. But not, oddly enough, lying down in my bag, à la Eskimo: I find I plain fail to produce. Such a block is apparently not uncommon among the house-trained.

REPLENISHING SUPPLIES

On extended trips you always face the problem of how to replenish your supplies. Generally speaking, you can't carry food for more than a week, or maybe two (page 34). Other items also need replacement: stove fuel, toilet paper, other toilet articles, perhaps powder and rubbing alcohol for your feet. You'll probably need additional film too, and new maps and replacement equipment and even special gear for certain sections of the trip.

* An ad in a recent issue of *Sierra*, the Sierra Club magazine, offers more than commiseration. "Sani-fem provides the lightest (1 ounce), most effective sanitation available in wilderness areas. Sani-fem lets women stand when nature calls. The mosquitoes, cold wind and nuisances of the old way are gone because standing cures them all. No undressing! Just unzip! . . . Nothing to empty or replace. Complete with case and instructions. Environmentally sound." (The Sani-fem Feminine Urinary Director, $7.99, or 2 for $13.98; from Sani-fem, 7415 Stewart and Gray, Downey, CA 90241. Attn: Ms. Linda Lee.)

Outposts of civilization

On my six-month California walk I was able to plan my route so that I called in every week or ten days at remote country post offices. Before I started the trip I had mailed ahead to each of these post offices not only a batch of maps for the stretch of country ahead but also items of special gear, such as warm clothing for the first high mountain beyond the desert. I wrote each postmaster explaining what I was doing and asking him to hold all packages for me until at least a reasonable time after my estimated date of arrival. At each post office I mailed to the old Ski Hut, back in Berkeley, a list of the food and equipment I wanted to pick up two weeks later; and a list of film and personal requirements went to a reliable friend. So at each post-office call-in I found waiting for me everything I needed for the next leg of the journey.

These calls at outposts of civilization provided a change of diet too: there was always a store near the post office, and usually a café—and a motel. I often stayed a day or two in the motel to write and mail a series of newspaper articles (and also to soak in several hot showers and cold beers). Exposed film went out in the mails, and completed notes, and sometimes equipment I no longer needed. All in all, the system worked very well. It could be adapted, with modifications to suit the needs of the moment, for many kinds of walking trips.

For an Eastern firm that offers such a supply service, see page 21.

In wild areas you have to replenish by other means. One way is to make

Caches.

On the California walk I put out several water caches at critical points, and at one or two of them I also left a few cans of food. Later I realized that I should have left at least a day's nondehydrated food, for a treat—and possibly some dehydrated food for the way ahead so that I could have cut down my load.

I was able to put those caches out by car, on little-used dirt roads, but on most wilderness trips you have to pack the stuff in ahead of time. On the two-month Grand Canyon trip I put out two caches of water, food and other supplies. From the purely logistic standpoint I should have carried these caches far down into the Canyon so that on the trip itself I would not have to detour. But there is, thank God, more to walking than logistics. I had been dreaming about the Canyon for a year, and one of the prime concerns in all my planning was to shield the dream from familiarity—that sly and deadly anesthetic. As I wrote in *The Man Who Walked Through Time*, "I knew that if I packed stores down into the Canyon I would be 'trespassing' in what I wanted to be unknown country; but I also knew that if I planted the caches outside the Rim I would in picking them up break both the real and symbolic continuity of my journey. In the end I solved the dilemma by siting each cache a few feet below the Rim." Recently, I more or less repeated this procedure for a midway cache on a two-week trip.

Such delicate precautions should, I think, always be borne in mind when one of the aims of a backpacking trip, recognized or submerged, is to explore and immerse yourself in unknown country. You must avoid any kind of preview. Before my Grand Canyon trip several people said, "Why not fly over beforehand, low? That's the way to choose a safe route." But I resisted the temptation—and in the end was profoundly thankful I had done so.

The best way to make, mark and protect a cache will depend on local conditions. Rain and animals pose the most obvious threats. But extreme heat has to be avoided if there is film in the cache, and extreme cold if there is water. (For the protection and refinding of water caches, and the best containers, see page 203. For precautions when caching dehydrated food in damp climates, see page 181.)

A cave or overhanging rockledge is probably the best protection against rain. Burying is the simplest and surest protection, especially in sandy desert, against temperature extremes and also against animals. For animals that can read, leave a note. On the California walk I put one with each cache: "If you find this cache, please leave it. I am passing through *on foot* in April or May, and am depending on it." Similar notes went on the Grand Canyon caches. But I feel fairly sure that none was ever read.

At each Grand Canyon cache all food and supplies went into a metal 5-gallon can. These cans are ideal for the job. Provided the lid is pressed firmly home the cans are watertight, something close to airtight and probably proof against all animals except bears and humans. I find that by packing the cans very carefully I can just squeeze in a full week's supply of everything. They are useful, too, for packing water ahead (page 203). They are also excellent for airdrops—and having them interchangeably available for caches or airdrops may help keep your plans conveniently fluid until the last possible moment. But metal cans are no longer easy to find. A good substitute for food caches: a 5-gallon plastic bucket with clip-on plastic lid of the kind now used for some foodstuffs and such construction materials as paint, adhesive and tar (about 1½ pounds, and anything from free to $5 from users).

Airdrops

Prearranged parachute airdrops are a highly efficient means of re-plenishment. But they are noisy. And I'm glad to know that in today's heavily used wilderness areas they have been banned as a normal supply method—as should all administrative, nonemergency overflights. After all, an object of going into such places—perhaps *the* object—is "to get away from it all"; and surely no one in his senses would want to inject "it" routinely in the form of low-flying aircraft. I have found, oddly enough, that the disturbance you suffer personally by having an airdrop is very small indeed; but once low-altitude flights—for any purpose at all—became anything more than very exceptional incursions they would disturb for everyone the solitude and sense of freedom from the man-world that I judge to be the essence of wilderness travel. As with sanita-tion, it is a matter of density.

But there are still places—especially in Alaska, Africa and South America—in which an occasional airdrop remains a reasonable supply method as well as the only practical one. So I retain almost intact this section from earlier editions.

Although airdrops are efficient, they are not perfect. On the ground, a practical disadvantage is that they tie you down to being at a certain place at a certain time. They are more dependable than most people imagine, but uncertainties do exist—above all, the uncertainty of weather—and I would prefer not to rely on an airdrop if there were any considerable danger that the plane might be delayed more than a day or two by storms or fog.

Airdrops have one important advantage over other means of supply: they act as a safety check. Once you've signaled "all's well" to the plane, everyone concerned soon knows you are safe up to that point. And if the pilot fails to locate you or sees a prearranged "in trouble—need help" signal then rescue operations can get under immediate and well-directed way.

Airdrops are not cheap—but neither are they ruinous. Most small rural charter outfits seem to charge around $70 for each hour of actual flying. If the base airport is within, say, 50 miles of the drop site you ought to get by on about 1 ¼ hours flying time, or under $90—provided the pilot has no trouble locating you. You may have to add the cost of the parachute—but see page 547.

Establishing contact is the crux of an airdrop operation.

First, make sure you've got hold of a good pilot. Unless there was no alternative I'd hesitate to depend on a man who had never done a drop before. It is essential too that he can map-read efficiently. (I suppose all pilots are more or less competent for the conditions they're used to; but that does not mean they can all pinpoint an agreed drop zone accurately enough in roadless wilderness.) Above all, satisfy yourself that you've got a careful and reliable man. Make local inquiries. And try to assess his qualities when you talk to him. Distrust a slapdash type whose refrain is "Just say where and when, and leave the rest to me." Feel reassured if he wants to cross all t's meticulously and to dot every last i and to have clear in his mind all alternative actions in case of delay for weather, failure to make contact with you or some such snafu as supplies falling into a river or smashing to pulp on rock because the parachute failed. I admit that it's a problem to know what to do if you decide, after discussing the minutest details with a pilot, that you just don't trust him. It's not easy to extricate yourself without gashing the poor fellow's feelings. The solution is probably to approach him first on a conditional basis: "Look, I find that I *may* need an airdrop at—" But perhaps you can dream up a better gambit.

Success in making contact depends only in part on the pilot. The man on the ground has a lot to do with it too. So make sure you know what the hell you are doing.

The first time I arranged an airdrop I was very conscious that I had no idea at all what the hell. The occasion* was the long Grand Canyon trip. I wanted three airdrops. The pilot and I, talking over details beforehand, decided that under expected conditions the surest ground-to-air signal was mirror-flashing. I would carry a little circular mirror, about 2 inches in diameter—the kind you could then pick up for 15 cents in any variety store. The pilot, who had been an Air Force survival instructor, assured me that such a mirror was just as good as specially made mirrors with cross-slits—and, at barely an ounce, was also appreciably lighter. The trick was to practice beforehand. I soon picked up the idea. You hold the mirror as close to one eye as you can and shut the other eye. Then you extend the free hand and aim the tip of the thumb at a point (representing the plane) that is not more than about 100 yards away. You move the mirror until the sun's reflection, appearing as a bright, irregular patch of light, hits the top of your thumb. Then you tilt the mirror up a bit until only the lowest part of the patch of light remains on your thumb. The rest of it should then show up exactly on the object that represents the plane. If it does not, keep practicing with fractional adjustments of mirror and thumb until you know exactly where to hold both so as to hit your target. You are now ready for the real thing. Ready, that is, to flash sunlight into the pilot's eyes.

"It's the surest way I know," said my Grand Canyon pilot. "On

* Described in rather different detail in The Man Who Walked Through Time, pp. 81–4.

survival exercises I've located guys that had nothing to flash with except penknife blades or even just sunglasses. When that flash hits my eye just once, the job's done. That's all I need to know: where to look. But without something to start me off, the expanse of ground I can see, especially in broken country like the Canyon, is just too damned big."

After a few minutes' practice I had complete confidence in the mirror routine; but we also arranged that I should spread out my bright orange sleeping bag as a marker, and would have a fire and some water ready so that when the plane had located me and came over low on a trial run I could send up a plume of smoke to indicate wind direction.

Because I was not sure how far I could travel across very rough country in a week, and because I did not want to be held back if I found I could move fast, we arranged primary and alternate sites for the first drop. We set zero hour at 10:00 A.M. on the eighth morning after I left an Indian village that would be my last contact with civilization. The chances were good that at ten o'clock no clouds would obscure the sun and that the day's desert winds would not yet have sprung up.

I made the alternate, farther-along site in time and, with complete confidence in the mirror signaling technique, decided for various reasons to take the drop about 2 miles from the prearranged place, out on a flat red rock-terrace. The plane arrived dead on schedule. But it failed to see my frantic flashings and, after an hour's fruitless search around the prime site and back along the way I'd come, was heading for home and passing not too far from me when I poured water on the waiting fire and sent a column of smoke spiraling up into the clear air. Almost at once the plane banked toward me, and within minutes my supplies were sailing safely down, suspended from a big orange parachute.

Later, a park ranger in the plane told me that he'd seen the smoke the moment it rose in the air. "But we didn't see the flashing until we were almost on top of you. At a guess, I'd say you didn't shake the mirror enough. You've got to do that to set up a good flashing. Oh, and your orange sleeping bag didn't show up at all against the red rock. We could hardly see it, even on the drop run."

So my first airdrop taught me a valuable lesson: unless it is absolutely unavoidable, don't change your prearranged drop site, even by a short distance. For the two later drops on that trip we had picked only one site, and each time I was in exactly the right place. I also had the white 8-by-9-foot plastic sheet (page 316) in my pack, and I spread it out beside the sleeping bag. Each time, the pilot saw the white patch as soon as he came within range, and although I had begun to flash with the mirror, the plane rocked its wings in recognition and I therefore stopped flashing before there was time to assess the mirror's worth. Both these later drops went off without a hitch.

Three years later, on the eighth morning of my seventeen-day hike-and-swim trip through Lower Grand Canyon, I had another airdrop. Because the route was untried I could not guarantee to be at the clearly defined riverside ledge that was the prime drop site, and on the scheduled morning I was still 3 miles upriver, on the most obvious and open ledge I could find—which was neither very obvious nor very open. Our plan was that if the pilot did not see me at the prime drop site he would fly upriver to my starting point and then return, still down in the Inner Gorge, between rockwalls more than 2000 feet high and, at their foot, barely 200 yards apart. It worked. The pilot missed me on the upriver run—because the early-morning sun was in his eyes and because I did not have time to generate much smoke from the fire I had ready. But on the return run he saw the now healthy smoke column from far upriver; and when he turned some way below me and came back for the drop, into the blinding sun, he had no difficulty knowing where I was because of the cloud of orange smoke from a day flare that I had carried for that specific purpose and had ignited as soon as I heard him returning downriver. The orange cloud persisted well and showed up clearly, he told me later. The parachute he used, by the way, was one he had made by stitching together two plastic windsocks. It worked fine.

So from my limited experience with airdrops I have come to the following tentative conclusions: The easiest and surest way to attract a pilot's attention under suitable conditions is by a fire-and-water smoke column. A good day flare may be even better, but is perhaps too valuable in an emergency (page 586) to be used in supply drops except when other methods have failed. Obviously, there are conditions under which any smoke signal may be ineffective: among very tall trees (where you'd hardly choose to take a parachute drop anyway), and probably in very high winds. For me, mirror-flashing remains an unproven but potentially valuable method. As for markers, I suspect that white is better than orange on most backgrounds other than snow. Finally, I grant now that it is dangerous to change your drop site unilaterally; but if you are going to be somewhere along an unmistakable line, such as a river, and the pilot is prepared to search along it, you can with reasonable safety leave a lot of latitude.

A reader writes that flashing is a much surer business with a double-sided mirror that has a central hole or cross-slits. You look at the plane through the hole. The sun, shining through the hole, casts a bright spot on your nose or face or maybe even hand. You adjust the mirror until the reflection that you see of this bright spot in the back of the mirror coincides with the hole—and is seen right on the plane. At that moment the mirror is flashing at the plane. I guess so. But I'd still waggle it about a lot. Nowadays I have a wristwatch that reflects a bright spot efficiently, and I might rely on that for signaling in an airdrop—as I do for possible rescue.

Several people have written asking what I did in the Canyon with the parachutes and other garbage. I packed the chutes and everything else into the metal 5-gallon cans that the supplies had been packed in (page 204); and I tucked the cans away out of sight.

Helicopters

Useful as they may be, helicopters are—at least in wilderness—disgusting bloody machines. And I feel sure that having one land and offload supplies—and also bring you into contact with "outsiders"—would be a far more disruptive event than an airdrop. What's more, the 'copters' fiendish clatter and the way they can mosey into every corner make them even less desirable as wilderness suppliers than conventional planes. Still, I suppose there are times and places . . .

Average charter rates for a small helicopter operating no higher than about 5000 feet run around $140 an hour. Supercharged 'copters for mountain work may cost $175 an hour, and the newer light-turbine versions as much as $375. (Comparable rates for small conventional plane: around $70.)

It's worth knowing—not so much for supply purposes but because most wilderness rescue work is now carried out by helicopters—that they cannot put down just anywhere. A slope of more than about 10 degrees is not a feasible landing place for even a small machine. In good conditions, though, on a clear surface, an expert pilot may be able to hover with one skid on a steeper slope long enough to pick up a casualty. But even for this method the slope cannot be more than about 25 degrees.

Pack animal or support backpacker

I have never tried replenishing supplies by either of these methods. Obviously, though, you must make cast-iron arrangements about the meeting place—and hardened-steel arrangements if someone else is going to plant a cache for you.

Auxiliary pack animal

Indoorsmen often ask why I never use a pack animal such as a burro on any of my long walks. Blame for the thought probably lies with Robert Louis Stevenson and his *Travels with a Donkey*—or maybe with TV prospectors who amble across parched Western deserts escorted by amiable burros.

Frankly, I've never even been tempted. For one thing, I can go places a burro can't. And I blench at the prospect of looking after a burro's food and water supply. Also, although I know nothing at first hand about managing the beasts, I mistrust their dispositions. Come to think of it, I do not seem to be alone in my distrust. Precious few people use burros these days. It is perhaps significant that on one of the only two occasions I have come across the man-beast combination, the man was on one side of a small creek pulling furiously and vainly at the halter of the burro, and the burro was planted on the far bank with heels dug resolutely in.

Most stock impinges heavily on the country, too—with their shod feet, large droppings, appetites, and even brayings. South American llamas, which have begun to appear as pack animals in the Sierra Nevada, though in small numbers, score well here: they leave very faint tracks, and small and inoffensive droppings; and they seem to make no noise. But I hear they have abrasive dispositions—and tend to spit at you.

DANGERS, REAL AND IMAGINED

For many wilderness walkers, no single source of fear quite compares with that stirred up by

Rattlesnakes.*

Every year an almost morbid terror of the creatures ruins or at least tarnishes countless otherwise delightful hikes all over the United States and Canada. This terror is based largely on folklore and myth, hardly at all on fact.

Now, rattlesnakes can be dangerous, but they are not what so many people fancy them to be: vicious and cunning brutes with a deep-seated hatred of man. In solid fact, rattlers are timid and retiring. They are highly developed reptiles but they simply do not have the brain capacity for cunning in our human sense. And although they react to man as they would to any big and threatening creature they could hardly have built up a deep-seated hatred: the first man that one of them sees is usually the

* Only two distinct kinds of poisonous snakes occur in the United States: the coral snakes and the pit vipers—a group that includes rattlesnakes, cottonmouths (or water moccasins) and copperheads.

Coral snakes, though highly poisonous, rarely bite humans; and they are restricted to the southeast corner of the country plus one sector of Arizona.

last. Finally, the risk of being bitten by a rattler is slight, and the danger that a bite will prove fatal to a healthy adult is small.*

In other words, ignorance has as usual bred deep and unreasoning fear—a fear that may even cause more harm than snakebite. Not long ago, near San Diego, California, a hunter who was spiked by barbed wire thought he had been struck by a rattler—and very nearly died of shock.

The surest antidote to fear is knowledge. When I began my California walk I knew nothing about rattlesnakes, and the first one I met scared me purple. Killing it seemed a human duty. But by the end of the summer I no longer felt this unreasoning fear, and as a result I no longer killed rattlers—unless they lived close to places frequented by people.

Later I grew interested enough to write a magazine article about rattlesnakes, and in researching it I read the entire 1500-odd pages of the last-word bible on the subject. As I read, the fear sank even further away. Gradually I came to accept rattlesnakes as fellow creatures with a niche in the web of life.

The book I read was *Rattlesnakes: Their Habits, Life Histories and Influence on Mankind* by Laurence M. Klauber (2 vols.; University of California Press, 2nd edition, 1973; $75. Abridged edition, 1981, 350 pages, $19.95). Dr. Klauber was the world's leading authority on rattlesnakes, and in the book he sets out in detail all the known biological facts. But he does more. He examines and exposes the dense cloud of fancy and folklore that swirls around his subject. I heartily recommend this fascinating book to anyone who ever finds his peace of mind disturbed by a blind fear of rattlesnakes—and also to anyone interested in widening the fields in which he can observe and understand when he goes walking. You should find the book in any university library, and in any medium-size or large public library.

Among the many folklore fables Dr. Klauber punctures is the classic "boot story." I first heard this one down in the Colorado Desert of Southern California—and believed it. "There was this rancher," the old-timer told me, "who lived not far from here. One day he wore some kneeboots belonging to his father, who had died ten years before. Next day the rancher's leg began to swell. It grew rapidly worse. Eventually he went to a doctor—just in time to avoid amputation from rattlesnake poisoning. Then he remembered that his father had been struck when wearing the same boots a year before he died. One of the snake's fangs

* In the United States more people are killed and injured in their bathtubs than by snakebite. Of 210 million Americans, perhaps 1200 a year are bitten. Twelve of these (or 1 percent) may die; but this figure includes people who have been badly frightened, those with weak hearts, and small children whose bodies cannot absorb the venom. In other words, even without treatment, the odds on survival are very, very long.

had broken off and lodged in an eyehole. Eleven years later it scratched the son."

Essentially the same story was read before the Royal Society of London by a New World traveler on January 7, 1714. That version told how the boot killed three successive husbands of a Virginia woman. Today the incident may take place anywhere, coast to coast, and the boot is sometimes modernized into a struck and punctured tire that proves fatal to successive garagemen who repair it. Actually, the amount of dried venom on the point of a fang is negligible. And venom exposed to air quickly loses its potency.

Then there is the legend of the "avenging mate": kill one rattler, and its mate will vengefully seek you out. Pliny, the Roman naturalist who died in A.D. 79, told this story of European snakes, and it's still going strong over here. In 1954, after a rattlesnake had been killed in a downtown Los Angeles apartment, the occupant refused to go back because a search had failed to unearth the inevitably waiting mate.

The legend probably arose because it seems as though a male may occasionally court a freshly killed female. Some years ago a geographer friend of mine and a zoologist companion, looking for specimens for research, killed a rattler high in California's Sierra Nevada. The zoologist carried the snake 200 yards to a log and began skinning it. My friend sat facing him. Suddenly he saw another rattler crawling toward them. "It was barely four yards away," he told me later, "and heading directly for the dead snake; but it was taking its time and seemed quite unaware of our presence. We killed it before it even rattled. It was a male. The first was a female." An untrained observer might well have seen this incident as proof positive that the second snake was bent on revenge.

Toward the end of my seventeen-day trip down the Colorado I saw with my own eyes just how another myth could have arisen. I was running very short of food, and after meeting four rattlers within four days I reluctantly decided that if I met another I would kill and cook it. I duly met one. It was maybe 3 feet long—about as big as they grow in that country. I promptly hit it with my staff a little forward of the tail, breaking its back and immobilizing it; but before I could put it out of its pain by crushing its head, it began striking wildly about in all directions. Soon—and apparently by pure accident—it struck itself half-way down the body. It was a perfect demonstration of how the myth arose that wounded rattlers will strike themselves to commit suicide. (Quite apart from the question of whether snakes can comprehend the idea of a future death, rattlesnakes are little affected by rattlesnake venom.)

After I had killed that snake I cut off the head, wrapped the body in a plastic bag, and put it in my pack; but I could not for the life of me remember what Dr. Klauber had said about eating rattlers that had struck themselves. As I walked on, thinking of the venom that was probably still circulating through the snake's blood system, I grew less and less hungry. After half an hour, feeling decidedly guilty about the unnecessary killing, I discarded the corpse.

Later I found that although people are often warned against eating a rattler that has bitten itself there is in fact no danger if the meat is cooked: the poisonous quality of snake venom is destroyed by heat. It's as well to cut out the bitten part, though, just as you cut away damaged meat in an animal that has been shot. Back in the 1870s one experimenter got a big rattler to bite itself three or four times. It lived 19 hours and seemed unhurt. The man then cooked and ate it without ill effect.

According to Dr. Klauber, rattler meat has been compared with chicken, veal, frog, tortoise, quail, fish, canned tuna and rabbit. It is, as he points out, useful as an emergency ration because it is easily hunted down and killed, even by people weakened by starvation. But there's only 1 pound of meat on a 4-foot rattler, 2½ pounds on a 5-footer and 4½ on a 6-footer.

Even straightforward information about rattlesnakes often gets hopelessly garbled in the popular imagination. For example, the only facts about rattlers that many people know for sure are that they grow an extra rattle every year, revel in blistering heat and are fast and unfailingly deadly. Not one of these "facts" is true. Number of rattles is almost no indication of age. A rattler soon dies if the temperature around it rises much over 100°. It crawls so slowly that the only dangerous rattler is the one you don't see. Even the strike is not nearly as fast as was once thought. Tests prove it to be rather slower than a trained man's punching fists. If you move first—as fast as you can, and clean out of range—you may get away with it, though avoiding the strike, even if you're waiting for it, borders on the impossible.

Accurate knowledge will not only help dispel many unreasoning fears (it is nearly always the unknown that we fear the most), but can materially reduce the chances that you will be bitten.

Take the matter of heat and cold, for example. Rattlesnakes, like all reptiles, lack an efficient mechanism such as we have for keeping body temperature constant, so they are wholly dependent on the temperature around them. In cold climates they can hibernate indefinitely at a few degrees above freezing, and have fully recovered after four hours in a deep freeze at 4° F. Yet at 45° F. they can hardly move, and they rarely choose to prowl in temperatures below 65°. Their "best" range is 80–90° F. At 100° they're in danger, and at 110° they die of heat stroke. But these, remember, are *their* temperatures—that is, the temperatures their bodies attain through contact with the ground over which they are moving and with the air around them. These temperatures may differ markedly from official weather readings taken in the shade, 5 feet above ground level. When such a reading is 60°, for example, a thermometer down on sunlit sand may record 100°, and in the lowest inch of air about 80°. (See pages 88 and 509.) In other words, a rattler in the right place may feel snugly comfortable in an "official" temperature of 60°. On the other hand, in a desert temperature of 80° in the shade the sunlit sand might be over 130° and the lowest inch of air around 110°, and any rattler staying for long in such a place would die.

Once you know a few such facts you find after a little practice that your mind almost automatically tells you when to be especially watchful, and even where to avoid placing your feet. In cool early-season weather, for example, when rattlers like to bask, you will tend to keep a sharp lookout, if the sun is shining but a cold wind is blowing, in sunlit places that are sheltered from the wind. And in hot desert weather you will know that there is absolutely no danger out on open sand where there is no shade. On the other hand, the prime feeding time for rattlers in warm weather is two hours before and after sunset, when the small mammals that are their main prey tend to be on the move; so if you figure that the ground temperature during that time is liable to be around 80° to 90° you keep your eyes skinned. I do not mean that you walk in fear and trembling. But you watch your step. Given the choice, for example, you tend to bisect the space between bushes, and so reduce the chances of surprising a rattler resting unseen beneath overhanging vegetation. Once you're used to it, you do this kind of thing as a natural safe operating procedure, no more directly connected with fear than is the habit of checking the street for traffic before you step off a sidewalk.

You'll also be able to operate more safely once you understand how rattlesnakes receive their impressions of the world around them. Their sight is poor, and they are totally deaf. But they're well equipped with other senses. Two small facial pits contain nerves so sensitive to heat that a rattler can strike accurately at warm-blooded prey in complete darkness. (Many species hunt mainly at night.) They're highly sensitive to vibration too, and have rattled at men passing out of sight 150 feet away. (Moral: in bad rattler country, at bad times, tread heavily.) Two nostrils just above a rattler's mouth furnish a sense of smell very like ours. And that's not all. A sure sign that a snake has been alerted is a flickering of its forked tongue: it is "smelling" the outside world. The tongue's moist surface picks up tiny particles floating in the air and at each flicker transfers them to two small cavities in the roof of the mouth. These cavities, called "Jacobson's organs," interpret the particles to the brain in terms of smell, much as do the moist membranes inside our noses.

In Biblical times, people wrongly associated snakes' tongues with their poison. Nothing has changed. Stand at the rattlesnake cage in any zoo and the chances are you'll soon hear somebody say, "There, did you see its stinger?" or even, "Look at it stick out its fangs!" It is true, though, that an alarmed snake will sometimes use its tongue to intimidate enemies. When it does, the forked tips quiver pugnaciously out at their limit, arching first up, then down. It's a chillingly effective display. But primarily, of course, a snake reacts to enemies with that unique rattle. Harmless in itself, it warns and intimidates, like the growl of a dog.

The rattle is a chain of hollow, interlocking segments made of the same hard and transparent keratin as human nails. The myth that each segment represents a year of the snake's age first appeared in print as early as 1615. Actually, a new segment is left each time the snake sheds its skin. Young rattlers shed frequently, and adults an average of one to three times each year. In any case, the fragile rattles rarely remain complete for very long.

In action the rattles shake so fast that they blur like the wings of a hummingbird. Small snakes merely buzz like a fly but big specimens sound off with a strident hiss that rises to a spine-chilling crescendo. Someone once said that it was "like a pressure cooker with the safety valve open." Once you've heard the sound you'll never forget it.

The biggest rattlers are eastern diamondbacks: outsize specimens may weigh 30 pounds and measure almost 8 feet. But most of the thirty different species grow to no more than 3 or 4 feet.

People often believe that rattlers will strike only when coiled, and never upward. It is true that they can strike most effectively from the alert, raised-spiral position; but they are capable of striking from any position and in any direction.

Rattlers are astonishingly tenacious of life. One old saying warns, "They're dangerous even after they're dead"—and it is true. Lab tests have shown that severed heads can bite a stick and discharge venom for up to 43 minutes. The tests even produced some support for the old notion that "rattlers never die till sundown." Decapitated bodies squirmed for as long as 7½ hours, moved when pinched for even longer. And the hearts almost always went on beating for a day, often for 2 days. One was still pulsating after 59 hours.

A rattlesnake's enemies include other snakes (especially king snakes and racers), birds, mammals and even fish. In Grand Canyon I found a 3-foot rattler apparently trampled to death by wild burros. Torpid captive rattlers have been killed and part eaten by mice put in their cages for food! Not long ago a California fisherman caught a big rainbow trout with a 9-inch rattler in its stomach. But only one species of animal makes appreciable inroads on the rattlesnake population. That species is man—

to whom the warning rattle is an invitation to attack. If man had existed in large numbers when rattlesnakes began to evolve, perhaps 6 million years ago, it is unlikely the newfangled rattlebearers would have succeeded and flourished.

In spite of stories to the contrary, a rattlesnake meeting a large animal such as man hardly ever attacks so long as the potential enemy stays outside its striking range. (Very rarely, when courting, it may just possibly attack; but then, so may a deer or even a rabbit.) It may move toward you, but that will be for other reasons, such as the slope of the ground. Its first reaction will most likely be to lie still and escape attention. Then it may crawl slowly for safety. Detected or alarmed, it will probably rattle and rise into its menacing defensive coil—a vibrant, open spiral quite distinct from the tightly wound pancake resting position. It may also hiss. Finally, it may strike. Usually, though by no means always, it will rattle before striking. Of course, none of these comments necessarily applies if a man treads on a snake or comes suddenly and alarmingly within its restricted little world. Then, not unnaturally, the frightened animal will often strike without warning.

But it's important to remember that rattlesnakes are as moody as men, as unpredictable as women. A man who for many years was rattle-snake-control officer of South Dakota concluded that they simply "are not to be trusted, for some will violate all rules." Certain individuals, even whole species, seem to be always "on the prod." A few habitually strike without warning. Others seem almost amiable.

Defense is not, of course, the main purpose of a rattler's venom and fangs. Primarily, they're for securing food.

The fangs, regularly replaced, are precision instruments. One slender, curving tooth on each side of the snake's upper jaw grows almost five times longer than its fellows. In large rattlers it may measure ¾ inch. A cunning pivot-and-lever bone structure ensures that when the mouth is closed these fierce barbs lie flat; but as the jaw opens wide to strike they pivot erect. Each fang is hollow. Its cavity connects with a venom sac beneath the eye, equivalent to our salivary gland. When the fangs stab into a prey the snake injects a controlled dose of venom through the cavity and out of an aperture just above the fang's point. In the small mammals that rattlers mostly feed on, the venom causes almost instant paralysis and rapid death.

A rattlesnake's venom—present from birth—is as unpredictable as its temperament. Quantity and toxicity seem to vary widely from species to species, from individual to individual. In general, though, the bigger the snake, the greater the danger: a big snake stabs deeper with its fangs and generally injects more venom. But there are other, quite unpredictable, factors in any case of snakebite. It's not just that a rattler can control, at least to some degree, the amount of venom it injects; the quantity in its sacs will vary markedly according to whether it has or has not expended venom recently in killing prey.

Treatment of snakebite

The greatest danger is probably hysteria; people bitten by harmless snakes have come close to dying from fright. What many snakebite patients need most, in fact, is rest and reassurance. But there seems little doubt that, in cases of bad bites from genuinely dangerous snakes, *quick* physical treatment, carefully applied, can prevent possibly severe illness and may even save a life—especially of a child, whose small body can absorb little venom. Remember, though, that even venomous snakes may inject little or no venom when they bite, particularly under back-packing conditions, when the snake is likely to have been surprised and to have struck defensively, perhaps almost haphazardly.

The ideal treatment is to get to a hospital as quickly as possible so that a full evaluation can be made and, if necessary, antivenin injected with the proper safeguards. Under normal modern conditions, in fact, where transportation is available, many authorities now decry both old first-aid methods—cut-and-suck and cryotherapy. "The best first aid," says one expert, "is a set of car keys."

That advice is worth bearing in mind, even for backpackers. If you are within an hour or so of roadhead and quick access to a hospital, or at least a doctor, the best response to being bitten may be to walk out "at a moderate pace, taking frequent rests, using a sling if the bite is on the hand, and abstaining from alcohol." Provided, that is, the day is not too hot and you are not too exhausted or panic-stricken. A companion who can provide physical support and also keep an eye on your condition makes walking out much more practical. And two companions can maybe rig up a makeshift stretcher. Unless roadhead is more than 36 hours away, small children weighing less than about 60 pounds should be carried out, on shoulders or stretcher, as soon as possible. But in such cases, when other people are available, the best action may be to send out one or more fast messengers for a helicopter.

Clearly, each case is different. Judgment on the correct response demands both some knowledge of the facts and a lot of cool. But even anti-first-aid experts still tend to agree that when a healthy adult or large child is bitten more than an hour or two away from outside help, first aid on the spot may be the only practical response. That may certainly be your forced choice if you are alone, or if the weather is very hot (and walking would markedly raise your metabolic rate, so that the venom would spread and be absorbed dangerously fast). In such a situation you simply have to sit the thing out in as cool a place as you can find. You may become "feverish," and vomit and retch and feel generally pretty damned bad for as long as 48 hours. You may also, especially soon after being bitten, feel dizzy and on the point of fainting. If so, simply lie down with your feet higher than your head.

It is still difficult to find two informed people who fully agree on the best first-aid treatment. But cryotherapy (making the site of the bite so cold that the body absorbs the venom slowly enough to neutralize its most serious effects) has, according to one authority, "been almost universally condemned . . . as being hazardous. Numerous amputations of limbs have resulted from ice and ice-water immersion." And keeping the venom local may be dangerous.

That leaves us with cut-and-suck therapy. To be useful, it must be applied as soon as possible—preferably within 30 seconds, certainly within 4 or 5 minutes. After that, the bulk of the venom will have begun to circulate, you will suck out virtually none, and the treatment will be not only useless but probably harmful. Cut-and-suck treatment should only be applied, of course, after a careful—though very quick—confirmation that venom has actually been injected (you know soon enough, because of rapid inflammation and extreme pain). The cutting instrument must be at least partially sterilized, even if only by being flamed. The standard and probably best cut-and-suck kit, by Cutter, comes with a small vial of sterilizing liquid. One of these neat little devices (1 ounce, $4.90) is no bigger than a 12-gauge shell. It includes three rubber suction cups. Two of these cups form the kit's outer shell and are indented on the outside so that they grip the bottom of any pocket. The interlocking suction cups contain, in addition to the vial of sterilizing liquid, a small but very sharp blade, a constrictive band (formerly called a tourniquet), and full instructions. Memorize at least the essence of the instructions. And always remember that in the unlikely event of your being bitten it's the first few seconds and minutes that count.

In snake country I always carry a Cutter kit in my pants pocket. I find its presence highly reassuring. Recently, though, the kits have had a bad press. "Snakebite suction is stupidity," blares one newspaper article. But the difficulty seems to lie in misuse rather than any intrinsic deficiency (given that if you can get to medical aid quickly enough, you should probably not apply any kind of first aid). Above all, use the constrictive band, if at all, only during the very short period of not more than 5 minutes during which you are actually sucking out venom. The band's sole purpose is to delay, briefly, the venom's spread. And it should be tied only tightly enough to depress the skin and so constrict lymph flow but not blood flow. You should be able to slip a finger under the band. In other words, it must not become a tourniquet. Cutting should be done carefully and sparingly. Make no more than two cuts, one beside each fang mark. Even in fleshy places the cuts should be no more than ⅛ inch deep and ⅛ to ¼ inch long, and should run along the axis of the blood supply. Do *not* make x cuts. If the bite lies over a shallow vein or artery—on the underside of the wrist, for example—make no cuts at all, just apply suction cups: the risk of damage is too great. Be warned that even these instructions, though probably approved by a reasonable majority, will draw howls of anguish from many apparently well-informed people. But then, so will *any* form of first-aid treatment.

The one emergency treatment that everyone now agrees is not merely useless but positively dangerous—because it stimulates your metabolism and therefore spreads the venom more quickly—is the old-timers' "snakebite cure": alcohol.

I must accent that everything I have said, except for the warning against alcohol, applies only to rattlesnakes and other pit vipers of the United States and Canada (page 549, footnote). All have comparatively low-toxicity venom. The rare and rather docile coral snakes of Arizona are so small that they're very unlikely to be able to bite a human, and even when they do the results are short of deadly. But the larger coral snakes of Florida present more of a problem. Anyone penetrating known coral-snake country there might consider inquiring *from a reliable authority* about the possibility of carrying an antivenin. Keep in mind, though, that many experts strongly advise against such a course—for the same reason that they say it would be sheer idiocy for the layman to take antivenin in rattlesnake country: the risk from injecting it without full medical safeguards is greater than from a rattlesnake bite. Where snakes are more deadly—as in Africa and, I understand, Central and South America—the only worthwhile snakebite kit is antivenin and a syringe. But some people are very seriously allergic to the horse serum used in the antivenin. Before you even consider carrying a kit, check your reaction with an allergist.

I hope this rather long discourse has convinced you that rattlesnakes, although dangerous, are not the vicious and deadly brutes of legend. If you have in the past felt, as so many people do, a deep and unreasoning fear of them, then I hope I have helped just a little in dispelling that fear—and have left you free to walk almost anywhere.

You may even find that your understanding of rattlesnakes passes at length beyond mere factual knowledge. I have described in *The Man Who Walked Through Time* (p. 166) how I was sitting naked one afternoon on a sandbar at the edge of a willow thicket when I saw a pale-pink rattlesnake come gliding over the sand, barely 6 feet away from me, clearly unaware of my presence. Sitting there watching it, I found that I felt curiosity rather than fear. Slowly, gracefully, the snake threaded its way through a forest of willow shoots. As its flank pushed past each stem I could see the individual scales tilt under the stem's pressure, then move back flush. Four feet from my left buttock the snake stopped, its head in a sun-dappled patch of sand beside a cluster of roots. Unhurriedly, it drew its body forward and curled into a flat resting coil. Then it stretched and yawned. It yawned a long and unmistakable yawn. A yawn so uninhibited that for many slow seconds I seemed to see nothing but the pale lining of its mouth and two matching arcs of small, sharp teeth. When the yawn was over at last the snake raised its head and twisted it slowly and luxuriously from side to side, as a man or a woman will do in anticipation of rest and comfort to come. Finally, with such obvious contentment that I do not think I would have been altogether surprised to hear the creature purr, it laid its head gently on the pillow of its clean and beautifully marked body.

And all at once, for the first time in my life, I found that I had moved "inside" a rattlesnake. Quite unexpectedly, I had shared its sleepiness and anticipation and contentment. And as I sat looking down at the sleeping snake coiled in its patch of sun-dappled shade, I found myself feeling for it something remarkably close to affection.

Frankly, the feeling has not lasted. I am still no rattlesnake aficionado. But my fear, helped by the moment of understanding, has now contracted to vanishing point. On my 1966 trip down Lower Grand Canyon, when I met five rattlesnakes in five days, one small specimen even struck from under a stone and hit my boot (no damage done). Yet even at that moment I do not think I felt much fear: it was more a matter of interest and curiosity. But—and it may be a very big "but"—the rattlesnakes of Grand Canyon do not grow more than about 3 feet long. Whether I would have been so consistently calm in country thick with big diamondbacks, I just don't know. I'm afraid I can guess, though.

Scorpions

A friend of mine who does a great deal of hiking in Arizona once told me that he worried more about scorpions than about rattlesnakes. "You can see the rattlers," he said.

In Arizona there is good reason for respecting scorpions: the sting of two quite small, sand-colored species that are found in that state—and only there—is always serious and can prove fatal. But the sting of other scorpions found in North America (except Mexico) is rarely much more serious than a bee sting. (Remember, though, that some people react violently to almost any venom. For them, even a bee sting may be fatal.)

But unless you go around turning up stones you are not very likely to see a scorpion. I have only come across two in the United States: one, rather surprisingly, was at an elevation of over 10,000 feet; the other, in my garden.

There is a well-known desert tradition that in scorpion country you always turn out your boots before putting them on in the morning. Before I went down into Grand Canyon I asked an experienced park ranger about it. "Oh, it always sounds to me like an old wives' tale," he said. Then a smile leaked slowly out over his face, and he added, "But I still do it."

In the United States the animals that pose the greatest real danger are, rather surprisingly, "bugs": that is, arachnids and true insects (spiders, ticks and chiggers are arachnids). Bugs apparently cause 60 percent of total U.S. deaths from venomous animals.

Spiders

All spiders are in a sense "poisonous." That is how they make a living: they kill or incapacitate their prey by injecting small amounts of venom. But almost all spiders found in the U.S. have injecting mechanisms too delicate to penetrate human skin; and even if their venom were injected it would be close to harmless. There are three exceptions: tarantulas, black widows and brown recluses.

Tarantulas that occur in the U.S. do not, in spite of their evil aspect and matching reputation, inflict a serious bite. No more serious, again, than a bee sting. And your chances of meeting a tarantula are small. Only in late fall, usually November, do they normally emerge from their subterranean homes and, with gleams in all eight eyes, prowl the overland world in search of mates. Even then they remain, as far as humans are concerned, unbelligerent creatures, almost passive.

But black widows are dangerous. Although they're very much smaller than tarantulas their bites are always serious and in very rare cases can prove fatal, even to adults. (Statistics are blurred, but black widows cause maybe one death a year in the U.S.)

If you are bitten the only sensation at first may be something like a mild pinprick, though the spider may still be adhering to your skin. Two or three hours may pass before you suffer serious pain. But then, for thirty-six hours, the pain may be severe. Muscles may also cramp severely. Aspirin or Tylenol-codeine (page 495) will relieve the pain. Beyond that there seems to be no first aid of any value. Cut-and-suck treatment is useless as well as dangerous: there's simply not enough venom (which is of a neurotoxic type). And cryotherapy is now mostly condemned. So, once again, the best action, where it's possible, is high-tailing (circumspectly) or being hightailed out to qualified medical treatment. If that's impractical you have, once again, to sit the thing out in a cool place—reassuring yourself with that one-death-a-year figure.

Black widows have spherical bodies about the size of a marble. They do not have particularly noticeable legs. They are entirely black except for a red patch on the underside, shaped like an hourglass.

Brown-recluse spiders were, rather surprisingly, unknown to science until the 1940s. Once only a threat in the South, they seem to be spreading—perhaps because they hole up in stored furniture and get shipped out. A brown recluse's bite is painless. The first symptom, appearing hours or even days later, may be a skin ulcer that can become gangrenous and slough off tissue several inches square. The ulceration is very slow-healing: it may last up to a year. An untreated bitee may also suffer a fever and pass dark urine. Children may even die. Beyond getting to a doctor, quick, no one seems to offer any sensible advice on field treatment for this fortunately rare little beauty.

I have never been introduced to a brown recluse but it is said to be a small, pale brown spider with a dark brown, violin-shaped spot on its back.

Ticks and chiggers

are mostly a pest rather than a danger. But three species commonly carry the misleadingly named Rocky Mountain Spotted Fever (95 percent of human cases now occur in the East). Untreated, RMSF can prove fatal. And the symptoms, which develop in three to ten days—severe head and muscle ache, fever and a measleslike rash that often starts on feet or hands and then spreads—are easily misinterpreted. If diagnosed early the disease can be quickly cured. But the best protection is swift removal of all ticks: to transmit RMSF a tick must remain attached to the skin for about two to six hours. As we shall see, tick removal is good practice anyway.

Tick time in most of the country is summer, though in drier and warmer parts of the Southwest, including California, it's winter, starting with the first rains. When conditions are right, ticks (and chiggers too) migrate to the tips of grass stems and other vegetation. If you look closely during prime time you can see battalions of the little bastards waiting for a warm-blooded host to pass. As you brush by they grasp skin or clothing (but not, I find, a cold staff). They may then spend hours crawling toward tick-Nirvanas: soft, warm sectors such as buttocks, waist and upper back where there's pressure from clothing. This crawling phase is what gives you a break. In bad times, check frequently. The crop can sometimes be astonishing. In a heavily infested little valley I often walk through I once plucked 35 ticks off my bare legs after a passage of barely 300 yards. And by the time I was out of the valley, thirty minutes later, I had harvested a total of 104. That morning I checked at least every hour. In any tick country you should examine yourself once or more a day. The most popular tick parking places are not all easy to examine by yourself, of course, and if you're not traveling solo mutual search may be advisable. The only danger is that this operation, artistically conducted in the right company, may lead to such delectable results that all thought of tick removal fades.

Crawling ticks are simple to pluck off. But once they burrow in and start sucking blood it is not easy to remove them without leaving heads and pincers embedded. In RMSF-bearing ticks these remnants can still transmit the disease. And remnants from even the "harmless" species may cause infection. Some years ago a left-behind tick head in my groin, apparently embedded in the lymph system, sent an angry red line running up my leg, and as a registered hypochondriac I had no choice but to abort the trip and head for a doctor. Maybe wisely too.

The current gospel on removing ticks is to avoid both cigarette butts applied to tick butts (as an encouragement toward withdrawal) and also the application of oil or grease (as a suffocant). Most likely result: an embedded corpse. Instead, grasp the body with tweezers or tissue-covered fingertips and "roll" it upward without jerk or twist. (Frankly, I've twisted counterclockwise for years, in the belief that ticks burrow in corkscrew-fashion, and have achieved considerable success.)

I am inclined to believe that some fly repellents, such as Muskol (page 490), at least reduce the tendency of ticks to grasp you. Apparently they work for chiggers too.

Chiggers—mostly found in the East and South—are tiny red larval forms of mites. Once beachheaded on a warm human body they head for the softest parts, such as wrists, armpits and behind the knees. They don't actually suck blood, like ticks, but do dissolve skin cells—and set up an unholy itching. I'm told they can sometimes be removed, tediously and painfully, with extremely sticky tape. But if left alone they drop off after three or four days, and although the itching is pesky it rarely becomes serious.

Other bugs

In the U.S., insects other than malaria-transmitting mosquitoes are mostly no worse than perishing nuisances, to be fought with tents, cheesecloth (page 489), repellents (page 490) or clothing (pages 422 and 491). The pain and irritating itches left by some bites can be neutralized, I'm told, with Sting-Eze (½-ounce plastic bottle, $2.50)—also said to help alleviate the pain of poison-oak and ivy rashes (page 572).

But the real danger from insect bites lies in allergic reactions. In severe cases they can lead within minutes to "anaphylactic shock," in which the patient first suffers inability to breathe properly—often along with hives, vomiting and dizziness—and occasionally, because the small air passages in his lungs close, may pass out and even die from asphyxiation. Bee stings are notoriously liable to produce life-threatening reactions in certain people. If you know or even suspect you are susceptible to reactions to any kind of bite or sting, get a doctor's prescription for an emergency insect-sting allergy kit (1½ ounces, $10), containing antihistamine tablets and an adrenalin-loaded syringe (the adrenalin needs replacing every two or three years). Get the doctor to explain the kit's use. I have carried such a kit ever since suffering a mildly dramatic reaction to a bite, probably inflicted by an assassin bug that failed by a decent margin in its attempt.

Mammals

Contrary to popular indoor opinion, there is almost no danger from such large and reputedly ferocious mammals as mountain lions and bobcats. Mountain lions (also called cougars) may follow you at a safe distance out of curiosity but they will not attack—unless, possibly, you have a dog with you. Bobcats are less dependable, especially when with kittens. But I have woken to find fresh bobcat tracks within 6 feet of my sleeping bag. And during a wilderness breakfast a few years ago I looked up to see, 30 paces away, a full-grown specimen—mistrustful, pointy-eared, exquisitely speckled—that appraised me for several minutes before turning and trotting away.

On the other hand, if you stumble on almost any animal and surprise and frighten it, it may react ferociously in self-defense. And thirst or hunger or the sex urge or mother love may turn a normally peaceful beast into a potentially dangerous one. The best-known example is probably the black-bear mother with cubs. But moose can be dangerous during the rut. And, as I have said, even rabbits, when courting, have been known to attack an interfering human intruder.

Grizzly bears* clearly form an exception to the general rule. They occasionally attack and kill people without provocation—provocation that the human is aware of, anyway. But you can take precautions:

1. Stay away.

2. Accept the risk—knowing that it's likely to be less in really remote areas than in places the bears have become used to human presence. (The answer to the question "How safe do we want our wilderness?" seems to be that we are willing to accept, perhaps even welcome, a small degree of risk but that beyond a certain point we will probably want to cry "Stop!" Try to bear that in mind as you read the next 7 pages.)

3. Follow the advice of my bear-biologist advisor for this edition: "Avoid dense brush and situations where visibility is obscure. Allow for mutual introductions at 50 meters or more." A reader elaborates: "Grizzlies, like most bears, are extremely shy animals. If in grizzly territory, a hiker can travel with more peace of mind by making a noise either by 'singing loudly' (35 calories per 100 pounds per hour) or perhaps by making a rattle out of a tin can and some stones and tying it to his foot (around the ankle). Some [people] fix bells to their horses and even carry transistor radios for this purpose." He goes on to tell of being chased by a grizzly with two cubs while hiking in the Canadian Rockies. "The poor bears had been surprised while taking a bath in a river [and] we had made no sound coming into their territory. . . . I now always use a tin-can rattle when in grizzly country."

4. Walk alertly and carry a big gun.

In the last edition I commented that "except in rare cases, this is a poor solution that could turn out to be the most dangerous of the lot." But when I made my first trip to Alaska a few years ago and spent three weeks alone in a remote mountain area, a concerned Fish and Game Department biologist more or less insisted that I carry his .357 magnum revolver. Several recent and well-authenticated reports of people being killed by grizzlies overcame my reluctance. The bulky revolver, carried in a shoulder holster on my left side, proved to be no impediment and quickly became forgettable—though I remained comfortingly aware of its psychological protection.

* The Big Brown, or Kodiak, bear of southern Alaska (Ursus middendorfi) has now been lumped as a single species with the grizzly (Ursus horribilis). That should ease a widespread and long-standing befuddlement. But the chaos quota has been deftly sustained: our new, conglomerated grizzly becomes Ursus arctos—which practically guarantees intermittent confusion with the polar bear (formerly Thalarctos maritimus, now Ursus maritimus).

Another fruitful source of confusion: many "black" bears, especially in the Southwest, come in shades of brown. (Brown/grizzly bears now exist only in the Yellowstone and Glacier ecosystems, and in Canada and Alaska.)

Toward the end of my trip I "used" the gun. Two cubs and their mama ambled over a low crest in open, treeless country, directly in my path and perhaps 100 yards away. As Mama stood up to get a clear view of me (brown and indestructible, enormous, towering against the sky) I knew that the two of us were standing on the brink of that pivotal moment that always arises when a wild animal unused to humans meets one of us without clear introduction: for a brief, agonizing interval you can see the animal making up its mind whether this new creature should be fled from, ignored or attacked. And I understood what I had to do. I drew the revolver. Then I reached down and unclipped the Sierra Club cup that hung from my belt, moved it across my body to meet the revolver (which had miraculously shrunk to the dimensions of a pea-shooter) and began tapping the two metal objects together. Metal against metal is an unknown and apparently scary sound to truly wild animals. I have seen elephants veer away from it.

There on the Alaska tundra the effect was almost instantaneous. Mama came down from the sky and in the same movement turned left. On all fours she began hurrying back the way she had come, over the crest and out of sight. The cubs followed.

Long afterward, when I had advanced beyond the crest, I glimpsed the family far downhill to the right, half a mile away, semiskulking behind a willow thicket and peering up toward me. A week later, on my first morning back in Anchorage, I woke to hear a radio report that a man had been killed and part-eaten by a grizzly less than 50 miles from where I had been.

You can, of course, draw all kinds of conclusions from my nonadventure. The Alaska Department of Fish and Game, in a free pamphlet they will send anyone contemplating a visit to their backcountry (*The bears and you, or . . . how to become a bear-wise sourdough in ten minutes*), comment that a .357 magnum revolver "is better than nothing." They also advise you not to turn and run from a bear but to depart *slowly*, facing it. My bear advisor does not altogether agree. "It is very difficult to stop a grizzly with a .357," he says. "The majority of grizzly biologists now work unarmed. And if the slow back-off fails and the bear continues to advance, their current most favored response is *not* to run, *not* to play dead, but to draw oneself up as large as possible, wave one's arms and yell ferociously. If there are several people, stand together as one creature. Since most mammals are astonishingly adept at detecting fear it is important to talk oneself into rage and bellicosity and to bury the fear. With practice, by the way, you can read bear expressions with great accuracy and distinguish threatening from nonthreatening animals."

Whether the metal-against-metal trick saved me, I do not know. "Ninety percent of the time," says my advisor, "nothing happens anyway, no matter what you do. It's the ten percent that's uncertain." And in assessing the trick's value, remember that the bear I met was, like most Alaskan grizzlies, a truly wild animal. In places where they have frequent contact with humans, as in Denali and Glacier National Parks and also in their few remaining sanctuaries in the lower 48 states, the sound of metal against metal, as in pot rattling, is more likely to attract than repel them.

Where grizzlies are becoming accustomed to humans they pose in spades a problem that is festering toward a head with black bears. My advisor insists that this problem is "anthropogenic, not ursogenic": The root cause is us, not the bears. Us and our food. "Black bears are almost never a problem where backpackers are a rarity, but repeated exposure to a nutritious and easily obtained food resource has converted local populations of them into nuisances."

Note that word "nuisances." Not "dangers." Black bears are powerful and potentially dangerous animals; but, unlike grizzlies, they rarely pose a threat to human life. North American fatalities have been very, very low—except, oddly, in Ontario and to a lesser extent Minnesota (none there in the last ten years). There are no records of anyone being killed by a black bear in the Sierra Nevada. But bears may learn to bluff. One female in Yosemite would apparently lie in wait beside a heavily used trail, bound out within 10 yards of a passing backpacker and woof menacingly. Mostly, the backpacker would drop his or her pack and flee. The bear got her meal—and encouragement to repeat the maneuver. The terrified backpacker reported an "attack." Why black bears do not in fact attack backpackers remains unclear. They know the food is there in the pack; and they have apparently learned that an unarmed human poses no threat. The answer may be that humans have taken the place of grizzlies, which used to live in the same places and which scared the living daylights out of the black bears. The fact is, anyway, that even where they have long been severe nuisances, black bears have not taken to attacking people. The occasional injuries are more in the nature of accidents than attacks (as in the case of an unfortunate woman asleep in her tent when a bear thrust its paw through the fabric in search of food: she instinctively raised her head, then turned to face the sound—and one of the bear's claws slashed and destroyed one of her eyes).

There's no doubt, of course, that the bear problem has grown in recent years, especially in national parks, where people cannot carry guns and bears have learned they need not fear them. But although the robbers' methods often grow more sophisticated (cars left at roadhead with food in them have been bear-bashed) the growth is essentially in extent, not intensity. As backpackers have become thicker on the ground, so more and more populations of bears have learned to steal their food. Yet where bears have long been a nuisance the problem has not grown. In fact, countermeasures have often lessened it.

The first Park Service countermeasures consisted of trapping nuisance bears and relocating them in remote but still protected wilderness areas. That solution proved an ecological disaster. Almost all the bears either found their way back home or failed to establish territories within the park, moved outside and vanished—probably shot. (They almost never became nuisance animals in the backcountry.)

The relocation policy eventually gave way to "aversive conditioning": reestablishing fear of man in nuisance bears by zapping them with some painful but nonlethal weapon. The policy had obvious drawbacks. Mace and Halt (a pepper gas) are typical weapon candidates, and the prospects of misuse by crazies of the initiating species seem only one step less violent and obscene than those almost guaranteed by guns. Besides, common sense cries out against introducing such crap-world sleaze into the backcountry. But the biggest drawback, now emerging, is the bottom line. As animal behaviorists discovered long ago, it is much harder to unlearn an acquired habit than it was to acquire it. Tests with Halt, which worked better than tear gas, incapacitated bears for maybe 10 minutes. At first they stayed away for about two days from the food set out to attract them; but after later sprayings they would return within 20 minutes. Even repeated firings of rock salt into bear backsides by sharpshooters with shotguns—leaving the backsides in a pretty painful state that lasts for about three days—have not kept the bears away from campgrounds. They simply become "even more adept at materializing out of thin air when there's food about." So researchers seem to be moving away from aversive conditioning toward a solution that will effectively eliminate sources of available food.

In places bears are a nuisance the Park Service has, of course, long been moving in this direction. Their recommendations to backpackers are far-reaching: Hang all food and garbage out of reach of bears, both at night and if you leave camp during the day. Always cook some distance from tent or sleeping place, and downwind of it, so that food odors do not drift over you all night. Clean pots and utensils after each meal. Don't wear clothes with spilled food on them.*

* Other recent literature has suggested three further no-nos:

1. Don't wear perfume or hairspray; they seem to attract bears. Current informed opinion tends to regard the attraction as real—but hardly likely to provoke attack.

2. Don't menstruate: the smell may also attract bears. But my advisor regards the data as scant and doubts the "speculative" conclusion. He agrees that predators tend to be attracted by the smell of blood but notes that Indian and even white women have been menstruating in bear country without apparent hazard for a long, long time.

3. Don't make love: that too may attract bears. My advisor's comments, which closely parallel those in 2 above, make bullish news for barish readers.

The current NPS advice on hanging food beyond bears' reach involves a counterbalance technique. It works well, even using ordinary nylon cord (page 518) and especially with a few refinements; but I suggest you do at least one dry run before your first attempt in the field.

Details of the technique: Balance food (and garbage) into two equal sacks, not more than 10 pounds in each. (Stuff sacks are best. If you must rely on plastic bags, use only the stoutest: some bears know that by shaking the tree they may cause bags to tear.) Find—if you can, chum—a tree with a living, downward-sloping branch 20 feet above the ground and 4 or 5 inches minimum diameter at the trunk, with nothing bear-climbable below it. Tie a stone or other weight to end of cord and toss over branch. Try to make cord cross branch at least 10 feet from trunk, where it will support food but no bear. If it crosses too close to trunk, try to move outward. Failing that, retrieve and throw again. Tie one sack (the sturdiest, if one is flimsy) to cord end, leaving a sizable loop hanging free, and pull up to branch. Tie other sack to free end of cord as high as possible, again with hanging loop, and tuck any spare cord into sack so that it does *not* hang down. Toss second sack upward. It should stop more or less level with first, which will have descended. If necessary, adjust sacks with long stick or staff. Sacks should hang at least

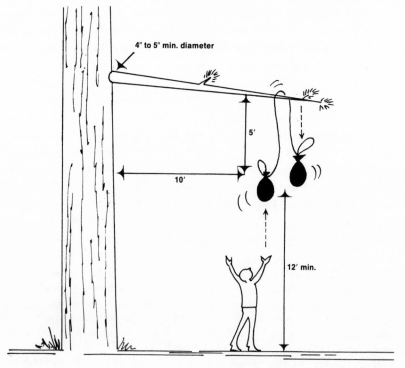

4" to 5" min. diameter

5'

10'

12' min.

Based on a National Park Service drawing

12 feet above ground. Retrieve cache by hooking loop at either sack with stick or staff (rubber tip a boon) and pulling down. (For small food caches, use one bag and a stone or log counterweight.)

An alternative that I've never tried is the small plastic Bear Block —a "unique locking device" with no movable parts that weighs 1 ounce alone—but 7 ounces together with the 50 feet of 3/16-inch nylon rope (1000-pound test) that comes with it. It works on a closed-loop system said to baffle even the brainiest bear ($7.50 each, including rope and 16-page brochure [*What you always needed to know about bears,* $.75 separately] from Bear Block, 20353 Lake Chabot Rd., Suite 103, Castro Valley, CA 94546). You use the same ideal branch as in the NPS method and can apparently hang up to 150 pounds. But my advisor reports that the lock may occasionally jam.

In heavily used, bear-rich backcountry you may find bear cables: either fixed ones that you toss your line over or deluxe models with pulleys that let you lower the cables and attach your food or pack with genuine ease. But the hassle-quotient of all other precautions is high: finding the right damned tree; hanging the food; not being able to camp at dusk without difficulty because of all the things that must be done; having the wind change so that, in spite of forethoughtfulness, you are sleeping dead downwind of the kitchen; and much, much more. Then there's weather. The distant-cooking, food-hanging routine—a pain at any time—becomes in torrential rain or driving sleet or snow a purgatory that you, or at least I, will be tempted to bypass. Yet the NPS say that beginner backpackers often seem enthralled by the whole "exciting" business. Alternatively, they're terrorized by the mere thought of the bear "menace." But before long most of them join experienced people in regarding all the precautions as a plain, perishing nuisance—a hassle that soon looms so large it sucks the joy out of the days. That is certainly how I see it. Much country in which you could not long ago use my in-bag eating system (page 270) without thought of danger has become so infested with camp-robbing bears that to do so is inviting trouble. Recently, visiting the backcountry of Sequoia National Park for the first time in years, I found that, unless you went above timber, it was regarded as crazy—and also unethical, because of the encouragement to bears—to disobey any of the Park Service's antibear instructions. So right now, from where I walk, there seem urgent reasons for solving the already extensive and spreading bear problem.

Fortunately, it begins to look as if a viable, low-hassle solution may at last be in the wings. Researchers at Sequoia–Kings Canyon and other parks have recently produced a prototype plastic canister that will fit into most big backpacks, weighs only 3 pounds, will accept about 20 pounds of dehydrated food and is bearproof. (Smeared with jam, it withstood bear-handling by Alaskan grizzlies.) Smaller versions for short trips are in the works. The canisters may soon be made commercially and weights may be pared, though costs remain uncertain. Now, having to fork out *x* extra dollars, lug 3 extra pounds along and make sure you keep all food battened down falls short of a perfect, hassle-free solution to the bear problem. But to me and a lot of other people it sounds better than anything else yet bruited. It may even lure me back into bear country.

(*Later:* It has so lured me. I carried a prototype canister on that 7-day snowshoe trek in late May. The heavy winter's snow meant that chances of meeting a bear were small—though a few had been seen up where I went; but I wanted to try the canister out, and I knew that the snow would record clear details of any bear/canister encounter.

I encountered no bears. In daily use, though, the device proved reasonably satisfactory. Once you get used to the recessed opening system, it raises no difficulties. But I found the reputed "5-day food capacity" overblown—except, perhaps, for a midget off his feed. I just managed to squeeze in 4 days' food—less one dinner, my milk squirter and margarine container. No room for garbage, either. Then one day when camped at the sloping lip of a 1000-foot escarpment I perceived that the cylindrical canister could, under the buffetings of a frustrated bear, all too easily begin to roll—and roll and roll and . . . The inventors are working on that problem.

The canister does not, of course, do anything to mitigate the dangers of in-tent or in-sleeping-bag eating. Not in the short term, anyway. The long-term hope is that by educating and equipping *all* backpackers so that their food no longer tempts bears, the robbers will slowly learn that they'll never find a meal at human campsites. In time, they'll leave backpackers alone. Things will return to the old "normal." Let us pray.

My brief trial confirmed two bonuses the canisters offer: they make fine camp seats; and they're useful for carrying garbage out to roadhead. They should be great for carrying water to camp too. And one park researcher wagers that someone will soon come up with a bucket game of some kind.)

I suspect that the bear problem is not really an isolated one. For decades now we have over wide areas desisted from shooting not only bears but all animals. And they too have learned. I hear reports of growing food thievery, East and West, by raccoons and porcupines. Perhaps the lessons of adequate food protection, if they work out, will stifle the recent drift—or, rather, surge—toward dangerous habituation of once-wild animals to mankind. I hope so—for the animals' good as well as ours. Otherwise, maddened people may try to impose harsher restraints.

Of course, less serious, old-style dangers remain. Backpacking in the Catskills some years ago, one reader became aware of a camp robber about four o'clock in the morning. "I moved slowly to check it out," he wrote me. "And it's just as well, because it was a rather large skunk. Right at my elbow. The disaster of a sudden move cannot be stressed too hard."

In spite of what I have written on page 515, there is still one other animal that puts the fear of God into me: *Homo sapiens nimrodamericanus*, the red-breasted, red-blooded, North American hunter. Every year, in the fall, the woods are alive with hunters, and every year a few more hunters fall dead. I know some of the massacre stories are probably apocryphal, but I play it safe: when the calendar springs the hunters loose I tend to stay at home—or at least to walk only in national parks, where hunters can't. But in the parks I must now hassle with bears. I'm sure hunters derive much sardonic amusement and also satisfaction—which may well be pragmatically sound—at the implicit ironies: we god-damned holier-than-thou backpackers must now choose between facing either marauding bears in parks or the marauding hunters who probably used to keep the bears from marauding.

Outside North America the general animal situation can be less reassuring. In East Africa, for example, many rhinos and some elephants and even perhaps a rare buffalo will charge without apparent provocation. (Or does trespass on another animal's territory constitute provocation? Remember the Cuban missile crisis.) Lions, if surprised, may also attack. See page 289 too. For appropriate action on meeting unicorns, see page 79.

A possible but low-level risk in certain places and at certain times is bubonic plague, contracted from fleas from rodents, including chipmunks and squirrels. To avoid, do not feed the live animals or pick up dead bodies. Another low-level risk, almost anywhere in the world, is attack by rabid animals. I have seen only one animal that I assumed was rabid: a jackal that in broad daylight walked openly across a wheatfield we were harvesting in Kenya. It seemed to be walking in a self-contained little world of its own, and it took no notice at all of either a combine or several people standing alongside. As it walked it kept twitching its head in a regular and demented fashion. It was, in other words, "acting contrary to general behavior patterns"—which is what rabid animals are described as habitually doing.

Now look, I hope you will hold in decent perspective all these pages I have written about possible dangers of attack by wild animals. The real point, and not only with rattlesnakes, is that knowledge reduces both fear and danger. Provided you behave sensibly, the risks are really very slight—probably a great deal less than those involved in getting to the wilderness, when some unprovoked animal traveling rapidly in the opposite direction may fall asleep or suffer a heart attack or burst a tire and slew across the dividing line and write an abrupt "finis" to your little game.

The only vegetable dangers you're likely to meet (assuming no gigantic Venus flytraps) are

Poison oak, ivy and sumac.

All these closely related plants cause rashes on some people—perhaps most people—if oil from leaf or stem comes in contact with the skin, directly or through transfer by clothes or other agents. The poison in all three plants is urushiol, an oil-soluble compound carried in canals *below* the surface of leaves and all other parts except pollen, which is nonpoisonous. So leaves or stems must be bruised in some way before you can be affected. In practice, though, almost all leaves are "bruised" by insects, weather, etc. Because urushiol's reaction with your skin begins within a minute of contact—though symptoms may take from 6 hours to a week to appear (commonly 2 days)—the sooner you start treatment after exposure the less severe the reaction is likely to be. But if you're highly susceptible and get a bad case you may spend 3 ghastly weeks in the hospital. (And never assume you're safe: one experienced friend of mine maintains that "the hospitals are full of people who thought they were immune." Although nobody can get a reaction on first contact, that contact—or the hundredth—may cause sensitization.) In less serious cases, affected skin reddens, swells and develops blisters. The rash is always liable to spread, and it itches like crazy. Scratch, and you increase the irritation. Urushiol is long-lived stuff that clings to clothing, tools, pets, etc., and unless washed off can cause reactions for years.

Folklore, purveyed by hearty souls who are probably immune, goes something like this: "Can't understand what all the fuss is about. Just a good wash down with soap and hot water afterward and you'll never get any rash worth talking about. Why, I've waded thigh deep through the stuff and never had any kind of a rash at all."

Washing, especially with cold water, to close the pores, and a good soaping and rinsing indeed seem to help, if done immediately after contact. Hot showers, later, alleviate the itching—though they may possibly prolong the symptoms. Calamine lotion or creams containing benadryl may also reduce itching. (See also Sting-Eze, page 563.) But there is still no known cure—or safe and reliable preventative. On the other hand, cortisone creams do a good job of suppressing symptoms if sparingly applied immediately after contact or at first blush of irritation.

They seem to hold the reaction down, prevent spread and almost eliminate itching. A mild rash may persist for as long as 3 weeks, but it never gets out of hand. At least, that has been my experience with Synalar, a cortisone-based prescription cream. In poison-oak country I always carry a small tube. You can now buy over-the-counter cortisone creams. Opinion on the effectiveness of prophylactics now available, including shots, covers the whole spectrum from "useless" to "miraculous," so I guess a lot depends on the individual. Note that people who react violently to urushiol may get some reaction to prophylactics. And if over-the-counter brands containing urushiol, such as ImmunOak, ImmunIvy and homeopathic pills, are taken during an attack they will only make it worse. I have no firsthand experience of any prophylactic, but have read recommendations for Kerodex 51 (Ayerst Laboratories) and Toxic-Guard barrier creams (Reynes Products Inc.); people who won't be able to avoid urushiol-bearing plants can apply them to bare skin before exposure.

Many Easterners now come West to backpack, and they're often confused about where to expect and how to recognize poison oak. No wonder. It's ubiquitous stuff. Although primarily a plant of low-altitude grasslands and forests, I've found it at nearly 7000 feet in the Sierra Nevada and, once, beside a desert creek in Southern California. And it's a botanical chameleon. Leaves are normally indented and oaklike; but they're variable. Their color is normally green; but they can be red, even in spring. Their surface is often shiny; but not always. The plant may be a single small stalk, standing on its own or lurking among others; it may climb, vinelike, far up a tree; or it may mass into dense clumps a dozen feet high and covering acres. Almost the only constant you can verbalize, in fact, is that its leaves, like those of poison ivy, *always* grow in clusters

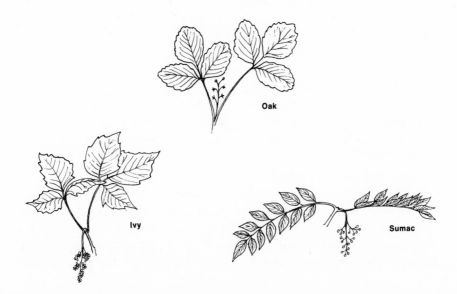

Oak

Ivy

Sumac

of three. Yet once you're familiar with the stuff you can recognize it readily enough; and in suspect country you soon learn to keep your eyes skinned in a barely conscious safe-operating procedure akin to that you adopt in rattler country (page 553).

Hypothermia

The little booklet I recommended in the last edition, by the late Dr. Theodore G. Lathrop—*Hypothermia: Killer of the Unprepared*—is unfortunately no longer in print. But recent years have brought a flood of publicity on the subject, so perhaps fewer people remain unprepared. Certainly, the salient points should be understood by anyone who lives a life unwrapped in cotton and who wishes to remain among the quick.

Hypothermia (= subnormal body temperature; often called "exposure") is not a danger restricted to high altitudes or bitter cold. Under certain conditions—wind, wetness and a victim who is exhausted or unprepared to protect himself—deaths have occurred at sea level and at temperatures no lower than 42° F.

The progressive steps that lead to severe hypothermia can, once begun, accelerate alarmingly. A person who is exhausted—from overexertion, sickness, lack of food or even extreme apprehension—and who becomes cold in wet, windy conditions may very quickly become colder and lose the capacity to rewarm himself. To generate heat, a cold body starts shivering—which in turn consumes a great deal of energy (page 157). Even apart from that, a cold body greatly elevates its metabolic demands (for oxygen and energy), and only a very fit person can meet them for long. In addition, hypothermia, like dehydration (page 189), quickly impairs judgment and so reduces chances of effective remedial action.

It is therefore vital that you understand the progressive symptoms of hypothermia. They are easy enough to recognize in someone else; difficult, but not impossible, to recognize in time in yourself. First, coldness and fatigue; then shivering that becomes uncontrolled; eventually—and this is the tip-off, and also the reason self-diagnosis is fiendishly difficult—increasing lethargy, until at last the patient plain gives up. In the early stages, heat loss from the central organs becomes too great for replacement by the metabolism; soon the nervous system ceases to function adequately; finally, the heart may stop.

Wet clothing is often the prime contributor. Clothing protects you by trapping body-warmed air between its layers and your skin. Water eliminates these air spaces—and conducts heat away from your body up to 240 times as fast as still, dry air. Wool used to be by far the best material when wet; but a soaked-through set of light hiking gear that includes a wool jersey, wool-cotton shirt and string vest but is unprotected by a windproof outer garment will, in a 9-mph wind, afford less than 10 percent of its dry insulating value. The new polypropylene underwear and pile garments that wick moisture away from your skin (pages 378–83) would seem to remove that danger. I guess there may be some increased heat loss through evaporation from the skin, but I doubt it. I have seen no informed comment on the matter.

Wind drastically increases chilling effect—and in theory two-thirds of the maximum increase occurs when the wind is blowing at only 2 mph. But the windspeed that counts is the one at your skin. If you're

WINDCHILL

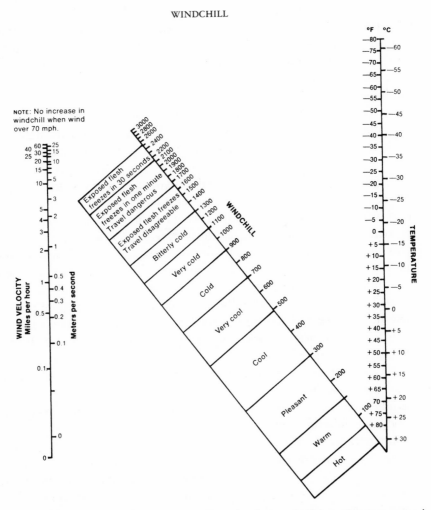

Line chart showing windchill and state of comfort under varying conditions of temperature and wind velocity. From Consolazio et al., Metabolic Methods (St. Louis: C. V. Mosby Company, 1951)

poorly dressed, that may approach or even equal the outside velocity. But proper windproof clothing can cut the effect to almost nil—though if the clothing is wet, wind will increase the evaporation and therefore the heat loss. The chart on the previous page gives values for almost the whole human operating range. To use it, join with a ruler the wind velocity on left scale and the temperature on right scale, then read off windchill factor on diagonal—and learn that absolutely calm air at 30° F. means a chill factor of 350 (cool, going on pleasant) and is the equivalent of a 2-mph wind at 58° F. (page 354). Play with the chart, and think; but remember the blunting effects of good clothing.

Aids to prevention. Try to avoid getting overfatigued: rest periodically, though not long enough to become chilled. Eat small amounts of food periodically too, to keep your metabolism fueled. Make every effort not to get wet—from rain or sweat; or wear "self-drying" synthetic clothes. Guard against anything that may cause sudden unnecessary cooling, such as ceasing to exercise and not readjusting or adding to your clothing.

Treatment. First reduce heat loss. Try to get out of wind and put on dry clothes, or at least a windproof shell. Above all, protect the head and back of the neck (see pages 347 and 417). If stationary, insulate body from ground.

Second, produce heat. It is vital to remember that you are trying to reheat the body core, not the peripheries. One of the body's responses to cold is to reduce circulation and therefore heat flow to feet, hands and all outlying areas, including the whole skin: as their temperature falls, so does the heat-dissipation rate. If you warm these precooled areas all you are likely to do, at least at first, is to increase the circulation and heat flow from core to periphery—and therefore to cool the already heat-starved core, perhaps even fatally. So doubt has been thrown on the old first-aid treatment for a hypothermic non-solo backpacker: have someone embrace him or her in a sleeping bag, with both bodies naked. It may do harm rather than good.

One alternative, immersion in a hot bath, is rarely possible in the field, except at hot springs, and even that may produce an immediate peripheral cooling effect. Hot drinks, if the patient can drink them, are good, especially if sweet (though *not* alcohol—Saint Bernard's kegs notwithstanding). But the best remedy is exercise. That is the one sure way to get the vital organs to produce heat. The companions of a person diagnosed as hypothermic should provide physical support and force him or her to walk, if necessary for as long as an hour. That, it seems, is the most likely way to keep the heart from passing the critical cold point—and also to warm it and the liver back to the point at which they can function well enough to begin reheating the whole body. If you are alone and can recognize your hypothermic plight early enough, the best thing you can do is force yourself to do the same: exercise as hard as possible. If you can manage to hike uphill with a heavy load, it may increase heat output sixfold. Clearly, such treatment for a solo backpacker depends on a diagnosis being made before the fires of determination have been banked. Which brings us back, unfortunately, to the beginning of this section.

Mountain sickness

An excellent little book, *Mountain Sickness: Prevention, Recognition and Treatment* by Peter H. Hackett, M.D. (1980, 3 ounces, $4.50, plus $1.25 handling, from American Alpine Club, 113 East 90th St., NYC 10028), presents the current gospel in practical form, for laymen and physicians. It is clearly dangerous for me to attempt a summary of what turns out to be a rather complicated subject; but it might be even more dangerous—for those going up high—if I failed to make the attempt. (For suggestions on acclimation for moderately high trips, see page 40; on walking methods up high, page 97.) Dr. Hackett—who is Director of Medical Research for the Himalayan Rescue Association, and also the fourth man (and first American) to climb to the summit of Everest alone —has kindly checked this summary and the related sections. He suggested a few alterations, now incorporated.

"Acute mountain sickness" (AMS) is a fairly specific and potentially fatal condition with well-recognized but somewhat variable symptoms. It is, says Dr. Hackett, "not a mysterious or terribly complex entity that can only be dealt with by experienced mountain doctors. In fact, it is quite simple to recognize and easy to treat if it is recognized early enough, and requires no special medical knowledge. What it does require, however, is a high index of suspicion—which can only be based on reading about the condition or on having experienced it. Undoubtedly, the most common cause of morbidity and mortality from mountain sickness is lack of recognition because of ignorance."

AMS rarely seems to occur below 10,000 feet, though a few healthy people may begin to suffer at about 8000 and those with heart or lung problems even lower. A person's "AMS threshold" may differ appreciably on different occasions; factors that affect it certainly include rate of ascent, degree of exertion and state of hydration.

Dr. Hackett says with obvious truth that AMS "is much better prevented than treated." Above all, he counsels careful acclimation. His measures are specifically tailored for newcomers to altitudes above 10,000 feet, but he recommends them for the experienced too: they may "mean the difference between a marginally enjoyable struggle and a comfortable, thoroughly enjoyable (and safe) trip. Why suffer?"

His main acclimating recommendations: If possible, start low and climb on foot. If you must drive or fly to above 10,000 feet, rest for 24 hours. Limit your net gain (i.e., camp to camp) to 1500 feet a day. Try to carry high (over passes, ridges) and sleep low. "It is the sleeping altitude that is critical." If continually moving higher, rest every third day.

Dr. Hackett's other recommendations: "Drink enough fluids (at least 3 quarts a day) to maintain a clear and copious urine." Do not take extra salt. Avoid overexertion. Eat a diet high in carbohydrates. And do not use medications as prophylactics: they may produce undesirable side effects and also a false sense of security. Exceptions: rescuers lifted abruptly to high elevations and people proven highly susceptible to AMS. (For them, "Diamox may be an alternative to giving up the mountains in favor of the beaches.") Another possible exception: people making a once-in-a-lifetime, limited-schedule trip up high, as to an Everest base camp, who have no time to linger and no second chance.

Headache is by far the most common AMS symptom. A mild headache that comes on after exertion and subsides after a rest or tea or coffee or maybe an aspirin, and which vanishes after a night's rest, is no more than an inconvenience. Deep breathing may help. So may massaging of the arteries at the temple. But a moderate-to-severe headache that persists after a night's rest, despite aspirin or acetaminophen and perhaps 30 mg. codeine, may be more serious. Stop ascending. If the headache persists after a second night's rest, descend—for at least 1000 feet.

Periodic breathing or Cheyne-Stokes syndrome (page 41) is not serious in itself but may increase insomnia, itself a common high-altitude occurrence that tends to disappear after a week. For treatment, see page 580.

Mild gastrointestinal disorders, including loss of appetite, are not in themselves an indication of AMS but in severe form, especially as nausea, and with other symptoms, may be serious. Reduced urinary output, though difficult to distinguish from straight dehydration, should be taken as a warning sign, especially if there are other symptoms. For pulmonary symptoms, see pulmonary edema, below.

The two most specific and crucial AMS symptoms are lassitude and ataxia. Lassitude may be distinguished from physical exhaustion, which responds to food, fluids and a night's rest. Lassitude typically deepens over a 24-to-48-hour period. And if someone gets to the stage where he "cannot get up for meals, will not talk to anyone and refuses to drink sufficient fluids, he soon cannot take care of himself" and may lapse into unconsciousness within 12 hours. Lassitude may be the only symptom of severe AMS. But it is usually accompanied by some degree of ataxia.

Ataxia (or loss of coordination) is another crucial sign of serious AMS—though it may occur in mild form with plain exhaustion or in hypothermia. Testing for ataxia is fortunately very simple, and every high-altitude backpacker should understand at least the heel-to-toe-walking-along-a-straight-line test often used by police to check sobriety. A normal person can "toe the line" without difficulty. Mildly ataxic people sway and show signs of difficulty in maintaining balance. In severe cases they may fall. An alternative test is the Romberg. Have the patient stand "at attention"—arms at sides, feet touching. Face him, place your arms around his upper body and tell him you won't let him fall. Then have him close his eyes. A normal person stands still. An ataxic person will start to sway within 10 to 15 seconds and may fall against your arms. The signs are obvious and impressive. Someone with ataxia can become a litter case within 6 hours and will usually do so within 24—unless sent down (never alone) for 1000 or even 3000 feet.

Peripheral edema (swelling of the face, hands or feet) does not cause pain but can be dramatic and unsettling. It is more common in women than in men. Swelling of hands or feet is rarely serious, though rings should be removed from fingers as soon as possible. Facial edema is more likely to be a sign of AMS but normally occurs along with other symptoms.

The two extreme and dangerous conditions resulting from AMS are cerebral edema and high-altitude pulmonary edema.

Cerebral edema (CE) takes several days to develop, and is therefore of concern only if you are staying up high. Symptoms are generally severe forms of those already described, though toward the end there will probably be confusion, disorientation, sometimes hallucinations and, ultimately, unconsciousness. "Descent is the only definitive therapy (as of 1980) . . . as rapidly . . . and as far down as possible. . . . Taking someone down in the middle of the night instead of waiting until morning may save a life or prevent long-term brain damage."

People developing high-altitude pulmonary edema (HAPE) usually exhibit at least some of the standard AMS symptoms. Specific signs include breathlessness even at rest, high breathing and pulse rates, decreased exercise capacity—and a cough. Distinguishing between a "normal" high-altitude cough due to dry air and a HAPE cough is difficult. But the former will probably ease during rests and be assuaged by cough lozenges or steam inhalation. A HAPE cough persists during rests and does not respond to treatment. But it too may be "dry" at first, and only in advanced cases be accompanied by "pinkish or rusty-colored frothy sputum." These uncertainties are what make HAPE dangerous. It is difficult to diagnose. And if left untreated, death may be only hours away. Once again, the treatment is prompt and rapid descent. (A thousand feet will probably be enough, 3000 feet almost certainly.) Oxygen, if available, is very helpful.

The basic problem of AMS seems to be "abnormal fluid shifts into the brain and lungs," so CE and HAPE often occur together. Distinguishing between them hardly matters, because treatment is the same: "When in doubt, go down!"

Treatment for milder forms of AMS includes various medications. Dr. Hackett recommends only Diamox, a prescription drug he judges useful in all forms except pulmonary edema. It need be taken only once every 8 or 12 hours, usually for only a few doses. A single tablet at bedtime will eliminate the Cheyne-Stokes periodic-breathing syndrome (page 578). Unlike some physicians, Dr. Hackett does not advocate Diamox as a prophylactic for everyone going high (for cases in which he does recommend it, see page 578). "The drug," he says, "has a number of side effects and should not be considered lightly. . . . Its effect on physical performance at altitude may also be detrimental [though] this is a subject of current controversy." Possible side effects include numbness and tingling in fingers, toes and face, increased frequency of urination, and nausea, vomiting and drowsiness.

In this brief summary, all I have been able to do is put out some signposts to the proper management of AMS so that no one remains totally ignorant of the basics. For full information, read Dr. Hackett's *Mountain Sickness*. But if you go above 10,000 feet be sure to maintain "a high index of suspicion." And remember that early diagnosis is the key and that descent, not medication, is the surest and safest cure.

Avalanches

are mostly a hazard to skiers and climbers, but backpackers may sometimes need to know something about them, especially when showshoeing. I am not much more competent an authority than your average Hottentot; in fact, it has been said that "the only avalanche experts are dead." But reportedly good sources of information include the Forest Service's *The Avalanche Handbook* (ID #76:489, 1 pound 3 ounces, 1978, $4.50 from the Superintendent of Documents, U.S. Government Printing Office, Washington, DC 20402), *The ABC of Avalanche Safety* by Edward R. La Chapelle (paperback, 2 ounces, $1.95 from The Mountaineers, Seattle, 1978), and *Avalanche and Snow Safety* by Colin Fraser (Scribner, 1978; other details lacking, but ISBN 0684147947 and Library of Congress #78-054594). *Ski Touring in California* by David Beck ($7.95

from Pike Press, Mammoth Lakes, CA, 1979) has an extensive section on avalanches, applicable to non-California too. See also an article in *Backpacker* Magazine #42, January 1981, page 36.

Lightning

Lightning is a low-risk danger worth learning something about: knowledge can reduce the hazard to vanishing point.

For walkers, mountains are the dangerous places. American Alpine Club statistics show that in a recent 22-year span there were 14 lightning accidents on U.S. mountains. Twenty-eight people were involved. Seven died. But mountains are by no means the most dangerous places. And even in other wild areas the risk remains low. (In the metal-rich man-world, though, it is surprisingly high: lightning kills about 150 Americans a year—more than tornadoes or hurricanes—and injures about 250, predominantly east of the Mississippi.)

If you are caught up high in a storm the first thing to remember is the old mountaineering maxim: "In a storm, get off peaks and ridges." Avoid steep inclines (where the current flows fastest) and seek out flat ledges or gentle slopes. If possible get near a pinnacle that will act as a lightning rod. Stay a little way out from its base but not farther away than its height. Crouch low, touching the ground only with your feet, or sit on some insulator such as a coiled climbing rope. Keep clear of metal, such as your packframe or an aluminum staff. A cave, though the obvious shelter, is probably the most dangerous place of all unless it is very deep and high-roofed. Stay resolutely clear of shallow, low-roofed caves that are really no more than overhanging ledges. On August 4, 1948, a party of four California climbers was surprised by a storm near the summit of Bugaboo Spire in British Columbia and took shelter in just such a "cave." Almost at once a bolt of lightning struck outside the entrance. Two of the party died; the other two, dazed and burned, barely managed to make their way down safely.

No matter how careful you are, of course, the element of luck remains. On Bugaboo Spire it was the chance positioning of the four members of that party at the moment of the strike that determined who would live and who would die. Remember, though, that near-strikes such as the Bugaboo party suffered are not always serious. That day three other parties of the same expedition were all "hit," out in the open, with no ill effects. And mountains are by no means the only dangerous places. On the same day as the Bugaboo accident two children were killed by lightning in an open field in Oklahoma.

Useful facts: To estimate the distance in miles to a thunderstorm (and gain some idea of how much time you have to get the hell out of there) count the number of seconds between lightning and thunder and divide by 5.

At roadhead, the inside of your car is almost certainly the safest place around.

First aid. Persons struck by lightning receive a severe electrical shock and may be burned, but they carry no electrical charge and can be handled safely. A person "killed" by lightning can often be revived by prompt mouth-to-mouth resuscitation, cardiac massage and prolonged artificial respiration. In a group struck by lightning, the apparently dead should be treated first; those who show vital signs will probably recover spontaneously, although burns and other injuries may require treatment. Recovery from lightning strikes is usually complete except for possible impairment or loss of sight or hearing. (Source: "Death from Lightning —and the Possibility of Living Again" by H. B. Taussig, *Annals of Internal Medicine,* Vol. 68, No. 6 [June 1968].)

Many experienced outdoorsmen—and all reasonable hiking organizations—contend that one of the greatest dangers in wilderness travel is a practice that permeates this book:

Walking alone.

They may have something too. But once you have discovered solitude—the gigantic, enveloping, including, renewing solitude of wild and silent places—and have learned to put it to creative use, you are likely to accept wihout a second thought such small additional dangers as the solitude imposes. Naturally, you are careful. You make darned sure that someone always knows where you are, and when you will be "out." You leave broad margins of safety in everything you do: hurrying (or not hurrying) over rough country to make up time; crossing (or not crossing) the creek on that narrow log; inching past (or not inching past) that perilously perched boulder. And when it comes to the all-important matter of luck you keep firmly in mind the Persian proverb I have already quoted: "Fortune is infatuated with the efficient."

But if you judge safety to be the paramount consideration in life you should never, under any circumstances, go on long hikes alone. Don't take short hikes alone either—or, for that matter, go anywhere alone. And avoid at all costs such foolhardy activities as driving, falling in love or inhaling air that is almost certainly riddled with deadly germs. Wear wool next to the skin. Insure every good and chattel you possess against every conceivable contingency the future might bring, even if the premiums half-cripple the present. Never cross an intersection against a red light, even when you can see that all roads are clear for miles. And never, of course, explore the guts of an idea that seems as if it might threaten one of your more cherished beliefs. In your wisdom you will probably live to a ripe old age. But you may discover, just before you die, that you have been dead for a long, long time.

A book like this should obviously have something to say about

SURVIVAL.

But I find to my surprise that I can rake up precious little—and that I've never really given the matter the thought it seems to deserve.

Hoping to fill this awkward and humiliating gap in my knowledge, I asked a friend of mine—an experienced hiker, a cross-country skier of repute and an expert climber who has been on Alaskan and Himalayan expeditions—for suggestions about books to read. "Oh, I dunno," he said. "I never read them. And I guess I never give the matter much thought."

Somewhat relieved but still uneasy, I turned for counsel to a practical outdoorsman who is in heavy demand as an instructor of survival and associated crafts. We talked for some time, but with each subject he brought up—water sources, signal flares, first-aid and snakebite kits, loosening waistbelt when wading rivers and so on—I found myself saying, "Oh, but I've discussed that in the book as part of normal operating procedure."

After four or five such answers my counselor paused. "Yes," he said slowly. "Come to think of it, I guess you could say, really, that if you know how to operate properly in wilderness, then you know most of what there is to know about survival.

"What it generally amounts to, anyway, with inexperienced people, is simply not giving in to terror. That's what usually happens: ignorance —then panic. If your partner breaks a leg, for instance, you're in bad shape if you start thinking, 'Is it safe to leave him here, with all these wild animals around?' Of course it's safe—provided he's warm and comfortable. But if you don't know that, and feel suddenly overwhelmed and alone, you're liable to give way to panic. Naturally, you must be able to find your way out to civilization or the nearest help, and then guide rescuers back unerringly to the right place . . . but here we're back with plain competence in operating. And this is the kind of survival problem that's most likely to arise with walkers in the United States. Almost anywhere, outside of Alaska, you can get out to civilization—if you can walk—within two days at most. The old idea of survival as the problem of having to look after yourself for six months, completely cut off, when you're in good physical shape just doesn't apply here any more. And the rest amounts in most cases to medical knowledge and common sense."

In other words, this kind of "survival" mostly amounts to "experience." But "experience" is not easy to assess. When I left the Mexican border at the start of my summer-long walk up California in 1958, at the age of thirty-five, I had never spent a night on my own, away from the man-world, dependent *entirely* on what I carried on my back. (It was only some years later, I think, that I registered this fact—with considerable surprise.) I'm more than a little leery, now, of admitting my "inexperience" at that time: I might encourage tyros to attempt stupid and dangerous things. But even on the day I walked north from the Mexican border I was no tyro. Not really. I had considerable experience, in war and peace, of walking with loads and also of being alone in the bush for days on end—in cabins, for example, and canoeing around a remote lake. Also, in addition to being drum-tight with determination, I knew the limitations of my experience. I knew I had a lot to learn as I went along. That was important. People often get into trouble because they unwittingly—often unthinkingly—bite off more than they know how to chew. And sometimes, then, they do not survive.

"Survival" in the sense of living off the land (page 151) poses a different problem. It's a real one all right, but most answers are specifically local. Knowing what to eat and what not to eat in the Sierra Nevada will get you nowhere in the Adirondacks, and even less place in the Mojave Desert. In each kind of country you have to learn it all again. Sometimes there are local books or pamphlets—often listed in equipment makers' catalogues (Appendix II). Useful sources include Explorer Scouts, hiking and mountaineering clubs (Appendix III) and universities (forestry departments might be good places to start). For less local information, see Euell Gibbons's *Stalking . . .* books: *. . . the Wild Asparagus; . . . the Healthful Herbs;* and *. . . the Blue-Eyed Scallop.* Also the card decks of *Edible and Poisonous Plants* (page 151).

If you want reassurance on the broader questions of survival, and if you're a reader of books on such matters (and I guess you are if you've come 580 pages with me), there's plenty of material. The list waxes and wanes, so consult your local library, or maybe *The Whole Earth Catalog.* Somewhat outside regular books, there is a neatly packaged little "Wilderness Pocket n' Pak Library" with five small booklets in a plastic folder —*Survival, Edible Plants* (3 vols.) and *Primitive First Aid* (8 ounces, $7.50 in color, $5.95 in black and white from "The Wilderness Is . . . ," P.O. Box 160, Post Falls, ID 83854). Also a set of five double-sided plastic cards, 3 by 5 inches, swivel-mounted with corner grommet, bearing over 300 items, including news of "edible plants and 40 first aid topics, covering temperate, desert, arctic and tropic zones" (½ ounce, $3.95, Survival Cards, P.O. Box 1805, Bloomington, IN 47402).

But perhaps, like me, you're lazy or a touch skeptical about such reading. If so, just remember, comfortably, that survival is 80 percent competence, 20 percent local knowledge and 100 percent keeping your cool.

"The best single survival item you can carry," an experienced backpacker once said to me, "is a

Space blanket."

These ultralightweight, aluminized Mylar sheets (56 by 84 inches; 2 ounces; $3) certainly have a lot going for them. Wrapped around as makeshift blanket, "they reflect up to 90% of a person's body heat back to him." They are wind- and waterproof. The original, high-quality versions remain flexible at 60° below and, unlike some counterfeits, are very difficult to tear. They fold down to 1½ by 2 by 4 inches. Proclaimed uses include: emergency blanket; lean-to protection against wind, rain or snow; sun awning; short-term groundsheet (though they'll soon puncture); litter for carrying injured person; heat reflector behind your back at campfire; reflector for ovens; fill-in reflector for photography (page 466, footnote); and a signal to aircraft or ground (sun reflection with the silver side, or color contrast with the orange side). For an occasion I was thankful I had gone back to carrying one—after a stretch when I didn't —see page 432. The blanket is almost always worth taking, I now feel, even if only as insurance on away-from-the-pack sidetrips. And I testify that as a pocket-stuffable item for covering your legs in frigid ballparks, nothing I know of can hold a candlestick to it.

A heavier, more durable space blanket (also 56 by 84 inches, but 12 ounces and $14.50) is a multiple laminate of polyethylene, aluminum and fiberglass, grommeted at each corner. One side is silvery metalized plastic, the other red or blue. Properties and uses as above. Very much tougher than the lightweight version, it is said to make a really viable groundsheet and also a reasonable makeshift over-the-shoulders poncho around camp.

Another rather similar blanket, based on Rip-stop nylon, is bright orange (visible up to 4 miles away) and proclaimed to be windproof, waterproof, light-, heat- and even radar-reflective (10 ounces, with protective plastic pouch, $18, Survival Blankets Inc., P.O. Box 11, Buzzards Bay, MA 02532).

Emergency signals

These days, almost any search operation for people believed lost in wild country is carried out, at least at first, from the air. So it pays to carry something that will enable you to signal to a search plane even if you are injured and can move very little or not at all. A mirror and a smoke flare are obvious candidates. But if you are able to build a fire and have water available, natural smoke may be the best bet. For details of flares and distress signals, see pages 499 and 500. For use and usefulness of mirror, flares, and smoke, see pages 545–7. For makeshift mirror-substitutes, see page 499.

The same signals can, of course, be used for establishing contact with search parties on the ground. So can a whistle (page 500).

For places a helicopter can and cannot land, see page 548.

Keeping an eye on the weather

is an ongoing and all-pervasive part of "survival." Yet it's surprisingly difficult to formulate satisfactory guidelines. In fact, I find it hard to focus anything really worth saying, beyond "In any but the safest places and seasons—and perhaps even then—don't forget to keep a corner of your mind ready to detect any hint of a change." Above all, watch the wind. It can tip you off to what the general high-low atmospheric patterns are doing at that moment in your corner of the planet, and they, more than anything else, control and convey the storms that are what we mostly mean when we say "weather" in this context. But the nature of the clouds, which are often what you use to detect the wind, can be highly significant too. A book by Walter F. Dabberdt, *Weather for Outdoorsmen* (Scribner, 1981, 14½ ounces, $4.95), has cloud-formation photographs as endpapers and some useful information in between. But a lot of the most vital weather lore is a local matter. In the Sierra Nevada, for example, any persistent wind with some south in it should be regarded as a warning signal, and at certain times of year, under certain conditions, as an almost explicit warning to run for lower ground. But that gem won't apply in many other places, of course.

Local weather books are rare, but *Weathering the Wilderness: The Sierra Club Guide to Practical Meteorology* by William F. Reifsnyder (1980, 10 ounces, $8.95) devotes less than half its 275 pages to weather in general, the rest to eight regional climates: Northern and Southern Appalachians, Great Lakes Basin, Northern and Southern Rockies, Cascades, Olympics, and Sierra Nevada. The book is, according to a harsh critic of my acquaintance, "a brave attempt at an impossible task." The best teachers are probably an alert awareness and years of experience. For weather radios, see pages 36 and 524.

But no matter how you get your knowledge, use it constantly. Watch the clouds, wind, temperature. Mark any changes. And remember that a bad storm can convert a smiling playground into a potential morgue. Avoiding that potential is, of course, survival.

PRESERVING THE WILDERNESS

In earlier editions of this book I wrote, "Once you become a walker, you become a conservationist: no one can walk for days on end through wild and unspoiled country and then stumble on some man-perpetrated horror without having his blood start to boil." I am less sure in my assertion than I used to be, but the principle stands.

Please do not misread me. On balance, I am in favor of man. At times, though, my vote might just go the other way—and such moments mostly come when I have stumbled on the atrocities of the feeble-minded. I still remember vividly, from twenty-five years ago, walking across a secluded forest glade and all at once finding myself standing stock-still beside an old campsite that was a carnage of beer cans and cardboard boxes and torn plastic sheeting and dirty aluminum-foil plates and crumpled, soggy newspapers. Once, deep in a sidecanyon that led to the Inner Gorge of the Grand Canyon of the Colorado, I passed half a dozen pale-pink boulders that the ages had worn into smooth and sensuous sculpture but which had recently been overprinted with crude black drawings and the timeless legend "Batman." Such droppings of bat-witted individuals are bad enough; but it angers me far more when a whole segment of society goes in for large-scale desecration. Many years ago, for two long and satisfying summers, I walked the virgin forests of western Vancouver Island, British Columbia, prospecting and staking claims for a mining company (and hoping, with some confidence, that the claims would never be developed). At intervals during those two summers I would emerge without warning from the coolness and cloistered calm of huge trees and green undergrowth into the glare and heat and desolation of gouged earth and splintered wood. I have never recovered from those moments: logging is still the one provocation that I acknowledge might drive me to murder.

Logging at least has some solid justifications: it generates both needed wood products and also a satisfying life for some people. The same cannot be said for an exploding, flippant, quintessentially modern scourge, only somewhat less destructive, that I see as man at his blind worst. Off-Road Vehicles (ORVs) undoubtedly give users a lot of pleasure. We must not forget that. In fact, we should try to empathize. But freedom to enjoy yourself is contingent on not harming your neighbors —your human and other neighbors. It's rather like freedom of speech, which does not include shouting "Fire!" in a crowded theater. For example, doing motorcycle slaloms around Arlington National Cemetery would no doubt be fun; but few people would condone such desecration. Yet many places beloved by ORV users and being desecrated by them— such as the California deserts—are just as beautiful and fragile as Arlington. For those with tuned-in eyes they carry at least as much significance. If left intact they will last a great deal longer. And we have no damned right to butcher them for brief bursts of fun. Now, ORVs are expensive toys. Makers have a huge stake in protecting their use, and the ORV lobby is therefore well organized and carries heavy political clout. Since 1968 the number of ORVs, in the U.S. alone, has zoomed from a handful to over 6 million. So their users' political influence is growing fast—and so is the butchery.

Make no mistake about the butchery. Accumulated results can be appalling. A single motorcycle or dune buggy crossing fragile desert or certain kinds of grassland leaves a compacted track. Scars can last for years, decades, even centuries. And where one wheel passes, others almost always follow. The increasingly popular cross-desert motorcycle races are only a part of the problem. On some grassy hills near Gorman, 50 miles north of Los Angeles, the ORV trail network can already be seen from a plane flying at 30,000 feet.

The physical butchery—butchery of precious places that were until recently free from the vehicular yoke that lies so heavy across most of our land—is the obvious and brutal part. But those of us who walk for pleasure and beyond know that the ORVs' stark, straight-line, engineering tracks—visible and invisible—crucify two of the essences of wilderness: silence; and nature's soft and subtle curves and rhythms. In other words, this relatively new scourge is, at root, yet another arm of a menace I have railed against before: the deadly tentacles of the engineering mind.

More and more, it seems, the engineers are gathering up the reins of power. And they are little men, most of them, with no concept at all of what their projects are doing to the face of the earth. They will, if it serves any half-baked economic purpose, slash a freeway through irreplaceable redwood groves. Driven by a perfectly understandable professional challenge and an equally understandable desire to have plenty of work in the years ahead (and also driven, even less consciously, by the built-in self-aggrandizement mechanism that rots into the structure of almost all our human institutions), they will concoct plans for gigantic, unnecessary dams. That particular urge now seems to have ebbed a little. But other, more recent tides have come and gone: such propositions as the MX race-course madness and oil rigs spattered through protected wildernesses. And as we look around the world today, it seems difficult to avoid the conclusion that many of our current problems stem from the application of engineering overlays to biological systems.*

Of course, the engineers do not always have their way. In recent decades we have protected many new wilderness areas from "progress." But we must not take for granted these precious, last unmammonized oases—or much that marches alongside them. (The late, unlamented Reagan-Watt tandem, though perhaps only a passing aberration, has shown that.) We must continue to respond, vigilantly, to the old shibboleth "You can't stop progress" by saying, "Sure, but you can redefine it." And we must remember that, in the end, the politicians are not necessarily the guilty ones. The enemy, as usual, is us—the whole damned clutch of homo insapiens. We all tend to get trapped in the human corner. We repeatedly forget—or, encouraged by most of our current religious systems, have never truly grasped—that there is more

---

* A Missouri engineer has written complaining of an attack, similar to the above, that I made against engineers in the second edition. He wrote civilly and cogently. He pointed out that we need technology—"a necessary evil"—to maintain any kind of progress, even to ward off starvation. He said he was a Sierra Club member and worked actively to protect and increase wilderness areas. He said a lot more, with eloquence and sincerity. "So you see," he concluded, "just because I am an engineer, I'm not necessarily a mad despoiler. I hope you will think twice before you again condemn an entire group of people in print."

He is dead right, of course. I do not back down an inch from my inveighings against the dangers of the mass engineering mind, but I should not have appeared to pour scorn on all engineers. And I apologize.

I am grateful to the man from Missouri for drawing my attention to this error—and also for underlining something else, at least as important, that I tried to say last time: my engineering outburst, left unqualified as it was, bordered on or even blundered into arrogant self-righteousness. And self-righteousness is an occupational hazard for all of us who call ourselves conservationists or preservationists—or, if you must, "ecologists."

Now, it does not matter much that self-righteousness begets crashing bores—the sort of people you're always slipping away from at parties. What does matter is that as soon as we raise our self-righteous banners we lose our effectiveness. The Sierra Club, of which I am a member, though hardly an active one, remains perhaps today's most effective U.S. conservationist voice. But, like cooperative societies and organized religious bodies, it tends to be a holier-than-thou organization. The maggot is built in. As a result, the words "Sierra Club" are liable to raise, even in neutral circles, a chorus of groans—not to mention such pungent bumper stickers as "Sierra Club, kiss my axe." You can see the same effect on a small scale when we who are rabid antilitter fiends forget that we are human (see, pointedly, page 269) and start throwing our holy weights around: the result may well be a hostile group strewing their every last can and food wrapper about the landscape, deliberately and gleefully.

So we must always be on guard against our self-righteousness. It is difficult, I know. I, too, am pretty damned sure that we *are* holier than the litterlouts and the blinder engineers. But we must try to suppress the conviction—not just because it may possibly be unfounded, or even because it is bad for our souls or something, but because it reduces the chances that we will achieve what we desperately want and need to achieve.

to the world than us. We become hopelessly homocentric, perceptually myopic. We say, for example, that the U.S. (or maybe the Western world) is in economic trouble, and that therefore we must make major fiscal and social adjustments. To me, it seems much truer and pragmatically more fruitful to say that humanity is in trouble because it has moved out of harmony with the rest of the world, and that the only response that makes any sense is striving to restore that harmony. "Hardheaded realists" tend to label those who voice such thoughts as "impractical dreamers." But Robert McNamara was once an archetypical hardheaded realist, and you should listen to him now. There are plenty of clear early-warning signs, anyway: acid rain, toxic spills, vanishing rainforests, carbon-dioxide build-up—and the dark, swelling shadow of nuclear war.

Yet even when we correct our myopia and shrug off the omens for a moment, the very signposts to the way ahead remain far from clear. Julian Huxley defined man as "nothing else than evolution become conscious of itself." Others consider us the brain of the planetary organism. It certainly seems not unreasonable to see ourselves as the current spearhead of evolution. And once you start trying to discern the spear's trajectory you eventually ask, "What are people for?" Huxley responded—rather surprisingly for a biologist—"The answer has something to do with their quality." But that thought, warm and socially seminal though it may be, is less relevant for our present purposes than Lewis Thomas's insight—equally surprising from a physician—that what we seem to do best, or at least better than any other organism, is communicate, and that perhaps we should therefore consider communication our "biological function." As a writer, I naturally tend to buy that. But I find myself unwilling even to rent one of Thomas's follow-up suggestions: "There may be some laws about [our] kind of communication, mandating a critical density and mass before it can function with efficiency. Only in this century have we been brought close enough to each other, in great numbers, to begin the fusion around the earth, and from now on the process may move very rapidly. . . . What we need is more crowding, more unrestrained and obsessive communication." This scenario meshes with my acceptance of the view that evolution seems to move in the direction of increasing complexity. But it runs head on into two opposing convictions. First, that there are already far too many of our species on the planet for its overall and necessary harmony, not to mention for our own health and safety, and that our most urgent need is, for starters, to cut our numbers, radically. We are unlikely to do this job ourselves—other than by nuclear war, which seems certain to impose gross, totally inharmonious and "unacceptable" side effects on the rest of the planet. (It is essential, of course, that we protect other gene pools with potential for alternative lines of progress should our spearhead shatter.) Yet if we are not culled in some relatively benign way, and soon—perhaps by some deadly, widespread and human-specific disease, such as Very Easily Acquired Immune Deficiency Syndrome—the human bubble seems in imminent danger of bursting. My second opposing conviction, strong and gut, and entwined with the first, is that we need more wide and protected reaches of the planet, still rich and complicated and harmonious, where we do not dominate everything so stunningly.

I have for some time struggled with these opposing and apparently contradictory views—the need for greater density and the needs for culling and for wild places—and at last I have, with a little help from my friends, come up with a possible reconciliation. What we may need is more crowding together in certain restricted but fluidly interconnected localities, so that we generate even tenser communications—but also, at the same time, an overall retrenchment that will allow us to protect those precious wild places where we can stand back and contemplate and gain at least a whiff of perspective. Frank Herbert's Dune dwellers understood: they knew that "polish comes from the cities, wisdom from the desert."

Perhaps you are complaining by now that these reflections are neither profound nor even very satisfactory. But I shall let them stand, even though I might do better tomorrow. I am still seeking—even if it is for solutions to insoluble problems. And perhaps that is the point. It could be that what I am really trying to say is: "Note that reflections like this are what seem to emerge in the end whenever you push hard at your worries about how to continue preserving the green world that opens up so richly once you have become a reasonably complete walker."

LEARN OF THE GREEN WORLD

Learn of the green world what can be thy place.

Ezra Pound

Learn of the Green World

The wilderness has a mysterious tongue,
which teaches awful doubt.

Quoted by Charles Darwin
in *The Voyage of the Beagle*

When I began this book it was my intention to examine, here at the end, the delights of walking in different kinds of country. For I was afraid that in the course of 600 fundamentally how-to pages we might have forgotten the feel-how—afraid that the ways and means might have masked the joys and insights that can come, in the end, from the simple act of walking. I am still afraid that such an eclipse may have occurred. But I see now that the delights of different places are not what I must write about. They too are only means to an end.

Now, I am the last person to deny that each kind of country—and also each season of the year and each hour of the day—has its own very special enchantments.

Mountains offer the slow unfolding of panoramas and the exhilaration of high places. Their summits, even the humble ones, are nearly always pinnacles of experience. And afterward you come back down. You ease back, step by step, from stark rock and snow into the world of observable life: first, a single tuft of vegetation in a windswept saddle; then the tracks of a small mammal; two hours later the first tree; then the first tree that can stand upright against the wind; then the tracks of a large two-footed animal that was wearing lug-sole boots; then undeniable soil; soon trees that would be trees in any company; finally, thick undergrowth beneath the trees—and you pat your pocket to make sure the snakebite kit is still there.

In the desert you rediscover, every time you go back, the cleanness that exists in spite of the dust, the complexity that underlies the apparent openness, and the intricate web of life that stretches over the apparent barrenness; but above all you rediscover the echoing silence that you had thought you would never forget.

Then there is untrodden snow country, silent with its own kind of silence. And the surging seashore. And other dominions too, each with its own signature: estuaries, the river worlds, marshland, farmlands, moors and the open plain.

But in the course of time the memories meld. For they come, all of them, from the green world.

When I open my own mind and let the memories spill out, I find a many-hued mosaic. I remember the odd excitement and the restricted yet infinitely open world I have moved through several times when I have clambered up—very late at night, and following the little pool from my flashlight beam—to the flat, grassy summit of the hill on which I wrote at last the opening chapter of this book. I remember a three-day walk along an unspoiled beach with the wind always barreling in from the Pacific and the sand dunes always humping up on my left; and I remember the ceaseless surging and drawing back of the sea, with its final, curving excursions into smooth sand—excursions that sometimes left stranded, high and almost dry, little fragments of transparent protoplasm (which set me thinking, "This is the stuff we came from") and sometimes cast up a bottle that I could peer at (laughing at myself for being so childlike) in the hope that it might contain a message. I remember standing on snowshoes outside my half-buried tent after a four-day storm, in a newly gleaming white world, and watching the guilty, cloud-bearing southwest wind trying to reassert itself; I remember feeling a northeast breeze spring up, and almost hearing it take a deep breath and say, "They shall not pass," and then begin to blow in earnest; and I remember watching, thankfully, as the line of dark clouds was held along a front, horizon to horizon, and then was driven back, slowly but inexorably, until at last it retreated behind the peaks and the sky was left to the triumphant northeast wind and the warm and welcome sun. I remember trying to clamber up a steep woodland bank after dark, somewhere in the deep South (I think it was in Alabama), and finding myself in an enchanted world of fireflies and twisted tree roots and fireflies and clumps of grass and fireflies and wildflowers and fireflies and fireflies and fireflies—a world suddenly filled with a magic that I had not glimpsed since I was ten, and had almost come to disbelieve in. I remember striding down a desert road as dusk fell, with the wind catching my pack and billowing out the poncho like a sail and carrying me almost effortlessly along before it; and I remember how, when the rain came, it stung my bare legs, refreshing without hurting. I remember, in a different, sagebrush desert, coming to the edge of a village and passing a wooden building with three cars and a truck parked outside, and a battered sign that said PENTECOSTAL CHURCH OF GOD, EVERYONE WELCOME; I remember that the church door stood open to the warm evening, and that I could hear a piano and the congregation following along, with only a hint of exasperation, a half-beat behind a contralto whom nature had endowed with the volume, tempo, rigidity and determination of a brass band. In another desert village—a long-dead ghost town, this one—I remember a clump of wild blue irises growing inside the worn wooden threshold of a once busy home. I remember red, red sunsets in a small desert valley when I was not alone. I remember, further back, a dead native cow in a clearing in the dry African bush; and, in the blood-softened soil beside its torn-out entrails, a single huge paw mark. I remember the small, round, furry heads of the hyraxes that would solemnly examine us from the boulders just behind our 13,000-foot camp up near Lewis Glacier on Mount Kenya. Further back still, I remember three otters cavorting across a moonlit Devonshire meadow; and a stag on a Scottish moor, silhouetted, elemental; and a shoal of small fish swimming slowly over a sloping bed of brown gravel that I can still see, stone fitting into stone, down a fifty-year tunnel. And now, vaulting back into yesterday, I find I am remembering an elk that stands regally among redwood trees and the last tendrils of morning mist, and a surprised beaver that crouches almost at my feet and eyes me for clues, and a solitary evening primrose that has prospered in a desolation of desert talus, and a rainbow that arches over a dark mountain tarn, and the huge and solemn silence that encompasses, always, the buttes and mesas and cliffs and hanging terraces of the Grand Canyon of the Colorado.

Everyone who walks has his own floodlit memories—his own fluttering windwheel of scenes and sounds and scents. (It is often the scents that linger longest, though you do not know it until they come again.) But no matter what the hue of the individual memories, they all come from the green world. And in the end, when you have learned to connect —only to connect—you understand that it is simply the green world that you seek.

I suppose you could say that going out into this older world is rather like going to church. I know that it is in my case, anyway. For me, praying is no good: my god, if I have one, is a kind of space-age Pan, and is not interested in what happens to me personally. But by walking out alone into wilderness I can elude the pressures of the pounding modern world, and in the sanctity of silence and solitude—the solitude seems to be a very important part of it—I can after a while begin to see and to hear and to think and in the end to feel with a new and exciting accuracy. And that, it seems to me, is just the kind of vision you should be hoping to find when you go to church.

Now, I do not want to suggest that out in the wilderness my mind —or, I suspect, anyone else's mind—is always soaring. Most of the time it operates on a mundanely down-to-earth level. In the course of a four-day hike taken primarily so that I could sort out ideas and directions for the first edition of this book, I tried to write down before they had faded away the thoughts that had run through my head while I was climbing one afternoon up a long and fairly steep hill. What I scribbled down was, in part: "Wonder how far now, over top and down to next creek. Maybe should have half-filled canteen from that last spring. . . . Oh hell, left heel again! Hope it's not a blister. Moleskin? No, not yet. Oh, look at that squirrel! Sun caught it beautifully, coming in from behind at an angle. Hm, horse tracks. Wonder how old. . . . Phew! Pretty damned hot for January. Better take off shirt at next halt. Almost time for rest anyway. Only five minutes. That should just get me to top of hill. . . . Hey, what's that on my leg? Oh, just water dripping off wet socks, on pack. . . . Oh my God, look! It'll be at least ten or fifteen minutes to top of bloody hill. Maybe more. . . . Say, your thoughts really do run on, don't they? Normally, don't notice it much, but . . . wait a minute, better jot down what I've been thinking, as accurately and as far back as I can. Might just be worth using in the walking book. Yes, out notebook right now. . . ."

Twice more on that four-day trip I jotted down odd islets of thought that jutted up from what was no doubt a continuous stream. Once, on a slightly less mundane but still distinctly unsoaring level, I found that as I walked I had concocted a mnemonic sentence ("King Philip, come out, for God's sake!") for a sequence that often leaves me groping: the hierarchy of categories into which biologists divide the living world (kingdom, phylum, class, order, family, genus, species). And one evening I was warming myself by a campfire and looking up at the dark pine trees silhouetted against a quarter-moon and beginning to think of beauty and life and death (or so my notes assure me) when I realized with some surprise that I was at the same time singing quietly to myself the soulful and almost immortal refrain from a song that was implanted in my mind somewhere deep in half-forgotten childhood: "And the captain sat in the captain's chair, and he played his ukulele as the ship went down."

But in trying to preclude a false impression I must not overcompensate. There are, of course, times when your mind soars or floats or hangs free and impartial—or dives into the depths.

For even in wilderness you may, very occasionally, plunge into despair—into the blackness that exists, I suppose, deep down in all our lives, waiting to blot out the underpinnings and so keep us honest. I remember a desert canyon in which, as I lay quiet beneath the stars, man was a pointless impostor on the bleak and ancient surface of the earth, and I knew I would never hope again. And I remember a night on a mountain when all that existed out in the blackness beyond my campfire was a small hemlock, and even the hemlock only flickered into and out of existence at the mercy of the fickle firelight; a night on which, for an endless, empty span, that little tree with its dark, stark needles was more lasting and more real than I was, and so claimed a crushing victory; a night on which, above all, the blackness beyond the tree was tragically and incontestably more real than the fragile tree, and therefore claimed the final, aching, desolate victory. Such interludes—in which the keepers of the void ensnare you and all, all is vanity—are rare in wilderness. But they happen. And, although I would like to deny it, they are worse than in the city. While they last, the blackness is blacker, more hopeless, more desolately victorious. This time you cannot appeal to a more profound reality.

But, far more often than despair, you find elation. A squirrel leaps across a gap in the trees, a hundred feet above your head, and your mind, caught by the beauty, leaps too—across the gap between the dragging everyday world and the universals. Two swallows, bound head to tail in tight and perfect formation, bank up and away from a cliff face in a joyous arc of freedom. A quartet of beavers browses by the margin of a backwater, silent and serene, a tableau from a calmer age. Or you sit, triumphant, on a rocky peak and look and look at the whole world spread out below; and for a while, though still human, you are no longer merely human.

At such moments you do not "commune with nature" (a trite phrase that seems to classify nature as something outside and separate from us humans). At such moments you know, deep down in your fabric, with a certainty far more secure than intellect can offer, that you are a part of the web of life, and that the web of life is a part of the rock and air and water of pre-life. You know the wholeness of the universe, the great unity. And if you keep walking long enough—for several weeks or for several months—you may with care and good fortune experience whole days or even series of days during which you exist in this happy, included state.

They do not last, of course, these rich cadenzas. But their echoes linger. When you first return to the world of man there is a period of readjustment, just as there was when you left it and went out into the wilderness. After that first glorious hot shower (which is always—and always to your new surprise—a great experience in itself) you may find that for a day, or perhaps three days, or even a week, you live an unreal, cut-off-by-a-screen-of-gauze sort of existence. But once you have readjusted to hot showers and radios and orthodox beds and automobiles and parking meters and sidewalks and elevators and other people and other people's points of view, you begin to find that you have regained thrust and direction and hope and wonder and other such vital intangibles whose presence or absence color so indelibly the tenor of our lives, but which are very difficult to discuss without sententiousness. You find yourself refreshed, that is, for the eternal struggle of trying to see things as you more or less know they are, not merely as other people tell you they are. Above all, you find that you have recomprehended—totally, so that it is there behind every thought—the knowledge that we have arisen from everything that has gone before. You know, steadily, that we are more than just a fascinating and deadly and richly promising species that has begun to take over the face of the earth. You know again, fully, that this species you belong to is the current spearhead of life—and that your personal meaning is that you are a part of the spearhead. And so you find that you can take up once more the struggle we all have to make in our own several and quirky ways if we are to succeed in living lives that are truly human—the struggle to discern some glimmering of sense in the extraordinary phenomenon that is man.

And that, I guess, is quite a lot to get out of such a simple thing as walking.

Check List of Equipment

Note: the jacket photo is keyed to this list.
For an explanation, see back flap of jacket.

Even if you have not already done so, you will in time probably develop your own check list (see page 37); but this one may be a useful starter. You can, of course, make your own idiosyncratic additions—and may also want to inject some minor items I have mentioned in the text but chosen to exclude, such as bootwax, squeeze tubes, pot scouring pad, snow anchors for tent, hammock, umbrella, razor, meat tenderizer (unseasoned) and even, if you really must, a trail guide.

Suggestion: Photocopy this list, rule columns in both margins, and before a trip check off each item as you put it ready (on an old groundsheet or whatever), perhaps again as you transfer each item to the pack—and possibly even once more, at trailhead, before you finally strike out and away from civilization.

This is a rather exhaustive list, including most of the items you will even want to consider, no matter what the conditions. *Your final selection for any trip will always fall far short of the complete list.* (Italics are in the hope of warding off the occasional misreaders' letters that bleat, "Surely you don't take *all* that stuff along with you?")

I give no weights this time around because the possible alternatives subsumed under many items have grown so numerous and diverse that sample or average weights would carry little meaning. For ranges or examples of weights (and, of course, for full details) see pages cited. For samples of gear I carried under specified conditions in earlier times, see *The Thousand-Mile Summer*, photographs between pp. 32 and 33, and *The Man Who Walked Through Time*, Appendix, p. 235.

Foundations

Page
65   Boots ✓
69   Gaiters
75   Socks ✓
77   Camp shoes ✓
81   Staff (and attachments?)
83   Ice axe
84   Crampons
85   Snowshoes
87   Rubbing alcohol
88   Footpowder
89   Moleskins ✓

Walls

101   Belt bag . ✓
113   Pack (also page 135) ✓

Kitchen

122   Food (see table, pages
        184–5)
180   Booze bottle ✓
196   Water purification tablets ✓
199   Solar still kit
204   Canteen(s) (empty)
207   Water bag
208   Rubber tubing
209   Cooking pots
210   Pot lifter
211   Fry pan
211   Cup ✓
214   Spoon ✓
214   Knife ✓
215   Knife sharpener
215   Salt-pepper shaker ✓
215   Sugar container ✓
216   Margarine container
217   Milk squirter
217   Bookmatches ✓
218   Matchsafe(s)
218   Magnifying glass

218   Can opener
219   Dish cloth ✓
229   Stove ✓
252   Fuel bottle(s) or spare ✓
        cartridge(s)
253   Stove filler ✓
255   Eyedropper
257   Priming paste
258   Stove windscreen
260   Foam pad for stove
260   Wundergauze
261   Stove cleaner

Bedroom ✓

290   Tent ✓
294   Fly sheet
293   Tent poles ✓
308   Tent pegs ✓
316   Polyethylene sheet
317   Visklamps
330   Groundsheet
332   Foam pad or air mattress ✓
335   Air mattress patch kit
357   Sleeping bag ✓
349   VB liner

Clothes Closet

383   Pile jacket ✓
388   VB jacket ✓
389   VB pants ✓
393   Undervest
395   Long johns ✓
395   Undershorts ✓
395   Shirt (? spare)
396   Sweater
398   Down jacket
400   Short pants
402   Long pants
402   Pile pants
403   Down pants
403   Belt or suspenders
411   Rain jacket
413   Poncho

APPENDIX 1A

Load details, sample one-week and overnight trips (page 27)

ONE-WEEK TRIP, LATE FALL, IN HIGH MOUNTAINS

	lbs.	ozs.
Pack and contents *	55	–
Boots (PMS Easy Hiker)	5	4
Clothing worn at start (see below)	2	5
Binoculars	1	2
Staff (Nomad, 27-inch handle)	1	2
Total: From Skin Out (FSO)	64	13

Clothing worn at start:	lbs.	ozs.
Wool shirt		9
Corduroy shorts (Jammers)		15
Bandanna		1
Jockey shorts		2
Outer socks (wool)		6
Inner socks (1 wool, 1 polypro, as test)		1
Hat		3
Total:	2	5

TWO-DAY, ONE-NIGHT TRIP UNDER EASY, FAMILIAR CONDITIONS

	lbs.	ozs.
Pack and contents (see below)	19	–
Clothing worn at start **	1	5

* Full pack weighed on scale that registered only in pounds, so FSO totals, here and below, are meaningful only to nearest pound.

Pack: Gregory Cassin (with all optional pockets and office-on-yoke, 8 pounds—and well worth it; see page 137). Pack contents not recorded in detail, but they included a Sierra Designs Sphinx tent (5½ pounds), MSR stove plus a full quart of gas, and around 15 pounds of food. Clothing in the pack ran only slightly heavier than in overnight kit, below.

** Savings from clothing worn on week-long trip (above): polypropylene vest (4 ounces) vice wool shirt; and Baggie shorts (6 ounces) vice both corduroy and jockey shorts.

	lbs.	ozs.
Boots (New Balance Rainier)	2	6
Binoculars	1	2
Staff (Nomad, 12-inch handle)	—	12
FSO load:	24	9

Pack and contents — lbs. — ozs.

		lbs.	ozs.
1	Spare set of socks		8
1	Moleskin		½
1	Pack (Sierra West Half Dome)	1	6
1	Waterproof pack cover		4
	Food (see below)	3	5
6	Potable Aqua tablets		—
2	Canteens (1 quart each)*		5½
1	Waterbag (1 gallon)		4
1	Salewa stove (incl. cartridge)		11
1	Salewa pot		7
1	Plastic cup (Palco)		½
1	Spoon (Lexan)		½
1	Knife (Swiss Army: "Tinker")		3
1	Milk squirter		1
1	Book matches		—
1	Matchsafe (plastic)		1
	Mautz fire paste		—
1	Magnifying glass		½
1	Plastic tarp	1	4
6	Visklamps and balls		6
1	Groundsheet †		2½
1	Foam pad (Blue Foam, hip-length)		10½
1	Sleeping bag (Blue Puma Bear Cub)	1	15
1	Sleeping bag vapor barrier liner		5
1	Sleeping bag stuff sack ‡		4
1	Pair gaiters		3½
1	Pair polypropylene long johns		3½
1	Vapor barrier shirt		6½
1	Pile jacket	1	6½
1	Gore-Tex jacket	1	3½
1	Pair Gore-Tex pants (Sierra West Lite)		8½
1	Pair wool gloves		2½
1	Silk balaclava		1
1	Pile balaclava		3½

* Needed because camp and work area far from water.

† Large plastic merchandise wrapping bag, about 1 mil, slit down edges to make 30-by-80-inch sheet—and doubling as protection for foam pad when lashed outside pack.

‡ Heavy stuff sack taken to ensure dryness of sleeping bag and/or because I couldn't find the right bloody one.

1 Garbage bag (Colin's kilt)	3½
1 Flashlight (Mallory 805) with batteries	3
1 Spare bulb	–
1 Pair sunglasses (clip-ons)	1
1 Compass	½
Toilet paper	½
1 Bottle fly dope (almost empty, for ticks)	1
1 First-aid kit (normal, incl. allergy kit)	6
1 Whistle	½
1 Notebook (half empty)	1
1 Pen	–
2 Pencils	–
1 Office-on-yoke	3
1 Thermometer	1
Rip-stop repair tape	–
1 Needle and thread	–
Nylon cord (several lengths)	4
1 Spare plastic bag	–
1 Smoke bomb	2
1 Space blanket	2
1 Elastic bandage	1½
Plastic bags (various) (estimated)	1
1 Small stuff sack (ultralight)	1

Total in pack: 19   –

Food   ozs. (net)

Instant oatmeal plus Familia (premixed) (breakfast)	4½
2 bars pemmican (Bear Valley) (lunches)	7½
Beef and Rice (Mountain House) } (dinner)	5½
Meat bar (Westland)	2
Beef jerky (2 sticks)	½
Sugar	2½
Milk (Milkman)	4
7 tea bags (Lipton)	1
Nuts	3
Gorp	6
2 bars semi-sweet chocolate (Ghirardelli)	8
Candies	5
Spirulina	½

Food total (net)   3 lbs.   2½ ozs.
Wrappings (estimated)   2½

Food total (gross)   3 lbs.   5   ozs.

Mail-Order Retailers of Backpack Equipment, Foods and Services

This list is as complete and current as I can make it. But please treat it as a guide, not a gospel. *And remember that many of the major, household-word suppliers do not accept retail mail orders.*

The *star grading* is an attempt, inevitably fallible, to indicate the *range* of equipment that each firm offers (in its catalogue, not necessarily in its store). For example, **** means "just about everything a backpacker could want, and a wide choice of models." The stars do not necessarily reflect *quality* of stock.

Additional symbols:
†Firms that specialize in a certain branch or branches of equipment— usually, though not always, of high quality.
‡Firms that operate a general-merchandise mail-order service, of which backpacking equipment typically forms only a minor part.

Where both a street address and P.O. Box number are given they indicate, respectively, a retail store location and a mail-order address.

UNITED STATES

Coast to Coast

‡Montgomery Ward.
‡Sears, Roebuck.

Arizona

†Teton Enterprises, Box 533, Bisbee, 85603. (Kodel/cotton sleeping bag liners. See page 365.)

California

**Adventure 16, 4620 Alvarado Canyon Road, San Diego, 92120. (Catalogue offers packs, tents, sleeping bags, clothing and some accessories. Store carries full range. Quarterly newspaper: *Footprints*. Also laundry service.)

†Air Lift, 2217 Roosevelt Ave., Berkeley, 94703. (Air mattresses.)

†Alpenlite, 3891 No. Ventura Ave., Ventura, 93001. (A wide range of packs. Expanding their range. Also Alpine Aid first aid kits.)

†Antelope Camping Equipment, 21740 Granada Ave., Cupertino, 95014. (Packs. Some accessories.)

†Black Forest Snowshoe Company, P.O. Box 1007, Nevada City, 95959. (Snowshoes—wood, aluminum, plastic—and snowshoe kits and accessories.)

†Blue Puma, 650 Tenth St., Arcata, 95521. (Sleeping bags, down and pile clothing, raingear.)

†Chouinard Equipment, 245 West Santa Clara/P.O. Box 90, Ventura, 93002. (Mainly hardware for alpinists; but some interesting items for backpackers, incl. VB liners and socks, small tent, tumpline.)

†Down Depot, The, 701 Shrader St., San Francisco, 94117. (Counter service and mail-order dry-cleaning of all down-filled articles [page 366]. Repairs, too. Soon to sell emergency repair kits, bulk down and accessories.)

†Granite Stairway Mountaineering, 2310 Laurel St., Napa, 94559. (Retail mail-order outlet for Black Ice equipment: tents, clothing, packs; see page 20. Further confusion caused by use of name that until recently belonged to totally different firm. No catalogue yet, but Black Ice fliers apply.)

†Gregory Mountain Products, 7420 Trade St., San Diego, 92121-2478. (Packs—I-frame and frameless. See page 136. Also down cleaning service.)

†Moonstone Mountaineering, P.O. Box 4206, Arcata, 95521. (Sleeping bags—hi-tech, synthetic-filled, organized in "modular sleeping systems." Clothing—vapor barrier, pile, other synthetics.)

†Mountain Equipment, 1636 S. Second St., Fresno, 93702. (Mail order only to areas not served by dealers. Packs of all kinds. PolarGuard sleeping bags.)

†Nature Company, The, P.O. Box 7137, Berkeley, 94707. Stores in Berkeley, San Francisco (2) and Palo Alto. (In no sense a real backpacking equipment source; but offers binoculars, altimeters, ultralight magnifying lenses [page 218], books and other pleasing furbelows.)

†Necksaver, Inc., 15 Castle Park Way, Oakland, 94611. (Chest harnesses for cameras and binoculars. See page 464.)

***North Face, The, 1234 Fifth St., Berkeley, 94710. 16 retail stores in California, Colorado, Arizona and Washington. (Catalogue distributed through dealers. Mail orders filled only from areas not served by dealers. Stores offer full range, catalogue only tents, packs, sleeping bags, clothing and a few accessories.)

†Patagonia, P.O. Box 150, Ventura, 93002. (Clothing.)

†Shelter Systems, P.O. Box 308, Carmel Valley, 93924. (Catalogue. Small dome tents. See page 303.)

†SI Equipment, P.O. Box 5509, Carson, 90479. Toll-free out-of-state phone: 800-421-2179. Store: 2322 Artesia Blvd., Redondo Beach, 90278. (Survival food and equipment, some of interest to backpackers. Catalogue $2.)

**Sierra West, 6 East Yananoli St., Santa Barbara, 93101. (Retail mail orders filled only from areas not served by dealers. A wide range of lightweight packs, tents and accessories, including first-aid kits.)

†Western Mountaineering, 550 South First St., San Jose, 95113. Also in Santa Cruz. (Mail order: down-filled sleeping bags and clothing only. Stores offer full range of gear.)

†Wheeler and Wilson Boots, 206 N. Main St., Bishop, 93514. (Boot repairs—hiking, climbing and welted ski boots.)

***Wilderness Experience, 20675 Nordhoff St., Chatsworth, 91311. (Phone from out of state, toll-free, 800-BACKPAK [800-222-5725] for catalogue or dealer addresses; mail orders filled for areas not served by dealers. Full range of packs, tents, sleeping bags and clothing.)

†ZZ Corporation, 10806 Kaylor St., Los Alamitos, 90720. (Zip and other stoves. See page 248.)

Colorado

†Bibler Tents, 954A Pearl St., Boulder, 80302. (Small, ultralight Gore-Tex tents; some climbing accessories.)

†Blue Spruce Jammers, P.O. Box 827, Fort Collins, 80522. (Corduroy shorts. See page 400.)

†Camp 7, 1275 Sherman, Longmont, 80501. (Sleeping bags; tents.)

‡Frostline, P.O. Box 339993, Denver, 80233-0583. (Kits. A few backpacking items. See page 21.)

†Komito Boots, Estes Park, 80517. (Boot repairs. See page 74. Some boots.)

†Madden Mountaineering, P.O. Box 1979, Boulder, 80306. (Packs. First-aid kits.)

**Marmot Mountain Works, 331 S. 13th St., Grand Junction, 81501. Other stores in Berkeley, CA, and Belleview, WA. (Stores offer full range; catalogue, only sleeping bags, tents and clothing. Specialty: ultralight gear.)

†Mountain Mend, 6595-D Odell Pl., Boulder, 80301. (Repairs and custom refits on all outdoor gear except boots and canvas articles. Also make custom gear to specifications, especially sleeping bags and gaiters.)

Mountain Sports, 821 Pearl St., Boulder, 80302. (No catalogue, but carry full range of established lines.)

†Robertson Harness/Synergy Systems, P.O. Box 217, Westminster, 80030. (Synergy packs, camera packs, climbing harnesses.)

Connecticut

†Cannondale, 9 Brookside Pl., P.O. Box 122, Georgetown, 06829-0122. (Fill mail orders only from areas not served by dealers. Catalogue. Packs, tents, sleeping bags, clothing.)

Ski Hut, The, Keeler Bldg., Wilton, 16897. Another store in Hamden, CT. (No catalogue, but stores carry full range of equipment. Also run "outdoor adventure trips.")

Illinois

†Grade VI, P.O. Box 8, Urbana, 61801. (Packs and accessories. Catalogue.)

†Todd's, 5 S. Wabash Ave., Chicago, 60603. (Boots and shoes, including some for backpacking.)

Indiana

**Indiana Camp Supply, P.O. Box 344, Pittsboro, 46167-0344. (Catalogue. Accent is on extended wilderness living, but much for the backpacker. Specialty: medical kits.)

Louisiana

*Delta Wilderness Outfitters, 1817 Veterans Blvd., Metairie, 70005. Two stores. (Stores apparently carry full range of gear, but catalogues only a small selection. Also offer outdoor trips, U.S. and Canada.)

Maine

**‡L. L. Bean, Freeport, 04033. Order phone: 207-865-3161, 24 hours. Store open 24 hours too, and 365 days. (Famous catalogue of general outdoor merchandise offers much for backpackers.)

Maryland

H & H Surplus and Campers' Haven, 424 N. Eutaw St., Baltimore, 21201. (No current catalogue, but offer "a very extensive range of backpacking equipment.")

Massachusetts

***Don Gleason's Campers Supply, Pearl St., Northampton, 01060. (Catalogue $.75. Good stock of backpacking as well as camping gear.)

**Moor & Mountain, 63 Park St., Andover, 01810. Credit-card orders, phone 616-475-3665. (Photocopy of current catalogue, $1. Specializes in sales to expeditions and institutions.)

Nebraska

*Cabela's, 812 13th Ave., Sidney, 69160. (Accent is on hunting and fishing, but some backpacking gear.)

New Hampshire

****Eastern Mountain Sports, Vose Farm Rd., P.O. Box 811, Peterborough, 03458. Also 21 stores: MA (5), NY (4), NH (2), ME (2), CT (2), PA (2), VT, NJ, MN and CO. (Range offered in catalogues varies: see page 21.)

**International Mountain Equipment, Box 494, Main St., North Conway, 03860. (Catalogue. Gear for mountaineering; but some high-quality stuff for backpackers.)

**Stephenson's, RFD 4, Box 145, Gilford, 03246. (1980 catalogue, with annual inserts, $3. Warmlite tents, sleeping bags, packs and clothing.)

New Jersey

****Campmor, 810 Route 17 North, P.O. Box 999, Paramus, 07652. Toll-free out-of-state phone orders: 800-526-4784. (Free, unfancy catalogue is probably the most complete and comprehensively indexed now around.)

‡Edmund Scientific, 101 E. Gloucester Pike, Barrington, 08007. 24-hour credit-card phone orders, toll-free: 800-257-6173; in NJ, 800-232-6677. ("Scientific" goodies, including a few of possible interest to backpackers.)

***Ramsey Outdoor, 226 Route 17 North, Paramus, 07652. (Catalogue similar to Campmor's, though less comprehensive.)

New York

ABC Sport Shop, 185 Norris Dr., Rochester, 14610. (No catalogue, but carry full range; and repair boots, stoves.)

†Down East (Leon Greenman's Down East Outdoor Service Center), 93 Spring St., New York, 10012. (Specialty: dry-cleaning down sleeping bags and garments [see page 366]. Also modify and repair them —and tents and backpacks. Resole boots. Sell do-it-yourself repair materials: down, nylon taffeta, webbing, etc. Also own Walking News [books and maps]—see below.)

†Freeman Industries, P.O. Box 415, Tuckahoe, 10707. (Trak soapless supersoap, dentifrice and kits. See page 488.)

‡Hudson's, 97 Third Ave., New York, 10003. (General gear, but a fair backpacking selection.)

Kreeger & Sons, 16 W. 46th St., New York, 10036.

†Tough Traveler, 1012 State St., Schenectady, 12307. (Packs, camera bags.)

†Travel Mini Pack, 10 S. Broadway, Nyack, 10960. (Brochure: "Toiletries and travel accessories in uniquely small sizes.")

†Walking News, P.O. Box 352, Canal St. Sta., New York, 10013. (Publish *The Great Outdoors Booklist*—abridged, 499 titles; free for 20-cent stamp. Also Hikers Region Maps and guide books, N.J. and Hudson River areas. All available at Down East, above.)

Oklahoma

‡P & S Sales, P.O. Box 45095, Tulsa, 74145. (Outdoor supplies, some of interest to backpackers.)

Oregon

†Beckel Canvas Products, 2232 S.E. Clinton, Portland, 97202. (Custom-made canvas tents and flies, for static camps or pack trips. Accessories too.)

†Down Home, Deadwood, 97430. (High-quality, custom-made down-filled sleeping bags and systems. Also mukluks and booties. Now sell only direct.)

Rhode Island

**North by Northeast (formerly Pak Foam), 181 Conant St., Pawtucket, 02862. Toll-free order phone: 800-556-7262. (Backpacking rain-gear, pile and bunting garments, gaiters, foam pads, bivvy sacks, accessories.)

Tennessee

**Mountain Camper, P. O. Box 291, Seymour, 37865. Credit-card order phone, toll-free: 800-251-1021 (in TN, 800-332-6006). 19 stores, from New Hampshire to Texas. (Catalogue aimed primarily at campers, but some gear for backpackers.)

Utah

**Kirkham's Outdoor Products (formerly AAA Tent and Awning), 3125 South State St., Salt Lake City, 84115. Toll-free order phone: 800-453-7756. (Catalogue. Tents, fair range other gear.)

Vermont

‡Orvis Company, The, 10 River Rd., Manchester, 05254. (Essentially fishing gear, but some accessories for backpackers.)

Washington

‡Early Winters, 110 Prefontaine Place South, Seattle, 98104. (Frequent-appearing catalogues always include some backpacking gear, often new and interesting.)

**‡Eddie Bauer, Fifth and Union, P.O. Box 3700, Seattle, 98130. Toll-free order phone: 800-426-8020 (AK, HI: 800-426-8020; WA: 206-885-3330). 29 stores, coast to coast and Canada. (For Canadian mail orders, see page 614.) (General outdoor catalogue offers limited amount of backpacking gear; but many stores carry excellent, very extensive range.)

†ELD Equipment, 111 N. Washington, P.O. Box 914, Olympia, 98507. (Brochure. Small, light, custom-made tents.)

†Feathered Friends, 2130 1st Ave., Seattle, 98121. (Catalogue. High-quality down-filled sleeping bags and systems.)

†QB Outfitters, 4210 E. 4th Plain Blvd., P.O. Box 2324, Vancouver, 98668. (Specialty: Danner boots. Will supply Danner catalogue.)

****REI (Recreational Equipment Inc.), P.O. Box C-88125, Seattle, 98188. A cooperative. 8 stores: Seattle; Portland, OR; Berkeley; Los Angeles (2); Minneapolis; Anchorage and Denver. Toll-free order phone: 800-426-4840 (except AK and HI); WA: 800-562-4894. (Excellent catalogue [page 22]. Now pay postage.)

†Yak Works, 2030 Westlake Ave., Seattle, 98121. 24-hour toll-free order phone: 800-426-9935 (except AK, HI and WA). (Frequent-appearing catalogues always include backpacking gear, often new and interesting.)

Wisconsin

‡Gander Mountain, Box 248, Wilmot, 53192. Toll-free order phone: 800-558-9410 (except AK, HI and WI). (Catalogue. Essentially for hunters, but some backpacking accessories.)

Laacke and Joys, P.O. Box 92912, Milwaukee, 53202. Stores: Milwaukee, Brookfield and Mequon. (No catalogue, but do mail-order business with full range of backpacking equipment. Also rent it.)

Wyoming

**Paul Petzold Wilderness Equipment, P.O. Box 489, Lander, 82520. (Catalogue. Specialty: PolarGuard-filled sleeping bags and garments; but a fair range of other gear.)

CANADA

Please note that this list is essentially for Canadians. Various financial imped-iments prevent most Canadian firms from being able to supply individual U.S. residents economically. Indeed, it is hardly reasonable to expect replies to other than exceptional U.S. mail orders.

Coast to Coast

Simpson-Sears. Head office: 22 Jarvis St., Toronto, M5B 2B8. Cata-logue distribution centers in Toronto, Regina, Halifax and Van-couver.

British Columbia

Woodward's. Head office: 101 West Hastings St., Vancouver, V6B 4G1. Branches elsewhere in British Columbia and Alberta. (No ca-talogue; but has "country shopping," a telephone ordering system.)

Ontario

***Black's Camping Equipment, 225 Strathcona and Bank, PO Box 4501, Ottawa, K1S 5H1. Stores in Ottawa, Toronto, Montreal and Quebec City (Ste. Foy). (Catalogue kit: a continually updated collection of brochures and fliers.)

**‡Eddie Bauer, 50 Bloor St. West, Toronto, M4W 1A1. Other stores in Calgary and Edmonton. (See U.S. entry, Washington.)

‡King Sol Outdoor Stores, 639–647 Queen St. West, Toronto, M5V 2B7. (Army/Navy surplus and camping gear; but some items of backpacking gear, especially accessories, at good prices.)

Lightweight Foods

Many of the retailers listed above (and especially those rated **** or ***) offer a wide range of lightweight foods for backpackers. Most of the foods are made by a few specialist firms. Some of these firms—including Richmoor and Oregon Freeze Dried Foods (Mountain House products)—will advise you of the major retail outlets handling their merchandise but do not them-selves operate retail mail-order services. Others do.

Some of the firms listed will mail only case lots. Others, understand-ably, find they cannot fill orders totaling less than $20 or $25. So study catalogues before ordering.

New "organic" food suppliers still keep sprouting in classified ads and other fertile fields; but it seems that they still tend, unfortunately, to fold their tents like the Arabs and as silently steal a whey.

UNITED STATES

California

AlpineAire, P.O. Box 926, Nevada City, 95959. ("Natural foods": no preservatives, sugar, m.s.g., or artificial ingredients. Welcome orders from long-trek hikers. Will supply latest information on drop points along Pacific Crest Trail.)

Dri-Lite Foods (Backpacker's Pantry), 1540 Charles Dr., Redding, 96003. (Discounts to nonprofit organizations.)

Intermountain Trading Company. P.O. Box 5019, Berkeley, 94705. (Bear Valley Pemmican and Meal Pack bars. See page 168.)

Trail Foods, P.O. Box 9309, North Hollywood, 91609. (Wide selection Mountain House, Dri-Lite and Richmoor foods. Also some tents and packs.)

Illinois

Ad. Seidel & Son, 2200 Lunt Ave., Elk Grove Village, 60007. (Case-lot orders to camps and groups only. Bulk quantities—25 pounds of a single vegetable, for example—to individuals for repackaging.)

Massachusetts

Stow-A-Way Industries, 166 Cushing Highway (Rt. 3-A), Cohasset, 02025. Toll-free order phone (outside MA): 800-343-3803. (Separate catalogues for backpacking and survival foods. Mountain House, Dri-Lite and Richmoor, in addition to their own Stow-Lite line. Some backpacking accessories. Bulk discounts—and to nonprofit organization members. Will supply long-trek hikers: see page 21.)

Nevada

Weepak, 155 North Edison Way, Reno, 89502. (Wide selection of both backpacking and bulk foods.)

Oregon

Natural Food Backpack Dinners, P.O. Box 532, Corvallis, 97330.

CANADA

Ontario

HarDee Freeze-Dry Foods, 579 Speers Rd., Oakville, L6K 2GA. (Good selection individual items in laminated foil pouches. Also bulk packs.)

Organizations That Promote Walking

Although the groups I've listed vary in size from a handful to the 350,000 of the Sierra Club and 500,000 of the Audubon Society, all of them, as far as I can confirm, include communal hikes among their activities—even when their names suggest otherwise. And you may, in spite of pages 5 (footnote) and 582, sensibly prefer to walk in company. In any case, communal hikes are a safe way of getting to know the ropes—for an afternoon nature stroll or a month's wilderness backpacking.

No amount of research is going to dredge up the name of every walking group in the country; and secretaries, not to mention entire organizations, come and go. So any list like this is sure to be incomplete, and it begins to die before it is born. But it should at worst offer leads for earnest seekers. If an address proves "dead," inquire for the current version from local libraries, newspapers, chambers of commerce or other sources your ingenuity smells out.

Please remember that secretaries—particularly of small local clubs—tend to be starved for funds and inundated with mail. If you write, it is only courteous to enclose a stamped, self-addressed #10 envelope.

UNITED STATES

Coast to Coast

The American Hiking Society, 1701 18th St., N.W., Washington, DC 20009.
Promotes the building and protection of foot trails, and serves other hiking interests. Organizes long-distance hikes to support aims. Open to individuals and to clubs, as affiliates. Chapter in San Francisco.

The American Lung Association: Treks for Life and Breath Program.
Branches in 45 states offer 3- to 9-day backpacking trips (as well as canoeing, winter camping and bicycling). These are low-cost fund-raising events to raise money for the ALA's environmental-quality and quality-of-

life programs. Anne Bolzoni, American Lung Association, 1740 Broadway, New York, NY 10019 will provide list of treks in your area.

The National Audubon Society.
  Headquarters: 950 Third Ave., New York, NY 10022.
  Western regional office: 555 Audubon Way, Sacramento, CA 95825.
  Nationwide: 600 chapters and affiliates.
  The society's walks are always nature walks and normally accent bird-watching; but do not forget that they are walks.

The Sierra Club.
  Headquarters: 530 Bush St., San Francisco, CA 94108 (415-981-8634).
  The Club now has 56 chapters, covering the entire U.S. and also Canada (2 chapters). See listings under each state and province. Some chapters embrace several states or parts of states, and some states have more than one chapter (California, 13). Each chapter is made up of one or more regional groups: write appropriate chapter for information about group in your area. Addresses and phone numbers inevitably change: if in trouble, you can get latest listings from Club headquarters in San Francisco (Leader Services Department). Chapters and groups sponsor local outings and conservation work.

National Campers and Hikers Association, 7172 Transit Rd., Buffalo, NY 14221. Primarily for car-campers, but also for walkers, tenters, etc. Has 2900 chapters and 252 "teen" chapters.

Many colleges and universities—perhaps most—have hiking clubs. If local inquiries prove fruitless, consider asking: Association of College Unions-International, 400 E. Seventh St., Bloomington, IN 47405.

And for possible local walking activities do not forget: American Youth Hostels, Boy Scouts, Campfire Girls, Four-H Clubs, Girl Scouts, Young Life Campaign, YMCA and YWCA; also churches, parks and recreation departments of some big cities, and national and state parks.

Several big cities now offer longish hiking trails within or around their boundaries. Among them:
  Atlanta: Stone Mountain Trail (6½ miles)
  Boston: Blue Hills Trails
  Chicago: Illinois Prairie Path (23 miles)
  Cleveland: Emerald Necklace Trail
  Columbus, OH: Scioto River Trails
  Denver: Highline Canal Trail (18 miles)
  New York: Harriman Long Path (16 miles; part of 214-mile Long Path, George Washington Bridge, NJ to Windham, in Catskills)
  Philadelphia: Fairmont Park Trail (8½ miles)
  Phoenix: North and South Mountain Trails (15 miles)
  San Francisco/Oakland: East Bay Skyline Trail (14 miles)

Domestic and Worldwide Trips with Nonprofit and Commercial Outfitters and Agencies: The field has burgeoned in recent years, but any list would probably be useless: the smaller outfits seem to come and go like desert rainpockets. For a current selection, see the ads, especially near the end, of relevant magazines—from club organs (*Audubon, Sierra*) to *Outside* and *Backpacker.* The ads reach out beyond backpacking and trekking to horsepacking, river rafting, canoeing and whatevering. And some outfits offer special angles of vision: wildlife, birdwatching, archeology, folkways. Many of the brochures list alluring itineraries, from Appalachia to the Zambezi. Most sumptuous and dream-inducing of them is the new annual by Mountain Travel of Albany, CA. A work of art—that costs $9.95.

Regional

The Appalachian Trail Conference.
   P.O. Box 807, Harpers Ferry, WV 25425 (304-535-6331).
   Thirty-one trail clubs affiliated to this conference maintain the 2138-mile, Maine–Georgia Appalachian Trail; 40-odd other clubs are non-maintenance affiliates. The conference is the surest source of up-to-date information on Eastern-seaboard walking activities. Listed clubs affiliated to the conference are marked ■.

The Federation of Western Outdoor Clubs.
   Secretary: Fay Ogilvie.
   5529 27th Ave. N.E., Seattle, WA 98105.
   The secretary will supply information on club addresses or membership but unfortunately cannot answer questions on trails or hiking details. Members clubs are marked ♦.

The New England Trail Conference.
   Secretary: Forrest E. House.
   33 Knollwood Dr., East Longmeadow, MA 01028.
   A valuable source of information on hiking activities in the area. Publishes *Hiking Trails of New England,* a source for guidebooks of New England and New York.

Alabama

Sierra Club: Alabama chapter, c/o Thomas Williams, 1371 Toney Dr., Huntsville, 35802 (205-881-5377).

Alaska

Mountaineering Club of Alaska, P.O. Box 2037, Anchorage, 99510.
Sierra Club: Alaska chapter, P.O. Box 2025, Anchorage, 99510 (907-479-7074).

Arizona

Sierra Club: Grand Canyon chapter, c/o D. Crook-Barc, 12433 N. 28th Dr., Apt P24, Phoenix, 85029 (602-933-7415).

Arkansas

Sierra Club: Arkansas chapter, P.O. Box 5927, N. Little Rock, 72119 (501-224-6063).

California

Berkeley Hiking Club, P.O. Box 147, Berkeley, 94701.
♦California Alpine Club, 562 Flood Bldg., 870 Market St., San Francisco, 94102.
♦Contra Costa Hills Club, 4000 Broadway, Oakland, 94611.
♦Desomount Club, 4930 Ranchito Ave., Sherman Oaks, 91423.
Sierra Club chapters:

>   Angeles, 2410 W. Beverly Blvd., Ste 2, Los Angeles, 90057 (213-387-4287).
>   Kern-Kaweah, 1000 Pebble Beach Dr., Bakersfield, 93309.
>   Loma Prieta, 2253 Park Blvd., Palo Alto, 94306 (415-327-8111).
>   Los Padres, P.O. Box 30222, Santa Barbara, 93105.
>   Mother Lode, P.O. Box 1335, Sacramento, 95806 (916-444-2180).
>   Redwood, P.O. Box 466, Santa Rosa, 95402.
>   San Diego, 1549 El Prado, San Diego, 92101 (619-233-7144).
>   San Francisco Bay, 6014 College Ave., Oakland, 94618 (415-658-7470).
>   San Gorgonio, P.O. Box 1023, Riverside, 92502.
>   Santa Lucia, Eco Slo, 985 Palm St., San Luis Obispo, 93401 (805-544-1777).
>   Tehipite, P.O. Box 5396, Fresno, 93755 (209-292-7036).
>   Toiyabe: See Nevada (includes part of eastern California).
>   Ventana, P.O. Box 5667, Carmel, 93921 (408-624-8032).

♦Tamalpais Conservation Club, Room 562, Flood Bldg., 870 Market St., San Francisco, 94102 (415-391-8021).

Colorado

♦American Wilderness Alliance, 4260 E. Evans Ave., Denver, 80222.
Sierra Club: Rocky Mountain chapter, 2239 E. Colfax #206, Denver, 80206 (303-321-7144).

Connecticut

■ Connecticut chapter, Appalachian Mountain Club: Judith K. Bensancon, 139 Milton St., West Hartford, 06119.

APPENDIX

Connecticut Forest and Parks Association Inc., Secretary: John E. Hibbard, 1010 Main St., P.O. Box 8537, East Hartford, 06108.
Sierra Club: Connecticut chapter, 118 Oak St., Hartford, 06106 (203-527-9788).

Delaware

■ Brandywine Valley Outing Club, P.O. Box 7033, Wilmington, 19810 (302-478-2853).
■ Wilmington Trail Club, P.O. Box 1184, Wilmington, 19899.
Sierra Club: See Potomac chapter, District of Columbia.

District of Columbia

■ Potomac Appalachian Trail Club, 1718 N St., N.W., 20036.
Sierra Club: Potomac Chapter, c/o Jim Clarke, 1916 Dundee Rd., Rockville, MD 20850. (Also includes Delaware, Maryland and West Virginia.)

Florida

Appalachian Trail Club of Florida, 5400 34th St., West, Morton Village 5L, Bradenton, 33503 (813-758-1227).
Florida Trail Association, P.O. Box 13708, Gainesville, 32604 (904-378-8823).
Sierra Club: Florida chapter, P.O. Box 2692, Tallahassee, 32316 (813-922-1645).

Georgia

■ Georgia Appalachian Trail Club, P.O. Box 654, Atlanta, 30301.
Sierra Club: Georgia chapter, c/o Mayhew, P.O. Box 38131, Atlanta, 30334 (404-633-0666).

Hawaii

Hawaiian Trail and Mountain Club, P.O. Box 2238, Honolulu, 96804.
Sierra Club: Hawaii chapter, P.O. Box 22897, Honolulu, 96822 (808-946-8494).

Idaho

♦ Idaho Alpine Club, P.O. Box 2885, Idaho Falls, 83401.
Sierra Club: Northern Rockies chapter, P.O. Box 424, Spokane, 99210. (Includes part of eastern Washington.)

Illinois

Sierra Club: Great Lakes Chapter, 53 W. Jackson, Suite 1064, Chicago, 60604 (312-431-0158).

Tazewell-Peoria Hiking Club, Peoria Park District, Glen Oak Pavilion, 2218 N. Prospect Rd., Peoria, 61603-2193 (309-688-3667).

Indiana

Sierra Club: Hoosier chapter, P.O. Box 40275, Indianapolis, 46240.

Iowa

Iowa Mountaineers, P.O. Box 163, Iowa City, 52240.

Sierra Club: Iowa chapter, The Thoreau Center, 3500 Kingman Blvd., Des Moines, 50311 (515-277-8868).

Kansas

Johnson County Outdoor Society, P.O. Box 95, Shawnee Mission, 66202 (913-362-3590).

Sierra Club: Kansas chapter, RR#2 Box 170, 5640 S. 103rd St. E., Derby, 67037 (316-788-0084).

Kentucky

Sierra Club: Cumberland chapter, c/o Graddy, Rt. 1, Hedden Rd., Versailles, 40383 (606-846-4907).

Louisiana

Sierra Club: Delta chapter, 111 S. Hennessey St., New Orleans, 70119 (504-345-2339).

Maine

■ Maine Appalachian Trail Club, Inc., Augusta Rd., RFD #3, Winslow, 04902.

Sierra Club: See New England chapter, Massachusetts.

Maryland

■ Maryland Appalachian Trail Club, Jim Rice, 440 N. Prospect St., Hagerstown, 21769.

■ Mountain Club of Maryland, c/o Thurston Griggs, 5128 Rolling Rd., Baltimore, 21227.

Sierra Club: See Potomac chapter, District of Columbia.

■ Terrapin Trail Club, Box 67, Univ. of Maryland, College Park, 20742.

Massachusetts

- Appalachian Mountain Club, 5 Joy St., Boston, 02108. (All Appalachian Trail maintenance in Massachusetts is under Berkshire chapter, A.M.C.: Ed Lewis, Chairman, Berkshire chapter, Appalachian Trail Committee, 40 Aubrey Dr., Dalton, 01267.)
- Metawampe (University of Massachusetts Faculty Outing Club), Univ. of Massachusetts, Amherst, 01002.
- Mt. Greylock Ski Club, Inc., P.O. Box 478, Pittsfield, 01201.
  Sierra Club: New England chapter, 3 Joy St., Boston, 02108 (617-227-5339). (Also embraces Maine, New Hampshire, Vermont and Rhode Island.)

Michigan

North Country Trail Association, P.O. Box 311, White Cloud, 49349. (Information and schematic maps of newly designated North Country [National Scenic] Trail, 3226 miles long.)
Sierra Club: Mackinac chapter, 135 Linden, East Lansing, 48823 (517-337-8247).

Minnesota

Sierra Club: North Star chapter, 2929 4th Ave. S., #N, Minneapolis, 55408 (612-827-3562).
Wilderness Inquiry Association, c/o Greg Lais, 2929 4th Ave. S., #O, Minneapolis, 55408.

Mississippi

Sierra Club: Mississippi chapter, P.O. Box 4335, 513 N. State St., Jackson, 39216 (601-355-7495).

Missouri

Sierra Club: Ozark chapter, P.O. Box 12424, Olivette, 63132 (314-727-2311).
See also Kansas: Johnson County Outdoor Society.

Montana

- Montana Wilderness Association, P.O. Box 635, Helena, 59624 (406-443-7350).
- Rocky Mountaineers, P.O. Box 4262, Missoula, 59807.
  Sierra Club: Montana chapter, P.O. Box 7315, Missoula, 59807 (406-549-4475).

Nebraska

Omaha Walking Club, 537 So. 50th Ave., Omaha, 68106.
Sierra Club: Nebraska chapter, 1602 Military Ave., Omaha, 68111 (402-553-4010).

Nevada

Sierra Club: Toiyabe chapter, P.O. Box 8096, University Stn., Reno, 89507. (Chapter includes sliver of eastern California.)

New Hampshire

■ Dartmouth Outing Club, Box 9, Robinson Hall, Dartmouth College, Hanover, 03755.
Lumberjack Outing Club, c/o Skimeister Ski Shop, North Woodstock, 03262.
Sierra Club: See New England chapter, Massachusetts.
Wonaloncet Out Door Club, c/o Mrs. Barbara Sidley, Box 15, Wonaloncet, 03897.

New Jersey

Adirondack Mountain Club: North Jersey chapter, P.O. Box 185, Ridgewood, 07451.
Cosmopolitan Club of Montclair, Dr. H. Meienhoffer, 35 Glenwood Rd., Upper Montclair, 07043 (201-744-2444).
■ Interstate Hiking Club, Herbert E. Snider, 6 Carl Dr., Fairfield, 07006.
■ New York–New Jersey Trail Conference—many New Jersey clubs: see New York.
Sierra Club: New Jersey chapter, 360 Nassau St., Princeton, 08540 (609-924-3141).
Woodland Trail Walkers, Mrs. Frances Grimes, 108 Cookman Ave., Ocean Grove, 07756.

New Mexico

Philmont Scout Ranch and Explorer Base, Cimarron, 87714 (505-376-2281). (Outdoor adventure, including backpacking, for youth groups. Run by Boy Scouts of America but "open to groups and organizations whose goals and aims are commensurate with those of the BSA—such as Church, 4-H, etc." Carefully controlled conditions outlined in brochure.)
Sierra Club: Rio Grande chapter, c/o Colburn, 1601 Lee Trevino Dr. #1049, El Paso, TX 79936 (915-592-4033). (Includes western tip of Texas.)

New York

Adirondack Forty-Sixers, Adirondack, 12810.

Adirondack Mountain Club, 172 Ridge St., Glens Falls, 12801. Chapters: Genesee Valley, Rochester; Knickerbocker, New York and vicinity; Long Island; Mid-Hudson, Poughkeepsie; New York, metropolitan area; Ramapo, Rockland County; Seneca, Canandaigua. See also New Jersey.

Adirondack Trail Improvement Society, Saint Huberts, 12943.

American Youth Hostels, 132 Spring St., New York, 10012 (212-431-7100).

■ Appalachian Mountain Club, New York chapter: 225 W. 34th St., 15th Floor, New York, 10001.

Ardsley Outing Club, Bob Sillman, 18 Larchmont St., Ardsley, 10502.

Catskill 3500 Club, Ken A. Shuker, 20 Cedar Lane, Cornwall, 12518.

Cayuga Trails Club, P.O. Box 754, Ithaca, 14850.

College Alumni Hiking Club, Mrs. E. E. Weitz, 290 Ninth Ave., New York, 10001.

Finger Lakes Trail Conference, Rochester Museum of Arts and Sciences, P.O. Box 18048, Rochester, 14618. Formed in 1961 to build a foot trail across southern New York State, from the Catskills to the Alleghenies, connecting the Bruce Trail of Canada with the Appalachian Trail. Now includes branch trails. Sponsor clubs and individuals seem to fluctuate. For further information on them, apply above address.

■ Nassau Hiking and Outdoor Club, Rodger W. Junk, 3 Rosedale Rd., Valley Stream, 11560.

■ New York Hiking Club, Harold Diamond, 404 E. 18th St., Brooklyn, 11226.

■ New York–New Jersey Trail Conference, 20 West 40th St., P.O. Box 2250, New York, 10001 (212-921-4025). A nonprofit federation of over 60 hiking and outdoor clubs and 3000 individual members who volunteer to build and maintain hiking trails. This maintenance network covers over 700 miles of marked trails in the New York metropolitan area, and includes the Appalachian Trail in New York and New Jersey from the Connecticut border to the Delaware Water Gap. Founded 1920. Member organizations include both local clubs and chapters of such major bodies as the Sierra Club, American Youth Hostels and Boy Scouts of America.

■ New York Ramblers, Anne H. Blumenstein, 4523 Broadway, Apt 3-C, New York, 10040.

New York State Department of Environmental Conservation, 50 Wolf Rd., Albany, 12233. (Hiking Information.)

New York State Office of Parks, Recreation & Historic Preservation, Empire State Plaza, Bldg. 1, Albany, 12238 (518-474-0414). (Hiking Information.)

Sierra Club: Atlantic chapter, 196 Morton Ave., Albany, 12202 (518-462-9812).

Suffern Historical Hikers, Gardner F. Watts, 15 Beech Rd., Suffern, 10901.

■ Torrey Botanical Club, Grace A. Dietz, New York Botanical Garden, Bronx, 10458.

■ Tramp and Trail Club of New York, Robyn Stockton, 229 E. 52nd St., New York 10022.

■ Westchester Trails Association, Linda Heilmann, 632 Warburton Ave., Apt 6-K, Yonkers, 10701.

■ Woodland Trail Walkers, John J. Cotter, 350 E. 65th St., New York, 10021.

North Carolina

■ Carolina Mountain Club, P.O. Box 68, Asheville, 28802.

■ Nantahala Hiking Club, Route 10, Box 322, Franklin, 28734.

■ Piedmont Appalachian Trail Hikers (PATH), President: Hazel Monroe, 422 Lee Ave., Wadesboro, 28107.

Sierra Club: North Carolina chapter, P.O. Box 2860, Winston-Salem, 27102 (919-725-2351).

North Dakota

Sierra Club: Dacotah chapter, c/o David Warren, P.O. Box 93, Pierre, SD 57501 (605-224-6940). (Chapter includes South Dakota.)

Ohio

Akron Metropolitan Park Hiking Club, c/o Bert Szabo, Metropolitan Park District, 975 Treaty Line Road, Akron, 44313.

Central Ohio Hiking Club, YMCA, 40 W. Long St., Columbus, 43215.

Sierra Club, Ohio chapter, 65 S. 4th St., Columbus, 43215 (614-461-0734).

Oklahoma

Sierra Club: Oklahoma chapter, P.O. Box 60882, Oklahoma City, 73146 (405-436-1400).

Oregon

♦ Angora Hiking Club, P.O. Box 12, Astoria, 97103.

♦ Chemeketans, 360½ State St., Salem, 97301.

♦ Crag Rats, 4720 Okenwood Dr., Hood River, 97031.

Mazamas, 909 N.W. 19th, Portland, 97209.

♦ Obsidians, Inc., P.O. Box 322, Eugene, 97440.

◆Oregon Coast Trail Association, c/o Jack Remington, Coordinator, 525 Trade St. S.E., Salem, 97310.

◆Santiam Alpine Club, Inc., P.O. Box 1041, Salem, 97308.

Sierra Club: Oregon chapter, 2637 S.W. Water St., Portland, 97201 (503-222-1963).

◆Trails Club of Oregon, P.O. Box 1243, Portland, 97207.

Pennsylvania

Keystone Trails Association, P.O. Box 251, Cogan Station, 17728. An association of hiking clubs, including the following:

■ Allentown Hiking Club, 3000 Parkway Blvd., Allentown, 18104.

Alpine Club of Williamsport, P.O. Box 501, Williamsport, 17701.

■ Appalachian Mountain Club: Delaware Valley chapter, Winfield W. Howe, 422 Dudley Ave., Narberth, 19072.

■ Back To Nature Hiking Club Of Philadelphia (Batona), John W. Kirker, 238 Taylor Rd., Springfield, 19064.

■ Blue Mountain Eagle Climbing Club and Wilderness Park Association, P.O. Box 3523, Reading, 19605.

Boondockers Hiking Club, Bernie McKenna, 553 Midland St., Pittsburgh, 15221.

■ Horse Shoe Trail Club, Robert Chalfont, Jenkintown, 19046.

■ Lancaster Hiking Club, Roy K. Albright, 45 Petersburg Rd., Neffsville, 17601.

■ Philadelphia Trail Club, Mrs. A. Peers Montgomery, 520 Fox Rd., Glenside, 19038.

■ Springfield Trail Club, John W. Kirker, 238 Taylor Rd., Springfield, 19064.

■ Susquehanna Appalachian Trail Club, Warren Sleighter, 102 Fifth St., New Cumberland, 17070.

■ York Hiking Club, Mrs. Frank V. Senft, 1957 Woodstream Dr., York, 17402.

■ Lebanon Valley Hiking Club, Richard C. Kimmel, 1020 Martin St., Lebanon, 17042.

Penn State Outing Club, Hiking Division, Intramural Bldg., University Park, 16802.

Sierra Club: Pennsylvania chapter, P.O. Box 135, Cogan Station, 17728.

Susquehanna Trailers Club, George Kupstas, 339 Ridge Ave., Kingston, 18704.

Rhode Island

Sierra Club: New England chapter. See Massachusetts.

South Carolina

Sierra Club: South Carolina chapter, P.O. Box 12112, Columbia, 29211 (803-799-0321).

South Dakota

Sierra Club: Dacotah chapter, c/o David Warren, P.O. Box 93, Pierre, 57501 (605-224-6940). (Chapter includes North Dakota.)

Tennessee

Bowater Southern Paper Company, Public Relations Dept., Calhoun, 37309. ("Pocket wilderness areas.")

Sierra Club: Tennessee chapter, c/o McCaleb, 100 Colonial Dr., Hendersonville, 37075 (615-822-4046).

■ Smoky Mountains Hiking Club, Rt. 3, Highway 95, Lenoir City, 37971.

■ TERC Hiking Club, c/o Tennessee Eastman Recreation Club, Box 511, Kingsport, 37662.

Texas

Sierra Club: Lone Star chapter, P.O. Box 1931, Austin, 78767 (512-478-1264). See also New Mexico, Rio Grande chapter, which includes western tip of Texas.

Utah

Sierra Club: Utah chapter, Central City Community Center, 615 South 3rd East, Salt Lake City, 84111 (801-363-9621).

♦ Wasatch Mountain Club, 1228 Bryan Ave., Salt Lake City, 84105.

Vermont

Country Inns Along the Trail: Eight inns organized to offer hiking on an 80-mile stretch of Vermont's Long Trail. Meals and beds at each day's end. Brochure from: Churchill House Inn, R.D. 3, Brandon, 05733.

■ Green Mountain Club, Inc., P.O. Box 889, Montpelier, 05602.

Sierra Club: See New England chapter, Massachusetts.

Virginia

■ Mt. Rogers Appalachian Trail Club, David Thomas, Route 37, Box 248, Abingdon, 24210.

■ Natural Bridge Appalachian Trail Club, P.O. Box 3012, Lynchburg, 24503.

■ Old Dominion Appalachian Trail Club, P.O. Box 25283, Richmond, 23260.

■ Roanoke Appalachian Trail Club, Mac MacDaniels, 2423 Lincoln Ave. S.W., Roanoke, 24015.

Sierra Club: Old Dominion chapter, c/o Holcomb, Rt. 2 Box 385, Blacksburg, 24060.

■ Tidewater Appalachian Trail Club, P.O. Box 8246, Norfolk, 23503.

■ University of Virginia Outing Club, PO Box 101X, Newcomb Hall Station, Charlottesville, 22903.
■ Virginia Tech Outing Club, Dave Jenkins, Faculty Advisor, PO Box 538, Blacksburg, 24060.

Washington

♦ Boeing Employees Alpine Society, P.O. Box 3703, M.S.4H-96, Seattle, 98124.
♦ Cascade Wilderness Club, P.O. Box 1547, Bellingham, 98227.
♦ Cascadians, P.O. Box 2201, Yakima, 98902.
♦ Hobnailers, P.O. Box 1256, Spokane, 99210.
♦ Intermountain Alpine Club, P.O. Box 505, Richland, 99352.
♦ Klahane Club, P.O. Box 494, Port Angeles, 98362.
♦ Mountaineers, The, 719 Pike St., Seattle, 98101.
♦ Mt. Baker Club, P.O. Box 73, Bellingham, 98227.
♦ Mt. St. Helena Club, P.O. Box 843, Longview, 98632.
♦ Olympians, Inc., P.O. Box 401, Hoquiam, 98550.
♦ Ptarmigans, P.O. Box 1821, Vancouver, 98668.
  Puget Sound Mycological Society, 2559 N.E. 96th, Seattle, 98115 (206-523-2892 or 522-5848).
♦ Seattle Audubon Society, 712 Joshua Green Bldg., Seattle, 98101.
♦ Sierra Club: Cascade chapter, c/o Ruth Weiner, 6837 51st Ave. N.E., Seattle, 98115 (206-527-4131). See also Idaho, Northern Rockies chapter, which includes part of eastern Washington.
  Signpost Magazine, Editor, Ann Marshall, 16812 36th Ave., Lynnwood, 98036. Extensive club and trail lists, etc. See page 000.
♦ Skagit Alpine Club, P.O. Box 513, Mt. Vernon, 98273.
♦ Spokane Mountaineers, Inc., P.O. Box 1013, Spokane 99210.
♦ Summit Alpine Club, c/o Mike Holt, 6542 4th Ave. N.E., #2, Seattle, 98115.
  Volunteers for Outdoor Washington (VOW), 3935 University Way N.E., Seattle, 98105.
  Wanderers, 5102 Mud Bay N.W., Olympia, 98502.
  Washington Alpine Club, P.O. Box 352, Seattle, 98111.

West Virginia

■ Kanawha Trail Club, Inc., c/o George Becker, P.O. Box 4474, Charleston, 25304.
  Sierra Club: See Potomac chapter, District of Columbia.

Wisconsin

  Sierra Club: John Muir chapter, 111 King St., Madison, 53703 (608-256-0565).
  Wisconsin Hoofers Outing Club, The Wisconsin Union, 800 Langdon St., Madison, 53706.

Wyoming

Sierra Club: Wyoming chapter, Rt. 62 Box 164, Lander, 82520 (307-738-2632).

CANADA

Coast to Coast

Alpine Club of Canada.
> Club Manager: R. Matthews, P.O. Box 1026, Banff, Alberta T0L 0C0.
> (Please note that this is essentially a *climbing* club—though it seems to offer some walking, too. Sections in Banff, Calgary, Edmonton, Montreal, Ottawa, Toronto, Vancouver, Vancouver Island and Winnipeg.)

Canadian Hostelling Association (Association canadienne de l'ajisme).
> National Office: 333 River Road, Tower A, 3rd Floor, Vanier City (Ottawa), Ontario, K1L 8H9.
> Twelve regional and provincial offices. See provincial listings. (A non-profit recreational and educational organization whose aim is to *help all* [no maximum age limit], but especially young people, toward a greater knowledge, care and love of the countryside by providing hostels or other simple accommodations for them on their travels. Activities in addition to hiking: cycling, canoeing, snowshoeing, skiing and mountain climbing. Hostel shops in Halifax, Montreal, Toronto, Ottawa, Calgary, Edmonton, Victoria and Vancouver, cooperatively operated, sell and rent camping, skiing and hiking equipment.)

Alberta

Canadian Hostelling Association:
> Northern Alberta District, 10926 88th Ave., Edmonton, T6G 0Z1 (403-432-7798).
> Southern Alberta District, 1414 Kensington Rd. N.W., Calgary, T2N 3P9 (403-283-5551).
Sierra Club: Western Canada chapter. See British Columbia.

British Columbia

British Columbia Hostelling Association, 3425 W. Broadway, Vancouver, V6R 4N6 (604-736-2674).
Federation of Mountain Clubs of British Columbia, P.O. Box 33768, Station D, Vancouver, V6J 4L6. Represents the following outdoor clubs:
> Alberni Valley Outdoor Club, P.O. Box 56, Port Alberni, V9Y 7M6
> Alpine Club of Canada—Vancouver Section, P.O. Box 2839, Vancouver, V6B 3X3

Alpine Club of Canada—Vancouver Island Section, c/o 311 Stevens Rd., Victoria V8X 3X3

British Columbia Mountaineering Club, P.O. Box 2674, Vancouver, V6B 3W8

Caledonia Ramblers, Box 26, Station A, Prince George, V2L 4R9

Chilliwack Outdoor Club, c/o 50885 Winona Rd., R.R. #8, Sardis, V0X 1Y0

Comox District Mountaineering Club, c/o 220 Back Rd., Courtenay, V9N 3W6

Fraser Valley Hikers, c/o 32285 Hillcrest Ave., Clearbrook, V2T 1S7

Hygh Tymers, c/o 955 Burrard St., Vancouver, V6Z 1Y2

Island Mountain Ramblers, P.O. Box 691, Nanaimo, V9R 5M2

Kelowna Outdoor Club, c/o #303–543 Rowcliffe Ave., Kelowna, V1Y 5Y8

Klister Outdoor Klub, c/o 7909 Patterson St., Burnaby, V5J 3P7

Kootenay Mountaineering Club, Box 3195, Castlegar, V1N 3H5

North Shore Hikers, P.O. Box 4535, Vancouver, V6B 4A1

Okanagan Similkameen Parks Society, P.O. Box 787, Summerland, V0H 1Z0

Outdoor Club of Victoria, c/o #225–1701 Cedar Hill Cross Rd., Victoria V8P 2P9

Outsetters Club, c/o 5899 132 St., Surrey, V3W 4K6

Outward Bound, c/o #101–1600 W. 6th Ave., Vancouver, V6J 1R3

Penticton Outdoor Club, c/o 171 Walden Crescent, Penticton, V2A 1R6

Sierra Club: Western Canada chapter, 620 View St., Room 314, Victoria, V8W 1J6 (604-386-5255).

Simon Fraser University Outdoor Club, Burnaby, V5A 1S6

Squamish Ski & Outdoor Club, Box 2317, Squamish, V0N 3G0

Timberline Trail & Nature Club, P.O. Box 779, Dawson Creek, V1G 4H8

Valley Outdoor Association, c/o 8681 Shepherd Way, Delta, V4C 4J9

Vancouver Natural History Society, P.O. Box 3021, Vancouver, V6B 3X5

Varsity Outdoor Club, University of British Columbia, Vancouver, V6T 1W5

Golden Agers Hiking Club, c/o 3556 Dundas, Burnaby, V5K 1S1.

Manitoba

Manitoba Hostelling Association, 1700 Ellice Ave., Winnipeg, R3H 0B1 (204-786-5641).

Sierra Club: Western Canada chapter. See British Columbia.

New Brunswick

Sierra Club: See Ontario chapter.

Newfoundland

Newfoundland Hostelling Association, P.O. Box 1815, St. John's, A1C
5P9 (709-753-8603).
Sierra Club: See Ontario chapter.

Nova Scotia

Nova Scotia Hostelling Association, Sport Nova Scotia Center, 5516 Spring
Garden Rd., P.O. Box 3010 South, Halifax B3J 3G6 (902-425-5450).
Sierra Club: See Ontario chapter.

Ontario

Bruce Trail Association, The, P.O. Box 857, Hamilton, L8N 3N9 (416-
689-7311). Nine Bruce Trail Clubs maintain the 430-mile Bruce Trail
along the Niagara Escarpment, Niagara to Tobermory.
Federation of Ontario Hiking Trail Associations, Box 422, Cambridge,
N1R 5V5. Formed in 1974 to coordinate concerns of all trail clubs in
the province. Includes, in addition to the Bruce Trail Association:
Avon Trail Assoc., Box 384, Stratford, N5A 6T3.
Elgin Hiking Trail Club, Box 11, St. Thomas, N5P 3T5.
Ganaraska Trail Assoc., Box 1136, Barrie, L4M 5E2.
Grand Valley Trails Assoc., Box 1233, Kitchener, N2G 4G8.
Guelph Trail Club, Box 1, Guelph, N1H 6J6.
Maitland Trail Assoc., Box 443, Goderich, N7A 4C7.
Quinte-Hastings Recreational Trail Assoc., Box 133, Belleville, K8N
5J1.
Rideau Trail Assoc., Box 15, Kingston, K7L 4V6.
Thames Valley Trail Assoc., Box 821, Terminal B, London, N6A 4Z3.
Voyageur Trail Assoc., Box 66, Sault Ste. Marie, P6A 5L2.
Great Lakes Hostelling Association, 223 Church St., Toronto, M5B 1Z1
(416-368-1848).
National Capital Hostelling Association, 18 The Byward Market, Ottawa,
K1N 7A1 (613-230-1200).
Sierra Club, Ontario chapter, 47 Colborne St., Suite 308, Toronto M5E
1E3 (416-366-6692). Includes all eastern Canada.

Prince Edward Island

Prince Edward Island Hostelling Association, P.O. Box 1718, Charlotte-
town, C1A 7N4 (902-894-9696).
Sierra Club: See Ontario chapter.

Quebec

Club de la Montagne Canadienne, 1431 rue Patrice Lasalle, Quebec, H8N
1P9.
Club Montafond Outdoors Activities, C.P. 399, Sutton VoE 2Ko.
Fédération québécoise de la Marche, La, 1415 Jarry St. East, Montréal, H2E
2Z7. For $5, including postage, will send list of over 100 hiking trails
throughout Quebec ("Repertoire des sentiers"): length, difficulty, location, facilities, managing organizations. "Easily understood even if
you don't read French."
Parc d'Environnement Naturel de Sutton, C.P. 809, Sutton, VoE 2Ko.
Quebec Hostelling Federation, 803 Mont-Royal Avenue East, Montreal,
H2J 1W9 (514-521-5230).

Saskatchewan

Saskatchewan Hostelling Association, Saskatchewan Sport and Recreation
Center, 2205 Victoria Ave., Regina, S4P 0S4 (306-522-3651).
Sierra Club: Western Canada chapter. See British Columbia.

Yukon

Sierra Club: Western Canada chapter. See British Columbia.

Pleasant Quotes for Contemplative Walkers

I nauseate walking.

WILLIAM CONGREVE

When you have worn out your shoes, the strength of the shoe leather has passed into the fiber of your body. I measure your health by the number of shoes and hats and clothes you have worn out. He is the richest man who pays the largest debt to his shoemaker.

EMERSON

The longing to be primitive is a disease of culture.

GEORGE SANTAYANA

Today I have grown taller from walking with the trees.

KARLE WILSON
(Mrs. Thomas Ellis Baker)

If you pick 'em up, O Lord, I'll put 'em down.

ANON.
The Prayer of the Tired Walker

Our mental make-up is suited to a life of very severe physical labor. I used, when I was younger, to take my holidays walking. I would cover 25 miles a day, and when the evening came I had no need of anything to keep me from boredom, since the delight of sitting amply sufficed. . . .

When crowds assemble in Trafalgar Square to cheer to the

echo an announcement that the government has decided to have them killed, they would not do so if they had all walked 25 miles that day.

BERTRAND RUSSELL

Walking is the best of panaceas for the morbid tendencies of authors.

LESLIE STEPHEN
In Praise of Walking

I drew my bride, beneath the moon,
Across my threshold; happy hour!
But, ah, the walk that afternoon
We saw the water-flags in flower!

COVENTRY PATMORE

I want a divorce.

BARBARA BAILEY MARCUS
Response suggested for
Mrs. Coventry Patmore

If you are ready to leave father and mother, and brother and sister, and wife and child and friends, and never see them again—if you have paid your debts, and made your will, and settled all your affairs, and are a free man, then you are ready for a walk.

THOREAU

The civilized man has built a coach, but he has lost the use of his feet.

EMERSON

Huh, your feet must be stronger than your head!

STRANGER
To Colin Fletcher,
during thousand-mile walk

Happiness is not a station you arrive at, but a manner of traveling.

MARGARET LEE RUNBECK

There is more to life than increasing its speed.
                              GANDHI

The swiftest traveler is he that goes afoot.
                              THOREAU

And the Lord said unto Satan, Whence comest thou? Then Satan
answered the Lord, and said, From going to and fro in the earth,
and from walking up and down in it.
                              JOB 1:7

Thou shalt have a place also without the camp, whither thou shalt
go forth abroad: and thou shalt have a paddle upon thy weapon;
and it shall be, when thou wilt ease thyself abroad, thou shalt dig
therewith, and shalt turn back and cover that which cometh from
thee.
                              DEUTERONOMY XXIII:13

The man who goes alone can start today; but he who travels with
another must wait till that other is ready, and it may be a long
time before they get off.
                              THOREAU

Now, to be properly enjoyed, a walking tour should be gone upon
alone. . . . because freedom is of the essence.
                              STEVENSON

He travels the fastest who travels alone.
                              KIPLING

A bore is a person who deprives you of solitude without providing
you with company.
                              JOHN MACDONALD (?)

            The true male never yet walked
            Who liked to listen when his mate talked.
                              ANNA WICKHAM
                              (Mrs. Patrick Hepburn)

I was never less alone than when by myself.
EDWARD GIBBON

In solitude
What happiness? Who can enjoy alone,
Or all enjoying, what contentment find?
MILTON
Paradise Lost

Solitude is as needful to the imagination as society is wholesome
for the character.
JAMES RUSSELL LOWELL

That inward eye which is the bliss of solitude.
WORDSWORTH

O Solitude! where are the charms
That sages have seen in thy face?
COWPER
*Verses Supposed to Be Written
by Alexander Selkirk*

Now my soul hath elbow room.
SHAKESPEARE

He went back through the Wet Wild Woods, waving his wild
tail, and walking by his wild lone. But he never told anybody.
KIPLING
The Cat That Walked by Himself

O why do you walk through the fields in gloves,
Missing so much and so much?
FRANCES CORNFORD
To a Fat Lady Seen from the Train

Oh, he's a genuine backpacker, all right. He's got a filed-down
toothbrush.
Overheard by Colin Fletcher

Who walks with beauty has no need of fear;
The sun and moon and stars keep pace with him;
Invisible hands restore the ruined year,
And time, itself, grows beautifully dim.

DAVID MORTON

There's night and day, brother, both sweet things; sun, moon, and stars, brother, all sweet things; there's likewise a wind on the heath. Life is very sweet, brother; who would wish to die?

GEORGE BORROW
Lavengro

Mountains are earth's undying monuments.

HAWTHORNE

You ask me:
    Why do I live
    on this green mountain?

This is
    another sky,
No likeness
    to that human world below.

LI PO

What men call gallantry, and gods adult'ry,
Is much more common where the climate's sultry.

BYRON
Don Juan

Three things there are that ease the heart—water, green grass, and the beauty of woman.

FRANK HERBERT
Dune

"Would you tell me, please, which way I ought to go from here?"

"That depends a good deal on where you want to go to," said the Cat.

"I don't much care where—" said Alice.

"Then it doesn't matter which way you go," said the Cat.

"—so long as I get *somewhere*," Alice added as an explanation.

"Oh, you're sure to do that," said the Cat, "if you only walk long enough."

LEWIS CARROLL
Alice in Wonderland

"I'm sure nobody walks much faster than I do."

"He can't do that," said the King, "or else he'd have been here first."

LEWIS CARROLL
Through the Looking-Glass

The Promised Land always lies on the other side of a wilderness.

HAVELOCK ELLIS

The walking stick serves the purpose of an advertisement that the bearer's hands are employed otherwise than in useful effort, and it therefore has utility as an evidence of leisure.

THORSTEIN VEBLEN
The Theory of the Leisure Class

Dear Uncle Colin: I'm haveing fun at camp My counselors he Read one of your Books anb he said it gave him sore Feet.

Postcard from honorary nephew

Hi-Rise Campsites, Inc., has announced plans to construct a 20-story campground in downtown New Orleans. . . . Plans for the $4 million project call for eight lower floors of parking and 12 upper stories with 240 individual sites equipped with utility hookups for campers . . . [and] campsites carpeted with artificial turf, and a rooftop pool

"This will be unique—the first of its kind anywhere," said Wesley Hurley of Hi-Rise. "It is designed for today's different kind of camping. People don't want the woodsy bit now; they want to camp in comfort near the city."

Associated Press report
[Sub-historical footnote: The facility was never built.]

All men who explore
Deplore
That frustrating hurdle,
The girdle.

COLIN FLETCHER
(Unpublished)

I find that the three truly great times for thinking thoughts are
when I am standing in the shower, sitting on the john or walking.
And the greatest of these, by far, is walking.

COLIN FLETCHER
(Unpublished)

It is interesting that in both Japanese Zen and Plains Indian
animism, there are walking and sitting forms of contemplation.

ROB SCHULTHEIS
The Hidden West

When I am not walking, I am reading; I cannot sit and think,
[but] books think for me.

CHARLES LAMB

Man is a thinking reed but his great works are done when he is
not calculating and thinking.

DAISETZ T. SUZUKI

He likes the country, but in truth must own,
Most likes it when he studies it in town.

WILLIAM COWPER

Thou canst not stir a flower
Without troubling of a star.

FRANCIS THOMPSON

The wonder that I feel is easy,
Yet ease is the cause of wonder.

T. S. ELIOT

To a person uninstructed in natural history, his country or seaside stroll is a walk through a gallery filled with wonderful works of art, nine-tenths of which have their faces turned to the wall.

THOMAS HUXLEY

The last word in ignorance is the man who says of a plant or animal, "What good is it?" If the land mechanism as a whole is good, then every part of it is good, whether we understand it or not.

ALDO LEOPOLD

Solvency is entirely a matter of temperament and not of income.

LOGAN PEARSALL SMITH

There is no cure for birth and death save to enjoy the interval.

GEORGE SANTAYANA

To understand life, man must learn to shudder.

Quoted by Loren Eiseley

Comedy is tragedy plus time.

Attributed to Carol Burnett's mother

Humor and knowledge are the two great hopes of civilization.

KONRAD LORENZ

I went to the woods because I wished to live deliberately, to front only the essential facts of life, and see if I could not learn what it had to teach, and not, when I came to die, discover that I had not lived.

THOREAU

To enjoy the full flavor of life, take big bites. Moderation is for monks.

ROBERT HEINLEIN
Time Enough for Love

Early and provident fear is the mother of safety.

EDMUND BURKE

The beginning of wisdom is a salutary shock.

ARNOLD TOYNBEE

All paths lead nowhere, so it is important to choose a path that has heart.

CARLOS CASTAÑEDA

Improvement makes straight roads; but the crooked roads without improvement are roads of genius.

WILLIAM BLAKE

Man . . . walks up the stairs of his concepts, [and] emerges ahead of his accomplishments.

JOHN STEINBECK

Man discovers that he is nothing else than evolution become conscious of itself.

JULIAN HUXLEY

. . . man, in his paranoid arrogance, has perpetrated the greatest blasphemy of all time by stating in the Bible, "So God created Man in his own image." . . . There is a God all around us which man has refused to accept but he abuses and exploits her forgetting that she of all deities is our own true God. . . . Man's greatest enemy is his own kind and upon an understanding of this fact depends his chances of survival in the future.

DR. PHILIP E. GLOVER
Former Director,
Tsavo Research Project, Kenya

The human race is bound to defile, I've often noticed it,
Whatever they can reach or name, they'd shit on the morning star
If they could reach. . . .
A day will come when the earth will scratch herself and smile and
rub off humanity.

ROBINSON JEFFERS

Anybody who pursues a grand design for the expansion of terrestrial life into the universe had better observe carefully the spirit and style of the people who succeed in living in harmony with nature in the wildernesses of earth.

> FREEMAN DYSON
> *Disturbing the Universe*

It is in the long run essential to the growth of any new and high civilization that small groups of people can escape from their neighbors and from their governments, to go and live as they please in the wilderness.

> FREEMAN DYSON
> *Disturbing the Universe*

Men and their works have been a disease on the surface of their planets before now. . . . Nature tends to compensate for diseases, to remove or encapsulate them, to incorporate them into the system in her own way.

> FRANK HERBERT
> *Dune* (set in the far future)

The . . . scientists were wrong . . . the most persistent principles of the universe were accident and error.

> FRANK HERBERT
> *Dune*

Let a man once overcome his selfish terror at his own finitude, and his finitude is, in one sense, overcome.

> GEORGE SANTAYANA

The concept of progress acts as a protective mechanism to shield us from the terrors of the future.

> FRANK HERBERT
> *Dune*

If one advances confidently in the direction of his dreams, and endeavors to live the life which he has imagined, he will meet with a success unexpected in common hours.

> THOREAU

Grow up as soon as you can. It pays. The only time you really live fully is from thirty to sixty. . . . The young are slaves to dreams; the old, servants of regrets. Only the middle-aged have all their five senses in the keeping of their wits.

HERVEY ALLEN

Walk while ye have the light, lest darkness come upon you.

ST. JOHN XII:35

I speak truth, not so much as I would, but as much as I dare; and I dare a little the more, as I grow older.

MONTAIGNE

Growing old isn't so bad—when you consider the alternative.

MAURICE CHEVALIER

We will go no more to the woods, the laurel-trees are cut.

THÉODORE DE BANVILLE

And as I turn me home,
My shadow walks before.

ROBERT BRIDGES

Acknowledgments

Injustice lurks in every list of acknowledgments: there is no really practical way to distinguish between major donators of time or expertise and those who kindly dotted a few "i"s. So I must single out three men who contributed mightily and steadily throughout the three years of work on this edition. Carl D. Brandt, as usual and from the earliest drafts, acted not only as my literary agent but also as both literary and backpacking critic. Steve Olson, formerly of Trailwise, counseled me—as he had with earlier editions—on virtually every aspect of backpacking. And Rich Davies of REI, Berkeley, furnished almost equal support. I wish to thank them all, very warmly.

The big supporting cast (other than those named in the text) is listed overleaf in four categories: advisors in specific fields; readers who sent valid ideas, comments or suggestions; staff members of commercial firms who lent helping hands; and those who produced the book.

The third category poses some problems. Naturally enough, the firms are mostly based near my home, and mentioning their names is in a sense unfair to others that chance to be distant. Besides, I would prefer to leave out all mention of commercial affiliation: I jealously guard the freedom from pressure that comes from being independent of all commercial sources, and I recognize that my independence must be not only real but also seen to be real. After considerable deliberation, I have settled on a compromise. In the commercial category I will include only individuals who reached out those helping hands repeatedly or beyond the call of duty, or who contributed particularly valuable, even glittering, ideas. And in these cases I will mention their parent organizations: all these firms donated time and displayed other generosities—which not every outfit did. This decision leaves me less than fully satisfied, but it's the best I can muster.

One other thing. Although I've striven to make each category complete, I feel unhappily sure that a few names will have slipped my memory or filtered through what passes for my filing system. If so, I'm sorry. I really appreciated the help.   C.F.

ADVISORS IN SPECIFIC FIELDS: Kirk R. Allen, DPM (feet); John J. D'Attilio, MD (sunglasses and goggles); John Davis (spiders); Bob and Dick DeWolf ("The New Wave"); Dean diPilla (spirulina, fasting); Boyd Evison (backcountry permits); Marc Fowler (cameras, binoculars); David Graber (bears); Janice Herald (nutrition); Donald B. Kunkel, MD (treatment of snakebite); John Larsen (photography); Bruce L. Meyer, MD (first aid and other medical matters); Ralph E. Retherford, MD (nutrition); Gail Robbins (nutrition); Em Scatteregia (backcountry permits); Bob and Janet Steinberg (future of the goddam species); and Joan Tinoco (nutrition—for this and previous editions).

READERS WHO WROTE OFFERING VALID IDEAS, SUGGESTIONS OR COMMENTS: *Alaska:* Sasha Wik. *California:* "A backpacker"; Norton and Mithoo Benner; Polly Black; Charles L. Clausen; Mike Grant: Richard Gross; Bob Harmon; Jeanie Hayes; Carl Hazen; Donald Henze; Eric L. Jowett; Douglas Kelt; Kelly S. Lassey; Vincent F. Lee; Sam G. Lutz; Kevin Mann; E. Phil Pister; Robert Silla; Janet Campbell Sorenson; Link Van Cleave. *Colorado:* Judy Moffett; Karl Williamson. *Connecticut:* Norman A. Greist. *Georgia:* Jeff Montgomery. *Hawaii:* Boyd Hill. *Illinois:* Charles Rufino; Michael R. Shaw. *Iowa:* Jim Dorian Rooks. *Kentucky:* Rodger K. Mathews; Dick Thornton. *Louisiana:* Ed Johnston. *Maine:* Scott Buxton. *Maryland:* Robert Hughes. *Massachusetts:* Jim DeMund; Steve Harvester. *Michigan:* John Hartranft; Steve Pawlowski. *Mississippi:* Louie Spencer. *Missouri:* Larry Horowitz: James P. Martineau; Stuart McElfresh; Paul J. Stamler. *Nebraska:* Warren Bosley. *New Jersey:* Paul Macghee. *New Mexico:* David Hysom. *New York:* Robert Benner; Gerard Bilquin; Clare Brandt; Robert S. Calese; Albert (Cap) Field; Dennis Fitzgerald; Chris Hawkins; John Ho; Bob Lefkowitz; B. Bailey Marcus; "Rigg and Maggie"; Paul Schueler. *Ohio:* Steve Courtright; Todd Woolf. *Oregon:* Dennis K. Marker. *Pennsylvania:* Michael Cannon; Jeff Hudson; Hendrick G. van Oss. *South Carolina:* Jerry Boyer. *Texas:* John W. Colburn; Bill McKenna; Mike Stabler; Deborah Wohlt. *Vermont:* Anne Mausolff. *Virginia:* Darrow Kirkpatrick; Jack Sawicki. *Washington:* Gary Lund; Alan E. Nourse. *Wisconsin:* Tim J. Kuchler; Jeffrey G. Wischer. *Virgin Islands:* Lee C. Gerhard. *Canada:* John LaBella; John Mansbridge. *Liberia:* Terry McGuire.

STAFF OF COMMERCIAL FIRMS: Pat Nims and Bob Power of Eddie Bauer; Scott Carpenter, Bill Pursley and Shelley Risko of Bugaboo; Justus Bauschinger of Class 5; George Rudolf and John Schelling of Donner Mountain Corporation; Bill Brackin, Eric Reynolds, Mike Scherer, Randy Verniers and Gordon Wing of Marmot Mountain Works; Fred Williams of Moonstone; Mark Erickson and Bob Howe of The North

Face; Diana Jagerski, Paul Kaprowski, Leslie Mandell, Gary Ranz, Kevin Washington and Gary Went-Bolgear of REI; Keith Roush of Royal Robbins; Al French, Paul Kramer and Mark Nadell of Sierra Designs; Carl Antholz, Kathy Larramendy, Dennis McCullah and Peter Noone of the old Ski Hut; and Joe Bevier, Mike Nelson and Gary Schaezlin of Western Mountaineering.

THOSE WHO PRODUCED THE BOOK: That is, everybody at Knopf. They once more managed to make me feel that we were always working *together* to ensure the best possible book. In particular, Ashbel Green, my editor, again supervised the whole rambling operation with cool competence and good humor. Peter Hayes, his assistant, fielded explosions of detail. Dorothy Schmiderer, designer, leaned over backwards to meet my wishes. And Melvin Rosenthal, production editor, labored long hours on and off the phone to accommodate my last persnickety demand. Finally, I want to thank Betty Berenson of San Francisco, who, as in earlier editions, built the index with T.L.C.

Index

In entries with two or more page references, **boldface type** indicates where the main discussion of the topic can be found.

acclimation:
for high altitude, 40–2, 97–8, 355–6, 577–8
and sleeping, 41, 354–6
Ace bandages, 403, 525
acute mountain sickness, 40, **577–80**
Adhesive Knit, 89–90
adhesive repair tape, 367, **511–12**
adhesive tape, 495
A-frame tents, 289, 291, 293, 295, **296–7**; see also tents
afternoons:
desert, 325
typical, 273–6
afternoon tea, 170–2, 275
agaves, uses of, 83, 265, 485
age, and conditioning, 39
Agricultural Handbook No. 8, 155, 177 *n.*
air mattress, 277, 331, 332, **334–6**, 358
as chair, 336
down-filled, 337
when floating pack, 535, 537
inflating, 335–6
as raft, 531–2, 533
see also Therm-a-Rest pads
air travel, packs in, 141
airdrops, **544–8**
costs of, 544
signaling for, 545–6, 547
airplanes, and protecting packs, 141
alarm clock, 508
Alaska, and grizzly bears, 564–6
alcohol, 180–1
contraindicated for snakebite, 558
for priming stoves, 257
alcohol, rubbing, 86, 87
alcohol stoves, 246–7

alkaline batteries, 447, 448, 449
allergic reactions:
to insect bites, 563
to poison oak, ivy, sumac, 572–4
allergies, first-aid supplies for, 495, 496, 572, 573
altimeters, 484
altitude:
acclimating to, 40–2, 97–8, 355–6, 577–8
and acute mountain sickness, 40, 577–80
and appetite, 154
and cooking, 280–1
and disciplining thoughts, 98–9
and getting in shape for, 41
and lightning, 581–2
problems of, 41, 98, 577–80
and Selective Awareness, 99
and skin protection, 492–3
and stoves, 236–7, 243–4
and sunglasses, necessity of, 456–60
and walking rhythm, 97–8
and zen, 99
aluminum foil, 211
anaphylactic shock, 563
animals:
dangerous, 289, 563, 564–6, 571
food stealers, 566–71
pack, 548–9
photographing, 472
rabid, 571
trails made by, 485–6
watching, 287, 458
anoraks, 410; see also rainwear: jackets
antibiotics, 495, 496
antifogging mists, 458–9

A NOTE ON THE TYPE

The text of this book was set in a digitized version of
Garamond No. 3, a modern rendering of the type first
cut in the sixteenth century by Claude Garamond
(1510–1561). He was a pupil of Geoffroy Troy and is
believed to have based his letters on the Venetian
models, although he introduced a number of important
differences, and it is to him we owe the letter which we
know as Old Style. He gave to his letters a certain
elegance and a feeling of movement which won for their
creator an immediate reputation and the patronage of
the French King Francis I.

Composed by Dix Type Inc., Syracuse, New York.
Printed and bound by The Murray Printing Company,
Westford, Massachusetts.

*Typography and binding based on designs
by Winston Potter*